PLANNING AND CONTROL USING ORACLE® PRIMAVERA® P6 VERSIONS 8.1 TO 15.2 PPM PROFESSIONAL

Planning and Progressing Project Schedules With and Without Roles and Resources in an Established Database

BY

PAUL EASTWOOD HARRIS

DISCLAIMER

The information contained in this publication is to the best of the author's knowledge true and correct. The author has made every effort to ensure accuracy of this publication, but may not be held responsible for any loss or damage arising from any information in this publication. Furthermore, Oracle Corporation reserves the right in their documentation to make changes to any products to improve reliability, function, or design. Thus, the application of Service Packs or the use of upgraded software may result in the software operating differently from the descriptions in this publication.

AUTHOR AND PUBLISHER

Paul E Harris
Eastwood Harris Pty Ltd
PO Box 4032
Doncaster Heights, 3109
Victoria, Australia

e-mail: harrispe@eh.com.au
Web: http://www.eh.com.au
Tel: +61 (0) 4 1118 7701

Please send any comments on this publication to the author.

ISBN 978-1-925185-27-0 – B5 Paperback
ISBN 978-1-925185-28-7– A4 Spiral
ISBN 978-1-925185-29-4 – eBook

15 July 2016

INTRODUCTION

This publication is an upgrade of the *Project Planning & Control Using Primavera P6 Version 7* and has been written to enable new users to learn the planning and scheduling functions of Primavera Version 8.1 to 15.2. Please note there are no versions 9 to 14 and Oracle changed their naming convention with the release of 15.1 so the name is the same as the year of the release. Due to the changes in the menus in this release, it is not possible to make the book backward compatible to earlier versions of the software.

Many users will have prior experience with SureTrak, P3, Asta Powerproject or Microsoft Project and the author explains where there are differences in the products' functionality.

The author would appreciate any constructive comments on how this publication may be improved.

SUMMARY

The publication may be used as:

- A training manual for a three-day training course, or
- A self-teach book, or
- A reference manual.

The screen shots for this publication are taken from Primavera Version 8.1 or 8.2 or 8.3 or 8.4 or 15.1 or 15.2.

One-, two-, or three-day training courses may be run using this publication and it includes exercises for the students to complete at the end of each chapter. After the course, students may use this publication as a reference book. Instructors' PowerPoint presentations are available from Eastwood Harris web sites.

This publication is ideal for people who would like to quickly gain an understanding of how the software operates and explains how the software differs from Primavera P3, SureTrak and Microsoft Project, thus making it ideal for people who wish to convert from these products.

CUSTOMIZATION FOR TRAINING COURSES

Training organizations or companies that wish to conduct their own training may have this publication tailored to suit their requirements. This may be achieved removing, reordering or adding content to the publication and by writing their own exercises. Please contact the author to discuss this service.

AUTHOR'S COMMENT

As a project controls consultant I have used a number of planning and scheduling software packages for the management of a range of project types and sizes. The first publications I published were user guides/training manuals for Primavera SureTrak, P3 and Microsoft Project users. These were well received by professional project managers and schedulers, so I decided to turn my attention to Primavera Enterprise, which is now called Primavera P6. This publication follows the same proven layout of my previous publications. I trust this publication will assist you in understanding how to use Primavera P6 on your projects.

APPRECIATION

I would like thank Michael Jack for his assistance in writing this book and Thomas Grant for his assistance in proof reading parts of the book.

CURRENT BOOKS PUBLISHED BY EASTWOOD HARRIS

99 Tricks and Traps for Microsoft Office Project - Including Microsoft Project 2000 to 2007
Planning Using Primavera Project Planner P3 Version 3.1 - Revised 2006
Planning Using Primavera SureTrak Project Manager Version 3.0 - Revised 2006
Project Planning and Scheduling Using Primavera Contractor Version 6.1 - Including Versions 4.1, 5.0 and 6.1
Planning and Scheduling Using Microsoft Office Project 2007 - Including Microsoft Project 2000 to 2003 - Revised 2009
Planning and Control Using Microsoft Project and *PMBOK® Guide* Fourth Edition
Planning and Control Using Microsoft Project 2010 and *PMBOK® Guide* Fourth Edition
Project Planning & Control Using Primavera P6 Version 7 - For all industries including Versions 4 to 7 Updated 2012
Planning and Scheduling Using Microsoft Project 2010 - Updated 2013 Including Revised Workshops
Planning and Control Using Microsoft Project 2010 & *PMBOK® Guide* Fifth Edition
Planning and Control Using Microsoft Project 2013
Planning and Control Using Microsoft Project 2013 & *PMBOK® Guide* Fifth Edition - No Subtitle
Planning and Control Using Oracle Primavera P6 - Versions 8.2 & 8.3 EPPM Web
99 Tricks and Traps for Microsoft Project 2013
Oracle Primavera P6 EPPM Web Administrators Guide
Planning and Control Using Oracle Primavera P6 Versions 8.1 to 15.1 PPM Professional
Planificación y Control Usando Oracle Primavera P6 Versiones 8.1 a 15.1 PPM Profesional
规划和控制 Oracle Primavera P6 应用 版本 8.1-15.1 PPM 专业版
Planning and Control Using Oracle Primavera P6 - Versions 8.2 to 15.1 EPPM Web

SUPERSEDED BOOKS BY THE AUTHOR

Planning and Scheduling Using Microsoft® Project 2000
Planning and Scheduling Using Microsoft® Project 2002
Planning and Scheduling Using Microsoft® Project 2003
Planning and Scheduling Using Microsoft® Office Project 2007
PRINCE2™ Planning and Control Using Microsoft® Project
Planning and Control Using Microsoft® Project and *PMBOK® Guide* Third Edition
Project Planning and Scheduling Using Primavera Enterprise® – Team Play Version 3.5
Project Planning and Scheduling Using Primavera Enterprise® – P3e & P3e/c Version 3.5
Project Planning and Scheduling Using Primavera® Version 4.1 for IT Project
Project Planning and Scheduling Using Primavera® Version 4.1 or E&C
Planning and Scheduling Using Primavera® Version 5.0 – For IT Project Office
Planning and Scheduling Using Primavera® Version 5.0 – For Engineering & Construction
Project Planning & Control Using Primavera® P6 – Updated for Version 6.2
Planning Using Primavera Project Planner P3® Version 2.0
Planning Using Primavera Project Planner P3® Version 3.0
Planning Using Primavera Project Planner P3® Version 3.1
Project Planning Using SureTrak® for Windows Version 2.0
Planning Using Primavera SureTrak® Project Manager Version 3.0
Planning and Control Using Oracle Primavera P6 - Version 8.1 Professional Client & Optional Client
Planning & Control Using Primavera® P6™ For all industries including Versions 4 to 7
Planning and Control Using Oracle Primavera P6 - Versions 8.2 EPPM Web
Planning and Control Using Oracle Primavera P6 - Versions 8.2 & 8.3 EPPM Web
Planning and Control Using Oracle Primavera P6 - Version 8.1 & 8.2 Professional Client & Optional Client
Planning and Control Using Oracle Primavera P6 - Version 8.1, 8.2 & 8.3 Professional Client & Optional Client
Project Planning and Control Using Oracle Primavera P6 - Versions 8.1, 8.2 & 8.3 Professional Client & Optional Client
Planificación y Control de Proyectos Usando Oracle Primavera P6 - Versiones 8.1, 8.2 y 8.3 Cliente Profesional y Opcional
项目规划和控制 ORACLE PRIMAVERA P6 应用 - 版本 8.1, 8.2 & 8.3 专业&可选客户端
Project Planning and Control Using Oracle Primavera P6 - Versions 8.1 to 8.4 Professional Client & Optional Client
Planning and Control Using Oracle Primavera P6 - Versions 8.2 to 8.4 EPPM Web
Planificación y Control de Proyectos Usando Oracle Primavera P6 Versiones 8.1 a 8.4 Cliente Profesional & Cliente Opcional
规划和控制 ORACLE® PRIMAVERA® P6 应用 版本 8.1-8.4 专业&可选客户端

1 INTRODUCTION

1.1 Purpose

The purpose of this book is to provide a method for planning, scheduling and controlling projects using Primavera P6 Version 8.1 to 15.2 Professional Client and Optional Client within an established Enterprise Project database or a blank database up to an intermediate level. Please note there are no versions 9 to 14 as Oracle has changed their naming convention with the release of 15.1, so the name is the same as the year of the release. There are differences between how the Professional Client (the term used when opening a PPM database) and Optional Client (the term used when opening a EPPM database) operate and these are identified throughout the book.

Due to the change in the menu system, it is not possible to make the menus in this book backward compatible to earlier versions of Primavera P6, but users of earlier versions should be able to use this book as most functions are the same once one has invoked a menu command.

This book covers the following topics:

- Understand the steps required to create a project plan and monitor a project's progress
- Understand the Primavera P6 environment
- Create a project and set up the preferences
- Define calendars
- Creating a Work Breakdown Structure and adding activities
- Format the display
- Add logic and constraints
- Use Filters, Group, Sort and Layouts
- Print reports
- Record and track progress of an un-resourced schedule
- User and Administration Preferences and Scheduling Options
- Create and assign roles and resources
- Resource optimization including leveling
- Update a project containing resources
- Other methods of organizing data and Global Change
- Managing the enterprise environment including multiple project scheduling

The book is not intended to cover every aspect of Primavera P6, but it does cover the main features required to create and update a project schedule. It should provide you with a solid grounding, which will enable you to learn the other features of Primavera 6 by experimenting with the software, using the help files and reviewing other literature.

This book was written to minimize superfluous text, allowing the user to locate and understand the information contained within as quickly as possible. If at any time you are unable to understand a topic in this book, it is suggested that you use the Primavera Version 6.0 Help menu or User Manuals, which are available on the software downloads in pdf format, or the Oracle website to gain a further understanding of the subject.

The "What Is New" chapters identify the major changes in the software from Versions 6.0 and 7. If you are using this book with an older version, you may find some features do not exist, but I have tried to indicate in which version the new features were introduced and/or removed. Primavera Systems Inc. and the new owners Oracle Corporation continually releases Service Packs for the software and there may be instances where the software operates differently due to the loading of a Service Pack.

1.2 Required Background Knowledge

This book does not teach you how to use computers or to manage projects. The book is intended to teach you how to use Primavera in a project environment. Therefore, to be able to follow this book you should have the following background knowledge:

- The ability to use a personal computer and understand the fundamentals of the operating system.
- Experience using application software, such as Microsoft Office, which would have given you exposure to Windows menu systems and typical Windows functions such as copy and paste.
- A sound understanding of how projects are managed, such as the phases and processes that take place over the lifetime of a project.

1.3 Purpose of Planning

The ultimate purpose of planning is to build a model that enables you to predict which activities and resources are critical to the timely completion of the project. Strategies may then be implemented to ensure that these activities and resources are managed properly, thus ensuring that the project will be delivered both **On Time** and **Within Budget**.

Planning aims to:

- Identify the total scope of the project and plan to deliver it,
- Evaluate different project delivery methods,
- Identify Products/Deliverables required to deliver a project under a logical breakdown of the project,
- Identify and optimize the use of resources and evaluate if target dates may be met,
- Identify risks, plan to minimize them and set priorities,
- Provide a baseline plan against which progress is measured,
- Assist in stakeholders' communication, identifying what is to be done, when and by whom and
- Assist management to think ahead and make informed decisions.

Planning helps to avoid or assist in evaluating:

- Increased project costs or reduction in scope and/or quality,
- Additional changeover and/or operation costs,
- Extensions of time claims against your customer or client,
- Loss of your client's revenue,
- Contractual disputes and associated resolution costs,
- The loss of reputation of those involved in a project, and
- Loss of a facility or asset in the event of a total project failure.

1.4 Project Planning Metrics

The components that are normally measured and controlled using planning and scheduling software:

- Scope
- Time
- Resource Effort/Work (these are called Units in Primavera P6)
- Cost

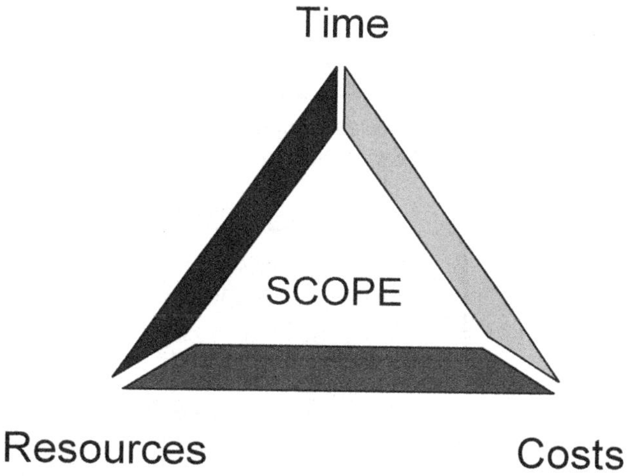

A change in any one of these components normally results in a change in one or more of the others.

Other project management functions that are not traditionally managed with planning and scheduling software but may have components reflected in the schedule include:

- Document Management and Control,
- Quality Management,
- Contract Management,
- Issue Management,
- Risk Management,
- Industrial Relations, and
- Accounting.

The development of Enterprise Project Management systems has resulted in the inclusion of many of these functions in project planning and scheduling software. Primavera includes modules for:

- Issue Management,
- Risk Management, and
- Document Management.

1.5 Planning Cycle

The planning cycle is an integral part of managing a project. A software package such as Primavera makes this activity much easier.

When the original plan is agreed to, the **Baseline** or **Target** is set. The **Baseline** is a copy of the original plan and is used to compare progress of an updated schedule. Earlier versions were limited 50 baselines but this restriction has been removed in later versions.

After project planning has ended and project execution has begun, the actual progress is monitored, recorded and compared to the **Baseline** dates.

The progress is then reported and evaluated against the Baseline.

The plan may be changed by adding or deleting activities and adjusting Remaining Durations, Logic or Resources. A revised plan is then published as progress continues. A revised Baseline may be set if the original Baseline becomes irrelevant due to the impact of project scope changes, a change in methodology or excessive delays.

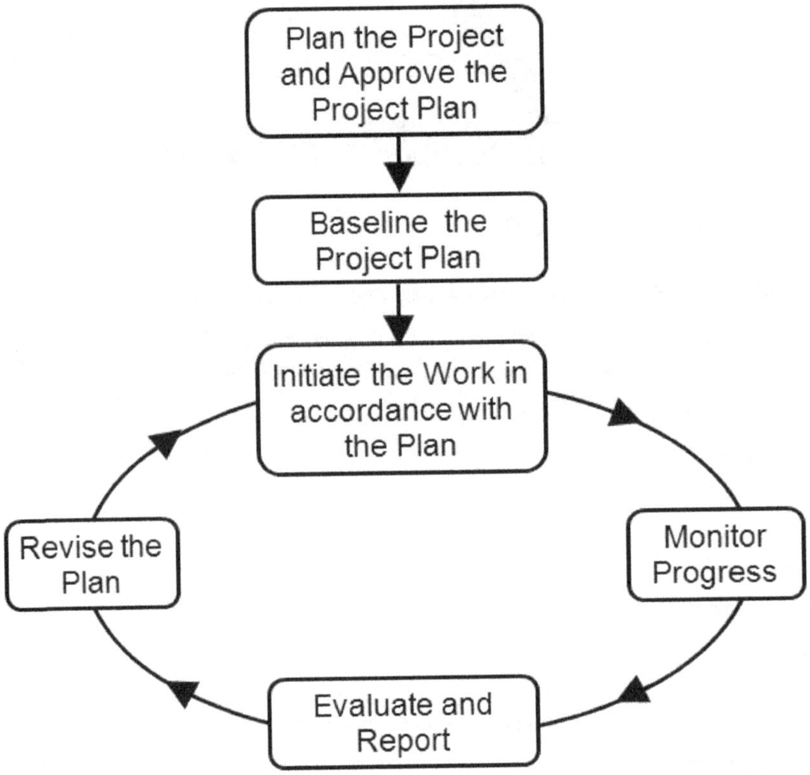

Updating a schedule assists in the management of a project by recording and displaying:

- Progress and the impact of project scope changes and delays as the project progresses,
- The revised completion date and final forecast of costs for the project,
- Historical data that may be used to support extension of time claims and dispute resolution, and
- Historical data that may be used in future projects of a similar nature.

1.6 Levels of Planning

Projects are often planned at a summary level and then at a later date detailed out before the work commences. Smaller projects may be scheduled in detail during project planning, but large or complex projects may require several iterations before the project plan is fully detailed out.

The main reasons for not detailing out a project early are that:

- There may not be enough information at that stage and
- Preparing detailed schedules wastes time, as they may be made redundant by unforeseen changes.

The following planning techniques discussed in other well-known project management books may be considered:

PMBOK® Guide

The *PMBOK® Guide*, which is a project management reference book published by the Project Management Institute, discusses the following techniques:

- The **Rolling Wave**. This technique involves adding more detail to the schedule as the work approaches. This is often possible, as more information is known about the scope of the project as work is executed. The initial planning could be completed at a high level in the **Work Breakdown Structure** (**WBS**). As the work approaches, the planning may be completed at a **WBS Component** and then to a **Work Package** level planning.
- The use of **Sub-projects**. These are useful in larger projects where more than one entity is working on the project schedule. This situation may exist when portions of projects are contracted out. A sub-project may be detailed out when the work is awarded to a contractor.
- The use of **Phases**. A Phase is different from a PRINCE2 Stage, as Phases may overlap in time and Stages do not. Phases may be defined, for example, as Design, Procure and Install. These Phases may overlap, as Procurement may commence before Design is complete. The Phase development of a schedule involves the detailing out of all the associated WBS elements prior to the commencement of that Phase.
- The *PMBOK® Guide* does not have strict definitions for levels of plans but assumes that this process is undertaken when decomposing the **Work Breakdown Structure** (**WBS**). There are some other models available that may be used as guidelines, such as the PMI "Practice Standard for Work Breakdown Structures."

PRINCE2 Plans

PRINCE2 is a project management methodology that was developed in the UK. This methodology defines the type of plans that a project team should consider.

Stages in PRINCE2 are defined as time-bound periods of a project, which do not overlap in time and are referred to as Management Stages. The end of a Stage may signify a major event, such as signing a major contract. Project Phases may overlap in time, but Stages do not. Under PRINCE2 a Project Plan is divided into Stages and a Stage plan is detailed out prior to its commencement. PRINCE2 defines the following levels of plans:

- **Programme Plan –** which may include Project Plans or one or more portfolios of multiple projects,
- **Project Plan –** this is mandatory and is updated through the duration of a project,
- **Stage Plan –** there is a minimum of two Stage Plans: an **Initiation Stage Plan** and **First Stage Plan**. There would usually be one Stage Plan for each Stage,
- **Exception Plan –** which is at the same level and detail as a Stage Plan and replaces a Stage Plan at the request of a Project Board when a Stage is forecast to exceed tolerances (contingent time), and
- **Team Plan –** which is optional and would be used on larger projects where Teams deliver Products that require detailed planning. A typical example is a contractor's plan, which would be submitted during the bid process.

Jelen's Cost and Optimization Engineering

This book defines the following levels of plans:

- Level 0: This is the total project and is, in effect, a single bar spanning the time from start to finish.
- Level 1: This schedules the project by its major components. For example, a level 1 schedule for a process plant may be broken into process area, storage and handling area, site and services, and utilities. It is shown in bar chart format.
- Level 2: Each of the level 1 components is further subdivided. For example, utility systems are broken into water, electrical, gas, sanitary, etc. In most cases, this schedule level can only be shown in bar chart format although a bar chart with key constraints may be possible.
- Level 3: The subdivision continues. This is probably the first level that a meaningful critical path network can be drawn. It is also a good level for the project's overall control schedule since it is neither too summarized nor too detailed.
- Levels 4–?: The subdivision continues to whatever level of detail is needed by the user. When operating at these more detailed levels, the planners generally work with less than the total schedule. In most cases these "look-ahead" schedules span periods of 30–180 days. The user may utilize either bar chart or CPM format for these schedules.

This paragraph was reproduced from Jelen's Cost and Optimization Engineering, *author F. Jelen, copyright 1983, ISBN 0-07-053646-5, with the written permission from the publisher McGraw-Hill.*

1.7 Monitoring and Controlling a Project

After a plan has been produced, it should be executed and the work authorized in accordance with the plan. If there is to be a change in the plan, then the plan should be formally changed. If necessary, the client should be informed and, if required by the contract, approval should be sought.

It may be difficult to obtain approval for extension of time claims when the plan is not followed then and furthermore this will make dispute resolution more difficult.

Monitoring a project records progress to date:

- Records the start and finish dates of completed activities,
- Confirms that the required quality is met,
- Thus confirms the deliverables/products that have been produced,
- Confirms that the deliverables/products are produced on time, with the planned resources and to budget,
- Records the progress of started activities,
- Applies the productivity to date for future similar activities,
- Add or amend schedule to reflect changes, and
- Historical data is recorded for use in planning future projects.

Controlling a project provides the next level of management with information that enables them to manage a project and make informed decisions on problems:

- Ensure that the project is being executed according to the plan,
- Compare the project's progress with the original plan,
- Reviews the productivity to date and how the current productivity will affect future activities,
- Forecast problems as early as possible which enables corrective action to be taken as early as possible,
- Review options to improve the schedule, and
- Obtain data required for preparing extension of time claims and for dispute resolution.

2 CREATING A PROJECT PLAN

The aim of this chapter is to give an understanding of what a plan is and some practical guidance on how a schedule may be created and updated during the life of a project.

2.1 Understanding Planning and Scheduling Software

Planning and scheduling software enables the user to:

- Enter the breakdown structure of the project deliverables or products into the software. This is often called a Work Breakdown Structure (WBS) or Product Breakdown Structure (PBS),
- Break a project down into the work required to create the deliverables and enter these into the software as Activities under the appropriate WBS,
- Assign durations, constraints, predecessors and successors of the activities and then calculate the start and finish date of all the activities,
- Assign resources and/or costs, which represent people, equipment or materials, to the activities and calculate the project resource requirements and/or cash flow,
- Optimize the project plan,
- Set Baseline Dates and Budgets to compare progress against,
- Use the plan to approve the commencement of work,
- Record the actual progress of activities and compare the progress against the Baseline and amend the plan when required, allowing for scope changes, etc.,
- Record the consumption of resources and/or costs and re-estimate the resources and/or costs required to finish the project, and
- Produce management reports.

There are four modes or levels in which planning and scheduling software may be used.

	Planning	**Tracking**
Without Resources	**LEVEL 1** Planning without Resources	**LEVEL 2** Tracking progress without Resources
With Resources	**LEVEL 3** Planning with Resources	**LEVEL 4** Tracking progress with Resources

As the level increases, the amount of information required to maintain the schedule will increase and, more importantly, your skill and knowledge in using the software will increase. This book is designed to take you from Level 1 to Level 4.

2.2 Enterprise Project Management

Primavera is an Enterprise Project Management software package that enables many projects to be managed in one database. These projects may be summarized under a hierarchical structure titled the Enterprise Project Structure (EPS). This function is similar to summarizing activities of a project under a Work Breakdown Structure (WBS).

An EPS is used for the following purposes:

- To manage user access to projects within the database.
- To manage activities over multiple projects that have a common interest, such as a critical resource.
- Top-down budgeting of projects and resources that may later be compared to the bottom-up or detailed project estimates.
- To allow standardized reporting of all projects in the database.

Individual projects must be created within an EPS database. Primavera has not been designed as a single project planning and scheduling software package and there is an administrative overhead in managing projects in an EPS database. You may wish to consider managing single projects using Primavera Contractor, which does not have the overhead of managing an Enterprise database but has activity limits.

Primavera has a function titled Portfolios that enables a limited number of projects to be viewed at a time. For example, Portfolio would enable you to view projects in a physical area, or of a specific type or client.

2.3 *Understanding Your Project*

Before you start the process of creating a project plan, it is important to have an understanding of the project and how it will be executed. On large, complex projects, this information is usually available from the following types of documents:

- Project charter or business case
- Project scope or contract documentation
- Functional specification
- Requirements baseline
- Plans and drawings
- Project execution plan
- Contracting and purchasing plan
- Equipment lists
- Installation plan
- Testing plan

Many project managers conduct a **Stakeholder Analysis** at the start of a project. This process lists all the people and organizations with an interest in the project and their interests or desired outcomes.

- Key success factors may be identified from the interests of the influential stakeholders.
- It is important to use the stakeholder analysis to identify all the stakeholder activities and include them in the schedule.

It is imperative to gain a good understanding of how the project is to be executed before entering any data into the software. It is considered good practice to plan a project before creating a schedule in any planning and scheduling software. These documents are referred to by many terms such as Project Execution Plan or Project Methodology Statement. You should also understand what level of reporting the project team requires, as providing either too little or too much detail will often lead to a discarded schedule.

There are three processes required to create or maintain a plan at each of the four levels:

- Collecting the relevant project data,
- Entering and manipulating the data in software, and
- Distributing, reviewing and revising the plan.

The ability of the scheduler to collect the data is as important as the ability to enter and manipulate the information using the software. On larger projects, it may be necessary to write policies and procedures to ensure accurate collection of data from the various people, departments, stakeholders/companies, and sites.

2.4 Level 1 – Planning Without Resources

This is the simplest mode of planning.

2.4.1 Creating Projects

To create a project in a Primavera database, you will need the following information:

- An EPS Node, OBS Node in the database to assign the project,
- Project ID (a code assigned to the project) and the Project Name,
- The Project Start Date (and perhaps the Finish Date), and
- The Rate Type. Primavera has five rates per resource and this option enables you to select a rate as the default resources rate.

It would also be useful to know other information such as:

- Client name, and
- Project information such as location, project number and stakeholders.

2.4.2 Defining the Calendars

Before you start entering activities into your schedule, it is advisable to set up the calendars. These are used to model the working time for each activity in the project. For example, a 6-day calendar is created for those activities that will be worked for 6 days a week. The calendar should include any public holidays and any other exceptions to available working days, such as planned days off.

Primavera has three types of calendars:

- **Global**– which may be assigned to activities and resources in any project,
- **Project**– these are project-specific calendars assigned to activities, and
- **Resource**– that are assigned to resources.

Project and Resource calendars may be linked to Global calendars, enabling any changes to holidays made to a Global calendar to be inherited by the associated Project and Resource calendars.

2.4.3 Defining the Project Breakdown Structures

A project breakdown structure (PBS) is a way of categorizing the activities of a project into numerous codes that relate to the project. The codes act as tags or attributes of each activity.

During or after the activities are added to the schedule, they are assigned their PBSs so that they may be grouped, summarized, and filtered in or out of the display.

Primavera has two principal methods of assigning a PBS to your project:

- The Work Breakdown Structure (WBS) function, which is comparable to the P3 and SureTrak WBS functions.
- The Activity Code function that operates in a way similar to P3 and SureTrak.

Before creating a project, you should design your PBSs by asking the following questions:

- Which phases are involved in the project (e.g., Design, Procure, Install and Test)?
- Which disciplines are participating (e.g., Civil, Mechanical and Electrical)?
- Which departments are involved in the project (e.g., Sales, Procurement and Installation)?
- What work is expected to be contracted out and which contractors are to be used?
- How many sites or areas are there in the project?

Use the responses to these and other similar questions to create the PBSs.

2.4.4 Adding Activities

Activities must be defined before they are entered into the schedule. It is important that you carefully consider the following factors:

- What is the scope of the activity? (What is included and excluded?)
- How long is the activity going to take?
- Who is going to perform it?
- What are the deliverables or output for each activity?

The project estimate is usually a good place to start looking for a breakdown of the project into activities, resources, and costs. It may even provide an indication of how long the work will take.

Activities may have variable durations depending on the number of resources assigned. You may find that one activity that takes 4 days using 4 workers may take 2 days using 8 workers or 8 days using 2 workers.

Usually project reports are issued on a regular basis such as every week or every month. It is recommended that, if possible, an activity should not span more than two reporting periods. That way the activities should only be **In-Progress** for one report. Of course, it is not practical to do this on long duration activities, such as procurement and delivery activities, that may span many reporting periods.

Good practice recommends that you have a measurable finish point for each group of activities. These may be identified in the schedule by **Milestones** and are designated with zero duration. You may issue documentation to officially highlight the end of one activity and the start of another, thereby adding clarity to the schedule. Examples of typical documents that may be issued for clarity are:

- Issue of a drawing package
- Completion of a specification
- Placing of an order
- Receipt of materials (delivery logs or tickets or dockets)
- Completed testing certificates for equipment or systems

2.4.5 Adding the Logic Links

The logic is added to the schedule to provide the order in which the activities must be undertaken. The logic is designated by indicating the predecessors to, or the successors from, each activity. There are two methods that software uses to sequence activities:

- Precedence Diagramming Method (PDM), and
- Arrow Diagramming Method(ADM).

Most current project planning and scheduling software, including Primavera, uses PDM. You can create a PDM diagram using the Network Diagram function.

There are several types of dependencies that may be used:

1. **Mandatory dependencies**, also known as **Hard Logic** or **Primary Logic**, are relationships between activities that may not be broken. For example, a hole has to be dug before it is filled with concrete, or a computer delivered before software is loaded.
2. **Discretionary dependencies**, also known as **Sequencing Logic** or **Soft Logic** or **Secondary Logic,** are relationships between activities that may be changed when the plan is changed. For example, if there are five holes to be excavated and only one machine available, or five computers to be assembled and one person available to work on them, then the order of these activities could be set with sequencing logic yet changed at a later date.

   Both **Mandatory dependencies** and **Discretionary dependencies** are entered into Primavera as activity relationships or logic links. The software does not provide a method of identifying the type of relationship because notes or codes may not be attached to relationships. A **Note** may be added to either the predecessor or the successor activity to explain the relationship.
3. **External dependencies** are usually events outside the control of the project team that impacts on the schedule. An example would be the availability of a site to start work. This is usually represented in Primavera by a Milestone that has a constraint applied to it. This topic is discussed in more detail in the next section.

The software will calculate the start and finish dates for each activity. The end date of the project is calculated from the start date of the project, the logic amongst the activities, any **Leads**(often referred to as **Negative Lag**)or **Lags** applied to the logic and durations of the activities. The following picture shows the effect of a lag and a lead on the start of a successor activity:

An example of a **Finish to Start** with positive lag:

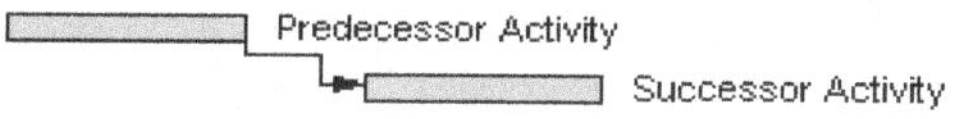

An example of a **Finish to Start** with negative lag:

2.4.6 Developing a Closed Network

It is good practice to create a **Closed Network** with the logic. In a **Closed Network**, all activities have one or more predecessors and one or more successors except:

- The project start milestone or first activity, which has no predecessors, and
- The finish milestone or finish activity, which has no successors.

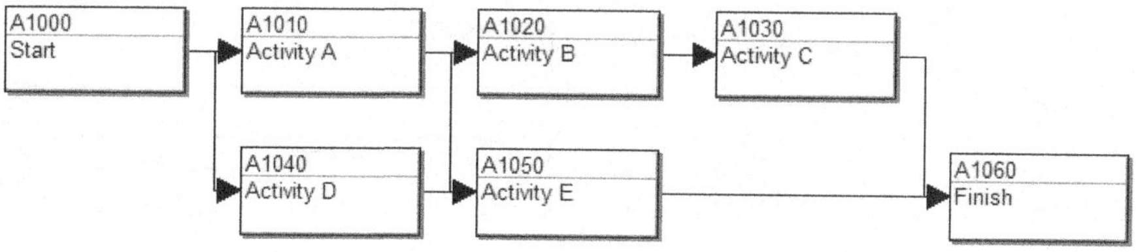

When a closed network is not established then the Critical Path, Total Float and Free Float will not calculate correctly

The project's logic must not loop back on itself. Looping occurs if the logic states that A preceded B, B preceded C, and C preceded A. That is not a logical project situation and will cause the software to generate an error comment during network calculations.

Thus, when the logic is correctly applied, a delay to an activity will delay all its successor activities and delay the project end date when there is insufficient spare slippage time to accommodate the delay. This spare time is normally called **Float** but note that Microsoft Project uses the term **Slack** for **Float**.

2.4.7 Scheduling the Project

The software calculates the shortest time in which the project may be completed, Activities are moved forward in time until they meet a Relationship or Constraint or a calendar nonwork time. Un-started activities without logic or constraints are scheduled to start at the Project Start Date or as permitted by calendar nonwork times.

Scheduling the project will identify the **Critical Path(s)** when there is a **Closed Network**. The Critical Path is the chain(s) of activities that takes the longest time to accomplish; a delay to any activity in the chain will delay the end date of the project. The calculated completion date depends on the critical activities starting and finishing on time. If any of them are delayed, the whole project will be delayed.

2.4.8 Critical Path

The Critical Path is the shortest duration that a project may be completed in and a delay to any activity will delay the end date of the project, activities A1000 to A1030 and A1060 below also shown in red are on the critical path:

Activity ID	Activity Name	Orig Dur	Start	Finish
A1000	Start	0d	01-Sep-14	
A1010	Activity A	5d	01-Sep-14	05-Sep-14
A1020	Activity B	5d	08-Sep-14	12-Sep-14
A1030	Activity C	5d	15-Sep-14	19-Sep-14
A1040	Activity D	2d	01-Sep-14	02-Sep-14
A1050	Activity E	2d	08-Sep-14	09-Sep-14
A1060	Finish	0d		19-Sep-14

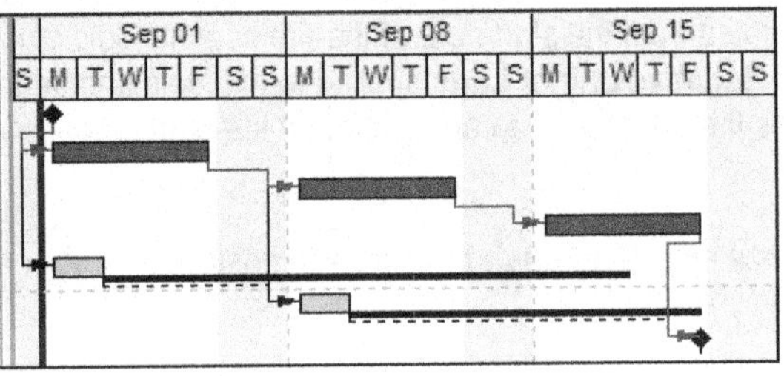

2.4.9 Total Float

Total Float is the amount of time an activity may be delayed without extending the project end date.

- An activity with Total Float may delay another activity,
- May be displayed in a column and in the Gantt Chart, as per the thin black bar below and
- May be negative.

Activity ID	Activity Name	Orig Dur	Start	Finish	Total Float
A1000	Start	0d	01-Sep-14		0d
A1010	Activity A	5d	01-Sep-14	05-Sep-14	0d
A1020	Activity B	5d	08-Sep-14	12-Sep-14	0d
A1030	Activity C	5d	15-Sep-14	19-Sep-14	0d
A1040	Activity D	2d	01-Sep-14	02-Sep-14	11d
A1050	Activity E	2d	08-Sep-14	09-Sep-14	8d
A1060	Finish	0d		19-Sep-14	0d

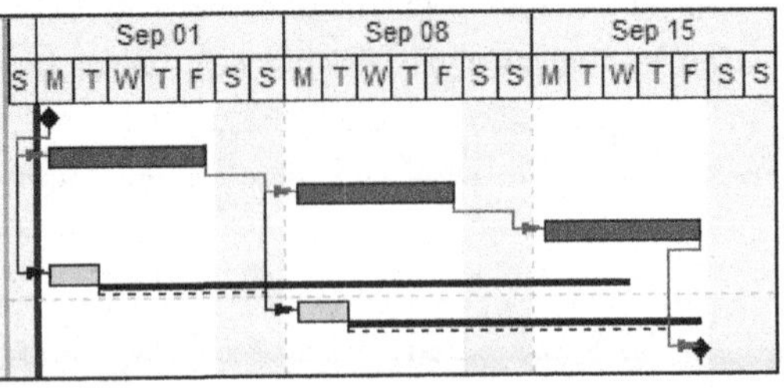

2.4.10 Free Float

The Free Float is the amount of time an activity may be delayed without delaying another activity.

- Displayed only in a column and
- Is never in the negative.

Activity ID	Activity Name	Orig Dur	Start	Finish	Total Float	Free Float
A1000	Start	0d	01-Sep-14		0d	0d
A1010	Activity A	5d	01-Sep-14	05-Sep-14	0d	0d
A1020	Activity B	5d	08-Sep-14	12-Sep-14	0d	0d
A1030	Activity C	5d	15-Sep-14	19-Sep-14	0d	0d
A1040	Activity D	2d	01-Sep-14	02-Sep-14	11d	3d
A1050	Activity E	2d	08-Sep-14	09-Sep-14	8d	8d
A1060	Finish	0d		19-Sep-14	0d	0d

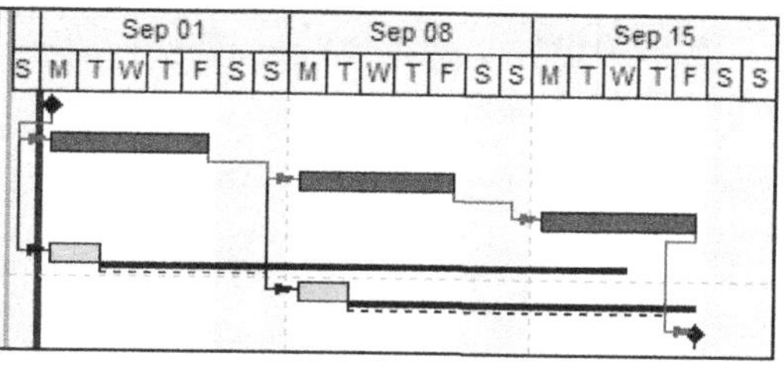

P6 does not display Free Float as a bar.

2.4.11 Relationship Colors

Relationship colors in P6 may not be formatted as with most other software:

- Solid Red are Critical and normally do not have Total Float,
- Solid Black are Driving Non-Critical and their successors have Total Float,
- Dotted Black are Non-Driving Non-Critical and their predecessors have Free Float.

Activity ID	Activity Name	Orig Dur	Start	Finish	Total Float	Free Float
A1000	Start	0d	01-Sep-14		0d	0d
A1010	Activity A	5d	01-Sep-14	05-Sep-14	0d	0d
A1020	Activity B	5d	08-Sep-14	12-Sep-14	0d	0d
A1030	Activity C	5d	15-Sep-14	19-Sep-14	0d	0d
A1040	Activity D	2d	01-Sep-14	02-Sep-14	11d	3d
A1050	Activity E	2d	08-Sep-14	09-Sep-14	8d	8d
A1060	Finish	0d		19-Sep-14	0d	0d

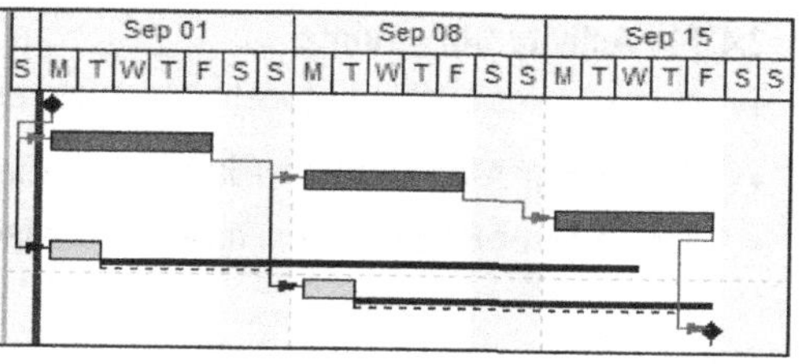

2.4.12 Constraints Types

There are two types of constraints:

- **Project Constraints** which includes the **Project Start Date** and **Project Finish Date**, and
- **Activity Constraints**; the two most common are **Start On or After** (Early Start) **and Finish On or Before** (Late Finish).

External dependencies are applied to a schedule using **Constraints** and these may model the impact of events outside the logical sequence of activities. A constraint would be imposed to specific dates such as the availability of a facility to start work or the required completion date of a project. Constraints should be cross-referenced to the supporting documentation, such as Milestone Dates from contract documentation, using the **Notebook Topics** function.

2.4.13 Project Constraints

A **Project Start Date** called **Project Planned Start** in P6 is the earliest date that any activity may be scheduled to start. An activity will start on the **Project Start Date** unless one of the following stop the activity starting on the **Project Start Date**:

- There is a Calendar Non Work time, or
- A constraint, or
- A relationship.

A **Project Must Finish Date**s optional, but once set this controls Total Float (often referred to as Float in P6).

When a **Project Must Finish Date** constraint is assigned then Total Float is calculated to this date.

- The picture shows a project with a Project Finish date on Friday 26 September developing 5 days Total Float.

Activity ID	Activity Name	Orig Dur	Start	Finish	Total Float
A1000	Start MS	0d	01-Sep-14		5d
A1010	Activity A	5d	01-Sep-14	05-Sep-14	5d
A1020	Activity B	5d	08-Sep-14	12-Sep-14	5d
A1030	Activity C	5d	15-Sep-14	19-Sep-14	5d
A1040	Activity D	2d	01-Sep-14	02-Sep-14	16d
A1050	Activity E	2d	08-Sep-14	09-Sep-14	13d
A1060	Finish MS	0d		19-Sep-14	5d

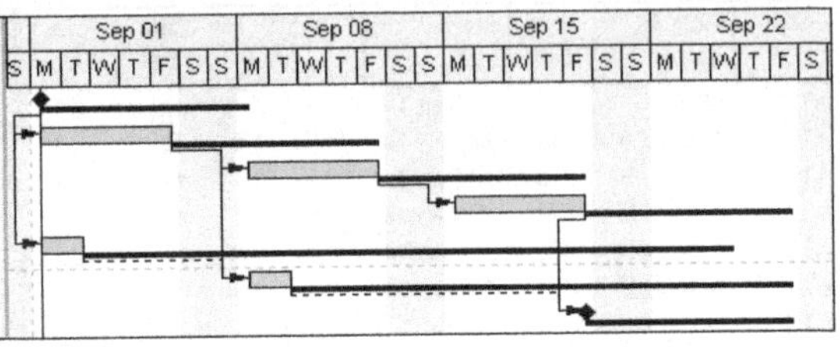

- The picture shows a schedule with a Project Finish date of Friday 12,
- This is earlier than the calculated finish date, thus calculating 5 days Negative Float:

Activity ID	Activity Name	Orig Dur	Start	Finish	Total Float
A1000	Start MS	0d	01-Sep-14		-5d
A1010	Activity A	5d	01-Sep-14	05-Sep-14	-5d
A1020	Activity B	5d	08-Sep-14	12-Sep-14	-5d
A1030	Activity C	5d	15-Sep-14	19-Sep-14	-5d
A1040	Activity D	2d	01-Sep-14	02-Sep-14	6d
A1050	Activity E	2d	08-Sep-14	09-Sep-14	3d
A1060	Finish MS	0d		19-Sep-14	-5d

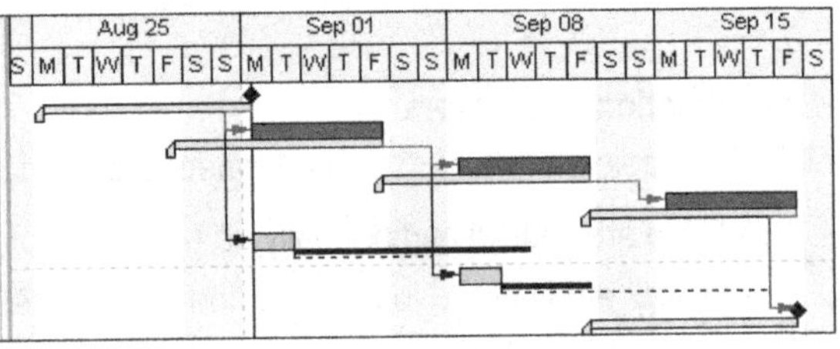

2.4.14 Activity Constraints

Typical examples of activity constraints would be:

- **Start on or After** for the availability of a site to commence work, and
- **Finish on or Before** for the date that a total project must be completed or handed over.

Activity Early Start Constraint

- An activity will no longer start on the Data Date when a **Start On or After** constraint is assigned
- This is more commonly known as an **Early Start** constraint.

Activity ID	Activity Name	Primary Constraint	Primary Constraint Date
A1000	Start	Start On or After	08-Sep-14 08
A1010	Activity A		
A1020	Activity B		
A1030	Activity C		
A1040	Activity D		
A1050	Activity E		
A1060	Finish		

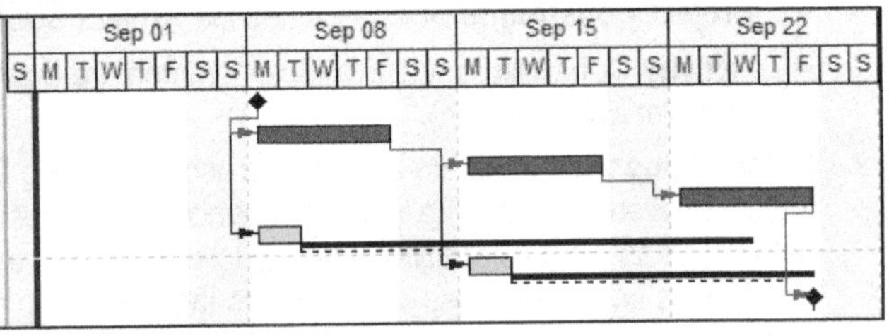

In P6 the time must always be displayed as P6 will often set constraints at 00:00hrs which is midnight and is not very often an appropriate time to set constraints.

Activity Late Finish Constraint

- This picture below shows a schedule with an additional **Finish Date On or Before** constraint assigned 4 days earlier than the calculated finish date,
- Thus Negative Float is created, representing the amount of time that needs to be caught up.
- This is more commonly known as a Late Finish constraint:

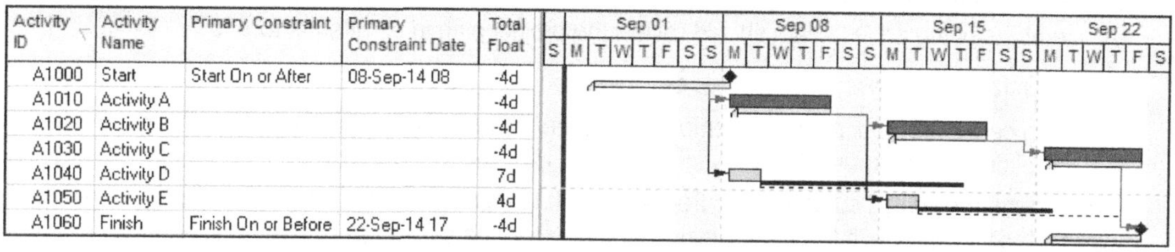

Activity ID	Activity Name	Primary Constraint	Primary Constraint Date	Total Float
A1000	Start	Start On or After	08-Sep-14 08	-4d
A1010	Activity A			-4d
A1020	Activity B			-4d
A1030	Activity C			-4d
A1040	Activity D			7d
A1050	Activity E			4d
A1060	Finish	Finish On or Before	22-Sep-14 17	-4d

- The picture below shows a schedule with a **Finish Date On or Before** constraint assigned after the calculated finish date,
- The Total Float is **NOT** calculated to the constraint date when the constraint date is **LATER** the calculated Early Finish.
- Positive Total Float is **NOT** created and a critical path of zero days float is maintained:

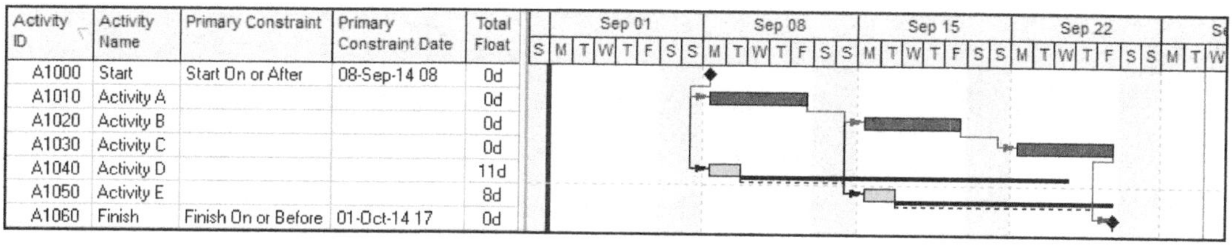

Activity ID	Activity Name	Primary Constraint	Primary Constraint Date	Total Float
A1000	Start	Start On or After	08-Sep-14 08	0d
A1010	Activity A			0d
A1020	Activity B			0d
A1030	Activity C			0d
A1040	Activity D			11d
A1050	Activity E			8d
A1060	Finish	Finish On or Before	01-Oct-14 17	0d

2.4.15 Risk Analysis

The process of planning a project may identify risks, so a formal risk analysis should be considered. A risk analysis may identify risk mitigation activities that should be added to the schedule before it is submitted for approval.

2.4.16 Contingent Time

The addition of contingent time should be considered when submitting a schedule for approval. Estimates usually have contingency and if this money is to be expended then an allowance for time to spend the contingent funds needs to be made. Contingent time may be added to a schedule in a number of ways:

- Insert one or more contingent time activities in the project. These would be adjusted in length as the project progresses to maintain the planned end date.
- Assign work days in the calendar nonwork days. For example, a building project could be scheduled on a 5-day per week basis, knowing that work will be undertaken on the Saturday.
- Increase the activity durations by a factor, this will affect either the resource Units per Timeperiod or total resource Units and should not be used on a resourced schedule.
- Assign positive lags between activities, although this is not recommended by the author.

2.4.17 Formatting the Display – Layouts and Filters

There are tools to manipulate and display the activities to suit the project reporting requirements. These functions are covered in the **Group, Sort and Layouts and the Filters** chapters.

2.4.18 Printing and Reports

There are software features that enable you to present the information in a clear and concise manner to communicate the requirements to all project members. These functions are covered in the **Printing and Reports** chapter.

2.4.19 Issuing the Plan

All members of the project team should review the project plan in an attempt to:

- Optimize the process and methods employed, and
- Gain consensus among team members as to the project's logic, durations, and Project Breakdown Structures.

Team members should communicate frequently with each other about their expectations of the project while providing each with the opportunity to contribute to the schedule and further improve the outcome.

2.5 *Level 2 – Monitoring Progress Without Resources*

2.5.1 Setting the Baseline

The optimized and agreed-to plan is used as a baseline for measuring progress and monitoring change. The software may record the baseline dates of each activity for comparison against actual progress during the life of the project.

2.5.2 Tracking Progress

The schedule should be **Updated** (progressed) on a regular basis and progress recorded at that point. The date on which progress is reported is known by a number of different terms such as **Data Date**, **Update Date**, **Time Now** and **Status Date**. The **Current Data Date** is the field Primavera uses to record this date. The **Data Date** is **NOT** the date that the report is printed but rather the date that reflects when the update information was gathered.

Whatever the frequency chosen for updating, you will have to collect the following activity information in order to update a schedule:

- Completed activities
  - Actual Start date
  - Actual Finish dates
- In-progress activities
  - Actual Start date
  - Percentage Completed
  - Duration or Expected Finish Date of the Activity
- Un-started work
  - Any revisions to activities that have not started
  - New activities representing scope changes
  - Revisions to logic that represent changes to the plan

The schedule may be updated after this information has been collected. The recorded progress is compared to the **Baseline** dates, either graphically or by using columns of data, such as the **Baseline Finish Variance** column:

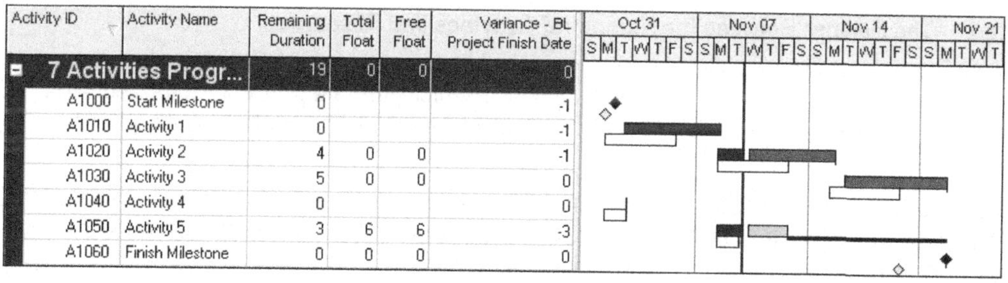

Activity ID	Activity Name	Remaining Duration	Total Float	Free Float	Variance - BL Project Finish Date
7 Activities Progr...		19	0	0	0
A1000	Start Milestone	0			-1
A1010	Activity 1	0			-1
A1020	Activity 2	4	0	0	-1
A1030	Activity 3	5	0	0	0
A1040	Activity 4	0			0
A1050	Activity 5	3	6	6	-3
A1060	Finish Milestone	0	0	0	0

2.5.3 Corrective Action

At this point, it may be necessary to further optimize the schedule to bring the project back on track by discussing the schedule with the appropriate project team members. The possible options are:

- Reduce the contingent time allowance.
- Assign a negative lag on a Finish to Start relationship, which enables a successor to commence before a predecessor is completed.
- Change relationships to allow activities to be executed in parallel.
- Reduce the durations of activities. In a resourced schedule, this could be achieved by increasing the number of resources assigned to an activity.
- Work longer hours per day or days per week by editing the calendars, or
- Reduce the scope and delete activities.

2.6 *Level 3 – Scheduling With Resources, Roles and Expenses*

2.6.1 Estimating or Planning for Control

There are two modes that the software may use at Level 3.

- **Estimating**. In this mode, the objective is to create a schedule with costs that are used only as an estimate. The schedule will never be updated. Activities may have many resources assigned to them to develop an accurate cost estimate and include many items that would never be updated in the process of updating a schedule.
- **Planning for Control**. In this mode, the intention is to assign actual units (hours) and costs to resources, then calculate units and costs to completion, and possibly conduct an Earned Value analysis. In this situation, it is important to ensure that the minimum number of resources are assigned to activities, and preferably only one resource assigned to each activity. The process of updating a schedule becomes extremely difficult and time consuming when a schedule has many resources per activity. The scheduler is then under threat of becoming a timekeeper and may lose sight of other important functions, such as calculating the forecast to complete and the project finish date.

2.6.2 The Balance Between the Number of Activities and Resources

When Planning for Control on large or complex schedules, it is important to maintain a balance between the number of activities and the number of resources that are planned and tracked. As a rule, the more activities a schedule has, the fewer resources should be created and assigned to activities.

When a schedule contains a large number of activities and a large number of resources assigned to each activity, the result may be that no members of the project team are able to understand the schedule and the scheduler is unable to maintain it.

Instead of assigning individual resources, such as people by name, consider using "Skills" or "Trades," and on very large projects use "Crews" or "Teams."

This technique is not so important when you use a schedule for estimating the direct cost of a project (by assigning costs to the resources) or if you are not using the schedule to track a project's progress (such as a schedule that is used to support written proposals).

Therefore, it is more important to minimize the number of resources in large schedules that will be updated regularly, because updating every resource assigned to each activity at each schedule update is very time consuming.

2.6.3 Creating and Using Resources

First, one would usually establish a resource pool by entering all the required project resources into a hierarchical table in the software. The required quantity of each resource is assigned to the activities. In an Enterprise environment these resources may already be defined for you.

Entering a cost rate for each resource enables you to conduct a resource cost analysis, such as comparing the cost of supplementing overloaded resources against the cost of extending the project deadline.

Estimates and time-phased cash flows may be produced from this resource/cost data.

2.6.4 Creating and Using Roles

Primavera has an additional function titled **Roles**, which is used for planning and managing resources.

- A Role is a skill or trade or job description and may be used as an alternative to resources during the planning period of a project.
- Roles are defined in a hierarchical structure and hold a **Proficiency Level**.
- Roles may be assigned to activities in a way similar to how resources are assigned. Roles can be replaced later by resources after it has been decided who is going to be assigned the work.
- Primavera Version 5.0 introduced a function allowing a Role to be assigned a rate.

2.6.5 The Relationship Between Resources and Roles

Primavera has the ability to define roles and associate them with resources. A role is a job title, trade or skill and may have many resources. A multi-skilled resource may have multiple roles. For example, a role may be a Clerical Assistant and there may be five clerical assistants in a company who would be assigned the Clerical Assistant Role. If one clerical assistant were also a data entry person, then this resource would be assigned two roles: Clerical Assistant and Data Entry.

2.6.6 Activity Type and Duration Type

Activities may be assigned an **Activity Type** and **Duration Type**,, which affect how resources are calculated. Additional software features enable the user to more accurately model real-life situations. These features are covered in the **Assigning Roles, Resources and Expenses** chapter.

2.6.7 Budgets

The Budget function enables Top-Down Budgeting at a summary level against each EPS Node in an accounting style. Budgets may be compared to the detailed estimates calculated after resources have been assigned to Activities. The Budget function is not covered in detail in this book.

2.6.8 Resource Usage Profiles and Tables

These features enable the display and analysis of project resource requirements both in tables and graphs.

The data may be exported to Excel or reports run for further analysis and presentation.

2.6.9 Resource Optimization

The schedule may now have to be resource optimized to:

- Reduce peaks and smooth the resource requirements, or
- Reduce resource demand to the available number of resources, or
- Reduce demand to an available cash flow when a project is financed by a customer.

Leveling is defined as delaying activities until resources become available. There are several methods of delaying activities, and thus leveling a schedule, which are outlined in the **Resource Optimization** chapter.

2.7 *Level 4 – Monitoring and Controlling a Resourced Schedule*

2.7.1 Monitoring Projects with Resources

When you update a project with resources, you will need to collect some additional information:

- The quantities and/or costs spent to date per activity for each resource, and
- The quantities and/or costs required per resource to complete each activity.

You may then update a resourced schedule with this data.

After a schedule has been updated, then a review of the future resource requirements, project end date, and cash flows may be made.

Updating a resourced project is time consuming and requires experience and a good understanding of how the software calculates a schedule. Ideally, this should only be attempted by experienced users or by a novice under the guidance of an experienced user.

2.7.2 Controlling a Project with Resources

At this point, it is possible to undertake a great deal of analysis and often Earned Value Performance Measurement techniques are used.

3 STARTING UP AND NAVIGATION

3.1 Logging In

After clicking on the icon or menu item on your desktop to start Primavera, you will be presented with the **Login** form.

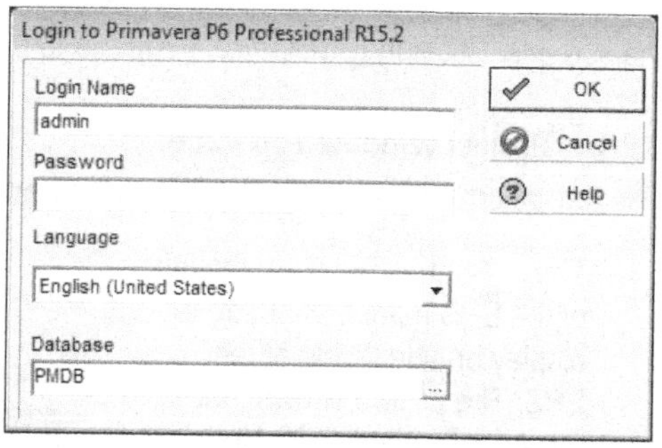

When you have more than one database to select from, you may click on the ... icon under **Database**. This opens the **Edit Database Connections** form where you may select an alternative database to open:

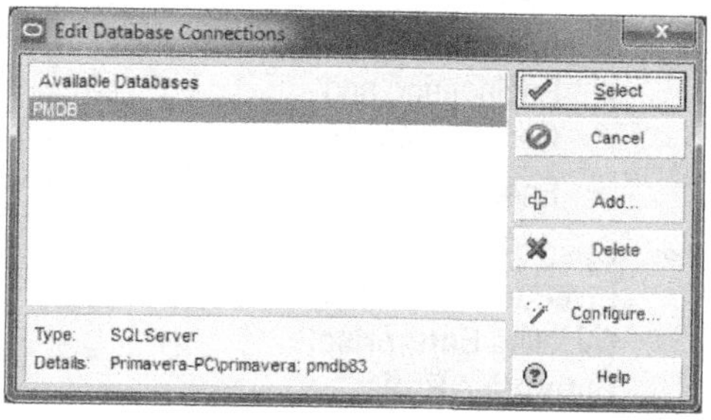

- Select the required database from the list of databases,
- Click the Select icon,
- Enter your Login Name and Password, which are case sensitive, and then
- Click OK to open the selected database.

Version 15.2 move the selection of the menu language from the **Tools** menu to the **Login screen**.

You screen may look like the picture below depending on what version of the software you have (EPPM Optional Client or Professional Project Manager), how your system has been configured, what industry version you are using. The Enterprise menu item has been opened in the Professional Project Manager:

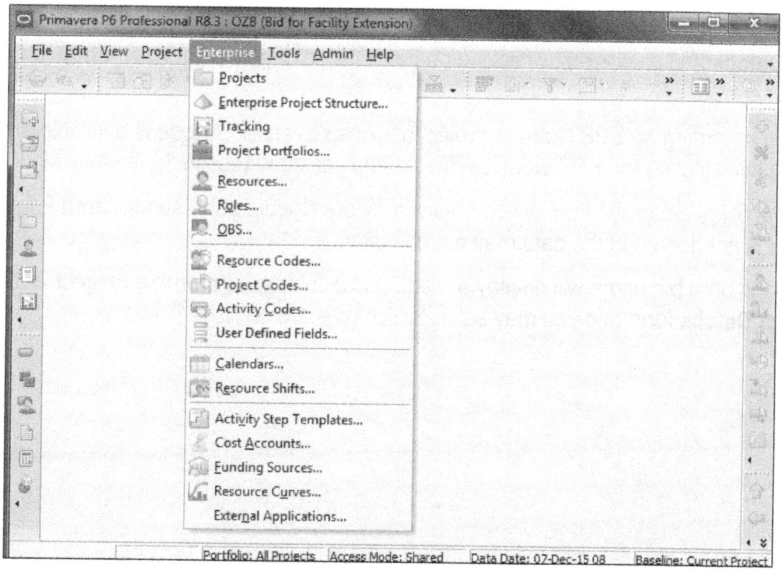

It is suggested that you select from the **User Preferences...**, **Application** tab either the **Projects** if you work on different projects all the time or the **Activities** option if you work on the same project all the time.

3.2 *The Projects Window*

The sample database supplied with Primavera will be used to demonstrate how to navigate around the screens. Click on **Enterprise**, **Projects** to open the **Projects Window**.

3.2.1 Project Window Top Pane

The top window displays the **Enterprise Project Structure** (EPS):

- The [+] and [-] icons to the left of the EPS names are used to display or hide levels of the EPS. The picture shows that the **All Initiatives** EPS Node has two projects.
  - ➢ Engineering and Construction, and
  - ➢ Energy Services.
- Open the **Enterprise Project Structure (EPS)** form by selecting **Enterprise, Enterprise Project Structure...** from the menu.

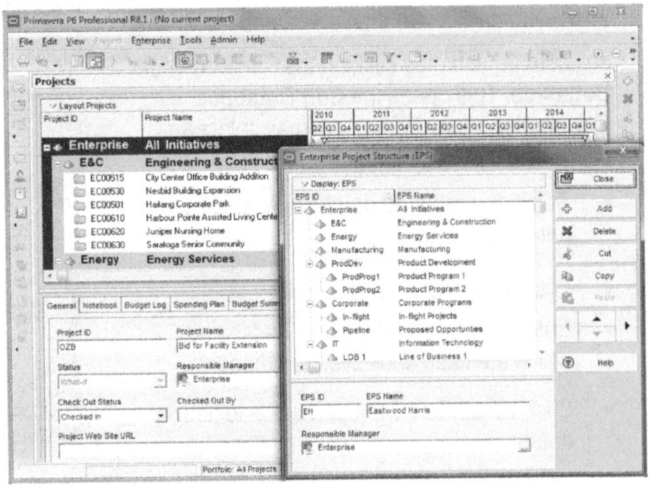

- It is now clear which entries are EPS Nodes and which are Projects.
- The menu commands **View**, **Expand All**, **Collapse All** and **Collapse To...** will summarize the bands to the required level in the EPS.

3.2.2 Project Window Bottom Pane Details Tab

The bottom window **Details** tab may be hidden by clicking on the icon or selecting **View, Show on Bottom**, **Details** and displayed by clicking on the icon or selecting **View, Show on Bottom**, **Details**.

Information regarding an EPS Node or project assigned to an EPS Node is available at the bottom of the screen by selecting the EPS Node or Project and selecting tabs in the bottom window.

Many of the fields are grayed out which means they are calculated or summarized from other data or the project is not open and the data may not be edited.

Right-clicking on a tab name will display a menu and selecting **Customize Project Details** will open the **Project Details** form and you may select which tabs are displayed.

3.3 Opening One or More Projects

Enterprise and Project data is accessed in the **Projects Window**.

To access Project activity information such as activities, resources and relationships, a project must be opened and the **Activities Window** displayed.

One or more projects may be opened at the same time by

- Selecting:
  - One or more projects and/or
  - One or more EPS Nodes,
- Then, right-clicking and selecting **Open Project**, or
- Selecting **Ctl+O**.

Alternatively select **File**, **Open...** to open the **Open** form:

- The **Open** form displays the access options for opening a project as **Exclusive**, **Shared or Read Only** which are not available with the other methods of opening projects:

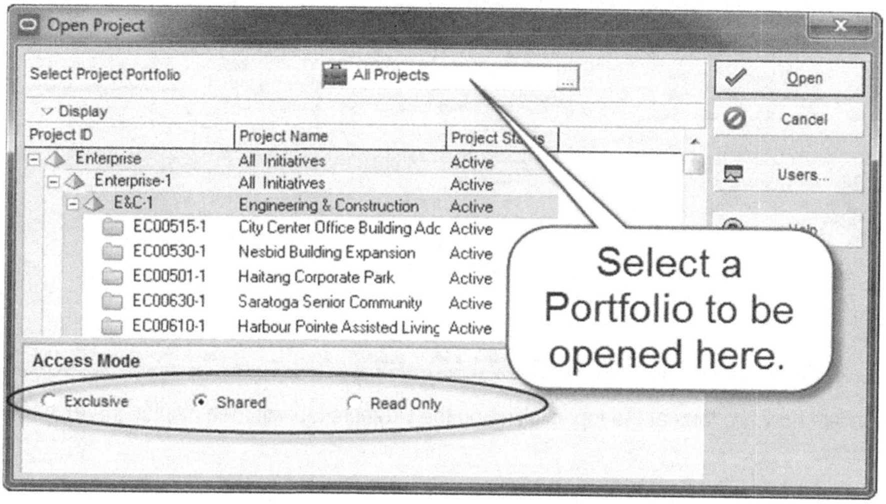

Recently opened projects may be opened from the **File, Recent Projects**, a new function in Version 8.1.

A project may only be opened as **Exclusive** (meaning that only the current user may edit it) by using the **File**, **Open**...form. All other methods will result in the project being opened in the **Shared** mode and all users with access to the project may open and edit the project(s) at the same time. The **Shared** option may result in one user's edits being overwritten by another user's edits, depending on who saved the project and when. A project that is opened in the **Shared** mode by multiple users with different **User Preferences Time Units** will result in the users calculating different values for Activity, WBS Nodes and Project durations in days.

If more than one project is to be opened at a time then it is **VERY IMPORTANT** that the **Multiple Project Scheduling** chapter is read and understood.

3.4 *Displaying the Activities Window*

To open the **Activities Window**:

- Select **Project**, **Activities**, or
- Click on the icon:

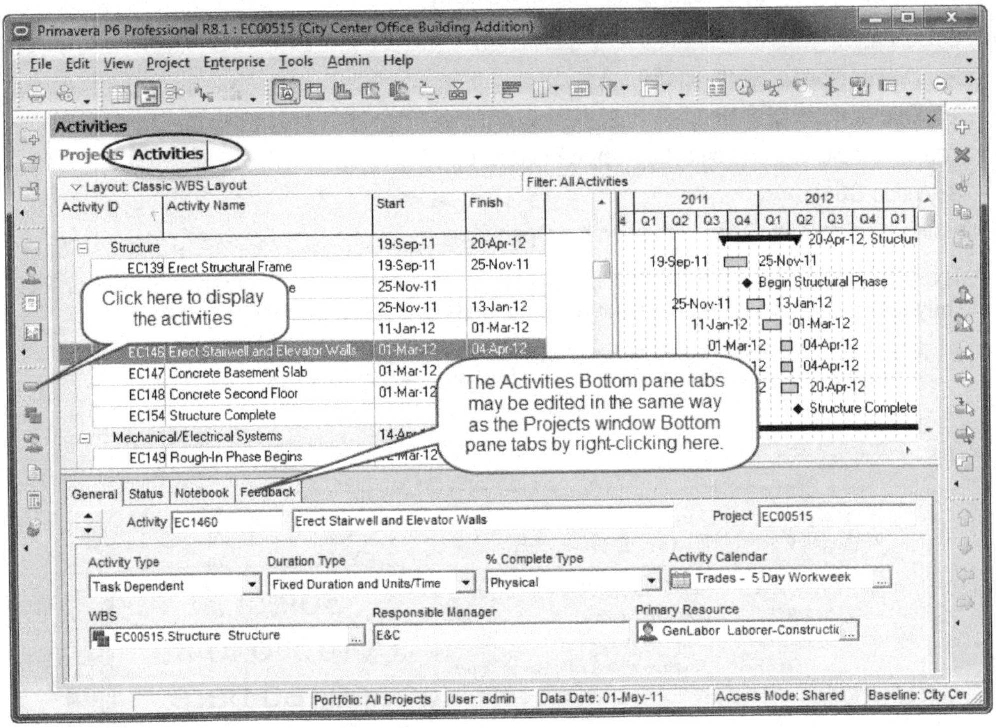

- There are now two tabs at the top; clicking on the Projects tab will then display the **Projects Window**.

3.5 *Opening a Portfolio*

The **Portfolio** function reduces the number of Projects that are viewed in the **Projects Window**:

- To create a **Portfolio** select **Enterprise**, **Project Portfolios...** and open the **Portfolio** form.
- Create a portfolio and add projects using the **Portfolio** form.
- A **Portfolio** may be **Global** and all users have access or **User** and just available to that user.
- The **File**, **Open...** (project) form also enables the selection of a **Portfolio** which reduces the number of projects that are displayed in the **Open** (project)form.
- After a **Portfolio** has been selected using **File**, **Select Project Portfolio...** only those projects in the Portfolio will be displayed in the **Projects Window**.

3.6 *Top and Bottom Panes of Windows*

Windows such as the **Projects**, **WBS**, **Activities**, **Resources** and **Resource Assignments** have **Top** and **Bottom Panes**, and these may be formatted to meet your requirements.

Layouts are similar to **Microsoft Project** views and are created to save most of the formatting in the **Top** and **Bottom Panes** in most windows, such as the **Activities** and **Project** windows. Attributes such displayed tabs, columns, Timescale, print settings, Grouping and Sorting, are saved as part of a **Layout**. These **Layouts** do not save the date and time formatting, which is set by each user from the **Edit**, **User Preferences**, **Time Units** and **Dates** tabs.

A **Layout** may be copied or opened by either:

- Selecting **View**, **Layout** and selecting the appropriate command,

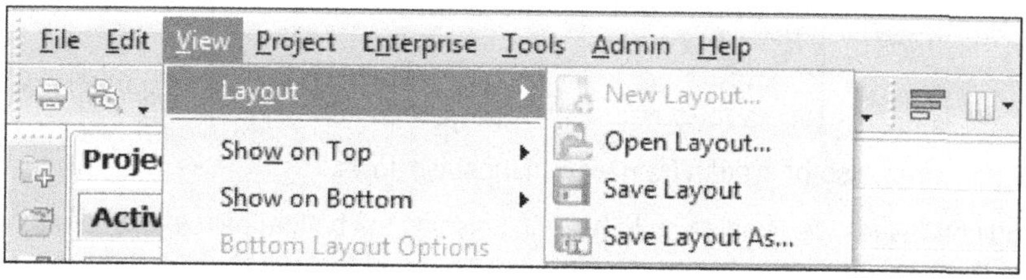

- Or clicking on the down arrow found under the Window tab name:

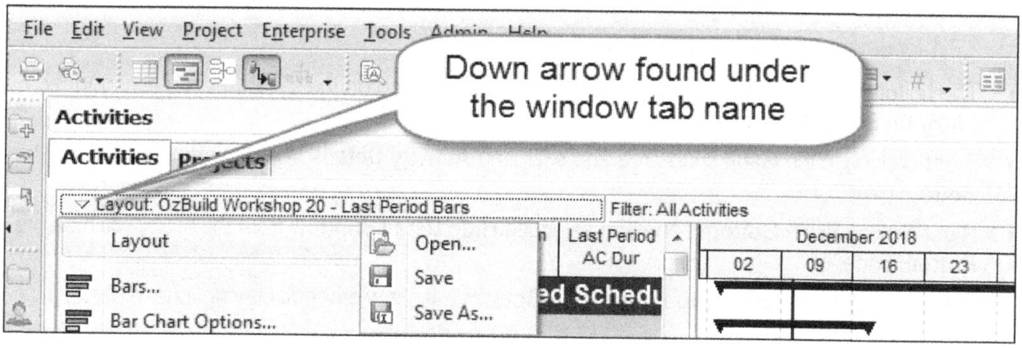

- The Open Layout command lists the available systems Layouts:

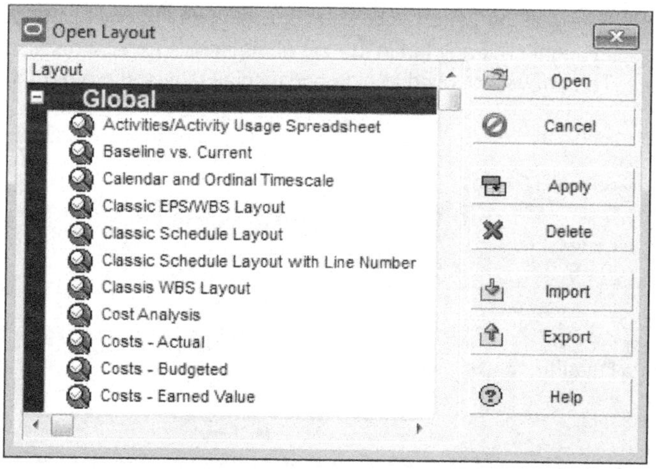

- The Save As Layout command allows Layouts to be saved as:
  - **All Users**, which makes them **Global Layouts** which are available to everyone,

- **Another User**, which allows you to transfer your layout to someone else,
- **Current User**, which allows a layout to be copied to create a new layout for the user, and
- **Project** layout, which creates a layout that is available to anyone who opens the project.

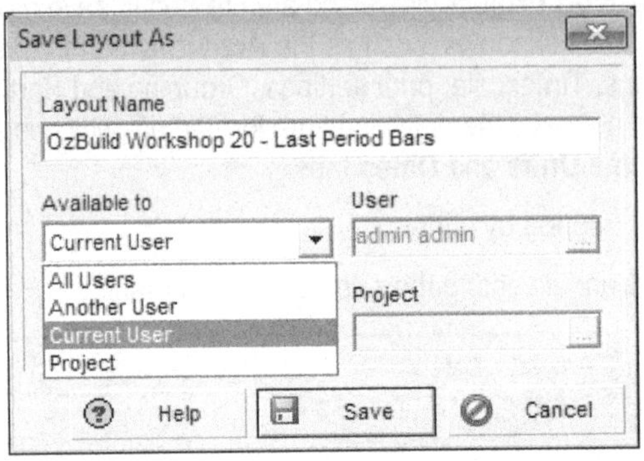

The Bottom pane may also be hidden from view in most windows.

The following commands will enable you to hide and display the bottom panes; they are the similar to the **Projects Window** discussed earlier.

- The bottom window **Details** tab may be hidden by clicking on the icon or selecting **View, Show on Bottom**, **No Bottom Layout**. You may need to add the buttons to your toolbar, see paragraph 3.7.1 for details on how to add buttons.
- The bottom window **Details** tab may be displayed by clicking on the icon or selecting **View, Show on Bottom**, **Details**.
- Right-clicking in the Gantt chart area and selecting **Activity Details** from the menu will display the **Bottom** pane, or
- Right-clicking in the **Bottom** pane and selecting **Hide Detail Window** from the menu will hide the **Bottom** pane, or
- Selecting **View, Show on Top** or **Show on Bottom** will show other display options for the top and bottom panes.

The following commands will enable you to format the top and bottom panes.

- Some **Details** forms may be formatted to display only the tabs that are of use to the scheduler.
- To format the display, right-click any tab in the top of the details pane and select **Customize Project Details....** The arrows are used to hide and display tabs and reorder them.

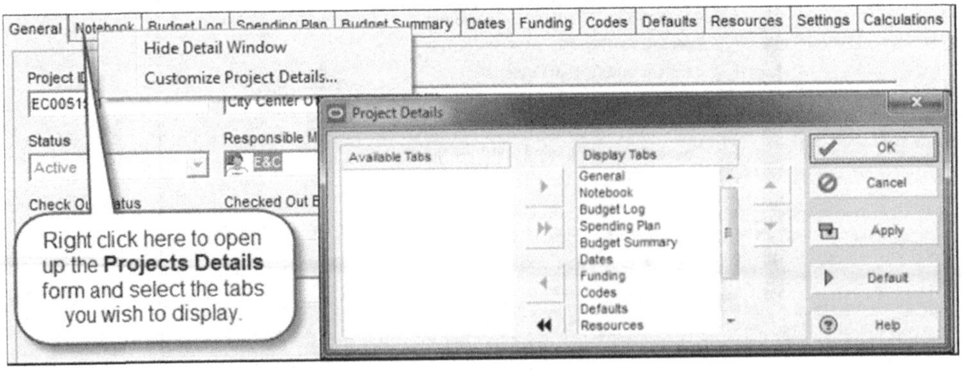

It is recommended that you remove all the tabs that you are not using so the screen is not so busy and it is simpler to find commands.

3.7 User Interface Update

The user interface in both client versions has been overhauled and now allows user defined toolbars and menus:

3.7.1 New Customizable Toolbars

All the old P6 toolbars have been removed. The new toolbars operate in a similar way to Microsoft Office 2003 and many toolbar icons have been changed.

Toolbars will not be covered in detail but significant productivity improvements may be made by ensuring that functions frequently used are available on a toolbar.

- There are many built-in toolbars in Primavera P6. These may be displayed or hidden by:
  - Using the command **View**, **Toolbars** or right-clicking in the toolbar area and then checking or un-checking the required boxes to display or hide the toolbars, or
  - Using the command **View**, **Toolbars**, **Customize...**, **Toolbars** tab and then un-checking the required boxes to display or hide the toolbars.

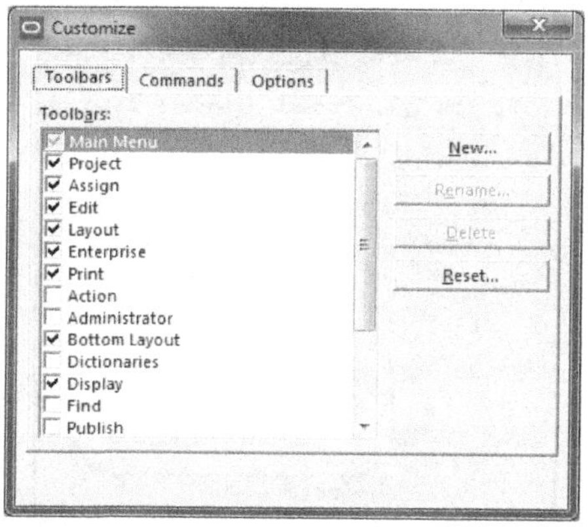

- Individual toolbar icons may be reset to default by selecting **View**, **Toolbars**, **Customize...**, **Toolbar** tab and clicking on Reset... .
- Icons may be added to a bar by selecting **View**, **Toolbars**, **Customize...**, **Toolbar** tab **Commands** tab. **Toolbar Icons** may be selected from the dialog box and dragged onto any toolbar.

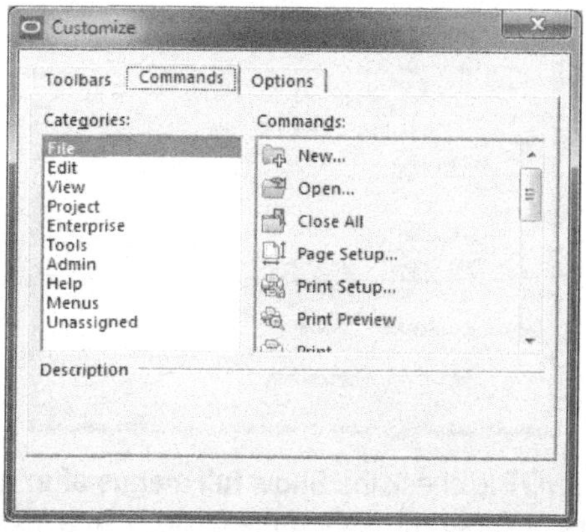

- Icons may be removed from the toolbars after the **Customize** (Toolbar) form is opened by holding down the left mouse button on the icon and dragging them off the toolbar.

- Icons may also be added or removed when a toolbar is dragged into the center of a window. This reveals a further menu for editing the icons:

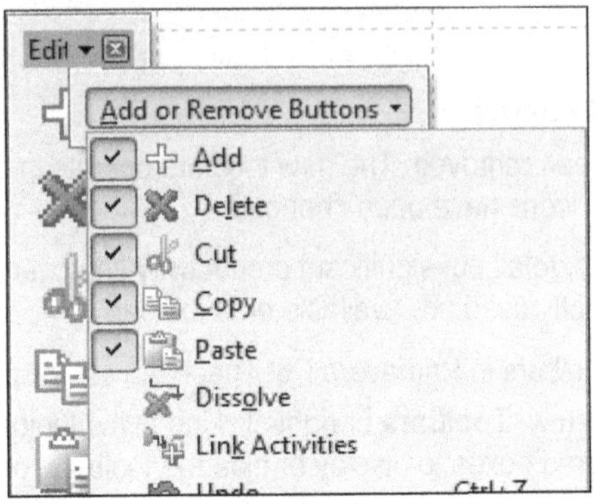

- Icons may also be added or removed by clicking on the down arrow at the right-hand end of each toolbar:

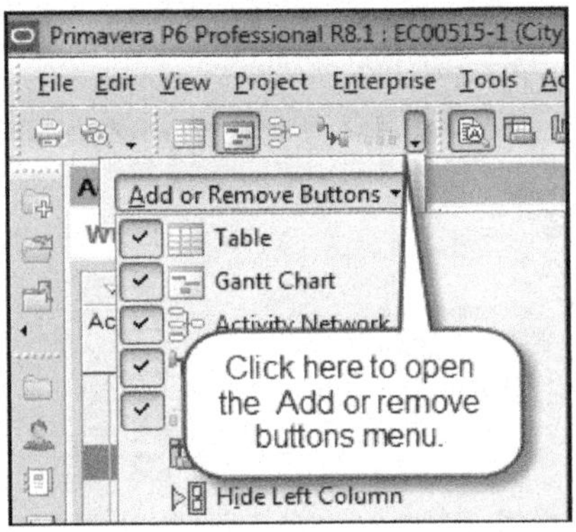

- All toolbar icons may be reset to default by selecting **View, Rest All Toolbars**.
- Toolbars may be locked so they may not be dragged by selecting **View, Lock All Toolbars**.
- Other toolbar display options are found under **View**, **Toolbars...**, **Customize** and then selecting the **Options** tab.

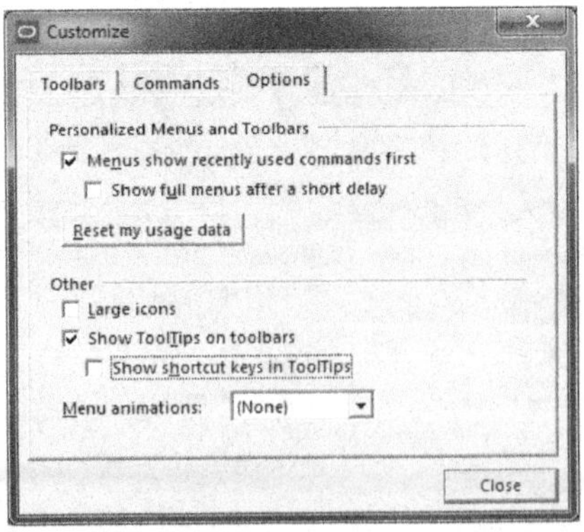

It is recommended **NOT** to check the S**how full menus after a short delay** option in the **View**, **Toolbars...**, **Customize**, **Options** tab to ensure full menus are always displayed. This saves time waiting for the menu item you require to be displayed. The author found that this function did not work at the time of writing this book.

3.7.2 Customizable menus

The menus may also be edited:

- Open the **Customize** Formby selecting **View**, **Toolbars...**, **Customize**,
- Then with the **Customize** form open move the mouse to the menu on the top left-hand side of the screen,
- Right-click on a menu header to reveal a menu:

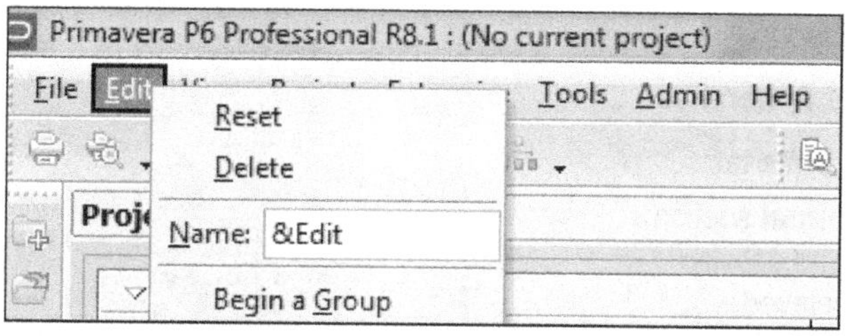

- Right-click on a menu item and you may now edit or drag the command up or down in order:

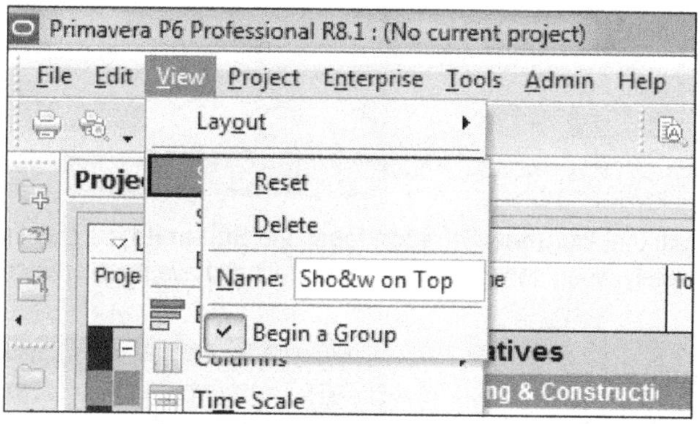

3.7.3 Status Bar

The Status bar is at the bottom of the screen and may be hidden or displayed by selecting **View**, **Status Bar**. It shows some useful information about the project you have open:

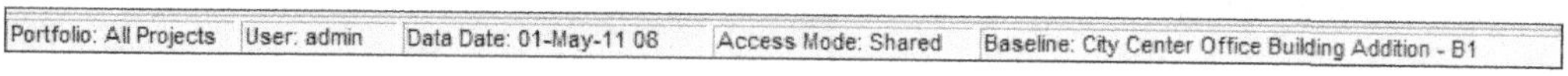

3.8 User Preferences

3.8.1 Time Unit Formatting

The **User Preferences** enable each user to select how some information is displayed or calculated. These are covered in detail in the **User and Administration Preferences and Advanced Scheduling Options** chapter.

To adjust how the date and time are displayed:

- Select **Edit**, **User Preferences...**,
- Select the **Time Units** tab,
- The **Duration Format** section determines how the activity durations are displayed,

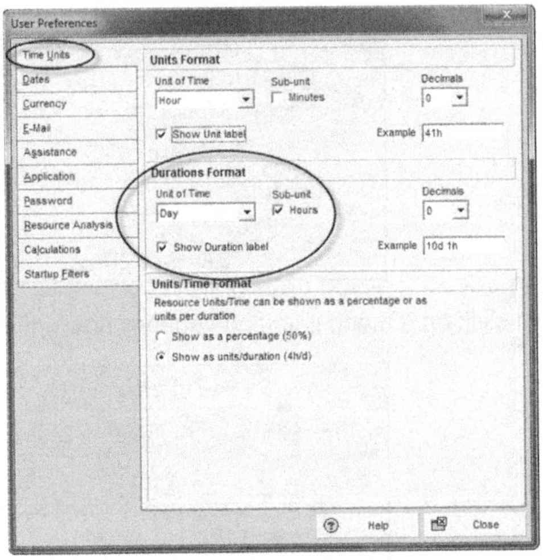

It is important that the **Show Duration label** and **Sub-units** are checked as you will see immediately when non round days for durations have been created.

3.8.2 Date Formatting

This is where you decide if the time is to be displayed:

- Select the **Dates** tab,
- Set the **Date Format**,
- Set the **Options**,
- Set the **Time** options.

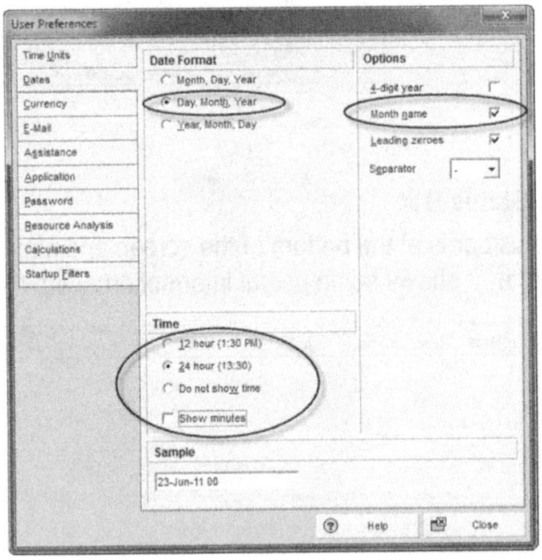

Date Format. It is strongly recommended using **Month name** on international projects so there is no confusion between the US mm/dd/yy format and the ROW (Rest of World) format of dd/mm/yy.

Time Units: It is **STRONGLY** recommended that the time is **ALWAYS** displayed in 24 hour format so the user knows the time of any selected date. This is because the software will often select 00:00,(the first minute of a day) when assigning dates. The author does not display minutes to keep the date column widths slightly narrower.

3.9 Starting Day of the Week

The default **First day of week** is often Sunday. Many people prefer to see Monday as the first day of the week because the calendar date in the weekly view is then Monday and is a work day, as per the picture below:

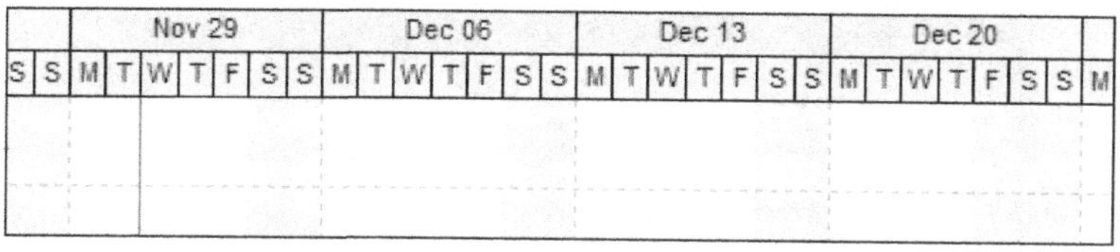

In the Professional Client the **Starting Day of the Week** may be set in the **Admin, Admin Preferences..., General** tab:

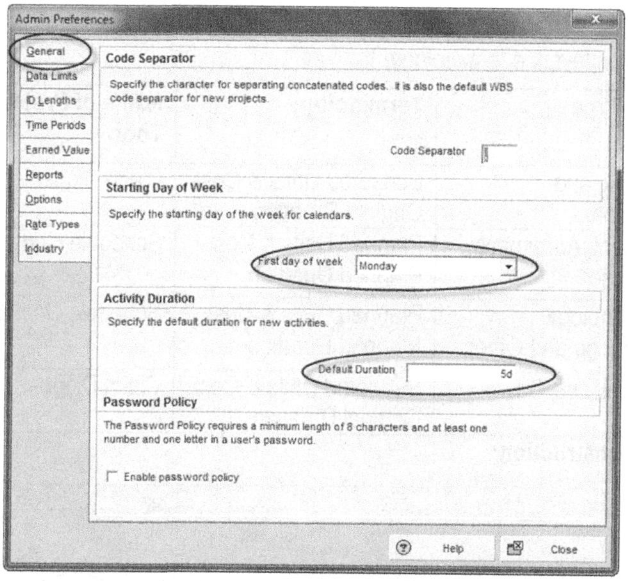

In the Optional Client the start day of the week is set by the database administrator from **Administer**, **Application Settings**, **General**:

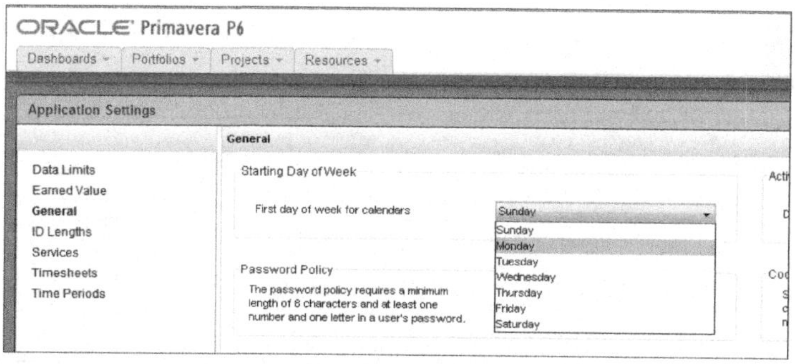

You must select **Save and Close** or your edits will be lost:

3.10 Admin Preferences – Set Industry Type

The Industry type determines the terminology used in some fields and in earlier versions was set when the software was loaded. This now may be set in the P6 Professional by selecting **Admin**, **Admin Preferences..., Industry** tab:

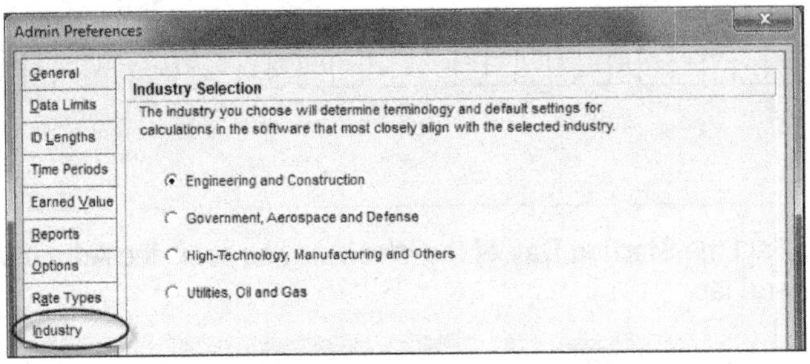

The following table displays the terminology:

Industry Type	Terminology	Name of Project Comparison Tool
Engineering and Construction	Budgeted Units & Cost Original Duration	Claim Digger
Government, Aerospace, and Defense	Planned Units & Cost Planned Duration	Schedule Comparison
High-Technology, Manufacturing and Others	Planned Units & Cost Planned Duration	Schedule Comparison
Utilities, Oil, and Gas	Budgeted Units & Cost Original Duration	Claim Digger

Engineering and Construction:

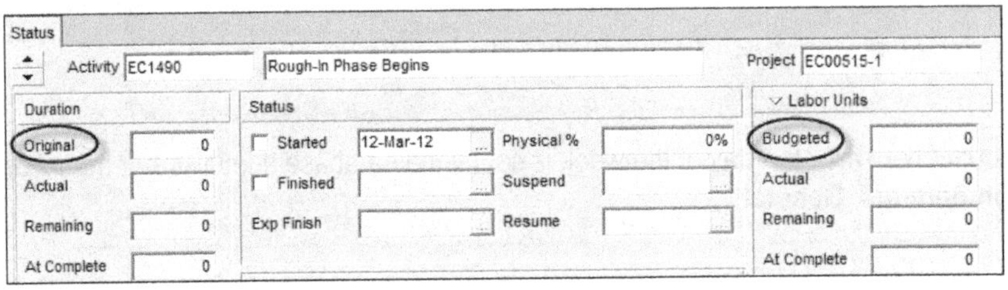

Government, Aerospace, and Defense:

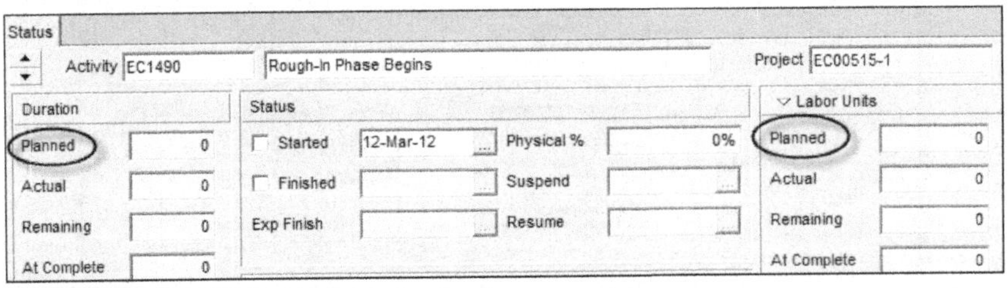

If a different Industry Type is selected then P6 has to be restarted to see the changes. The EPPM Web Client only uses Planned Units & Cost, Planned Duration and Schedule Comparison.

3.11 Application of Options within Forms

Primavera is consistent in the way the data in most forms may be Grouped, Sorted and Filtered. After the basics are understood, then as these principles may be applied to most forms you will find it easier to navigate around the software.

After the format or options have been selected within forms such as Bars, Filters and Group and Sort, click:

- The [✔ OK] icon to apply the formatting and close the form, or
- The [Apply] icon to apply the format and leave the form open.

This is useful for checking if the option displays as required before closing the form.

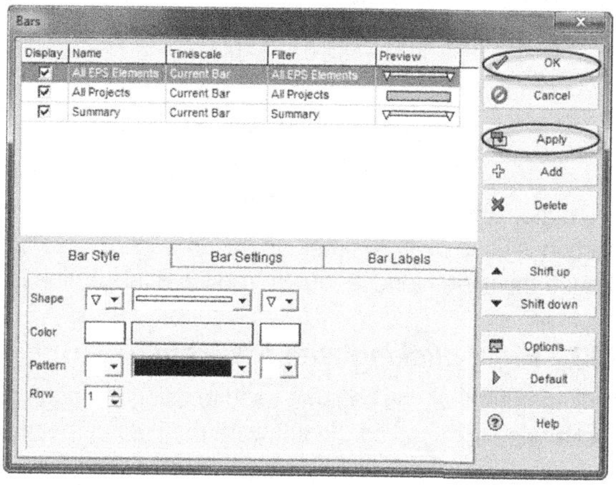

Often there is an arrow [▽] in a box and this indicates that there is a menu that may be opened by clicking on the arrow. Data in a form may be formatted and filtered from this menu.

The picture on the right shows the **Enterprise, User Defined Fields...** form:

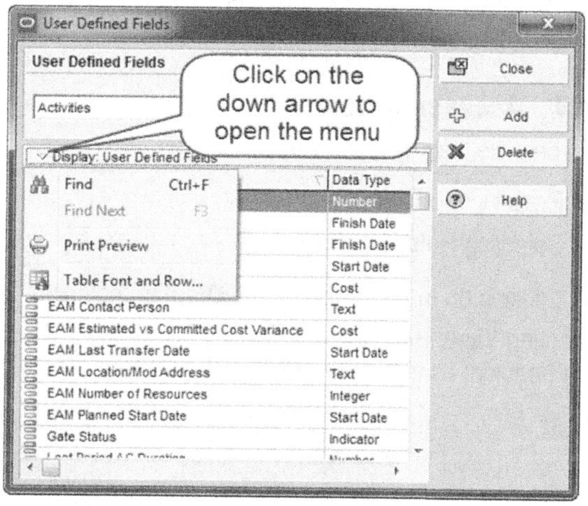

Sorting data within windows and forms such as Activities, Resources, OBS, may be achieved by clicking on the title above the first data item. Clicking on the **Resource ID** box will rotate the sort from hierarchical to alphabetical to reverse alphabetical.

If there is a filter applied, then this data may not be sorted.

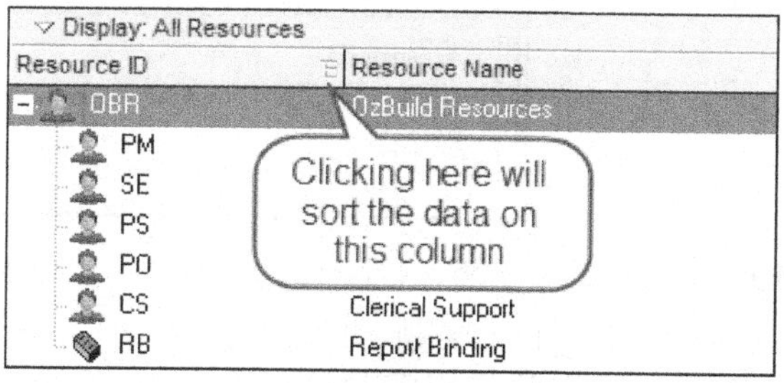

3.12 *Do Not Ask Me About This Again*

Many forms have a check box **Do not ask me about this again**.

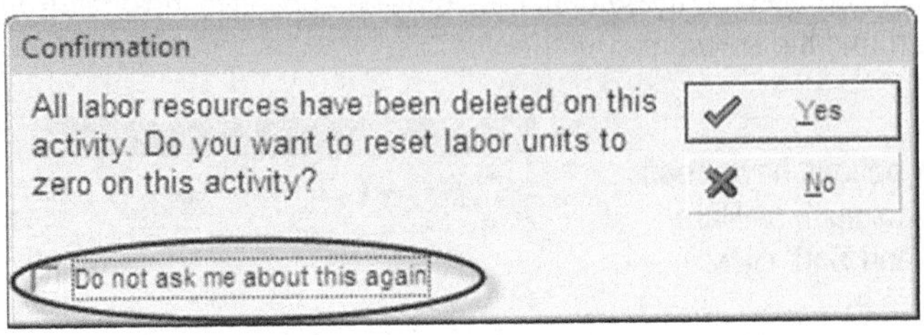

This option will hide the form when the function is used the next time, thus saving time when a function is used multiple times. In earlier versions of P6 it was not to possible to see this form again through the user interface, but in Version 8 this option is reset the next time you run the application.

3.13 *Right-clicking with the Mouse*

It is important that you become used to using the right-click function of the mouse as this is often a quicker way of operating the software than using the menus.

The right-click function will usually display a menu, which is often different depending on the displayed View and Active Pane selected. It is advised that you experiment with each view to become familiar with the menus.

3.14 *Accessing Help*

The help file may be accessed by:

- Pressing the F1 key,
- Selecting **Help**, **Contents...**
- Clicking on the icon on the **Display** toolbar.

Selecting **View**, **Hint Help** will display information about a field when the mouse is moved over the field heading, as in the preceding picture. This is useful for understanding how the fields calculate.

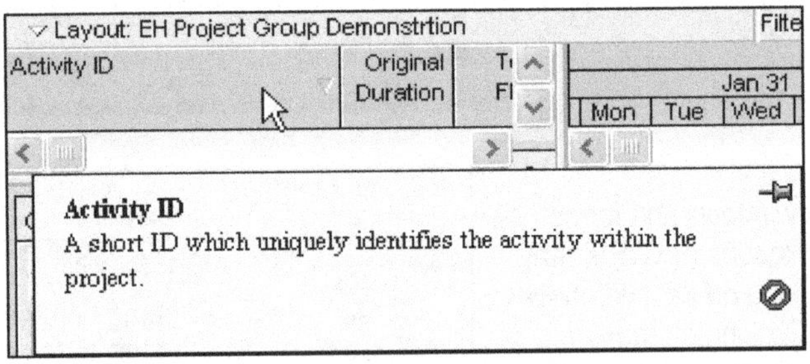

Many articles are available at the author's web sites **www.primavera.com.au** and **www.eh.com.au**.

You may also log in to the Oracle Support web list, a link available from www.primavera.com.au, and access the Oracle Support database.

The Help menu in P6 Version 8.3 has an additional menu option titled **Online Help** which will display the information in HTML format assisting people with disabilities who may access additional browser functions.

The **Admin Preferences**, **Options** tab has a new P6 Online Help section which sets the default for the F1 key. The URL is set to the Oracle Technology Network (OTN):

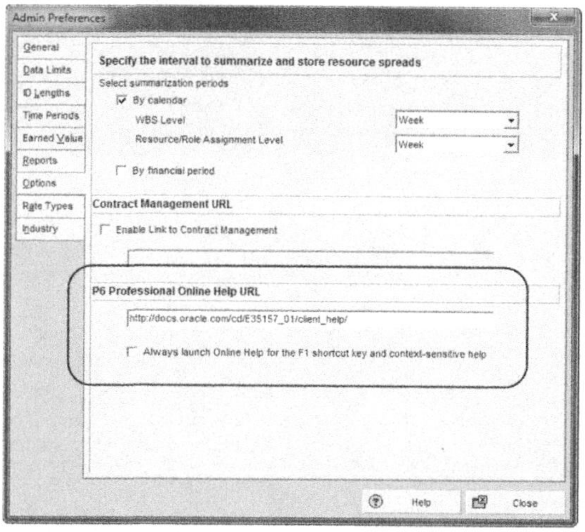

3.15 Refresh Data – F5 Key

The author found that sometimes changes made in one place would not be reflected somewhere else; such as relationships added but not visible in columns or WBS Nodes edited in the WBS Window but the changes not reflected in the Activities Window.

If this happens then select **File**, **Refresh Data** or press the **F5** key which:

- Writes your data to the database,
- Reads changes that other users may have made to your schedule,
- Puts the Data Date vertical line on the Gantt chart in the correct place when the system does refresh correctly and
- Corrects other display issues discussed above.

3.16 Commit Changes – F10 Key

The **File**, **Commit Changes** command writes any changes you have made to the database. These may then be read by other users by the Refresh Data command.

3.17 Send Project

The **File**, **Send Project...** should create an XER file (an export file) automatically and attach it as an attachment to an email.

3.18 Closing Down

The closing down options are:

- Select **File**, **Close All** or **Ctrl+W** to close all **Projects**.
- Select **File**, **Exit** or click the  icon in the top right side of the Primavera window to shut down all projects and close Primavera.

If you close down the system leaving one or more projects open, then these projects will be open the next time you log in. Go to the **Edit**, **User Preferences...**, **Application** tab and set the **Application Startup Window** to **Activities** so the software will open with your last project **Activities Window** displayed.

3.19 *Workshop 1 – Navigating Around the Windows*

Background

To become familiar with Primavera you will open your database and navigate around the windows.

Note: Your windows may look different from the one used in this publication which uses a demonstration database provided by Oracle Primavera.

Assignment

1. Open your database. If a project is open, select **File**, **Close All** to close the project.
2. Select **Edit**, **User Preferences...** select the **Application** tab and select the **Application Startup Window** as **Projects**. This will ensure the database opens at the **Project Window** each time you start up Primavera.
3. Close the **User Preferences** form.
4. Hide and display the **Status Bar** by using the **View**, **Status Bar** menu.
5. Select **Enterprise**, **Projects** to open the **Projects Window**.
6. Scroll up and down and inspect the Enterprise Project Structure and the projects.
7. Expand and close the EPS using the [+] and [-] buttons to the left of the project descriptions.
8. From the **Projects Window**, hide and display the bottom pane **Projects Details** form by clicking on the **View**, **Show on Bottom, No Bottom Layout** and **View**, **Show on Bottom,** Details.
9. Use the and buttons on the **Bottom Layout** toolbar to hide and display the bottom pane **Projects Details** form. You may need to display the toolbar and/or add the buttons to the toolbar.
10. Double click in the Gantt Chart area in line with a project to bring the project bar into view.
11. Open the **Bars** form by clicking on the button, uncheck all the bars in the **Display** column, click [Apply] and the bars will disappear without closing the form.
12. Now check all the bars in the **Bars** form and click on the [OK] button and the bars will appear and the form will close.
13. Open the **Projects Details** form, right-click on a tab in the **Projects Details** form and select **Customize Project Details...** then hide and display some tabs. Leave only the **General**, **Dates**, **Defaults** and **Notebook** tabs displayed. We will reveal the remainder as we need them:

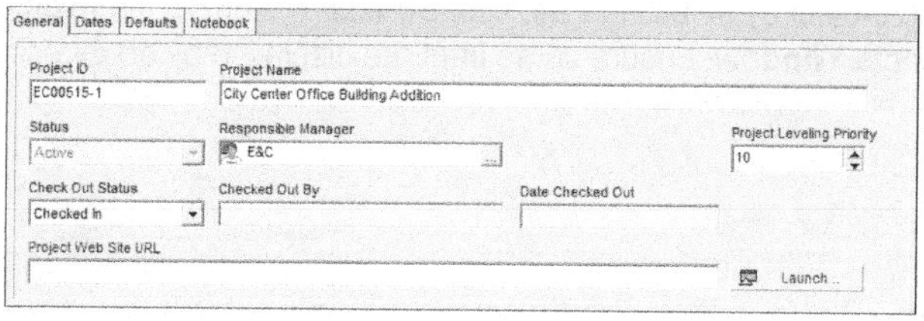

14. Select a project you have access to (possibly the City Center Office Building Addition project if you are operating in the Primavera Demonstration database) and open the **Project** by right-clicking on the project and selecting **Open Project**.

15. Click on the **Activities** tab or the icon if the **Activities Window** does not open automatically and display the project activities.

16. Double-click in the Gantt Chart area in line with a activity to bring the activity bar into view.

17. Click on the Activity ID column title multiple times and see the activities reorder, then click on other column titles and see the activities reorder based on the column data. Leave the activities ordered by Activity ID.

18. Adjust the timescale using the buttons.

19. Check above the Activity ID column and ensure that it displays **Layout: Classic WBS Layout**. If it does not select View, **Layout**, **Open Layout**, do not save changes; select the Classic WBS Layout and click on Open.

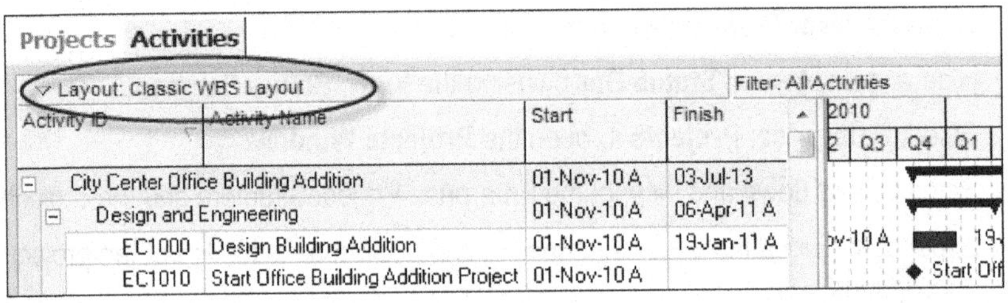

20. Move back to the **Projects Window** and then back to the **Activities Window** using the tabs at the top of the window.

21. From the **Activities Window** display the **Activity Details** form in the **Bottom** pane by selecting View, **Show on Bottom**, **Details** and then hide it by selecting View, **Show on Bottom**, **No Bottom Layout**.

22. From the **Activities Window** hide and display the bottom pane **Activity Details** form by clicking on the and buttons on the **Bottom Layout** toolbar.

23. Open the **Activity Details** form, right-click on a tab in the **Activity Details** form and select **Customize Activity Details...** then hide and display some tabs. Leave only the **General** and **Status** tabs displayed. We will reveal the remainder as we need them:

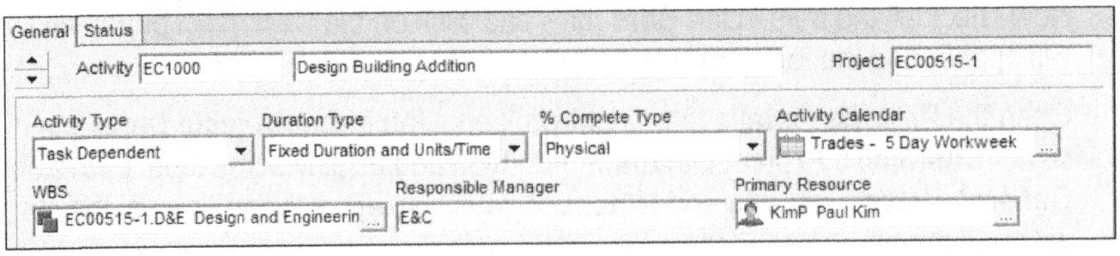

24. Close the project by selecting File, **Close All** and return to the **Projects Window**. From the **Projects Window**, ensure some bars are displayed by double-clicking in the bar area.

25. Open the **User Preferences** form by selecting **Edit**, **User Preferences...**and select the method you wish to display the date from the **Dates** tab and set your options as per below, showing the time in hours:

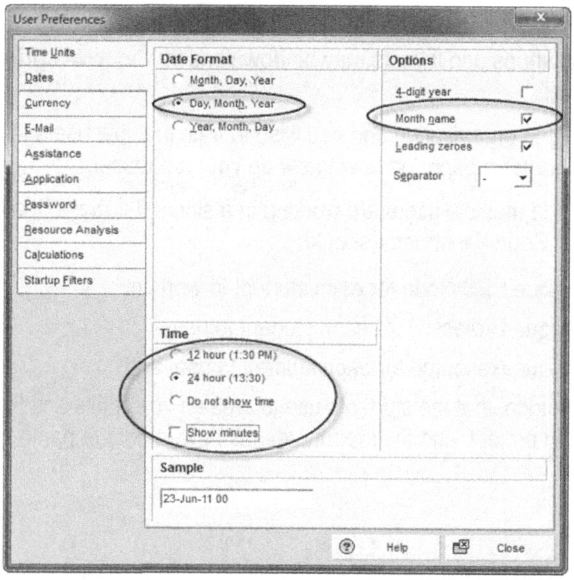

NOTE: It is strongly recommended that the time is always displayed as per the picture above so the user knows the time when Actual Starts, Actual Finish and Constraints are applied because the software will often select 00:00, first minute of a day.

26. Open the **User Preferences** form by selecting **Edit**, **User Preferences...**and select the **Time Units** tab and set your options as shown below:

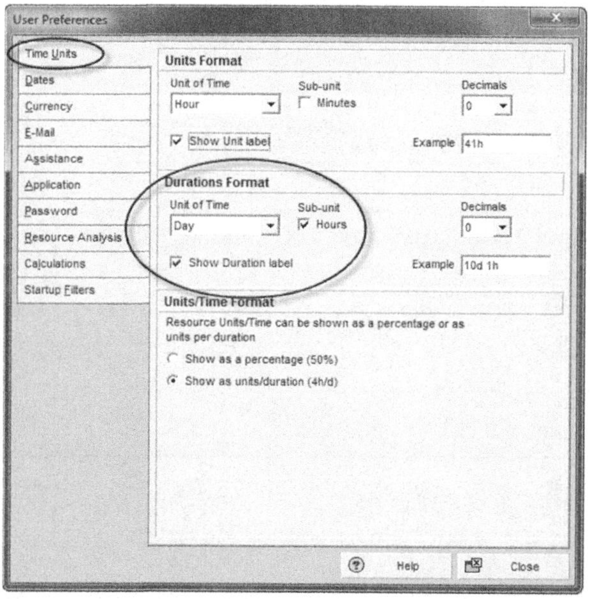

27. Close the **User Preferences** form.

28. Ensure all projects are closed by selecting **File**, **Close All**.

NOTES FOR TRAINING COURSE INSTRUCTORS AND/OR DATABASE ADMINISTRATORS:

1. Training course instructors and/or administrators may consider purchasing the instructor's PowerPoint presentation from **www.primavera.com.au** or **www.eh.com.au**. This slide show is fully editable and a sample in pdf format may be downloaded from this web site.
2. Completed workshops and layouts may be downloaded from **www.primavera.com.au** or **www.eh.com.au**.
3. If you are a training organization and you wish to train multiple users in one database, please contact the author for a paper on how to set up your database.
4. In summary, when multiple users are working in a single database, the Database Administrator or Course Instructor should:
   - Create a unique EPS Node for each student to work in,
   - Assign a unique Project ID for each student to use,
   - Create a unique Resource for each student to use, and
   - Assign a protocol that the students use to create Project IDs and Resource IDs so that each student project, and their resources, all have a unique name.

4 CREATING A NEW PROJECT

There are several methods to create a new project from the **Projects Window**:

- Run the **Create New Project** wizard, or
- Copy an existing project and edit it, or
- Import a project created from another Primavera database or created with another software program such as P3, SureTrak or Microsoft Project, or Asta Powerproject.

Primavera P6 Enterprise Project Portfolio Management Version 8 Web has introduced project templates and dropped Methodology Manager/Project Architect.

4.1 Creating a Blank Project

You may create a new project at any point in time by selecting **File**, **New...** from the menu or clicking on the icon on the **Edit** toolbar. You will be guided through the **Create a New Project** wizard which will require the following information:

- The **EPS** Node the project is to be assigned to.
- The **Project ID**, a code to represent the project (a maximum of 20 characters), and **Project Name**.
- A **Planned Start** date, which is the earliest date any un-started activity will be scheduled to commence and an optional **Project Must Finish By** date.
  NOTE: Be sure to check the Start Time.
- When a **Project Must Finish By** date is set the project float will be calculated to this date and not to the latest activity finish.

It is even more important to check the finish time as it often defaults to 00:00 which is midnight of the Finish day, giving you one less day than planned:

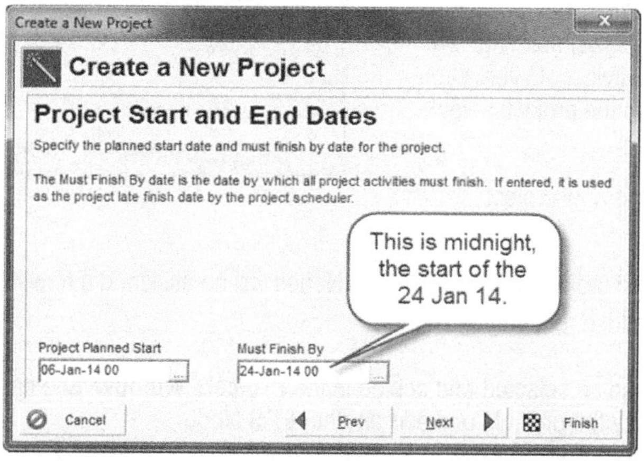

- The **Responsible Manager** is selected from the OBS structure. If the OBS has not been defined or the responsibility not assigned then Enterprise may be selected as the Responsible Manager.
- The **Resource Rate Type**. Each resource may have five different rates. This is where the default rates are selected but may be changed after a resource has been assigned to an activity.

It is a normal practice to copy and paste projects to keep a copy of a project at a specific point in time, normally after each update. When copying projects you should consider utilizing the Primavera defaults for the renumbering of the Project ID.

4.2 Copy an Existing Project

A Project or Projects may be copied in the **Projects Window** by:

- Highlighting the project(s) you wish to copy and select **Edit**, **Copy** or **Ctrl+C**,
- Highlighting the EPS Node that you wish to associate the new project with and select **Edit**, **Paste** or **Ctrl+V**,
- The first **Copy Project Options** form will then be displayed, enabling you to choose which Project data items you wish to copy with the project; select ,

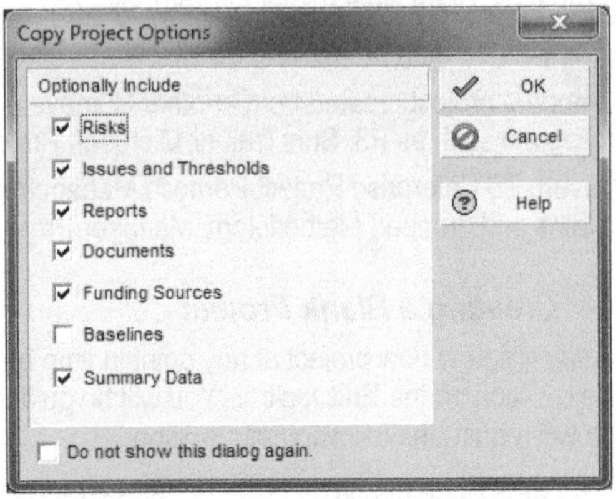

- The second **Copy WBS Options** form will be displayed, allowing you to choose which WBS data items you wish to copy with the project;
- After making a selection, click :

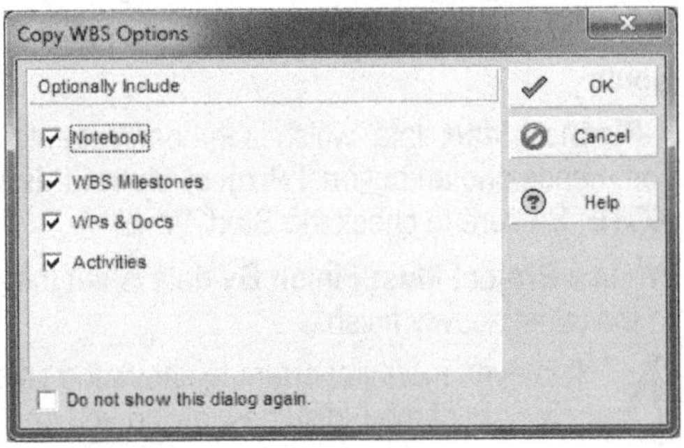

- The third **Copy Activity Options** form will be displayed, allowing you to choose the Activity data items you wish to copy with the project; select ,
- Open and edit the new project.

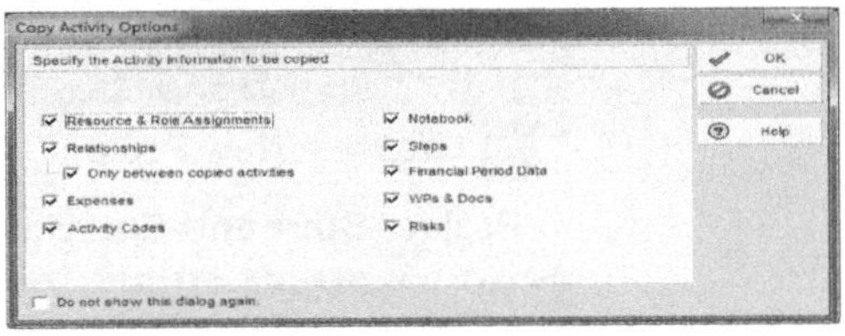

The copied projects and copied EPS Nodes will be assigned a new ID with a sequential number added to the Original ID.

An EPS Node may also be selected and copied in the **Projects Window**, and pasted to another location which will copy the projects and add another EPS Node.

4.3 Importing a Project

Different Versions of Primavera run on different databases including Oracle and Microsoft databases. Primavera will only operate with the database format with which it has been installed and set up.

Primavera will not open a standalone project file, does not supply a reader, and all project data has to be imported into a database before it may be opened.

You may be required to import a project that has been created in another program supplied by someone from within or outside your organization. Primavera is equipped with a set of tools for importing projects from other sources.

4.3.1 Primavera File Types

There are several Primavera proprietary file formats that you need to be aware of:

- **XER** – Used to exchange one or more projects between Primavera databases regardless of the database type in which it was created and exports all project data. Earlier versions of **XER** files may be imported into later version databases. A layout (formatting) is not part of an XER file.
- **PLF** – Used to exchange **Layouts** between Primavera databases regardless of the database type in which it was created. In Primavera Version 15.1 PLF files may now be imported into Visualizer.
- **ANP** – Used to save the position of activities in an **Activity Network**.
- **ERP** – Used to exchange **Reports** between Primavera databases regardless of the database type in which it was created.
- **XML** – A format introduced with Primavera Version 6.0 which is used to import data from the Project Manager module. This is the same software language but a different format to a Microsoft Project XML file. Version 15.1 introduced the ability to import and export Baseline projects.
- **PCF** – Used to exchange **Global Changes** between Primavera databases.
- **VLF** - Visualizer Layout File allows the import and export of Visualizer Layouts between users.

4.3.2 Non Primavera File Types

Select **File**, **Import...** to open a wizard that will guide you through the process of importing projects into your database.

Project (*.mpp).This is the default file format that Microsoft Project uses to create and save files. Microsoft Project 2016 – 2010, Microsoft Project 2007 and Microsoft Project 2000 – 2003 are three different formats.

Earlier versions of Primavera will not import any mpp file when Microsoft Project 2007 or later was installed as these disable the mpp import function. The import and export of mpp files in versions of Microsoft Project that are currently used is no longer supported.

Primavera will import and export to the following non Primavera file types using the wizards found under the menu commands **File**, **Import...** and **File**, **Export...**:

- **MPX (*.mpx).** This is a text format created by Microsoft Project 98 and earlier versions. MPX is a format that may be imported and exported by many other project scheduling software packages.
- Microsoft Project **XML** format is supported in Version 6.2 and later. This allows import of a file created by Microsoft Project 2000 and later without the installation of Microsoft Project. The file needs to be saved from Microsoft Project in XML format.
- **Primavera Project Planner P3** and **SureTrak** files saved in **P3** format. A SureTrak project in SureTrak format should be saved in Concentric (P3) format before importing.

To import files saved in **P3** format you need Btrieve loaded on your PC. Btrieve is loaded when P3 is installed. A demonstration version of P3 will load Btrieve onto your machine and enable P3 files to be imported. P3 may not be loaded on more recent operating systems such as Windows 7 make the use of this function difficult without an old operating system.

- **UN/CEFACT XML** format . P6 Version 8.3 introduced the support of format from the **File**, **Export** menu. This format is mandated by many US Government agencies.
- **XLS**. Primavera Version 5.0 introduced a function allowing the import and export of data in Excel format. It is best to export some sample data first and then update the data and import it. See the UTILITIES chapter for more information.

Read the Administrators Guide carefully before importing a project as this is a very complex operation and may import unwanted data into your database. It is recommended that you establish a sacrificial database into which you import projects so that corporate databases are not filled up with unwanted data.

4.4 Setting Up a New Project

To review or modify some of the basic Project or EPS information entered when a project was created, ensure that the **Project Details** form is displayed in the bottom of the screen:

- Highlight a project or EPS Node,
- The project must be open to edit some project data,
- You must also have the appropriate access rights to edit data,
- Select **View**, **Show on Bottom**, **Details** and click on the **General** tab:

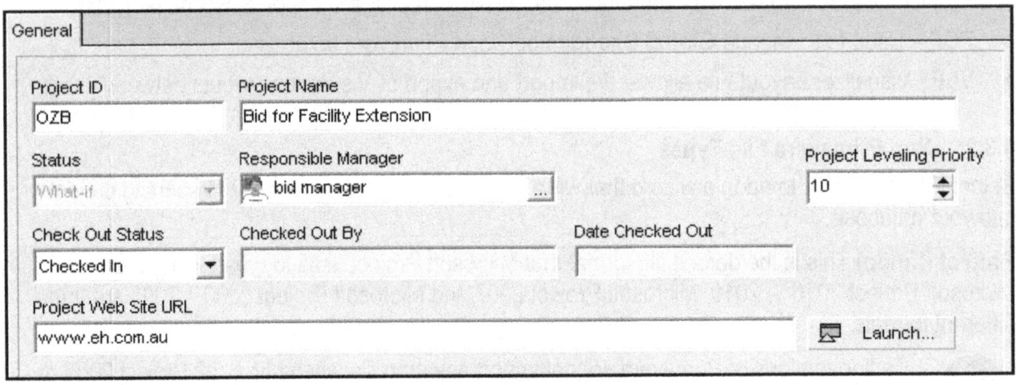

- The **Project Leveling Priority** is used when leveling a project to reduce peaks in resource requirements. Value of 1 is the highest and 100 the lowest.
- **Check Out Status** enables the user to determine if the project is checked in or checked out (New to Version 4.1). **Checked Out By** and **Date Checked Out** enables the user to establish if the project is currently checked out.

4.5 *Project Dates*

At this point, a project would not have normally started and you would set the project start date sometime in the future using the **Planned Start** field in the **Projects Window**, **Details** form, **Dates** tab. To open this form:

- Highlight your new project,
- Select **View**, **Show on Bottom**, **Details** and click the **Dates** tab:

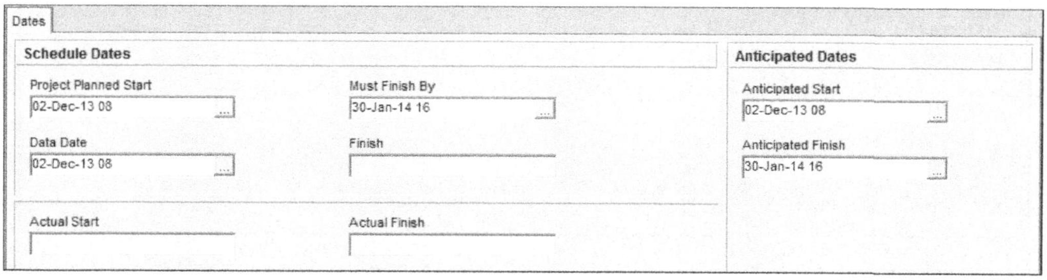

- **Scheduled Dates**
  - The **Planned Start** is the date before which no activity will be scheduled to start.
  - The **Must Finish By** date is an optional date. When this date is entered it is used to calculate the **Late Finish** of activities, thus all **Total Float** will be calculated to this date. This topic is covered in the **Adding Relationships** chapter.
  - The **Finish date** is a calculated date and is the date of the completion of the last activity.
  - The **Data Date** is used when updating a project. This topic is covered in the **Tracking Progress** chapter. Unlike Microsoft Project, all incomplete work is scheduled to take place after this date.
  - The **Actual Start** date is inherited from the earliest started activity.
  - The **Actual Finish** date is inherited from the latest completed activity when all activities are complete.
- **Anticipated Dates**
  - The **Anticipated Start** and **Anticipated Finish** dates may be assigned before a WBS structure and Activities have been created. The start and finish dates columns and bars at the EPS level adopt these dates when there are no activities. After Activities have been created, they may remain as a historical record only and are not displayed or inherited anywhere else.
  - **Anticipated Dates** may also be assigned to **WBS Nodes** in the **WBS Window**.

4.6 Saving Additional Project and EPS Information – Notebook Topics

Often additional information about a Project or EPS Node is required to be saved with the project such as location, client and type of project. This data may be saved in the **Projects Window**, **Details** form, **Notebook** tab.

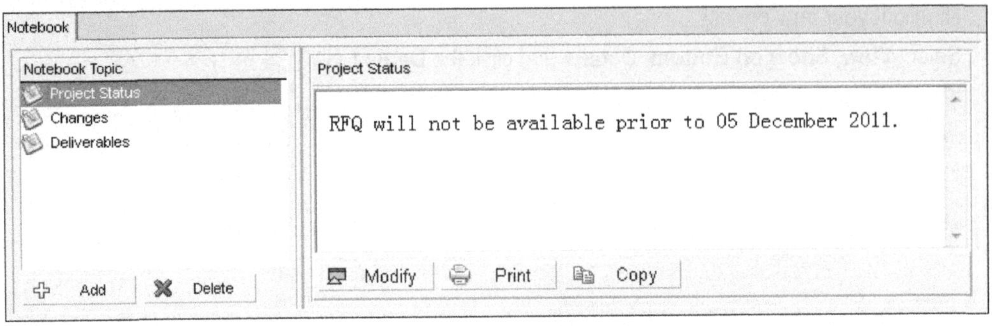

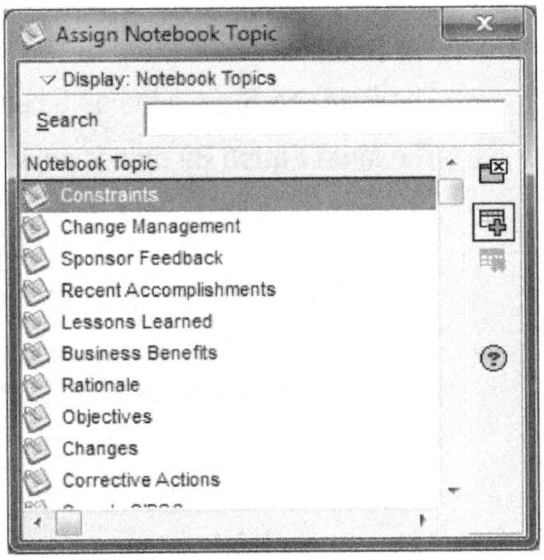

To add a **Note** to a Project:

- Click Add to open the **Assign Notebook Topic** form.
- Select a **Topic** from the list by clicking on the **Notebook Topic** you wish to select and click on the icon to add the topic to the Notebook.
- Close the form by clicking on the icon.
- You may now add notes to the selected **Project Notebook Topic** by clicking on the Modify **Modify** button,
- Notes may be added to **EPS** Nodes, **Activities** and **WBS Nodes** in the same way as Projects.
- Primavera version 6.0 introduced the search facility when assigning Notes.

To create a new **Notebook Topic**:

- Select **Admin**, **Admin Categories...** to open the **Admin Categories** form and select the **Notebook Topics** tab.
- The check boxes make the Categories available to EPS Nodes and/or Projects.

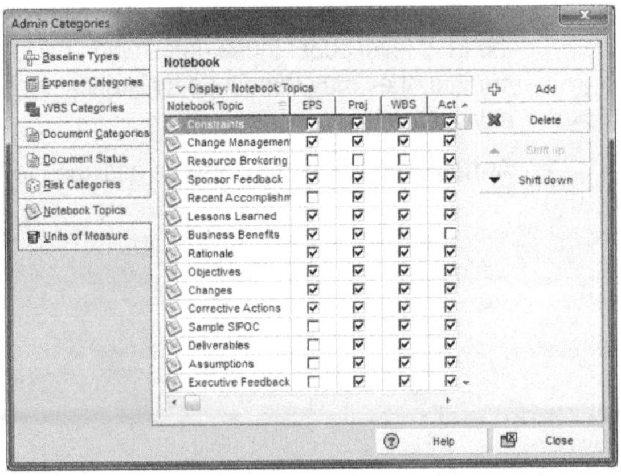

4.7 Workshop 2 – Creating Your Project

Background

You are an employee of Wilson International and are responsible for planning the Bid preparation required to ensure that a response to an RFQ (Request For Quote) from OzBuild Pty Ltd is submitted on time. While short-listed, you have been advised that the RFQ will be available on 03 December 2018 at 8:00 hrs (8:00 am) and you will be required to submit 3 bound copies of the proposal before 28 January 2019 at 16:00 hrs (4:00 pm).

NOTE: When multiple users are working in a single Professional database or using the Optional Client then:

- The Database Administrator or Instructor should create a unique EPS Node for each student to create their projects under.
- Each student should also be assigned a unique Project ID to use when creating their projects.

Assignment

1. Create a new project with the following information by selecting **File**, **New...** to open the **Create a New Project** wizard:
   - Select an appropriate EPS Node in your database to create the project or your nominated node when working in a shared database.
   - Project ID – OZB.

     NOTE: This Project ID may not be accepted if you are working in a shared database when there is another project with this Project ID. You may need to use another Project ID in this situation, such as OZB plus your initials.
   - Project Name – Bid for Facility Extension
   - Planned Start Date – 03 December 2018 at 08:00

     NOTE: Ensure that the 08:00 (8:00 AM) is added in this step. Forgetting to check and, if required, setting the time when assigning dates may lead to the schedule not calculating correctly.
   - Must Finish By – Leave Blank
   - Responsible Manager – Accept the default
   - Rate Type – Accept the default which is usually Price/Unit or Standard Rate
   - Click Finish to create the project.
2. The project should now be open. Check the text in the top left side of the screen; the project name should be displayed.
3. Ensure you are in the **Projects Window**.
4. Ensure the project is selected by clicking on it.

5. Add the following project information in **Project Details** in the **Bottom Pane**:
   - Select your project in the **Project Window** by clicking on it.
   - In the **General** tab set the **Status** to **What-if**, the project needs to be open to change the **Status**.
   - **Dates** tab
     - ➢ Set the Data Date to 03 December 2018 at 08:00
     - ➢ Anticipated Start 03 December 2018 at 08:00
     - ➢ Anticipated Finish 28 January 2019 at 16:00

     You should now see a bar in the Bar Chart above spanning these dates although there are no activities in the schedule. If no bar is displayed double-click in the Gantt Chart area level with the project.
   - Add a Notebook Topic using a suitable topic such as Constraints, Project Status or Issues stating, "RFQ will not be available prior to 03 December 2018."
6. Your project should look like this:

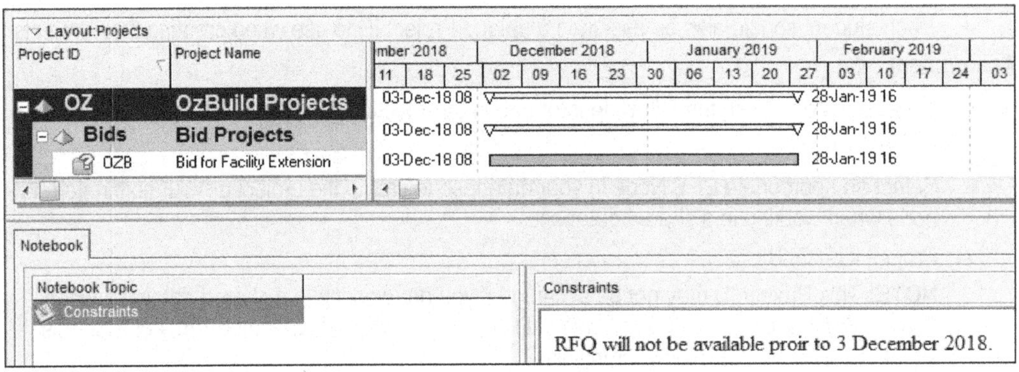

NOTES:

The date format will be displayed according to the **User Preferences** settings by selecting **Edit**, **User Preferences...** and selecting the **Dates** tab. Your date format should display the time as per the picture above.

The **First day of week** dates are displayed in the Timescale are normally a Sunday or Monday. This display option is set by the Administrator. In the picture above the Start of week has been set as Sunday and in the picture below this has been set as a Monday:

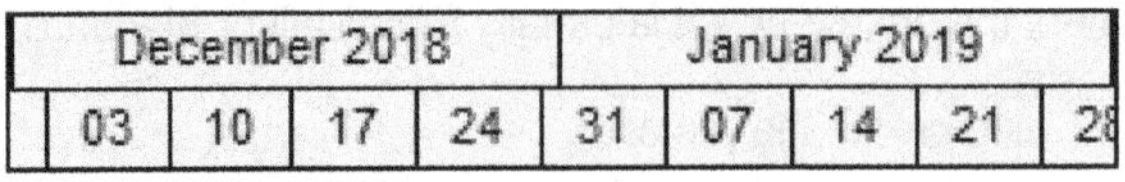

5 DEFINING CALENDARS

The finish date (and time) of an activity is calculated from the start date (and time) plus the duration of the calendar associated with the activity. Therefore, a five-day duration activity that starts at the start of the workday on a Wednesday, and is associated with a five-day workweek calendar (with Saturday and Sunday as nonwork days) will finish at the end of the workday on the following Tuesday.

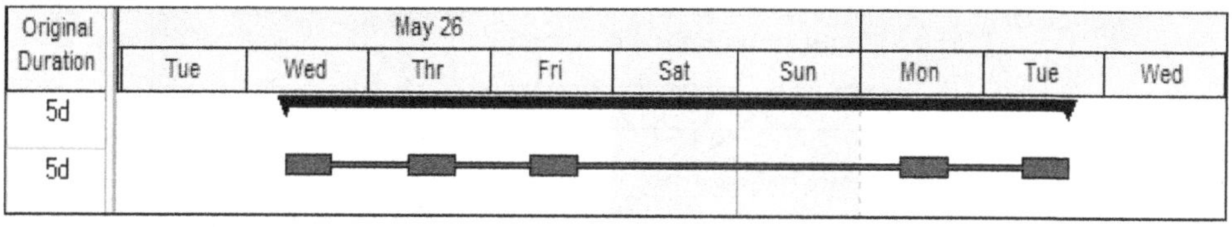

Primavera has three categories for calendars:

- **Global** – These calendars are available to all Projects and Resources.
- **Project** – These calendars are only available to the projects they are created in. These may only be created for a project when that project is open.
- **Resource** – There are now two types of resource calendars: **Personal**, new to Primavera Version 8.1, and **Shared**, which is the same as the earlier Resource calendar.
  - ➢ A **Personal** calendar is created for a specific individual resource.
  - ➢ A **Shared** Resource calendar may be assigned to one or more Resources, which in turn may be assigned to an activity in any project.

A Resource will be scheduled according to a Resource Calendar when the **Activity Type** is set to **Resource Dependent**; otherwise the activity is scheduled according to the Activity calendar.

⚠ When an activity is made **Resource Dependent**, unlike in some other software, it still acknowledges the Activity Calendar for calculating the start of the resource work. Some software ignores the Activity Calendar and ONLY acknowledges the resource calendars when an activity is made resource-driven. You may wish to consider placing resource-driven activities on a 24-hour, 7-day per week calendar in circumstances when resource calendars have start times that are earlier in the day than the activity calendar start times. This prevents a delay to start of resource-driven activities by an Activity Calendar.

You may create a new, or edit an existing, calendar to reflect your project requirements, such as adding holidays or additional workdays or adjusting work times. For example, some activities may have a 5-day per week calendar and some may have a 7-day per week calendar.

This chapter covers the following topics:

Topic	**Menu Command**
• Database **Default Calendar**	Select **Enterprise**, **Calendars...**and select the database **Default Calendar** from the **Default** column.
• Assigning the **Default Activity/Project Calendar**	This calendar is assigned to new activities. From the **Projects Window**, click the **Defaults** tab in the **Details** form.
• Creating, copying, editing or deleting calendars	**Enterprise**, **Calendars...**,select the **Global**, **Project**, or **Resource** button then click [Add] (to create a new calendar by copying an existing calendar) or [Modify...], or [Delete].
• Renaming an existing calendar	**Enterprise**, **Calendars...**,select **Global**, **Project**, or **Resource**, click the description and then modify it.

5.1 Database Default Calendar

The **Database Default Calendar** is selected in the **Enterprise**, **Calendars...** form and is used to display the Nonworking times in all views and all projects in a database.

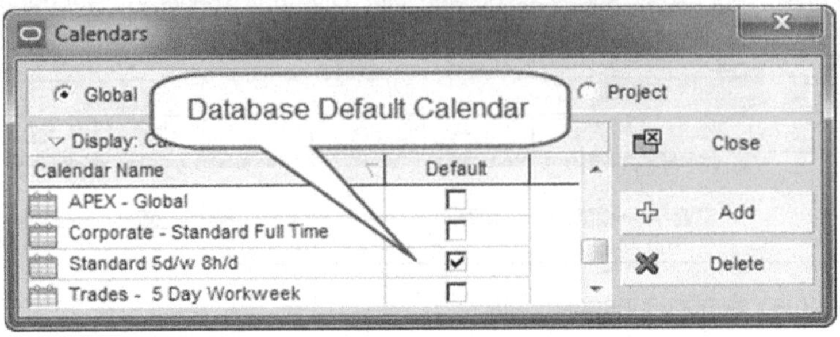

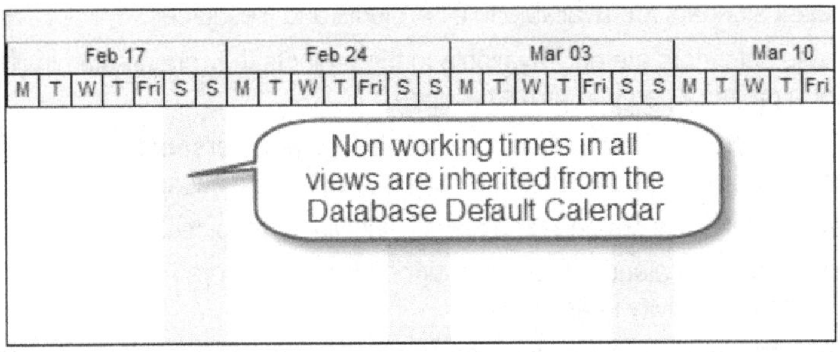

It is not possible for users to display different nonwork periods for different projects or views, as in most other scheduling software packages, without affecting all other projects in a database. This may become an issue with projects that have different work periods and may be solved by creating another database with a different **Database Default Calendar**.

5.2 Accessing Global and Project Calendars

Calendars may be accessed from the **Calendars** form for copying, editing and deleting by selecting **Enterprise**, **Calendars...**.

The following rules dictate when you are able to access the calendars:

- **Global** and **Resource Calendars** may be accessed with or without any projects open.
- A **Project Calendar** may only be copied, edited, and deleted when the project has been opened.
- To list, create, and edit more than one existing **Project Calendar** at the same time all the projects in question must be open.

5.3 The Project Default Calendar

5.3.1 Understanding the Project Default Calendar

A project is assigned a **Default Project Calendar** which may be either a **Global** or **Project** calendar:

- All new activities are assigned the project **Default Project Calendar** when they are created. Unlike in Microsoft Project, changing the **Default Project Calendar** will **NOT** affect the calendar assigned to any tasks.
- The **Default Project Calendar** may be selected for calculating leads and lags in the **Tools...**, **Schedule...**, **Options** form.

5.3.2 Assigning a Default Project Calendar

To assign or change the **Default Project Calendar** a project must be open:

- Open the **Projects Window** by selecting **Enterprise**, **Projects** and highlight the project,
- Click on the **Defaults** tab in the **Details** form; you will see the current **Default Project Calendar** in the **Calendar** box.
- Click the icon to the right of the heading **Calendar** to open the **Select Default Project Calendar** form:

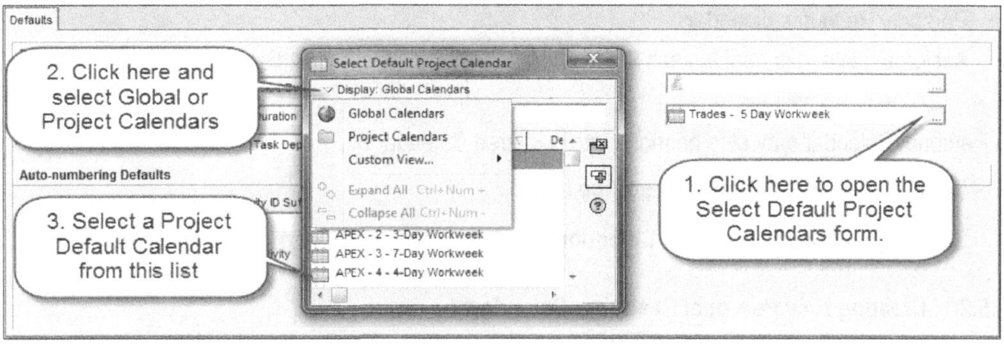

- Select either the **Global Calendars** or **Project Calendars** menu item from the drop down box under the Display: Project Calendars heading,
- Select the calendar to be the **Default Project Calendar**,
- Click the icon or **Double-Click** on the calendar to assign the new calendar.

5.4 Creating a New Global or Project Calendar

A project must be active to create a **Project Calendar**. You can create a new **Project Calendar** by copying an existing Global Calendar. You **MAY NOT** copy an existing Project or Personal Resource calendar to create a **Project Calendar**.

To create a new calendar:

- Select **Enterprise**, **Calendars...**,
- Select the **Global**, or **Project** button, depending on the type of calendar required,
- Then click on the Add icon to create a new calendar, or
- Select an existing Global calendar to copy. You may not copy an existing Project or Personal Resource calendar,
- Assign a name. It is best to keep these short as they are then easily displayed in a column.

5.5 Resource Calendars

A **Resource** or a **Global** calendar may be assigned to one or more resources. This is different from the philosophy of Microsoft Project, P3 and SureTrak, where each resource has its own calendar based on a project calendar and many resources are not able to share one calendar.

A Resource will be scheduled according to the assigned **Resource Calendar** when the **Activity Type** is set to **Resource Dependent**; otherwise, the activity is scheduled according to the **Activity Calendar**.

Resource availability is displayed in **Resource Usage Profiles** and is based on the Resource Calendar even when it is assigned to a **Task Dependent** activity.

5.5.1 Creating a New Shared Resource Calendar

To create a new Shared Resource calendar:

- Select **Enterprise**, **Calendars...**,
- Select the **Resources** button,
- Click on an existing Shared Resource Calendar,
- Then click either the [Add] icon to create a new calendar, or
- Select an existing Global or Shared calendar to copy. You may not copy an existing Project or Personal Resource calendar,
- Assign a name. It is best to keep these short as they are then easily displayed in a column.

A Personal Calendar may also be made into a Shared Calendar by:

- Opening the **Calendar** form, **Resource** button,
- Selecting an existing **Personal Calendar** and clicking on the [To Shared] **To Shared** icon.

5.5.2 Creating New Personal Resource Calendars

These may be created from the **Calendars** form by:

- Selecting **Enterprise**, **Calendars...**,
- Clicking on **Personal Resource Calendars**,
- Clicking on [Add] to open the **Select Resource** form to select the resource to be assigned the calendar, and
- Clicking on [Modify...] to modify the calendar in the normal way.

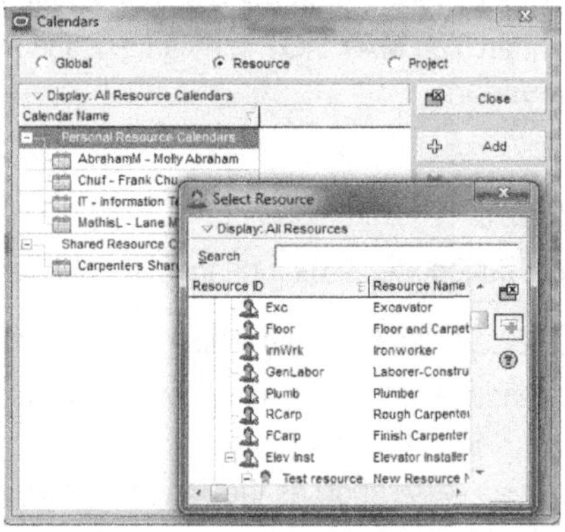

A Shared Calendar may also be made into a Personal Calendar by:

- Opening the **Calendar** form, **Resource** button,
- Selecting an existing **Shared Calendar** and clicking on the [To Personal] **To Personal** icon.

Or from the **Resources Window** by

- Opening the **Resources Window**, **Details** tab,
- Selecting the resource,
- Clicking on the 

icon to open the **Resource Calendar** form and edit the calendar in the normal way.

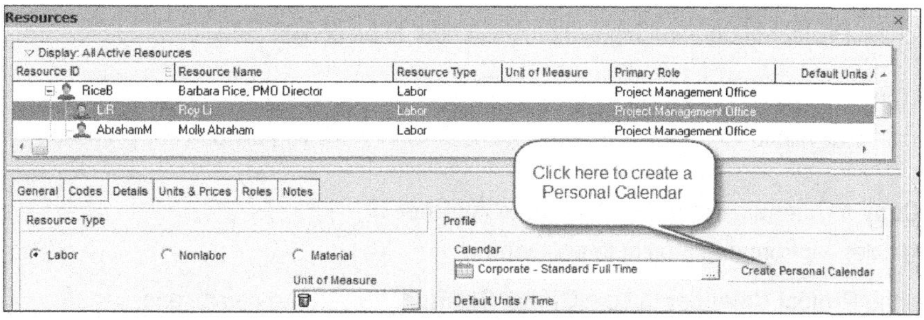

5.5.3 Personal and Shared Calendars Calculation and Display

The picture below displays three activities each 5 days long:

- A1000 is **Task Dependent and** acknowledges the 5-day per week activity calendar and ignores all resource calendars,
- A1010 and A1020 both acknowledge their respective Personal or Shared Resource Calendars for scheduling the work, but
- A1010 and A1020 both ignore Resource Calendars for Bar Necking:

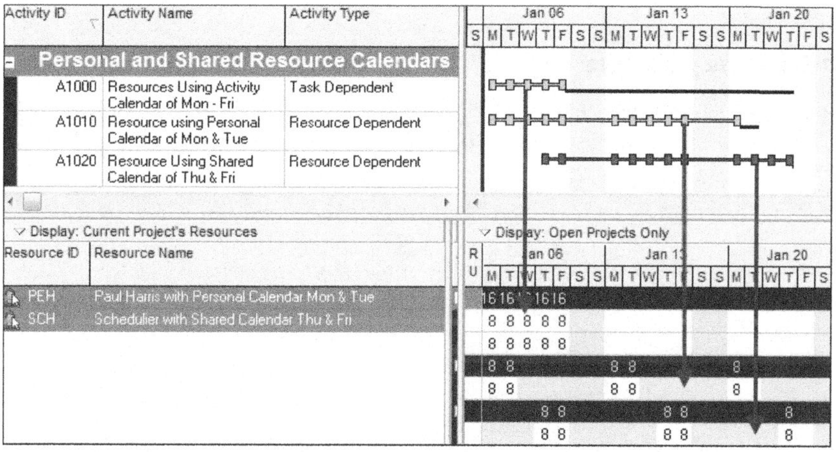

Bar Necking is based on Activity Calendar not resource working times.

When an activity is made **Resource Dependent**, unlike in some other software, it still acknowledges the Activity Calendar for calculating the start of the resource work.

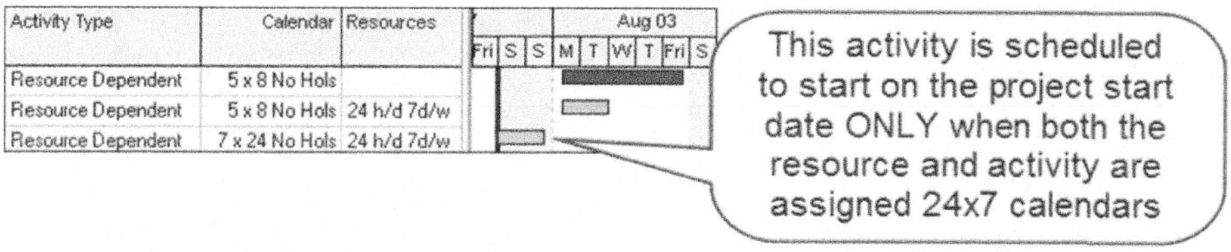

5.6 Move, Copy, Rename and Delete a Calendar

5.6.1 Moving a Project Calendar to Global

A **Project Calendar** may be moved to become a **Global Calendar**:

- Open the project that the calendar currently resides in,
- Select **Enterprise**, **Calendars...**,
- Select the **Project** button and highlight the calendar to be copied, and
- Click the 

icon.
- The calendar will no longer be a Project calendar so this function is not a copy function.

5.6.2 Copy a Calendar from One Project to Another

To copy a calendar from one project to another:

- Move the **Project Calendar** to be a **Global Calendar** as detailed above, and
- Create a new **Project Calendar** in both projects by copying the new **Global Calendar**.

5.6.3 Renaming a Calendar

To rename a calendar:

- Select **Enterprise**, **Calendars...**,
- Double-click the calendar description to edit in the same way as renaming a directory in Explorer.

5.6.4 Deleting a Calendar

To delete a calendar:

- Select **Enterprise**, **Calendars...**,
- Select the calendar and click the 

icon.

5.7 Editing Calendar Working Days

Prior to editing a calendar, particularly if it is a global calendar, click the [Used By...] icon to open the **Calendar Used By** form to determine which other Projects and Resources also use the calendar.

To edit a calendar:

- Select **Enterprise**, **Calendars...**,
- Select the **Global**, **Project**, or **Resource** button,
- Then click [Modify...] to open the **Calendar** form and modify an existing calendar:

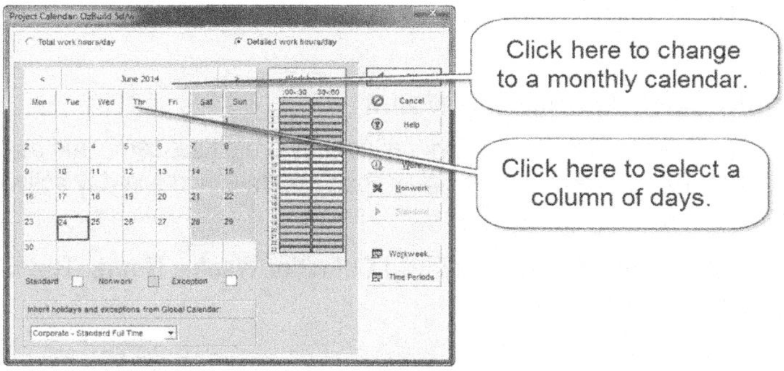

- Click in the month name to change the calendar view to monthly. This makes it quicker to navigate around the calendar and works in the other calendar view:

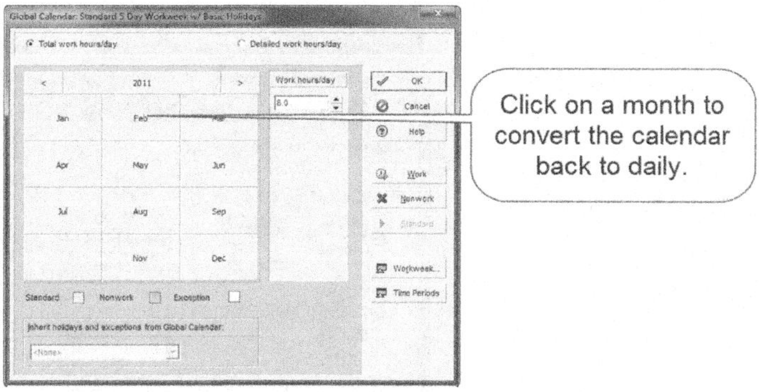

- To make **Nonwork Days** into **Work Days**, highlight the day(s) you want to edit by:
  - Clicking on an individual day, or
  - Ctrl-clicking to select multiple days, or
  - Clicking on a column or columns of days by clicking the day of the week box, which is located below the month and year. Ctrl-click will allow multiple columns to be selected.
  - Then click the [Work] icon to make these days working and **CHECK THE HOURS**.

⚠ When making a **Nonwork Day** into **Work Day** ensure you check that the working hours are the same as the rest of the calendar working days as the default is 08:00 to 16:00 which does not suit every calendar.

- To make **Work Days** into **Nonwork Days**, highlight the day(s) you want to edit as described in the paragraph above and then click the [Nonwork] icon to make these days nonworking days.
- To return individual days to the default setting, select the day and click the [Standard] icon.

5.8 Inherit Holidays and Exceptions from a Global Calendar

When creating a new Project or Resource calendar, a Global Calendar may be selected from the drop down box and this function will link the calendar holidays from the selected Global Calendar into the displayed calendar.

The Global and the new Project or Resource calendars will remain linked (in the same way as a Global Calendar in SureTrak and P3) and a change to a Global calendar holiday will be reflected in a calendar with Inherited Holidays.

It is suggested that this option never be used so each calendar is created as standalone without inheriting holidays from another calendar, and therefore will not change if another calendar has holidays changed.

5.9 Adjusting Calendar Working Hours

It is strongly recommended that the working hours per day are all the same and have the same start and finish time; otherwise, one-day activities may span two days and two-day activities may span three days, etc.

The working hours of a standard week are termed **Calendar Weekly Hours**. The working hours of selected individual days may be edited.

5.9.1 Editing Calendar Weekly Hours

There are two methods of editing the hours of every weekday of a calendar:

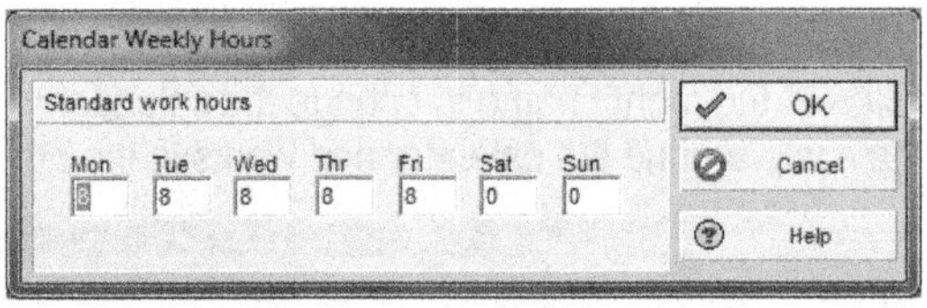

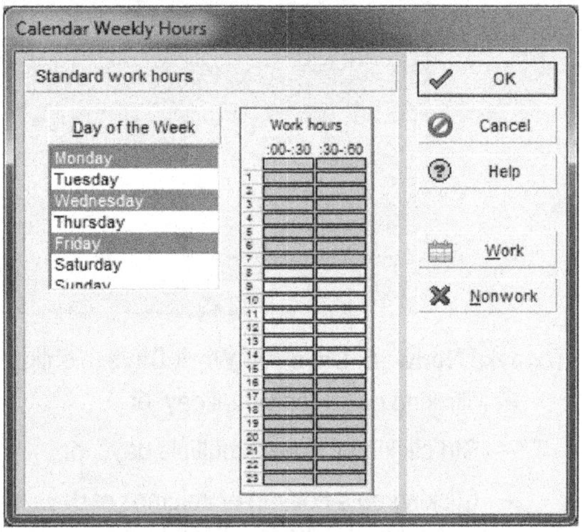

- From the **Calendar** form:
  - ➢ Select **Total work hours/day** and then
  - ➢ Click Workweek... to open the **Calendar Weekly Hours** form.
  - ➢ See warning below.
- Or from the **Calendar** form:
  - ➢ Select **Detailed work hours/day** and then
  - ➢ Click Workweek... to open the second Calendar Weekly Hours form.
  - ➢ Individual days of the week may be selected using Ctrl-click and then the work hours for multiple days edited simultaneously.
- Adjust the hours for the selected days in this form and click OK to accept the changes.

It is suggested that the **Total work hours/day** is not used as you will not know what start and finish time the software has selected for you.

5.9.2 Editing Selected Days Working Hours

To edit the working hours of individual days using **Total work hours/day**:

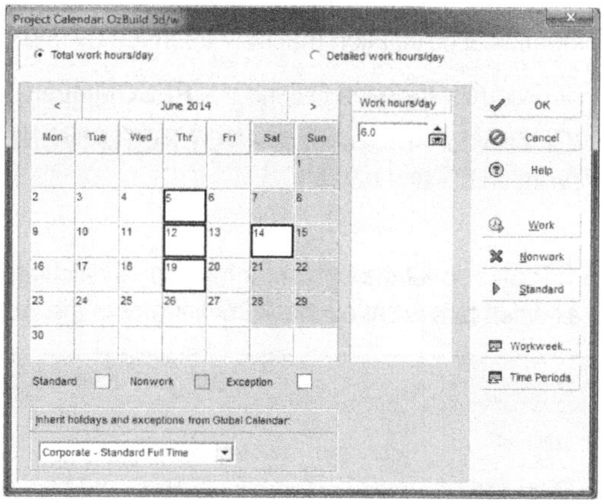

- Select the days you wish to edit by Shift-clicking, Ctrl-clicking individual days, or selecting one or more columns,
- Adjust the hours in the box below the title **Work hours/day**.
- The edited days will now adopt the color of the **Exception** days.
- Nonwork days may be made into Workdays by selecting the day and clicking on .

Ensure you check that the working hours are the same as the rest of the calendars' working days when making a **Nonwork Day** into **Work Day**. This is because P6 uses the default hours (08:00 to 16:00) which may be different from the calendar you are editing.

5.9.3 Editing Detailed Work Hours/Day

To edit the **Detailed work hours/day** of individual days:

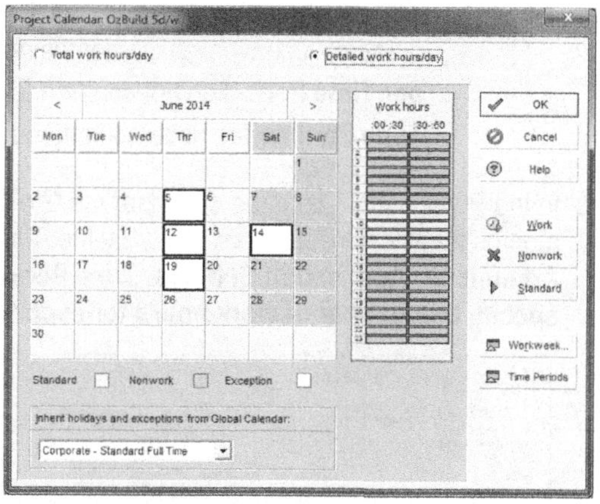

- Select the days to edit by Shift-clicking, Ctrl-clicking individual days, or selecting one or more columns,
- Click the **Detailed work hours/day** radio button,
- Adjust the hours to the nearest half hour by double-clicking on the table below the title **Work hours** to change them from working to nonworking.
- The edited days will now adopt the color of the **Exception** days.

When any calendar is changed or edited, the end date of all activities assigned with the calendar will be recalculated based on the new calendar. This may make a considerable difference to your project schedule dates.

When calendars have different start and end times some activities will span one day more than the duration of the activity because, for example, the last hour of the activity will roll into the next day.

It is recommended that the **Total work hours/day** form not be used as there is no control over the start and finish time of the day. It has been the author's experience that the software will assign some unpredictable start times, such as on the half hour. Users should use the **Detailed work hours/day** form.

When using the  function, the hours per day are set to the Database Calendar hours per day and this function does not use the hours set in the Workweek form of the calendar being edited. Therefore non work days made into working days with this function may have different working hours than other working days.

5.10 Calculation of Activity Durations in Days, Weeks or Months

P6 records durations in hours and the display of durations in days, weeks, or months of activities is a mathematical calculation that may be made by one of two methods:

- Individually for each Calendar – **RECOMMENDED METHOD**, or
- Globally for All Calendars – **NOT RECOMMENDED** (this was the only method used by P6 Version 6.2 and earlier).

In P6 Professional the option for the Global calculation of the durations in days, weeks, and months for all calendars is set by the Administrator in the **Admin**, **Admin Preferences...**, **Time Periods** tab.

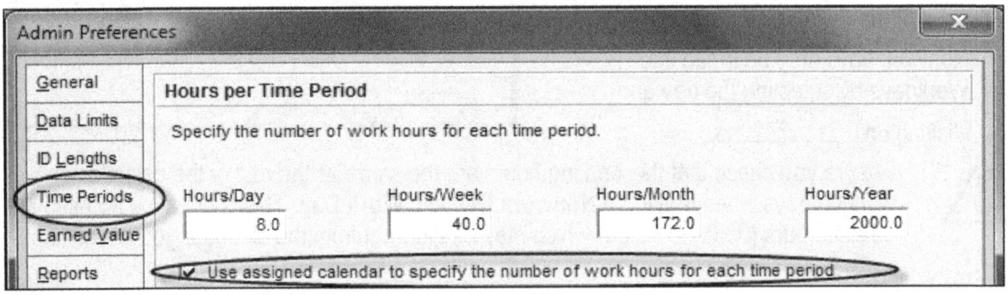

Un-checking the **Use assigned calendar to specify the number of work hours for each time period** check box disables individual calendar settings and therefore the activity durations in days weeks, months and years calculate incorrectly when the calendar **Hours per Time Period** do not conform to the settings in the **Admin**, **Admin Preferences...**, **Time Periods** tab. It is recommended that this never left unchecked.

In the P6 Optional Client the option for the Global calculation of the durations in days, weeks, and months for all calendars is set either by the Administrator through the Web Interface by selecting **Administer**, **Application Settings**, **Time Periods and** un-checking the **Use assigned calendar to specify the number of work hours for each time period** check box:

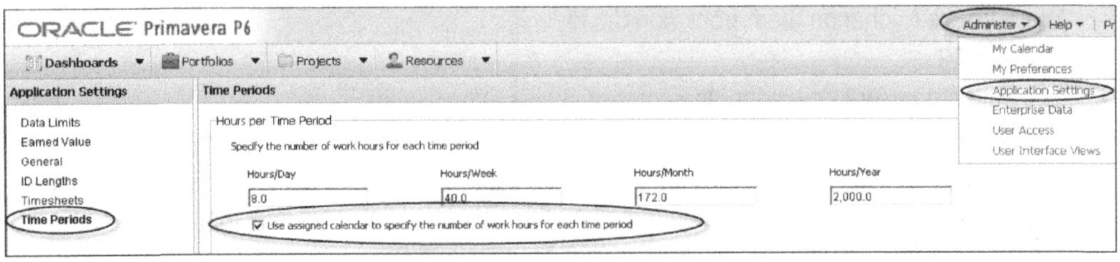

Individually for each Calendar – RECOMMENDED

In this situation the **Use assigned calendar to specify the number of work hours for each time period** box is checked and each calendar has its own set of parameters which are set in the **Hours per Time Period** tab when creating or editing a calendar. To set these parameters:

- Select **Enterprise**, **Calendars...**,
- Select the calendar to be edited,
- Click on the 

icon to open the **Calendar** form,
- Click on the 

icon to open the **Hours per Time Period** form:

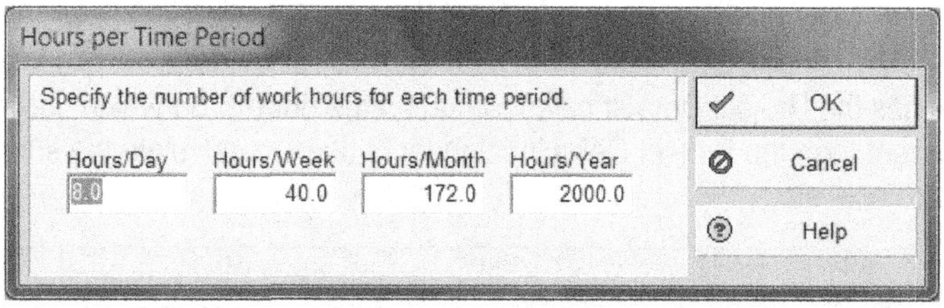

- This form allows the definition of the number of hours per day for each calendar, which in turn will enable the activity durations in days to be calculated and displayed correctly as long as the number of hours per day is the same for each work day in the calendar.

This is not an automated system and you will need to calculate each cell manually based on how your calendar is defined.

For the **Hours/Day** parameters to work it is advisable that each working day in a calendar has the same number of hours per day.

Therefore in the situation where a project is working a different number of hours per day it is recommended that you use an average hours per day and set both the **Work Hours per Day** in the **Hours per Time Period** form for every work day and the **Hours/Day** in the **Hours per Time Period** form to the one average number of hours per day.

For example; if you have a project that works 10 hours per day for Monday through Thursday, 8 hours on Friday and 6 hours on Saturday then each working day should be set to 9 hours per day.

Globally for All Calendars – NOT RECOMMENDED

With this option all calendars use the same parameters and these are set by the database administrator, in the **Hours per Time Periods** form which in turn sets the calculation for all calendars in the database to the same values.

This is **NOT** recommended unless all calendars in a database have exactly the same number of hours per day, days per week, and weeks per year which is very unusual.

When all the calendars do not have exactly the same number of hours per day, days per week, etc. then the durations in days, weeks, or months will not calculate correctly for calendars that do not comply with the setting in the **Admin Preferences**, **Time Periods** form. It is strongly recommended that this option is **NEVER UNCHECKED**.

5.11 Calendars for Calculating Project, WBS and Other Summary Durations

In Primavera Version 7 and later the summary durations of bands projects in the **Projects Window** are calculated based on the **Database Default Calendar** from the first activity Start to the last activity Finish from all the project in that band.

The summary duration of WBS bands and other bands created by Grouping activities by User Defined Fields or Activity Codes are calculated by:

- When all the activities in a band share the same calendar then the summary duration is calculated on the calendar of the activities in the band and the calendar name is displayed in the Calendar column, and
- When the calendars for the activities are different the summary duration is calculated on the Project Default calendar and the calendar field is blank.

The picture below has the Project Default calendar set as the 8hr/d & 5d/w and shows that when the calendars are different then the Project Default calendar is used to calculate the summary duration for WBS Nodes, Projects etc.:

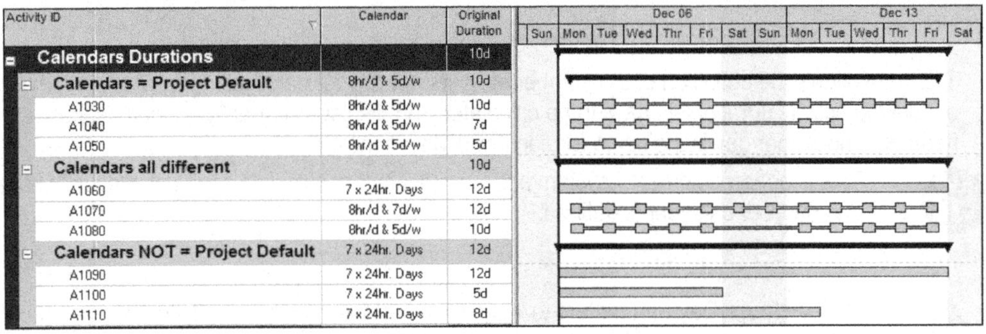

5.12 Tips for Mixed Calendar Schedules

When a project has mixed calendars, say an 8- and 10-hour per day, then a change of calendar from a predecessor on an 8-hour per day calendar to successor on a 10-hour calendar, the successor activity may have one hour of work on the same day as the predecessor and span 2 days. This situation leads to interesting Float calculations and confusion to schedulers.

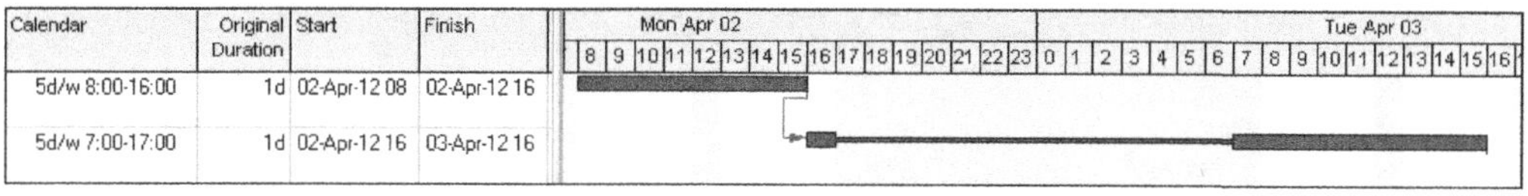

Primavera P6 does not have a "Start on a New Day" function found in other products such as Asta Powerproject, but which in itself brings on a new set of calculation issues. Techniques that may be considered to ensure one-day activities span one day and two-day activities span two days, etc. are:

- Apply an appropriate lag to the relationship, or
- When the Start and Finish Times are not an important scheduling consideration then assign all the calendars the same Start and Finish time but adjust the duration of the lunch break so the days have the desired number of hours. For example, a 10-hour day calendar could start at 07:00 and finish at 17:00 without any lunch break and an 8-hour calendar could start at 07:00 and finish at 17:00 and be assigned a 2-hour lunch break.

The picture below shows how 8-hour a day and 12-hour a day calendars in the same project may be set up to ensure all activities start and finish on the same day:

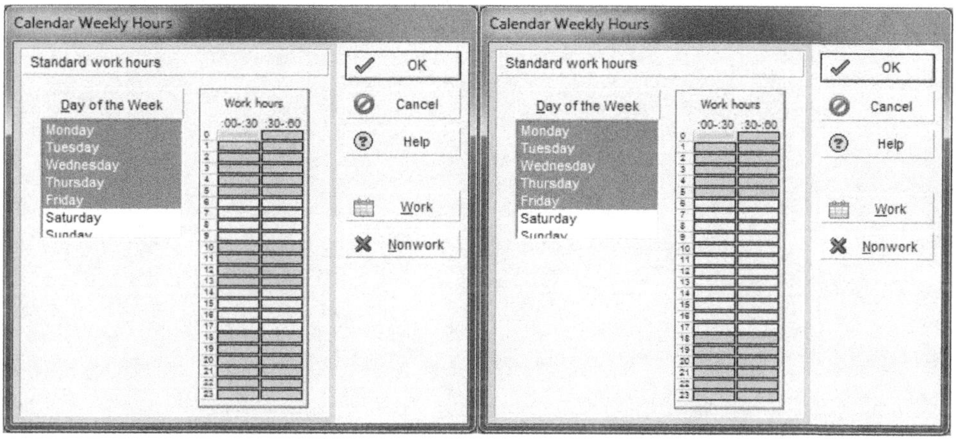

5.13 *Workshop 3 – Maintaining the Calendars*

Background

The normal working week at OzBuild Pty Ltd is Monday through Friday, 8 hours per day excluding public holidays. The installation staff works Monday through Saturday, 8 hours per day and the company observes the following holidays:

	2016	2017	2018	2019
New Year's Day	1 January	2 January*	1 January	1 January
Easter	25 - 28 March	14 - 17 April	30 March - 2 April	19 - 22 April
Christmas Day	27 December*	25 December	25 December	25 December
Boxing Day	26 December	26 December	26 December	26December

* These holidays occur on a weekend and the dates have been moved to the next weekday.

NOTE: Boxing Day is a holiday the day after Christmas celebrated in many countries.

Assignment

Although we could use a standard calendar we will create two new calendars for this project.

1. Ensure your new OzBuild Bid project is open.
2. Select **Enterprise**, **Calendars...** to open the **Calendars** form.
3. Click on the **Project** radio button.
4. Create a new Project Calendar titled "OzBuild 5 d/w" by clicking on the [Add] button and copying an appropriate calendar.
5. Click on the [Modify...] button to open the **Calendars** form.
6. Select the **Detailed work hours/day** radio button.
7. Click on the [Workweek...] button to open the **Calendar Weekly Hours** form.
8. Make the work hours from 08:00 to 16:00 without a lunch break from Monday to Friday and close the form.
9. Select **<None>** for **Inherit holidays and exceptions from Global Calendar**.
10. Click on the [Time Periods] button and check the Hours per Time Period are the same as in the diagram below, if not then edit them and then close the form:

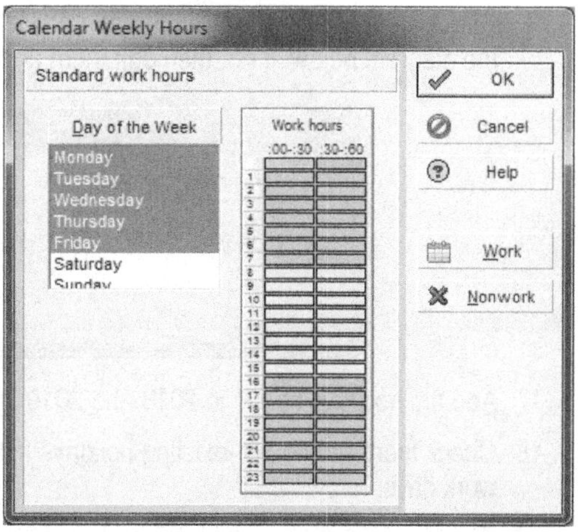

continued...

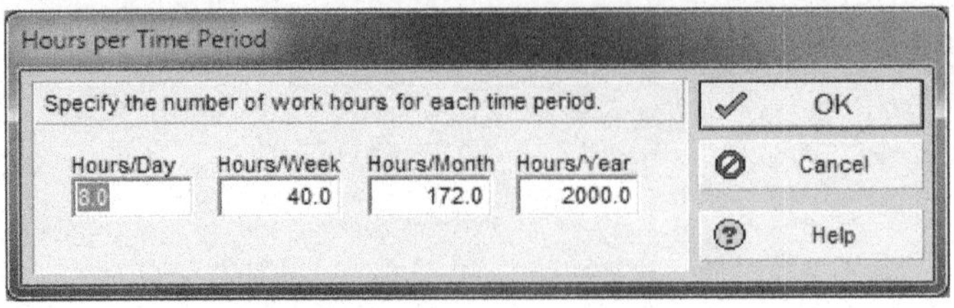

11. Add the holidays above in 2018 and 2019 only.
12. Check there are no pre-existing holidays in the calendar you copied that need to be made into work days.

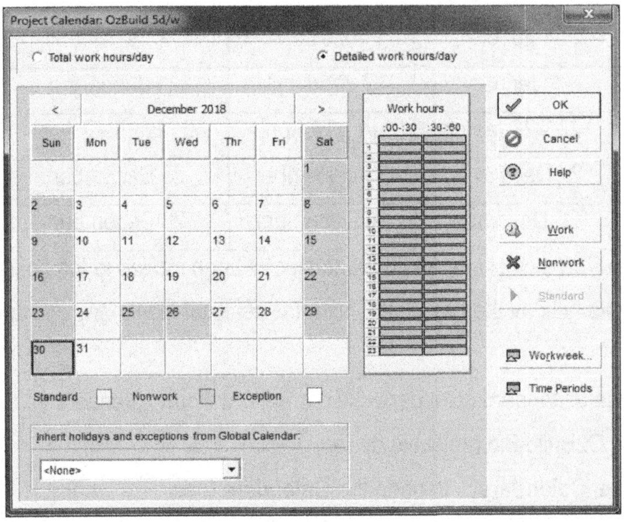

13. Create a new calendar titled "OzBuild 6 d/w" for the 6-day week by copying the same Global calendar.
14. Make the work hours from 8:00 to 16:00 from Monday to Saturday and close the form.
15. Select **<None>** for **Inherit holidays and exceptions from Global Calendar**.
16. Click on the  button and check the Hours per Time Period are the same as in the diagram below, if not then edit them and then close the form:

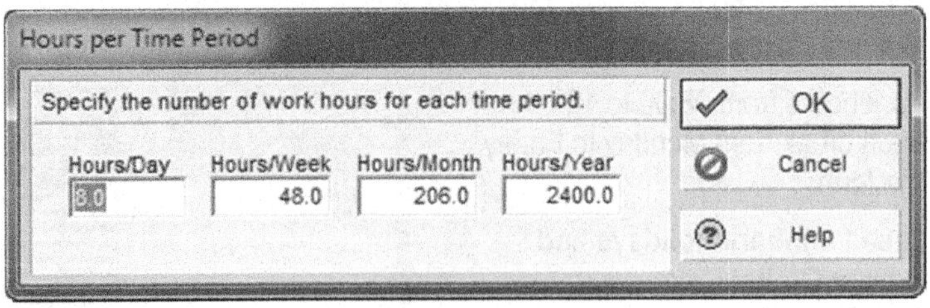

17. Add the holidays above in 2018 and 2019 only.
18. Check there are no pre-existing holidays in the calendar you copied that need to be made into work days.
19. Should you wish to make the first day of the week a Monday then select **Admin**, **Admin Preferences**, **General** tab and change the Starting Day of Week to Monday.
    NOTE: The workshop pictures in this book use the Primavera default and have not had the Starting Day of Week changed to Monday.

6 CREATING A PRIMAVERA PROJECT WBS

This chapter outlines how to create a WBS structure to enable activities to be assigned to a WBS Node so a schedule may be created.

The **Project WBS** function is designed to record a hierarchical WBS that has been developed on a traditional basis as outlined in many project management documents. A well-structured WBS should:

- Include all the project deliverables, and
- Be set at the appropriate level for summarizing project activities and reporting project progress.

The **Project WBS** function is used to group and summarize activities under a hierarchical structure in the same way as the WBS function in P3 and SureTrak, and the Custom Outline Codes in Microsoft Project. It is also similar to Outlining in all versions of Microsoft Project; however, in Primavera the Activities are assigned to a hierarchical WBS Node and are not demoted under a Parent task as with Outlining with Microsoft Project. The WBS structure is used to organize and summarize your project activities, including costs and resources during the planning, scheduling, and updating of Projects.

The project should be granulated (broken down) into manageable areas by using a project breakdown structure based on attributes of the project such as the Phases or Stages, Systems and Subsystems, Processes, Disciplines or Trades, and Areas or Locations of work. These headings are normally the basis of the project breakdown structure and are used to create the Primavera WBS structure, and the WBS should present the primary view of your project.

Defining the project breakdown structure may be a major task for project managers.

Primavera also has an **Activity Code** function similar to the **Activity Code** function in Primavera P3 and SureTrak software, Codes in Asta Powerproject and the Custom Outline Codes in Microsoft Project. This feature enables the grouping of activities under headings other than the "WBS Structure." Unlike in Primavera P3 and SureTrak software, **Activity Codes** are not the primary method of organizing activities in Primavera. They are covered in the **Activity Codes and Grouping Activities** chapter.

Topic	Menu Command
• Creating and Deleting a WBS Node	The menu commands **Add**, **Delete**, **Copy**, **Cut** and **Paste** all work to create, delete, move, and copy WBS Nodes.
• WBS Categories	WBS Categories are created in Professional P6 using the **Admin**, **Admin Categories...**, **WBS Categories** tab and are assigned to WBS Nodes by inserting the **WBS Categories** column in the **WBS Window**.

A **WBS Node** is a term used by Primavera that is often called a **WBS Code** and is a single point in the WBS structure that activities are assigned to. A Primavera WBS Node may record more information than P3, SureTrak, or Microsoft Project including the following data:

- **Anticipated Dates**, which are used to create a bar in the **WBS Window** when there are no activities under the WBS Node, but do not summarize in the **Projects Window**.
- **Notes**, which are recorded under **Notebook Topics**,
- **Budget**, **Spending Plan** and **Budget Change Log**,
- **WBS Milestones**, which may be used for assigning progress at WBS Node,
- **WP & Docs** that provide links to documents, and
- The rules for calculating **Earned Value** for each WBS Node.

The start and finish dates of a WBS Node are adopted from the earliest start date and latest finish date of the detailed activities under that WBS Node and use the **WBS Anticipated Dates** to create a bar when there are no activities assigned to a WBS Node.

The duration of a WBS Node is calculated from the start and finish dates, the database **Default Calendar** and the **User Options**.

A WBS Node may not have costs or resources assigned directly to the node. All costs and quantities are calculated from the activities associated with the WBS Node.

6.1 Opening and Navigating the WBS Window

To view, edit, or create a **WBS** structure:

- The project must be open.
- The **WBS Window** is displayed by selecting **Project**, **WBS** or by clicking on the **WBS** icon on the **Project** toolbar.
- The following picture is of the City Center Office Building Addition project showing the WBS Nodes on the left side of the screen and the WBS bars on the right side of the screen.
- The icons in the **Top Layout** toolbar enable different views of the WBS. Click on each icon to see its purpose.

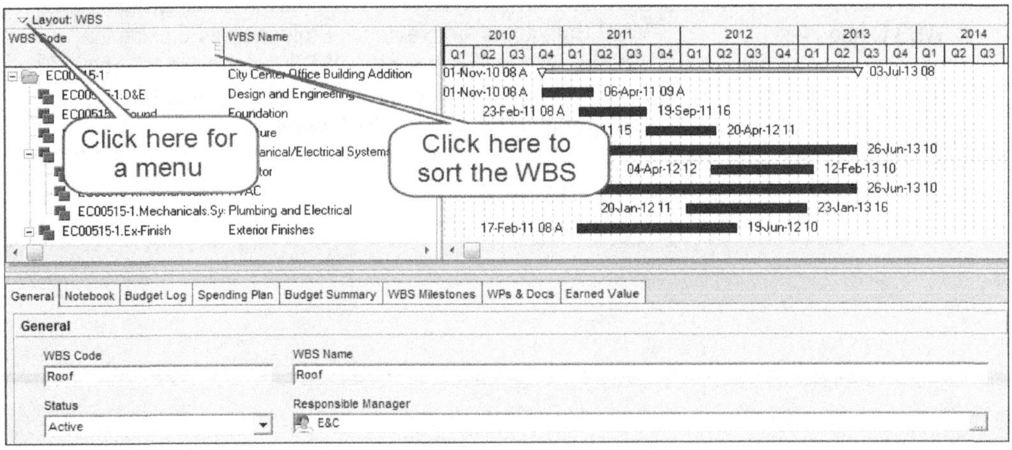

6.2 Creating and Deleting a WBS Node

To create a new WBS Node:

- Select a WBS Code or Name and right-click to display the menu, or
- Select the **Edit** menu command, or
- Use the icons from the **Edit** toolbar ,
- Use the  icons on the **Move** toolbar to put the WBS Nodes at the right level or to reorder them.

The commands **Add**, **Delete**, **Copy**, **Cut** and **Paste** all work to create, delete, move, and copy WBS Nodes.

- **Add** will add a new WBS Node under the level currently highlighted.
- **Delete** will delete the WBS Node. When a WBS Node has been assigned activities you will be given the option to either delete the activities or reassign the activities by selecting the **Merge Element(s)** option in the **Merge or Delete WBS Element(s)** form.

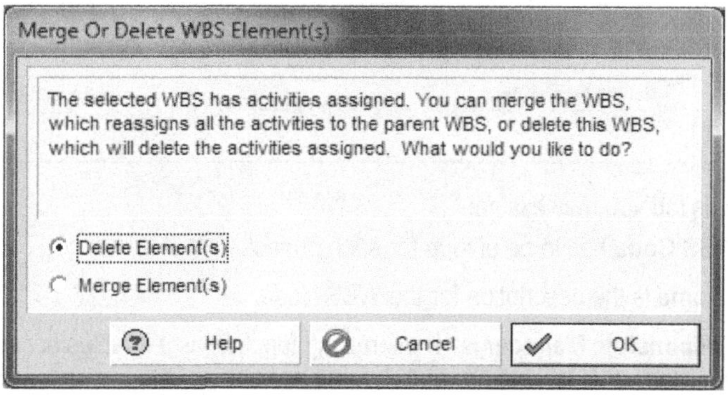

- **Copy** copies a WBS Node and the associated activities.
- **Cut** prepares to move a WBS Node and the associated activities to another location.
- **Paste** pastes a **Cut** or **Copied** WBS Node. After selecting **Paste**, the **Copy WBS Options** form, **Copy Activity Options** form, and **Renumber Activity IDs** form may be presented which enables the selection of the data to be pasted with the WBS Node. You will also be asked to renumber activities.

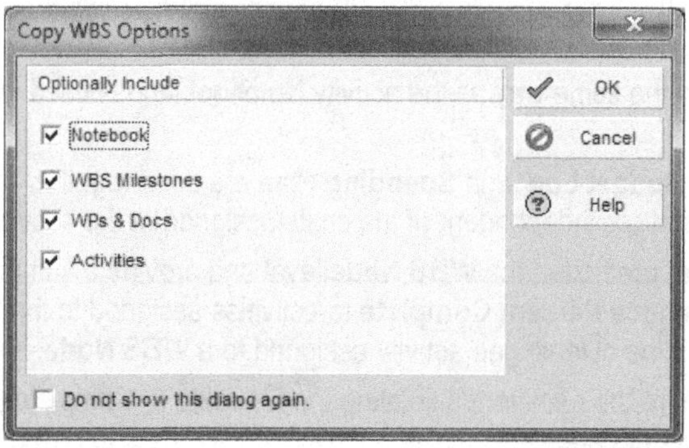

The **High Level Resource Planning Assignments** option was added in Primavera Version 6.0 web access software and now called Primavera P6 Enterprise Project Portfolio Management (earlier versions were called myPrimavera) and is web-based.

6.3 *WBS Node Separator*

The Default WBS Node Separator is assigned in the **Admin**, **Admin Preferences...**, **General** tab.

Each individual project WBS Node separator is defined in the **Projects Window**, **Project Details** form, **Settings** tab and overrides the default set in the **Admin Preferences** form, **General** tab.

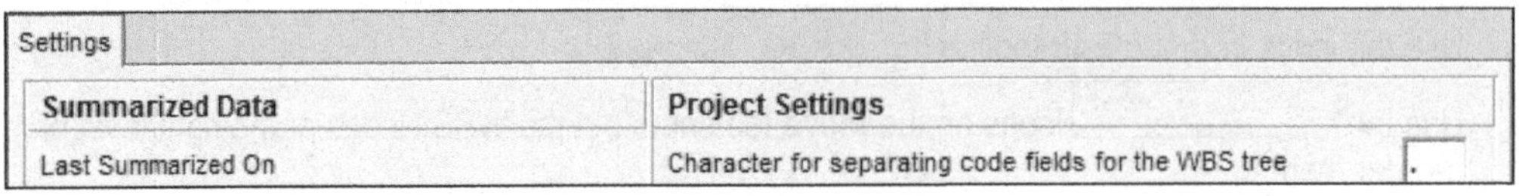

6.4 *Work Breakdown Structure Lower Pane Details*

The lower pane has a number of tabs that may be hidden or displayed.

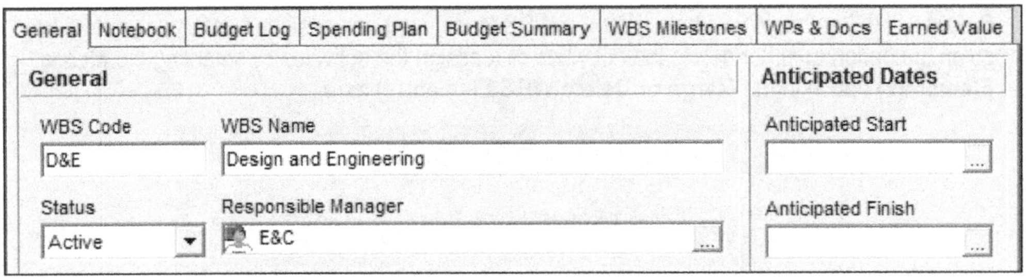

- **General** – in this tab you may assign:
  - The **WBS Code** has to be unique for each project.
  - **WBS Name** is the description for the WBS Node.
  - The **Responsible Manager** is an interesting function as it enables access to data to be controlled at the WBS Node level. When a User has access to change data in one WBS Node only then they are able to see the whole project but may only change data in the one node.
  - **Anticipated Dates**, as with the Project Anticipated Dates, will display a bar when the WBS Node has no activities but does not summarize in the **Projects Window**.
  - The **Status** – there are four WBS Status types: **Planned**, **Active**, **Inactive**, and **What-if**. The status of a WBS Node controls viewing and access to the Nodes and Activities assigned to the nodes by Primavera Timesheet users. These may be used in filtering and reporting.
- **Notebook** is used in the same way as the activity Notebook and is used to record notes about the WBS Node.
- **Budget Summary**, **Budget Log**, and **Spending Plan** are used together as a top-down method of assigning budgets and are independent of the costs assigned at the activity level.
- **WBS Milestones** are created at the **WBS Node** level and provide a summary method of assigning a **Performance Percent Complete** to activities assigned to that node. For this function to operate there must be at least one activity assigned to a **WBS Node**.
- **Earned Value** is where the rules for calculating the Estimate to Complete (ETC) and other Earned Value parameters are set.
- **WPs & Docs** enables the assignment of documents to a WBS Node and operates in the same way as the activities **WPs & Docs** tab.
- Displaying **Planning Resources** that may be assigned to WBS Nodes using **Primavera Web** (earlier versions were called myPrimavera), the web interface.

6.5 WBS Categories

WBS Nodes may be assigned categories, which enable WBS Nodes within an EPS to be grouped and sorted in different ways. WBS Categories are to WBS Nodes as Activity Codes are to Activities. In earlier P6 versions these were referred to as **Project Phases**.

- WBS Categories are created using:
  - In the Professional version in the **Admin**, **Admin Categories...**, **WBS Categories** tab, and
  - In the Optional Client **Administer**, **Enterprise Data, Projects BS Categories**.
- WBS Categories are assigned to and removed from WBS Nodes by inserting the **WBS Categories** column into the **WBS Window**.

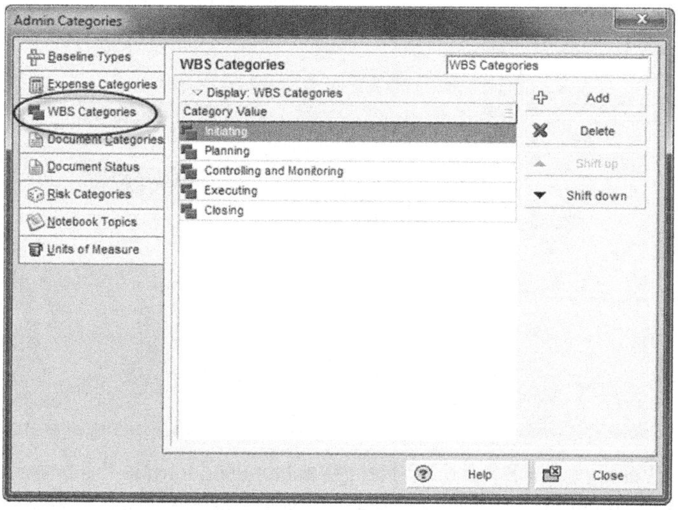

One use of a WBS Category could be, for example, to tag the WBS Nodes with the phases such as Design, Procure and Install and then the Activities may be grouped by WBS Category and then WBS or some other Activity Code.

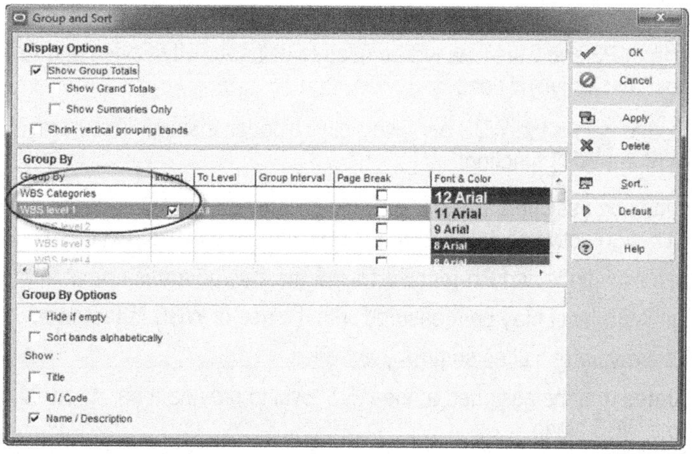

This topic is covered in more details in the **Grouping, Sort and Layouts** chapter.

WBS Categories may also be used in the **Tracking Window**.

6.6 Displaying the WBS in the Activity Window

On moving back to the Activity window the WBS may be displayed if an applicable Layout is selected or the View is Grouped by WBS.

If the WBS in not displayed then select **View**, **Group and Sort by**, click on the 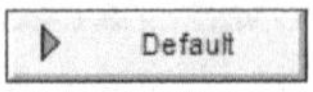

button or under the **Group By** box select **WBS** as in the form below:

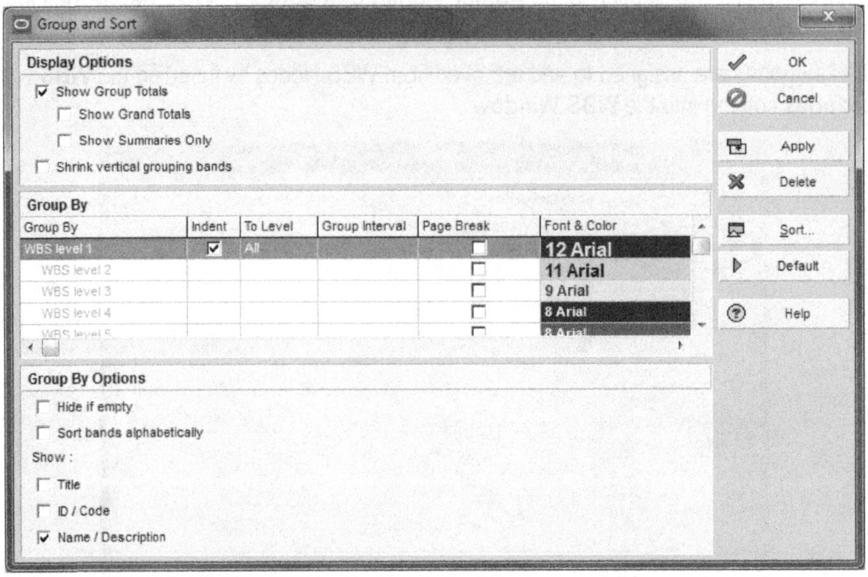

In P6 Versions 8.1, 8.2 and 8.3 that the author used to write this book, he found that after closing the Group and Sort form that the WBS bands were not displayed correctly and the user should press the F5 key to refresh the screen allowing the bands to be correctly displayed

6.7 Why a Primavera WBS is Important

People converting from P3 and SureTrak will be used to using Activity Codes and Activity ID Codes. Primavera does not have Activity ID codes.

You may be tempted to ignore the WBS and use Activity Codes instead. This paragraph will explain the main purposes of the WBS function:

- **User Access** may be assigned at this level, so two schedulers may open the same project and one may only change activities in WBS Nodes that have been assigned to that user.
- **Earned Value** calculations and **Project Performance** may be measured at this level.
- Progress at the WBS level may be measured with the use of **WBS Milestones**.
- WBS Activities are very useful as summary activities.
- **Anticipated Dates** may be assigned at the WBS level to provide a bar when no activities have been added to a WBS Node.
- The **Tracking Window** operates down to WBS Node level.
- There are a number of standard **Reports** that function at WBS Node level.

6.8 Workshop 4 – Creating the Work Breakdown Structure

Background

A review of the scope identifies three deliverables:

- Technical Specification
- Delivery Plan
- Bid Document

Assignment

1. With your OzBuild project open click on the button to open the **WBS Window**.
2. Click in the WBS field header until the sort indicator is displayed as three horizontal bars, as displayed in the picture below. The WBS will now be displayed hierarchically now:

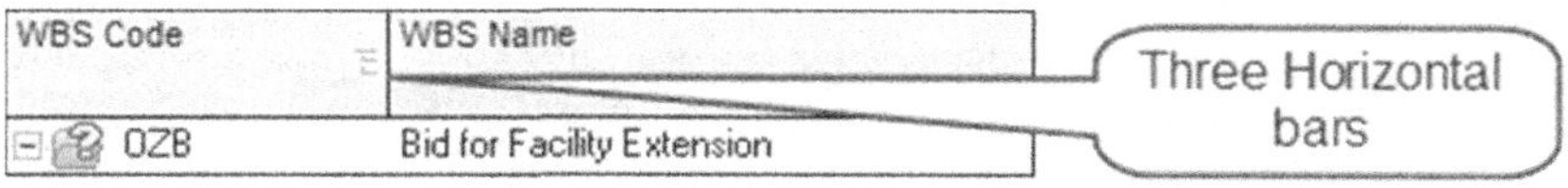

3. Select the Project Node and press the **Ins** key, or right-click and select **Add** to add the WBS Nodes and continue to add all three WBS Nodes for the three Phases above.
4. If the WBS Nodes are not indented, click the **WBS Code** heading as described in paragraph 2, until they are indented.
5. Use the arrows on the **Move** toolbar (right side of screen) to put them in the correct order and indent.
6. Your result should look like the following picture:

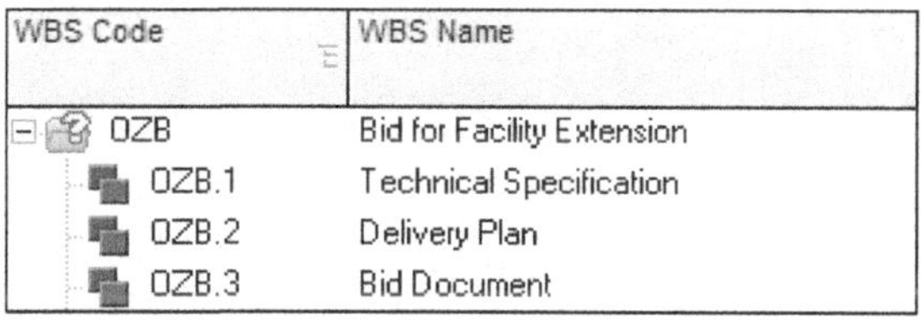

7. Move to the **Activities Window** by clicking on the icon on the **Project** toolbar or clicking on the **Activities** tab. Your screen may look like this:

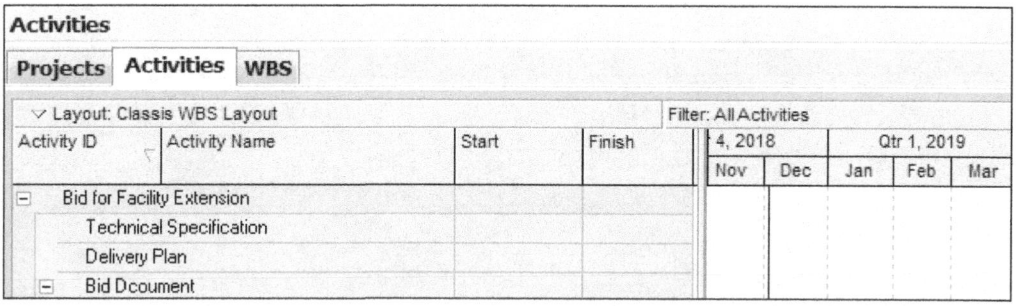

NOTE: Users may have to press the F5 key to refresh their data if the WBS is displayed incorrectly.

continued...

8. If your view looks different, select View, Layout, Open Layout..., select the **Classic WBS Layout** and click the Open button.
9. Depending on the Layout that your software has loaded, your data may be displayed in different columns, colors, and bar formatting. Layouts are covered in the **Group, Sort and Layouts** chapter. Should your layout not enable you to review your data entry, try selecting a different layout using the command **View**, **Layouts**, **Open Layout...**and selecting another layout from the list such as the Classic or Default WBS Layout.
10. If it is still not displayed correctly select **View**, **Group and Sort by**, click on the Default button and then under the **Group By** box select **WBS** as in the form below:

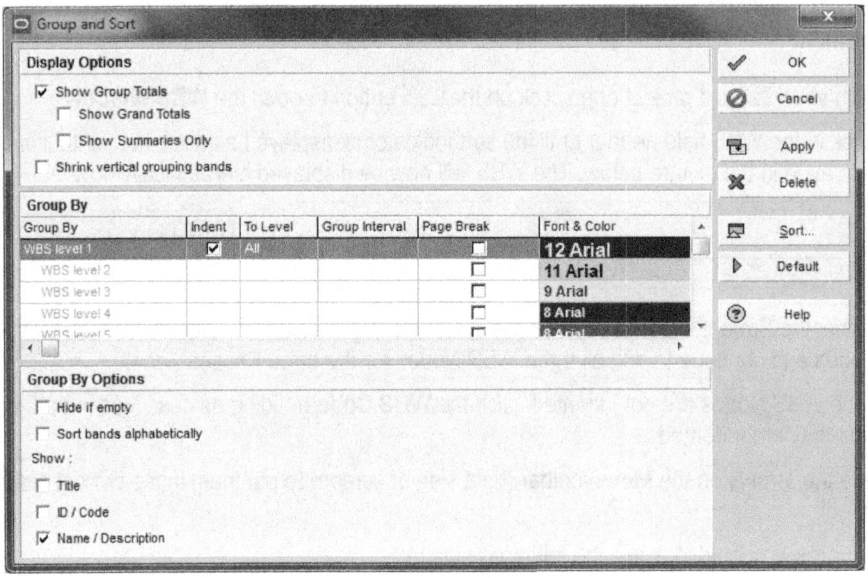

7 ADDING ACTIVITIES AND ORGANIZING UNDER THE WBS

Activities should be well-defined, measurable pieces of work with a measurable outcome. Activity descriptions containing only nouns such as "Bid Document" have confusing meanings. Does this mean read, write, review, submit or all of these? Adequate activity descriptions always have a verb-noun structure to them. A more appropriate activity description would be "Write Bid Document" or "Review and Submit Bid Document." The limit for activity names is 120 characters, but try to keep activity descriptions meaningful yet short and concise so they are easier to print.

When activities are created they are normally added under a WBS Node but may be organized under other coding structures such as Activity Codes or User Defined Fields.

This chapter will cover the following topics:

Topic	Menu Command
• Setting **Auto-numbering Defaults** and other defaults for new Activities	Select the **Defaults** tab from the **Bottom** pane in the **Project Window**.
• **Adding New Activities**	Select a line in the schedule and strike the **Ins** (**Insert Key**) or right-click and select the **Add** menu item.
• **Activity Details** form	May be displayed in the bottom pane by selecting **View**, **Show on Bottom**, **Details**.
• **Copying** activities in **Primavera**	Select the activities and copy and paste to the required location.
• **% Complete Type**	Use the **% Complete Type** drop down box in the **General** tab of the **Activity Details** form.
• **Milestones**	Use the **Activity Type** drop down box in the **General** tab of the **Activity Details** form.
• Assigning **WBS Nodes** to activities	• Create an activity in an existing WBS band, • Drag one or more activities into the desired band, • Display the WBS column and click the WBS cell to display the **Select WBS** form, or • Open the **General** tab in the lower window.

7.1 *New Activity Defaults*

After creating a new project and before adding activities it is important to set the defaults such as the Activity ID Numbers and Calendars. By setting them correctly before adding activities you will save a significant amount of time because you will not have to change a number of attributes against all activities at a later date. These defaults are set in the **Defaults** tab of the **Project Details** form:

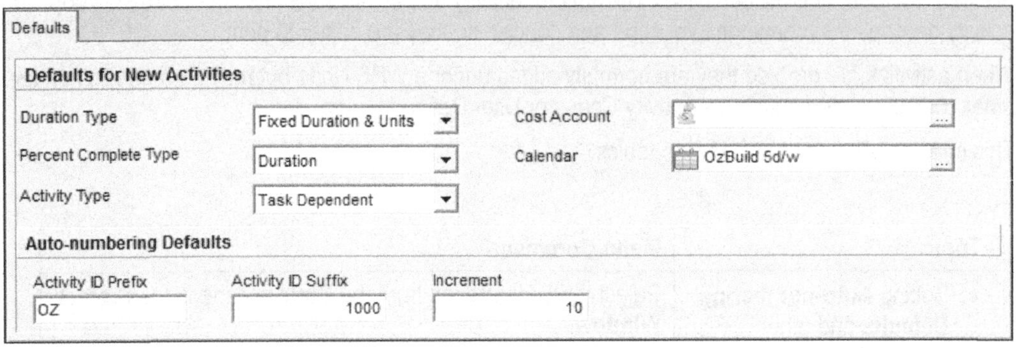

7.1.1 Duration Type

None of the **Duration Type** options affects how the schedule calculates until one or more resources is assigned to an Activity. The following options are available:

- **Fixed Units**
- **Fixed Duration & Units/Time**
- **Fixed Units/Time**
- **Fixed Duration & Units**

If you do not plan to add resources to Activities, then you do not need to assign a **Duration Type** and it may be left as the default.

This topic will be covered in detail in the **Assigning Roles and Resources Expenses** chapter.

7.1.2 Percent Complete Type

The **Percent Complete** type should be understood if it is intended to be used to update (status or progress) the schedule. This option may be set for each activity individually in Primavera and the default for new activities is set in the **Percent Complete Type** drop down box. Primavera has many Activity Percent Complete fields that may be displayed in columns and we will discuss four of them now:

Activity % Complete, which may be linked to only one of the three following % Complete fields and is always linked to the % Complete displayed on the Gantt Chart bars:

- **Physical % Complete**, which is independent of activity resources and durations,
- **Duration % Complete**, which is linked to activity durations, and
- **Units % Complete**, which is linked to resource units.

There are three percent complete options; each new activity is assigned the project default **Percent Complete Type** and then this may be edited for each activity as required.

Therefore, for example, when the option of **Physical % Complete** is selected for an activity then the **Activity % Complete** and the **Physical % Complete** are linked and a change to one will change the other and this value would be displayed on the Gantt Chart.

Default Percent Complete Type

The **Default Percent Complete Type** for each new activity in each project is assigned in the **Defaults** tab of the **Details** form in the **Project Window**:

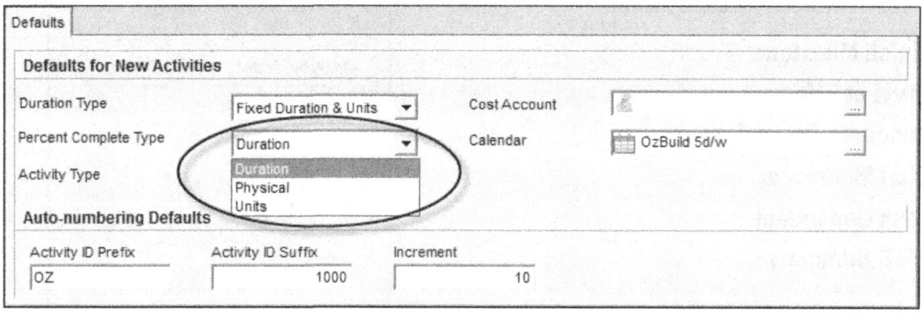

- A new activity Percent Complete Type is set to the Default Percent Complete when created and may be changed at any time.

Percent Complete Types

- **Physical % Complete** – This field enables the user to enter the percent complete of an activity and this value is independent of the activity durations. This is similar to the way P3 and SureTrak calculates the % Complete when the **Link Remaining Duration and Percent Complete** option is NOT selected.
- **Duration % Complete** – This field is calculated from the proportion of the **Original Duration** and the **Remaining Duration** and they are linked. A change to one value will change the other. When the **Remaining Duration** is set to greater than the **Original Duration** this percent complete is always zero. This is similar to the way P3 and SureTrak calculate the % Complete when the **Link Remaining Duration and Percent Complete** option is selected
- **Units % Complete** – This is where the percent complete is calculated from the resources' Actual and Remaining Units of Labor and Non Labor resources only. A change to one value will change the other and when more than one resource is assigned then all the Actual Units for all resources will be changed proportionally. This will be covered further in the **Updating Resources** chapter. This is similar to the Microsoft Project % Work Complete.

Activity % Complete

The **Activity % Complete** field is linked to the **% Complete Type** field assigned to an activity in the **General** tab of the **Details** form in the **Activities Window** or the **% Complete Type** column:

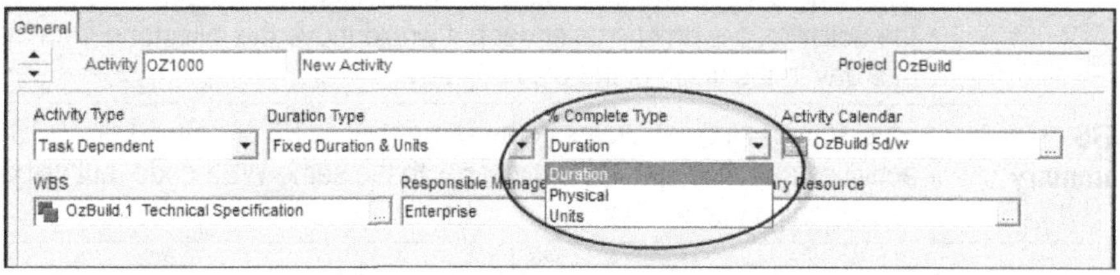

The **Activity % Complete** is also linked the **% Complete Bar** and this value is represented on the **% Complete** Bar.

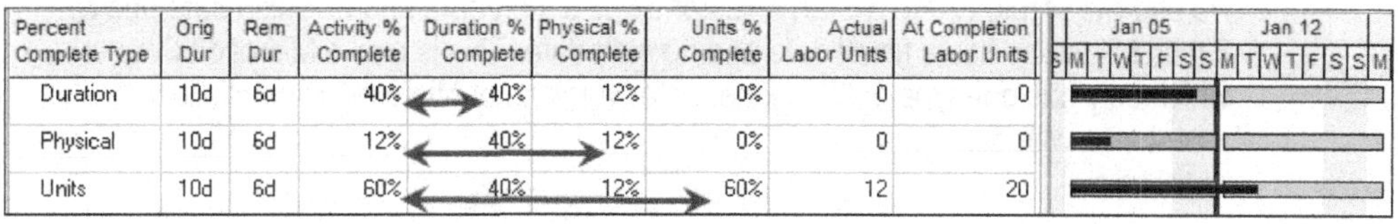

Percent Complete Type	Orig Dur	Rem Dur	Activity % Complete	Duration % Complete	Physical % Complete	Units % Complete	Actual Labor Units	At Completion Labor Units
Duration	10d	6d	40%	40%	12%	0%	0	0
Physical	10d	6d	12%	40%	12%	0%	0	0
Units	10d	6d	60%	40%	12%	60%	12	20

7.1.3 Activity Types and Milestones

An Activity may be assigned one of the following default Activity Types using the drop down box in the Project Defaults tab:

- **Finish Milestone**
- **Level of Effort**
- **Resource Dependent**
- **Start Milestone**
- **Task Dependent**
- **WBS Summary**

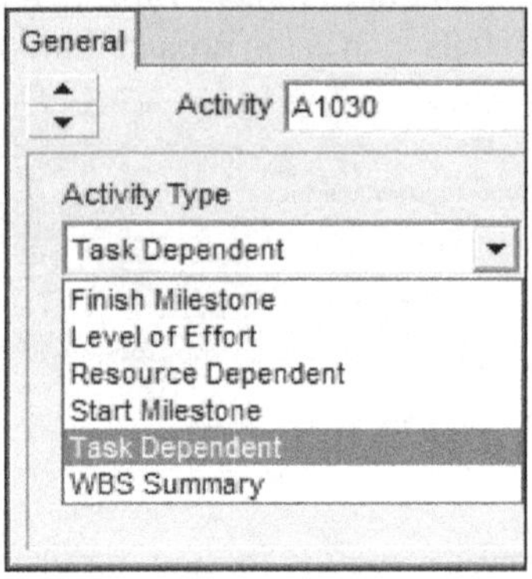

Activity Type	Description
• **Task Dependent**	These Activity Types have a duration and will only calculate the duration using the assigned calendar even when one or more resources are assigned to an activity.
• **Resource Dependent**	These Activity Types have a duration and will calculate the duration only using the calendar assigned to the activity when NO resources are assigned to the activity. These activities acknowledge Resource Calendars when resources are assigned. This is similar to an Independent Activity Type in P3 and SureTrak. They acknowledge the Activity calendar to calculate the Early Start date.
• **Level of Effort – LOE**	This Activity type is similar to P3 and SureTrak Hammock activities. It spans from the start or finish of one or more predecessor activities to the start or finish of one or more successor activities which are linked by relationships.
• **Start Milestone**	A Start Milestone has a start date and no finish date and is scheduled at the start of a time period and may not be assigned Resources.
• **Finish Milestone**	A Finish Milestone has a finish date, no start date and is scheduled at the end of a time period and may not be assigned Resources. Changing a milestone from Start to Finish would not affect a schedule when all the activities are on one calendar but would move the milestone from the start of a day to the finish of the previous day.
• **WBS Summary**	This Activity type calculates in the same way as P3 and SureTrak WBS activities and they span all activities with the same WBS code, but without relationships that are used with LOEs.

A Milestone has zero duration and is used to mark the start or finish of a major event. Primavera differentiates between **Start** and **Finish Milestones** in the same way as P3 and SureTrak, where a Start Milestone has a start date and no finish date and a Finish Milestone has a finish date and no start date. This is unlike Microsoft Project, which only has one type of Milestone. Later versions of Microsoft Project allow milestones with durations.

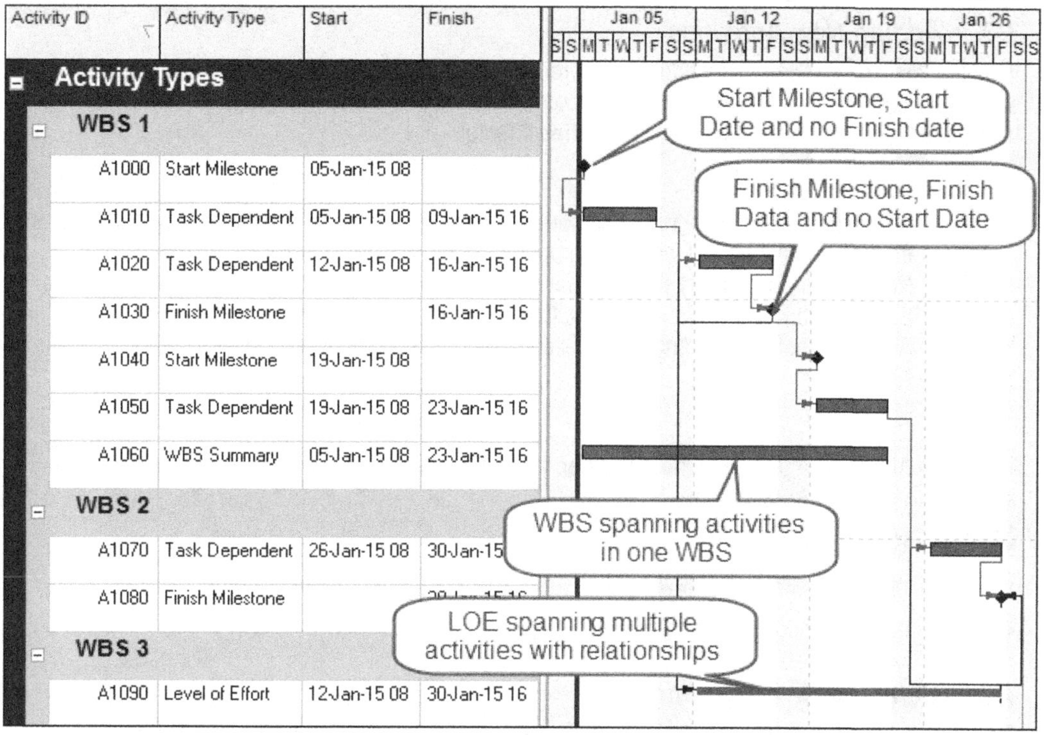

7.1.4 Cost Account

This selects the default Cost Account for all new Resources and Expenses and is blank by default. Cost Accounts are covered in detail in the **Other Methods of Organizing Activities** chapter.

7.1.5 Calendar

This topic was covered in detail in the **Calendars** chapter. This drop down box is used to select the default calendar for an activity. A **Default Project Calendar** is assigned to each project from the **Global** or **Project** calendar list.

All new activities are assigned the project **Default Project Calendar** when they are created; however, individual calendars may be assigned for each activity.

7.1.6 Auto-numbering Defaults

The **Auto-numbering Defaults** decides how new activities are numbered. The first activity added to a new project will be based on the defaults set in this form.

- The **Increment Activity ID based on selected activity** check box controls which of the **Auto-numbering Defaults** rules are acknowledged after the first activity is added:
  - ➢ When checked, new activities will inherit the number of the highlighted activity plus the **Increment** number, and
  - ➢ When unchecked, new activities will use the **Activity ID Prefix,** plus the **Activity ID Suffix** plus the Increment from the last activity.

i There are no Activity ID Codes allowing logic to be automatically embedded into the Activity IDs, which are a powerful features of both P3 and SureTrak.

7.2 Adding New Activities

It is often quicker to create a schedule in a spreadsheet and import the data into the scheduling software. Primavera offers a spreadsheet import function found under **File**, **Import...** which is very user friendly. This is covered in detail in **Utilities** chapter.

Some data associated with an imported activity must exist before the activity is imported from Excel otherwise it will not be imported. This includes items such as Roles, Resources, and Activity Codes. These data items may be imported using the Primavera SDK (which is loaded from the installation CD and instructions are available on the Administration Guide) and an Excel spreadsheet available from the Oracles Primavera Knowledgebase.

To add an Activity to a project in the **Activities Window** you must first open the project, select the appropriate WBS Node and then:

- Select **Edit**, **Add**, or
- Press the **Insert** key on the keyboard, or
- Click on the Add icon on the **Edit** toolbar.

7.3 Default Activity Duration

The default activity duration for newly created activities is specified in the **Admin**, **Admin Preferences...**, **General** tab **Activity Duration cell**.

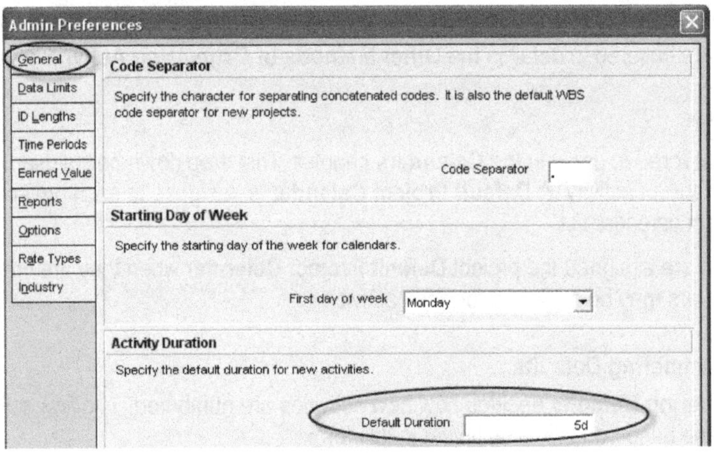

7.4 Copying Activities from other Programs

Activity data may NOT be copied from or updated from other programs (such as Excel) by cutting and pasting.

7.5 Copying Activities in P6

Activities may be copied from another project when both projects are open at the same time or copied from within the same project using the normal Windows commands **Copy** and **Paste**, by using the menu commands **Edit, Copy** and **Edit, Paste**, or by using **Ctrl+C** and **Ctrl+V**.

One or more activities may be selected to be copied by:

- **Ctrl-**clicking, or

- Holding the **shift** key and clicking on the first and last activity in a range, or
- Dragging a range with the mouse. With this operation be sure to select the whole activity or activities, not just a cell.

The **Copy Activity Options** form will be displayed. These options are self-explanatory:

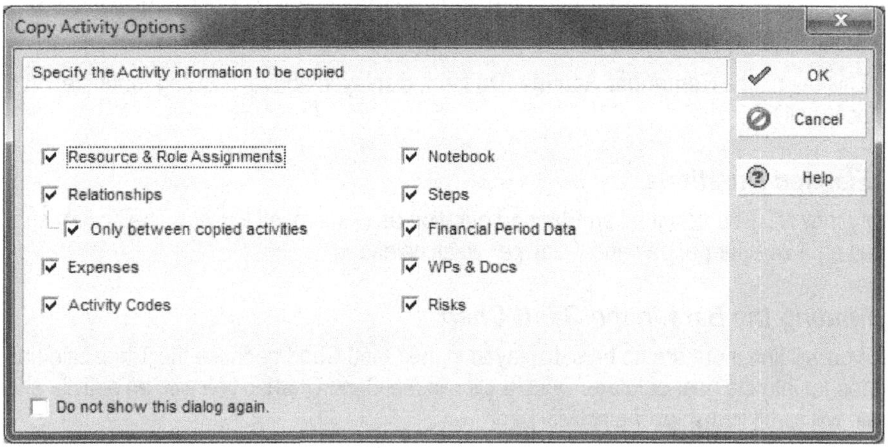

P6 Version 7 introduced a new function that allows the renumbering of pasted activities. The **Renumber Activity IDs** form is displayed next:

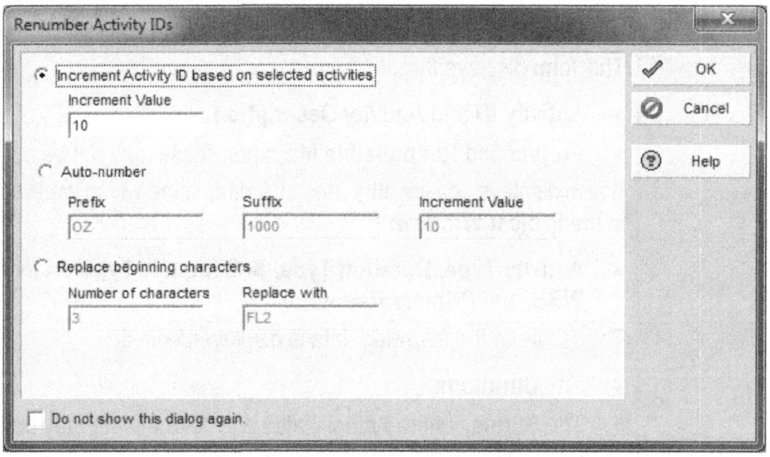

Should you attempt to renumber to Activity IDs that already exist then a further form is presented to allow manual renumbering by entering the new Activity Id in the **New Activity ID** column:

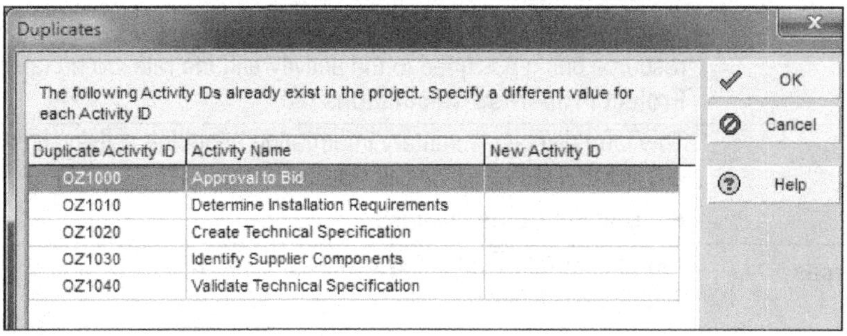

7.6 Renumbering Activity IDs

There is a new function in P6 Version 7 allowing the renumbering of activities. To use this function:

- Select the activities that are to be renumbered,
- Select from the menu **Edit**, **Renumber Activity IDs** or right-click in the columns area and select **Renumber Activity IDs**,
- This opens the **Renumber Activity IDs** form, displayed above, allowing renumbering of the activity IDs.

7.7 Elapsed Durations

An activity may NOT be assigned an **Elapsed** duration as in Microsoft Project. The activity should be scheduled on a 24-hour per day and 7-day per week calendar.

7.8 Finding the Bars in the Gantt Chart

At times you will find there are no bars displayed in the Gantt Chart because the Timescale has scrolled too far into the past or future. Double-click in the Gantt Chart in line with an activity and the Timescale will scroll to display the activity bar.

7.9 Activity Information – Bottom Layout

The Bottom Layout has a number of tabs where information about the highlighted activity may be viewed and edited. (These are not in any specific order as the tabs may be reordered on the screen.)

• **General**	This form displays the: • **Activity ID** and **Activity Description**. • **Project** and **Responsible Manager**, these may not be edited here. It also displays activity attributes including some which were set as defaults in the **Project Window**: • **Activity Type**, **Duration Type**, **% Complete Type**, **Activity Calendar**, **WBS**, and **Primary Resource**.
• **Status**	This is where the following data is displayed/edited: • The **Durations**, • The **Status**, where Actual Dates and % Complete may be entered, • Where **Constraints** are entered, and • By selecting from the drop down box the **Labor** and **Nonlabor Units** or **Costs** and **Material Costs** may be displayed. **NOTE:** It is possible to assign resource Units in the **Status** tab without a resource being assigned to the activity and the rate will be taken from the **Project Properties Calculations** tab.
• **Summary**	This form displays summary information about the activity. It has three buttons that select which data will be displayed: • **Units** or **Costs** or **Dates**.
• **Resources**	**Resources** and **Roles** may be assigned to activities and assignment information displayed.

• **Expenses**	**Expenses** may be added and edited here. These are intended for one-off costs that do not require a resource to be created. **NOTE:** These are often used for material costs on construction and maintenance projects to prevent clogging up the **Resource Window**.
• **Notebook**	Notes about activities may be made here by adding a **Notebook Topic** and then adding notes about the topic.
• **Steps**	This function enables an activity to be broken down into increments titled **Steps** that may be marked as complete as work on the Activity progresses.
• **Feedback**	This is where comments made in the timesheet module may be viewed.
• **WPs & Docs**	This is where files that have been listed in the **Work Products and Documents Window** may be associated with activities and then opened from this form.
• **Codes**	Project Codes may be created and activities associated with these codes with this form. These codes are similar to P3 and SureTrak Activity Codes and activities may be organized in a similar way.
• **Relationships**, **Predecessors** & **Successors**	This is where the activity's predecessors and successors are added, edited, and deleted. This is covered in the **Adding the Relationship** chapter.

7.10 Assigning Calendars to Activities

Activities often require a different calendar from the default **Project Calendar** that is assigned in the **Project Information** form. Primavera enables each activity to be assigned a unique calendar. An **Activity Calendar** may be assigned by the **General** tab of the **Bottom Layout** or by displaying the **Calendar** column.

7.10.1 Assigning a Calendar Using General Tab of the Bottom Layout Form

- Select one activity that you want to assign to a different calendar. Multiple activity selection may not be used. Open the **General** tab of the **Bottom Layout**,
- Click on the icon in the **Activity Calendar** box to open the **Select Activity Calendar** form,
- Select either **Global** or **Project** from the drop down list in the top left menu, and
- Select an Activity calendar by clicking the icon.

7.10.2 Assigning a Calendar Using a Column

You may also display the **Calendar** column and edit the activity calendar from this column. The process of displaying a column is covered in the **Formatting the Display** chapter.

Edit, **Fill Down** may be used to assign a new calendar to multiple selected activities.

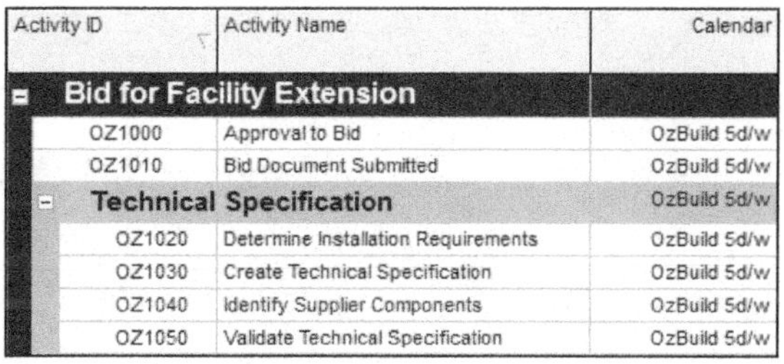

Activity ID	Activity Name	Calendar
Bid for Facility Extension		
OZ1000	Approval to Bid	OzBuild 5d/w
OZ1010	Bid Document Submitted	OzBuild 5d/w
Technical Specification		OzBuild 5d/w
OZ1020	Determine Installation Requirements	OzBuild 5d/w
OZ1030	Create Technical Specification	OzBuild 5d/w
OZ1040	Identify Supplier Components	OzBuild 5d/w
OZ1050	Validate Technical Specification	OzBuild 5d/w

7.11 Assigning Activities to a WBS Node

Activities are assigned to a WBS Node from the Activities Window. They may be assigned using the following methods:

- A new activity will inherit the WBS Node that is highlighted when an activity is created.
- A new activity will inherit the WBS Node of a selected existing activity when the project is organized by WBS Nodes and an activity is created.
- Select the activity and click the WBS box in the **General** tab in the lower window. This will open the **Select WBS** form where you may assign the WBS Node.
- The + and the - are used to expand or roll up the WBS structure. Click on the icon to assign the node.

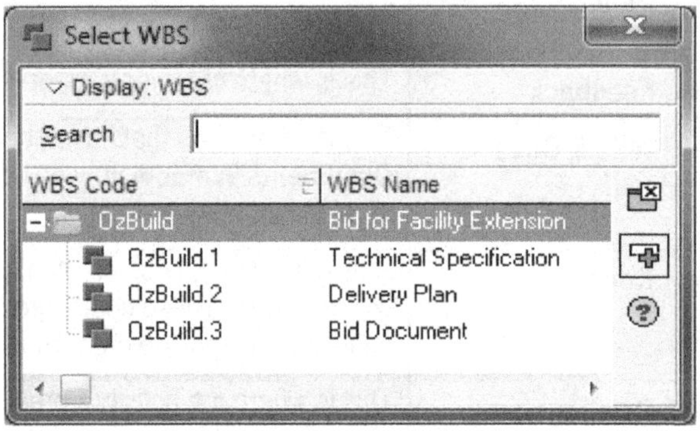

- Select one or more activities and move the mouse to the left of the activity description and the mouse will change into the shape displayed in the following picture. You may then drag the activities to another WBS Node.

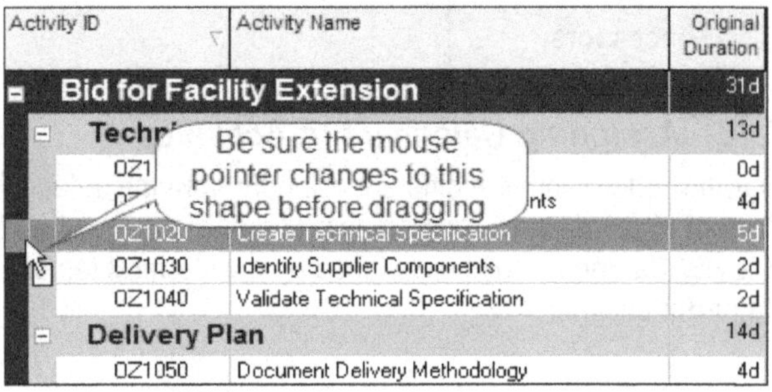

- Insert the WBS column by clicking on the icon and selecting WBS from the Columns form under General. Clicking in the WBS column of an activity will open the Select WBS form.

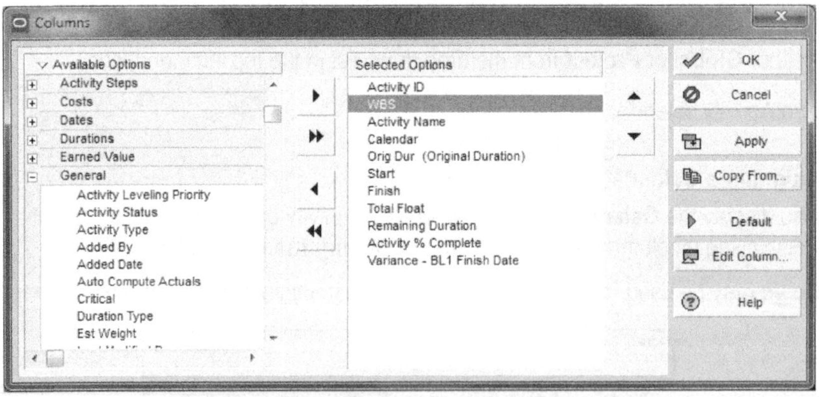

7.12 Reordering or Sorting Activities

The sort order of activities within a band is set by an order from one or more columns and you may not drag activities up or down the schedule in the same way as other products.

There are two principal methods of ordering activities after they have been added:

- Using the **Sort** function. To open the **Sort** form:
  - ➢ Select **View**, **Group and Sort by**, **Customize...** and click the Sort... icon, or
  - ➢ Click on the icon and click the Sort... icon to open the **Sort** form.

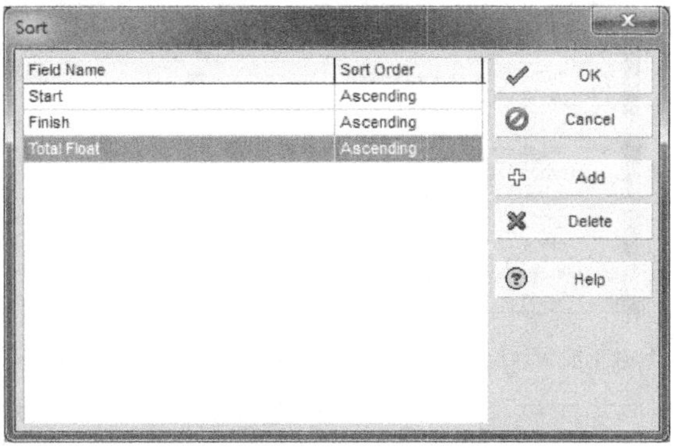

It is unfortunate that with Primavera, as soon as you use the option below to sort activities then without any warning the sorting fields entered into the **Sort** form above are overwritten by the column that has been used to sort the activities.

- Highlighting a column title and clicking with the mouse. The activities within a band will be reordered within that band in the order indicated with an arrow in the right side of the column header. The order will be either Ascending or Descending:

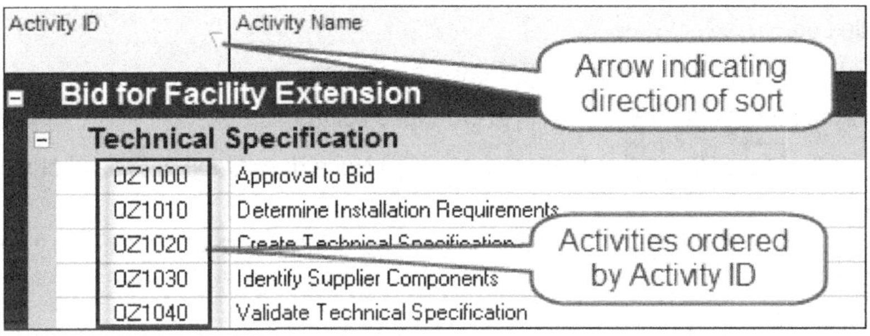

This function changes all the settings made in the **Sort** form on a permanent basis.

The Activities IDs are not renumbered when they have been reordered as they are with Microsoft Project.

7.13 Undo

Primavera Version 5.0 introduced a multiple **Undo** function that operates on Resources, Resource Assignments, and Activities Windows, but no **Redo** function.

There are many functions that will erase the Undo memory such as scheduling, summarizing, importing, opening a project, opening Code forms, opening User and Admin Preferences and closing the application.

7.14 Summarizing Activities Using WBS

The WBS bands may be summarized in the same way as in other project planning and scheduling software. The following picture shows the activities displayed under the WBS Nodes:

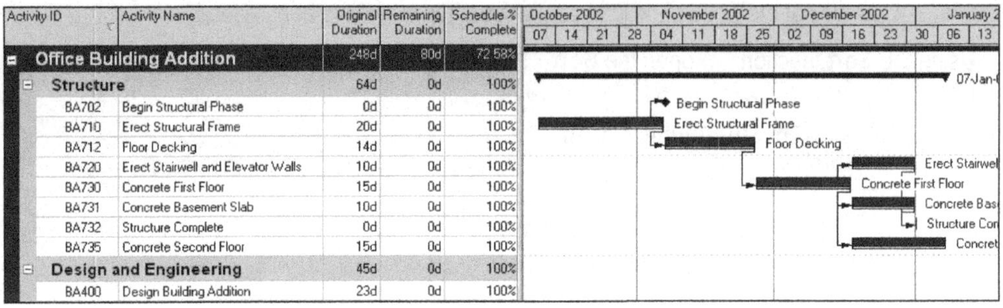

Activity ID	Activity Name	Original Duration	Remaining Duration	Schedule % Complete
Office Building Addition		248d	80d	72.58%
Structure		64d	0d	100%
BA702	Begin Structural Phase	0d	0d	100%
BA710	Erect Structural Frame	20d	0d	100%
BA712	Floor Decking	14d	0d	100%
BA720	Erect Stairwell and Elevator Walls	10d	0d	100%
BA730	Concrete First Floor	15d	0d	100%
BA731	Concrete Basement Slab	10d	0d	100%
BA732	Structure Complete	0d	0d	100%
BA735	Concrete Second Floor	15d	0d	100%
Design and Engineering		45d	0d	100%
BA400	Design Building Addition	23d	0d	100%

The following picture shows the activities summarized under the WBS Nodes:

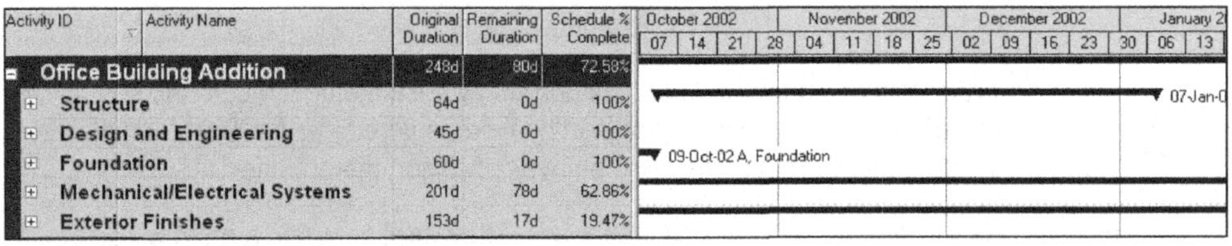

Activity ID	Activity Name	Original Duration	Remaining Duration	Schedule % Complete
Office Building Addition		248d	80d	72.58%
Structure		64d	0d	100%
Design and Engineering		45d	0d	100%
Foundation		60d	0d	100%
Mechanical/Electrical Systems		201d	78d	62.86%
Exterior Finishes		153d	17d	19.47%

WBS Nodes may be summarized or expanded by:

- Double-clicking any WBS band description. The band will either roll up when expanded or expand when rolled up.
- Selecting **View, Expand All** or **View, Collapse All** from the menu.
- Right-clicking and selecting **Expand All** or **Collapse All** from the menu.
- Clicking on the ⊟ or the ⊞ to the left of the WBS Node description to expand or collapse the WBS Node.

WBS Nodes may be reordered by clicking the arrow icons in the **Command** toolbar to the right side of the WBS Window.

7.15 Spell Check

To spell check a project, open the **Spell Check** form:

- Select **Edit**, **Spell Check**, or
- Hit the **F7** key.

This form is simple to use and does not use the operating system dictionary.

7.16 Workshop 5 – Adding Activities

Background

We need to set up the defaults and add the activities to the schedule.

Assignment

1. Go to the **Projects Window**, highlight the OzBuild project and select the **Defaults** tab in the **Activity Details** pane. If required, adjust all the following parameters.

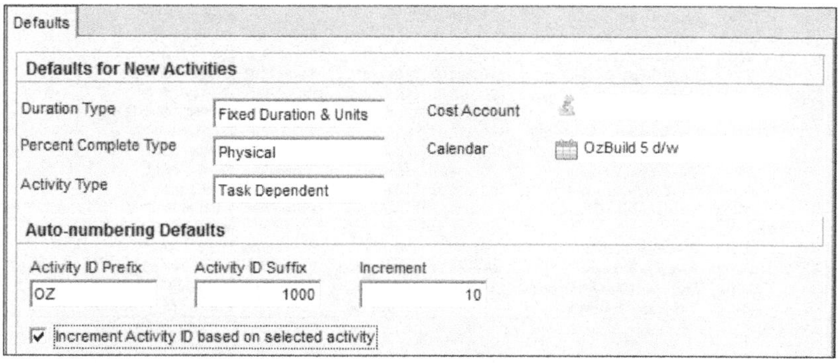

2. Open the **Activities Window** and add the following activities under the appropriate WBS.

NOTE: If the **New Activity** wizard appears select the "do not show this wizard again."

3. Click on the Activity ID column header if the activities become out of order.

Activity ID	Activity Name	Orig Dur	Calendar	Activity Type
	Technical Specification			
OZ1000	Approval to Bid	0d	OzBuild 5d/w	Start Milestone
OZ1010	Determine Installation Requirements	4d	OzBuild 5d/w	Task Dependent
OZ1020	Create Technical Specification	5d	OzBuild 5d/w	Task Dependent
OZ1030	Identify Supplier Components	2d	OzBuild 5d/w	Task Dependent
OZ1040	Validate Technical Specification	2d	OzBuild 5d/w	Task Dependent
	Delivery Plan			
OZ1050	Document Delivery Methodology	4d	OzBuild 5d/w	Task Dependent
OZ1060	Obtain Quotes from Suppliers	8d	OzBuild 5d/w	Task Dependent
OZ1070	Calculate the Bid Estimate	3d	**OzBuild 6d/w**	Task Dependent
OZ1080	Create the Project Schedule	3d	**OzBuild 6d/w**	Task Dependent
OZ1090	Review the Delivery Plan	1d	OzBuild 5d/w	Task Dependent
	Bid Document			
OZ1100	Create Draft of Bid Document	6d	OzBuild 5d/w	Task Dependent
OZ1110	Review Bid Document	4d	OzBuild 5d/w	Task Dependent
OZ1120	Finalise and Submit Bid Document	2d	OzBuild 5d/w	Task Dependent
OZ1130	Bid Document Submitted	0d	OzBuild 5d/w	Finish Milestone

continued.....

4. Assign the **Activity Calendar** a **6-day per week calendar** to Activity IDs OZ1070 and OZ1080 in the **General** tab of the **Activity Details** form.
5. Reschedule the project by pressing **F9** and check that the Data Date is set at 3 December 2018 at 08:00.
6. Your answer should look like the following picture, but you may have different columns displayed and there may be different text on the bars.
7. Ensure the sort order is by Activity ID by clicking on the Activity ID Heading:

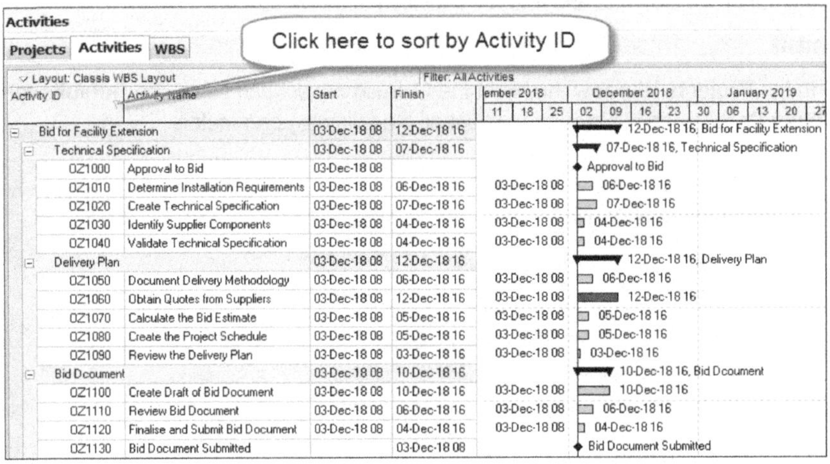

NOTE:

1. The picture above was created using the **Classic WBS Layout** that was loaded with the sample Oracle P6 Database.
2. Depending on the layout that your software has loaded, your data may be displayed with different columns and bar formatting. Should your layout not enable you to review your data entry, try selecting a different layout using the command **View**, **Layouts**, **Open Layout...**and select another layout from the list, such as the **Classic** or **Default WBS** Layout, which may be similar to the picture above. If this does not solve your problem then refer to the Layouts and Formatting sections of this book.
3. If your timescale week start date is different to the one above, for example the first day in the timescale is 3 Dec whereas the first day above is 2 Dec, then you may change this for all projects in the database if you have the access rights:
   - From the Professional Client (EPM) select **Admin**, **Admin Preferences** form, **General** tab, **Starting Day of Week** section and select Monday:

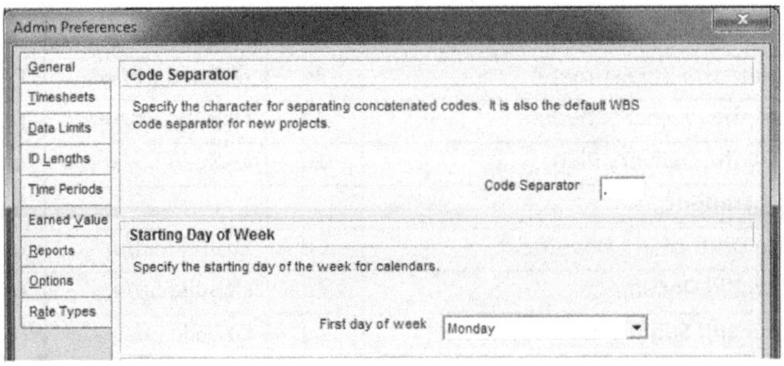

   - From the Web Client (EPPM) for the Optional Client, log into the web and select **Administer**, **Application Settings**, **General tab**, **Starting Day of the Week** section.

8 FORMATTING THE DISPLAY

This chapter shows you how to set up the on-screen presentation so that the schedule will be easier to read and more consistent. This chapter covers the following display and customizing topics:

Topic	Menu Command
• Formatting Columns	Open the **Column** form: • Select **View, Columns**, **Customize...**, or • Click on the icon.
• Formatting Activity Bars	Open the **Bar** form: • Select **View, Bars**, Options..., or • Click on the icon.
• Format Gridlines	**Bar Chart Gridlines** are formatted in the **View, Bar,** Options... form, **Sightlines** tab.
• Format Data Date	The **Data Date** is formatted in the **Bar Chart Options** form, **Data Date** tab.
• Formatting Row Height	Open the **Table, Font and Row** form by: • Selecting **View, Table Font and Row.**
• Formatting Colors	There are limited options for formatting colors: • **Text** colors are formatted in the **Color** form accessed from the **Table, Font and Row** form which is opened by selecting **View, Table Font and Row**, AaBbYyZz icon. • **Bar Colors** are covered in the **Formatting the Bars** paragraph of this chapter. • **Band** colors are selected as part of the formatting of the layout by selecting **View, Group and Sort by** or clicking on the icon.
• Formatting Fonts	There are limited options for formatting fonts: • **Text** fonts are formatted in the **Font** form accessed from the **Table, Font and Row** form which is opened by selecting **View, Table Font and Row**, AaBbYyZz icon. • **Notebook** entries may be formatted when edited.
• Format Timescale	• Click on the icon, or • Select **View, Timescale**, or • Right-click in the Bar Chart area and select **Timescale**.

The formatting is applied to the current **Layout** and this formatting may be automatically saved as part of the Layout when another Layout is selected; the system will prompt. Views are covered in the **Group, Sort and Layouts** chapter.

Beware of clicking the Default button in any form; this does not save your edits, but re-sets the form back to the Primavera defaults, destroying your hard work.

8.1 Formatting the Project Window

The formatting of the Project Window is very similar to the formatting of the **Activities Window** and will not be covered separately. Formatting, Filters and Layouts all work in the same way, except one is dealing with projects and not activities.

8.2 Understanding Forms

Unlike many software packages, Primavera has sorting and filtering functions in most forms and the principles are the same in most forms. This section will demonstrate some of the functions but you must be prepared to experiment with each form to see how they operate.

- Clicking in the **Resource ID** column of the **Resources Window** takes the formatting from hierarchical to alphabetical to reverse alphabetical and back to hierarchical. This function works in other forms with a hierarchical structure.

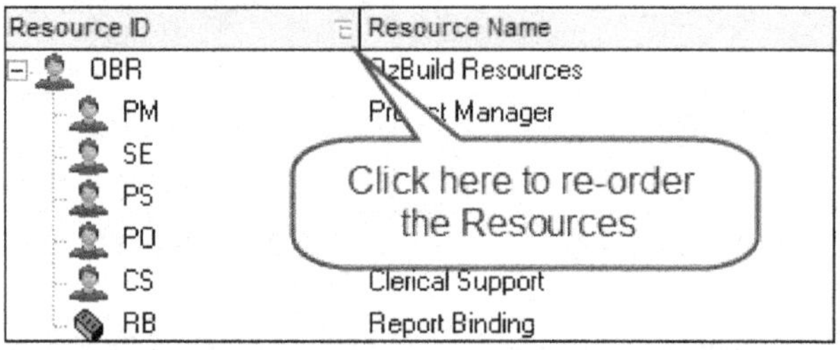

- The **Assign Successors** form has **Filter By** and **Group and Sort By** options that affect how data is grouped.

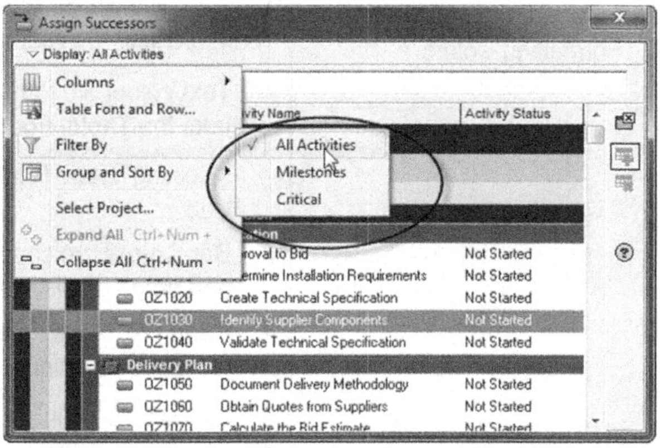

- The **Assign Resource** form has **Columns**, **Filter By**, and **Group and Sort By** options that affect what data is available.
- Ctl+F will also allow you to search for Resources matching a specific criteria.

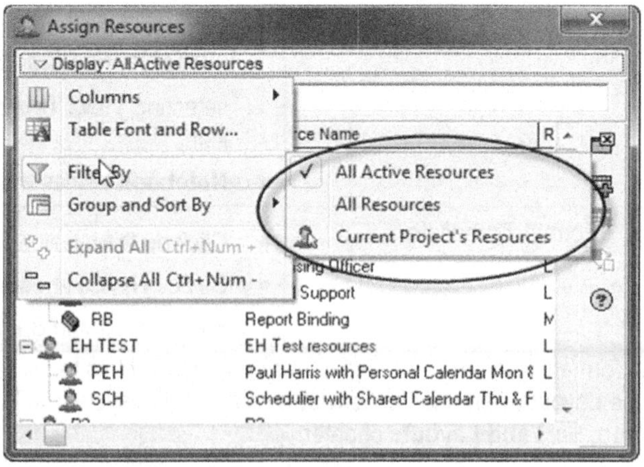

8.3 *Formatting the Bars*

The bars in the Gantt Chart may be formatted to suit your requirements for display. Primavera does not have the option to format individual bars but is able to assign a filter to a bar style so that a style is applied to activities that meet a filter definition.

At the time of writing this book the author had placed a layout on **www.primavera.com.au** or **www.eh.com.au** under Technical Papers that has the bar formatting issues discussed below fixed. It is suggested that downloading this layout will save users a significant amount of formatting time.

8.3.1 Formatting Activity Bars

To format all the bars you must open the **Bar** form:

- Select **View, Bars**, or
- Click on the  icon, or
- Right-click in the bars area and select **Bars** from the menu.

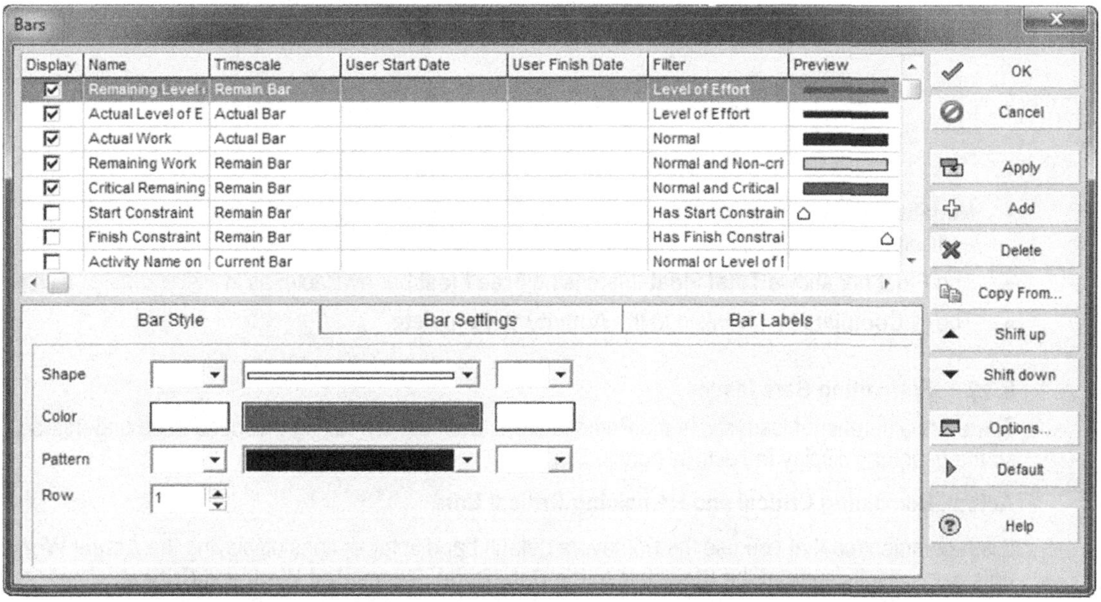

The following notes are the main points for using this function. Detailed information is available in the Help facility by searching for "Bar styles dialog box."

- Each bar listed in the table may be displayed on the bar chart by checking the box in the **Display** column.
- New bars may be added by clicking on the 

icon and deleted by clicking on the 

icon.
- The bar at the top of the list is placed on the screen and then the one below drawn over the top of it, so it would be simple to hide one bar with a second. The 

and 

icons are used to move the bars up or down the list and therefore determine which bar is drawn on top of the next.
- The **Name** is the title assigned to the bar and may be displayed in the printout legend.

- The **Timescale** option is similar to the **Show For ..., Tasks** option in the Microsoft Project **Bar Styles** form or the **Data Item** in the SureTrak **Format Bars** form, and enables the nomination of a predefined bar which is selected from the drop down box.
- Double-clicking on a cell in the **Filter** column opens the **Filters** form where you are able to select the filter/s which will determine which activities are displayed with the assigned bar format. Filters will be covered in detail in the **Filters** chapter.

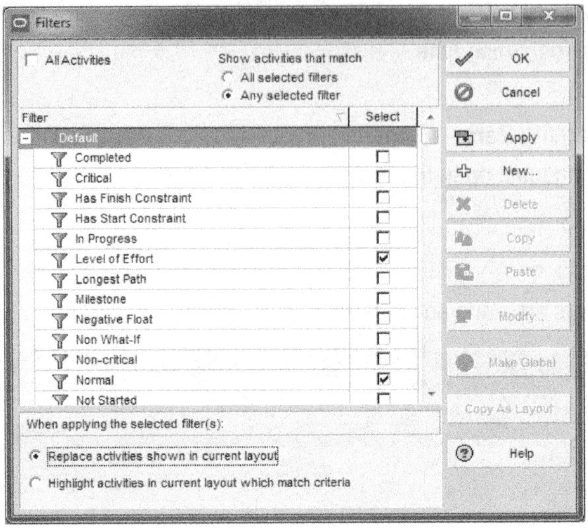

- **Negative Float** is displayed in a similar way as in Microsoft Project and requires another bar in addition to the **Positive Float** bar with both the **Timescale** and **Filter** selected as Negative Float.
- The **Float** bar shows **Total Float**; there is no **Free Float** bar available, as in P3.
- The **% Complete** bar is linked to the **Activity % Complete**.

8.3.2 Formatting Bars Issues

There are a number of issues with the Primavera standard bar formatting that need to be understood so the user may display the activity bars logically:

Actual, Remaining Critical and Remaining Critical Bars

It is recommended that you use the Primavera default bar display options displaying the **Actual Work** (this bar is displayed from the **Start** date to the **Data Date**), **Remaining Work** and **Critical Remaining Work** bars (these bars are displayed from the **Data Date** to the **Finish** date with the appropriate filter). This is because the **Early** bar will not display actual progress as in other software packages. Please read the **Understanding Dates** section in the **Tracking Progress** chapter to understand how the dates are calculated that are used to draw each bar.

Total Float Bar

The Total Float Bar is called the Float Bar in the Bars form which is inconsistent terminology.

By default a Total Float bar is displayed on a completed task, but the Float value is set to "Null" (which is displayed as a blank). It is not logical to display a float bar when there is no float value:

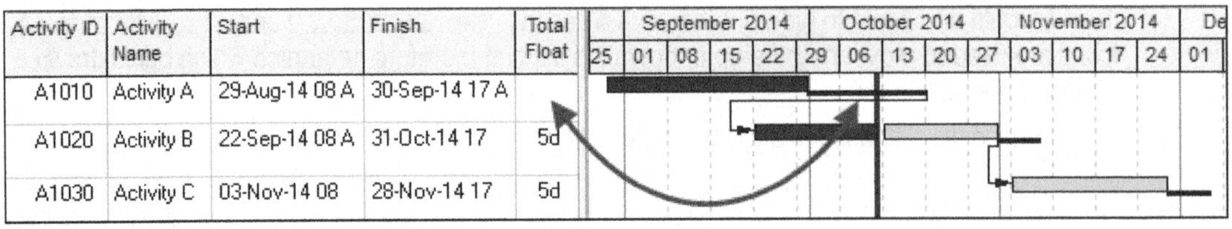

Activity ID	Activity Name	Start	Finish	Total Float
A1010	Activity A	29-Aug-14 08 A	30-Sep-14 17 A	
A1020	Activity B	22-Sep-14 08 A	31-Oct-14 17	5d
A1030	Activity C	03-Nov-14 08	28-Nov-14 17	5d

- To prevent this from happening you should edit the total **Float Bar Filter** in the **Bars** form so it is only displayed for Not Started or In Progress activities:

Display	Name	Timescale	User Start Date	User Finish Date	Filter	Preview
☑	Float Bar	Float Bar			Not Started or In Progress	

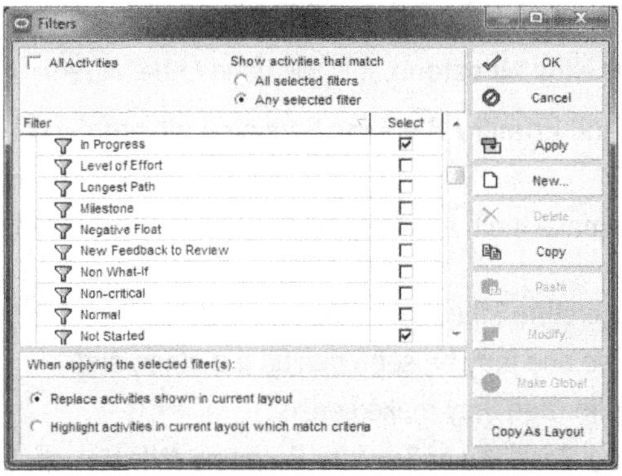

- This is what it should look like now:

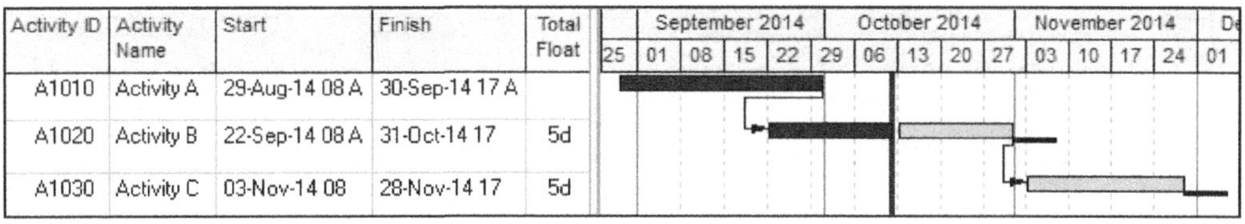

Free Float Bar

This may not be easily displayed.

A Baseline Bar is Displayed when NO Project Baseline set

A Baseline Bar is displayed when a Baseline has not been set. The Planned Dates are displayed as the Baseline Bar. Ensure you have a Baseline set before displaying a Baseline Bar.

Relationships displayed on Baseline Bars

By default the relationships are displayed on the Baseline Bar, which is not a normal method of displaying them:

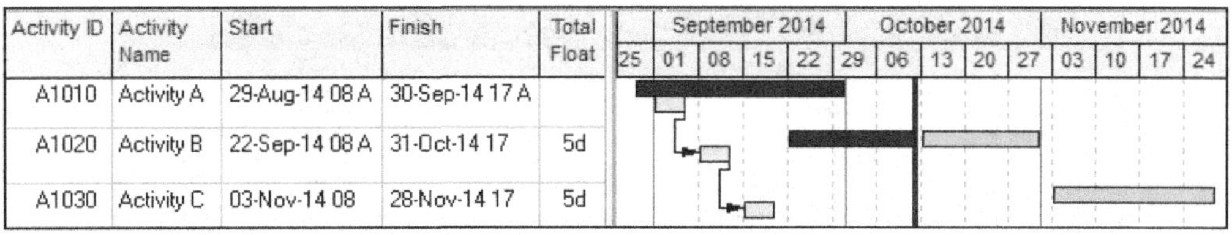

To remove relationships on the Baseline Bar, move all the Baseline Bars and Baseline Milestones to the bottom of the Bars form:

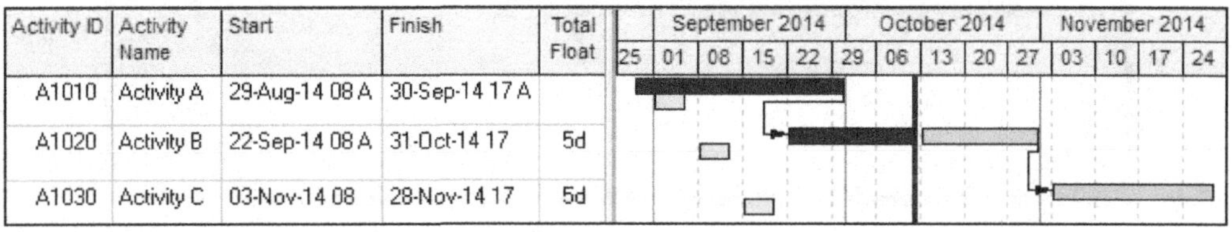

Remaining Level of Effort and Actual Level of Effort Bars

These are by default hidden and when these Activity Types are used then the activity bar will disappear. You should check both these bars so they are always displayed.

Baseline Bar Formatting

After you have moved all the baseline bars to the bottom:

- There is no **Project Baseline Milestone**; this will need to be added,
- The **Project Baseline** and **Primary Baseline** bars are both narrow yellow bars, the same as the Negative Float,
  - ➢ It is suggested you make them a different color and put them as thicker bars on the top and bottom of row 2,
  - ➢ Then change the **Baseline Milestone** colors to match,
  - ➢ Change the shape so one may be seen behind the other, and
  - ➢ Change the descriptions so they make sense,
- There are no **Secondary Baseline** or **Tertiary Baseline Milestones**. If you are not using these then delete the **Secondary Baseline** or **Tertiary Baseline** bars:

Display	Name	Timescale	User S	User F	Filter	Preview
☐	Project Baseline Bar	Project Baseline Bar			Normal	
☐	Project Baseline Milestone	Project Baseline Bar			Milestone	▽ ▽
☐	Primary Baseline	Primary Baseline Bar			Normal	
☐	Primary Baseline Milestone	Primary Baseline Bar			Milestone	△ △

Bar Text

There is text on many bars and it is difficult to add or remove text from bars with the current configuration.

It is suggested that text be removed from all bars, except from the **Current Bar Labels** bar by:

- Clicking on the **Bar Labels** tab at the bottom,
- Clicking on one bar at a time and using the ✖ Delete button at the bottom (NOT SIDE) of the screen to delete the text line,
- Changing the **Current Bar Labels** bar filter to read All Activities.

Now if you display the **Current Bar Labels** bar then text will be displayed on all bars and when this bar is hidden then all text will be removed from bars, thus making it simpler to add or remove bar text:

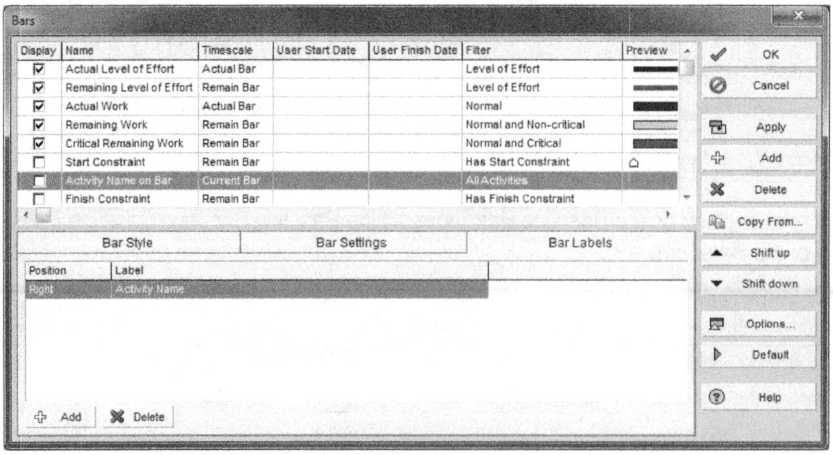

Creating a Summary Bar

It is not obvious how to create a Summary Bar:

- To create a new Summary Bar you will see that you may not select **Summary** from the filter drop down box,
- You must check the **Bar Settings** tab, **Show bar for grouping bands** to create a Summary Bar:

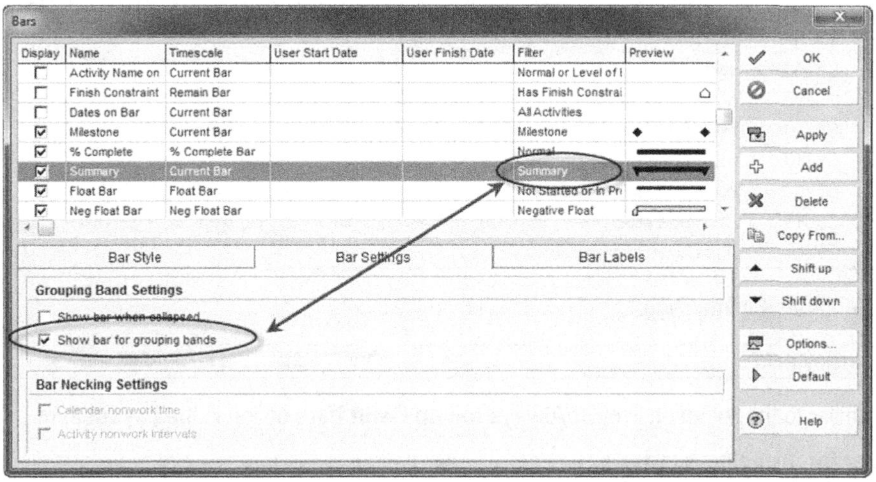

At the time of writing this book the author had placed a layout on **www.primavera.com.au** or **www.eh.com.au** under Technical Papers that has these bar formatting issues fixed. It is suggested that downloading this layout will save users a significant amount of formatting time.

8.3.3 Bar Style Tab

The appearance of each bar is edited in the lower half of the form. The bar's start, middle, and end points may have their color, shape, pattern, etc., formatted.

The bars may be placed on one of three rows numbered from 1 to 3, from top to bottom, one bar above the other. If multiple bars are placed on the same row, the bar at the top of the list will be drawn first and the ones lower down the list will be drawn over the top.

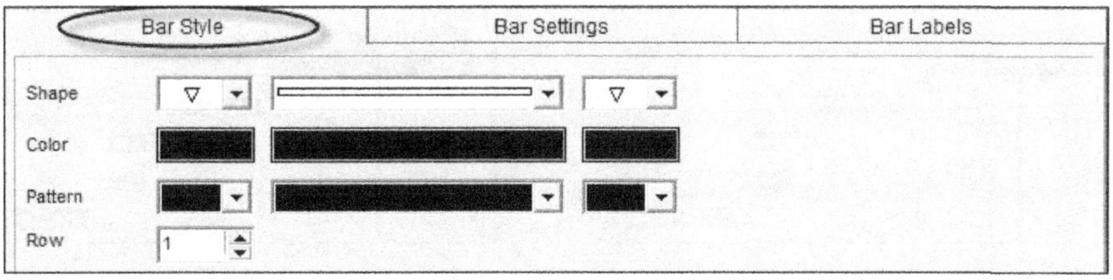

8.3.4 Bar Settings Tab

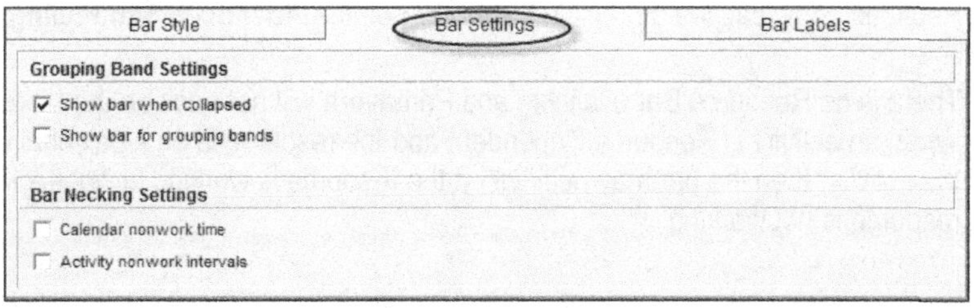

Show bar when collapsed

- **Show bar when collapsed** option displays the detailed bars on a single line when the WBS Node has been summarized; see the two pictures following:
  - Before summarizing:

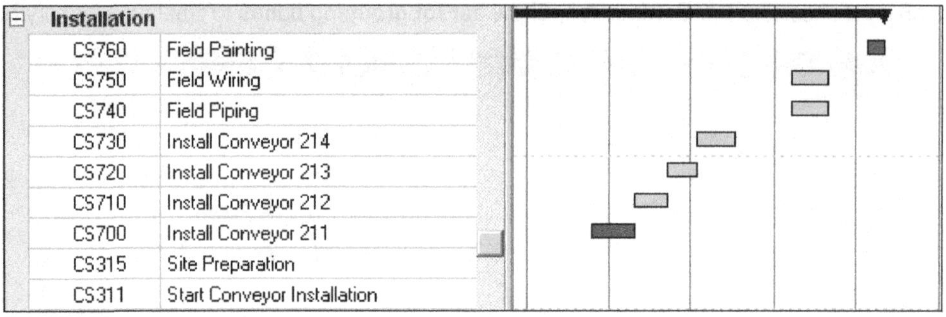

  - After summarizing:

This is similar to the Microsoft Project **Always roll up Gantt bars** option in the **Layout** form.

Show bar for grouping bands

This shows a summarized bar all the time and converts the filter automatically to "Summary" bars only.

When formatting the **Bar Settings** for Milestones it is important to take note of the checked boxes and Filter format. If the box **Show bar for grouping bands** is checked, Milestones will appear at the ends of Summary Bars and not in line with the actual activities they belong to. The filter in this case will read **Summary** and not **Milestone**.

Bar Necking Settings

Bar Necking displays a thinner bar during times of inactivity such as weekends and holidays and applies only to the Current Bar setting column in the **Bars** form:

Un-necked bars

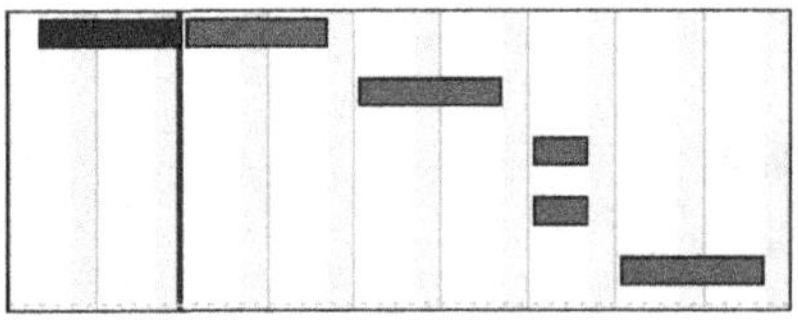

Necked bars

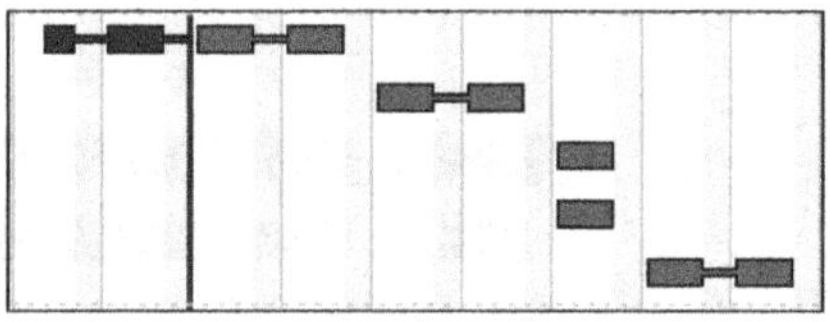

- **Calendar nonwork time** necks the bar based on the activity's calendar.
- **Activity nonwork intervals** necks the bar when Out of Sequence Progress options of Actual Dates or Retained Logic causes a break in the work. See the **Advanced Scheduling Options** paragraph.

There is no Resource Bar available and Primavera will not neck on the resource calendar. When an activity is Resource Dependent and the resource is on a calendar different from the activity, then the bar may neck when the resource is working or not neck when the resource is not working.

8.3.5 Bar Labels Tab

This tab enables the placement of text with a bar above, below, to the left, and to the right. The following pictures show how the start and finish dates are formatted and displayed on the bar chart:

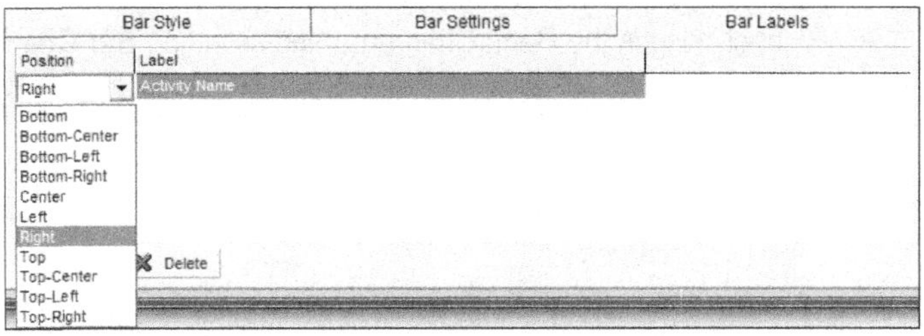

- Select the bar that you wish to add the label to.
- Click on the 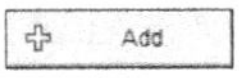 and the 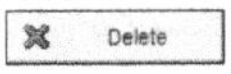 icons at the bottom of the **Bars** form to add and delete a **Label** item.
- Select the **Position** and **Label** from the drop down boxes in the **Bar Labels** tab.

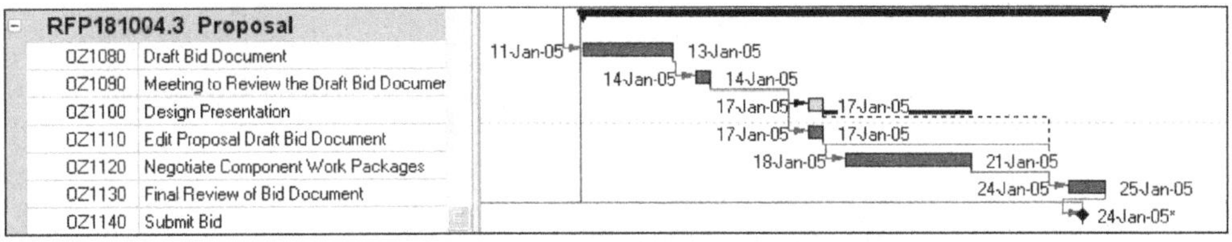

- The dates on the bar chart are adopted from the **User Preferences** and may not be formatted separately.

> *i* It is often useful to create a bar that only displays the text. This bar may be displayed or not displayed as required, which is much simpler than reformatting a bar to show text.

- Each **Notebook Topic** may be displayed on a bar one at a time by selecting the topic in the **Bar Labels** tab. After the box containing the label is displayed on the screen it may be adjusted in size by dragging.

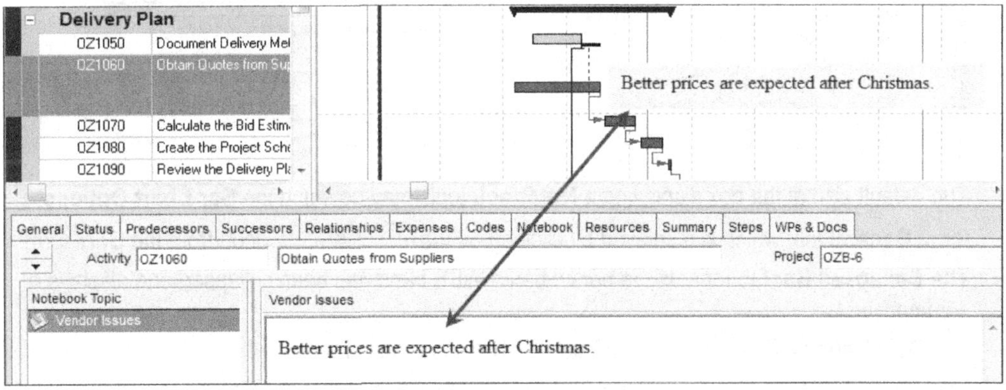

8.3.6 Bar Chart Options Form

- The **Bar Chart Options** form is displayed by:
  - Clicking on the Options... icon from the **Bars** form, or
  - By selecting **View, Bar,** Options..., or
  - Right-clicking in the Gantt Chart area and selecting **Bar Chart Options...**:

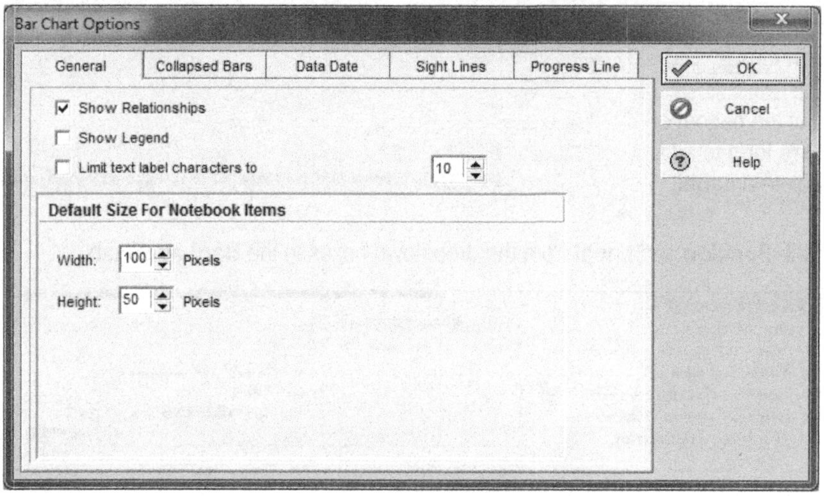

- The **General** tab has a variety of options for formatting the bar chart which are mainly self-explanatory.
  - **Show Relationships** has the same result as clicking on the icon and displays the relationships.
  - **Show Legend** displays a legend on the bar chart in the Activities View; see the following picture:

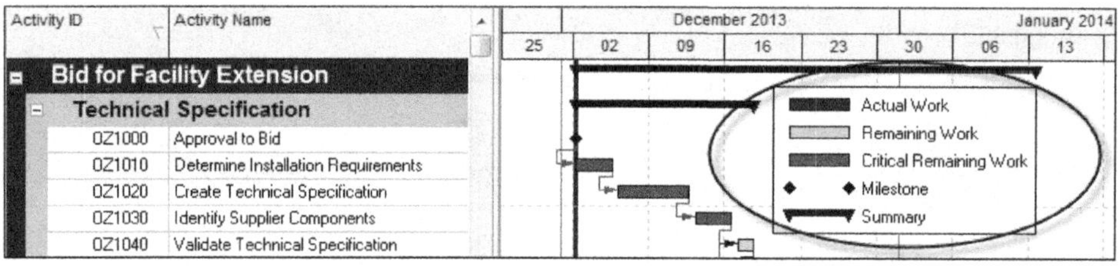

- The default size of the box displaying a **Notebook** topic may be set in the **Bar Chart Options** form, **General** tab, which is displayed by clicking on the Options... icon from the **Bars** form.
- The **Collapsed Bar** tab formats the bars when a WBS band has been collapsed and displays a summarized bar.
- The **Data Date** tab formats the Data Date, its style, color and size.
- Primavera Version 5.0 introduced the **Sight Lines** tab which enables the specification of both Major and Minor vertical and horizontal Sight Lines, which brings this functionality up to match P3, SureTrak and Microsoft Project.
- Primavera P6 Version 7 introduced the **Progress Line** Display on the Gantt Chart which is covered in detail in the next paragraph.

8.4 Progress Line Display on the Gantt Chart

A progress line displays how far ahead or behind activities are in relation to the Baseline. Either the Project Baseline or the Primary User Baseline may be used and there are four options:

- Difference between the Baseline Start Date and Activity Start Date,
- Difference between the Baseline Finish Date and Activity Finish Date,
- Connecting the progress points based on the Activity % Complete,
- Connecting the progress points based on the Activity Remaining Duration.

There are several main components of displaying a Progress Line in P6:

- First the progress line is formatted using the **View, Bar,** Options... , form, **Progress Line** tab, which may also be opened by right-clicking in the Gantt Chart area:

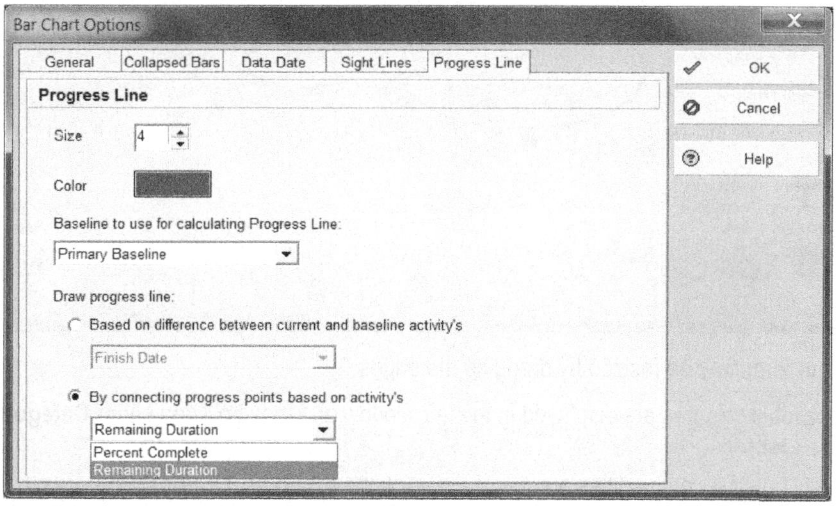

- Selecting **View, Progress Line** to hide or display the **Progress Line**.
- If you use either of the options of Percent Complete or Remaining Duration then you must display the appropriate Baseline Bar that has been selected as the **Baseline to use for calculating Progress Line:**
- The picture below shows the option highlighted above of **Percent Complete**:

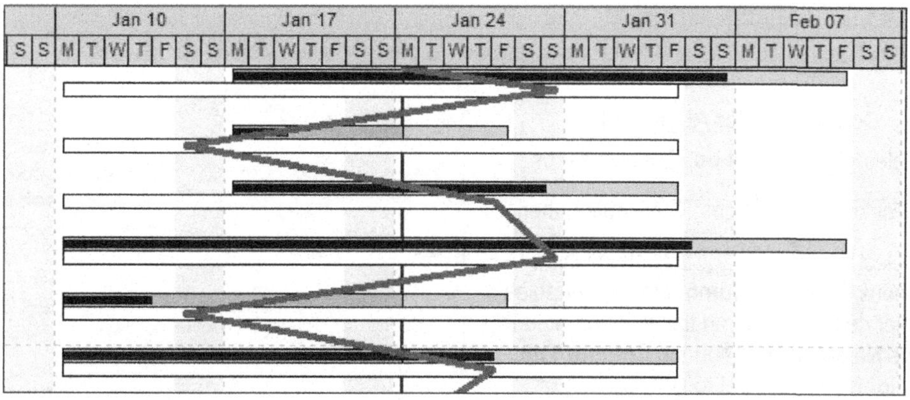

8.5 Formatting Columns

8.5.1 Selecting the Columns to be Displayed

The columns are formatted through the **Columns** form which may be opened by:

- Select **View, Columns**, **Customize**, or
- Click on the  icon, **Customize**, or
- Right-click in the Columns to open a menu and select **Columns**:

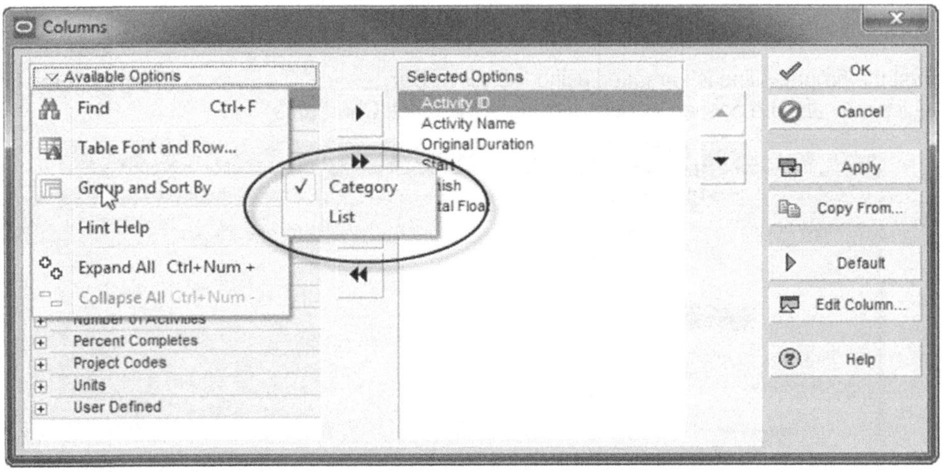

The **Column** form may be resized by dragging the edges.

- The available columns are displayed in the left window and may be listed under **Categories** or as a single **List**.
- To select how the column titles are displayed, click the **Available Options** drop down box and then select **Group and Sort By** to choose either **List** or **Categories**, as per the picture above.
- The columns to be displayed are listed in the right **Selected Options Window** and are copied from **Available Options** to and from **Selected Options** using:
  - ➢ The icons , or
  - ➢ Dragging, or
  - ➢ Double-clicking.
- The 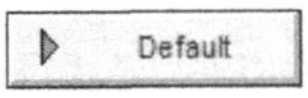 icon sets the columns back to the Primavera default column display.

8.5.2 Column Header Alignment

- Select **View, Columns**, **Customize**, or
- Click on the  icon, **Customize**, then
- Select the  option which opens the **Edit Column** form and enables a user definable column title to be created in the **New Title:** cell and the **Column Title Alignment** to be set to Left, Center, or Right.

8.5.3 Adjusting the Width of Columns

You may adjust the width of the column in two ways:

- By dragging the column title separator: move the mouse pointer to the nearest vertical line of the column. A mouse pointer will then appear and enable the column to be adjusted by click, hold and dragging.

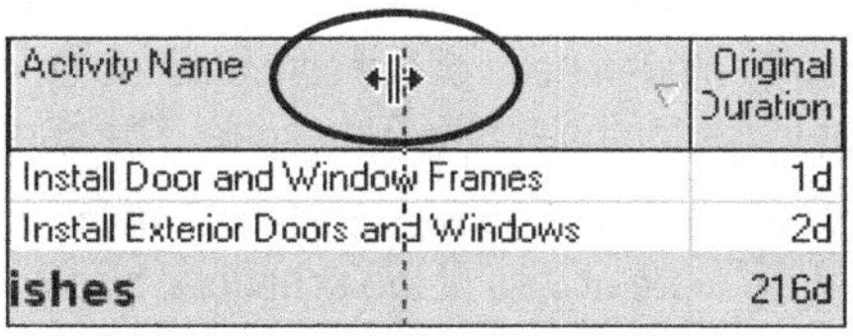

- From the **Column** form select Edit Column... to open the **Edit Column** form and enter the width of the column in pixels.

8.5.4 Setting the Order of the Columns from Left to Right on the Screen

The order of the columns on the screen, from left to right, is the same as the order in the **Columns** form **Selected Options Window** from top to bottom. The order of the columns may be altered:

- Highlight the column in the **Columns** form **Selected Options Window** and use the and icons, or
- Click and hold the column title in a window and drag the column.

8.6 Row Height and Show Icon

Row heights may be adjusted to display text that would otherwise be truncated by a narrow column.

- The height of all rows may be formatted by selecting **View, Table Font and Row** to open the **Table, Font and Row** form. The options in this form are self-explanatory.
- The **Show Icons** option will display a different icon in front of the Activity and WBS.
  - In the **Projects Window** indicates a **What-if** project, a **Unopened** project, and an **Opened** project.
  - In the **Activities Window** indicates a WBS Node, a blue a complete activity, a blue and green an in-progress activity, and a green an un-started activity.

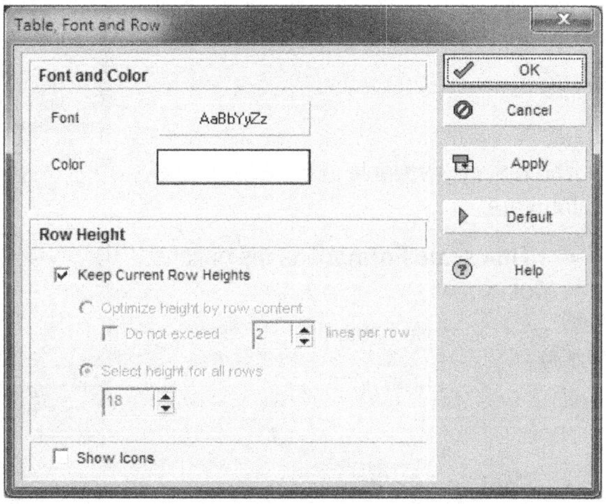

- The height of a single row may be manually adjusted in a similar way to adjusting row heights in Excel: click the row; the pointer will change to a double-headed arrow; then drag the row with the mouse. These manually adjusted rows are not saved with a Layout.

8.7 Format Timescale

8.7.1 Moving and Rescaling the Timescale

To display hidden parts of the schedule the timescale may be grabbed and moved by placing the cursor in the top half of the Timescale. The cursor will turn into a ; left-click and drag left or right.

The timescale may be rescaled, therefore increasing or decreasing the length of the bars and displaying more or less of the schedule, by placing the cursor in the bottom half of the Timescale. The cursor will turn into a ; click, hold and drag left to make the bars shorter and right to make the bars longer.

When there are no bars in view when you are viewing a time ahead or behind the activity dates, you may double-click in the **Gantt Chart** area to bring them back into view.

8.7.2 Format Timescale Command

The **Timescale** form provides a number of options for the display of the timescale, which is located above the Bar Chart. To open the **Timescale** form:

- Click on the icon, or
- Select **View, Timescale**, or
- Right-click in the Bar Chart area and select **Timescale**.

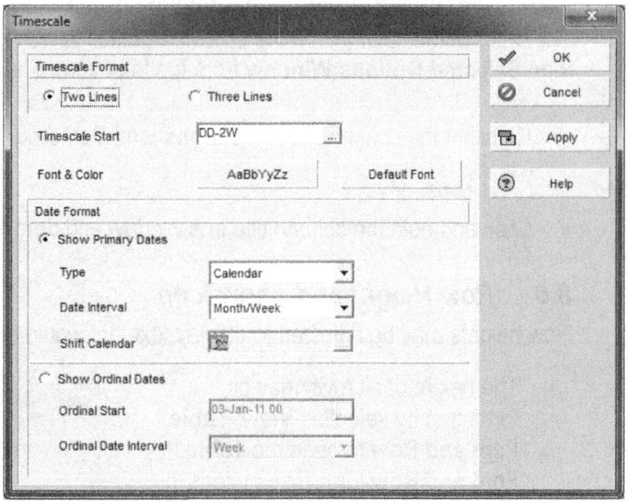

The options available in the **Timescale** form are:

- **Timescale Format** has the options of:
  - Two lines, or
  - Three lines

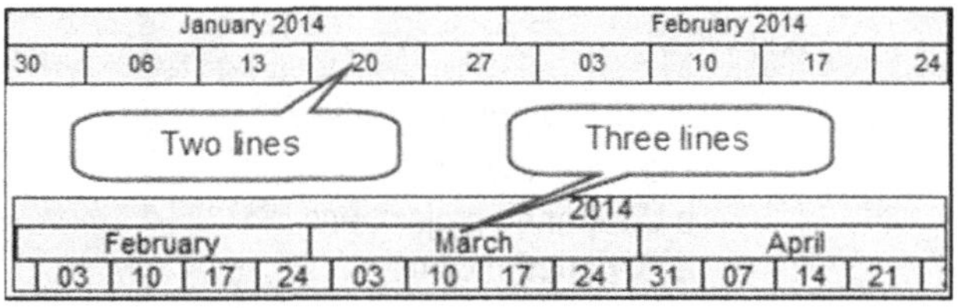

- **Font and Color**
  - The AaBbYyZz icon opens the **Edit**, **Font and Color** form which enables the timescale and column headers font and color to be changed.
  - By clicking on the Default Font icon all changes will be reversed.

Date Format

- **Type**
  - ➢ **Calendar** displays a normal calendar.
  - ➢ **Fiscal Year** displays the fiscal year in the year line. The Fiscal Year Start Month is set in the **Settings** tab of the **Project Details** form in the **Projects Window**.
  - ➢ **Week of the Year** displays the week of the year starting from "1" for the first week in January and is often termed **Manufacturing Week**.

- **Date Interval** sets the timescale and has the options in the picture to the right:

  - ➢ The **Week/Day 1** displays the days like this:

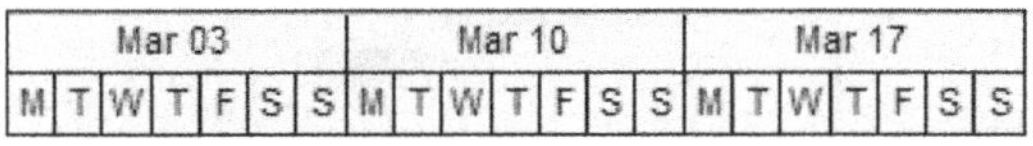

  - ➢ The **Week/Day 2** displays the days like this:

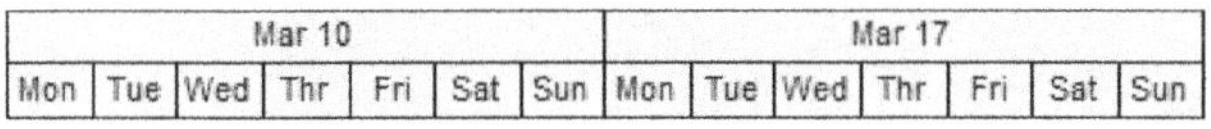

  - ➢ The **Date Interval** may also be adjusted by clicking on the or the , which moves the timescale setting up and down the list shown above.

- **Shift Calendar** breaks the day into time intervals to suit the shift intervals when the **Day/Shift** option has been selected.
- **Show Ordinal Dates** displays the timescale to be counted by the unit selected in the **Date Interval**. This is useful for displaying a schedule when the start of the project is unknown. Ordinal dates display the timescale by counting in the selected units starting from a user definable start date. This option works in a similar way to the P3 function where the ordinal start date may be selected. When 3 lines are displayed the ordinal dates and calendar dates may be displayed:

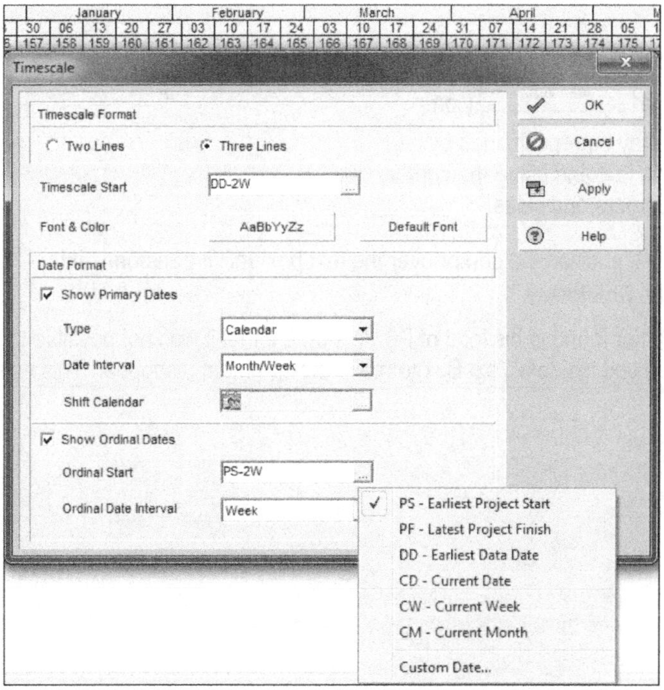

8.7.3 Nonwork Period Shading in Timescale

The nonwork period shading behind the bars is set by the database **Default Calendar** and is selected by:

- In the Professional Version selecting **Enterprise**, **Calendars...**and checking a calendar in the **Default Column**, and
- In the Optional Client this is set through the Web under **Administer**, **Enterprise Data**.

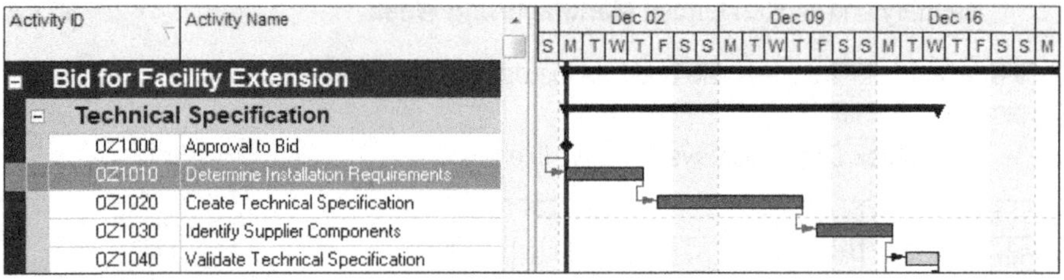

8.8 *Inserting Attachments – Text Boxes and Curtain*

8.8.1 Adding and Deleting a Text Box

A text box may be inserted in a bar chart area:

- Select the Activity which the new Text Box is to be associated with, either
- Right-click in the Bar Chart to open the menu, select **Attachments**, **Text**,

Or:

- Select **View, Attachments**, **Text**, and
- The **Text Attachment** form will be displayed.

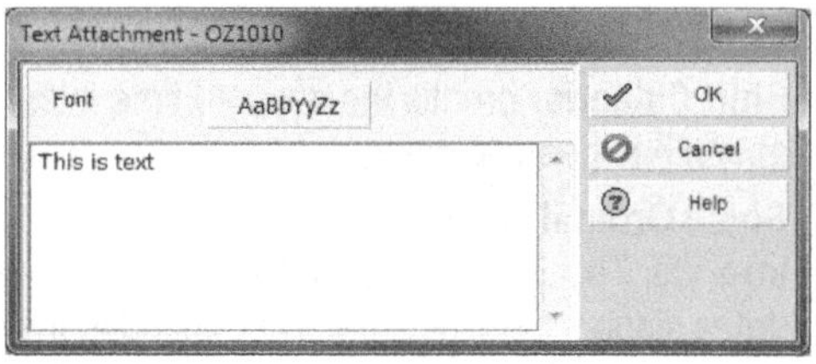

Then:

- Type in the text and format the font by clicking on the  icon.
- A **Text Box** may be repositioned by clicking on the text and using the cursor to drag the corners and sides.

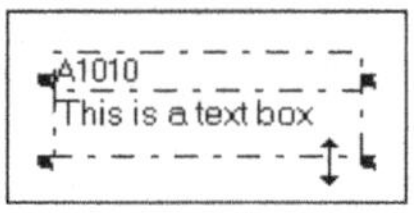

To delete a Text box, position the cursor over the text box until it transforms into a + then click and you may now hit the **Delete** key.

The author found in his load of P6 Version 8.2 that it was not possible to delete a Text Box, only the text inside a Text Box to make the comment disappear. This was fixed in Version 8.3.

8.8.2 Adding and Deleting a Curtain

Primavera Version 5.0 introduced a function allowing the placing of multiple curtains on the Gantt Chart which may be all hidden or displayed. A **Curtain**, used to highlight periods of time over part of the bar chart, may be displayed in a similar way to P3 and SureTrak.

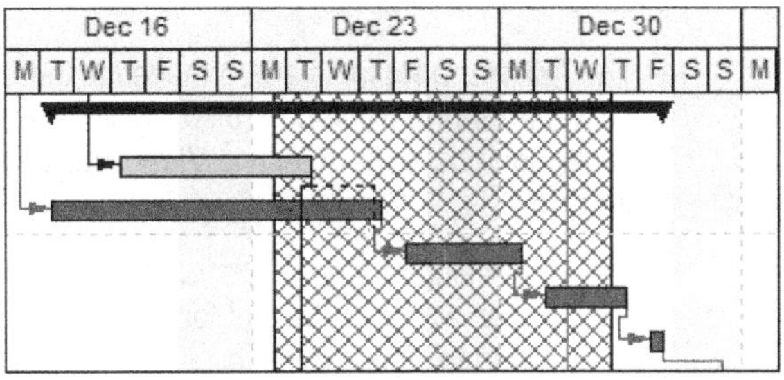

Select **View, Attachments** to display the **Curtain** menu or right-click a bar and select **Attachments, Curtain**:

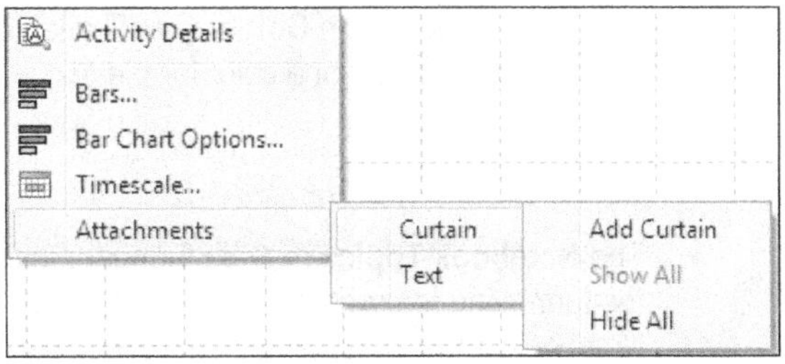

- **Add Curtain** opens the **Curtain Attachment** form used to create a curtain,
- **Show All** shows all the curtains,
- **Hide All** hides all the curtains, and
- Double Clicking on a curtain in the Gantt Chart also opens the **Curtain Attachment** form where individual curtains may be deleted or hidden.
- Using the **Start Date** and **Finish Date** boxes, or
- Grabbing the left or right edge of the Curtain in the Bar Chart (the cursor will change to a) and dragging the start or finish date, or
- Grabbing the Curtain in the center (the cursor will change to a) and dragging the whole Curtain.

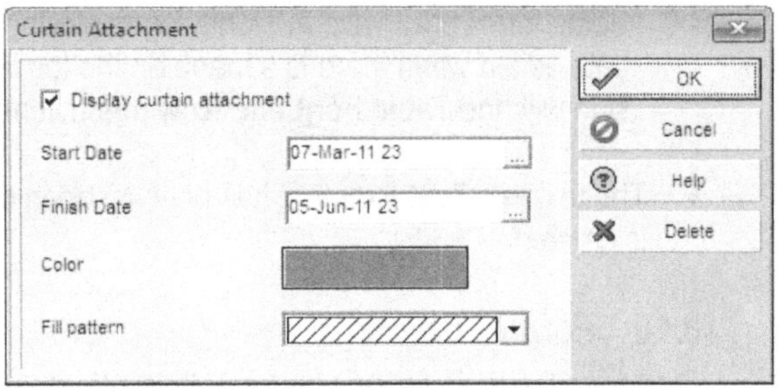

A curtain is deleted by double clicking on the curtain to open the **Curtain Attachment** form and clicking on the Delete button.

8.9 Format Fonts and Font Colors

The format font options are:

- The **Activity Data** fonts are formatted in the **Table, Font and Row** form (displayed in the paragraph above) by selecting **View, Table Font and Row**.
  - Clicking on AaBbYyZz, the **Font** icon will open the font form where normal Windows functions are available.
  - Clicking on the **Color** icon will enable the selection of a color for the text.

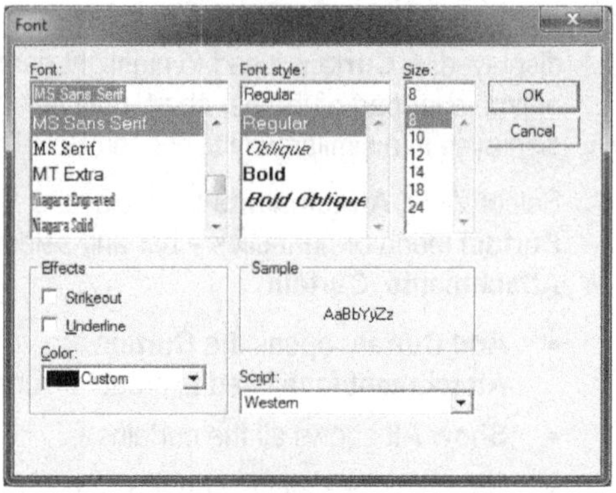

- The **Notebook Topics** may be formatted using the formatting features above where the Notebook items are entered in the lower pane.
- Some forms may have the fonts for displaying data edited when there is a menu on the top left side with the **Table Font and Row** menu item.

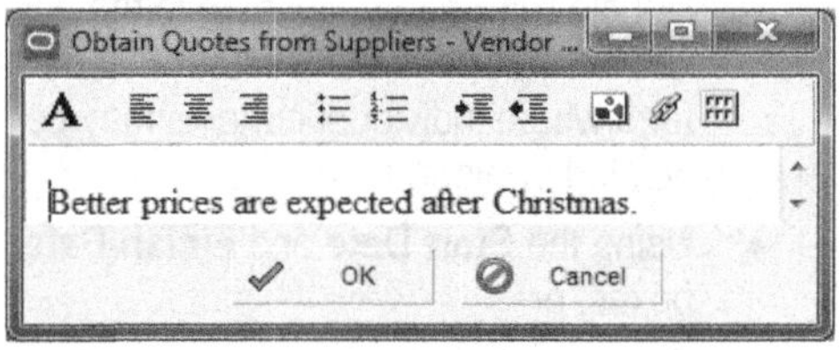

- The text in a **Text Box** that has been inserted onto the Bar Chart may be formatted when the box is created.

8.10 Format Colors

These are the main options for formatting colors:

- **Band** colors in layouts are formatted in the **Group and Sort** form by clicking on the icon or selecting **View, Group and Sort by**.
- **Text** colors are covered in the **Format Font and Colors** paragraph.
- **Bar Colors** are covered in the **Formatting the Bars** paragraph.
- **Timescale** and **Column Headers** are covered in the **Format Timescale Command** paragraph.
- **Sight Lines (Gridline)** colors may not be formatted.
- The **Progress Line** color is selected in the **Bar Chart Options** form, **Progress Line** tab.
- The **Data Date** is formatted in the **Bar Options** form, **Data Date** tab.
- The **Relationship Lines**, also known as **Dependencies**, **Logic**, or **Links**, may not be formatted and are displayed with the following characteristics:
  - Solid Red for Critical,
  - Solid Black for Driving,
  - Dotted Black for Non-driving, and
  - Blue when selected and may be deleted.

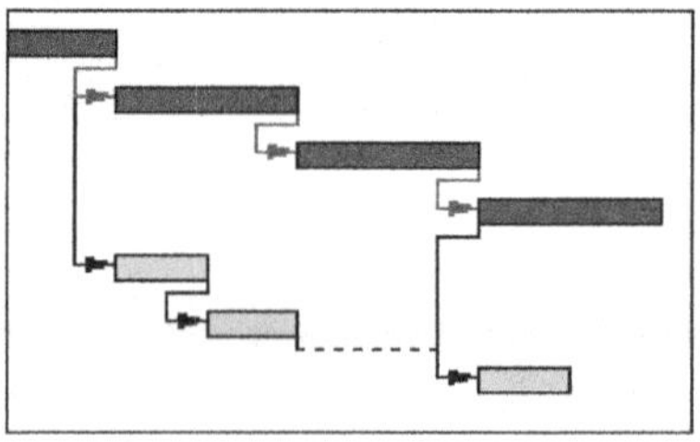

8.11 Line Numbers

Version 8.2 introduced a Microsoft Project style **Line Numbers**. Select **View**, **Line** Number to display or hide the Line Number.

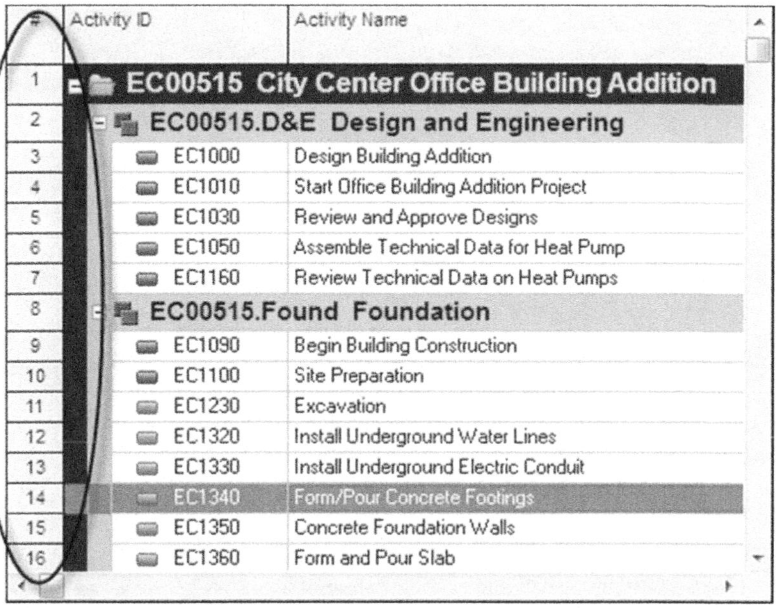

This is a very useful feature for reviewing a schedule to ensure that everyone in a meeting is looking at the same activity.

But as in Microsoft Project this is an order and the number will change if the schedule is reordered.

8.12 Workshop 6 – Formatting the Bar Chart

Background

Management has received your draft report and requests that some changes be made to the presentation.

Assignment

Format your schedule as follows, but depending on the default settings, your Gantt Chart View may differ from that shown, e.g., there may be no summary bars:

1. You will not have to complete the Step 3 of this workshop if you have internet access and are able to download a layout from www.primavera.com.au.
2. Download a layout:
   - Download the **www.primavera.com.au_Layout.plf** layout to your desktop from www.primavera.com.au, Technical Papers tab, or wwww.eh.com.au.
   - Import the Layout as a Project Layout by selecting **View**, **Layout**, **Open**.
   - Do not save your Layout.
   - Select 

, select the layout from your desktop, import and save it:

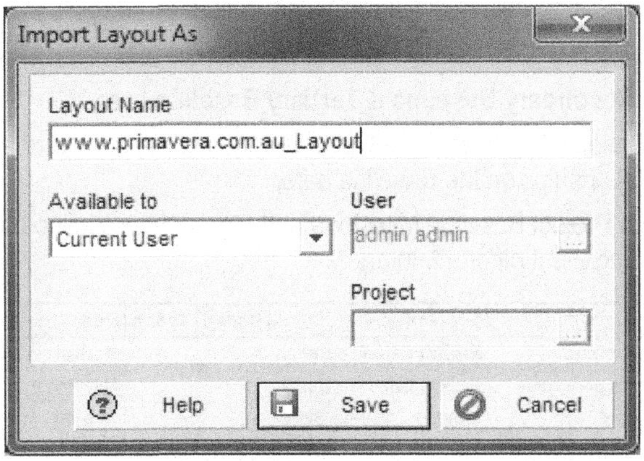

   - Select 

 to apply the layout.
   - Open the **Bars** form and review the settings.
   - Close the **Bars** form.
   - Now move to Step 4, DO NOT COMPLETE Step 3.

continued...

3. Format Bars, if you are unable to download the **www.primavera.com_Layout.plf** layout then:

   - To format the bars open the **Bars** form,
   - Click on the [Default] button to set the bars to the Primavera default settings,
   - Edit the **Float Bar** Filter (**Total Float** bar) so it only shows float for Not Started or In Progress activities. Ensure you select the **Any selected filter** in the **Filters** form:

Display	Name	Timescale	User Start Date	User Finish Date	Filter	Preview
☑	Float Bar	Float Bar			Not Started or In Progress	

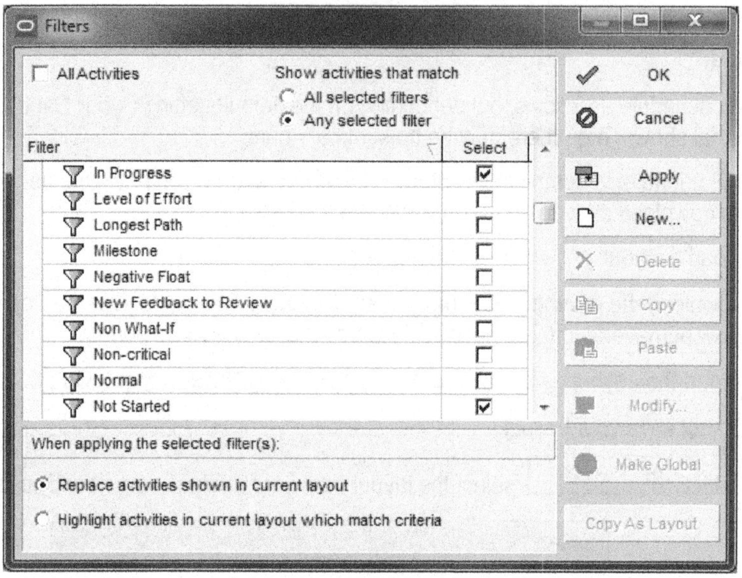

   - Delete the **Secondary Baseline** & **Tertiary Baseline** bars,
   - Move the Baseline bars and Baseline Milestones to the bottom of the Bars form to remove relationships on the Baseline bars,
   - Add missing Project Baseline Milestone and format the Baseline bars as per the picture below, making them different colors:

Display	Name	Timescale	User S	User F	Filter	Preview
☐	Project Baseline Bar	Project Baseline Bar			Normal	
☐	Project Baseline Milestone	Project Baseline Bar			Milestone	▽ ▽
☐	Primary Baseline	Primary Baseline Bar			Normal	
☐	Primary Baseline Milestone	Primary Baseline Bar			Milestone	△ △

   - Remove all text from all bars, except from the **Current Bar Labels** bar, by:
     - ➢ Clicking on the **Bar Labels** tab at the bottom,
     - ➢ Clicking on one bar at a time and using the [Delete] button at the bottom (NOT SIDE) of the screen to delete the text line,
     - ➢ Change the **Current Bar Labels** bar filter to read All Activities and do not display.

4. Display the following bars:
   - Remaining Level of Effort
   - Actual Level of Effort
   - Actual Work
   - Remaining Work
   - Remaining Critical Work
   - Milestones
   - % Complete
   - Summary Bar
   - Float Bar (Total Float)
   - Negative Float Bar
5. Adding Columns:
   - Add **Calendar** and **Activity Type** columns, from the **General** section of the **Columns** form, to the right of the Activity Name column.
   - Adjust the column widths to a best fit by dragging the column header divider lines.
   - Display the **Total Float** column if not displayed.
6. Press the **F9** key and click the  button which will schedule the project and calculate the float.
7. Adjusting Row Heights:
   - Change the Row Height to 30 points by selecting **View, Table Font and Row** and apply,
   - Now check the **Optimize height by row content** box, not exceeding 1 line per row and apply,
   - Now change the setting to 18 point height for all rows and apply.
   - Click on  to close the form.
8. Format Timescale to Year and Month, then Week and Day (two options), then Month and Week by using the  buttons.
9. Format the Vertical lines with a solid Major line every month and a Minor line every week by selecting **View**, **Bars** and clicking on the 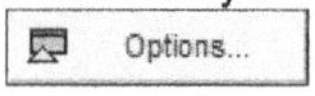 button and selecting the **Sight Lines** tab, or right-clicking in the Gantt Chart area and selecting **Bar Chart Options...** and selecting the **Sight Lines** tab.
10. Expand and contract the timescale and adjust it so that all the bars are visible.

continued...

11. See below for the expected results:

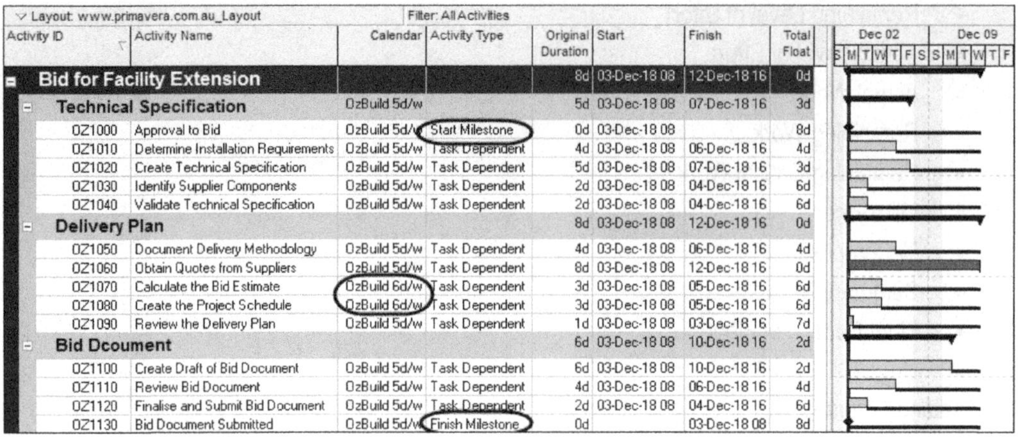

Layout: www.primavera.com.au_Layout — Filter: All Activities

Activity ID	Activity Name	Calendar	Activity Type	Original Duration	Start	Finish	Total Float
	Bid for Facility Extension			8d	03-Dec-18 08	12-Dec-18 16	0d
	Technical Specification	OzBuild 5d/w		5d	03-Dec-18 08	07-Dec-18 16	3d
OZ1000	Approval to Bid	OzBuild 5d/w	Start Milestone	0d	03-Dec-18 08		8d
OZ1010	Determine Installation Requirements	OzBuild 5d/w	Task Dependent	4d	03-Dec-18 08	06-Dec-18 16	4d
OZ1020	Create Technical Specification	OzBuild 5d/w	Task Dependent	5d	03-Dec-18 08	07-Dec-18 16	3d
OZ1030	Identify Supplier Components	OzBuild 5d/w	Task Dependent	2d	03-Dec-18 08	04-Dec-18 16	6d
OZ1040	Validate Technical Specification	OzBuild 5d/w	Task Dependent	2d	03-Dec-18 08	04-Dec-18 16	6d
	Delivery Plan			8d	03-Dec-18 08	12-Dec-18 16	0d
OZ1050	Document Delivery Methodology	OzBuild 5d/w	Task Dependent	4d	03-Dec-18 08	06-Dec-18 16	4d
OZ1060	Obtain Quotes from Suppliers	OzBuild 5d/w	Task Dependent	8d	03-Dec-18 08	12-Dec-18 16	0d
OZ1070	Calculate the Bid Estimate	OzBuild 6d/w	Task Dependent	3d	03-Dec-18 08	05-Dec-18 16	6d
OZ1080	Create the Project Schedule	OzBuild 6d/w	Task Dependent	3d	03-Dec-18 08	05-Dec-18 16	6d
OZ1090	Review the Delivery Plan	OzBuild 5d/w	Task Dependent	1d	03-Dec-18 08	03-Dec-18 16	7d
	Bid Dcoument			6d	03-Dec-18 08	10-Dec-18 16	2d
OZ1100	Create Draft of Bid Document	OzBuild 5d/w	Task Dependent	6d	03-Dec-18 08	10-Dec-18 16	2d
OZ1110	Review Bid Document	OzBuild 5d/w	Task Dependent	4d	03-Dec-18 08	06-Dec-18 16	4d
OZ1120	Finalise and Submit Bid Document	OzBuild 5d/w	Task Dependent	2d	03-Dec-18 08	04-Dec-18 16	6d
OZ1130	Bid Document Submitted	OzBuild 5d/w	Finish Milestone	0d		03-Dec-18 08	8d

12. Check the following:

- Click on Activity ID to make sure they are ordered correctly,
- The dates and times of all activities should start and finish at the same time of the day,
- Activity OZ1060 bar should be colored red as it is the Critical activity representing the shortest duration that the project may be completed,
- All other activities should have Float.

9 ADDING RELATIONSHIPS

The next phase of a schedule is to add logic to the activities. There are two types of logic:

- **Relationships** (**Dependencies** or **Logic** or **Links** between activities), and
- Imposed **Constraints** to activity start or finish dates. These are covered in the **Constraints** chapter.

The Primavera Help file and other texts use the terms **Relationships** and **Logic** for **Relationships** but do not use the terms **Dependencies** or **Links**.

We will look at the following techniques in this chapter:

Topic	Notes for creating a SF Relationship
• Graphically in the Bar Chart.	Drag the mouse pointer from one activity to another to create a dependency.
• By opening the **Activity Details** form.	Predecessor and Successors may be added and deleted from the **Relationships**, **Predecessor** or **Successor** tabs.
• By editing or deleting a dependency using the **Edit Relationship** form.	Double-click an activity link in the **Bar Chart** or **Activity Network** View.
• Opening the **Assign Predecessor** form or the **Assign Successor** form from the menu.	• Select **Edit**, **Assign**, **Predecessors...**, or • Select **Edit**, **Assign**, **Successors....**
• By displaying the **Predecessor** and/or **Successor** columns.	Double-clicking in the Predecessor or Successor cells will open the **Assign Predecessor** form or the **Assign Successor** form.
• Chain Linking or Automatically Linking activities with a Finish-to-Start relationship.	Select the activities in the order they are to be linked using the **Ctrl** key, right-click and select **Link Activities**.

Relationships

There are two types of dependencies that are discussed in scheduling:

- **Hard Logic**, also referred to as **Mandatory** or **Primary Logic**, are dependencies that may not be avoided: for example, a footing excavation has to be prepared before concrete may be poured into it.
- **Soft Logic**, also referred to as **Sequencing Logic**, **Discretionary Logic**, **Preferred Logic**, or **Secondary Logic**, may be changed at a later date to reflect planning changes: for example, determining in which order the footing holes may be dug.

There is no simple method of documenting which is hard logic and which is soft logic as notes may not be attached to relationships. A schedule with a large amount of soft logic has the potential of becoming very difficult to maintain when the plan is changed. As a project progresses, soft logic converts to hard logic due to commitments and commencing activities.

Microsoft Project allows one relationship between two activities, SureTrak and P3 two relationships between two activities and P6 four relationships between two activities.

9.1 Constraints

Constraints are applied to Activities when relationships do not provide the required result and are often a result of **External Dependencies**. Typical applications of a constraint are to constrain an activity to a date for:

- The availability of a site to commence work.
- The supply of information by a client.
- The required finish date of a project.

Constraints are often entered against Milestone activities to represent contract dates and may be directly related to contract items using Notebook Topics.

Constraints are covered in detail in the **Constraints** chapter.

9.2 Understanding Relationships

There are four types of dependencies available in Primavera P6:

- Finish-to-Start (**FS**) (also known as conventional)
- Start-to-Start (**SS**)
- Start-to-Finish (**SF**)
- Finish-to-Finish (**FF**)

Two other terms you must understand are:

- **Predecessor**, an activity that controls the start or finish of another immediate subsequent activity.
- **Successor**, an activity where the start or finish depends on the start or finish of another immediately preceding activity.

The following pictures show how the dependencies appear graphically in the **Bar Chart** and **Activity Network** (also known as PERT, Network Diagram and Relationship Diagram Views):

The **FS** (or conventional) dependency looks like this:

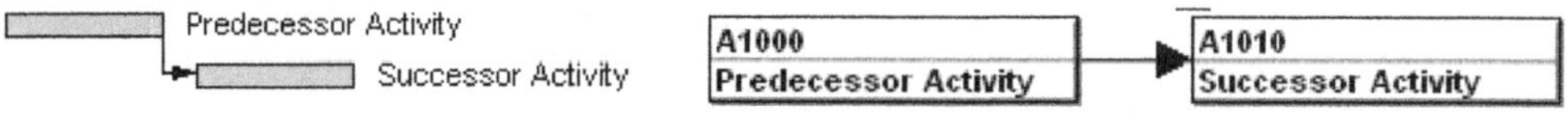

While the **SS** dependency is like this:

The **SF** dependency looks like:

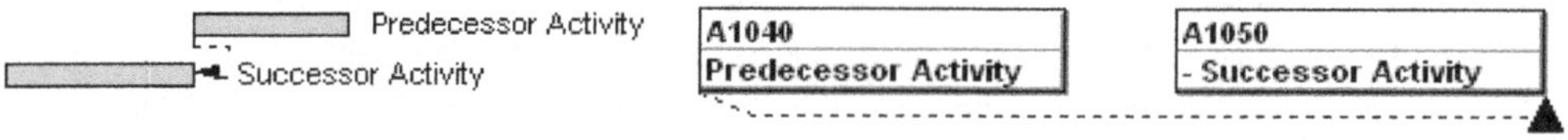

The **FF** dependency would be:

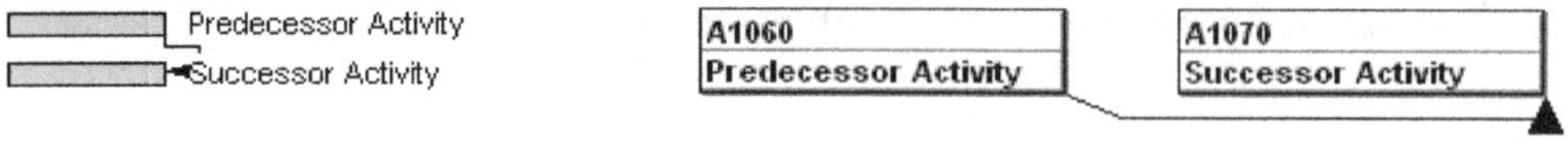

9.3 Understanding Lags and Leads

A **Lag** is a duration that is applied to a dependency to make the successor start or finish earlier or later.

- A successor activity will start later when a positive **Lag** is assigned. Therefore, an activity requiring a 3-day delay between the finish of one activity and start of another will require a positive lag of 3 days.
- Conversely, a lag may be negative when a new activity may be started before the predecessor activity is finished. This is called a **Lead** or **Negative Lag**.
- **Leads** and **Lags** may be applied to any relationship type.

An example of a **FS** with positive lag:

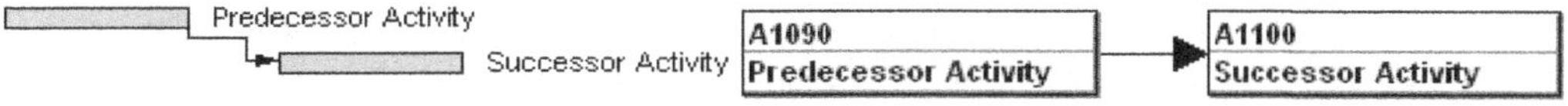

An example of a **FS** with negative lag:

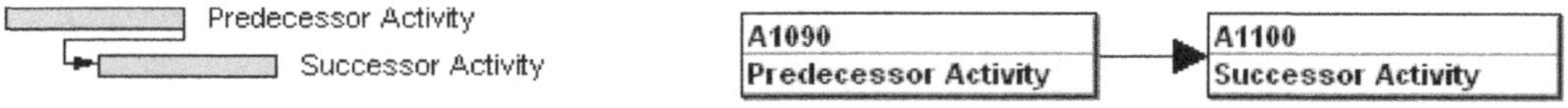

Here are some important points to understand about Lags:

- The lag duration is calculated on the lag as in Microsoft Project and other Primavera products. A lag is not assigned to one or both of the Predecessor and Successor activities as in Asta Powerproject.
- Lags may be assigned one of four calendars from the **Calendar for Scheduling Relationship lag** drop down box in the **General Schedule Options** form. This form is opened by selecting **Tools**, **Schedule...** and clicking on the Options... tab. The four Lag Calendar options are:
  - Predecessor Activity Calendar,
  - Successor Activity Calendar,
  - 24-Hour Calendar, and
  - Project Default Calendar.

Lags are calculated by Primavera P3 and SureTrak software using the Predecessor activity Calendar. Microsoft Project 2003 to 2010 uses the Successor Calendar or may have an Elapsed Duration Lag. Earlier versions of Microsoft Project used the Project Calendar. Asta Powerproject assigns the lag to either or both the predecessor or successor thus allowing either the Predecessor or Successor Calendar to be selected for each relationship.

You must be careful when using a lag to allow for delays such as curing concrete when the Lag Calendar is not a seven-day calendar. Because this type of activity lapses nonwork days, the activity could finish before Primavera calculated finish date.

You must be extremely careful when opening multiple projects when the Lag Calendar option is different for each project. This is because all the project options are changed permanently to be the same as the **Default Project** and therefore some of your projects may not calculate the same way as they did before opening the projects together. Please read the **Multiple Project Scheduling** chapter for more details on this topic.

9.4 *Formatting the Relationships*

Relationships lines may not be formatted like in SureTrak, but unlike Microsoft Project they do not adopt the color of the predecessor activity which is often misleading.

- The relationships may be displayed or hidden by clicking on the icon on the **Activity** toolbar or by checking and un-checking the **Show Relationships** box in the **Bar Chart Options** form, **General** tab.
- The color of the relationship represents:
  - Red - Critical and therefore a Driving relationship,
  - Solid Black - Non-Critical Driving relationship and therefore has Total Float,
  - Dotted Black - Non-Critical Non-Driving relationship and has Free Float, and
  - Blue - a selected relationship and may be deleted.
- A relationship is displayed on the **Baseline** bar, as discussed in paragraph 8.3, when the Baseline bar is above the Actual and Remaining bars in the **Bars** form. To place the relationships onto the Early bar, which is more logical, you should move the Baseline bars in the **Bars** form to below the Actual and Remaining bars in the **Bars** form.

Relationships on the Baseline Bar

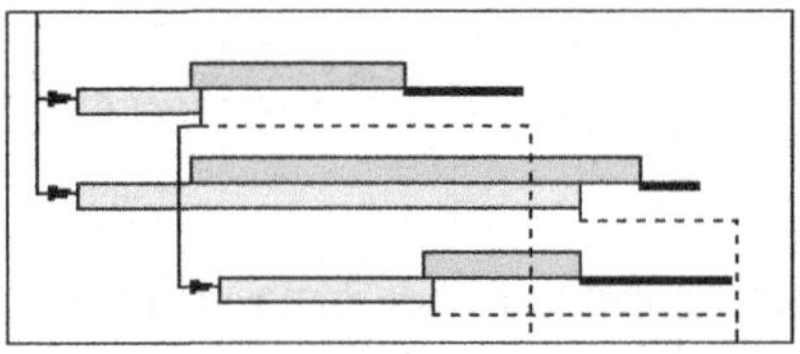

Relationships on the Current Bar

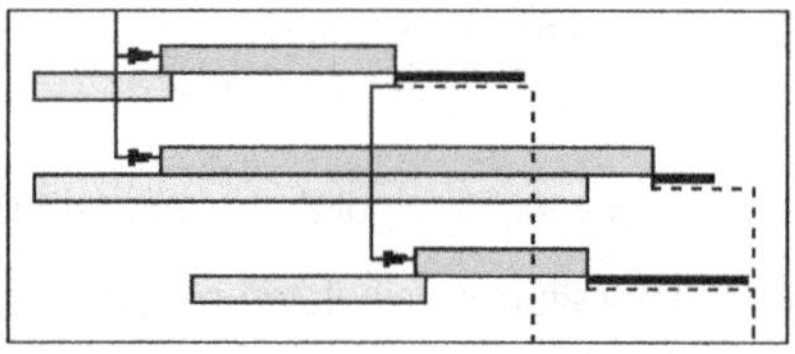

9.5 *Adding and Removing Relationships*

9.5.1 Graphically Adding and Deleting a Relationship

To add relationships move the mouse pointer to end of the predecessor activity bar, which will change the mouse arrow to a ↳. Then simply hold down the left mouse key, drag to the start of the successor activity and release the mouse button.

To create other relationships such as **Start to Start**, drag from the beginning of the predecessor to the beginning of the successor bar.

To confirm or edit the link or add lag after a link has been added, the **Edit Relationship** form may be opened:

- Select a relationship line by clicking and it will turn to blue and an arrow ↑ will appear, then
- Double-click to open the **Edit Relationship** form:

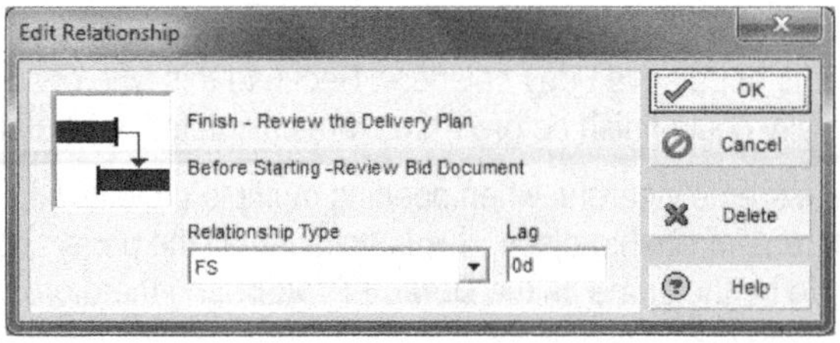

- Click on 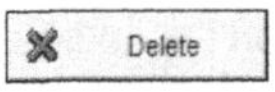

to delete a relationship.

9.5.2 Graphically Deleting a Relationship

Select a relationship and when it turns blue strike the **Delete** key to delete it and select Yes.

Another relationship may turn blue and if you wish to delete this relationship then you may strike the **Delete** key again and select Yes.

Multiple relationships may be deleted by striking the **Delete** key and select Yes multiple times. Once the last relationship has been deleted then you will start deleting activities, so be careful!

The author found in his load of P6 Version 8.2 that it was no longer possible to delete a relationship as in earlier P6 versions and this was fixed in Version 8.3.

9.5.3 Adding and Deleting Relationships with the Activity Details Form

The **Activity Details** form in the lower pane may be used for adding and deleting relationships.

Opening the Form

- Select either the **Predecessor,** or **Successor** or the **Relationship** tab (they all operate in a similar way). The **Successor** tab is displayed in the following picture:

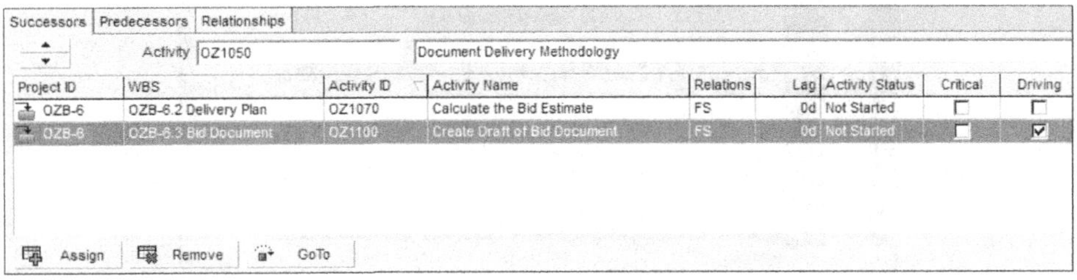

Editing the Form

- The **Predecessor** and **Successor** tabs may both be formatted and the columns you require may be displayed:
  - ➢ Right-click in the **Predecessor** or **Successor** tab, and
  - ➢ Select Customize Successor Columns... to open the **Predecessor** or **Successor Columns** form.
  - ➢ The following picture displays the fields that are available:

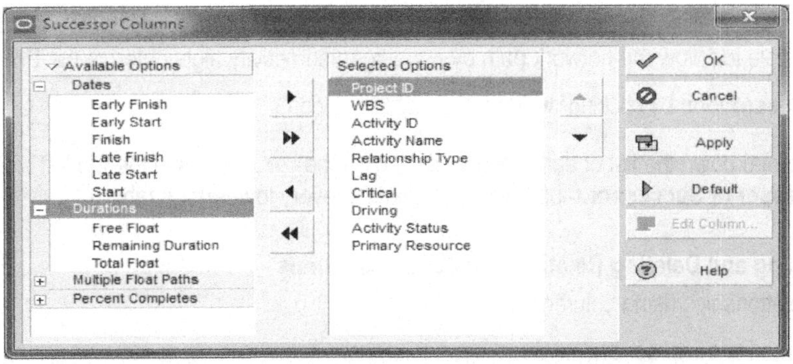

  - ➢ The data fields you require are added, deleted, and reordered using the arrows.
  - ➢ The title may also be edited using the **Edit Column Titles** form by clicking on the Edit Column... icon.

Adding a Relationship

- To **Add** a predecessor or successor:
  - ➢ Click on the icon **Assign Predecessor** in the **Assign Predecessor** form, or icon **Assign Successor** in the **Assign Successor** form, or
  - ➢ Format the form as required by clicking on the Display: All Activities icon,
  - ➢ Then select the relationship from the list:

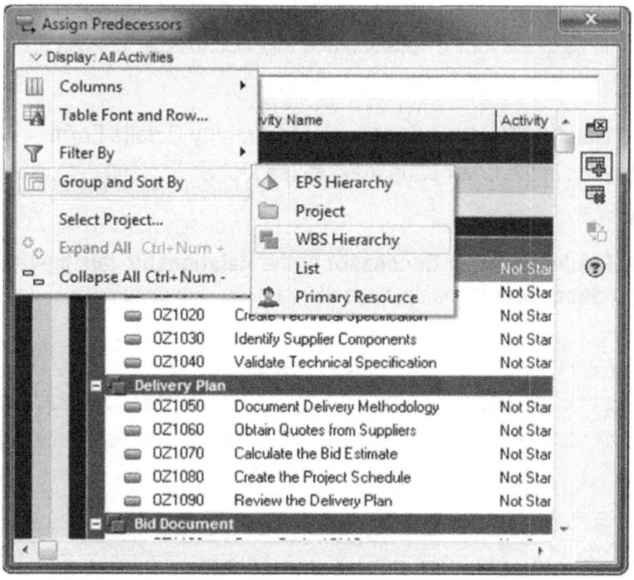

  - ➢ You may use the **Search** function and type in the first characters of either the Activity ID or the Description to narrow down your search.
  - ➢ Double-click the Activity or click the icon to assign the predecessor or successor.
- Enter the Relationship Type from the **Relationship Type** drop down list and the lag, if required, from the **Lag** drop down list.
- To enter another relationship, click the next activity line. The **Assign Predecessor** or **Successor** form will remain open.
- **Delete** a relationship by selecting a relationship and clicking on the **Remove** icon.
- It is possible to follow the network path by jumping to an activity highlighted in the **Predecessor** or **Successor** form by clicking on the GoTo icon.
- Move up and down the list of activities by clicking on the icons in the top left side of the **Predecessor** or **Successor** tabs. This icon exists in every lower pane tab.

9.5.4 Adding and Deleting Relationships Using Columns

To assign relationships using columns:

- Display the Predecessor and/or Successor columns,
- Double-click in the Predecessor or Successor column of an activity to open the **Assign Predecessor** or **Successor** form, and
- Proceed as above.

9.5.5 Chain Linking

Activities may also be linked by selecting two or more activities using the Ctrl key in the order you wish them to be linked, right-click and select **Link Activities:**

- This option will only create Finish-to-Start relationships.
- This option does not enable the user to Chain Unlink.

9.5.6 Using the Assign Toolbar Icons to Assign Relationships

The **Assign Predecessors** icon may be used to open the **Assign Predecessors** form and the **Assign Successors** icon may be used to open the **Assign Successors** form.

9.6 Dissolving Activities

When an activity is deleted then a chain of logical activities may be broken. The **Edit**, **Dissolve** command and the right-click **Dissolve** command will delete an activity but join the predecessors and successors with a Finish-to-Start relationship.

9.7 Circular Relationships

A **Circular Relationship** is created when a loop is created in the logic. When you reschedule you will be presented with the **Circular Relationships** form, which identifies the loop. If a loop is detected when scheduling a project, the **Circular Loop** form is displayed identifying any loops.

To remove a circular relationship either select the first activity in the list and remove the offending predecessor, which is the last Activity in the list, or go to the last activity in the list and remove the offending successor, which is the first activity in the list.

9.8 Scheduling the Project

After you have your activities and the logic in place, Primavera calculates the activities' dates/times. More specifically, Primavera **Schedules** the project to calculate the **Early Dates**, **Late Dates**, **Free Float** and the **Total Float**. This will enable you to review the **Critical Path** of the project. (Microsoft Project uses the term **Slack** instead of the term **Float**.) To schedule a project:

- Select **Tools**, **Schedule...**, or
- Strike the **F9** key to open the **Schedule** form:

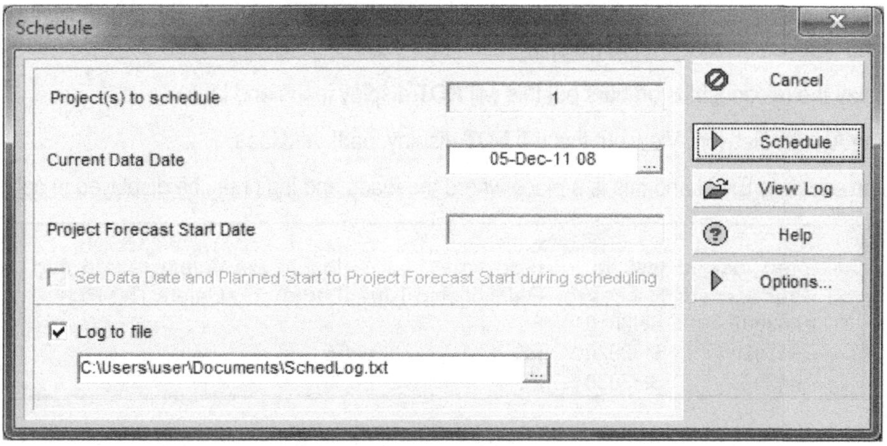

- Check the **Current Data Date**, which before a schedule is progressed should be the start date of the project.
- Click on the 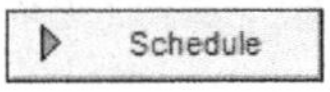

icon.

Ensure the "Log to file" check box is checked to display the scheduling log report. After scheduling a project, reopen the scheduling form and click the "View Log" to review the log report.

To turn on automatic calculation, select **Tools**, **Schedule...**, 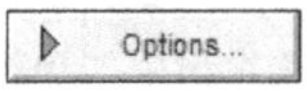

icon. Select **Schedule automatically when a change affects dates**.

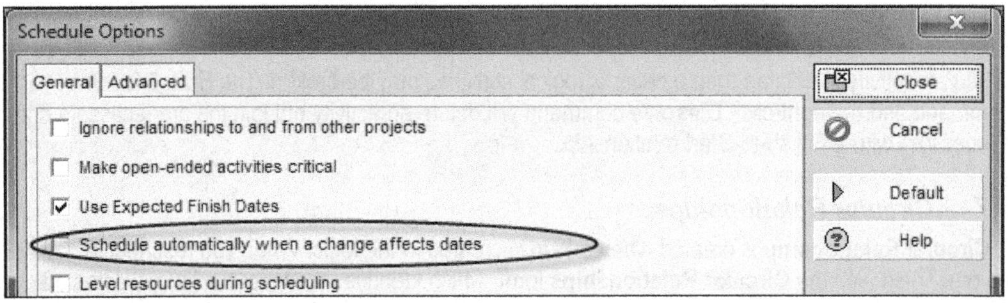

Sometimes it is preferable to have the software recalculate the schedule each time an edit is made to an activity which affects any activity dates. Often the response time with large schedules running on remote servers through Citrix or Terminal Server respond slowly and this option is best schedule left unchecked.

The default calculation setting for Microsoft Project and SureTrak is Automatic Calculation and Manual for P3 and Primavera P6.

9.9 Reviewing Relationships, Leads and lags

It is it is not possible to view all the leads and lags in columns from the user interface as in Microsoft Project or Asta Powerproject. Relationships may be viewed in the following methods:

- In the relevant Activity Details form tabs, where the Leads and Lags may be reviewed one activity at a time.
- By displaying the predecessor or successor column, but this will **NOT** display leads and lags.
- In the "Schedule Report - Predecessors & Successors", but the standard report supplied will P6 on the author's system will **NOT** display leads and lags.
- Display the relationships on bars but this will **NOT** display leads and lags.
- In the Activity Network View but this will **NOT** display leads and lags.
- As an export to Excel and this is a place where the leads and lags may be displayed in columns:

	A	B	C	L	M
1	pred_task_id	task_id	pred_type	lag_hr_cnt	delete_record_flag
2	Predecessor	Successor	Relationship Type	Lag(d)	Delete This Row
3	SH2002	SH2010	FS	-5	
4	SH2010	SH2020	FS	-5	
5	SH2020	SH2030	FS	-5	

9.10 Workshop 7 – Adding the Relationships

Background

You have determined the logical sequence of activities, so you may now create the relationships.

Assignment

1. Display the **Predecessor** column from the **Lists** section of the **Columns** form, to the right of the Activity Name.
2. Input the logic below using several of the methods detailed in this chapter:

Activity ID	Activity Name	Predecessors
Bid for Facility Extension		
Technical Specification		
OZ1000	Approval to Bid	
OZ1010	Determine Installation Requirements	OZ1000
OZ1020	Create Technical Specification	OZ1010
OZ1030	Identify Supplier Components	OZ1020
OZ1040	Validate Technical Specification	OZ1030
Delivery Plan		
OZ1050	Document Delivery Methodology	OZ1040
OZ1060	Obtain Quotes from Suppliers	OZ1030
OZ1070	Calculate the Bid Estimate	OZ1050, OZ1060
OZ1080	Create the Project Schedule	OZ1070
OZ1090	Review the Delivery Plan	OZ1080
Bid Document		
OZ1100	Create Draft of Bid Document	OZ1050
OZ1110	Review Bid Document	OZ1090, OZ1100
OZ1120	Finalise and Submit Bid Document	OZ1110
OZ1130	Bid Document Submitted	OZ1120

3. Press **F5** – **Refresh Data** if the relationships do not appear in columns.
4. Press **F9** or click on the Schedule button to schedule.
5. Hide and display the Logic Links using the icon. Leave them displayed.

continued...

Answer to Workshop 7

6. Format the columns as per the following picture:

Activity ID	Activity Name	Predecessors	Successors	Orig Dur	Start	Finish	Total Float
Bid for Facility Extension				31d	03-Dec-18 08	17-Jan-19 16	0d
Technical Specification				13d	03-Dec-18 08	19-Dec-18 16	2d
OZ1000	Approval to Bid		OZ1010	0d	03-Dec-18 08		0d
OZ1010	Determine Installation Requirements	OZ1000	OZ1020	4d	03-Dec-18 08	06-Dec-18 16	0d
OZ1020	Create Technical Specification	OZ1010	OZ1030	5d	07-Dec-18 08	13-Dec-18 16	0d
OZ1030	Identify Supplier Components	OZ1020	OZ1040, OZ1060	2d	14-Dec-18 08	17-Dec-18 16	0d
OZ1040	Validate Technical Specification	OZ1030	OZ1050	2d	18-Dec-18 08	19-Dec-18 16	2d
Delivery Plan				14d	18-Dec-18 08	09-Jan-19 16	0d
OZ1050	Document Delivery Methodology	OZ1040	OZ1070, OZ1100	4d	20-Dec-18 08	27-Dec-18 16	2d
OZ1060	Obtain Quotes from Suppliers	OZ1030	OZ1070	8d	18-Dec-18 08	31-Dec-18 16	0d
OZ1070	Calculate the Bid Estimate	OZ1050, OZ1060	OZ1080	3d	02-Jan-19 08	04-Jan-19 16	0d
OZ1080	Create the Project Schedule	OZ1070	OZ1090	3d	05-Jan-19 08	08-Jan-19 16	0d
OZ1090	Review the Delivery Plan	OZ1080	OZ1110	1d	09-Jan-19 08	09-Jan-19 16	0d
Bid Dcoument				31d	03-Dec-18 08	17-Jan-19 16	0d
OZ1100	Create Draft of Bid Document	OZ1050	OZ1110	6d	28-Dec-18 08	07-Jan-19 16	2d
OZ1110	Review Bid Document	OZ1090, OZ1100	OZ1120	4d	10-Jan-19 08	15-Jan-19 16	0d
OZ1120	Finalise and Submit Bid Document	OZ1110	OZ1130	2d	16-Jan-19 08	17-Jan-19 16	0d
OZ1130	Bid Document Submitted	OZ1120		0d		17-Jan-19 16	0d

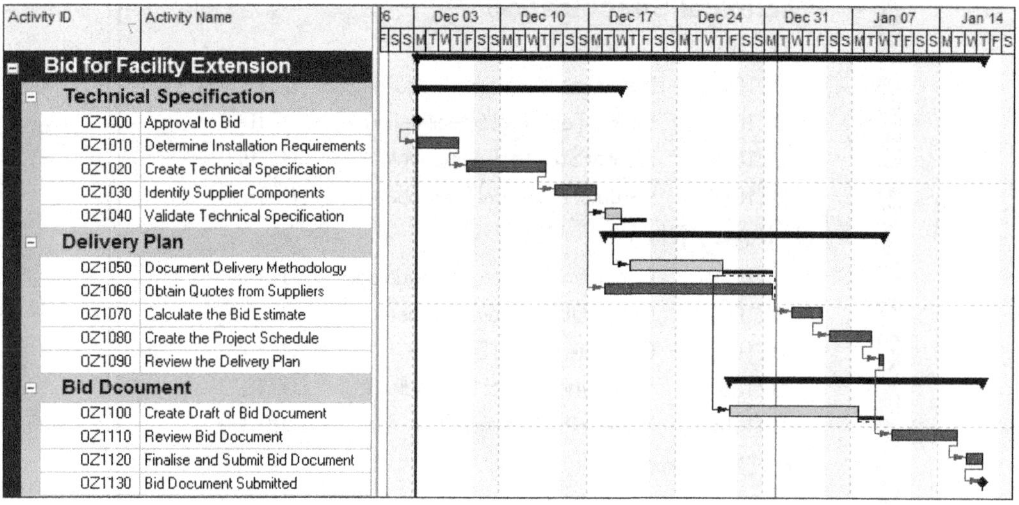

10 ACTIVITY NETWORK VIEW

The **Activity Network**, also known as the **PERT View**, displays activities as boxes connected by the relationship lines. See the following picture:

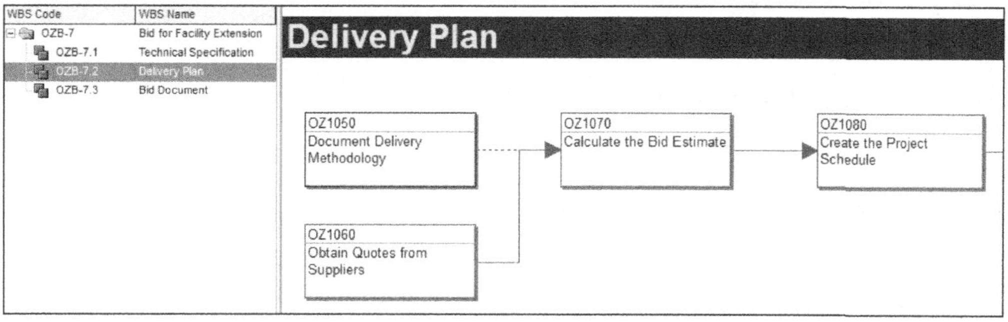

This chapter will not cover this subject in detail but will introduce the main features.

Many features available in the **Gantt Chart View** are also available in the **Activity Network View**, including:

Topic	Menu Command
• Viewing a Project Using the **Activity Network View**.	• Click on the **Top Layout** toolbar button, or • Select **View, Show on Top**, **Activity Network**.
• Adding and Deleting Activities in the **Activity Network** View.	• Use the **Insert** and **Delete** keys, or • Use the **Edit** toolbar, **Add** and **Delete** buttons, or • Use the menu commands **Edit**, **Add** and **Delete**.
• Adding, Editing and Deleting Relationships.	• Graphically drag from one activity to another, or • Use the **Predecessor**, or **Successor**, or **Relationship** tabs in the **Activities Window**, **Details** form.
• Formatting the Activity Boxes.	• Select **View, Activity Network**, **Activity Network Options...**,or • Right-click in the **Activity Network** area and select **Activity Network Options....**

10.1 Viewing a Project Using the Activity Network View

To view your project in the **Network View** either:

- Click on the **Top Layout** toolbar button, or
- Select **View, Show on Top, Activity Network**.

10.2 Adding and Deleting Activities

10.2.1 Adding an Activity

A **New Activity** may be created without a relationship by:

- Using the **Insert** key, or
- Use the **Edit** toolbar, **Add** button, or
- Selecting **Edit**, **Add**.

10.2.2 Deleting and Activity

Activities may be deleted by:

- Using the **Delete** key, or
- Use the **Edit** toolbar, **Delete** button, or
- Selecting **Edit**, **Delete**.

10.3 Adding, Editing and Deleting Relationships

Relationships may be added, deleted or edited using the following methods:

10.3.1 Graphically Adding a Relationship

- To create a FS relationship, move the mouse to the right side of the predecessor activity box (the pointer will change to a ↳) and drag to the left side of the successor activity. Selecting the left or right side of the predecessor and successor activity box will determine the type of relationship that is created.
- To edit the relationship, select the relationship (it will change to blue), double-click to open the **Edit Relationship** form, and edit the relationship.

10.3.2 Using the Activity Details Form

Open the **Relationships** tab in the **Activity Details** form:

- When the **Activity Details** form is not displayed, select **View, Show on Bottom**.
- Then add, edit, and delete activities in the same way as with the Gantt Chart.

10.4 Formatting the Activity Boxes

Activity Boxes may be formatted from the **Activity Network Options** form, which is displayed when an Activity Network View is displayed. The formatting affects both the **Trace Logic** and **Activity Network Window** formatting for the layout that is being formatted:

- Select **View, Activity Network**, **Activity Network Options...**,or
- Right-click in the PERT area and select **Activity Network Options...**:
  - A selection of box templates are available from the drop down box under the Activity Box Template title. These templates display different data in the box.
  - Click on Font & Colors... to format the text font and colors,
  - Click on Box Template... to edit the template or add and remove data items from the activity boxes.

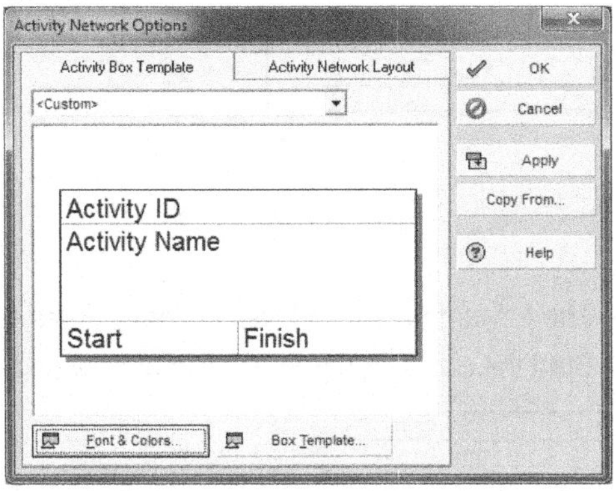

NOTE: This option also formats the **Trace Logic** boxes with the same format.

- Click on the **Activity Network Layout** tab to display further options which are self-explanatory:
  - **Show progress** will place a diagonal line through an in-progress activity and a cross through a completed activity.
  - The **spacing factors** are a percentage of the box sizes.

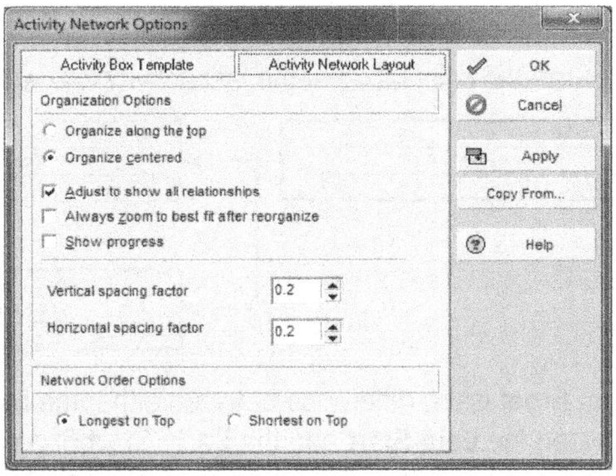

10.5 Reorganizing the Activity Network

Activities in the **Activity Network** view may be repositioned by dragging. There are two functions available when right-clicking in the **Activity Network** view:

- **Reorganize** will reposition activities that have not been manually positioned, and
- **Reorganize All** will reposition all activities including those that have been manually positioned.

10.6 Saving and Opening Activity Network Positions

When activities are manually dragged into new positions on the screen for presentation purposes, it is possible to save and reload these positions at a later date:

- **View, Activity Network**, **Save Network Positions...** will create an *.**anp** file, and
- **View, Activity Network**, **Open Network Positions...** will enable an *.**anp** file to be located and loaded which will reposition the activities as they were saved.

10.7 Early Date, Late Date and Float Calculations

To help understand the calculation of late and early dates, float and critical path, we will now manually work through an example. The boxes below represent activities.

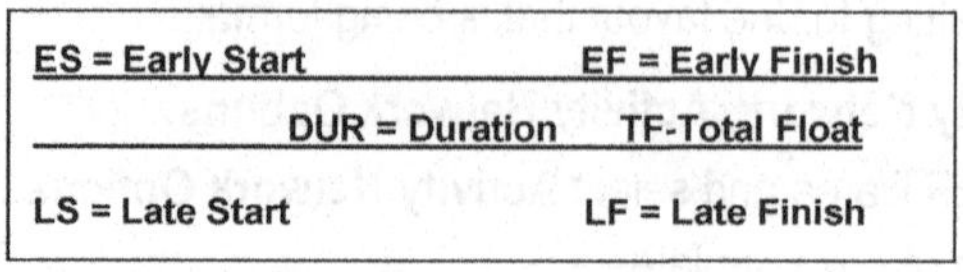

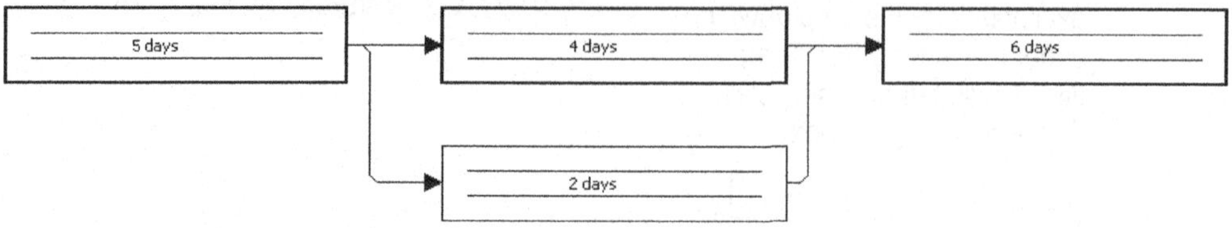

- The forward pass calculates the early dates: EF = ES + DUR – 1
  Start the calculation from the first activity and work forward in time.

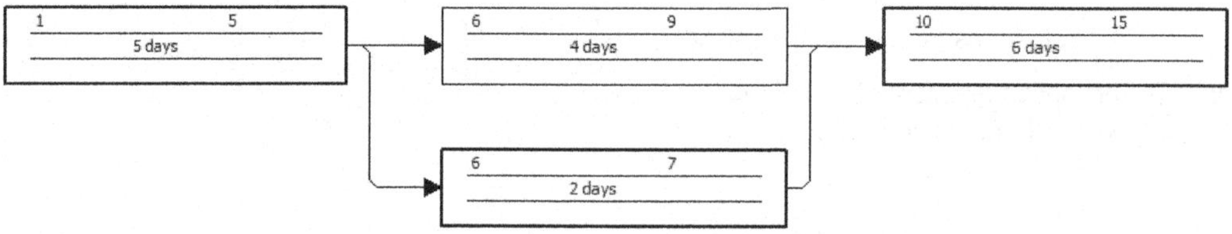

- The backward pass calculates the late dates: LS = LF – DUR + 1
  Start the calculation at the last activity and work backwards in time.

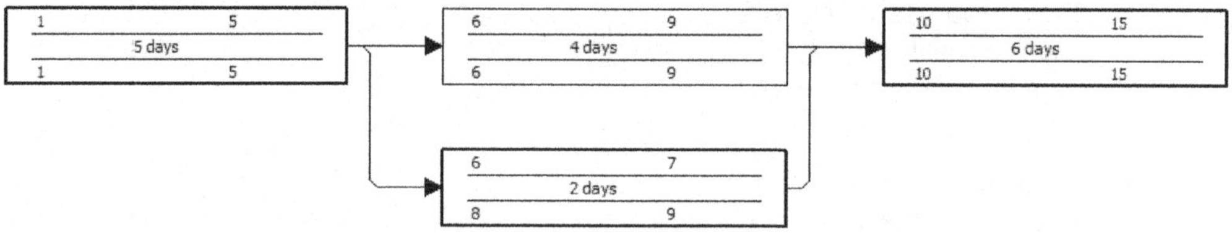

Total Float is the difference between either the **Late Finish** and the **Early Finish** or the difference between the **Late Start** and the **Early Start** of an activity. The lower 2 days' activity has float of 9 – 7 = 2 days. None of the other activities has float.

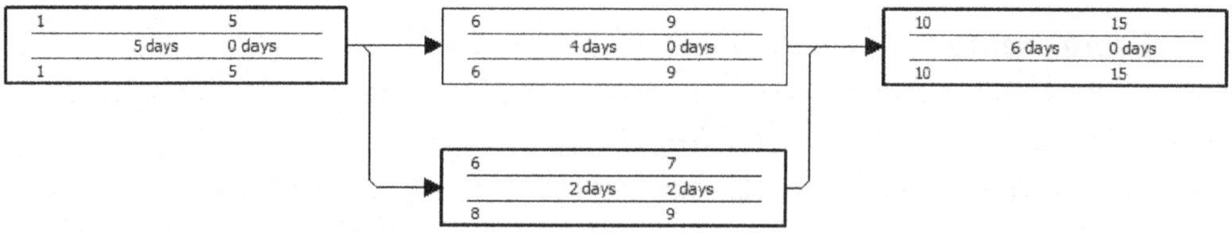

The **Critical Path** is the path where any delay causes a delay in the project and runs through the top row of activities. **Free Float** is the difference between the Predecessor Early Finish and the Successor Early Start.

An activity may not be on the Critical Path and may have more than one predecessor. A **Driving Relationship** is the predecessor that determines the Activity Early Start.

10.8 Workshop 8 – Scheduling Calculations and Activity Network View

Background

We want to practice calculating early and late dates with a simple manual exercise.

Assignment

1. Apply the Activity Network View of your OzBuild schedule by clicking on the icon.
2. Click on each node of the WBS and notice how only activities assigned to each node are displayed.
3. Click on the three Zoom icons and notice their effect on the schedule.
4. Calculate the Early Dates, Late Dates, and Total Float for the following activities, assuming a Monday-to-Friday working week and the first activity starting on 1 Apr 19.

ES = Early Start	**EF = Early Finish**
DUR = Duration	**TF - Total Float**
LS = Late Start	**LF = Late Finish**

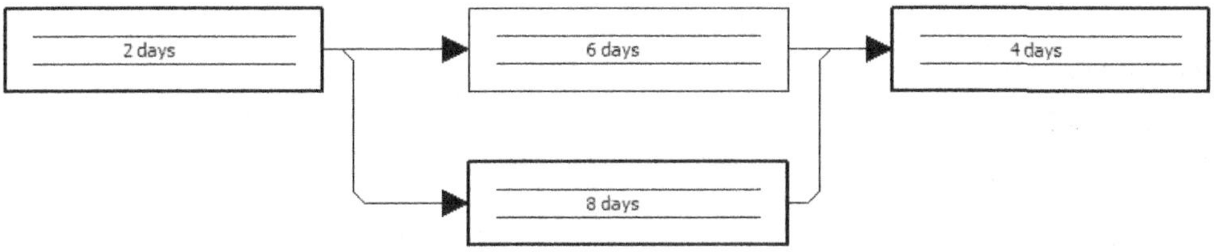

<	April 2019					>
Sun	Mon	Tue	Wed	Thr	Fri	Sat
	1	2	3	4	5	6
7	8	9	10	11	12	13
14	15	16	17	18	19	20
21	22	23	24	25	26	27
28	29	30				

5. See over the page for the answer:

Answer to Workshop 8

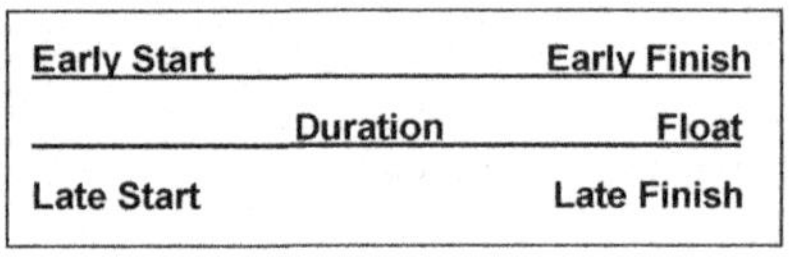

Forward Pass $EF = ES + DUR - 1$

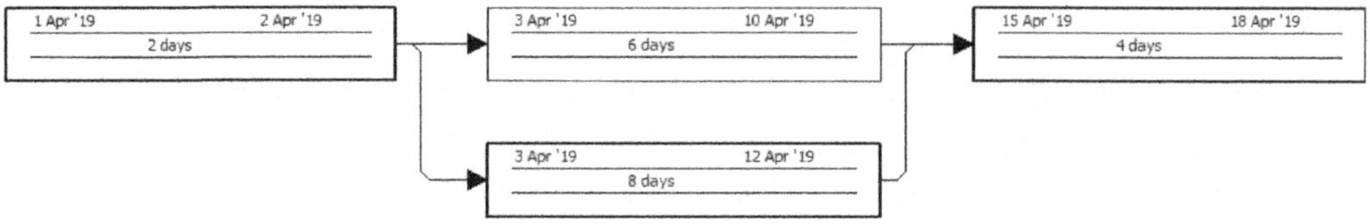

Backward Pass $LS = LF - DUR + 1$

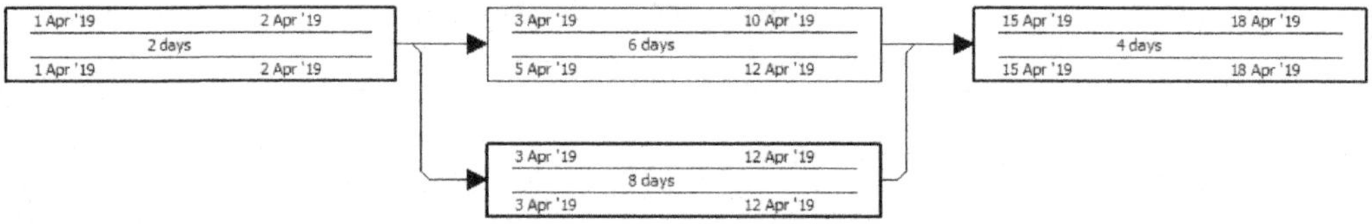

Float Calculation $TF = LS - ES$

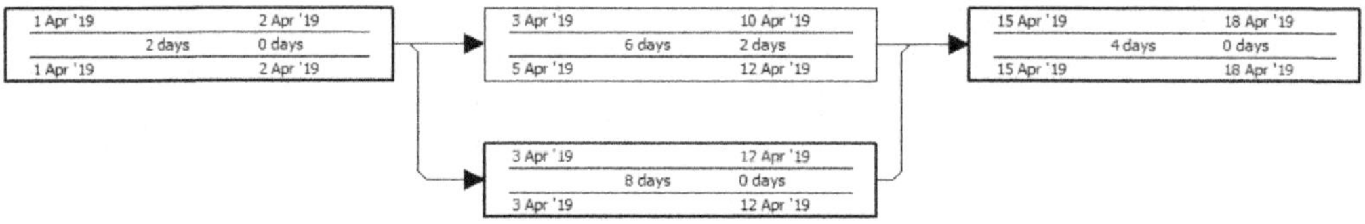

The Early Bar is the upper bar, the Late Bar the lower bar and the end of the Total Float bar, which is the thin bar, ends at the Late Finish date.

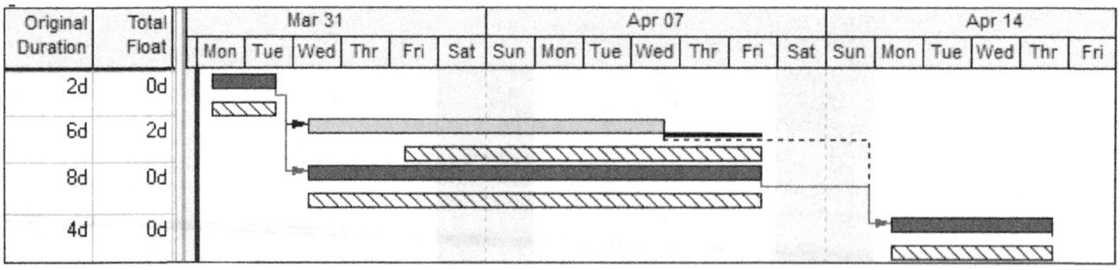

11 CONSTRAINTS

Constraints are used to impose logic on activities that may not be realistically scheduled with logic links. This chapter will deal with the following constraints in detail:

- **Start On or After**
- **Finish On or Before**

These are the minimum number of constraints that are required to effectively schedule a project.

Start On or After (also known as an "Early Start" or "Start No Earlier Than" constraint as it only affects the Early dates calculation) is used when the start date of an activity is known and does not have a predecessor. Primavera will not calculate the activity early start date prior to this date.

Finish On or Before (also known as "Late Finish" or "Finish No Later Than" constraint as it only affects the Late dates calculation) is used when the latest finish date is stipulated. Primavera will not calculate the activity's late finish date after this date.

The following table summarizes the methods used to assign Constraints to Activities or how to add notes to activities:

Topic	Notes for Creating a Constraint
• Setting a **Primary** and **Secondary** constraint with the **Activity Details** form.	Open the **Status** tab on the **Activity Details** form.
• Setting Constraints using columns.	The following columns may be displayed and the constraints assigned or edited: • Primary Constraint • Primary Constraint Date • Secondary Constraint • Secondary Constraint Date • Expected Finish Date
• Dragging an Activity in the Gantt Chart.	Dragging an Activity in the Gantt Chart will open the **Confirmation** form where the user is able to confirm the setting of a **Start On or After** constraint.
• Adding Notes, these could be about constraints or other activity information.	The **Activity Details** form has a **Notebook** tab, which enables Notes to be assigned to **Notebook Topics**.

Primavera will permit two constraints to be assigned to each activity. Asta Powerproject, P3, and SureTrak also allow two constraints but Microsoft Project only permits one except when a Deadline constraint is applied.

A full list of **constraints** available in Primavera:

- **<None>** This is the default for a new activity. An activity by default is scheduled to occur **As Soon As Possible** and does not have a Constraint.
- **Start On** Also known as **Must Start On** and sets a date on which the activity will start. Therefore, the activity has no float. The early start and the late start dates are set to be the same as the Constraint Date.
- **Start On or Before** Also known as **Start No Later Than** or **Late Start**, this constraint sets the late date after which the activity will not start.
- **Start On or After** Also known as **Start No Earlier Than** or **Early Start**, this constraint sets the early date before which the activity will not start.
- **Finish On** Also known as **Must Finish On**, this constraint sets a date on which the activity will finish and therefore has no float. The early finish and the late finish dates are set to be the same as the Constraint Date.
- **Finish On or Before** Also known as **Finish No Later Than** or **Late Finish**, this sets the late date after which the activity will not finish.
- **Finish On or After** Also known as **Finish No Earlier Than** or **Early Finish**, this sets the early date before which the activity will not finish.
- **As Late As Possible** Also known as **Zero Free Float**. An activity will be scheduled to occur as late as possible. It consumes Free Float only and does not have any particular Constraint Date. The Early and Late dates have the same date.
- **Mandatory Start** This constraint prevents float being calculated through this activity and effectively breaks a schedule into two parts. This is also sometimes called a Hard Constraint.
- **Mandatory Finish** This constraint prevents float being calculated through this activity and effectively breaks a schedule into two parts. This is also sometimes called a Hard Constraint.
- **Expected Finish** An **Expected Finish** sets the Early Finish to the Expected Finish constraint date and calculates the Remaining Duration from the Early Start date for an un-started activity, or Data Date if the activity is in-progress to the Expected Finish date.

Earlier Than constraints operate on the **Early Dates**, and **Later Than** constraints operate on **Late Dates**. The following picture demonstrates how constraints calculate Total Float of activities (without predecessors or successors):

Activity ID	Primary Constraint	Primary Constraint Date	Total Float	Free Float
A1000	As Late As Possible		5d	0d
A1010	Finish On	16-Jan-15 17	0d	0d
A1020	Finish On or After	16-Jan-15 17	5d	0d
A1030	Finish On or Before	16-Jan-15 17	5d	5d
A1040	Mandatory Finish	16-Jan-15 17	0d	0d
A1050	Mandatory Start	12-Jan-15 08	0d	0d
A1060	Start On	12-Jan-15 08	0d	0d
A1070	Start On or After	12-Jan-15 08	5d	0d
A1080	Start On or Before	12-Jan-15 08	5d	5d

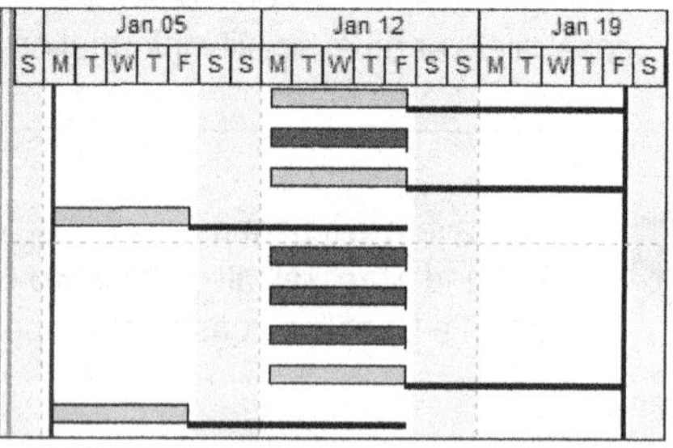

An activity assigned an **As Late as Possible** constraint in Primavera P6, Primavera Contractor, Primavera P3, and SureTrak software will schedule the activity so it absorbs only **Free Float** and will not delay the start of any successor activities, this is normally called a **Zero Free Float** constraint. In Microsoft Project, an activity assigned with an **As Late as Possible** constraint will be delayed to absorb the Total Float and delay all its successor activities which have float, not just the activity with the constraint.

11.1 Assigning Constraints

When setting constraints sometimes the constraint time will not be set at the start or finish of the activity calendar but set at 00:00 or some other irrelevant time. Therefore when setting constraints you should always display the time by selecting **Edit**, **User Preferences ...**, **Dates** tab to ensure the constraint time is compatible with the activity calendar.

11.1.1 Number of Constraints per Activity

Two constraints are permitted against each activity. They are titled Primary and Secondary Constraint. After the Primary has been set, a Secondary may be set only when the combination is logical and therefore a reduced list of constraints is available from the Secondary Constraint list after the Primary has been set.

11.1.2 Setting a Primary Constraint Using the Activity Details Form

To assign a constraint using the **Activity Details** form:

- Select the activity requiring a constraint,
- Open the **Status** tab on the **Activity Details** form,
- Select the **Primary Constraint** type from the **Date** drop down list to the right of **Primary Date**:

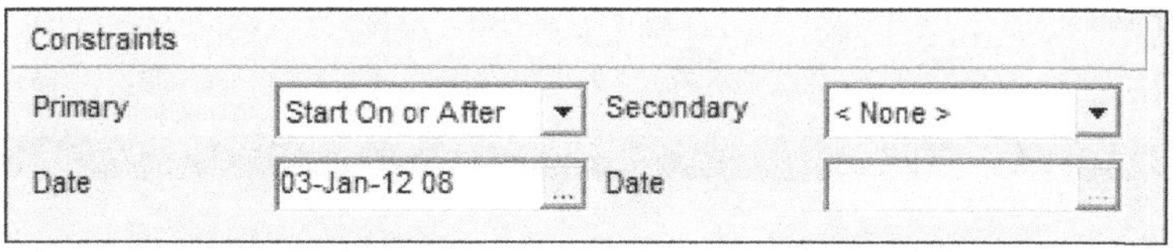

11.1.3 Setting a Secondary Constraint Using the Activity Details Form

To assign a constraint using the **Activity Details** form:

- Select the activity requiring a constraint,
- Open the **Status** tab on the **Activity Details** form,
- Select the **Secondary Constraint** type from the **Date** drop down list to the right of **Secondary Date**:

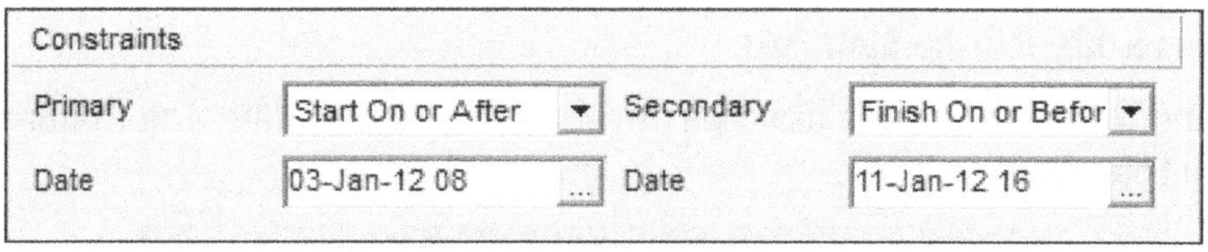

The picture above shows that after a **Primary Start On or After** constraint is set there are only two Secondary Constraints available. After a constraint is set the date will have an asterisk "*" next to it.

- Start Constraints will have the "*" next to the Start Date, and
- Finish Constraints will have the "*" next to the Finish Date.
- Unlike P3 and SureTrak one does not have to display the Late Dates to see a Late Constraint "*".

11.1.4 Expected Finish Constraint

This constraint is set in the dates **Status** area above the **Constraints** area and will only work if the **Tools**, **Schedule...**, 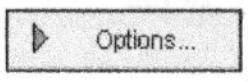

, **Use Expected Finish dates** check box is checked.

This constraint is set in the **Status** section of the **Activity Details**, **Status** tab, not under the **Constraints** section as one would expect:

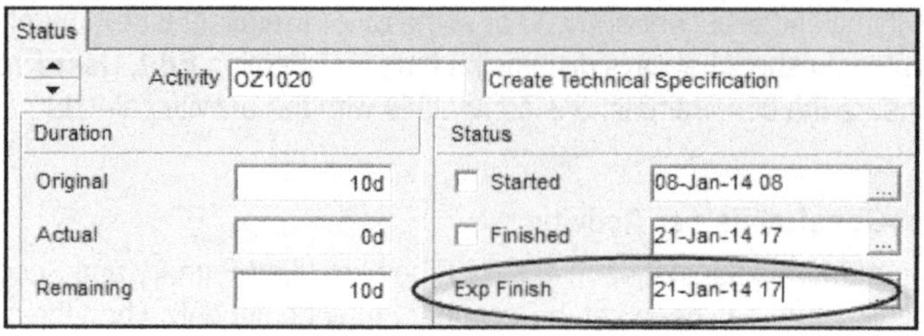

11.1.5 Setting Constraints Using Columns

The following constraint columns may be displayed and the Constraints edited or assigned using these columns:

- Primary Constraint
- Primary Constraint Date
- Secondary Constraint
- Secondary Constraint Date
- Expected Finish

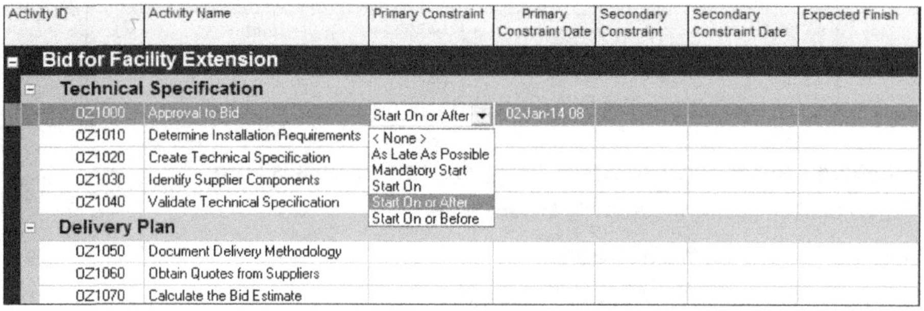

11.1.6 Typing in a Start Date

A **Start On or After** constraint may be assigned from the **Activity Status** tab or the **Start Date** column by typing a date into the **Start** field:

- A **Start On or After** constraint is assigned by overtyping the Start date. The **Confirmation** form will confirm this action.

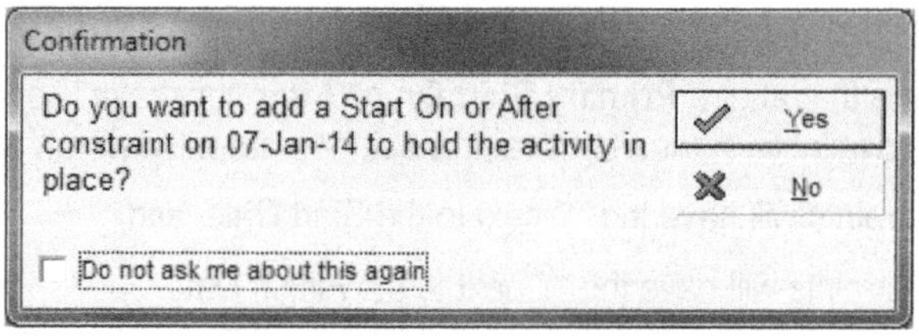

A date typed into the finish date will not assign a Finish Date constraint but will adjust the duration of the activity. In Microsoft Project, a date typed into either the Start or the Finish field will set a constraint; Primavera does not operate in this way.

Beware of clicking **Do not ask me about this again** as you will be unable to turn this option back on again using the user interface with earlier versions of P6.

11.2 Project Must Finish By Date

An absolute finish date may be imposed on the project using the **Project Window**, **Dates** tab:

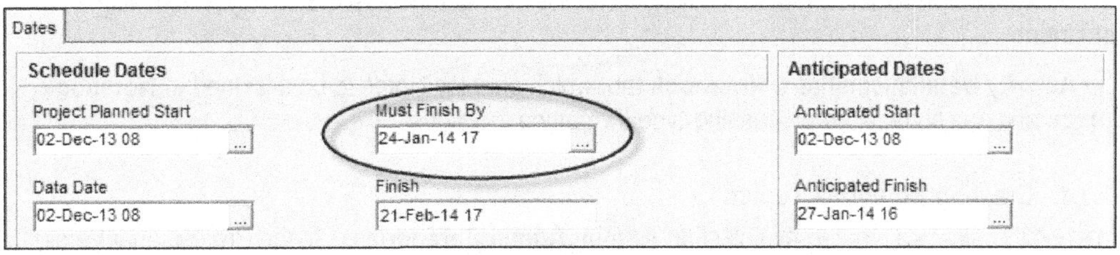

Imposing a **Must Finish By** date makes Primavera calculate the late dates from the **Must Finish By** date rather than the calculated early finish date. This will introduce positive float to activities when the calculated **Early finish** date is prior to the **Must Finish By** date:

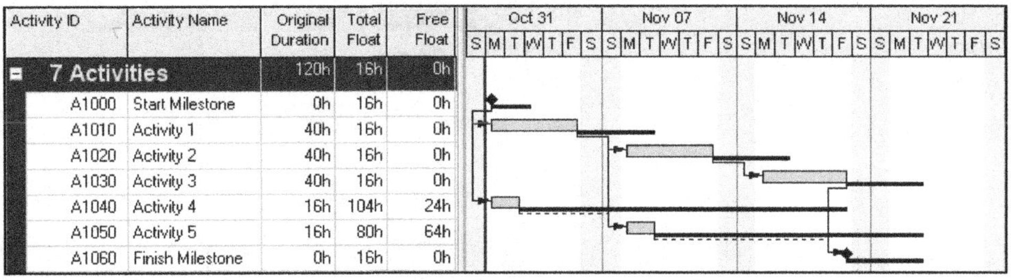

This will also create negative float when the activity's calculated early finish date is after the **Must Finish By** date, but it is not obvious where the negative float is being driven from as there are no constraints assigned to activities:

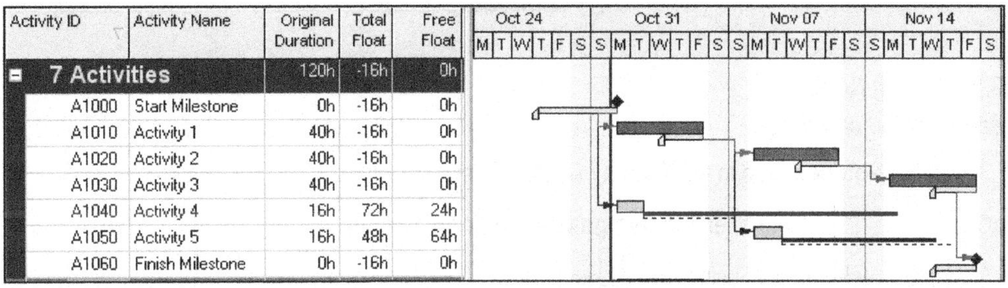

When opening multiple projects some further issues need to be considered when a **Project Must Finish By** date is set and these are covered in the **Multiple Project Scheduling** chapter.

To remove a **Project Must Finish By** date, highlight the date, press the **Delete** key and then the **Enter** key or tab out of the cell to ensure the date is removed.

This function is similar to the P3 and SureTrak function but very different from the way Microsoft Project "Project Information, Finish Date" operates. After a Finish Date is set in Microsoft Project all new Tasks are set with an As Late As Possible constraint and the Start Date is calculated. Primavera does not set As Late As Possible constraints after a **Must Finish By** date is set and the Project Start Date is still editable.

It is not obvious where the float is being generated after a **Must Finish By** date is imposed on a project. This is often confusing to people new to scheduling and it is recommended that you do not use a **Must Finish By** date. Instead, tie all activities to a **Finish Milestone** which has a **Late finish** constraint.

11.3 Activity Notebook

It is often important to note why constraints have been set. Primavera has functions that enable you to note information associated with an activity, including the reasons associated for establishing a constraint.

The **Activity Details** form has a **Notebook** tab, which enables Notes to be assigned to **Notebook Topics** and has some word processing-type formatting functions.

11.3.1 Creating Notebook Topics

Notebook Topics are created by selecting **Admin**, **Admin Categories…** in the Professional Version, and through the Web tool for the Optional Client and then selecting the **Notebook Topics** tab. After a topic has been created this topic may be made available to the following data fields by checking the appropriate box:

- EPS
- Project
- WBS
- Activities

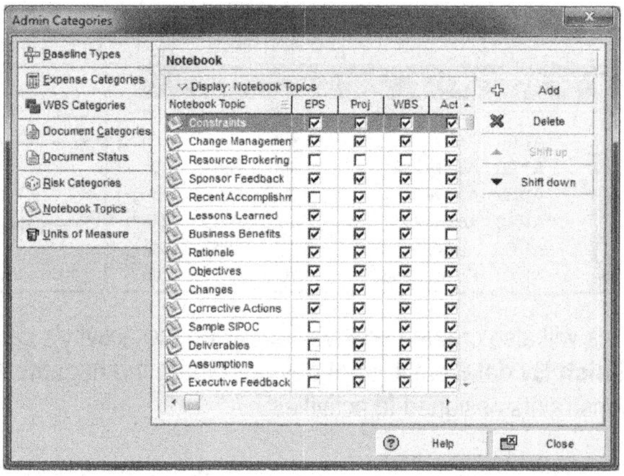

11.3.2 Adding Notes

To add a note to an activity:

- Select the **Notebook** tab in the **Activity Details** form,
- Click [Add] to open the **Assign Notebook Topic** form,
- Assign a Notebook topic using the icon, and
- Click [Modify...] to open a form where you may type in your note:

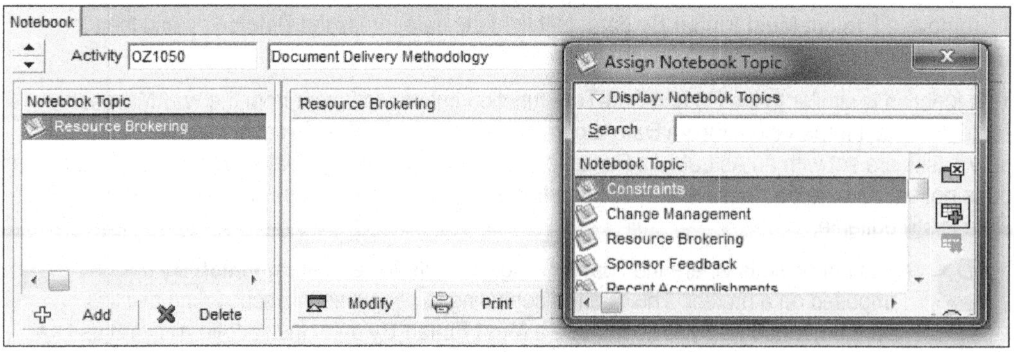

11.4 Workshop 9 – Constraints

Background

Management has provided further input to your schedule as the client has said that they require the submission on or before 28 Jan 2019.

Assignment

1. Go to the **Activities Window** and observe the calculated finish date and the critical path of the project before applying any constraints.
2. Bars – Display the **Float Bar (Total Float Bar)** and **Neg Float Bar (Negative Float Bar)**.
3. Columns – display the columns as per the picture below.
4. The client has said that they require the submission on 28 Jan 2019. Apply a **Finish On or Before** constraint and assign a constraint date of 28 Jan 2019 16:00 to the **Bid Document Submitted** activity from the **Status** tab.

   NOTE: The author has in the past found that constraint times have not always matched the activity calendar start times (e.g., 08:00) and finish times (e.g., 16:00) and have been set to 00:00. If you find the floats do not calculate correctly then open the **User Preferences** form and display the time. Review if the times are correct and if not edit them to suit your calendar.

4. Schedule the project. There should be no change in the Total Float as a **Finish On or Before** constraint will not develop Positive Float.
5. Remove the **Finish On or Before** constraint from the **Bid Document Submitted** activity.
6. Now move to the **Project Window**, **Dates** tab and assign a **Project Must Finish By** constraint of 28 Jan 2019 16:00. Return to the **Activities Window** and reschedule. All activities now have their float calculated to this date and have positive float.

Activity ID	Activity Name	Original Duration	Start	Finish	Total Float	Free Float
Bid for Facility Extension		31d	03-Dec-18 08	17-Jan-19 16	7d	0d
Technical Specification		13d	03-Dec-18 08	19-Dec-18 16	9d	0d
OZ1000	Approval to Bid	0d	03-Dec-18 08		7d	0d
OZ1010	Determine Installation Requ	4d	03-Dec-18 08	06-Dec-18 16	7d	0d
OZ1020	Create Technical Specifical	5d	07-Dec-18 08	13-Dec-18 16	7d	0d
OZ1030	Identify Supplier Componen	2d	14-Dec-18 08	17-Dec-18 16	7d	0d
OZ1040	Validate Technical Specific	2d	18-Dec-18 08	19-Dec-18 16	9d	0d
Delivery Plan		14d	18-Dec-18 08	09-Jan-19 16	7d	0d
OZ1050	Document Delivery Method	4d	20-Dec-18 08	27-Dec-18 16	9d	0d
OZ1060	Obtain Quotes from Supplie	8d	18-Dec-18 08	31-Dec-18 16	7d	0d
OZ1070	Calculate the Bid Estimate	3d	02-Jan-19 08	04-Jan-19 16	8d	0d
OZ1080	Create the Project Schedul	3d	05-Jan-19 08	08-Jan-19 16	8d	0d
OZ1090	Review the Delivery Plan	1d	09-Jan-19 08	09-Jan-19 16	7d	0d
Bid Dcoument		14d	28-Dec-18 08	17-Jan-19 16	7d	0d
OZ1100	Create Draft of Bid Docume	6d	28-Dec-18 08	07-Jan-19 16	9d	2d
OZ1110	Review Bid Document	4d	10-Jan-19 08	15-Jan-19 16	7d	0d
OZ1120	Finalise and Submit Bid Doc	2d	16-Jan-19 08	17-Jan-19 16	7d	0d
OZ1130	Bid Document Submitted	0d		17-Jan-19 16	7d	0d

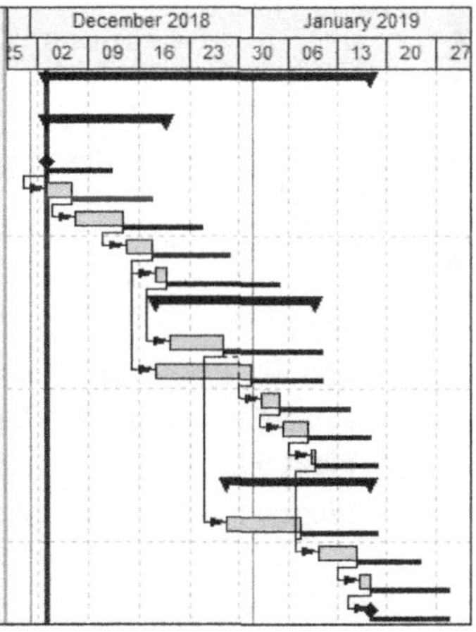

7. Remove **Project Must Finish By** constraint of 28 Jan 2019 16:00 (by highlighting the date and pressing the **Delete** key and tab out of the cell to ensure the date has been deleted.
8. Schedule the project and the Critical Path should return.

continued...

9. Apply a **Finish On or Before** constraint and assign a constraint date of 28 Jan 2019 16:00 to the **Bid Document Submitted** activity and schedule, the Critical Path will remain.

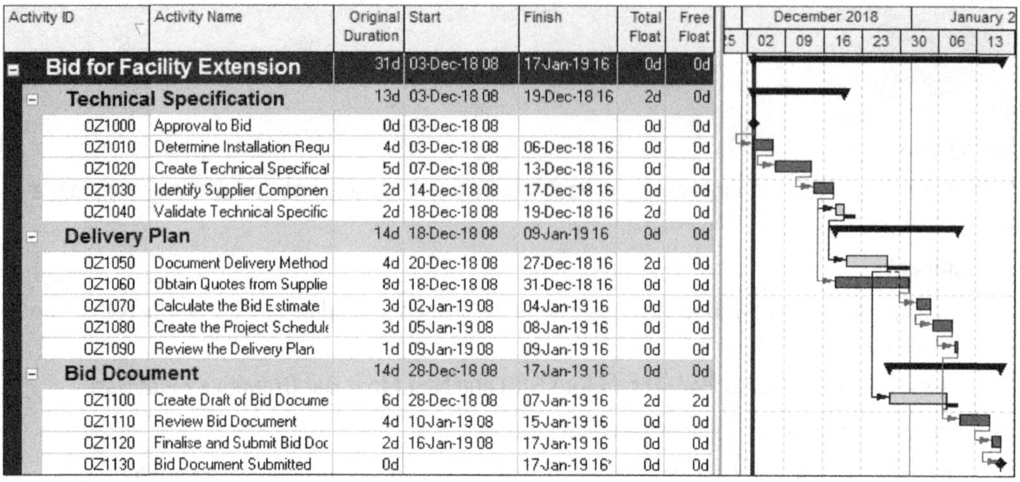

Activity ID	Activity Name	Original Duration	Start	Finish	Total Float	Free Float
Bid for Facility Extension		31d	03-Dec-18 08	17-Jan-19 16	0d	0d
Technical Specification		13d	03-Dec-18 08	19-Dec-18 16	2d	0d
0Z1000	Approval to Bid	0d	03-Dec-18 08		0d	0d
0Z1010	Determine Installation Requ	4d	03-Dec-18 08	06-Dec-18 16	0d	0d
0Z1020	Create Technical Specifical	5d	07-Dec-18 08	13-Dec-18 16	0d	0d
0Z1030	Identify Supplier Componen	2d	14-Dec-18 08	17-Dec-18 16	0d	0d
0Z1040	Validate Technical Specific	2d	18-Dec-18 08	19-Dec-18 16	2d	0d
Delivery Plan		14d	18-Dec-18 08	09-Jan-19 16	0d	0d
0Z1050	Document Delivery Method	4d	20-Dec-18 08	27-Dec-18 16	2d	0d
0Z1060	Obtain Quotes from Supplie	8d	18-Dec-18 08	31-Dec-18 16	0d	0d
0Z1070	Calculate the Bid Estimate	3d	02-Jan-19 08	04-Jan-19 16	0d	0d
0Z1080	Create the Project Schedule	3d	05-Jan-19 08	08-Jan-19 16	0d	0d
0Z1090	Review the Delivery Plan	1d	09-Jan-19 08	09-Jan-19 16	0d	0d
Bid Dcoument		14d	28-Dec-18 08	17-Jan-19 16	0d	0d
0Z1100	Create Draft of Bid Docume	6d	28-Dec-18 08	07-Jan-19 16	2d	2d
0Z1110	Review Bid Document	4d	10-Jan-19 08	15-Jan-19 16	0d	0d
0Z1120	Finalise and Submit Bid Doc	2d	16-Jan-19 08	17-Jan-19 16	0d	0d
0Z1130	Bid Document Submitted	0d		17-Jan-19 16*	0d	0d

10. Due to the proximity to Christmas, management has requested that you delay the **Obtain Quotes from Suppliers** until first thing in the New Year (03 Jan 2019). Consensus is that a better response and sharper prices will be obtained after the Christmas rush.

 - To achieve this, set a **Start On or After** constraint date of 03 Jan 2016 08:00 on the **Obtain Quotes from Suppliers** activity.
 - Now reschedule. Observe the impact on the critical path and end dates.

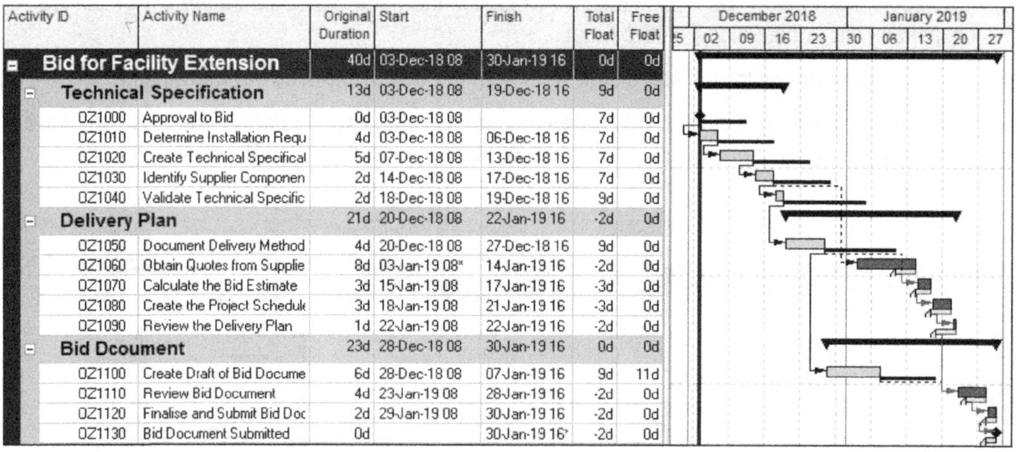

Activity ID	Activity Name	Original Duration	Start	Finish	Total Float	Free Float
Bid for Facility Extension		40d	03-Dec-18 08	30-Jan-19 16	0d	0d
Technical Specification		13d	03-Dec-18 08	19-Dec-18 16	9d	0d
0Z1000	Approval to Bid	0d	03-Dec-18 08		7d	0d
0Z1010	Determine Installation Requ	4d	03-Dec-18 08	06-Dec-18 16	7d	0d
0Z1020	Create Technical Specifical	5d	07-Dec-18 08	13-Dec-18 16	7d	0d
0Z1030	Identify Supplier Componen	2d	14-Dec-18 08	17-Dec-18 16	7d	0d
0Z1040	Validate Technical Specific	2d	18-Dec-18 08	19-Dec-18 16	9d	0d
Delivery Plan		21d	20-Dec-18 08	22-Jan-19 16	-2d	0d
0Z1050	Document Delivery Method	4d	20-Dec-18 08	27-Dec-18 16	9d	0d
0Z1060	Obtain Quotes from Supplie	8d	03-Jan-19 08*	14-Jan-19 16	-2d	0d
0Z1070	Calculate the Bid Estimate	3d	15-Jan-19 08	17-Jan-19 16	-3d	0d
0Z1080	Create the Project Schedule	3d	18-Jan-19 08	21-Jan-19 16	-3d	0d
0Z1090	Review the Delivery Plan	1d	22-Jan-19 08	22-Jan-19 16	-2d	0d
Bid Dcoument		23d	28-Dec-18 08	30-Jan-19 16	0d	0d
0Z1100	Create Draft of Bid Docume	6d	28-Dec-18 08	07-Jan-19 16	9d	11d
0Z1110	Review Bid Document	4d	23-Jan-19 08	28-Jan-19 16	-2d	0d
0Z1120	Finalise and Submit Bid Doc	2d	29-Jan-19 08	30-Jan-19 16	-2d	0d
0Z1130	Bid Document Submitted	0d		30-Jan-19 16*	-2d	0d

You will notice that the Finish Constraint on the **Bid Document Submitted** activity has created some negative float, which is displayed in the **Total Float** column and the **Negative Float** bar.

11. Display the Notebook tab in the **Activities Window**.

12. Add a Notebook Topic against the **Obtain Quotes from Supplier** activity indicating why there is a constraint on 03 Jan 2019.

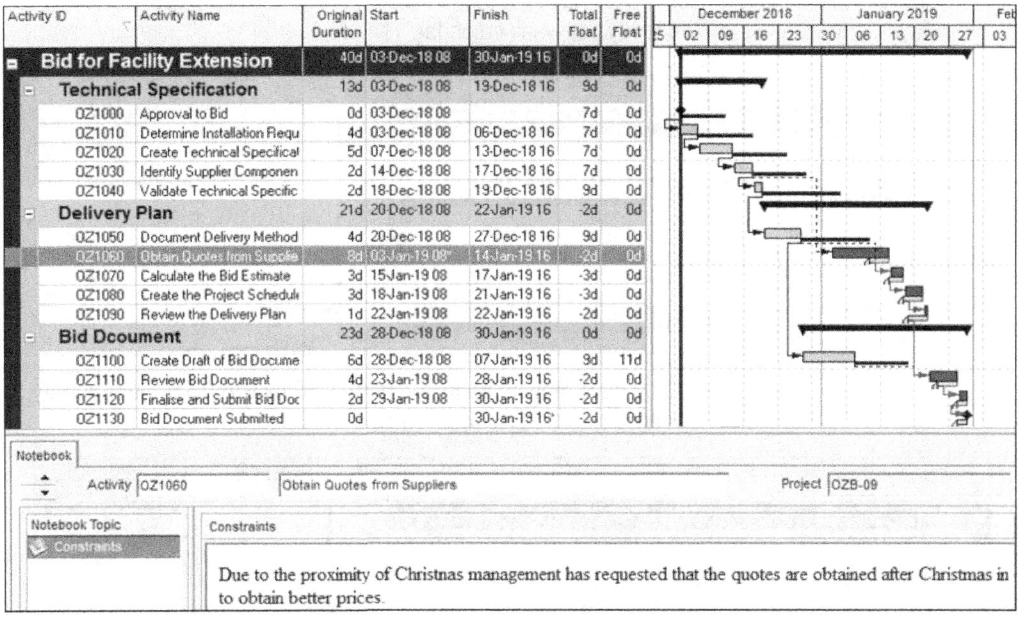

13. Open the **Group and Sort** form by clicking on the icon and group by **Total Float** and close the form.

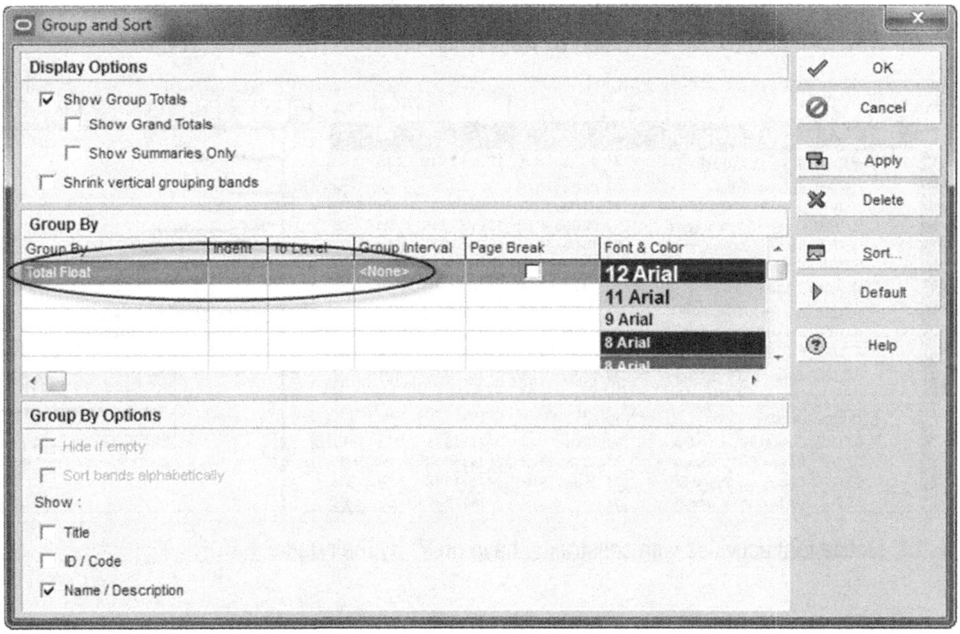

continued...

14. Sort on duration (by clicking in the **Original Duration** column) to bring the longest activity to the top. It is normally the longest activity that may be shortened.
    NOTE: Not all the activities are displayed in the two pictures below and the activities with 3 days Total Float are on the 6 day per week calendar:

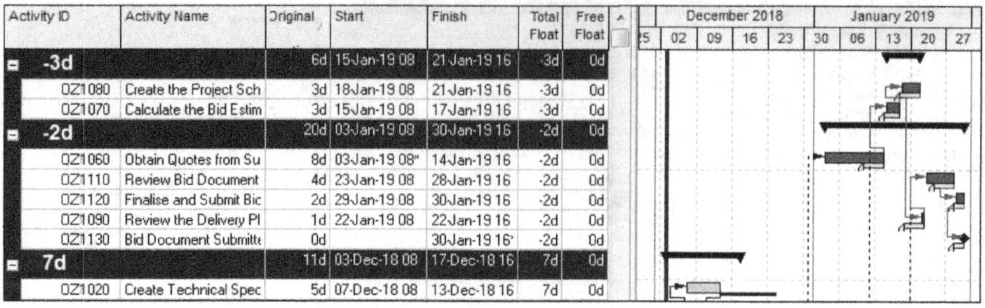

Activity ID	Activity Name	Original	Start	Finish	Total Float	Free Float
-3d		6d	15-Jan-19 08	21-Jan-19 16	-3d	0d
0Z1080	Create the Project Sch	3d	18-Jan-19 08	21-Jan-19 16	-3d	0d
0Z1070	Calculate the Bid Estim	3d	15-Jan-19 08	17-Jan-19 16	-3d	0d
-2d		20d	03-Jan-19 08	30-Jan-19 16	-2d	0d
0Z1060	Obtain Quotes from Su	8d	03-Jan-19 08*	14-Jan-19 16	-2d	0d
0Z1110	Review Bid Document	4d	23-Jan-19 08	28-Jan-19 16	-2d	0d
0Z1120	Finalise and Submit Bic	2d	29-Jan-19 08	30-Jan-19 16	-2d	0d
0Z1090	Review the Delivery Pl	1d	22-Jan-19 08	22-Jan-19 16	-2d	0d
0Z1130	Bid Document Submitte	0d		30-Jan-19 16*	-2d	0d
7d		11d	03-Dec-18 08	17-Dec-18 16	7d	0d
0Z1020	Create Technical Spec	5d	07-Dec-18 08	13-Dec-18 16	7d	0d

15. After review, it is agreed that 2 days may be deducted from **Review Bid Document** activity. Change the duration of this activity to 2 days, reschedule:

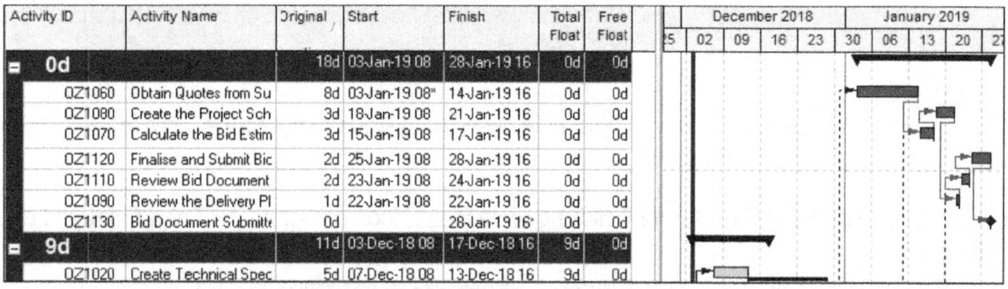

Activity ID	Activity Name	Original	Start	Finish	Total Float	Free Float
0d		18d	03-Jan-19 08	28-Jan-19 16	0d	0d
0Z1060	Obtain Quotes from Su	8d	03-Jan-19 08*	14-Jan-19 16	0d	0d
0Z1080	Create the Project Sch	3d	18-Jan-19 08	21-Jan-19 16	0d	0d
0Z1070	Calculate the Bid Estim	3d	15-Jan-19 08	17-Jan-19 16	0d	0d
0Z1120	Finalise and Submit Bic	2d	25-Jan-19 08	28-Jan-19 16	0d	0d
0Z1110	Review Bid Document	2d	23-Jan-19 08	24-Jan-19 16	0d	0d
0Z1090	Review the Delivery Pl	1d	22-Jan-19 08	22-Jan-19 16	0d	0d
0Z1130	Bid Document Submitte	0d		28-Jan-19 16*	0d	0d
9d		11d	03-Dec-18 08	17-Dec-18 16	9d	0d
0Z1020	Create Technical Spec	5d	07-Dec-18 08	13-Dec-18 16	9d	0d

16. Now organize by WBS and sort by Activity ID:

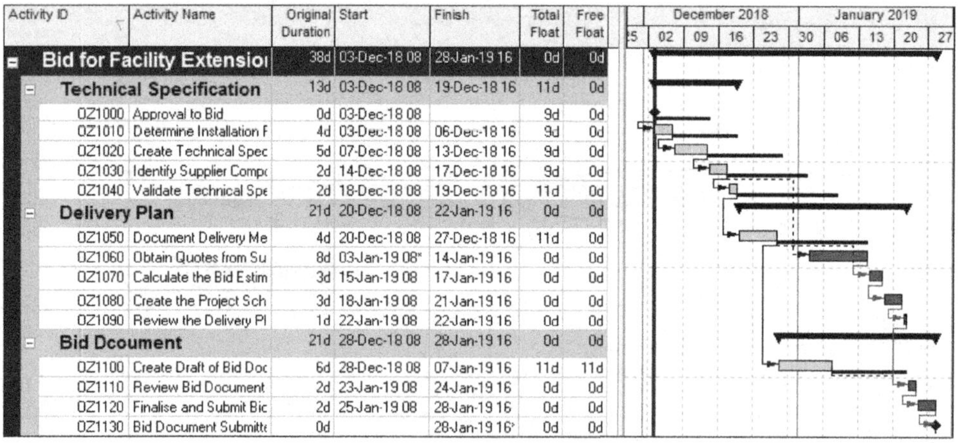

Activity ID	Activity Name	Original Duration	Start	Finish	Total Float	Free Float
Bid for Facility Extensio		38d	03-Dec-18 08	28-Jan-19 16	0d	0d
Technical Specification		13d	03-Dec-18 08	19-Dec-18 16	11d	0d
0Z1000	Approval to Bid	0d	03-Dec-18 08		9d	0d
0Z1010	Determine Installation F	4d	03-Dec-18 08	06-Dec-18 16	9d	0d
0Z1020	Create Technical Spec	5d	07-Dec-18 08	13-Dec-18 16	9d	0d
0Z1030	Identify Supplier Compo	2d	14-Dec-18 08	17-Dec-18 16	9d	0d
0Z1040	Validate Technical Spe	2d	18-Dec-18 08	19-Dec-18 16	11d	0d
Delivery Plan		21d	20-Dec-18 08	22-Jan-19 16	0d	0d
0Z1050	Document Delivery Me	4d	20-Dec-18 08	27-Dec-18 16	11d	0d
0Z1060	Obtain Quotes from Su	8d	03-Jan-19 08*	14-Jan-19 16	0d	0d
0Z1070	Calculate the Bid Estim	3d	15-Jan-19 08	17-Jan-19 16	0d	0d
0Z1080	Create the Project Sch	3d	18-Jan-19 08	21-Jan-19 16	0d	0d
0Z1090	Review the Delivery Pl	1d	22-Jan-19 08	22-Jan-19 16	0d	0d
Bid Dcoument		21d	28-Dec-18 08	28-Jan-19 16	0d	0d
0Z1100	Create Draft of Bid Doc	6d	28-Dec-18 08	07-Jan-19 16	11d	11d
0Z1110	Review Bid Document	2d	23-Jan-19 08	24-Jan-19 16	0d	0d
0Z1120	Finalise and Submit Bic	2d	25-Jan-19 08	28-Jan-19 16	0d	0d
0Z1130	Bid Document Submitte	0d		28-Jan-19 16*	0d	0d

17. Notice that activities with constraints have an "*" by their dates.

12 GROUP, SORT AND LAYOUTS

Group and Sort enables data such as activities in the **Activities Window**, WBS Nodes in the **WBS Window**, projects in the **Project Window**, and many other data items to be sorted and organized under other parameters such as **Dates** and **Resources** or user defined **Activity** and **Project Codes**. This function is similar to **Organize** in P3 and SureTrak and **Grouping** in Microsoft Project and Asta Powerproject.

Layouts is a function in which the formatting of parameters such as the **Group and Sort**, **Columns** and **Bars** is saved and reapplied later. This function is similar to **Layouts** in P3 and SureTrak or **Views** in Asta Power Project and Microsoft Project. A **Layout** may be edited, saved, or reapplied at a later date and may have a **Filter** associated with it. Layouts contain the formatting for all options of both the top and bottom pane.

Although Group and Sort is available in many forms, Layouts are only available in a few places including the following Windows:

- Projects
- WBS
- Activities
- Tracking

This chapter will concentrate on how **Group and Sort** and **Layouts** are applied in the **Activities Window** but the same principles apply to the other windows. This chapter covers the following topics:

Topic	Notes on the Function
• Reformat the Grouping and Sorting of projects in the **Projects Window** or activities in the **Activities Window** by opening the **Group and Sort** form	• Click on the icon, or • Select **View, Group and Sort by**, **Customize**.
• Create, save or edit a Layout	Select either: • From the menu **View, Layout**, **Save Layout As...**, or • From the **Layout** bar **Layout**, **Save As....**

The **Layout** bar location is indicated in the following picture:

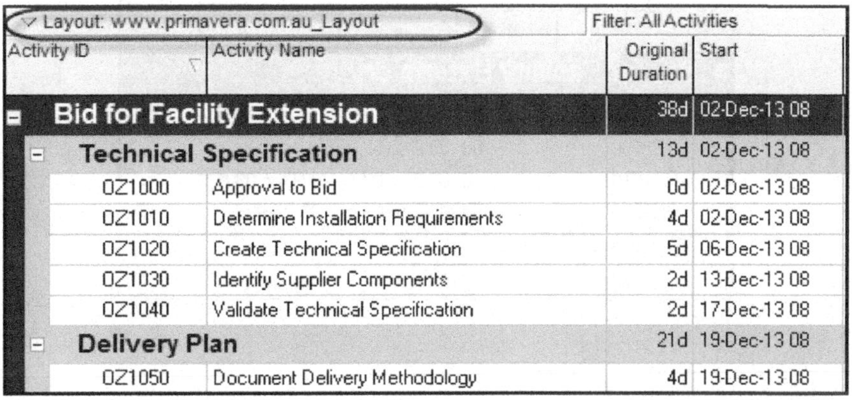

12.1 Group and Sort Activities

The **Group and Sort** function has been used in this publication to group activities under WBS bands.

To Group and Sort activities open the **Group and Sort** form by:

- Clicking the toolbar icon, or
- Selecting **View, Group and Sort by, Customize**.

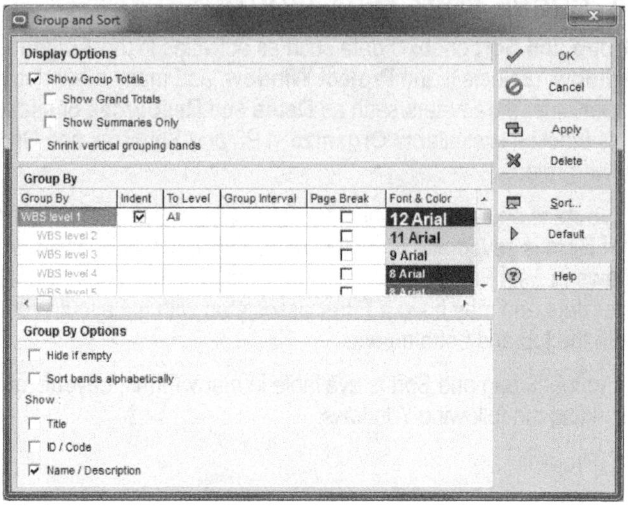

12.1.1 Display Options

Show Group Totals

Show Group Totals is a new function in Primavera Version 6.0 which when unchecked hides the summary data in the bands, which prevents the truncating of Band titles.

Summary Data Displayed

Activity ID	Original Duration	Start	Finish	Total Float
Bid for Fac	139d	08-Dec-09 A	22-Jan-10	0d
Research	31d	08-Dec-09 A	21-Dec-09	6d
OZ1000	0d	08-Dec-09 A		
OZ1010	1d	08-Dec-09 A	08-Dec-09 A	
OZ1020	8d	09-Dec-09 A	21-Dec-09	2d
Estimate	52d	22-Dec-09	08-Jan-10	3d
OZ1070	2d	07-Jan-10	08-Jan-10	0d

Summary Data Hidden

Activity ID	Original Duration	Start	Finish	Total Float
Bid for Faciliity Extension				
Research				
OZ1000	0d	08-Dec-09 A		
OZ1010	1d	08-Dec-09 A	08-Dec-09 A	
OZ1020	8d	09-Dec-09 A	21-Dec-09	2d
Estimate				
OZ1070	2d	07-Jan-10	08-Jan-10	0d

Show Grand Totals

Show Grand Totals provides a total of all the activities in a band at the top of a page and is similar to inserting a Project band in P3, or SureTrak with Organize, or displaying a Project summary task in Microsoft Project.

This displays a Summary band for multiple projects and adds up all the costs and hours for a project, displays the earliest and latest dates and a summary duration for all the data displayed. This feature is very useful:

- When the project is not organized by WBS and therefore has no project total line, or when multiple projects have been opened to calculate all the projects' values, and
- When multiple projects are open and thereby enables the total for multiple projects to be displayed.

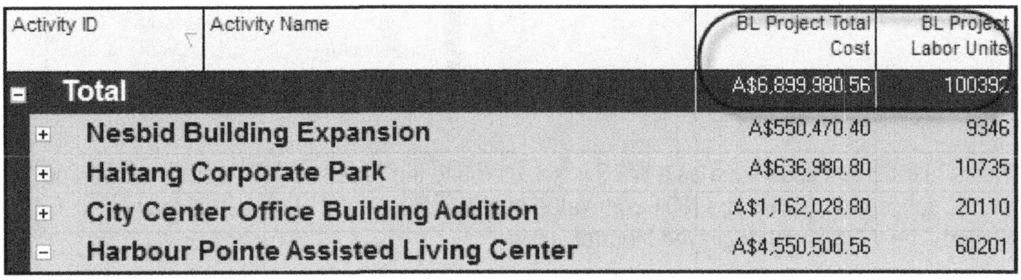

Show Summaries Only

Show Summaries Only hides all the activities and displays only the WBS or Codes that have been used to summarize the activities:

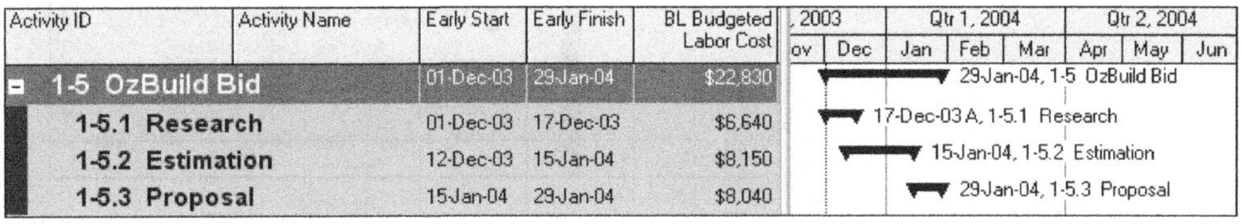

Shrink Vertical Grouping Bands

Shrink vertical grouping bands is new to Primavera Version 6.0 and narrows the Vertical Bands on the left of the screen. This is useful in projects with a number of levels in the WBS as this provides more usable screen space and paper width for printing.

Option Unchecked

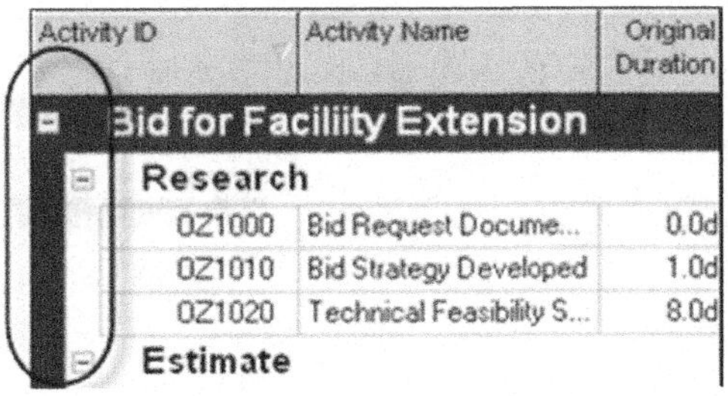

Option Checked

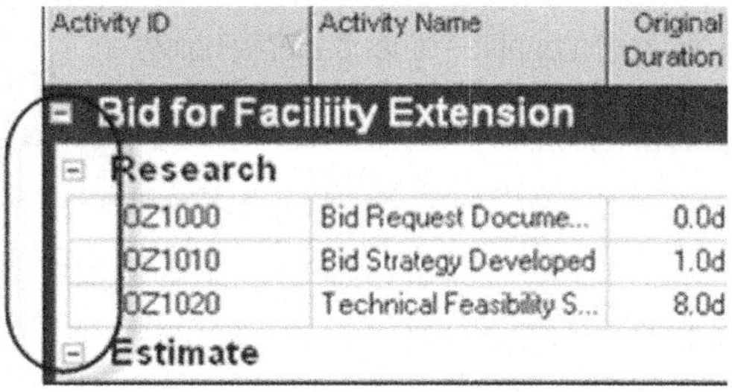

12.1.2 Group By

The **Group By** box has several options:

- **Group By and Indent**

When a hierarchical code such as a **WBS** and the **Indent** are selected, the subsequent bands are completed by the software and there are no other banding options available. The WBS is then displayed hierarchically:

Group By	Indent	To Level	Group Interval	Font & Color
WBS level 1	☑	All		12 Arial
WBS level 2				11 Arial
WBS level 3				9 Arial
WBS level 4				8 Arial

Activity ID	Activity Name	Early Start	Early Finish
Bid for Facility Ext...		06-Dec-04	24-Jan-05
Research		06-Dec-04	21-Dec-04
OZ1010	Bid Strategy M...	06-Dec-04	06-Dec-04
OZ1020	Investigate Te...	07-Dec-04	16-Dec-04
OZ1030	Document Inst...	17-Dec-04	21-Dec-04
OZ1000	Bid Request D...	06-Dec-04	
Estimation		17-Dec-04	10-Jan-05
OZ1040	Request Comp...	04-Jan-05	06-Jan-05

When a hierarchical code such as a **WBS** is selected and the **Indent** is **NOT** selected on a line then the subsequent bands are **NOT** completed by the software and other bands may be selected. The WBS is not displayed hierarchically:

Group By	Indent	To Level	Group Interval	Font & Color
Early Start			Week	12 Arial
WBS	☐	All		11 Arial
Resources				9 Arial
				8 Arial

Activity ID	Activity Name	Early Start	Early Finish
01-Dec-03		01-Dec-03	11-Dec-03
Research		01-Dec-03	11-Dec-03
Sales Engineer, System Engin...		01-Dec-03	01-Dec-03
A1010	Bid Strategy Meeting	01-Dec-03	01-Dec-03
System Engineer		02-Dec-03	11-Dec-03
A1020	Investigate Techni...	02-Dec-03	11-Dec-03
08-Dec-03		12-Dec-03	15-Jan-04
Research		12-Dec-03	17-Dec-03
Sales Engineer, System Engin...		12-Dec-03	17-Dec-03
A1030	Document Installati...	12-Dec-03	17-Dec-03

- **To Level**

The **To Level** option decides how many levels of the hierarchical code structure such as the WBS will be displayed. All activities are displayed under the lowest level of WBS, as chosen from the **To Level** drop down box.

This option enables other banding below the select level which is not permitted with the **All** option.

Group By

Group By	Indent	To Level	Group Interval	Font & Color
WBS	☐	2		12 Arial
		All		11 Arial
		1		9 Arial
		2		8 Arial

Group By

Group By	Indent	To Level	Group Interval	Font & Color
WBS	☐	2		12 Arial
Resources				11 Arial
				9 Arial
				8 Arial

- **Group Interval**

  This option is available with some fields such as **Total Float**, where the interval may be typed in, and **Date** fields, where a drop down box enables the selection of the time interval used to group activities:

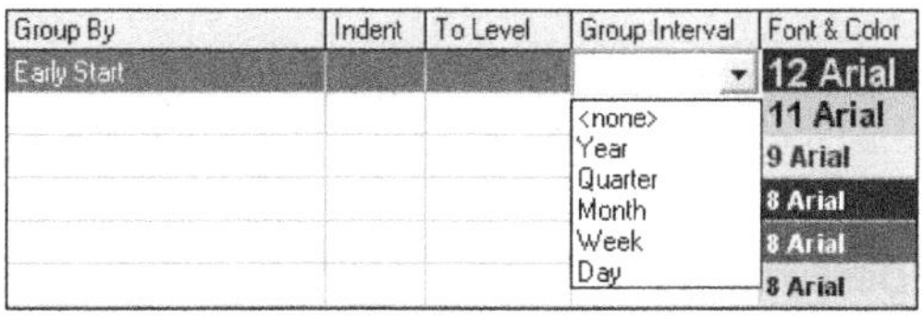

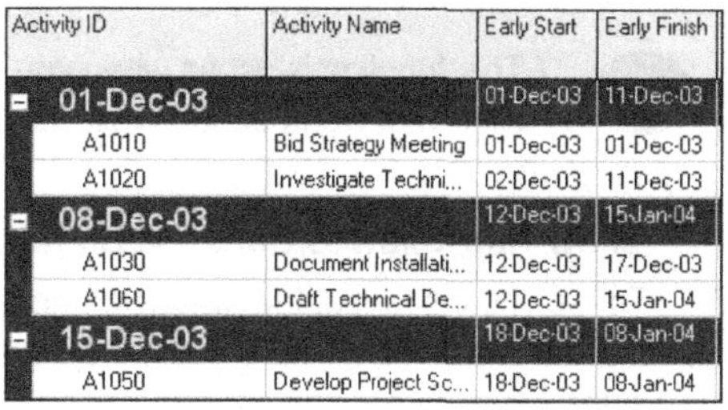

- **Font and Color**

  Double-click these boxes to open the **Edit Font and Color** form to change the font and color of each band.

12.1.3 Group By Options

- **Sort Banding Alphabetically**

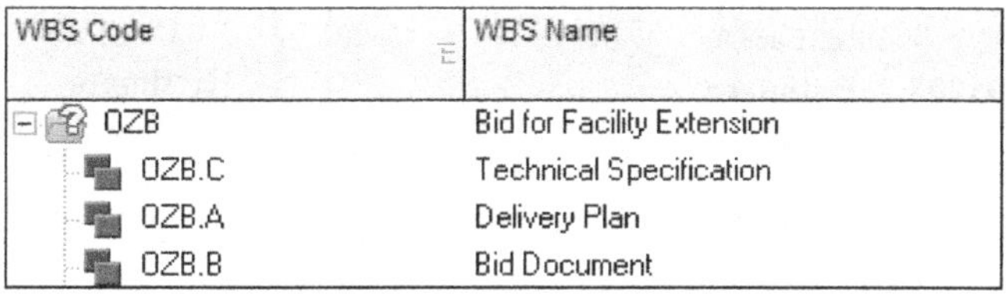

When unchecked they are sorted naturally per the picture above:

When this is checked the bands are sorted by the code assigned to the Activity Code or WBS Code:

This function is extremely useful for providing two sort orders for coding structures such as the WBS when the coding is entered, but only operates when the coding in the WBS Window is not in a natural sort order.

- **Hide if empty**

  Check this box to hide bands that:

  - Have not been assigned an activity, or
  - When activities have been filtered out and only the bands remains.

This function is useful when you have filtered on a couple of activities and the screen is filled with blank bands. This will remove all the blank bands.

- **Show Title**, **Show ID/Code** and **Show Name/Description**

  These options format the display of the band title. It is not possible to uncheck all the options as there then would not be a title in the band. The options change depending on the data displayed in the band:

With All Options Checked

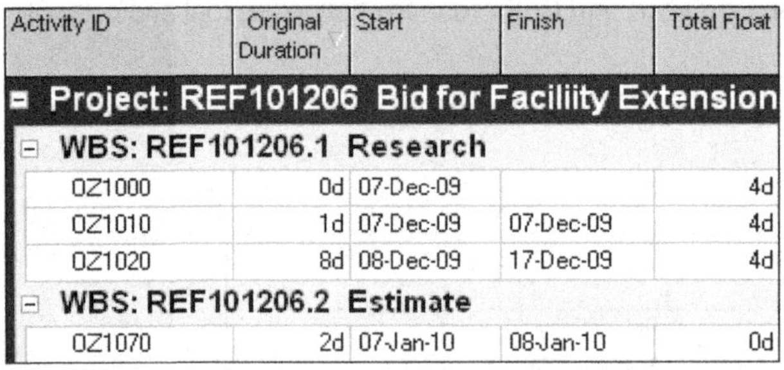

Activity ID	Original Duration	Start	Finish	Total Float
Project: REF101206 Bid for Faciliity Extension				
WBS: REF101206.1 Research				
0Z1000	0d	07-Dec-09		4d
0Z1010	1d	07-Dec-09	07-Dec-09	4d
0Z1020	8d	08-Dec-09	17-Dec-09	4d
WBS: REF101206.2 Estimate				
0Z1070	2d	07-Jan-10	08-Jan-10	0d

With Only Description Checked

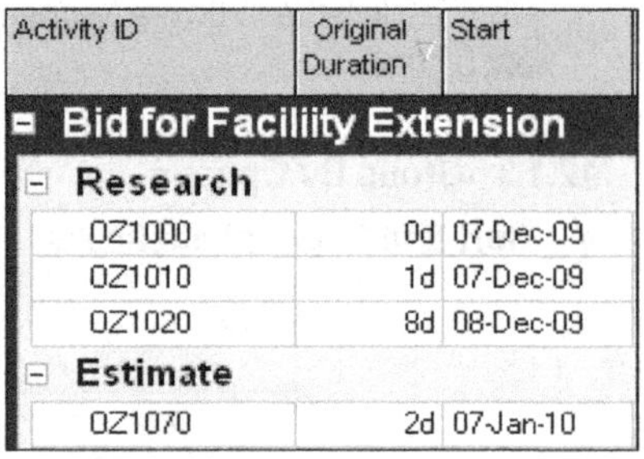

Activity ID	Original Duration	Start
Bid for Faciliity Extension		
Research		
0Z1000	0d	07-Dec-09
0Z1010	1d	07-Dec-09
0Z1020	8d	08-Dec-09
Estimate		
0Z1070	2d	07-Jan-10

NOTE: These options are set for each band individually.

12.1.4 Sorting

The 

icon opens the **Sort** form where the order of the activities in each band may be specified.

The order shown in the picture provides a good natural "Waterfall" order to activities:

This order may be easily overridden by clicking on the column titles to reorder activities and therefore the use of this option is problematic as clicking on the column header is very simple and will override options set here.

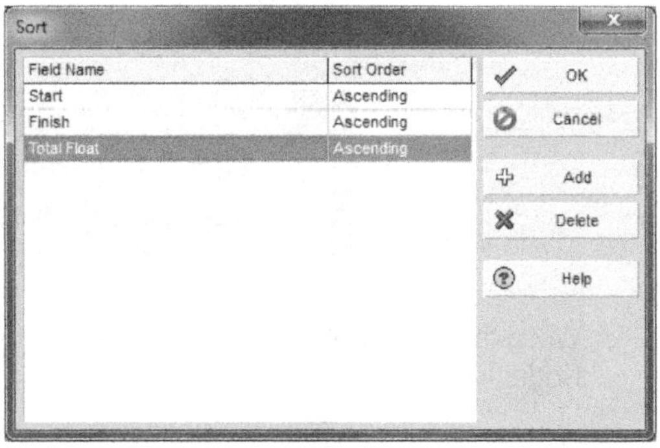

12.1.5 Reorganize Automatically

Primavera Version 4.1 introduced a function titled Reorganize Automatically in the **User Preferences** form and this was removed from the **User Preferences** form in Version 8. This function is now titled **Auto-Reorganization** which is covered next.

12.1.6 Auto-Reorganization

This function reorganizes data based on the current **Group and Sort** order when an activity's attributes are changed.

For example, when an activity's WBS code is re-assigned in the Activity Details pane, then the activity will automatically be moved to the newly assigned WBS band where the activities are grouped by WBS when this option is turned on.

This has now been moved to the menu and may be turned on and off and is uniquely set for each window. To activate or de-activate this function:

- Select **Tools**, **Disable Auto-Reorganization**, or
- Click on the **Tools** toolbar icon.

When the icon is a dark shade then the function is disabled and the command on the menu erroneously still states **Disable Auto-Reorganization** when it actually means **Enable Auto-Reorganization.**

When a new Layout or Filter is applied then the data is also automatically reorganized.

12.1.7 Set Page Breaks in the Group and Sort Form

In earlier versions of P6 page breaks could only be set at the first band in the **Group and Sort** form from the **Page Setup**, **Options** tab. The option of being able to set page breaks at any level has been added to P6 Version 8.1.

Select **View**, **Group and Sort by**, **Customize** or click on the icon and select **Customize** to open the **Group and Sort** form:

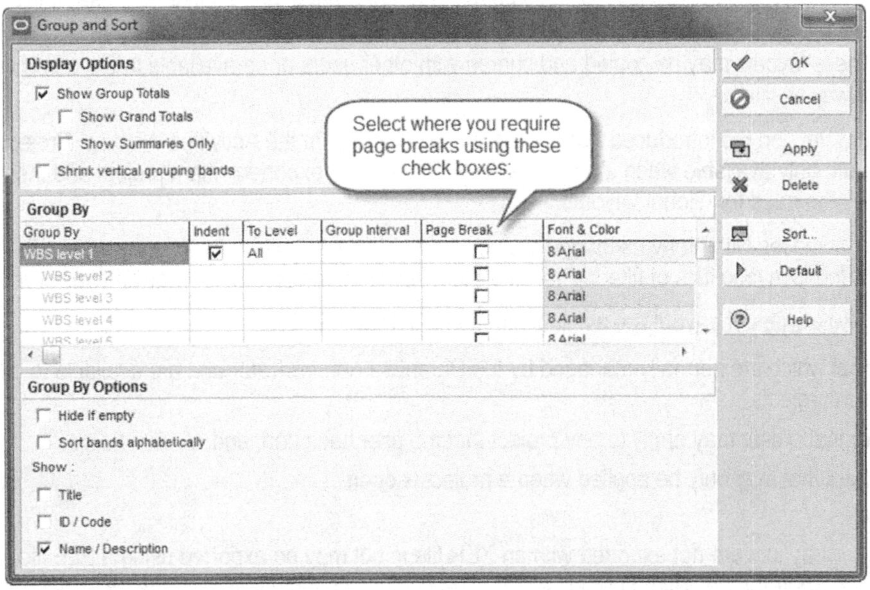

12.1.8 Group and Sort Projects at Enterprise Level

Projects in the **Projects Window** may be Grouped and Sorted in a similar way to the Grouping and Sorting of activities.

When a database is opened, the projects are by default displayed under the Enterprise Project Structure (EPS) in the **Projects Window**.

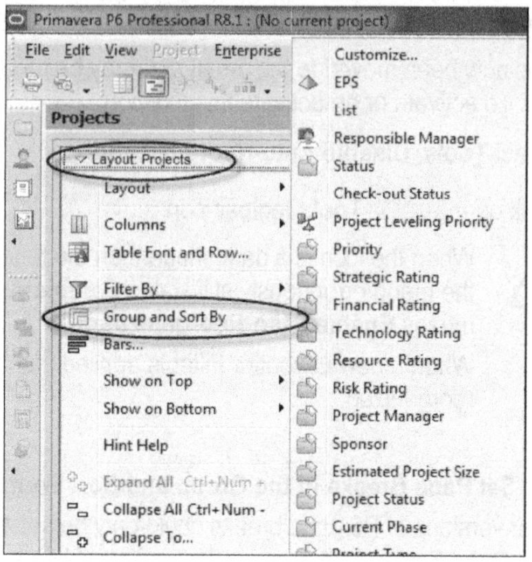

The projects may be Grouped and Sorted under a number of different headings by:

- Selecting **Layout**, **Group and Sort by**, **Customize**, or
- Right-clicking in the columns area and selecting **Group and Sort ...**, or
- Selecting **View, Group and Sort By**

Then selecting the option from the drop down list.

The **Customize**... option will open the project's **Group and Sort** form which operates in a similar way to the Activity's **Group and Sort** form.

12.2 Understanding Layouts

A standard load of Primavera is supplied with a number of predefined Layouts for some of the windows which are defined by default as **Global Layouts** and any user on the system may apply these. These layouts may be copied and shared with other users or be available to the current user in a similar way as filters.

Primavera Version 6.0 introduced Project Layouts available from the Activities Window. Project Layouts are only available when a project is open and may be exported with a project and therefore minimizes the need for Global Layouts.

In large databases with many users and projects there becomes a need to code layouts so they may easily be found in long lists of filters. Prefixing them with the project number may be considered.

The following types of Layout are available in the **Activities Window**:

- **Global** which are normally managed by the Database Administrator and are available to all users and all projects,
- **User** that a user may apply to any project that the user has open, and
- **Project** that may only be applied when a project is open.

Layouts are not exported with an XER file in but may be exported using a PLF file. Therefore to send a person a complete project schedule you may need to include the layout as a PLF file so the other user may easily reproduce your view of the data.

12.2.1 Applying an Existing Layout

Layouts may be applied from the **Open Layout** form by:

- Selecting the **Open** option from the **Layout Options** bar:

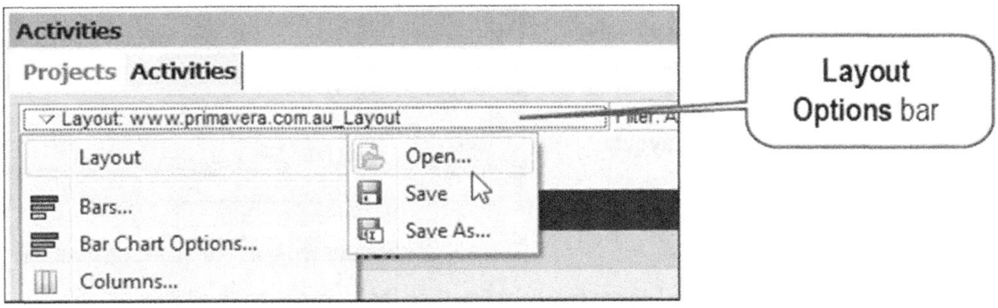

- Or, by selecting **View, Layout, Open Layout....**

When a Layout has been edited by changing any parameter, such as column formatting, a form will be displayed allowing the confirmation of the changes that have been made to the layout.

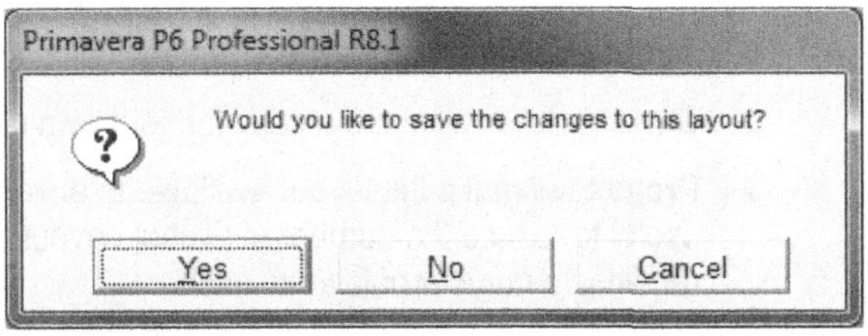

The **Open Layout** form will be displayed and an alternative layout may be selected from the list. The list has three headings after a project layout has been created, **Global**, **User**, and **Project**:

- Click on the  icon to apply the layout. This will leave the form open but allow the effect to be viewed, or
- Click on the 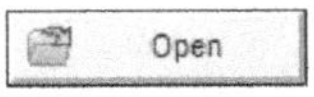 icon to apply the layout and close the form:

Click on the  icon to reorder the Layouts.

12.2.2 Creating a New Layout

A new layout may be created by saving an existing layout with a new name and editing it. To create a new Layout:

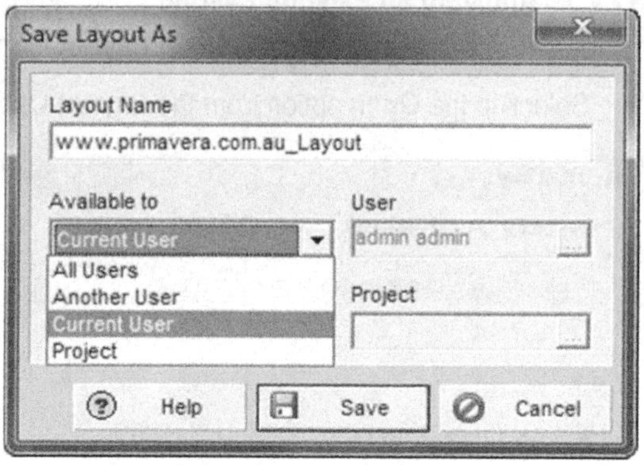

- Apply the layout that closely matches the requirements of the new layout and apply.
- Select either:
  - From the menu **View, Layout, Save Layout**, or
  - From the Layout Options bar **Layout**, **Save As…**:
- Type in a new **Layout Name** and select to whom you wish the layout to be available.
  - **All Users** will make the layout Global and therefore available to all users and you will need the appropriate security access to be able to create a Global Layout.
  - **Another User** will make the layout available to a nominated user.
  - **Current User** will make a copy for your own use.
  - **Project** will make the layout available to anyone who has the project open. This option is useful to reduce the number of Global Layouts in a database with a number of projects requiring a number of layouts each.
- Click on the  toolbar icon.

12.2.3 Saving a Layout after Changes

This layout may now be edited and the edits saved by selecting:

- From the menu **View, Layout**, **Save Layout As**, or
- From the Layout bar **Layout**, **Save**.

12.2.4 Layout Types

A layout is comprised of a **Top Pane** and a **Bottom Pane**. Each **Pane** may be assigned a **Layout Type**. This is a list of **Layout Types** and the panes that may be applied to the **Activities Window**:

Layout Name	Available in Top Pane	Available in Bottom Pane
• Gantt Chart	Yes	Yes
• Activity Details		Yes
• Activity Table	Yes	Yes
• Activity Network	Yes	
• Trace Logic		Yes
• Activity Usage Profile		Yes
• Resource Usage Spreadsheet		Yes
• Resource Usage Profile		Yes
• Activity Usage Spreadsheet	Yes	Yes

The available layouts vary depending on the window open. This chapter will predominately discuss the Activities Window but experimentation will show the options available in the other windows.

12.2.5 Changing Activity Layout Types in Panes

The **Toolbars** have icons for the display options in the top and bottom pane. Placing the mouse over each icon will display the function of each:

- 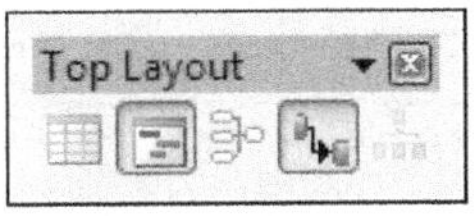

are the **Top Layout** toolbar icons, and
- 

are the **Bottom Layout** toolbar icons.

To change a **Layout Type** in a pane select from the menu:

- **View, Show on Top**, or

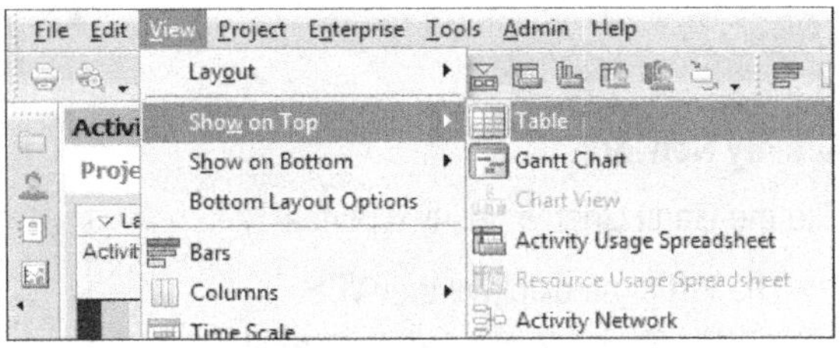

- **View, Show on Bottom.**

Then select the Layout Type required from the list.

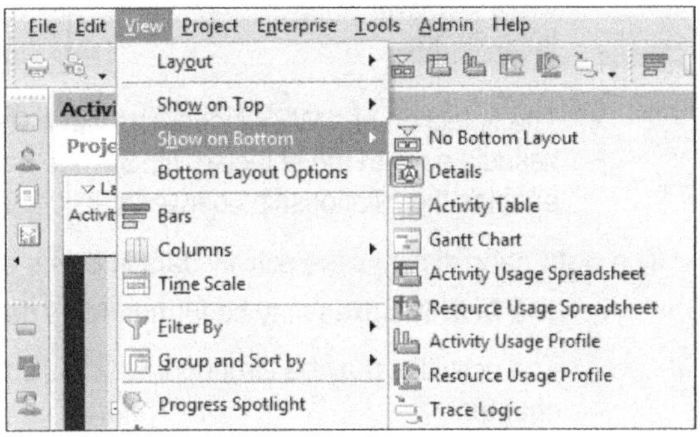

12.2.6 Activities Window Layout Panes

Each Layout Type has a number of options and the formatting of these has been discussed in earlier chapters.

Gantt Chart

The Gantt Chart has two sides:

- The left side where the columns are displayed may be formatted with the **Columns**, **Sorting** and **Grouping** functions.
- The right side may be formatted using the **Timescale**, **Bars** and **Gridlines** functions.

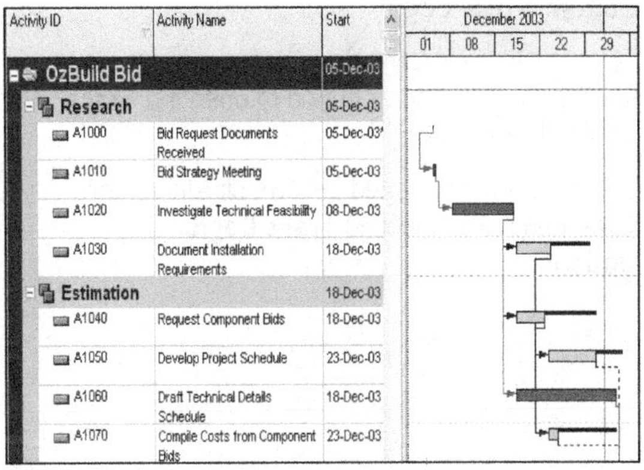

Activity Details

These may be displayed at any time in the Bottom Pane with any of the tabs hidden or displayed.

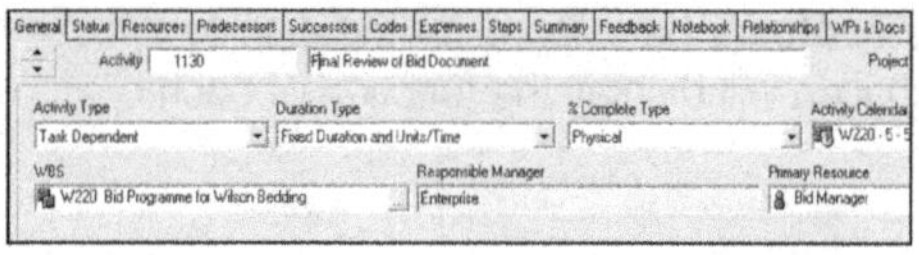

Activity Table

This layout is the same as the left side of the Gantt Chart and has no Bars and Timescale on the right side.

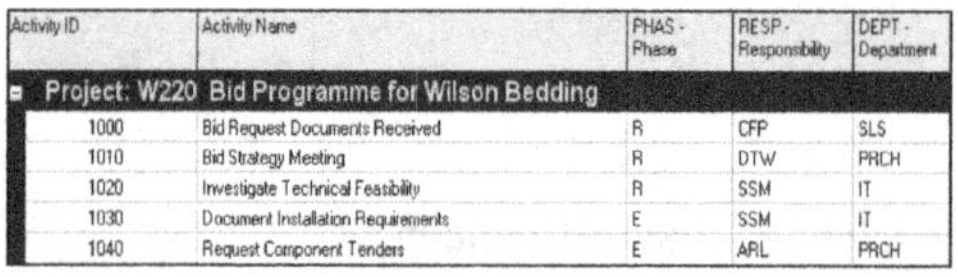

Activity ID	Activity Name	PHAS - Phase	RESP - Responsibility	DEPT - Department
Project: W220 Bid Programme for Wilson Bedding				
1000	Bid Request Documents Received	R	CFP	SLS
1010	Bid Strategy Meeting	R	DTW	PRCH
1020	Investigate Technical Feasibility	R	SSM	IT
1030	Document Installation Requirements	E	SSM	IT
1040	Request Component Tenders	E	ARL	PRCH

Activity Network

Like the Gantt Chart it has two panes:

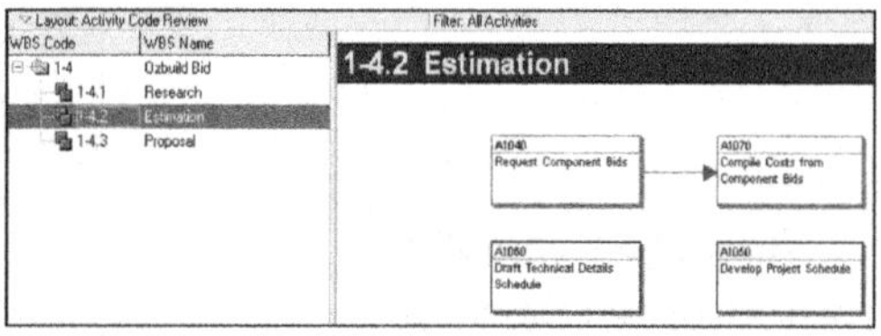

- The **left** pane displays the WBS:
  - This side may not be formatted except by adjusting the width of the columns.
  - The selection of a WBS Node acts like a filter and will only display activities that are associated with the selected WBS Node and lower level member WBS Nodes. This enables the relationships between activities within one WBS Node to be checked.
- The **right** pane displays the activity data in boxes and is organized under headings:
  - The Activity Boxes may be formatted as described in the **Activity Network** chapter.
  - The activities may be Grouped, which is covered in the **Grouping** section of this chapter.

Trace Logic

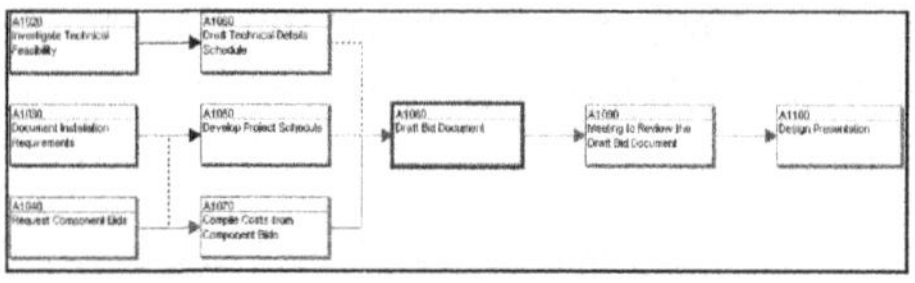

The Trace Logic options allow the selection of the number of predecessor and successor levels.

This is achieved by selecting **View, Show on Bottom**, **Trace Logic**.

To select the number of levels of predecessors to be displayed you are required to open the **Trace Logic Options** form.

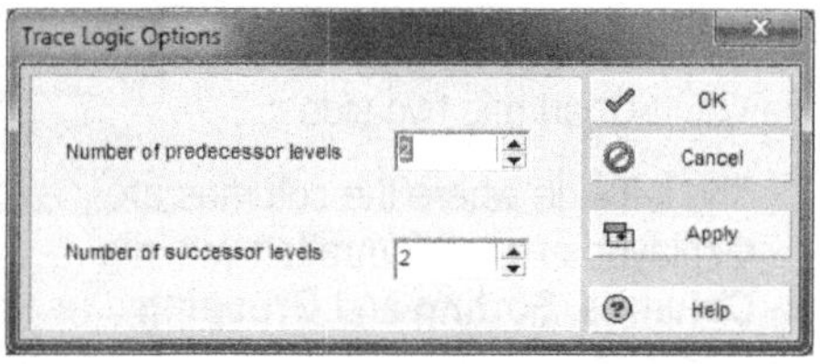

The form is then opened by right-clicking in the lower pane and selecting **Trace Logic Options...**.

Formatting Trace Logic and Activity Network

Formatting of these boxes in both of these panes is linked to the formatting in the **Activity Network**. The boxes are formatted by right-clicking in the right screen of the **Activity Network** pane and selecting **Activity Network Options....**

Resource Analysis Panes

The **Activity Usage Profile**, **Resource Usage Spreadsheet**, **Resource Usage Profile**, **Activity Usage Spreadsheet** views display resource information and will be discussed in the **Resource Optimization** chapter.

12.2.7 WBS and Projects Window Panes

The WBS and Projects Windows have three icons for the top pane:

-  shows a table without bars,
-  shows a table with bars, and
-  displays a Chart View of the WBS and the boxes may also be formatted by right-clicking and selecting **Chart Box Template**:

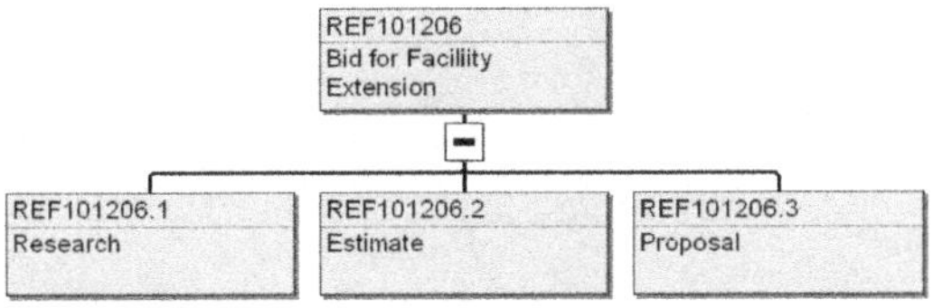

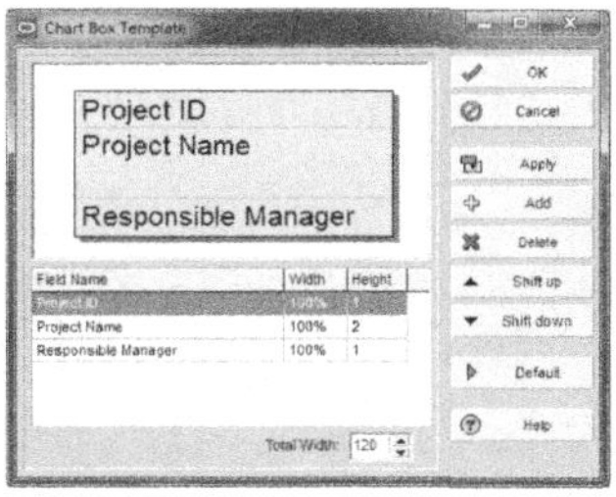

12.3 Copying a Layout To and From Another Database

A layout from any **Window** may be copied to another database by using the Import and Export functions from the **Open Layout** form. The layout is saved in a **Primavera Layout File (*.PLF)** format as a stand-alone file and is then imported into another database.

Layouts that include User Defined Fields and Codes may not display the UDF or Code information, or display incorrect information when a project and layout are imported because the UDFs and Codes are assigned a different database index number on import and these index fields are used to display the UDF data.

12.4 Workshop 10 – Organizing Your Data

Background

Having completed the schedule, you may report the information with different Layouts.

Assignment

Display your project in the following formats, noting the different ways you may represent the same data.

1. Hide and display the relationships, use the icon.
2. Display the **Activity Network**, use the icon.
3. Select **Zoom in**, **Zoom out** and **Best fit** using the icons.
4. Scroll up and down or click the **WBS** Nodes on the left side of the screen. You will notice that only the Activities associated with the highlighted WBS are displayed.
5. Ctl-click and select two WBS Nodes and you will see the relationships between the activities in each WBS Node.
6. Display the **Activity Table** by clicking on the icon.
7. Now display the Gantt Chart by clicking on the icon
8. Hide and display the **Bottom** pane by clicking on the and icons; you may need to add these icons to your toolbar.
9. With the bottom pane displayed click the icon to show the **Trace Logic** form.
10. Right-click in the **Trace Logic** form, select **Trace Logic Options...** and change the number of Predecessor and Successor Levels displaying 1, 2 and 3 levels and note the change in the layout.
11. Click on the predecessors and successors in each option and observe the changes.
12. Click on different activities in the upper pane and see the effect on the **Trace Logic** form.
13. Click on the icon to display the **Activity Details** form.

continued....

14. Create a new layout titled **OzBuild Workshop 10 – Without Float**, making it a User Layout, displaying the columns and formatting the bars per the following picture; the Total Float and Negative Float bars are not displayed:

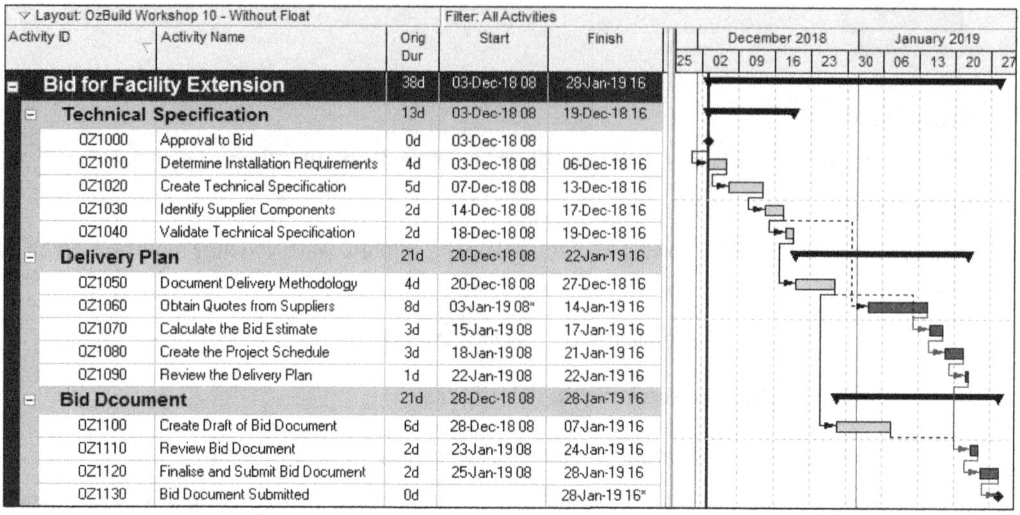

Activity ID	Activity Name	Orig Dur	Start	Finish
Bid for Facility Extension		38d	03-Dec-18 08	28-Jan-19 16
Technical Specification		13d	03-Dec-18 08	19-Dec-18 16
OZ1000	Approval to Bid	0d	03-Dec-18 08	
OZ1010	Determine Installation Requirements	4d	03-Dec-18 08	06-Dec-18 16
OZ1020	Create Technical Specification	5d	07-Dec-18 08	13-Dec-18 16
OZ1030	Identify Supplier Components	2d	14-Dec-18 08	17-Dec-18 16
OZ1040	Validate Technical Specification	2d	18-Dec-18 08	19-Dec-18 16
Delivery Plan		21d	20-Dec-18 08	22-Jan-19 16
OZ1050	Document Delivery Methodology	4d	20-Dec-18 08	27-Dec-18 16
OZ1060	Obtain Quotes from Suppliers	8d	03-Jan-19 08*	14-Jan-19 16
OZ1070	Calculate the Bid Estimate	3d	15-Jan-19 08	17-Jan-19 16
OZ1080	Create the Project Schedule	3d	18-Jan-19 08	21-Jan-19 16
OZ1090	Review the Delivery Plan	1d	22-Jan-19 08	22-Jan-19 16
Bid Dcoument		21d	28-Dec-18 08	28-Jan-19 16
OZ1100	Create Draft of Bid Document	6d	28-Dec-18 08	07-Jan-19 16
OZ1110	Review Bid Document	2d	23-Jan-19 08	24-Jan-19 16
OZ1120	Finalise and Submit Bid Document	2d	25-Jan-19 08	28-Jan-19 16
OZ1130	Bid Document Submitted	0d		28-Jan-19 16*

15. Save this layout.

16. Make a copy of it titled **OzBuild Workshop 10 – With Float**, making it a User Layout, displaying the columns and formatting the bars per the following picture; this is displaying the **Total Float** and **Negative Float** bars:

17. Save this layout.

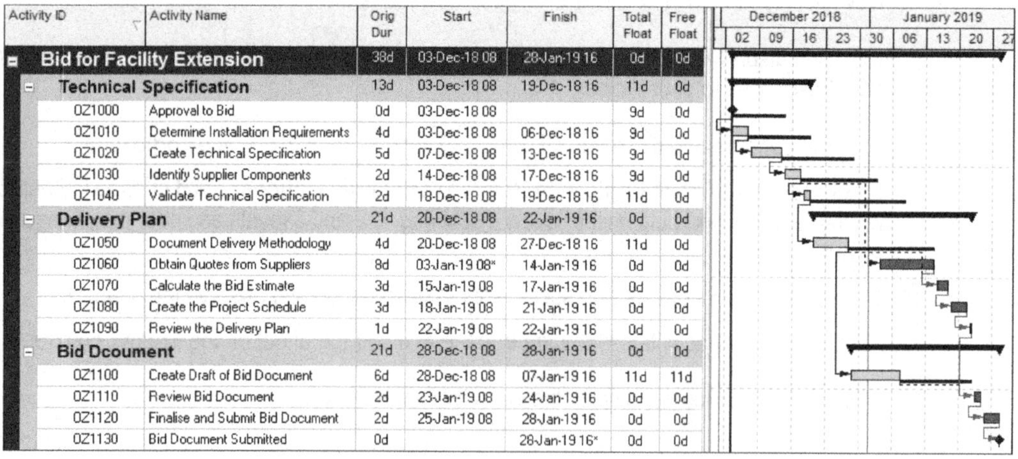

Activity ID	Activity Name	Orig Dur	Start	Finish	Total Float	Free Float
Bid for Facility Extension		38d	03-Dec-18 08	28-Jan-19 16	0d	0d
Technical Specification		13d	03-Dec-18 08	19-Dec-18 16	11d	0d
OZ1000	Approval to Bid	0d	03-Dec-18 08		9d	0d
OZ1010	Determine Installation Requirements	4d	03-Dec-18 08	06-Dec-18 16	9d	0d
OZ1020	Create Technical Specification	5d	07-Dec-18 08	13-Dec-18 16	9d	0d
OZ1030	Identify Supplier Components	2d	14-Dec-18 08	17-Dec-18 16	9d	0d
OZ1040	Validate Technical Specification	2d	18-Dec-18 08	19-Dec-18 16	11d	0d
Delivery Plan		21d	20-Dec-18 08	22-Jan-19 16	0d	0d
OZ1050	Document Delivery Methodology	4d	20-Dec-18 08	27-Dec-18 16	11d	0d
OZ1060	Obtain Quotes from Suppliers	8d	03-Jan-19 08*	14-Jan-19 16	0d	0d
OZ1070	Calculate the Bid Estimate	3d	15-Jan-19 08	17-Jan-19 16	0d	0d
OZ1080	Create the Project Schedule	3d	18-Jan-19 08	21-Jan-19 16	0d	0d
OZ1090	Review the Delivery Plan	1d	22-Jan-19 08	22-Jan-19 16	0d	0d
Bid Dcoument		21d	28-Dec-18 08	28-Jan-19 16	0d	0d
OZ1100	Create Draft of Bid Document	6d	28-Dec-18 08	07-Jan-19 16	11d	11d
OZ1110	Review Bid Document	2d	23-Jan-19 08	24-Jan-19 16	0d	0d
OZ1120	Finalise and Submit Bid Document	2d	25-Jan-19 08	28-Jan-19 16	0d	0d
OZ1130	Bid Document Submitted	0d		28-Jan-19 16*	0d	0d

13 FILTERS

This chapter covers the ability of Primavera to control which activities are displayed, both on the screen and in printouts, by using **Filters**.

13.1 Understanding Filters

Primavera has an ability to display activities that meet specific criteria. You may want to see only the incomplete activities, or the work scheduled for the next couple of months or weeks, or the activities that are in-progress.

Primavera defaults to displaying all activities. There are a number of pre-defined filters available that you may use or edit. You may also create one or more of your own.

A filter may be applied to display or to highlight only those activities that meet a criteria.

There are four types of filters:

- **Default** filters which are supplied with the system and may not be edited or deleted but may be copied and then edited or modified and are often used in conjunction with the display of bars.
- **Global** filters which are made available to anyone working in the database, and
- **User Defined** filters which are defined by a user and available only to that user unless it is made into a **Global** filter,
- **Layout** filters which make the filter only available when the current layout is applied. **NOTE:** If the current layout is a **Project** layout then this effectively makes the **Layout** filter a project filter.

The following types of filters are not available:

- Drop down or Auto filters as in Excel and Microsoft Project.
- Interactive filters as available in SureTrak and Microsoft Project. This is when a filter is applied and the user is offered choices from a drop down list. The lack of this function may result in an excessive quantity of filters being generated or the user continually editing frequently used filters.

On the other hand, P6 does allow multiple filters to be applied at the same time.

There are no dedicated project filters (except by creating a Layout filter) available in Primavera, so you might consider placing the project name or number at the start of a filter name so you may identify which filters belong to which projects. This is especially helpful when you have a number of **User Filters** or there are a number of **Global Filters**.

Topic	Menu Command
• To apply, edit, create, or delete a filter open the **Filters** form.	• Click on the icon, or • Select **View, Filter By..., Customize**, or • Right-click in the columns area and select **Filters...**.

13.2 *Applying a Filter*

13.2.1 Filters Form

Filters are applied from the **Filters** form which may be opened by:

- Clicking on the icon, or
- Selecting View, Filters..., Customize...or
- Right-clicking in the columns area and selecting **Filters...**
- **NOTE:** If the **All Activities** check box is not checked then there is a filter applied.

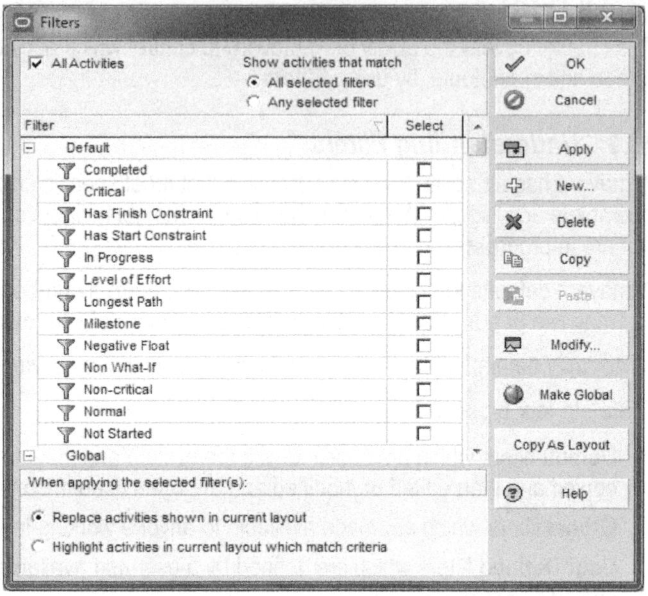

13.2.2 Applying a Single Filter

A single filter is applied by:

- Checking the **Select** check box beside one filter, and
- Clicking on the Apply icon to apply the filter and not close the form. If the result is undesirable another option may be selected, or
- Clicking on OK to apply the filter and close the form.
- When applying the selected filter(s):
  - Only activities that comply to the filter criteria will be displayed when the **Replace activities shown in the current layout** button is checked.
  - These activities will be highlighted in the **Select Activity** color when the **Highlight activities in current layout which match criteria** button is checked.

13.2.3 Applying a Combination Filter

A combination filter has two or more filters selected and has two options under **Show activities that match**:

- **All selected filters** where an activity to be displayed or highlighted has to match the criteria of **ALL** the filters, or
- **Any selected filters** where an activity to be displayed or highlighted has to match the criteria of **ONLY ONE** filter.

In many places in the software there will be an option of either clicking on the OK icon or the Apply icon:

- The Apply icon applies the format yet leaves the form open.
- The OK icon applies the format and closes the form.

13.3 Creating and Modifying a Filter

13.3.1 Creating a New Filter

Filters may be created from the **Filters** form by:

- Clicking on the New... icon in the **Filter** form and create a new filter, or
- Copying an existing filter using the Copy and Paste icons and then editing the new filter.

New filters will be created in the **User Defined** filter area at the bottom of the list.

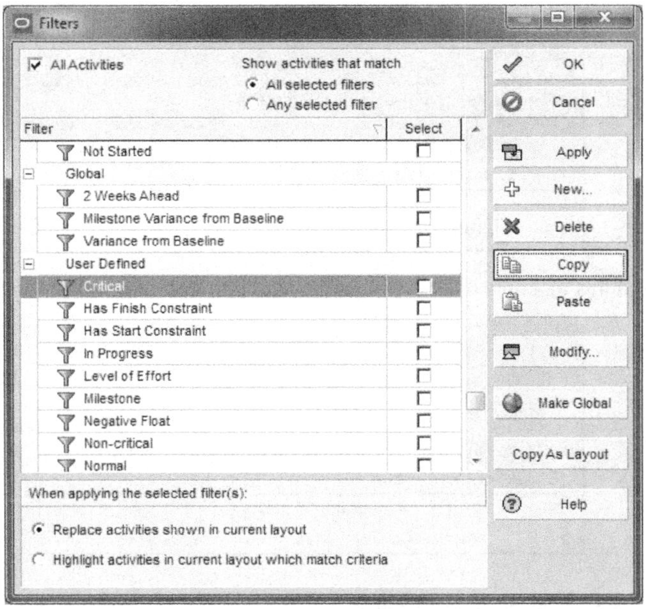

There are a large number of options available to create a filter and from the following examples you should be able to experiment and add your own filters. To modify an existing filter, select it from the **Filters** form and click the Modify... icon.

13.3.2 One Parameter Filter

The following example is a filter to display incomplete activities:

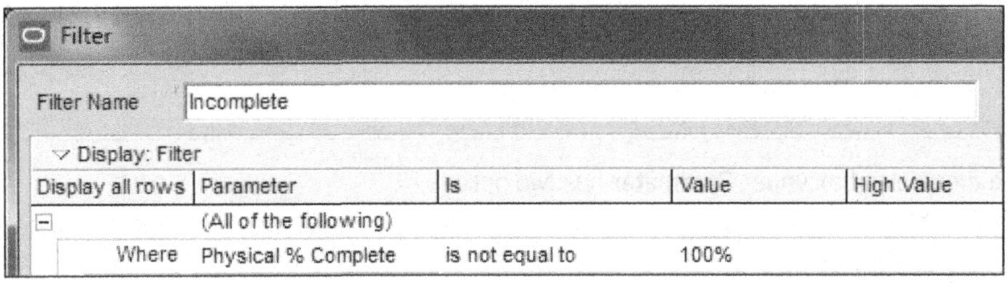

- **Parameter** is used to select any of the available database fields:
- Select one of the options from the **Is** drop down box:
- The parameter selected in the **Is** box determines if:
  - Only one **Value** is required, which is entered into the **Value** field, or
  - A range is required and two values are to be entered; then the **Value** and **High Value** are entered.

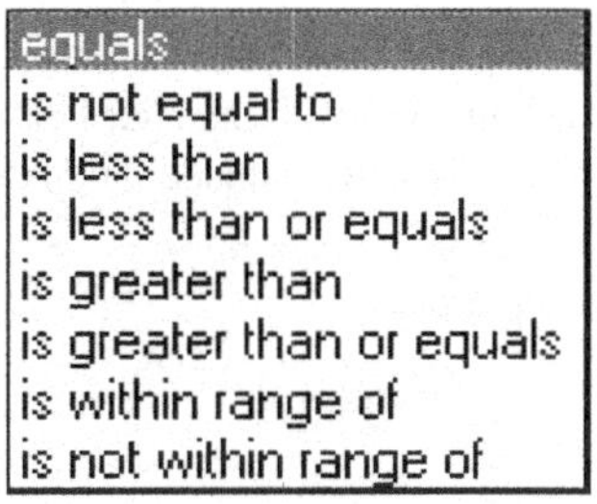

The following example is a filter to display in-progress activities using the **is not within range of** and **Value** and **High Value** options:

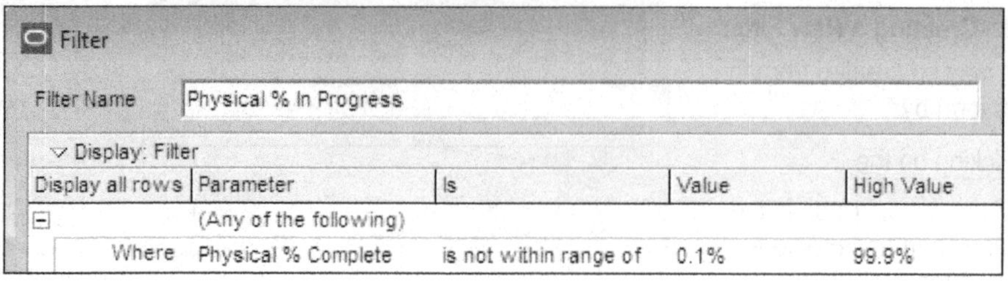

And this example uses the **equals** parameter and only the **Value** field is completed:

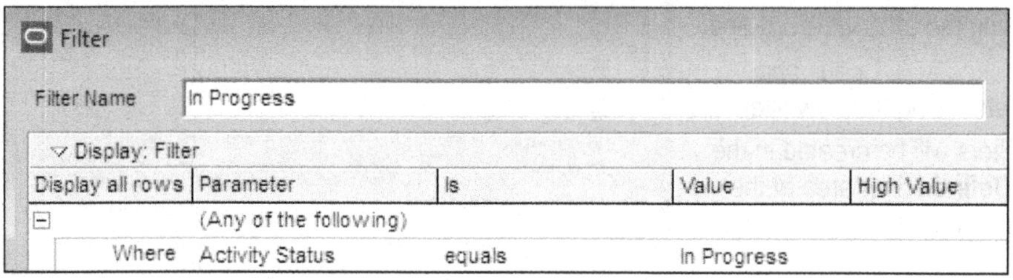

13.3.3 Two Parameter Filter

The following example is a filter to display all critical path activities and activities assigned the PM resource:

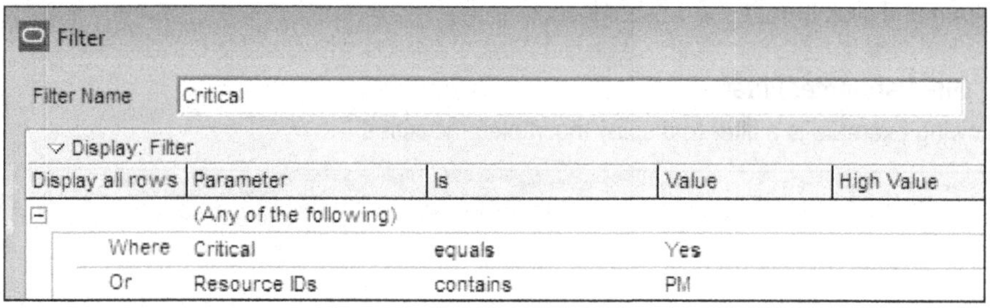

- The drop down box under **Parameter** has two options:
  - **(All of the following)**. This is used when an activity must meet all of the parameters selected below.
  - **(Any of the following)**. This is used when an activity must meet any of the parameters selected below.

When the first parameter is change to **All of the following** the **Display all rows** option changes to an **AND**. Therefore with the filter below there would normally be fewer activities displayed as the activities have to be critical and assigned the resource PM:

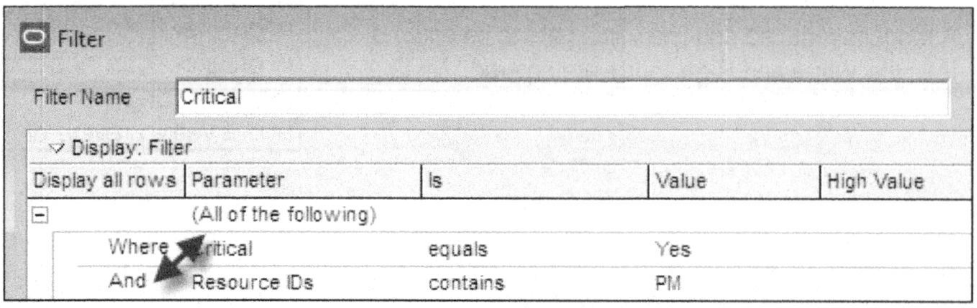

13.3.4 Multiple Parameter Filter

The following example is a filter to display incomplete activities on the critical path with resources PEH and SEH:

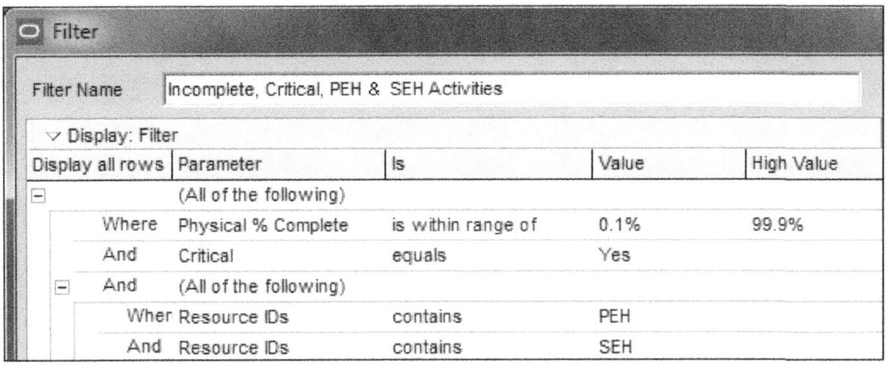

- In this example, **(All of the following)** was selected from the **Parameters** drop down box which enables a nesting effect of filter parameters.
- This function is similar to the filter levels in P3.

13.3.5 Editing and Organizing Filter Parameters

Lines in a filter are added, copied, pasted, and deleted using the appropriate icons in the **Filters** form.

The arrows allow the filter lines to be moved up and down and indented to the left and outdented to the right in a similar way to indenting and outdenting tasks in Microsoft Project.

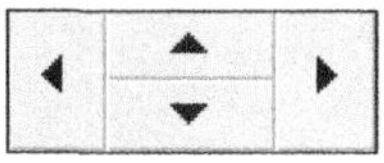

A filter may be optimized to delete the redundant filter lines using the **Optimize** command:

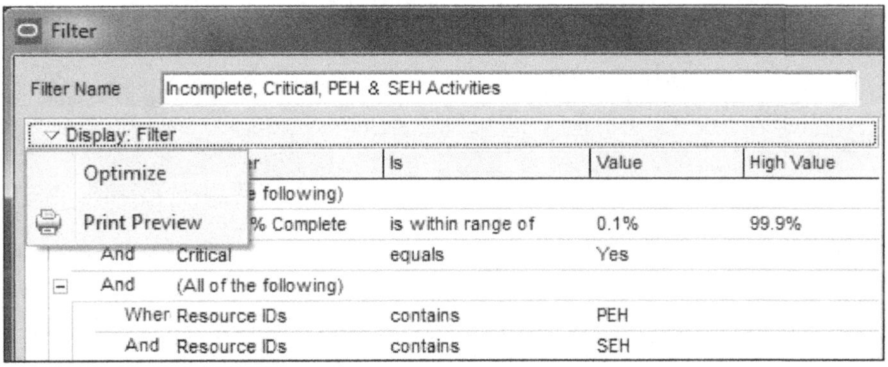

13.3.6 Understanding Resource Filters

NOTE: THIS IS A VERY IMPORTANT POINT FOR RESOURCE FILTERING

When filtering on resources the filter must use the option of **contains** in the **Is** column and not **equals**, as in the picture above, otherwise when an activity has been assigned more than one resource, then the activity will not be selected with a filter using the **equals** parameter.

13.4 *Workshop 11 – Filters*

Background

Management has asked for reports on activities to suit their requirements.

Assignment

Ensure your **OzBuild Bid** project is open.

1. Apply the **OzBuild Workshop 10 – With Float** layout.
2. They would like to see all the critical activities.
   - Ensure a column showing the **Total Float** is displayed, and
   - Apply the **Critical** activities filter.

   You will see only activities that are on the critical path and their associated summary activities.

Activity ID	Activity Name	Orig Dur	Start	Finish	Total Float	Free Float
Bid for Facility Extension		18d	03-Jan-19 08	28-Jan-19 16	0d	0d
Technical Specification		0d			0d	0d
Delivery Plan		14d	03-Jan-19 08	22-Jan-19 16	0d	0d
OZ1060	Obtain Quotes from Suppl	8d	03-Jan-19 08*	14-Jan-19 16	0d	0d
OZ1070	Calculate the Bid Estimate	3d	15-Jan-19 08	17-Jan-19 16	0d	0d
OZ1080	Create the Project Sched	3d	18-Jan-19 08	21-Jan-19 16	0d	0d
OZ1090	Review the Delivery Plan	1d	22-Jan-19 08	22-Jan-19 16	0d	0d
Bid Dcoument		4d	23-Jan-19 08	28-Jan-19 16	0d	0d
OZ1110	Review Bid Document	2d	23-Jan-19 08	24-Jan-19 16	0d	0d
OZ1120	Finalise and Submit Bid D	2d	25-Jan-19 08	28-Jan-19 16	0d	0d
OZ1130	Bid Document Submitted	0d		28-Jan-19 16*	0d	0d

3. Open the **Group and Sort** form and check the **Hide if empty** box and notice the **Technical Specification** band is hidden.

Activity ID	Activity Name	Orig Dur	Start	Finish	Total Float	Free Float
Bid for Facility Extension		18d	03-Jan-19 08	28-Jan-19 16	0d	0d
Delivery Plan		14d	03-Jan-19 08	22-Jan-19 16	0d	0d
OZ1060	Obtain Quotes from Suppli	8d	03-Jan-19 08*	14-Jan-19 16	0d	0d
OZ1070	Calculate the Bid Estimate	3d	15-Jan-19 08	17-Jan-19 16	0d	0d
OZ1080	Create the Project Schedu	3d	18-Jan-19 08	21-Jan-19 16	0d	0d
OZ1090	Review the Delivery Plan	1d	22-Jan-19 08	22-Jan-19 16	0d	0d
Bid Dcoument		4d	23-Jan-19 08	28-Jan-19 16	0d	0d
OZ1110	Review Bid Document	2d	23-Jan-19 08	24-Jan-19 16	0d	0d
OZ1120	Finalise and Submit Bid Dc	2d	25-Jan-19 08	28-Jan-19 16	0d	0d
OZ1130	Bid Document Submitted	0d		28-Jan-19 16*	0d	0d

continued...

4. Management would like to see all the activities with float less than or equal to 9 days:
   - Create a new filter titled: **Total Float Less Than or Equal to 9 Days**, and
   - Add the condition to display a total float of less than 9 days.

Filter Name: Total Float Less Than or Equal to 9 days

Display: Filter

Display all rows	Parameter	Is	Value	High Value
⊟	(All of the following)			
Where	Total Float	is less than or equals	9d	

   - Close the Filter form,
   - Click on the All Activities check box to ensure all activities are displayed,
   - Apply the new filter,
   - You should find that activities with more than 9 days' float are hidden:

Activity ID	Activity Name	Orig Dur	Start	Finish	Total Float	Free Float
Bid for Facility Extension		38d	03-Dec-18 08	28-Jan-19 16	0d	0d
Technical Specification		11d	03-Dec-18 08	17-Dec-18 16	9d	0d
OZ1000	Approval to Bid	0d	03-Dec-18 08		9d	0d
OZ1010	Determine Installation Rec	4d	03-Dec-18 08	06-Dec-18 16	9d	0d
OZ1020	Create Technical Specific	5d	07-Dec-18 08	13-Dec-18 16	9d	0d
OZ1030	Identify Supplier Compone	2d	14-Dec-18 08	17-Dec-18 16	9d	0d
Delivery Plan		14d	03-Jan-19 08	22-Jan-19 16	0d	0d
OZ1060	Obtain Quotes from Suppl	8d	03-Jan-19 08*	14-Jan-19 16	0d	0d
OZ1070	Calculate the Bid Estimate	3d	15-Jan-19 08	17-Jan-19 16	0d	0d
OZ1080	Create the Project Sched	3d	18-Jan-19 08	21-Jan-19 16	0d	0d
OZ1090	Review the Delivery Plan	1d	22-Jan-19 08	22-Jan-19 16	0d	0d
Bid Dcoument		4d	23-Jan-19 08	28-Jan-19 16	0d	0d
OZ1110	Review Bid Document	2d	23-Jan-19 08	24-Jan-19 16	0d	0d
OZ1120	Finalise and Submit Bid D	2d	25-Jan-19 08	28-Jan-19 16	0d	0d
OZ1130	Bid Document Submitted	0d		28-Jan-19 16*	0d	0d

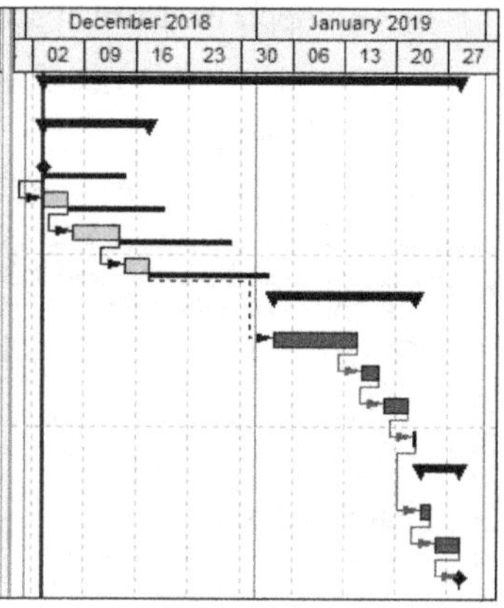

5. They would like to see all the activities that are critical or contain the word “Bid”.
   - Copy the **Critical** filter,
   - Edit the filter title to read: **Critical or Contains “Bid”**
   - Edit the top line to read **(Any of the following)**,
   - Add the condition: **Or** Name (Activity Name) contains **Bid**, and

Filter Name: Critical or Activity Name Contains "Bid"

Display: Filter

Display all rows	Parameter	Is	Value	High Value
⊟	(Any of the following)			
Where	Critical	equals	Yes	
Or	Activity Name	contains	Bid	

   - Apply the filter.

Activity ID	Activity Name	Orig Dur	Start	Finish	Total Float	Free Float
Bid for Facility Extension		38d	03-Dec-18 08	28-Jan-19 16	0d	0d
Technical Specification		0d	03-Dec-18 08	03-Dec-18 08	9d	0d
OZ1000	Approval to Bid	0d	03-Dec-18 08		9d	0d
Delivery Plan		14d	03-Jan-19 08	22-Jan-19 16	0d	0d
OZ1060	Obtain Quotes from Supplie	8d	03-Jan-19 08*	14-Jan-19 16	0d	0d
OZ1070	Calculate the Bid Estimate	3d	15-Jan-19 08	17-Jan-19 16	0d	0d
OZ1080	Create the Project Schedul	3d	18-Jan-19 08	21-Jan-19 16	0d	0d
OZ1090	Review the Delivery Plan	1d	22-Jan-19 08	22-Jan-19 16	0d	0d
Bid Dcoument		21d	28-Dec-18 08	28-Jan-19 16	0d	0d
OZ1100	Create Draft of Bid Docum	6d	28-Dec-18 08	07-Jan-19 16	11d	11d
OZ1110	Review Bid Document	2d	23-Jan-19 08	24-Jan-19 16	0d	0d
OZ1120	Finalise and Submit Bid Do	2d	25-Jan-19 08	28-Jan-19 16	0d	0d
OZ1130	Bid Document Submitted	0d		28-Jan-19 16*	0d	0d

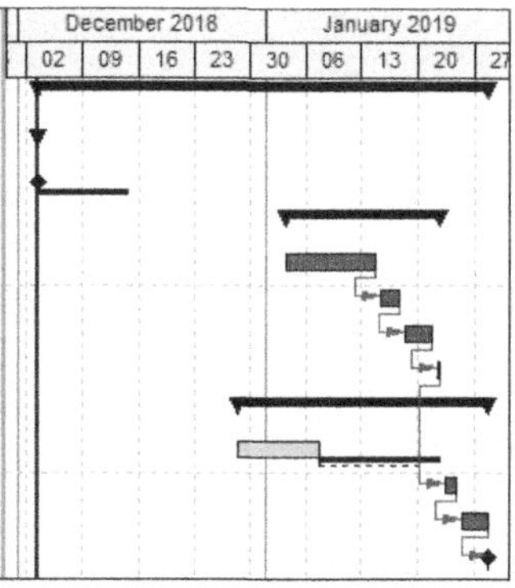

6. Now change the **(Any of the following)** option to **(All of the following)** and see the effect.

Activity ID	Activity Name	Orig Dur	Start	Finish	Total Float	Free Float
Bid for Facility Extension		10d	15-Jan-19 08	28-Jan-19 16	0d	0d
Delivery Plan		3d	15-Jan-19 08	17-Jan-19 16	0d	0d
OZ1070	Calculate the Bid Estimate	3d	15-Jan-19 08	17-Jan-19 16	0d	0d
Bid Dcoument		4d	23-Jan-19 08	28-Jan-19 16	0d	0d
OZ1110	Review Bid Document	2d	23-Jan-19 08	24-Jan-19 16	0d	0d
OZ1120	Finalise and Submit Bid Do	2d	25-Jan-19 08	28-Jan-19 16	0d	0d
OZ1130	Bid Document Submitted	0d		28-Jan-19 16*	0d	0d

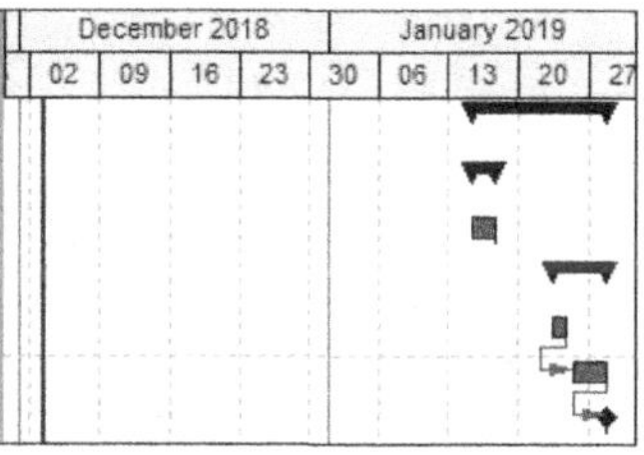

7. There should be fewer activities as it is now displaying activities that meet both conditions.
8. Now apply the **All Activities** filter to display all the activities.

14 PRINTING AND REPORTS

This is the stage at which the schedule is printed so people may review and comment on it. This chapter will examine some of the options for printing your project schedule.

There are several tools available to output your schedule:

- The **Printing** function prints the data displayed in the current Layout.
- The **Reporting** function prints reports, which are independent of the current Layout. Primavera supplies a number of predefined reports that may be tailored to suit your own requirements. Reports will not be covered in detail in this publication.
- The **Project Web Site Publisher** to publish the schedule to a web site using the **Tools**, **Publish** command.
- You may also copy and paste text data from columns and some tables into Excel and other products.

It is recommended that you consider using a product such as Adobe Acrobat to output your schedule in pdf format. You then will be able to e-mail high quality outputs that recipients may print or review on screen without needing a copy of Primavera.

14.1 Printing

When a Layout is split, the lower pane may be printed with the upper pane, with the exception of the **Activity Details** pane. This is similar to P3 and SureTrak, but different from Microsoft Project where only the Activity View may be printed. Other products, such as Asta Powerproject and Tilos, allow multiple resource histograms to be printed in one printout, which is not possible in P6.

Print settings, such as headers and footers, are applied to the individual Layouts and the settings are saved with that Layout.

The following normal print commands may be used when printing:

- **File**, **Page Setup...**
- **File**, **Print Setup...**
- **File**, **Print Preview**
- **File**, **Print...** or **Ctrl+P**

Each of these functions will be discussed only for printing the Gantt Chart. Printing all other Layouts is a similar process. Some Layouts will have different options due to the nature of the data being displayed. These other options should be easily mastered after the basics covered in this chapter are understood.

Each time you report to the client or management, it is recommended that you save a copy of your printout or report and a pdf file is an excellent method of saving this data. In conjunction with a robust file-naming convention that includes the project title and Data Date, a pdf file will enable you to reproduce these reports at any point in time in the future and have available a copy of the project schedule for dispute resolution purposes.

It is good practice to keep a copy of the project after each update, especially if litigation is a possibility. A project may be copied either by creating a Baseline, by exporting the project as an XER file or by using the project copy function, then making the **Status** inactive in the **General** tab of the **Projects Window**. It is important to note that although the project may be marked as inactive it may still be opened and modified.

14.2 Print Preview

To preview the printout, use the Primavera **Print Preview** option. Select **File**, **Print Preview** or click the icon on the **Print** toolbar:

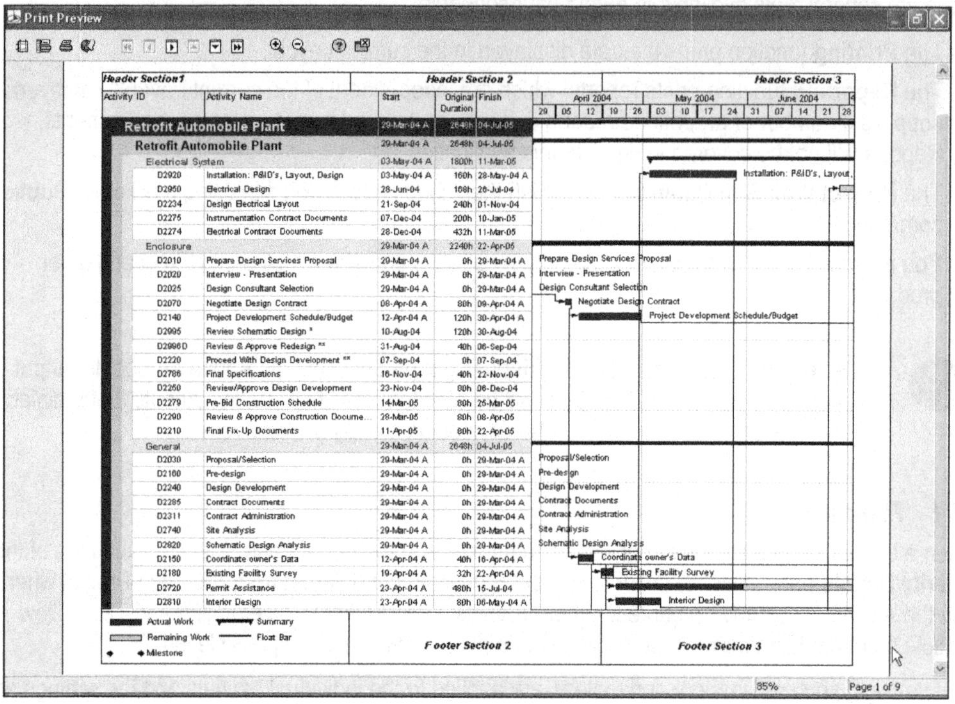

The following paragraphs describe the functions of the icons at the top of the **Print Preview** screen from left to right:

- The icon opens the **Page Setup** form to be covered in the next paragraph.
- The icon opens the **Print Setup** form where the printer and paper size, etc., may be selected.
- The icon opens the **Print** form where the printer, the pages to be printed, and the number of copies to be printed may be selected.
- The icon opens the **Publish to HTML** form and saves the view in HTML format where both the tables and bar charts are converted.
- The first six icons on the left, , allow scrolling when a printout has more than one page.
- The magnifying glass icons zoom in and out. You may also click in the **Print Preview** screen to zoom in.
- The button opens the Help file.
- The icon closes the **Print Preview** screen.

14.3 Page Setup

To open the **Page Setup...** form:

- Click the **Page Setup** icon on the **Print** toolbar, or
- Select **File**, **Page Setup...** to display the **Page Setup** form:

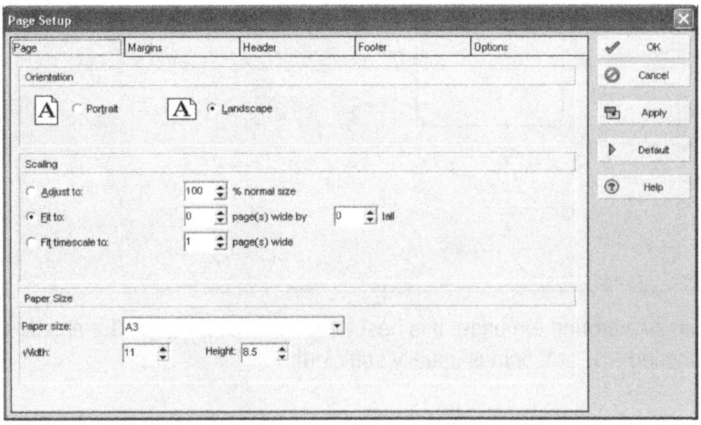

The **Page Setup** form contains the following tabs: Page, Margins, Header, Footer and Options.

When changes are made to a header or footer then the icons on the right side may be used:

- Apply – Applies the changes so they are visible without closing the form.
- Default – Resets the Page Setup settings to default.
- OK – Accepts the changes and closes the form.
- Cancel – Cancels the changes and closes the form.

14.3.1 Page Tab

The Primavera options in the **Page** tab are:

- **Orientation** enables the selection of **Portrait** or **Landscape** printing.
- **Scaling** enables you to adjust the number of pages the printout will fit onto:
  - **Adjust to:**– enables you to choose the scale of the column text and then the horizontal scale of the bars is adjusted to fit the remaining space.
  - **Fit to:** – enables you to choose the number of pages across and down and Primavera should scale the printout to fit.
  - **Fit timescale to:** – enables the user to select the number of pages the Gantt Chart is scaled over but leaves the font of the columns un-scaled. This will often be the best setting with 1 page(s) wide selected.

  These options work in conjunction with each other and can get quite difficult to operate. The author recommends that a good starting point for print options is to first set the **Adjust to:** to 100% so the text is printed out in a legible size and then set the **Fit timescale to:** is set to 1 page wide.

- Pages are numbered first across and then down, and does not follow the P3 and SureTrak convention of numbers down and letters across, or the Microsoft Project convention of numbering pages down and then across.

14.3.2 Margins Tab

With this option, you may edit the margins around the edge of the printout.

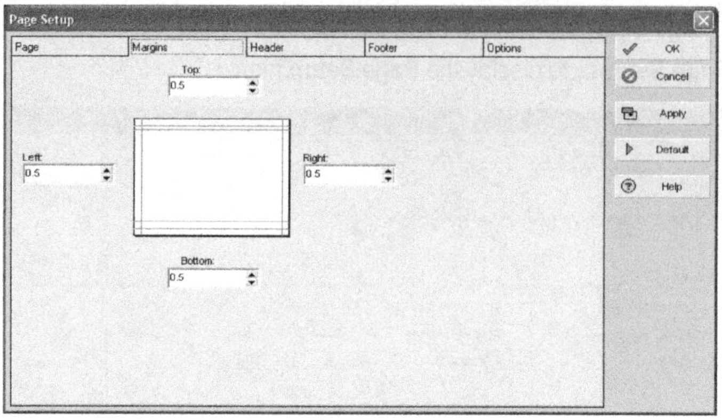

Type in the margin size around the page. It is best to allow a wider margin for an edge that is to be bound or hole punched – 1" or 2.5cm is usually sufficient.

14.3.3 Header and Footer Tabs

Headers appear at the top of the screen above all schedule information and footers are located at the bottom. Both the headers and footers are formatted in the same way. We will discuss the setting-up of footers in this chapter.

Click on the **Footer** tab from the **Page Setup** form. This will display the settings of the default footers and headers. You should modify the output to suit your requirements.

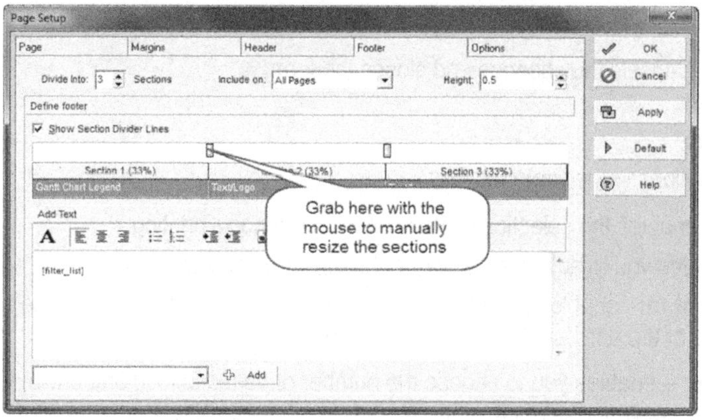

- **Divide Into:** – determines the number of sections the Header/Footer is divided into from 1 to 5 sections.
- **Include on:** – determines on which pages the Header/Footer is to appear: First Page, Last Page, All Pages, or No Pages.
- **Height:** – enables the user to select the height of the Header/Footer.
- **Define Footer**
  - **Show Section Divider Lines** check box – hides or displays the divider lines between the sections.
  - The sections may be sized by manually moving the divider lines with the mouse and the slide underneath the **Show Section Divider Lines**.

- **Section Content**

  This may be selected by clicking on the icon under the **Section** title and a subject type to be displayed selected.

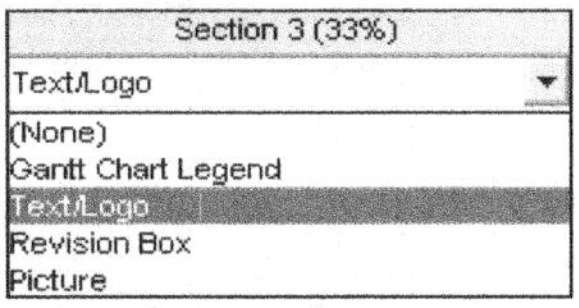

  - **(None)** – leaves the section blank.
  - **Gantt Chart Legend** – displays all the bars checked in the display column of the **Bars** form and only the fonts may be edited by clicking on the little Font icon at the bottom.
  - **Text/Logo** – enables many types of data to be displayed including text, a data item selected from the drop down box, fonts formatted by clicking on the formatting icons, a Logo inserted by clicking on the icon, Tables added by clicking on the icon, and a Hyperlink added by clicking on the link icon which opens the **Hyperlink** form.

When adding text it has been found by the author that the letter "s" may not be typed into the Header and Footer. Some people are able to cut and paste the required text with an "s" from another program or you may create an image and insert the image into the header or footer. This may be rectified with a service pack.

  - **Revision Box** has a **Revision Box Title:** – the following information may be entered manually: Date, Revision, Checked, Approved.
  - **Picture** – enables a picture to be placed in the footer and it may be manually adjusted to fit the space or automatically adjusted by checking the **Resize picture to fit the selection** box.

- The Add button allows the insertion of database fields from the drop down list which automatically update with from the current project. The following fields may be set for the whole organization: **Custom Label 1 to 3**, **Footer Label 1 to 3**, and **Header Label 1 to 3** and defined in P6 Professional in the **Admin, Admin Preferences..., Reports** tab and in the Primavera EPPM Optional Client **NOT FROM THE WEB** but from **Tools**, **Reports**, **Report Preferences**.

The Add button is a very useful feature as it allows for standard layouts to be created that update automatically from database fields such as Project ID and Project Name and therefore are always valid when you open a different project.

14.3.4 Options Tab

The Options tab has three sections:

- **Timescale Start:** and **Timescale Finish:** These options enable the **start and finish** point of the timescale to be set. Click on the icon and select a date from the drop down list. A **Custom Date...** may be selected from the menu and a calendar is opened to select the date.

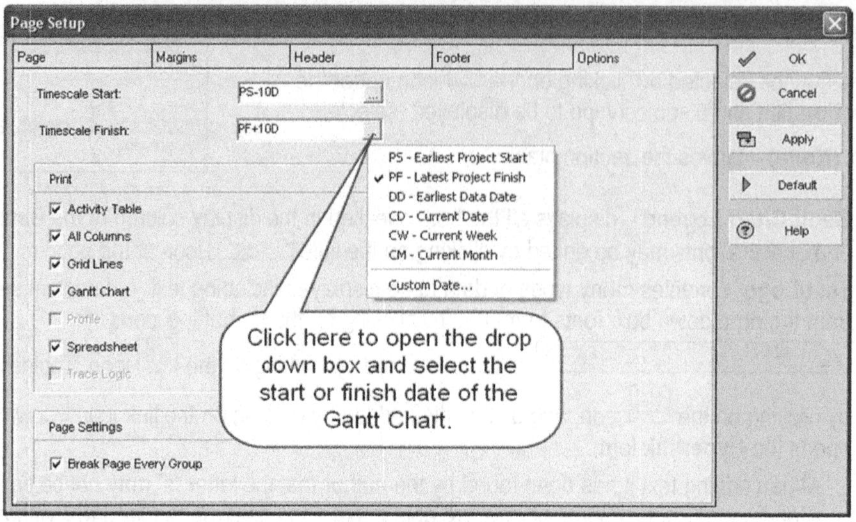

- A lag from the nominated dates may be specified, see the picture above where the timescale starts 10 days before the Project Start date and ends 10 days after the Project Finish date. This function works in a similar way to P3 and SureTrak
- The **Print** options alter depending on the Layout. The check boxes allow a selection of the data to be printed.

Only one resource histogram or a resource table may be printed at a time.

- The **Break Page Every Group** puts a page break at each change of heading in the first group in the **Group and Sort** form.

  P6 Version 8.1 has also added a function in the **Group and Sort** form that now allows a page break at any select level in Grouping of activities which in a way make this option redundant:

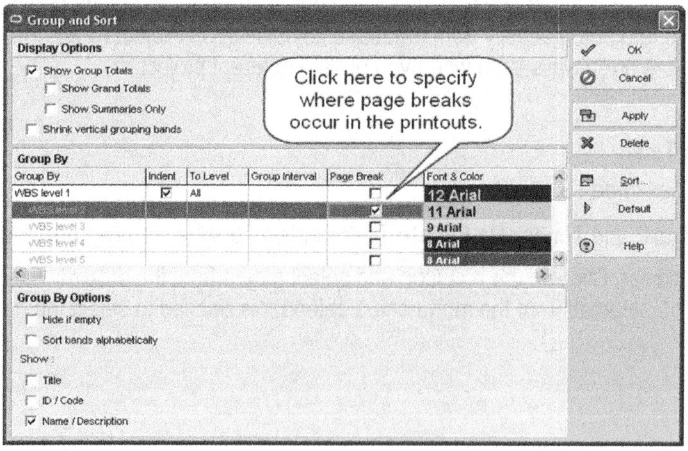

14.4 Print Form

The **Print** form is be opened by:

- Selecting **File**, **Print...**, or
- Executing the keystrokes **Ctrl+P**, or
- Clicking on the print icon in the **Print Preview** screen.

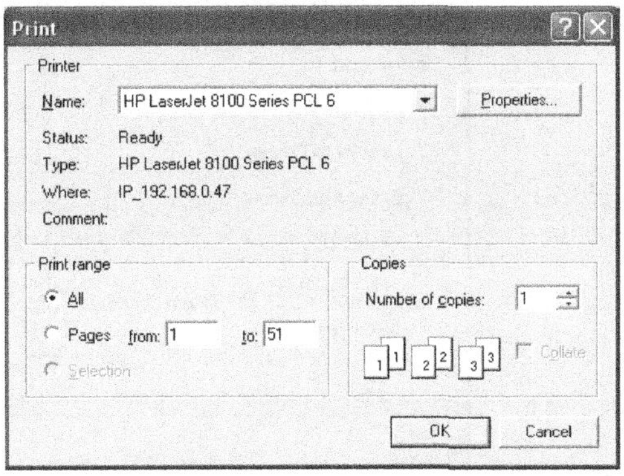

14.5 Print Setup Form

The **Print Setup** form is be opened by:

- Selecting **File**, **Print Setup...**, or
- Clicking on the print icon in the **Print Preview** screen.

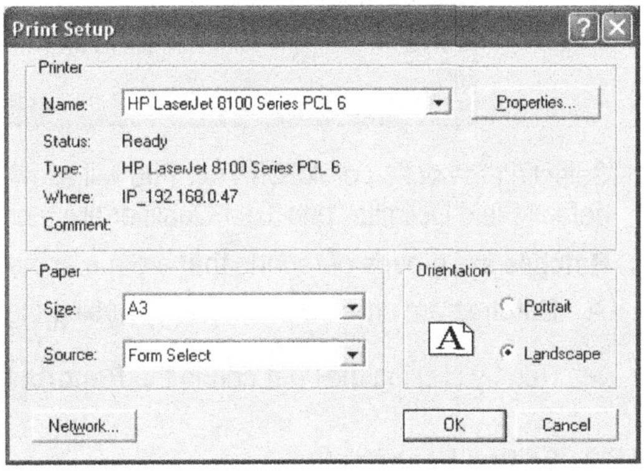

14.6 Reports

Click the icon on the **Enterprise** toolbar or select **Tools**, **Reports, Reports** to open the **Reports Window**:

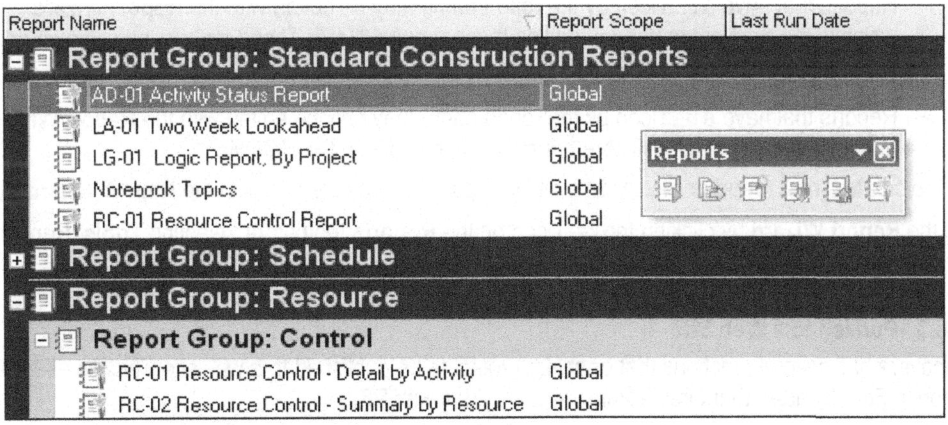

- The reports are grouped under a hierarchical structure that may be modified by opening the **Tools**, **Reports, Reports Groups** form or right-clicking and using the menu.

14.6.1 Running Reports

- A single report may be run by right-clicking on a report and selecting **Run**, **Report...** or clicking the icon on the **Reports** toolbar. This will open the **Run Report** form:

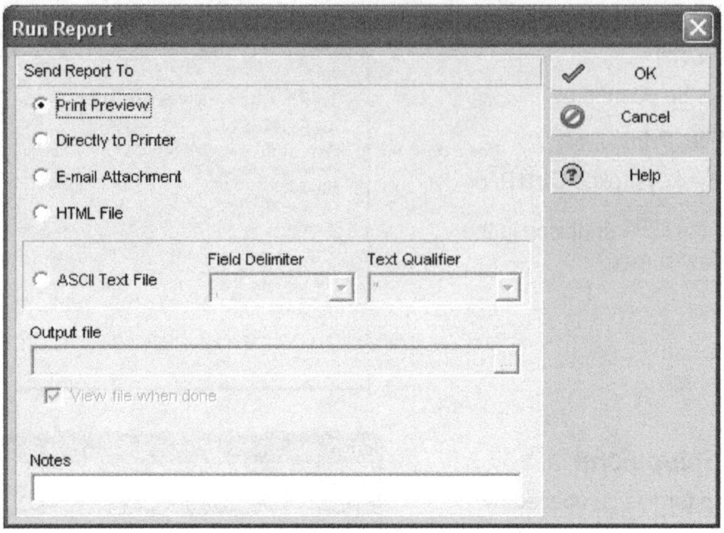

- Selecting the option of **ASCII Text File** will allow the report to be opened and edited in Excel. The default Field Delimiter and Text Qualifier are usually suitable for Excel.
- **Batches** are groups of reports that are run at the same time:
  - **Batches** are created and edited by using the **Tools**, **Reports, Batch Reports...**form, and
  - Run by clicking the icon in the **Reports** toolbar.

14.6.2 Editing Reports

- Reports may be cut, copied, and pasted using the **Edit** toolbar icons or right-clicking.
- They may be renamed by clicking on the description.
- Some reports may be edited with the **Report Wizard** and all may be edited with the **Report Writer**.
  - Reports that have a icon by the report name may be edited with the **Report Wizard**, which is the simplest method of editing these reports. **Note:** These reports may also be edited with the **Report Writer**.
  - Reports that have a icon by the report name may only be edited with the **Report Writer** and this is quite complex. There are basic instructions in the Help file.
- To create a new report or modify an existing report that was created with the **Report Wizard**, run the **Report Wizard** by clicking the icon on the **Reports** toolbar, or selecting **Tools**, **Report Wizard...**.

14.6.3 Publish to a Web Site

Primavera has several functions that enable a project to be published to a web site which is effectively the only "Free Reader" that Oracle Primavera provides with P6.

The **Tools**, **Publish,** menu has three options for creating a web site for a currently opened project:

- **Project Web Site...** creates a complete web site with any Reports or Layouts that have been created. This is a very useful function if it is required to publish a large amount of data.
- **Activity Layouts...** creates a web site with just the selected Activity Layout.
- **Tracking Layouts...** creates a web site with just the selected Tracking Layout.

14.7 Visualizer

14.7.1 Understanding Visualizer

Visualizer is new to P6 Version 8.3 and is an update of the P6 Version 8.2 **Timescale Logic Diagram** module. It is a separate piece of Windows Client software that reads your Oracle Primavera database and allows a higher level of Gant Chart customization than available from the Activities Window in either Professional or Web Client.

The screen dumps used in this section of the book are mainly taken from P6 Version 15.1 and 15.2, but as Visualizer evolves, the menus change and your version may not be the same as these pictures.

Visualizer may be run from within P6 or from the Windows Start Menu:

- Timescale Logic Diagrams (TSLD) and
- Gantt Charts.

It includes the following functions:

- Printing of Layouts imported from P6 and the creation of new Visualizer layouts,
- Notebook Topics and Steps may be displayed as fields in the activity table or as bar labels,
- Show Lead or Lag on relationships,
- Stack columns and use word wrapping in the Gantt chart,
- Show Multiple Activities on one row in the TSLDs, thus reducing the number of rows,
- Formatting of fields and labels,
- Use functions such as Baseline Bar display, Filters, Group and Sort,
- The Enterprise, Activity Code form allows Activity Codes colors to be defined. These colors may be assigned to bars, bar Start and Finish points in Visualizer, but these colors may not be assigned to bars in the Activity window Bars form.
- More shape choices and other formatting options for bars,
- Run reports in batches using programs like Windows Scheduler,
- Primavera Version 15.1 has enabled the ability to import and export PLF Layout files which are created in P6 Professional. Also, user may exchange Visualizer Layouts using the import and export of a VLF file.

Understanding how Visualizer operates:

- It is a separate piece of Windows Client software that is installed on a PC,
- It uses the same security as PPM,
- It may not be used to manipulate data, therefore it is just for presentation,
- The user is required to select an existing layout or create a new layout which will either display a Gantt Chart or TSLD, before selecting the project to report,
- Then the projects to report on are selected, and
- The layout is formatted and saved, if required,
- Visualizer layouts may be created and saved as Global, Project or User layouts,
- Visualizer uses P6 Admin Preferences for Calendar Start Day of the week, and on line help settings.

14.7.2 Starting Visualizer

To start Visualizer either select:

- From P6 PPM select **Tools**, **Visualizer**, and Visualizer will start without the need to log in again, or
- Open from the Windows Start Menu without opening P6, but you will need to use your P6 login name and password:

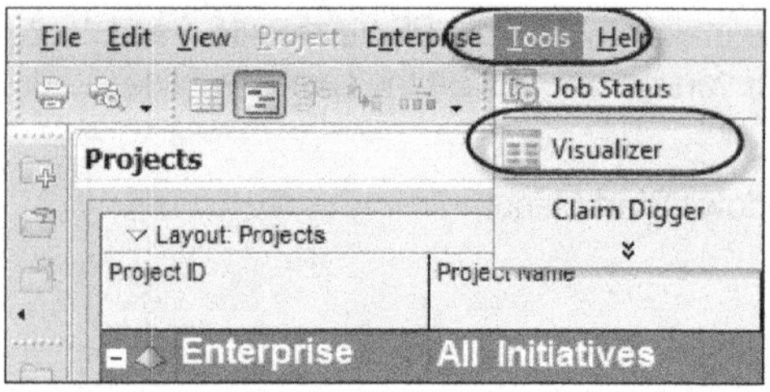

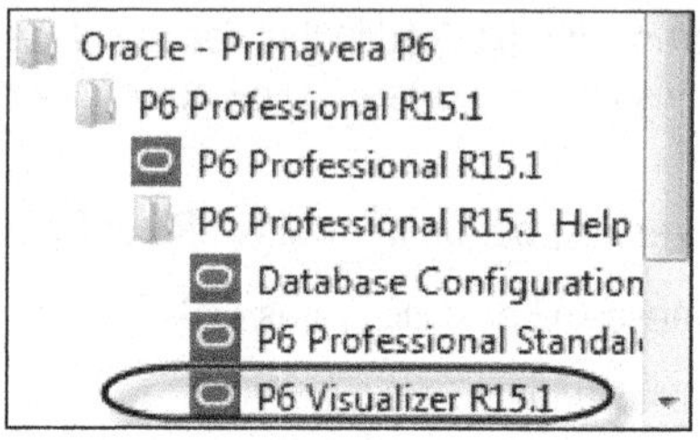

There are initially 4 or 5 buttons at the top of the screen and the additional printing button was available on earlier version of Visualizer:

-  - to create a New TSLD or New Gantt (chart)
-  - to open an Existing TSLD or Gantt (Chart)
-  - print, removed from later version of Visualizer
-  - to access Help, both local and Local or Online
- 

 - to Manage, and in later versions, import and export layouts.

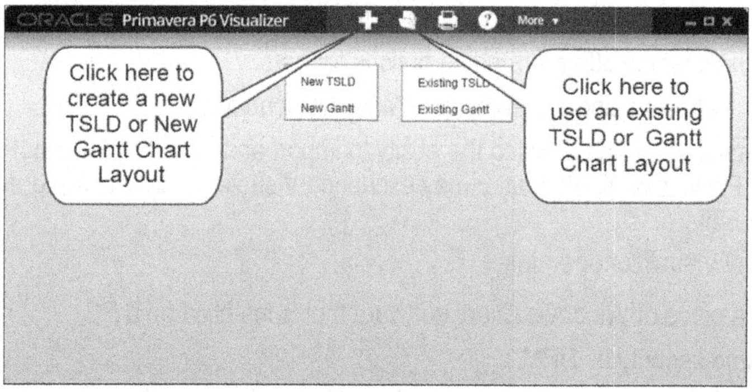

Version 8.4 introduced some new functions, including:

- Display **Shifts** as a **Date Interval**. This function is accessed from the **Timescale** tab **Date Interval** list.
- The ability to add a customized legend in headers and footers. This function is accessed from **Page Setup** tab, **Title Block** tab.
- Multiple Layouts may be selected and moved from one grouping to another in the **Manage Layouts** form.
- Bar Setting may now be copied from one layout to another. This function is accessed in the **Bars & Labels** tab, **Available Bars** section.

14.7.3 Create a New TSLD – Time Scaled Logic Diagram

To create a new TSLD select , **New TSLD**:

- You will then select which projects to report on, the picture below displays the options available to create a new TSLD:

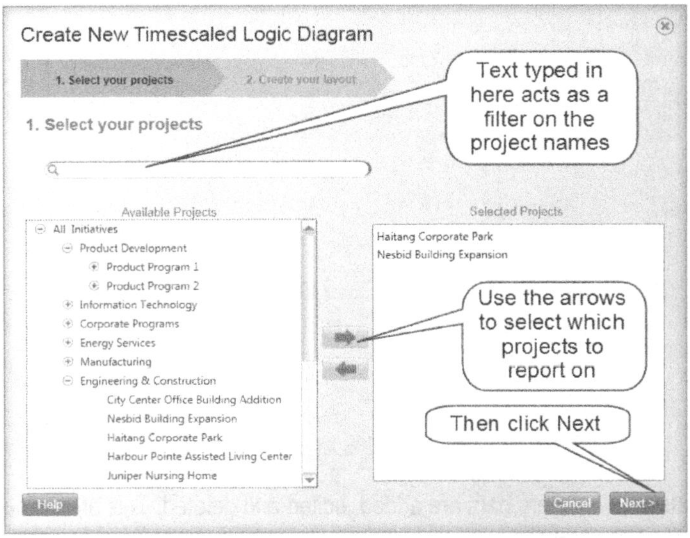

- Name the layout with an appropriate name,
- Use the radio buttons to either:
  - Select to copy an existing TSLD and select from the list below, or
  - To create a new TSLD,
- Select **Draw** to see the result or click **Options** to edit the layout:

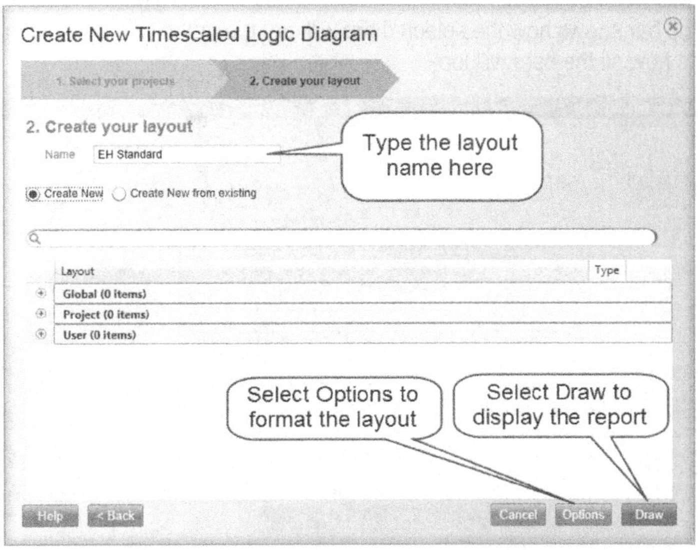

The **Options** form allows a large number of formatting options, which are similar to other P6 formatting functions, but graphically richer:

- **Timescale** is for formatting all aspects of the timescale, plus the gridlines on the body of the diagram:

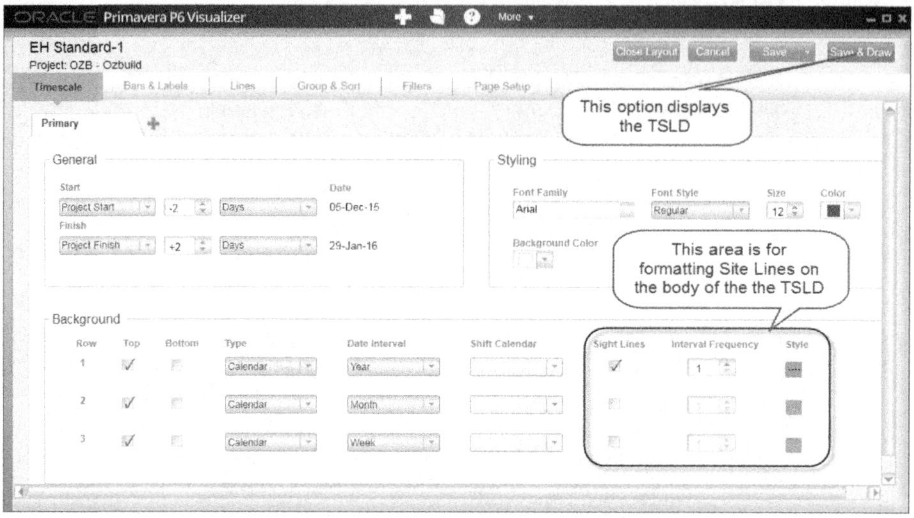

The **Bars & Labels** form is where bars are added, edited and deleted. This area is not intuitive so follow these instructions carefully:

- The **Available Bars** form is where bars are added, edited and deleted.
- You must name the bar with a name that makes sense, Visualizer does not name bars,
- The bar at the top of the list is drawn first and the second one in the list is drawn on top of the first, when it is on the same line,
- A bar selected under **Available Bars** is then formatted in the options on the right hand side,
- The middle top bar shows how the selected bar will be formatted and the bars in the middle bottom shows how all the bars will look:

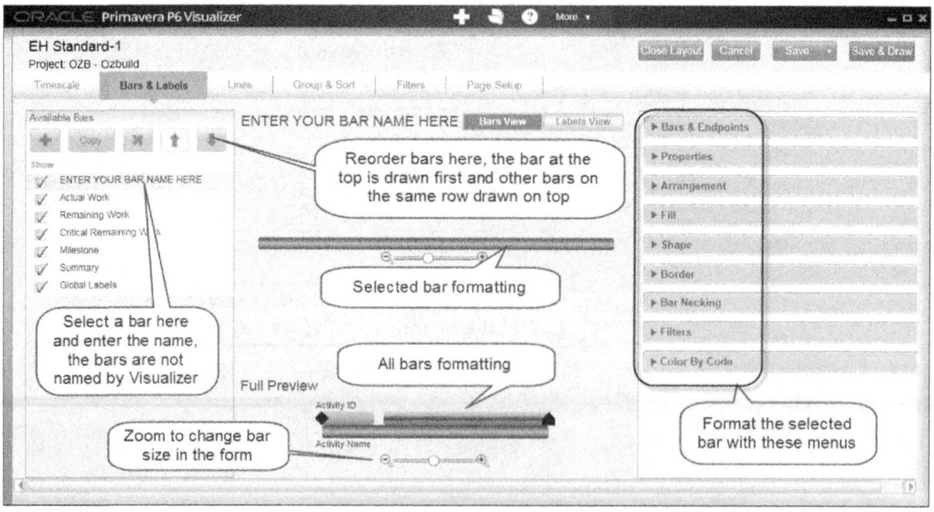

- **Lines** tab is where the Relationships, Data Date and Activity Group bands are formatted:
  - **Relationships** tab is where the relationships to be displayed are selected,
  - **Connections** tab is where Lead and Lag may be displayed,
  - **Data Date** allows formatting of the Data Date,
  - **Activity Group** allows the placing of a line around a group of bars that are associated with one activity:

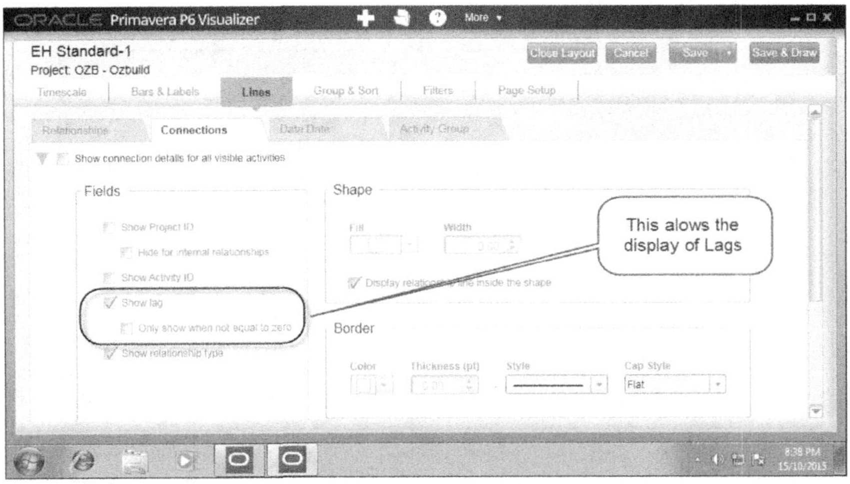

Group & Sort and **Filters Page Setup forms** work in the same way as other P6 products and will not be covered here, but still does not allow grouping on single resource when multiple resources are assigned to an activity.

Filters with the normal filtering functions,

Page Setup is a little different to other P6 products:

- To understand what is going on it is important to check **Show section borders**,
- **Sections** are effectively boxes that may be placed in the header or footer and project data may be typed in or read from the P6 database,
- Sections may be added deleted or adjusted in size,
- Headers and Footers are formatted the same way:

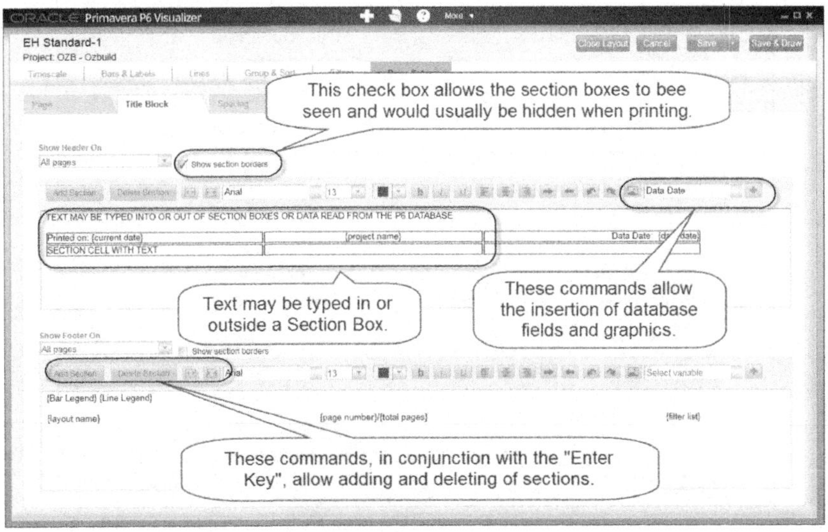

14.7.4 Create a New Gantt Diagram

Most of the options in the tabs are self-explanatory and the Gantt Diagram layout functions are similar to formatting in PPM and EPPM.

To create a new Gantt Chart select , **New Gantt**:

- You will then select which projects to report on, the picture below displays the options available to create a new Gantt Chart:

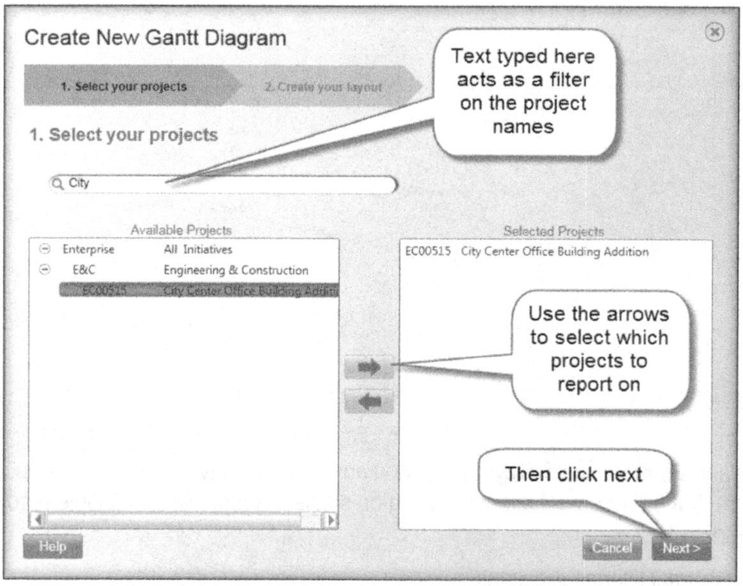

- Name the layout with an appropriate name,
- Use the radio buttons to either:
  - Select to copy an existing Gantt Diagram and select from the list below, or
  - To create a new Gantt Diagram,
  - The new Gantt Diagram is created as a User Layout.

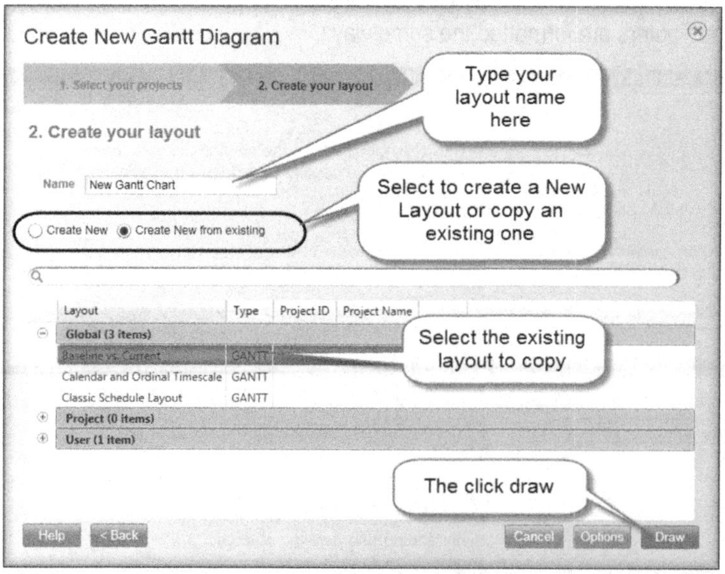

- Select **Draw** to see the result or click **Options** to edit the layout:

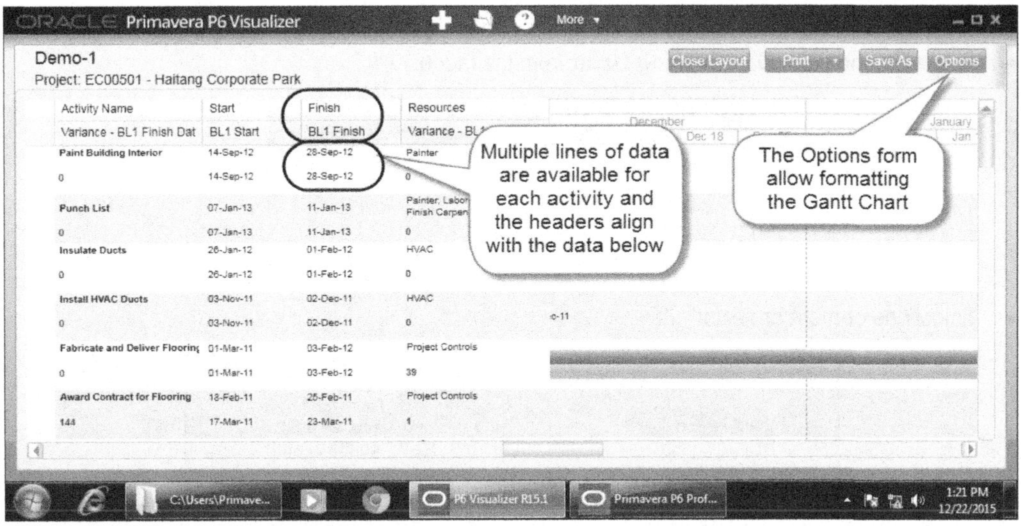

The **Options** form allows a large number of formatting options which are similar to other P6 formatting functions, but graphically richer:

- **Chart & Grid**
  - ➢ **Content** tab allows formatting of the columns and text.

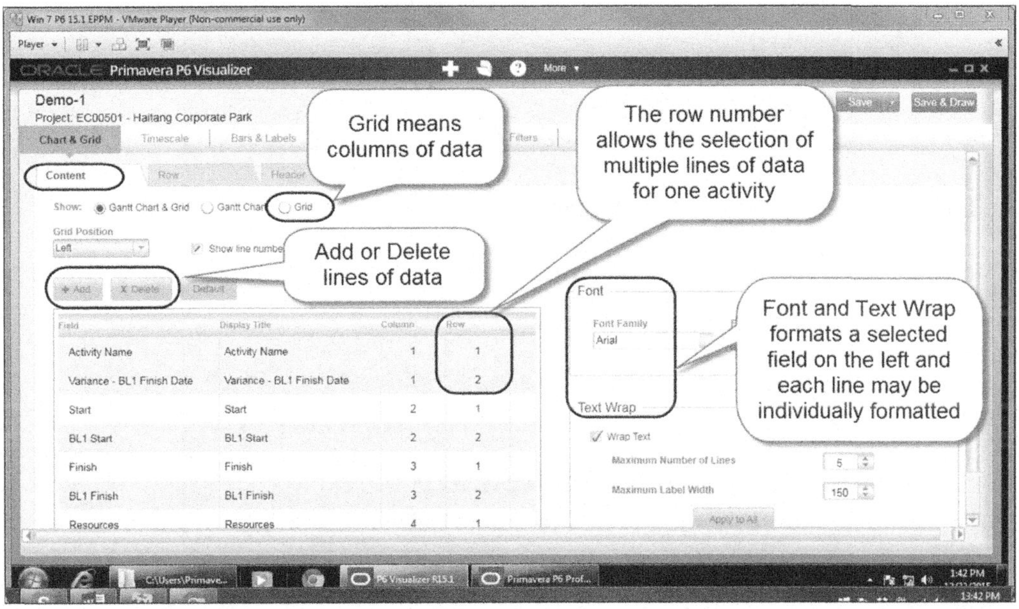

  - ➢ **Row** allows alternate coloring of rows,
  - ➢ **Header** is used to format the column headers.

Timescale, Bars & Labels Lines, Group & Sport ,**Filters**, and **Page Setup** all work in the same way as the TSLD and will not be covered a second time.

14.7.5 Open an Existing TSLD or Gantt Chart

To open an existing TSLD or Gant Chart is very similar to creating a new one:

- Select **Existing TSLD** or **Existing Gantt** from the menu:

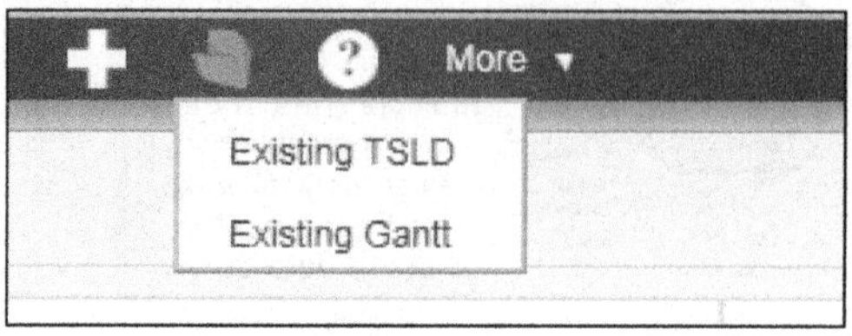

- Select one or more projects:

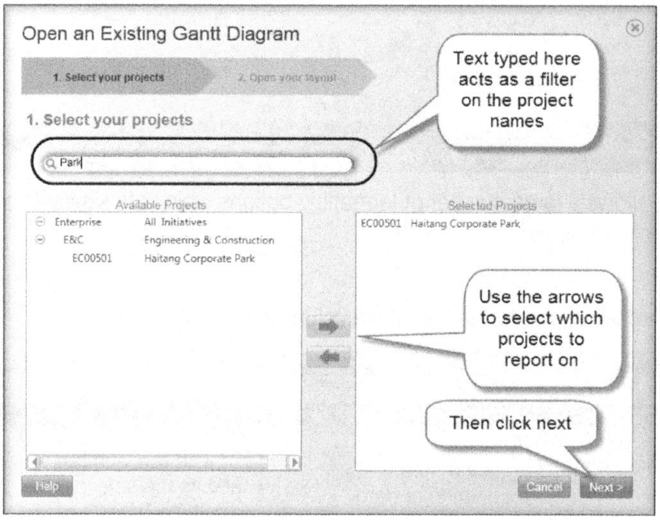

- Select an existing layout and click on draw:

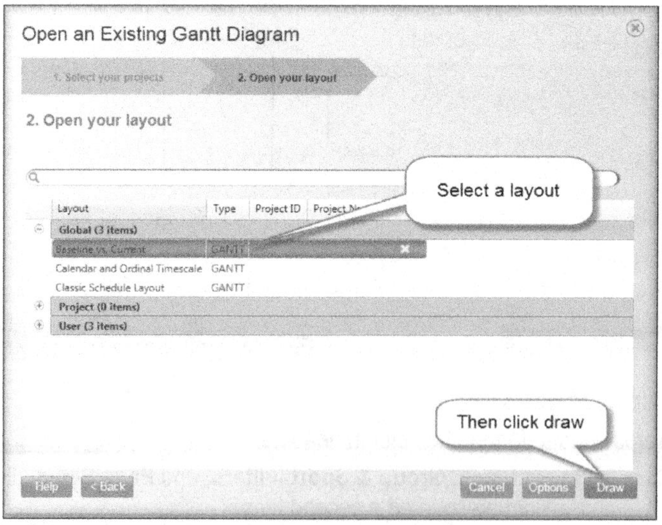

Use the **Options** to edit the layout and **Print** to print the report.

14.7.6 Manage Layouts

The **More** menu has options for managing Layouts:

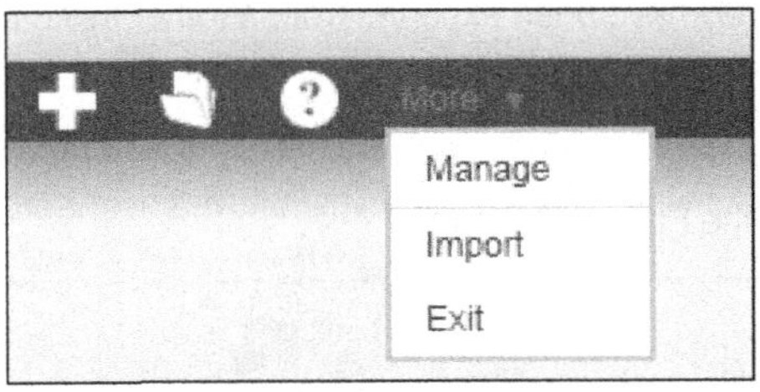

A New Gantt Chart or TSLD is created as a User Layout.

The **Manage** option allows a user to make any existing Layout a Project or Global layout:

- **Filter** allows the selection of **Gantt Chart** or **TSLD** layouts,
- Layouts may be copied and pasted to and from Global, Project and User.
- **Renaming** a layout is achieved by clicking on a Layout name and this will allow editing of the name:

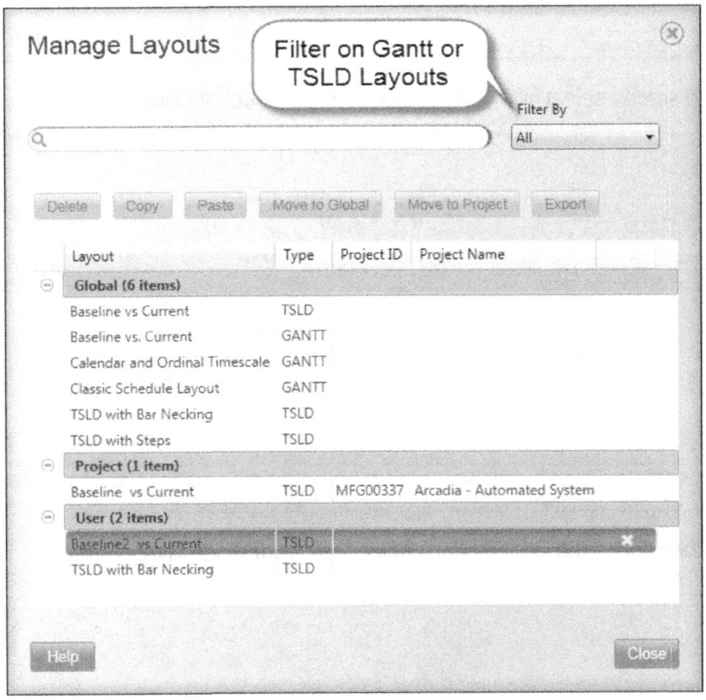

- **Exporting** a Visualizer Layout in VLF format is achieved by:
  - Selecting the layout,
  - Clicking the Export button,
  - Selecting a destination directory.

The **Import** function allows the import of:

- An existing Professional View that has been exported from the Professional client as a *.PLF or
- A Visualizer report that may have been exported from another system.

To import a layout:

- Select **More**, **Import**,
- In the first screen select the PLF or VLF file:

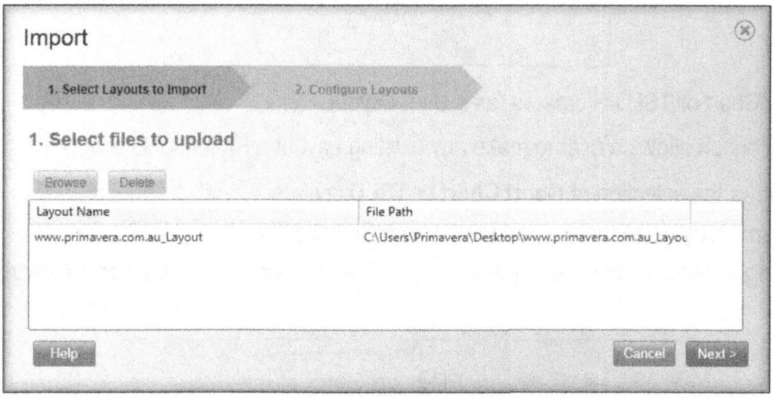

- In the second screen select from the options Global, Project or User.

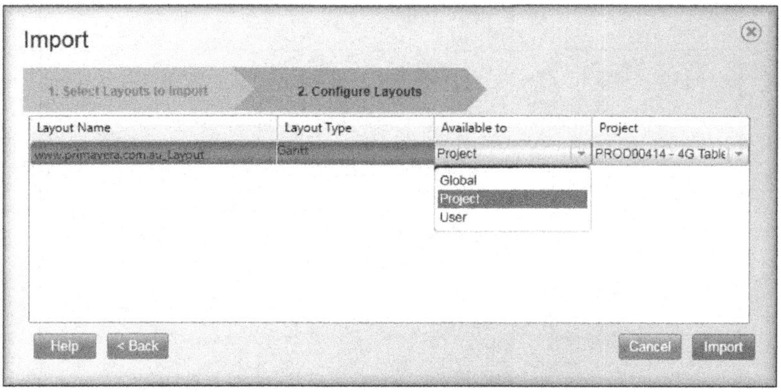

- You should then check the Options to optimize the layout in Visualizer.

14.8 Workshop 12 – Printing

Background

We want to issue a report for comment by management.

Assignment

Open your **OzBuild Bid** project from the previous workshop and complete the following steps:

1. Remove any filter.
2. Apply the **OzBuild Workshop 10 – With Float** layout.
3. Select **File**, **Print Preview** and click the icon on the **Print toolbar** to open the **Page Setup** form.
4. In the **Page** tab select:
   - **Orientation** – Landscape
   - **Adjust to** – 100%
   - **Fit to** – 0 page(s) wide by 0 pages tall
   - **Fit timescale to:** – 1 page wide
   - **Paper size:** – A4 or Letter
5. In the **Margins** tab set all the settings to 0.5", except for the **Top:** settings which should to be set to 0.75" to allow space for binding.
6. In the **Header** tab:
   - Divide Into: 3 Sections
   - Include on: All Pages, so this will repeat on every page
   - Height: 0.5
   - Section 1, insert as Text/Logo – **Printed on: [date] [time]** – Arial Regular 8 to the left
   - Section 2, insert as Text/Logo – **[project_name]** – Arial Bold 12 in the middle
   - Section 3, insert as Text/Logo – **Page [page_number] of [total_pages]** – Arial Regular 8, aligned to the right
7. In the **Footer** tab:
   - Divide Into: 3 Sections
   - Include on: First Page, so this will only be printed on the first page
   - Height: 1.25
   - Section 1 – Gantt Chart Legend
   - Section 2 – Picture – Find a suitable picture to put in
   - Section 3 – Revision Box
   - Adjust widths as required.

continued…

8. In the **Options** tab:
   - Set the Timescale Start: from the Project Start minus 5 days and Timescale Finish: to the Project Finish plus 5 days,
   - Show the Activity Table, All Columns, Grid Lines and Gantt Chart.
9. Apply the Layout and click OK
10. Compare your result with the picture below:

Answer to Workshop 12

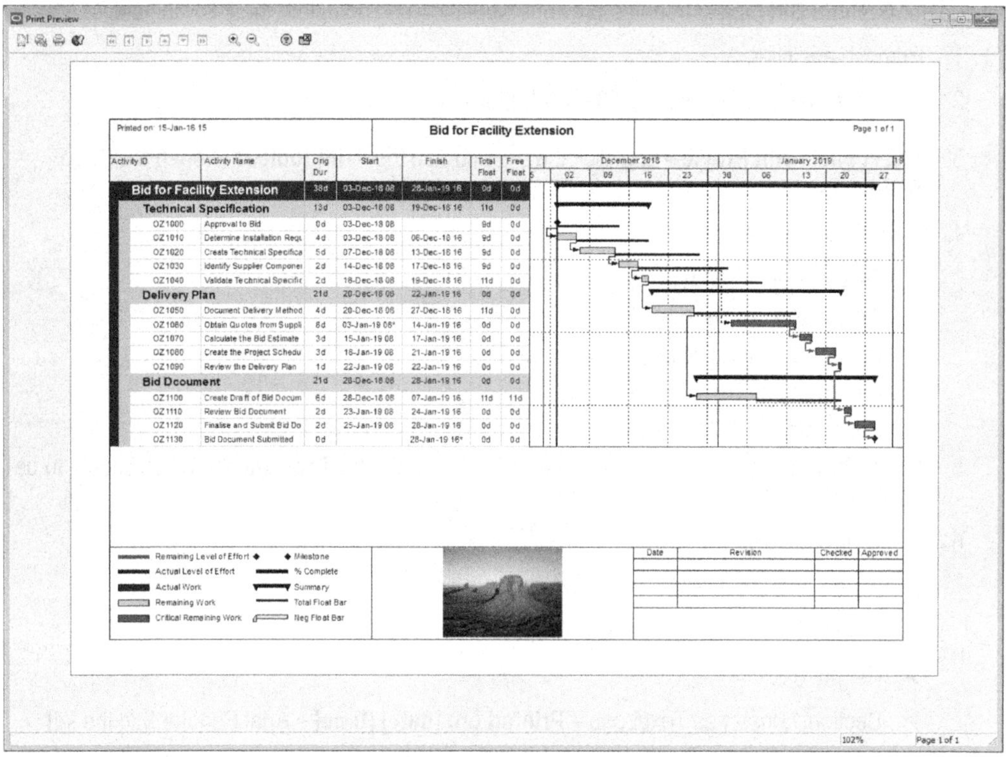

15 SCHEDULING OPTIONS AND SETTING A BASELINE

Tracking Progress is used after you have completed the plan, or have completed sufficient iterations to reach an acceptable plan, and the project may be progressing. Now the important phase of regular monitoring and control begins. This process is important to help catch problems as early as possible, and thus minimize their impact on the successful completion of the project. The main steps for monitoring progress are:

- Saving a **Baseline** schedule, also known as a **Target**. This schedule holds the dates against which progress is compared. The current project may be copied and used as a baseline or an existing project may be assigned as a baseline.
- Recording or marking-up progress as of a specific date, titled the **Data Date**. This date is also known as the **Status Date**, **Update Date**, **Current Date**, **Report Date**, and **As-Of-Date**.
- **Updating** or **Progressing** the schedule.
- Scheduling the project and at the same time moving the **Data Date** to the new **Data Date** and recalculating all the activities dates.
- Comparing and Reporting actual progress against planned progress and revising the plan and schedule, if required.

Comparing the status of an activity against more than one baseline is useful; for example:

- The original plan could be represented as one of the Baselines, to see the slippage against the original plan.
- Last Period, which could be another Baseline, to see the changes since the last update.

Primavera has the following functions:

- Primavera allows an unlimited number of baseline project files to be saved with a project.
- A baseline project may not be opened and viewed. It must be restored to the database to open and edit where it will no longer be a baseline.
- Up to four Baselines may be shown against a current schedule at one time either as bars on the Gantt Chart or in columns of data.
- Baseline comparison is displayed at Activity level in the **Activities Window**, not at resource level. Resource level comparison is available in resource views such as the **Resource Assignments Window**.

Shortcuts:

Topic	Menu Command
• Saving and Deleting and Setting a **Baseline**	To save a Baseline, select **Project**, **Maintain Baselines...** to display the **Maintain Baselines** form
• Setting a Baseline project	The baselines are assigned from the **Project**, **Assign Baselines...** form
• Update a Baseline	• Select **Project**, **Maintain Baselines**...and select the  icon to open the **Update Baseline** form.

15.1 Understanding Date Fields

Primavera has many more date fields for the current schedule than P3, SureTrak or Microsoft Project. This section explains how these date fields calculate.

There is very little documentation available on how these dates are calculated and the author has ascertained the information contained in this chapter by trial using an unresourced schedule.

After you understand these date fields, you should look again at the **Bar Timescale** options in the **Bars** form and it will be easier for you to understand how the bar formatting works.

15.1.1 Early Start and Early Finish

These are always the earliest dates that un-started activities or the incomplete portions of in-progress activities may start or finish based on calendars, relationships and constraints.

- The **Early Start** of the completed activity A1010 is set to the **Data Date** date and time after the activity has commenced, not to the **Actual Start**, as in most other software,
- The **Early Finish** of the completed activity A1010 is set to the **Data Date** date and time when the activity is complete, not to the **Actual Finish**, as in most other software,
- The **Early Start** of an in-progress activity is set to the **Activity Calendar** start after the activity has commenced, not to the **Actual Start**, as in most other software.

NOTE: Look carefully at the activity A1010 Early Start and Early Finish dates and then look at the Actual Start and Finish of the bar; they are very different:

Activity ID	Activity Name	Early Start	Early Finish
A1010	Activity A	12-Oct-14 00	12-Oct-14 00
A1020	Activity B	13-Oct-14 08	24-Oct-14 17
A1030	Activity C	27-Oct-14 08	21-Nov-14 17

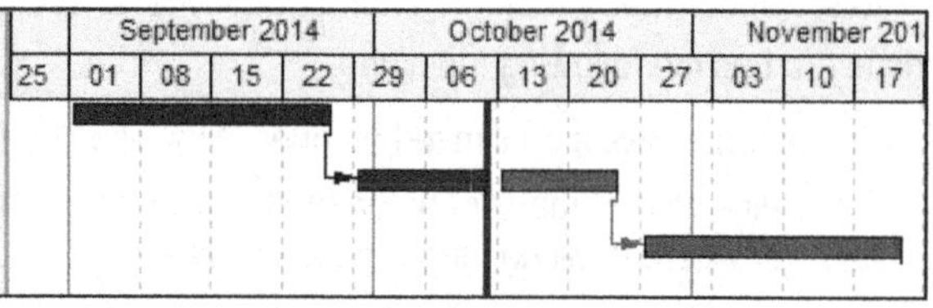

Thus the Early Start and Early Finish dates of completed activities and Early Start of in-progress activities is not displayed in other software in this way and often leads to confusion when converting from other software.

This is the reason why the **Early Bar** is not displayed by default in the Gantt Chart, as the **Early Bar** will not display Actual progress in the same way as other software.

15.1.2 Late Start and Late Finish

- These are the latest dates that **Un-started** activities or the incomplete portions of **In-progress** activities may start or finish based on calendars, relationships, and constraints.
- The **Complete** activity has the Late Dates set the date that is equivalent to the latest point in time that the activity could be restarted.
- The Total Float on the Complete Activity is "Null" but the default Layout shows a Float Bar.

NOTE: The end of the Total Float bar is the same date and time as the Late Finish and used to calculate Total Float.

Activity ID	Activity Name	Late Start	Late Finish	Total Float
A1010	Activity A	20-Oct-14 08	20-Oct-14 08	
A1020	Activity B	20-Oct-14 08	31-Oct-14 17	5d
A1030	Activity C	03-Nov-14 08	28-Nov-14 17	5d

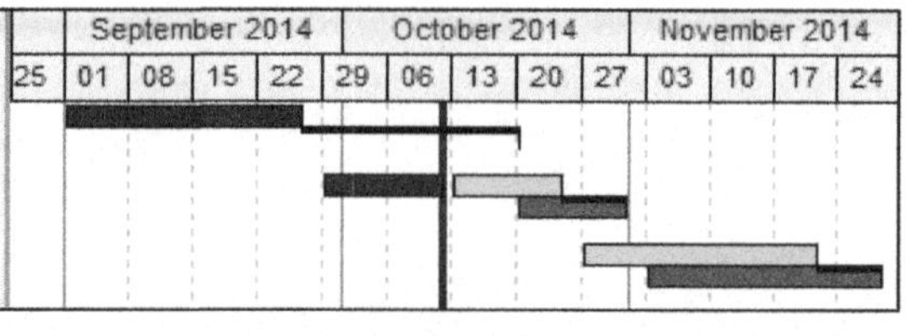

15.1.3 Actual Start and Finish

These dates are manually applied, representing when an activity started or finished, and override constraints and relationships. These dates should be set in the past in relation to the **Data Date**.

Activity ID	Activity Name	Actual Start	Actual Finish
A1010	Activity A	01-Sep-14 08	26-Sep-14 17
A1020	Activity B	29-Sep-14 08	
A1030	Activity C		

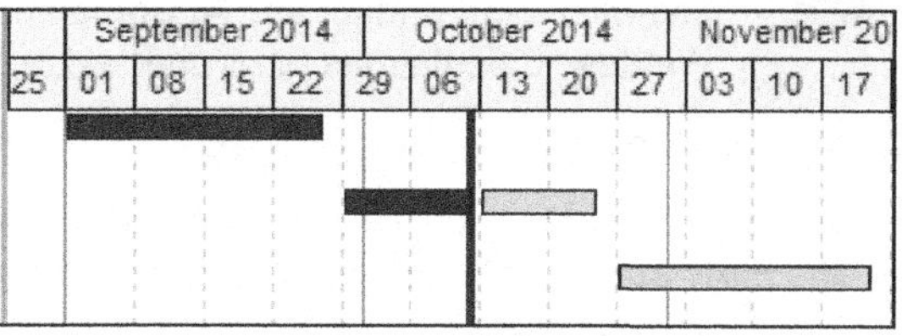

Actual dates should never change after they are assigned but both the **Apply Actuals** when activities are set to **Auto Compute Actuals**, and **Update Progress** functions may change Actual Dates. These functions must be used with extreme caution.

15.1.4 Start and Finish

The **Start** is set to the **Early Start** when the activity has not started and the **Actual Start** when it has started.

The **Finish** is set to the **Early Finish** when the activity has not started or is in-progress and the **Actual Finish** when it is complete.

- An "A" is placed after the date when an **Actual Start** or **Actual Finish** has been set,
- An "*" is placed after the date when a start constraint has been applied to the activity,
- These date fields allow the Early and Actual Start and Finish dates to be displayed as expected when the activity has not started, is in-progress, or complete:

Activity ID	Activity Name	Start	Finish
A1010	Activity A	01-Sep-14 08 A	26-Sep-14 17 A
A1020	Activity B	29-Sep-14 08 A	24-Oct-14 17
A1030	Activity C	27-Oct-14 08	21-Nov-14 17

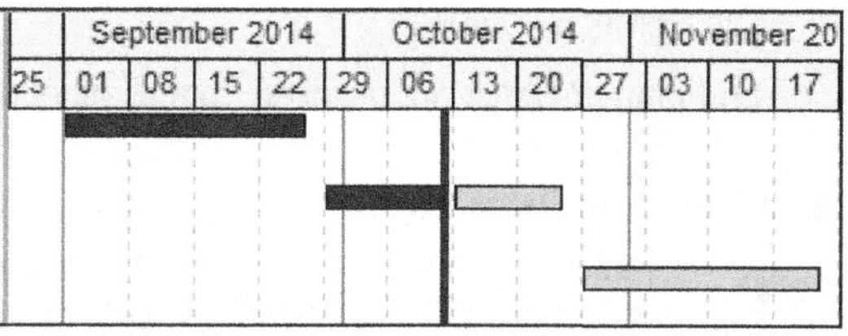

Users converting from P3 and SureTrak will be used to displaying the Early Start and Early Finish dates, but the Early Start and Early Finish dates should not be displayed when a schedule has progress, as this will give misleading information. The Start and Finish dates should always be displayed under normal scheduling conditions.

15.1.5 Planned Dates

The **Planned Finish** is calculated from the **Planned Start** plus the **Original Duration**. The **Original Duration** is labeled **Planned Duration** in some Industry Versions. These fields are always linked, therefore:

- A change to the **Planned Start** will change the **Planned Finish** via the **Original Duration**,
- A change to the **Planned Finish** will change permanently the **Original Duration,** and
- A change to the **Original Duration** will change the **Planned Finish**.

When an activity has **NOT** started:

- The **Planned** dates **ARE** normally linked to the **Start** and **Finish** when an activity has not started.

The **Original** and **At Completion** durations are **ONLY** linked when an activity has not started and when **Link Budget and At Completion for not started activities** box in the **Projects Window**, **Calculations** tab is checked.

- They are **NOT** linked to the Early Dates.
- A **Planned Start** may be manually edited and as the **Start** date is linked it is also changed, but the **Early Start** is **NOT** changed. The **Planned Start** and **Start** are reset to the Early Dates when a project is scheduled.
- The **Planned Finish** may be edited and is linked to the **Finish** date and the **Original Duration**. A change to the **Planned Finish** will change the **Finish** date and **Original Duration**. Rescheduling will recalculate the schedule using the new **Original Duration** and set the **Planned Finish**, **Finish**, and **Early Finish** to the same date.
- Thus a change to the **Planned Start** is reversed by rescheduling, but a change to the **Planned Finish** affects the **Original Duration** and is not reversed by rescheduling.

When an activity is in-progress:

- The **Planned Start** date remains unchanged when an **Actual Start** date is set which is different from the **Planned Start**. Therefore the **Planned Start** remains the same as the **Start Date** before the **Actual Start** was set.
- The **Planned Finish** is calculated from the **Planned Start Date** plus the **Original Duration**.
- After an activity has commenced, the **Remaining Duration** may be edited independently from the **Original Duration**. The **Planned Finish** may have a different date from the **Finish**, which is now set to equal the **Early Finish**.

When an activity is complete:

- The **Planned Dates** are unlinked from all other date fields.

15.1.6 Planned Dates Issues

This is one of the most important paragraphs in this book and you must be certain that you understand the Planned dates and how to avoid the issues associated with them.

The Planned Dates are very complex to explain and understand, so please read carefully. To summarize the statements above:

- When an activity has **Not Started** the Planned Dates match the Early Start and Early Finish.
- When an activity is **Complete** or **In-progress** the Planned Dates match the status of the activity immediately before it was marked as Started.

In the situation where a schedule is in the process of being updated:

- Assume the Data Date has been moved to the new Data Date and the project scheduled,
- Now all un-started activities will have their Start and Finish dates in the future,
- At this point every activity that is marked In-progress by assigning an Actual Start (which should be in the past in relation to the **Data Date**) will have **Planned Dates** that neither:
  - Match the status of the activity before the activity was marked as Started, nor
  - Match the status of the activity after the activity was marked as Started and possibly finished.

Thus in this situation and at this point in time the Planned Dates are now holding irrelevant dates that should never be displayed or used for any purpose.

Unfortunately the Planned Dates are used by default in several places and Database Administrators and Users must be aware of where they are used and how to avoid displaying them.

- The Planned dates are displayed as the **Project Baseline** bars and **Primary User Baseline** bars when no baseline has been assigned,

  Never display a Baseline Bar or columns unless a baseline project has been created and assigned, otherwise the Baseline bar and columns may represent irrelevant data.

- These Planned dates are used by the **Apply Actuals** function, when activities are set to **Auto Compute Actuals**, and the **Update Progress** function. Thus **Actual Start** dates and **Early Finish** dates of in-progress activities will be changed to the Planned Date values without warning.

  Ensure you never ever use the **Update Progress** function on a schedule that has been progressed, otherwise **Actual Start** dates and **Early Finish** dates of in-progress activities will be changed to the Planned Date values without warning.

- The **Planned Dates** from a Baseline schedule will be displayed as the Baseline Bars when the **Admin**, **Admin Preferences...**, **Earned Value** tab is set to **Budget values with planned dates**. Thus the Baseline Bars from an in-progress schedule will be incorrect.

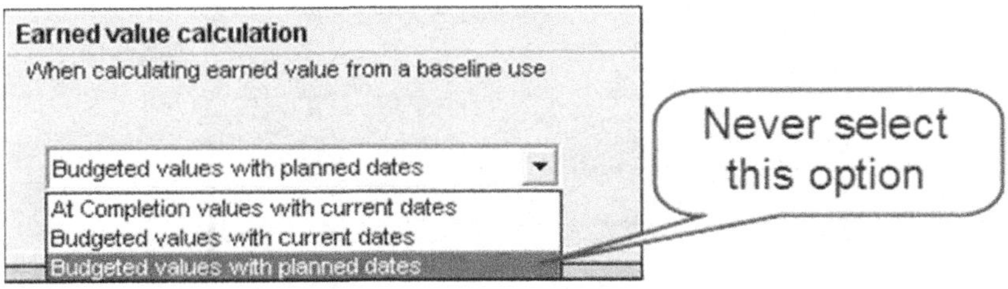

Ensure **Admin**, **Admin Preferences...**, **Earned Value** tab has this value set as **At Completion values with current dates** or **Budget Values with current dates**. When the schedule is not resource- or cost-loaded it does not matter which of these two you use. More details on these settings in paragraph 17.3.6.

15.1.7 Remaining Early Start and Finish

These are the earliest dates that the incomplete portions of un-started or in-progress activities may start and finish.

- They are blank when an activity is complete.
- They may be edited in the same way as Planned Dates.
  - When a **Remaining Early Start** is edited to a later than scheduled date, there is an option for constraining the **Remaining Early Start** with a **Start on or After Constraint**. If this is not set then the activity will move forward to its original position when scheduling.
  - When a **Remaining Early Finish** is edited, the **Remaining Duration** is also edited and the change is permanent. Scheduling does not take the schedule back to the original position.

Activity ID	Activity Name	Remaining Early Start	Remaining Early Finish
A1010	Activity A		
A1020	Activity B	13-Oct-14 08	31-Oct-14 17
A1030	Activity C	03-Nov-14 08	28-Nov-14 17

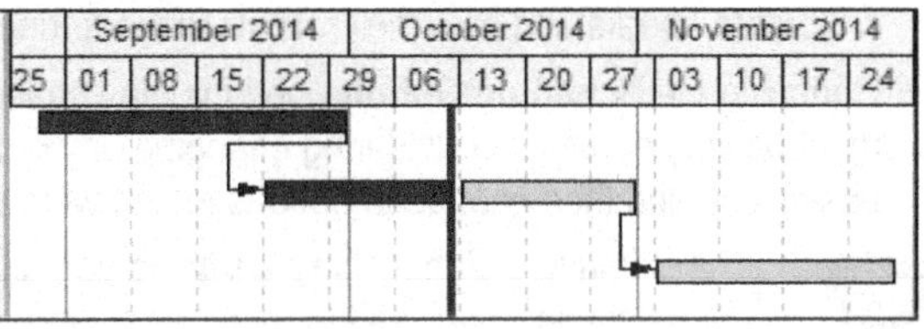

15.1.8 Remaining Late Start and Finish

These are the latest dates that the incomplete portions of activities may start and finish.

- They are blank when an activity is complete and may not be edited,
- They may not be displayed as a bar,
- They are set to equal the **Late Dates**.

Activity ID	Activity Name	Remaining Late Start	Remaining Late Finish
A1000	Activity A		
A1010	Activity B	13-Oct-14 08	07-Nov-14 17
A1020	Activity C	10-Nov-14 08	05-Dec-14 17

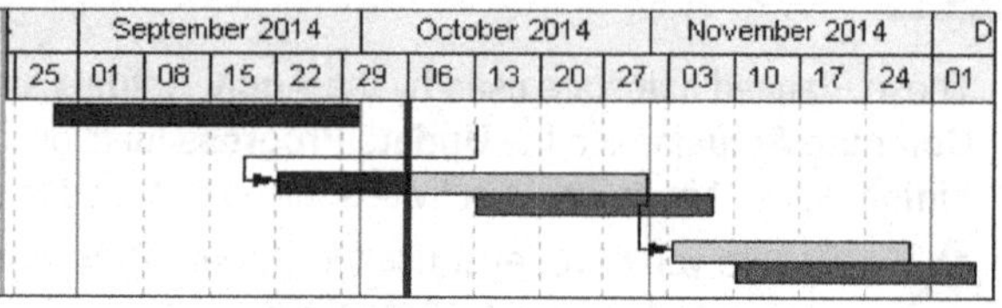

15.2 *Scheduling Options – General Tab*

When a project is rescheduled there are some options available in the **Schedule Options** form which is opened by selecting **Tools**, **Schedule...**, **Options**:

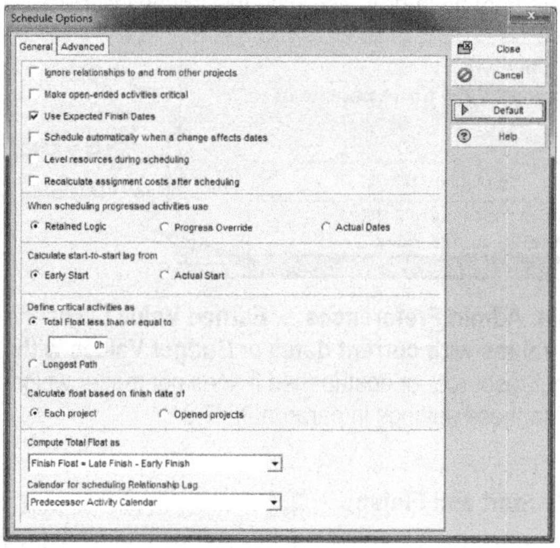

- Pressing the **Default** button will set the options back to the P6 defaults, not save yours as the default as in Microsoft Project.
- The default options are good defaults but some need to be changed to suit specific situations.
- These options apply to all activities in the currently opened schedule.
- When more than one schedule has been opened then you should read carefully the **Multiple Project Scheduling** chapter to understand how the **Default Project** function operates.
- If you export a schedule to another database it is prudent to send a copy of the current options so they may be checked when imported into another databbase, especially if the schedule is to be opened with other projects. Again, you should read carefully the **Multiple Project Scheduling** chapter to understand how the **Default Project** function operates.
- Changing the **Schedule Options** options may change the way the schedule calculates and users must be very careful if considering changing any of them. You may wish to copy the schedule, baseline it, and then change to options to see what the effect is on the schedule calculation.

The Primavera **Scheduling Options** defaults are good and it is suggested that they should not be changed unless the user has good reason to change them.

15.2.1 Ignore relationships to and from other projects

Check this in the **Tools**, **Schedule...**, **Options** form to ignore relationships with other projects that are currently not open.

These relationships may be created between two projects when:

- Two or more projects are opened together, or
- When assigning a relationship another project is opened and a relationship is created to an activity in another project.

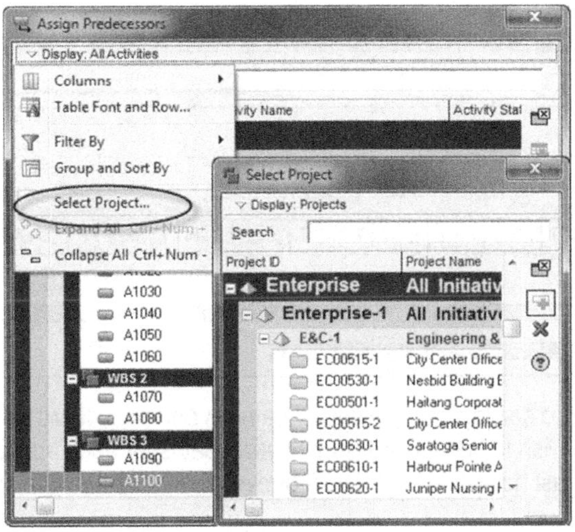

This option will also ignore **External Dates**, which are the **External Early Start** and **External Late Finish** dates.

External Dates are constraints created when a project is exported from Primavera Contractor and/or another P6 database and imported into P6. They act like Early Start and Late Finish Constraints and are used to represent the relationships that would have originally provided the Early Start and Late Finish dates to the Critical Path calculations of the imported schedule.

These dates can be very confusing if one is not aware that they have been created or how they operate. The negative float in the picture below is created by these dates after an activity's duration was increased by 34 days:

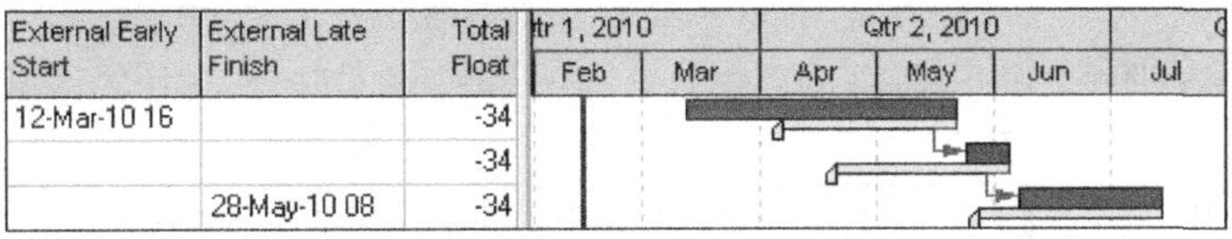

When you import a project from another database ensure you **ALWAYS** check for External Dates and understand how they operate.

If you export and then import back into the same database then External dates are not normally created but the relationships are re-established with the original schedule they were linked with.

On the other hand, if the original schedules have been deleted then these External Dates may be created.

15.2.2 Make open-ended activities critical

An open-ended activity is an activity without a successor and which has float to the end of the project. Checking the box makes these activities critical with zero total float when they do not have a successor.

- Open-ends Not Critical:

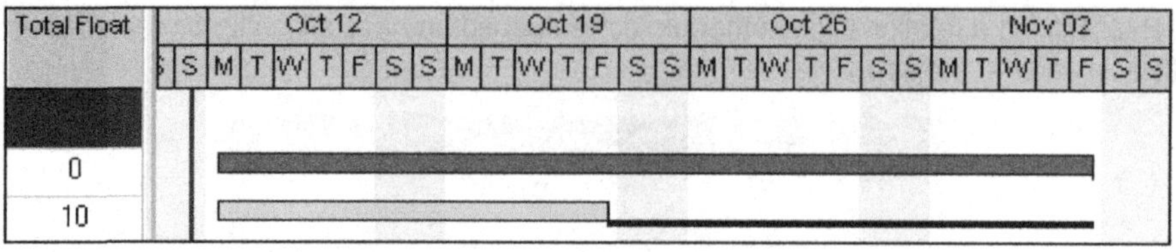

- Open-ends Critical:

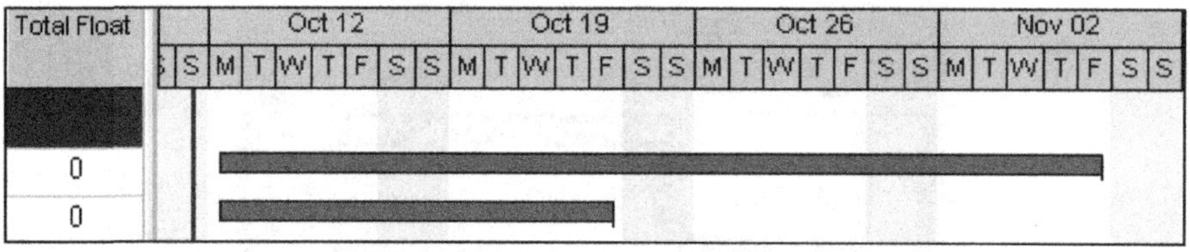

This also allows the user to display multiple critical paths in one project without the use of constraints and is useful should you wish to see the individual critical paths for each area of a project. In order for this function to work the last activity in each chain or events must not have a successor:

- Open-ends Not Critical:

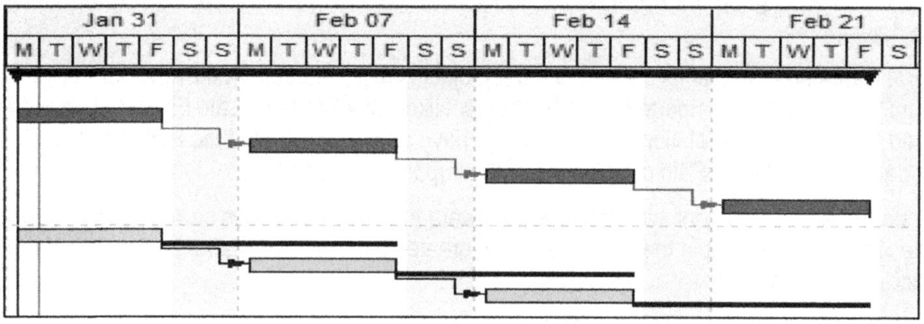

- Open-ends Critical:

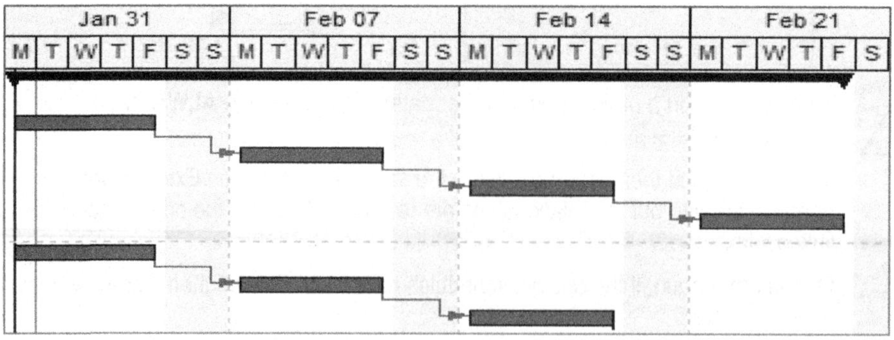

15.2.3 Use Expected Finish Dates

The intention of this option is for people using timesheets to be able to set an Expected Finish constraint for an activity.

Once an Expected Finish date is set then the software calculates the Remaining Duration from:

- The Early Start when an activity has not started, or
- The Data Date when an activity has started, or
- A Resume date if a Suspend and resume date has been set.

Therefore Expected finish dates may be assigned from the Timesheets module and this option allows the project manager to ignore these dates submitted with the timesheets.

This is always checked by default and will disable or enable Expected Finish constraints assigned in the **Status** tab of the **Activities Details** tab or from a column.

This is usually not turned off and the pictures below show the effect of this constraint before and after scheduling an activity with an Expected Finish Constraint assigned:

- Before scheduling:

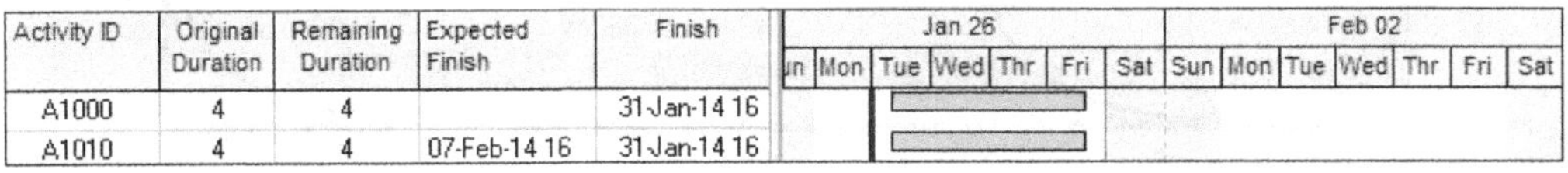

- After scheduling:

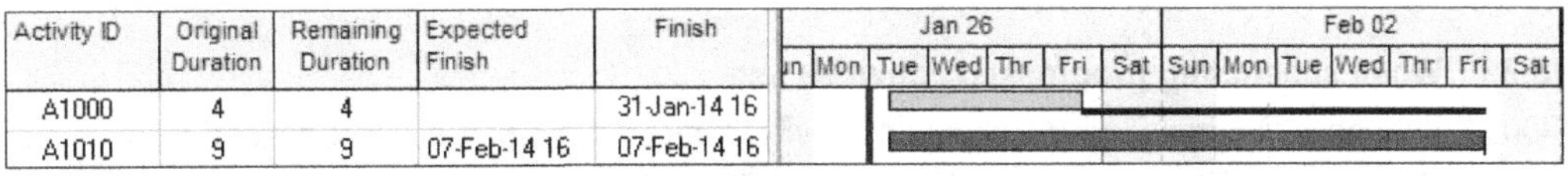

15.2.4 Schedule automatically when a change affects dates

This is similar to automatic recalculation in other products and this recalculates the schedule when data that affects the timing of the schedule is changed.

P6 is a database product and Schedule Automatically will result in the schedule recalculating every time you make a change. This may slow down your work significantly; this option is usually left off.

15.2.5 Level resources during scheduling

Leveling a schedule delays activities until resources become available. This is a form of resource optimization and this option levels the project resources each time it is scheduled. Resource leveling is covered in paragraph 20.6.

This is **NOT** recommended as it slows down the schedule calculation and the schedule often changes each time it is scheduled.

15.2.6 Recalculate resource costs after scheduling

Resource Unit Rates may be set to change over time in the **Units & Prices** tab of the **Resources Window**:

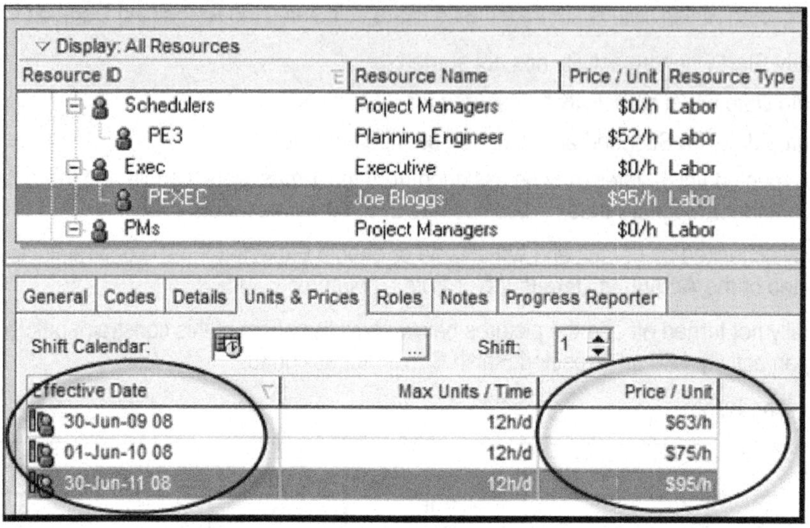

This option recalculates a resource cost when a resource is scheduled into a different cost rates time bracket.

15.2.7 When scheduling progressed activities use

"Out of Sequence Progress" occurs when an activity starts before a predecessor defined by a relationship has finished. Therefore the relationships have not been acknowledged and the successor activity has started out of sequence. There are three options in P6 for calculating the finish date of a successor when the successor activity has started before the predecessor activity is finished:

- Retained Logic
- Progress Override
- Actual Dates

The selected option is applied to all activities in a schedule when it is calculated. Open the **Schedule Options** form by selecting **Tools**, **Schedule...** and clicking on the 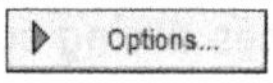

icon where the options are found under **When scheduling progressed activities use**:

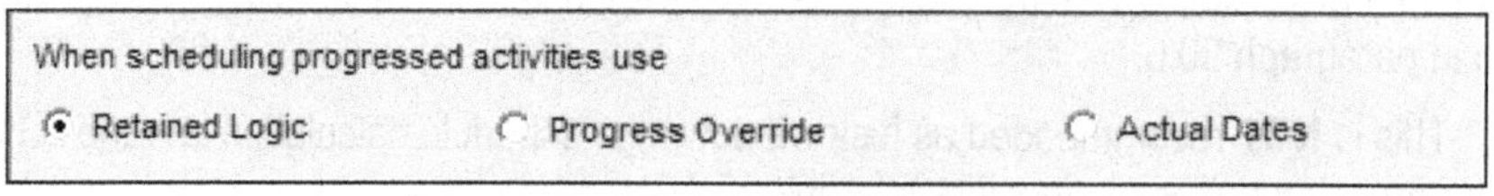

The picture below represents the status of the activities before updating the schedule:

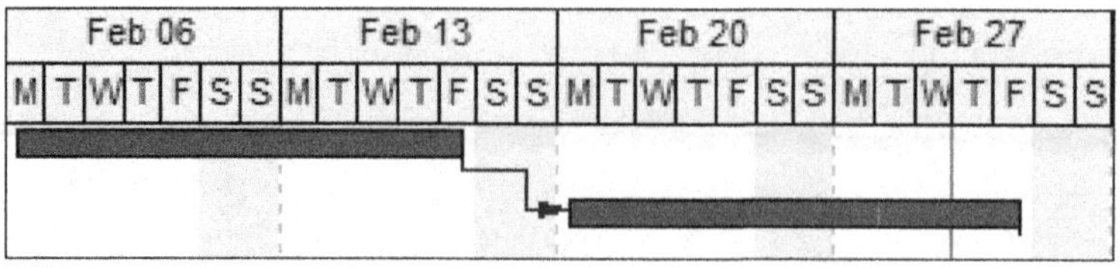

- **Retained Logic.**
  In the example following, the relationship is maintained between the predecessor and successor for the unworked portion of the activity (the Remaining Duration) and continued after the predecessor has finished. The relationship forms part of the critical path and the predecessor has no float.
  NOTE: This is the recommended option:

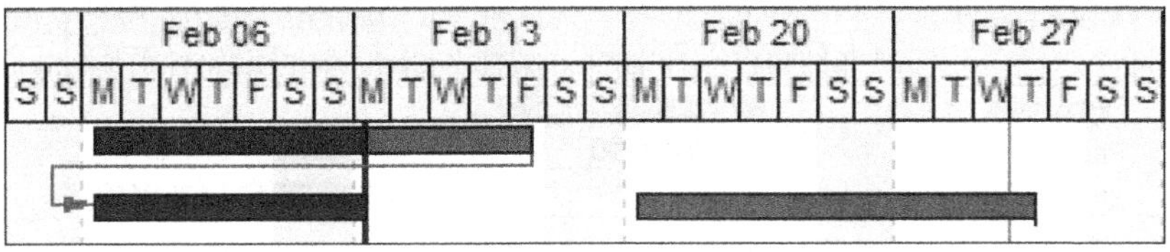

- **Progress Override.**
  In the example following, the Finish-to-Start relationship between the predecessor and successor is disregarded, and the unworked portion of the activity (the Remaining Duration) continues before the predecessor has finished.
  NOTE: The relationship is not a driving relationship and DOES NOT form part of the critical path in the example below and the predecessor has float:

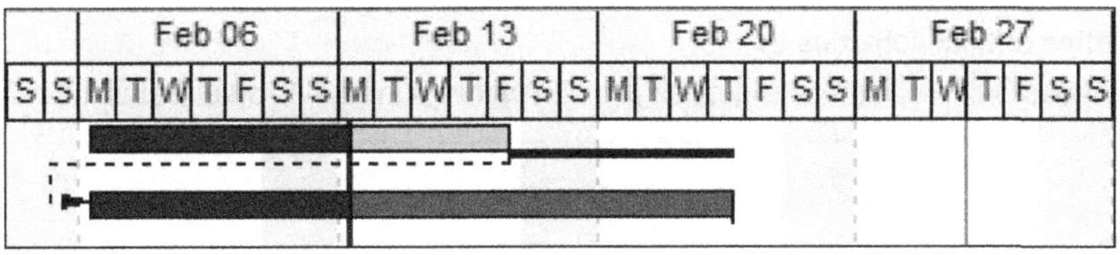

- **Actual Dates.**
  This function operates when there is an activity with Actual Start Dates in the future, which is not logical. With this option the remaining duration of an in-progress activity is calculated after the activity with actual start and finish in the future:

When there are no Actual Dates in the future this option calculates as Retained Logic.

This situation with Actuals in the future may happen when two projects open together and have different Data Dates. This situation is best avoided and it is best to make the Data Dates of all projects the same.

Retained Logic and Progress Override are not terms used by Microsoft Project but are used in P3 and SureTrak and operate in the same way in Primavera. Retained Logic produces a more conservative schedule (a longer duration schedule) and is more likely to place an out-of-progress relationship on the critical path and adjustments may be made as required.

If your schedule has Actual dates in the future of the Data Date (which may occur when the update information is collected at different times and the earlier date is used as the Data Date or multiple projects are open) then the use of Actual Dates would calculate the most conservative schedule.

15.2.8 Calculate start-to-start lag from

The successor of an activity with a Start-to-Start and positive lag would start after the lag has expired. When the predecessor commences out of sequence the lag may be calculated from the predecessor calculated Early Start or the Actual Start.

- The Actual Start gives a less conservative schedule:

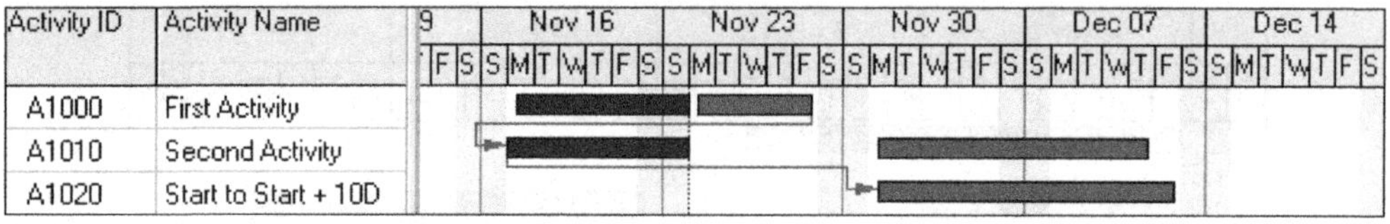

- The Early Start gives a more conservative schedule:

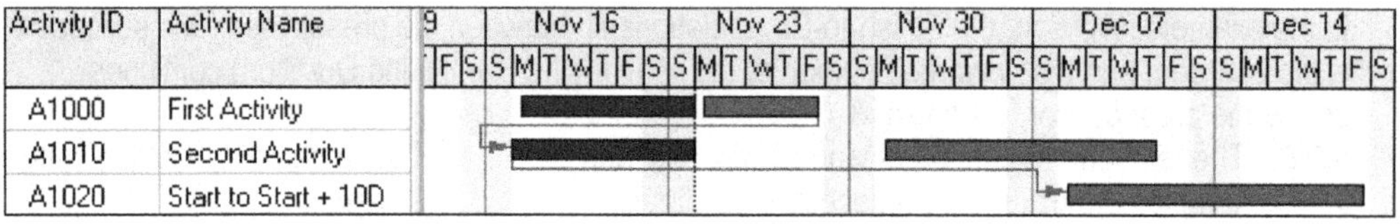

15.2.9 Define critical activities as

Critical Activities Definition criteria is defined in the **Projects Window**, **Project Details**, **Settings** tab:

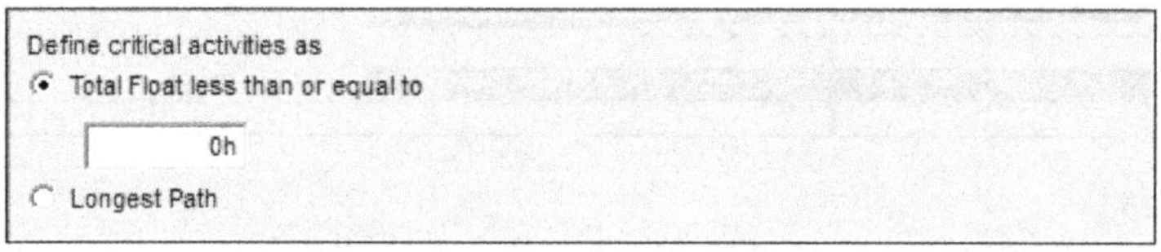

These options are used for analyzing schedules that utilize multiple calendars which may result in activities on the critical path possessing float.

- **Total Float less than or equal to** – Activities may be marked as critical and with a chosen float value. Sometimes a small positive value is used to isolate the near critical activities on schedules or displaying the full critical path on multiple calendar schedules.
- **Longest Path** – This option isolates the longest chain of activities in a schedule and should be used when multiple calendars are in use and some activities, which form part of the critical path, still have float when the successor is assigned a calendar with fewer or different working days.
- In the example below the Total Float has been set to **Total Float less than or equal to zero** and the critical path has disappeared:

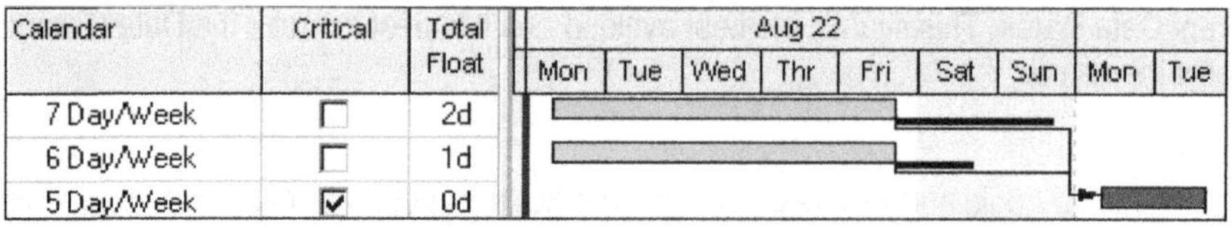

- When the Total Float is then set to less than or equal to 1 day results in the picture below:

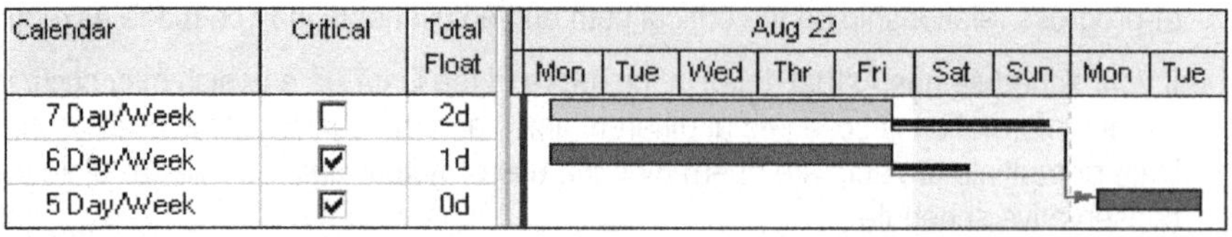

- When the Total Float is then set to **Longest Path** results in the picture below:

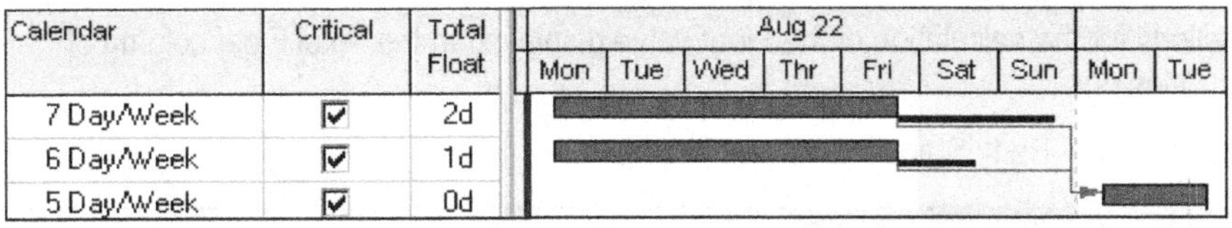

ACTION: Longest path is recommended for projects with multiple calendars.

15.2.10 Calculate float based on finish date

This is a new function to Version 6.2. When more than one project is opened the Total Float may be calculated based on each individual project or the longest project:

- Each project – used when each project's critical path is required:

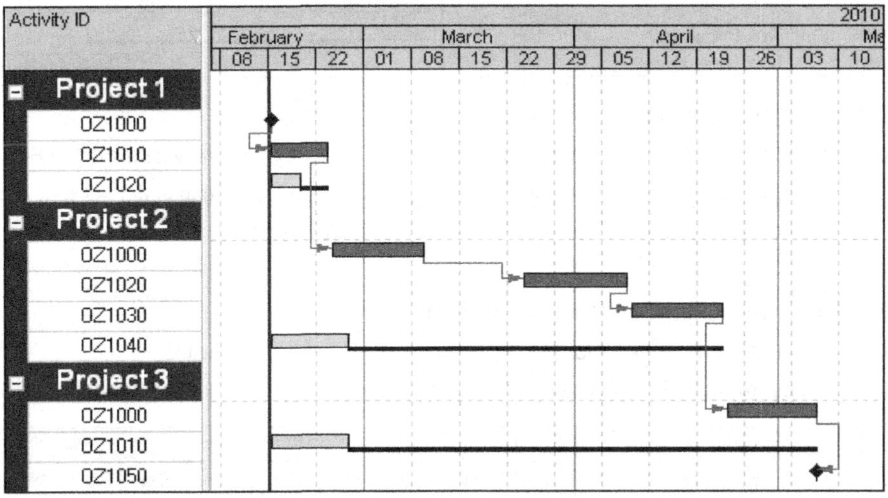

- Opened projects – used when all the P6 projects are related and float is required to be based on the longest project:

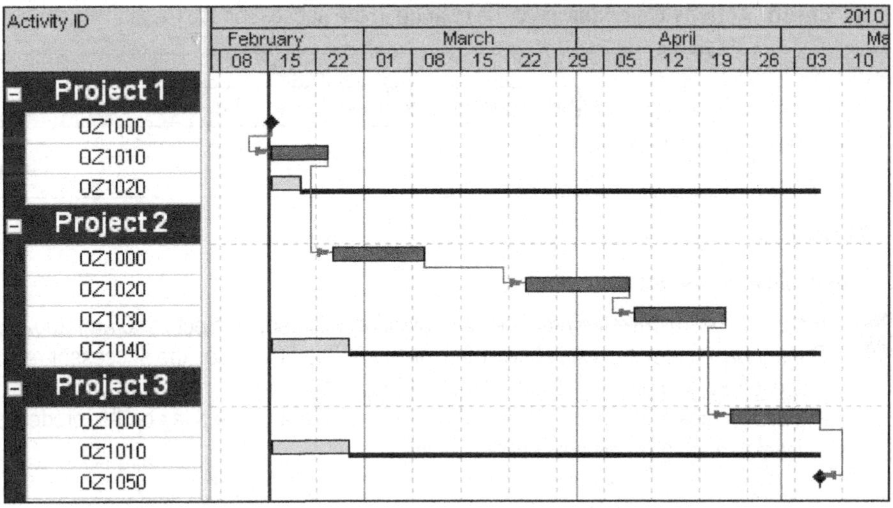

15.2.11 Compute Total Float as

There are three options for the calculation of the Float value displayed in the Total Float column of WBS and LOE activities only:

- Start Float = Late Start – Early Start

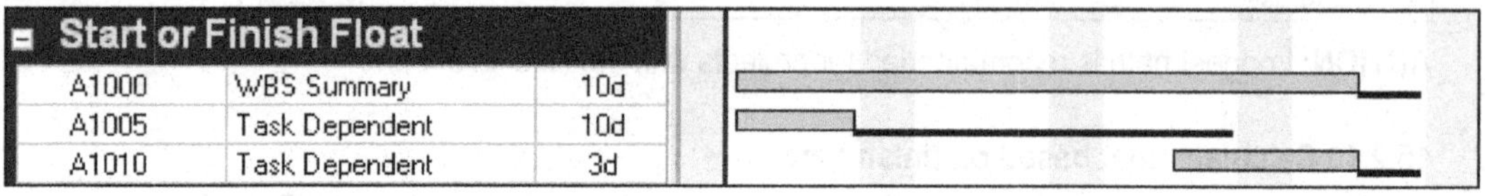

- Finish Float = Late Finish – Early Finish

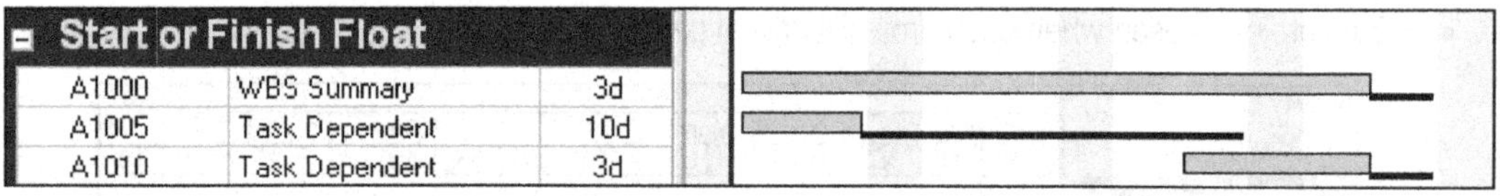

- Smallest of Start Float and Finish Float

It can be seen from the pictures above that the Total Float bar only displays the Finish Float.

The Smallest of Start Float and Finish Float is the most conservative but the Finish Float will always give an answer that is the same as the Total Float bar.

15.2.12 Calendar for scheduling Relationship Lag

- There are four calendar options for the calculation of the lag for all activities:
  1. **Predecessor Activity Calendar** is the default, The example below has a 40-hour lag, or

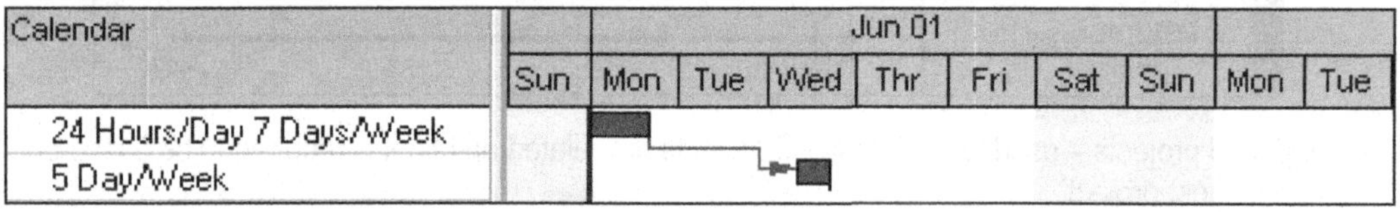

  2. **Successor Activity Calendar**. note the change in the successor start, or

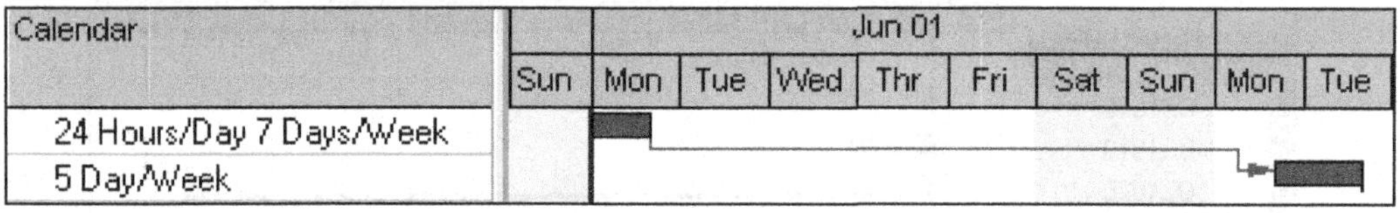

  3. **24-Hour,** or
  4. **Project Default Calendar**.

P3 and SureTrak use the predecessor calendar, Microsoft Project 2000 and 2002 uses the Project Base calendar, and Microsoft Project 2003 to 2007 uses the successor calendar. Microsoft Project also has the option of an Elapsed lag duration. Asta Powerproject does not assign lags to the relationship but a relationship may have a lag on the predecessor activity and a lag on the successor activity.

15.2.13 Scheduling Options – Advanced Tab

This tab selects the options for calculating multiple critical paths and is covered in detail in the **Utilities** chapter.

15.3 Setting the Baseline

Setting the Baseline makes a complete copy of a project, including relationships, notebook entries and codes. You are then able to compare the current project's progress against the baseline.

There are two types of Baselines that are often saved with scheduling software such as P6 – Management and Last Period Status:

Management Baselines

These are usually a copy of an original unprogressed schedule that has been contractually agreed to as the Baseline or Target schedule and are used to:

- Evaluate progress and report progress to a client or customer,
- Provide a base for Extension of Time claims and other contractual claims that may be made based on these Baseline schedules.

Last Period Status Baselines

These are copies of a schedule at a point in time and are used for the management of a project:

- Usually they are used to measure the loss in time from one reporting period to another,
- They allow management to ascertain performance and make decisions on how to manage the project,
- They are displayed in exactly the same way as Management Baselines with the software,
- These Baselines usually, after the first period update, have progress.

Up to 50 baselines per project may be saved in a database in earlier versions but in Version 6.0 and later an unlimited number may be saved.

There is still a restriction of copying a maximum of 50 Baselines when copying a project.

- The number of baselines that may be saved is set in the **Admin Preferences** form by selecting **Admin**, **Admin Preferences...**, **Data Limits** and setting the number in the **Maximum baselines per project** box.
- The number of baselines that may be copied when copying a project is set in the **Admin Preferences** form by selecting **Admin**, **Admin Preferences...**, **Data Limits** and setting the number in the **Maximum baselines copied with project** box.
- Up to four baselines, one **Project Baseline** and three **User Baselines**, may be displayed and compared to the current project.

If another user opens the project, they will only see the one **Project Baseline** and not the other **Users Baseline**.

- A baseline project may be restored back into a database as a normal project. Then it may be edited and resaved as a baseline project.

After the Baseline is set, it is possible to compare the progress with the original plan. You will be able to see if you are ahead or behind schedule and by how much. The Baseline schedule should be established before you update the schedule for the first time.

15.3.1 Creating a Baseline

To create a Baseline, ensure the project is open and select **Project**, **Maintain Baselines...** to display the **Maintain Baselines** form:

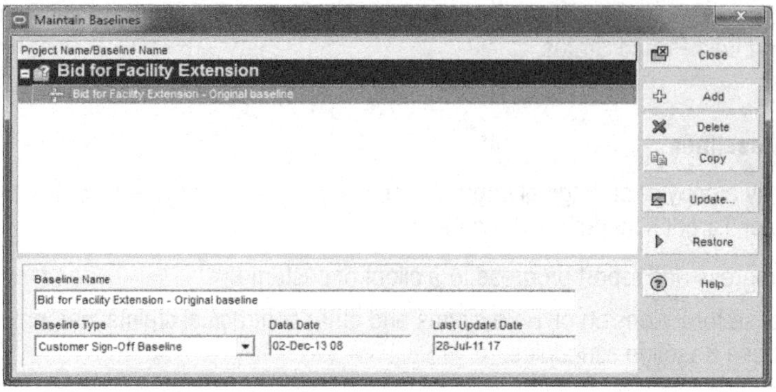

- To create a new baseline click the  icon to open the **Add New Baseline** form:

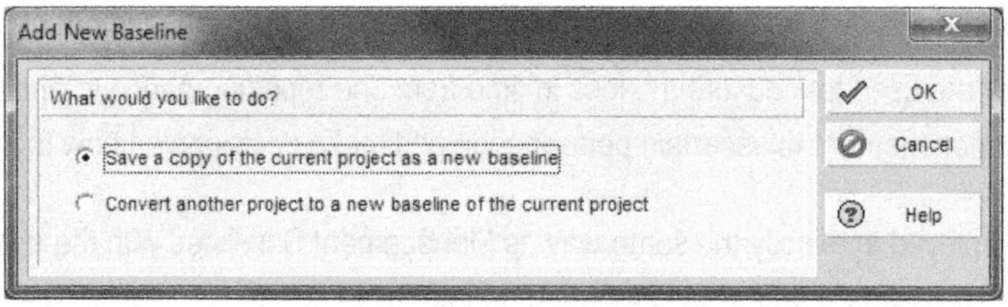

- Select either of the two options in the form:
  - **Save a copy of the current project as a new baseline** will make a copy of the currently open project. P6 adds B1, B2, etc., after the name and returns you to the **Baselines** form, or
  - **Convert another project to a new baseline of the current project** will open the **Select Project** form where another project may be selected to be a baseline. This project will then move from the current projects window into the **Maintain Baselines** form and is not available to be opened from the **Projects Window**.
- Assign a **Baseline Type** from the drop down box. Baseline Types are defined in the **Admin**, **Admin Categories...** form, **Baseline Type** tab.

15.3.2 Deleting a Baseline

To delete a project baseline from the database:

- Open the **Maintain Baselines** form by selecting **Project**, **Maintain Baselines...**,
- Select the baseline project to be deleted, and
- Click on the  icon.

15.3.3 Restoring a Baseline to the Database as an Active Project

To restore a project back to the database so it may be edited or used as a current project:

- Open the **Maintain Baselines** form by selecting **Project**, **Maintain Baselines...**,
- Ensure the baseline is not assigned as any baseline in the **Baselines** form,
- Select the baseline project to be restored, and
- Click on the  icon.

15.3.4 Update Baselines

The new Primavera Version 5.0 **Update Baseline** function is similar to the P3 function and enables the Baseline schedule to be updated with data from the current schedule or deleting activities that are no longer in the current schedule without restoring the Baseline schedule:

- Select **Project**, **Maintain Baselines...** and select the Update... icon to open the **Update Baseline** form:

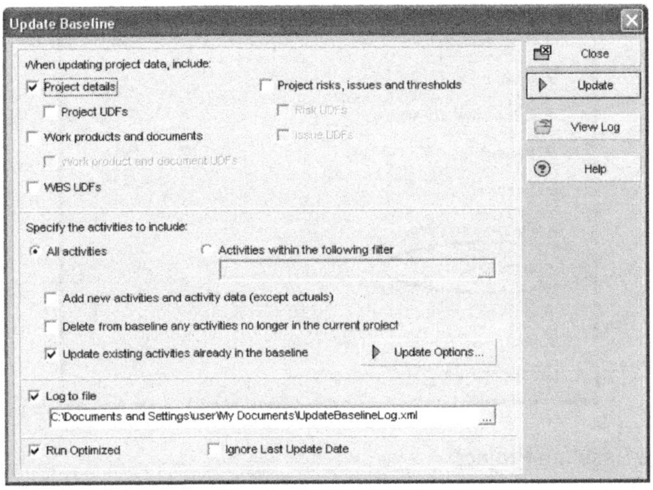

- When **Run Optimized** is not checked then an error log is kept during the updating process.
- **Ignore Last Update Date** may be used when a project is updated at different times and the last Baseline Update may not be valid for the current schedule although the Baseline has been updated with more recent data.
- Select Update Options... to open the **Update Baseline Options** form to select which data items are updated.

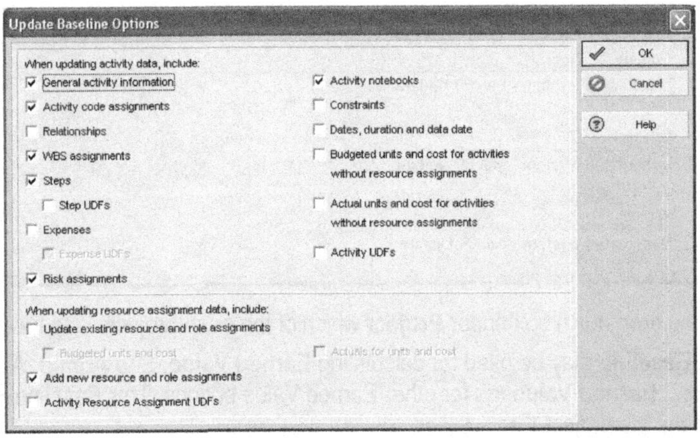

This is a very powerful feature but it is the opinion and experience of the author that the Update Baseline is often the fastest way to destroy a good baseline. A backup of the baseline should be taken before using this function. Furthermore, it is probably best to open edit and review the changes to a Baseline rather than risk using the Update Baseline function.

15.3.5 Copying a Project with Baselines

Primavera Version 6.0 introduced the option of being able to copy baselines when a project is copied in the **Projects Window** using Copy and Paste.

You must manually reassign the baselines after the project has been copied.

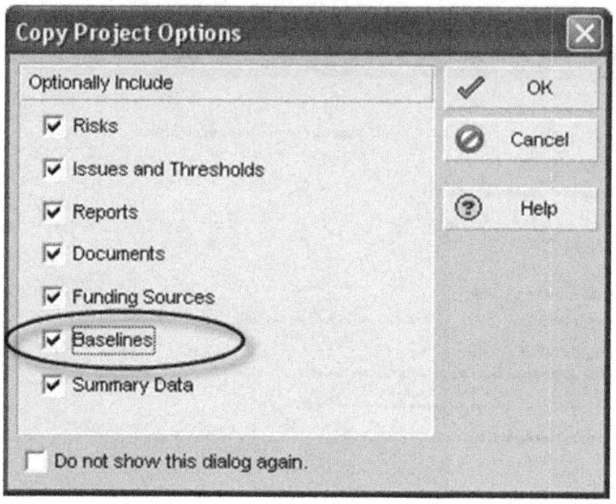

15.3.6 Setting the Baseline Project

The baselines are assigned from the **Project**, **Assign Baselines...** form:

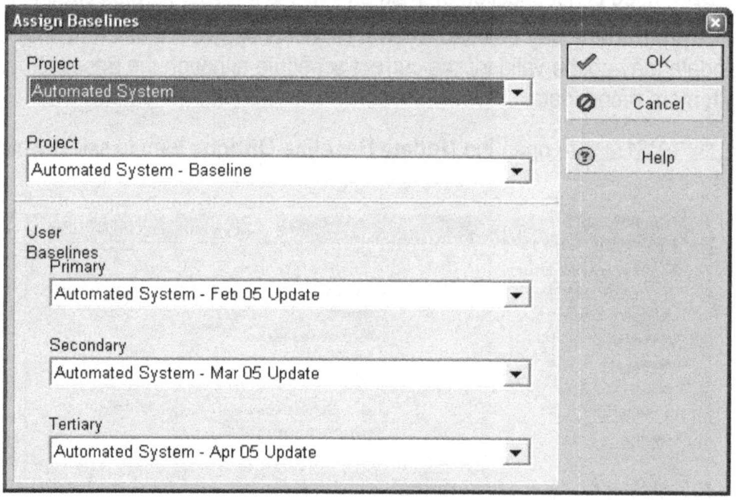

- Select from the drop down box under **Project** which of the open projects is to have a baseline set.
- The **Project Baseline** may be used for calculating **Earned Value**. See **Admin**, **Admin Preferences...**, **Earned Value** tab for other Earned Value options. This Baseline is seen by any User who opens the project.
- Select which other baseline projects are required to be displayed using the drop down boxes under **User Baselines**, the options are **Primary**, **Secondary** and **Tertiary** User Baselines.

User Baselines are only seen by the User who has set the Baseline. So other users who open a project and apply, for example, a Project Layout that displays a User Baseline, will have to also make sure that they set the same baseline as the original user.

- Earned Value calculations may be performed using either the **Primary Baseline** values or the **Baseline** values from the current project. Select the **Settings** tab in the **Projects Window**. This is similar to the P3 option **Tools**, **Options**, **Earned Value**.

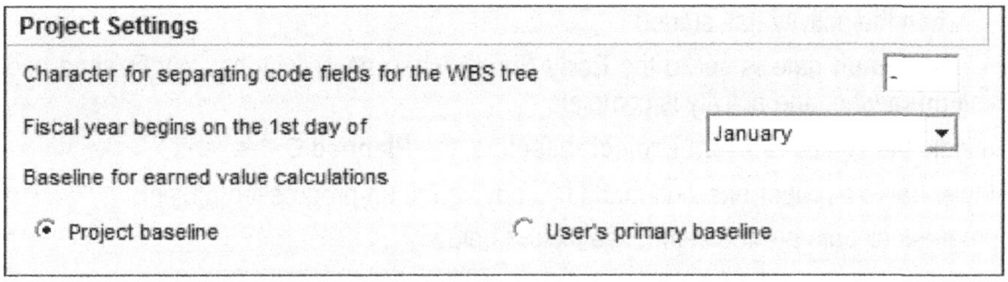

- The **Admin**, **Admin Preferences...**, **Earned Value** tab, **Earned value calculation** section has three options. These options decide which Baseline schedule values are read to calculate the Earned Value fields and which bars are displayed as Baseline Bars. The **At Completion values with current dates** is the author's preferred option when resources are assigned.

When the **Budget values with planned dates** is selected, which is often the default value when the software is loaded, then the planned dates are displayed as a baseline bar. This is undesirable when a progressed schedule is displayed as a Baseline, say, for comparing this period's date values with last period's date values. This is because the **Planned Dates** often hold irrelevant data.

15.3.7 Understanding the <Current Project> Baseline

Because **Planned Dates** are difficult to understand and may lead to misinterpretation of the schedule baselines, it is important that you understand the following points:

- The **Planned Dates** are used by the <**Current Project> Baseline** in the **Assign Baseline** form.
- The <**Current Project> Baseline** is the default baseline for both the **Project Baseline** and **Primary User Baseline**.
- When **NO** baseline has been set by a user then the **<Current Project> Baseline** and therefore the **Planned Dates** are displayed as the **Baseline Bars**.
- The <**Current Project> Baseline** is not a true baseline, the dates may change each time a schedule is updated and may hold irrelevant data in a schedule that has been updated.
- The term **Current Schedule** is normally used to describe the activities as they are currently scheduled, and the term **<Current Project> Baseline** is confusing as it is not the **Current Schedule** but the **Planned Dates**, which may be different from the **Current Schedule**.

The following picture has three bars:

- The upper bar represents the Start and Finish dates:
  - The **Start** date is set to the **Early Start** when an activity has not started and **Actual Start** when the activity has started.
  - The **Finish** date is set to the **Early Finish** when an activity has not finished and **Actual Finish** when the activity is complete.
- The middle bar is the **<Current Project>baseline**, the **Planned Dates**, and
- The lower bar is a proper baseline made by copying the un-progressed project.

With no progress all bars are the same, see picture below:

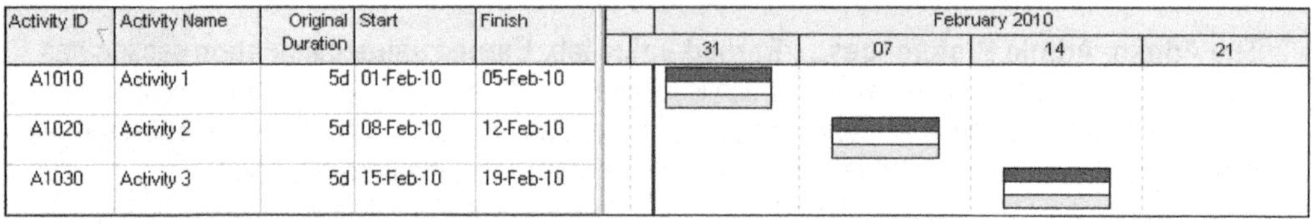

Activity 1 has been marked complete and the Data Date moved. The Planned Dates equal the Start and Finish date before the activity was marked as started. The un-started activities, Activity 2 and 3, in the **<Current Project> baseline** have changed their dates to equal the Start and Finish, see picture below:

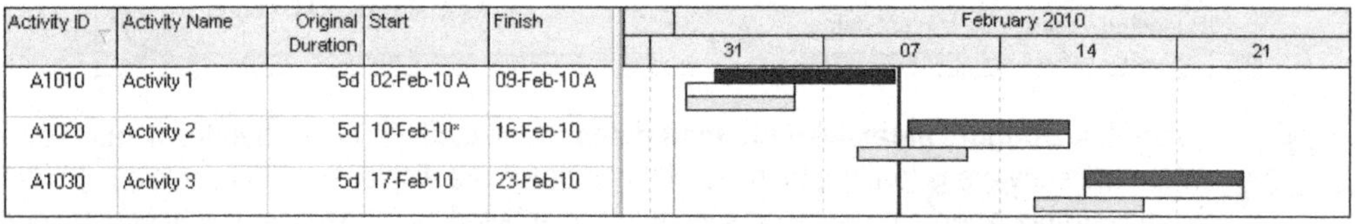

Activity 2 has been marked in-progress and the Data Date moved, delaying Activity 3. Activity 2 Planned Dates (represented by the **<Current Project> baseline**) match the status of the activity before it was marked Started, not a Baseline. Activity 3 Planned Dates represented by the **<Current Project> baseline** bars have changed a second time and match the new Start and Finish:

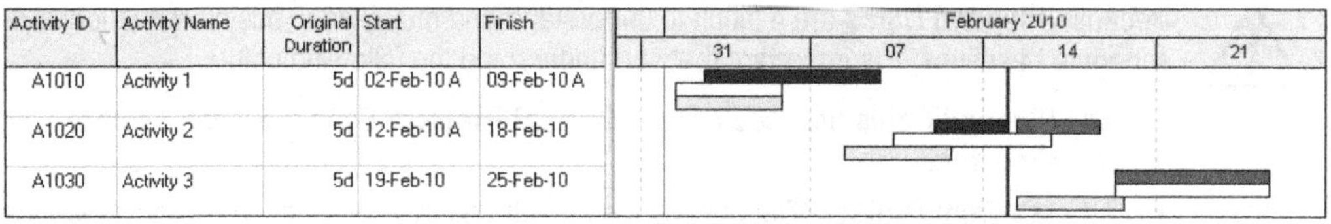

When no Baseline is set by the user, the project will **DISPLAY** the **<Current Project>** (from the Planned Dates, not the Current Schedule Start and Finish dates) as the Baseline bars and, in effect:

- All un-started activities are "re-baselined" at each update, and
- Started and Complete activities Planned Dates match the Start and Finish dates of the activity just before an activity was marked as started. Therefore, the Planned Dates of these activities could contain irrelevant data. This happens when a project has been rescheduled and the Data Date moved forward and then activities marked as Started. At this point the Planned Dates now do not represent either a Baseline, or the last period status or the next period status of a task. They contain irrelevant data that should never be displayed.

This is generally not accepted as a good practice.

There are some significant issues here that need to be carefully managed:

- If no Baseline is set and a layout that displays a baseline bar is applied, then a baseline bar that the user did not set and may contain irrelevant dates from the Planned Dates will be displayed. This may create confusion and these bars may change on each schedule update.
- If one user sets a Primary Baseline, which is a User Baseline and therefore only seen by that user, and a different user opens a project, then this second user will see only the **<Current Project> baseline** and not the other user's Primary Baseline. This will result in one user seeing something different from another user when two users open a project.

You may wish to restrict the access (see paragraphs 17.2 and 24.4) to a project schedule to prevent the **<Current Project> baseline** being displayed inadvertently.

15.3.8 Displaying the Baseline Data

The Baseline Dates may be displayed by:

- Displaying the **Baseline** columns; there are fewer predefined columns for the **Secondary User Baseline** and **Tertiary User Baseline**:
  - **BL** is the **Project Baseline**
  - **BL1** is the **Primary User Baseline**
  - **BL2** is the **Secondary User Baseline**
  - **BL3** is the **Tertiary User Baseline**

Activity ID	Activity Name	Start	Finish	BL Project Finish	BL Project Start	BL1 Finish	BL1 Start
Bid for Facility Extension		02-Dec-13	27-Jan-14	27-Jan-14	02-Dec-13	27-Jan-14	02-Dec-13
Technical Specification		02-Dec-13	18-Dec-13	18-Dec-13	02-Dec-13	18-Dec-13	02-Dec-13
OZ1000	Approval to Bid	02-Dec-13			02-Dec-13		02-Dec-13
OZ1010	Determine Installation Req...	02-Dec-13	05-Dec-13	05-Dec-13	02-Dec-13	05-Dec-13	02-Dec-13
OZ1020	Create Technical Specific...	06-Dec-13	12-Dec-13	12-Dec-13	06-Dec-13	12-Dec-13	06-Dec-13
OZ1030	Identify Supplier Compone...	13-Dec-13	16-Dec-13	16-Dec-13	13-Dec-13	16-Dec-13	13-Dec-13
OZ1040	Validate Technical Specifi...	17-Dec-13	18-Dec-13	18-Dec-13	17-Dec-13	18-Dec-13	17-Dec-13
Delivery Plan		19-Dec-13	21-Jan-14	21-Jan-14	19-Dec-13	21-Jan-14	19-Dec-13

- Showing a baseline bar on the Bar Chart by selecting the appropriate bars in the **Bars** form:

Display	Name	Timescale	User Sta...	User Fi...	Filter	Preview
☐	Project Baseline MS	Project Baseline Bar			Milestone	△ △
☐	Primary Baseline Bar	Primary Baseline Bar			Normal	
☐	Primary Baseline MS	Primary Baseline Bar			Milestone	▽ ▽
☐	Secondary Baseline Bar	Secondary Baseline Bar			Normal	
☐	Secondary Baseline MS	Secondary Baseline Bar			Milestone	▲ ▲
☐	Tertiary Baseline Bar	Tertiary Baseline Bar			Normal	
☐	Tertiary Baseline MS	Tertiary Baseline Bar			Milestone	▽ ▽

15.4 *Workshop 13 – WBS, LOEs and Setting the Baseline*

Background

We will first look at how WBS and LOE activities work and then set a Baseline.

Assignment - WBS Activity

Open your **OzBuild Bid** project file and complete the following steps:

1. Apply the **OzBuild 10 – With Float** layout
2. Create a new activity under the **Bid Document** WBS Node:
   - Activity ID OZ1140
   - Titled **WBS Activity** and
   - Assign it an Activity Type of **WBS Summary** using the **Activities Window**, **General** tab.
3. Schedule to see how it calculates the Float Bar length.
4. Drag the WBS activity to the **Delivery Plan** WBS Node and schedule to see how it operates.
5. Drag the WBS activity to the **Technical Specification** WBS Node and schedule:

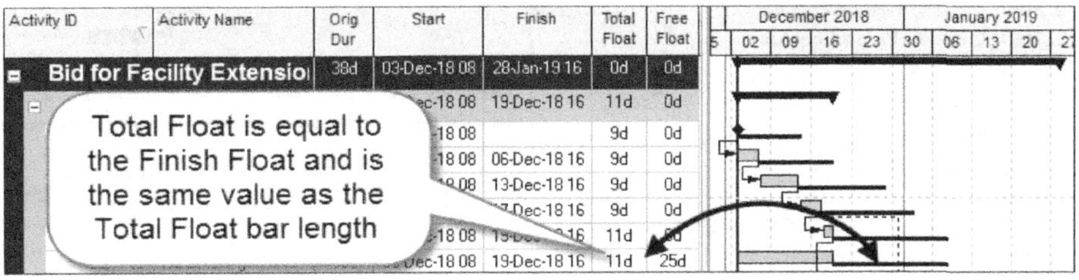

6. Select **Tools**, **Schedule...**, **Options** and change the **Compute Total Float** to **Start Float**: = Late Start – Early Start

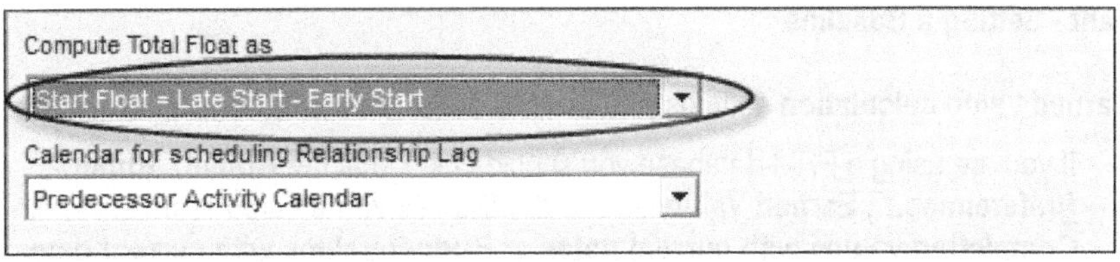

7. Schedule and you will see that the float value is now the same value as the Start Float, but the Float Bar still shows the Finish Float Value:

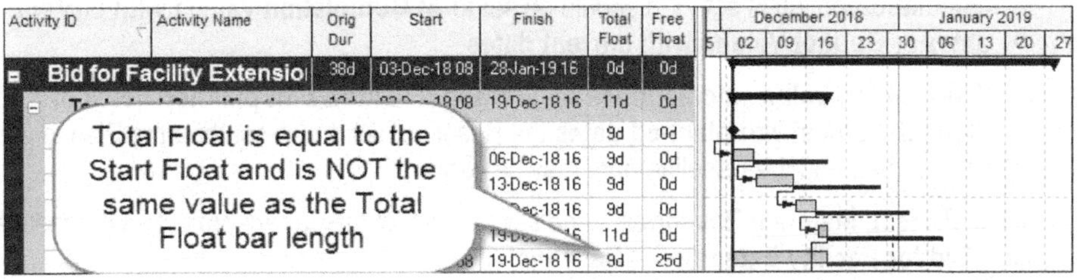

continued...

8. Go to the Scheduling Options form and change the **Compute Total Float** to **Finish Float** and schedule.

Assignment - LOE Activity

9. Apply the **OzBuild 10 – Without Float** Layout
10. Change the **Activity Type** of the WBS Activity to a **Level of Effort** and rename it to **LOE Activity**,
11. Open the Bars form and ensure LOE bars are displayed,
12. Drag activity OZ1140 to the **Delivery Plan** WBS Node and sort on Activity ID,
13. Add OZ1060 SS OZ1140 and OZ1140 FF OZ1070 relationships and see how it calculates.

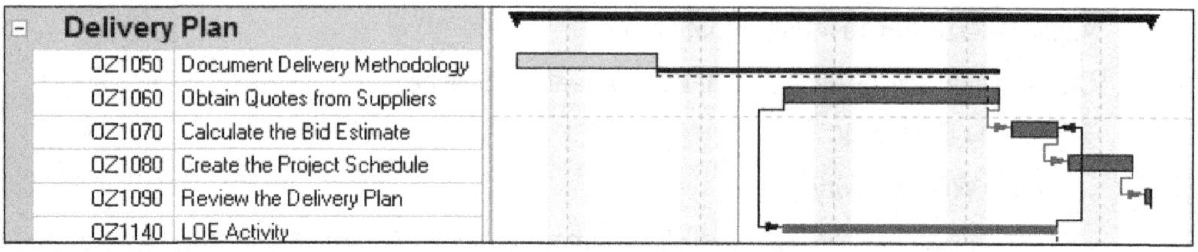

14. Add OZ1050 SS OZ1140 and OZ1140 FF OZ1110 relationships and see how it calculates.

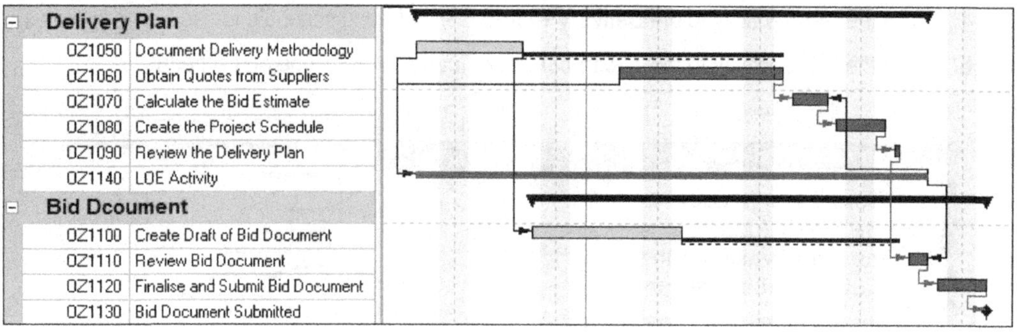

15. Delete the LOE activity.

Assignment - Setting a Baseline

16. **Earned value calculation** settings:
    - If you are using a PPM database you should check that the **Admin**, **Admin Preferences...**, **Earned Value** tab has the **Earned value calculation** set to **At Completion values with current dates or Budget Values with current dates**. You may not be able to change this if you do not have the necessary access.
    - If you are using a EPPM database you should find out what the **Earned value calculation** option is set to. It should be set to **At Completion values with current dates** or **Budget Values with current dates.**
    - If the **Earned value calculation** is set to **Budget values with planned dates** or **Planned values with planned dates** the Baseline has progress, then the Planed Dates will be read and the Baseline bars may be wrong.
17. Select **Project**, **Maintain Baselines...** and save a copy of the current project as a Baseline and title it **Bid for Facility Extension – Baseline**.

18. Assign an appropriate **Baseline Type**, such as **Customer Sign-Off**, (the options may vary depending on your database) and close the form.
19. Select **Project**, **Assign Baselines...** and make this your **Project Baseline** and **Primary Baseline** and close the **Assign Baselines** form. This ensures that any baseline bar will show a real baseline and not the Planned Dates.
20. Apply the **OzBuild 10 – With Float** layout, do not save the current layout, and save this as a new layout titled **OzBuild Workshop 13 – Baseline**.
21. Create, if required, and display the following bars:
    - All current schedule bars which are Actual Work, Remaining Work and Critical Remaining Work, Milestones and Summary,
    - % Complete Bar,
    - Float Bar (Total Float) and Neg Float Bar (Negative Float),
    - The Project Baseline Bar and Project Baseline Milestones,
    - For clarity ensure no text is displayed.
22. Display the following columns:
    - Activity ID
    - Activity Name
    - Activity % Complete
    - Original Duration
    - Remaining Duration
    - Start
    - Finish
    - Total Float
    - Variance - BL Project Finish Date
23. Make sure the Timescale is daily or weekly.
24. Show the time in 24-hour format, but do not show the minutes by selecting **Edit, User Preferences...**, **Dates** tab.
25. Save your layout.

continued...

26. Check your answer against the diagrams below:

Activity ID	Activity Name	Activity % Complete	Orig Dur	Rem Dur	Start	Finish	Total Float	Variance - BL Project Finish Date
Bid for Facility Extension			38d	38d	03-Dec-18 08	28-Jan-19 16	0d	0d
Technical Specification			13d	13d	03-Dec-18 08	19-Dec-18 16	11d	0d
OZ1000	Approval to Bid	0%	0d	0d	03-Dec-18 08		9d	0d
OZ1010	Determine Installation	0%	4d	4d	03-Dec-18 08	06-Dec-18 16	9d	0d
OZ1020	Create Technical Spe	0%	5d	5d	07-Dec-18 08	13-Dec-18 16	9d	0d
OZ1030	Identify Supplier Comp	0%	2d	2d	14-Dec-18 08	17-Dec-18 16	9d	0d
OZ1040	Validate Technical Sp	0%	2d	2d	18-Dec-18 08	19-Dec-18 16	11d	0d
Delivery Plan			21d	21d	20-Dec-18 08	22-Jan-19 16	0d	0d
OZ1050	Document Delivery Me	0%	4d	4d	20-Dec-18 08	27-Dec-18 16	11d	0d
OZ1060	Obtain Quotes from Su	0%	8d	8d	03-Jan-19 08*	14-Jan-19 16	0d	0d
OZ1070	Calculate the Bid Estin	0%	3d	3d	15-Jan-19 08	17-Jan-19 16	0d	0d
OZ1080	Create the Project Sch	0%	3d	3d	18-Jan-19 08	21-Jan-19 16	0d	0d
OZ1090	Review the Delivery P	0%	1d	1d	22-Jan-19 08	22-Jan-19 16	0d	0d
Bid Dcoument			21d	21d	28-Dec-18 08	28-Jan-19 16	0d	0d
OZ1100	Create Draft of Bid Do	0%	6d	6d	28-Dec-18 08	07-Jan-19 16	11d	0d
OZ1110	Review Bid Document	0%	2d	2d	23-Jan-19 08	24-Jan-19 16	0d	0d
OZ1120	Finalise and Submit Bi	0%	2d	2d	25-Jan-19 08	28-Jan-19 16	0d	0d
OZ1130	Bid Document Submitt	0%	0d	0d		28-Jan-19 16*	0d	0d

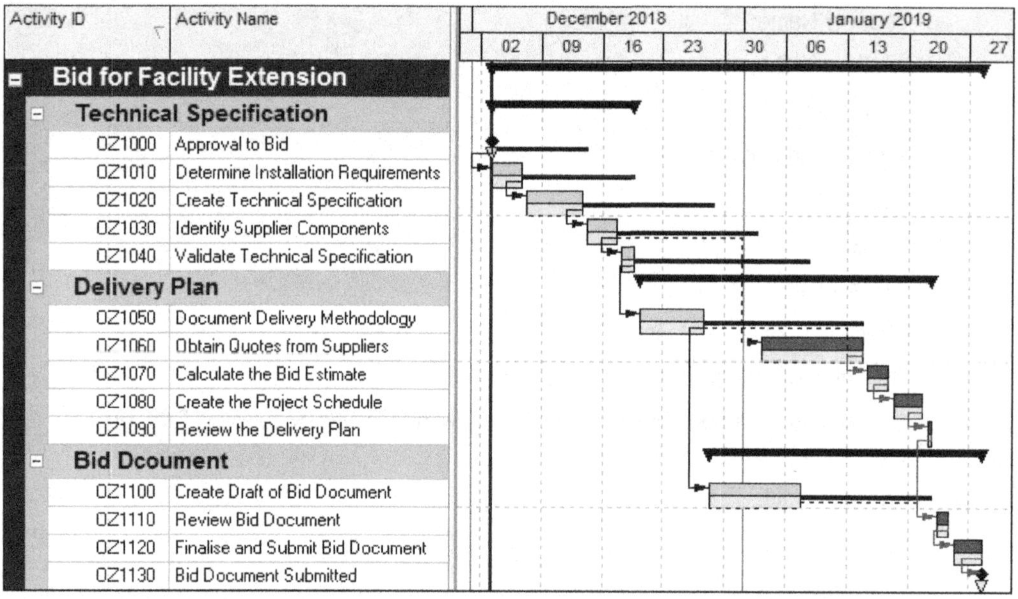

Note: For clarity the baseline above has been made thicker than would be viewed using the primavera.com.au layout and displayed in yellow for people viewing the book in black and white.

16 UPDATING AN UNRESOURCED SCHEDULE

Now that the Baseline has been set we can start tracking progress and the important phase of regular monitoring and control begins. This process is important to help catch problems as early as possible, and thus minimize their impact on the successful completion of the project. The main steps for monitoring progress are:

- Saving a **Baseline** schedule, covered in the last chapter,
- Recording or marking-up progress at the **Data Date**.
- **Updating** or **Progressing** the schedule:
  - Completed activities are assigned **Actual Start** and **Actual Finish** dates,
  - In-progress activities are assigned **Actual Start** dates, and the activity's **Remaining Durations** and **Percent Completes** are adjusted,
  - Adjustments are made to un-started work based on the productivity to-date, and
  - Project scope changes should be added as new activities.
- Scheduling the project and at the same time moving the **Data Date** to the new **Data Date** and recalculating all the activities dates. The **Data Date** may also be moved before updating the activities from the **Project Window**, **Dates** tab.
- Comparing and Reporting actual progress against planned progress and revising the plan and schedule, if required.

Comparing the status of an activity against more than one baseline is useful; for example:

- The original plan could be represented as one of the Baselines, to see the slippage against the original plan.
- Last Period, which could be another Baseline, to see the changes since the last update.

By the time you get to this phase you should have a schedule that compares your original plan with the current plan, showing where the project is ahead or behind. If you are behind, you should be able to use this schedule to plan appropriate remedial measures to bring the project back on target.

This chapter covers the following topics:

Topic	Menu Command
• Saving and Deleting and Setting a **Baseline**	To save a Baseline, select **Project**, **Maintain Baselines...** to display the **Maintain Baselines** form.
• Assigning a Baseline project	The baselines are assigned from the **Project**, **Assign Baselines...** form.
• Recording Progress	Guidelines on how to record progress.
• **Retained Logic** and **Progress Override**	Open the **General Schedule Options** form by selecting **Tools**, **Schedule......** and clicking the Options... icon.
• Setting the **Current Data Date** and **Scheduling** the project	Open the **Schedule** form by: • Selecting **Tools**, **Schedule...**, or • Pressing the **F9** key, or • Clicking the icon.

16.1 Practical Methods of Recording Progress

Normally a project is updated once a week, bi-weekly, or monthly. Very short projects could be updated daily or even by the shift or hour. As a guide, a project would typically be updated between 12 and 20 times in its lifetime. A high risk project should be updated more often than a low risk project. Progress is recorded on or just after the **Data Date** and the scheduler updates the schedule upon the receipt of the information.

The following information is typically recorded for each activity when updating a project:

- The activity start date and time if required,
- The number of days or hours required to complete the activity or the date and time the activity is expected to finish,
- The percentage complete, and
- If complete, the activity finish date and time.

A printout of the schedule may be used for recording the progress of the current schedule and is often produced prior to updating the project. Ideally progress should be recorded by a physical inspection of the work or by a person who intimately knows the work, although that is not always possible. It is good practice to keep this marked-up record for your own reference. Ensure that you note the Data Date of the mark-up and, if relevant, the time.

Often a Status Report or mark-up sheet, such as the following illustration, which has a 4-week look-ahead filter applied, is distributed to the people responsible for marking up the project progress. The marked-up sheets are returned to the scheduler for data entry into the software and then filed for dispute resolution.

A page break could be placed at each responsible person's band in the **Group and Sort** form, and when the schedule is printed each person could have their own page of activities that are either in-progress or due to commence. This is particularly useful for large projects.

Activity ID	Activity Name	Rem Dur	Orig Dur	Phy % Comp	Start	Actual Start	Suspend Date	Resume Date	Finish	Actual Finish
Bid for Facility Ext...		34d	38d		03-Dec-13 08 A	03-Dec-13 08			27-Jan-14 16	
Technical Specific...		9d	13d		03-Dec-13 08 A	03-Dec-13 08			18-Dec-13 16	
OZ1000	Approval to Bid	0d	0d	100%	03-Dec-13 08 A	03-Dec-13 08				
OZ1010	Determine Ins...	0d	4d	100%	03-Dec-13 08 A	03-Dec-13 08			05-Dec-13 16 A	05-Dec-13 16
OZ1020	Create Techni...	5d	3d	40%	05-Dec-13 08 A	05-Dec-13 08			12-Dec-13 16	
OZ1030	Identify Suppli...	2d	2d	0%	13-Dec-13 08				16-Dec-13 16	
OZ1040	Validate Tech...	2d	2d	0%	17-Dec-13 08				18-Dec-13 16	

Other electronic methods, discussed next, may be employed to collect the data. Irrespective of the method used, the same data needs to be collected.

There are several methods of collecting data for the project status:

- By sending a printed sheet to each responsible person to mark up by hand and return to the scheduler.
- By cutting and pasting the data from Primavera into another document, such as Excel, and E-mailing the document to them as an attachment.
- By giving the responsible party direct access to the schedule software to update it. This approach is not recommended, unless the project is broken into sub-projects. By using multiple projects with one scheduler accessing each project, or assigning access through WBS Nodes, only one person updates each part of the schedule.
- When the Primavera timesheets have been implemented this process may be used to update the activities.

Some projects involve a number of people. In such cases, it is important that procedures be written to ensure that the update information is collected:

- In a timely manner,
- Consistently,
- Completely, and
- In a usable format.

It is important for a scheduler to be aware that some people have great difficulty in comprehending a schedule. When there are a number of people with different skill levels in an organization, it is necessary to provide more than one method of updating the data. You even may find that you have to sit down with some people to obtain the correct data, yet others are willing and comfortable to E-mail you the information.

16.2 Understanding the Concepts

There are some terms and concepts used in scheduling and some that are specific to Primavera that must be understood before updating a project schedule.

Users must always display the time when updating a project, otherwise the time of 00:00 is sometimes selected by P6 as the Start or Finish time which is usually not desirable.

16.2.1 Activity Lifecycle

There are three stages of an activity lifecycle:

- **Not Started –** The **Early Start** and **Early Finish** dates are calculated from the **Predecessors**, **Constraints**, and **Activity Duration**.
- **In-Progress –** The activity has an **Actual Start** date but is not complete.
  - Assigning an **Actual Start** date overrides the **Start Constraints** and **Start Relationships** which are used to calculate the **Early Start**.
  - The **Finish Date** may be calculated from the **Data Date** or **Resume Date** and the **Remaining Duration**, or an **Expected Finish Constraint**, or a **Finish Relationship**.
- **Complete –** The activity is in the past, the **Actual Start** and **Actual Finish** dates have been entered into Primavera, and they override all logic and constraints.

16.2.2 Assigning an Actual Start Date and Time of an Activity

This section will explain how Primavera assigns the **Actual Start** of a **Complete** or an **In-Progress** activity.

- **Actual Start** date is assigned in the **Actual Start** field by checking the **Started** check box, or
- Entering a date in the **Actual Start** column.

This date overrides the **Early Start date**.

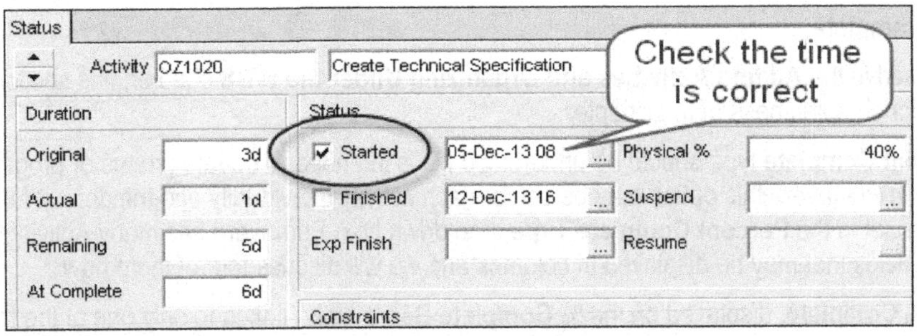

- The activity **Actual Start** date is set to equal the **Start** date when this box is checked.

- The **Actual Start** date calendar is opened by clicking on the ... icon to the right of the **Started** check box and a different start date may be assigned. This date should not be in the future of the project Data Date. It would not be logical to have an activity assigned a start date in the future.
- An **Actual Start** may also be assigned in an **Actual Start** column.

16.2.3 Assigning an Actual Finish Date and Time of an Activity

This is assigned in the same way as an Actual Start and this should be in the past. An **Actual Finish** date overrides an **Early Finish** date and finish date constraints and finish relationships are ignored.

16.2.4 Calculation of Durations of an In-Progress Activity

Durations

The Primavera has many duration fields, we will discuss four duration fields below:

- An activity **Original Duration** (**Planned Duration**) in some Industry Versions) is the duration from the **Early Start** to the **Early Finish** calculated over the **Activity Calendar** and is calculated when an activity has not yet started. When an **Actual Start** is entered, this duration is no longer recalculated or directly used for scheduling, but may be edited.
- The **Actual Duration** is the activity's worked duration and is either the duration from:
  - The **Actual Start** to the **Data Date** of an **In-progress** activity, or
  - The **Actual Start** to the **Suspend Date** of a suspended **In-progress** activity, or
  - The **Actual Start** to the **Actual Finish** of a **Completed** activity.
- The **Remaining Duration** is the unworked duration of an **In-progress** activity and is the duration from the **Data Date** or **Resume Date** to the **Early Finish** date of an activity.
- The **At Completion Duration= Actual Duration + Remaining Duration**. Before an activity has started, the **Actual Duration** is zero and the **Remaining Duration** equals the **Original Duration**.
- The **Original Duration** is linked to the **Remaining Duration** when an activity is un-started and **Link Budget and At Completion for not started activities** box in the **Calculations** tab of the **Projects Window** is checked.
- The Remaining bar is based on the **Remaining Duration**, and the Remaining Duration may commence a period of time after the **Data Date** so there is often a gap between the **Data Date** and the **Remaining Start** of an in-progress activity.

The in-built proportional link between **Original Duration**, **Actual Duration**, **Remaining Duration**, and **% Complete** that exists in Microsoft Project does not exist in Primavera.

Percent Complete

As discussed in the **Adding Activities and Organizing Under the WBS** chapter, this section is repeated for completeness of this chapter.

The **Percent Complete** type should be understood if it is intended to update (status or progress) a schedule. In Primavera this option may be set for each activity individually and the default for new activities is set in the **Percent Complete Type** drop down box. Primavera has many Activity Percent Complete fields that may be displayed in columns and we will discuss four of them now:

Activity % Complete, displayed on the **% Complete Bar**, may be linked to only one of the three % Complete following three fields:

- **Physical % Complete**

- **Duration %Complete**
- **Units % Complete**

There are three Percent Complete options; each new activity is assigned the project default **Percent Complete Type** and then this may be edited for each activity as required.

Therefore if the option of **Physical % Complete** is selected for an activity then the **Activity % Complete** and the **Physical % Complete** are linked and a change to one will change the other.

Default % Complete

The **Default % Complete Type** for each new activity in each project is assigned in the **Defaults** tab of the **Details** form in the **Project Window**:

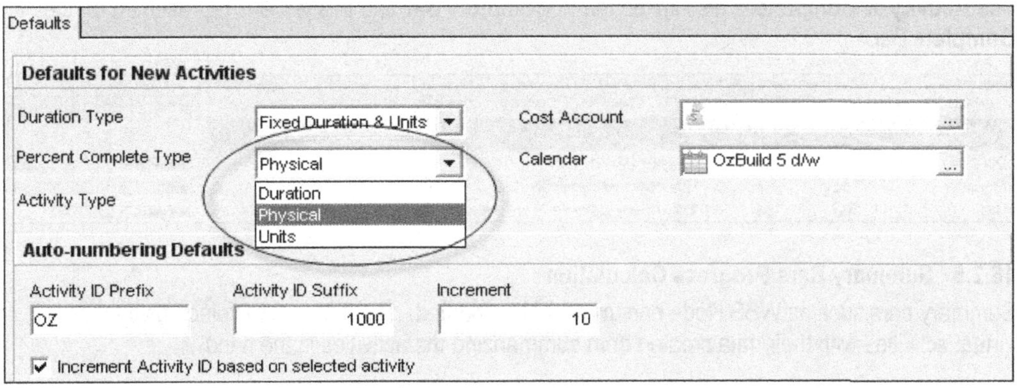

- Each new activity **Percent Complete Type** is set to the **Default Percent Complete** and may be changed at any time.

Percent Complete Types

- **Duration % Complete** – This field is calculated from the proportion of the **Original Duration** and the **Remaining Duration** and they are linked and a change to one value will change the other. When the **Remaining Duration** is set to greater that the **Original Duration** this percent complete is always zero. This is similar to the way P3 and SureTrak calculates the % Complete when the **Link Remaining Duration and Percent Complete** option is selected
- **Physical % Complete** – This field enables the user to enter the percent complete of an activity and this value is independent of the activity durations. This is similar to the way P3 and SureTrak calculates the % Complete when the **Link Remaining Duration and Percent Complete** option is NOT selected.
- **Units % Complete** – This is where the percent complete is calculated from the resources Actual and Remaining Units. A change to one value will change the other and when more than one resource is assigned then all the Actual Units for all resources will be changed proportionally. This will be covered further in The **Updating Resources** chapter. This is similar to the Microsoft Project % Work Complete.

The Units % Complete is calculated from the value of all the Labor and Non-Labor Resources, so be careful when more than on type of resource is assigned to an activity. For example the software could be adding concrete volumes with labor hours and excavator hours.

Activity % Complete

The **Activity % Complete** field is linked to the **% Complete Type** field assigned to an activity in the **General** tab of the **Details** form in the **Activities Window** or the **% Complete Type** column:

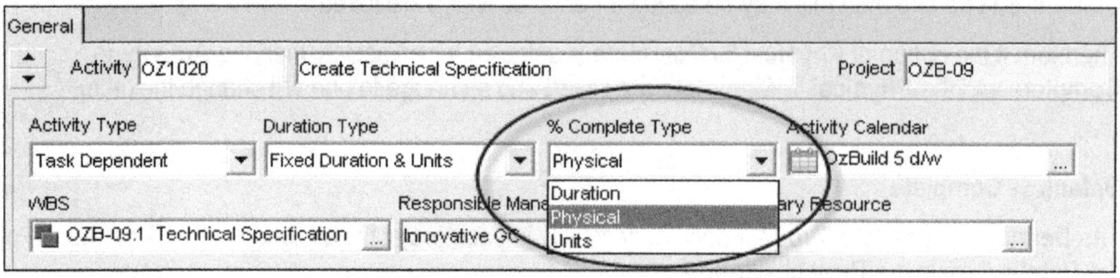

The **Activity % Complete** is also linked the **% Complete Bar** and this value is represented on the **% Complete** Bar.

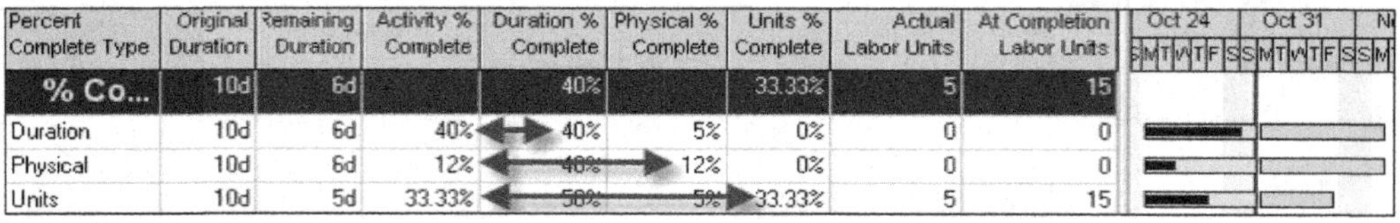

Percent Complete Type	Original Duration	Remaining Duration	Activity % Complete	Duration % Complete	Physical % Complete	Units % Complete	Actual Labor Units	At Completion Labor Units
% Co...	10d	6d		40%		33.33%	5	15
Duration	10d	6d	40%	40%	5%	0%	0	0
Physical	10d	6d	12%	40%	12%	0%	0	0
Units	10d	5d	33.33%	50%	5%	33.33%	5	15

16.2.5 Summary Bars Progress Calculation

Summary bars such as WBS Node bars may not be updated, as in Microsoft Project, as they are virtual activities with their data created from summarizing the activities in the band.

16.2.6 Understanding the Current Data Date

The **Current Data Date** is also known as the **Data Date**, **Update Date**, **Status Date**, **Progress Date**, **As At Date**, **Time Now**, **Report Date** and the **Project Data Date**. Primavera has one **Data Date**, titled **Current Data Date,** which operates in a similar way to the **Data Date** in P3 and SureTrak.

The Primavera **Current Data Date** is displayed as a vertical line on the schedule; this Data Date vertical line may be formatted in the **Bar Chart Options** form.

In P6 the function of the **Current Data Date** is to:

- Separate the completed parts of activities from incomplete parts of activities.
- Calculate or record all costs and hours to-date before the **Current Data Date**, and to forecast costs and hours to go after the **Current Data Date**.
- Calculate the **Finish Date** of an in-progress activity from the **Current Data Date** plus the **Remaining Duration** over the **Activity Calendar**, when the Suspend and Resume function has not been used.

16.3 Updating the Schedule

The next stage is to update the schedule by entering the mark-up information against each activity.

When dealing with large schedules it is normal to develop a look-ahead schedule by creating a filter to display incomplete and un-started activities commencing in the near future only.

The schedule may be updated using the following methods:

- Using the fields in the **Status** tab of the **Details** form in the lower pane, or
- Displaying the appropriate tracking columns by:
  - Creating your own layout, or
  - Inserting the required columns in an existing layout.

16.3.1 Updating Activities Using the Status Tab of the Details Form

Ensure you are showing the time and then open the **Status** tab:

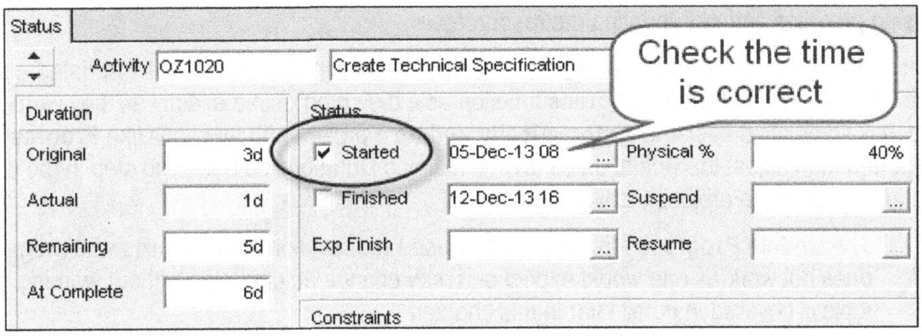

Updating a Complete activity:

- Check the **Started** box and enter the actual **Start Date and Time** if different from the displayed date.
- Check the **Finished** box and enter the actual **Finish Date and Time** if different from the displayed date.

Updating an In-progress activity:

- Check the **Started** box and enter the actual **Start Date and Time** if different from the displayed date.
- When the **Duration Type** is **% Duration** the **% Duration Complete** and **Remaining Duration** are linked, then either:
  - The **Remaining Duration** is edited and the **% Complete** is calculated, or
  - The **% Complete** is entered and the software calculates the **Remaining Duration**, or
  - A **Remaining Duration** greater than the **Original Duration** may be entered and the **% Duration** will remain at zero, until the **Remaining Duration** is less than the **Original Duration**.

Irrespective of the method used to calculate the **Remaining Duration**, after the schedule is recalculated the end date of the activity is calculated from the **Current Data Date** plus the **Remaining Duration** over the **Activity Calendar**.

⚠ Be careful that the % Duration Complete does not change the Remaining Duration to a non-round day and that activity then finishes halfway through a day. This results in all the successor activities starting and finish in the middle of the day.

Updating an **Un-started** activity:

- The **Original Duration**, **Relationships** and **Constraints** of an un-started activity should be reviewed.

16.3.2 Updating Activities Using Columns

An efficient method of updating activities is by displaying the data in columns. This may be achieved by:

- Inserting the required columns in an existing layout, or better:
- Creating a Layout with the required columns and updating the schedule using these columns.

16.4 Progress Spotlight and Update Progress

Primavera Version 5.0 introduced a new function for highlighting the activities that should have progressed in the update period. This function is titled **Progress Spotlight** and is similar to the P3 and SureTrak Progress Spotlight function; however, it does not have the additional SureTrak features of reversing progress and not updating the resources.

The user then has the option of selecting some or all of the activities that should be updated and updating them using the **Update Progress** function as if they progressed exactly as they were Planned. It is sometimes easier to **Automatically update** a project with functions like **Progress Spotlight** and then adjust the Actual dates and Remaining Durations as a second step in the updating process, especially if the project is going to plan.

⚠ The **Update Progress** function must be used with caution on schedules with progress as it does not work as one would expect and may change actual dates without warning. This topic is covered in detail later in this chapter.

The Spotlight may be moved to reflect the new Data Date by either:

- Dragging the Data Date, or
- Using the **Tools** toolbar, **Spotlight** icon.

16.4.1 Highlighting Activities for Updating by Dragging the Data Date

To highlight activities that should have been progressed in the last period by dragging the Data Date:

- Hold the mouse arrow on the Data Date line and display the double-headed arrow ↔, and
- Press the left mouse and drag the Data Date line to the required date.
- All the activities that should have been worked in the time period are highlighted:

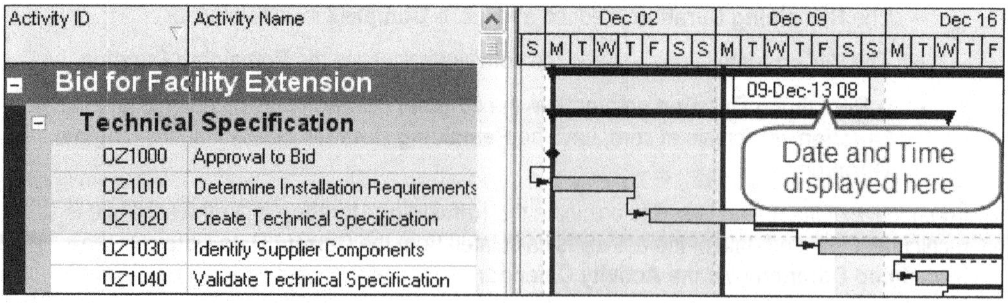

16.4.2 Spotlighting Activities Using Spotlight Icon

The Spotlight facility highlights all activities that should have progressed in one minor time period of the timescale settings. To use **Progress Spotlight**:

- Set the Timescale to be the same as your Update Periods. If you are updating weekly then set the time period to weeks in the **Timescale** form.
- Select **View, Progress Spotlight** or click the icon and the next period of time (one week if your scale is set to one week) will be highlighted.
- Click the **Progress Spotlight** icon a second time to return the Spotlight back to the Data Date.

You are now ready to update progress.

16.4.3 Updating a Project Using Update Progress

To update a schedule using the **Update Progress** form, select **Tools, Update Progress**:

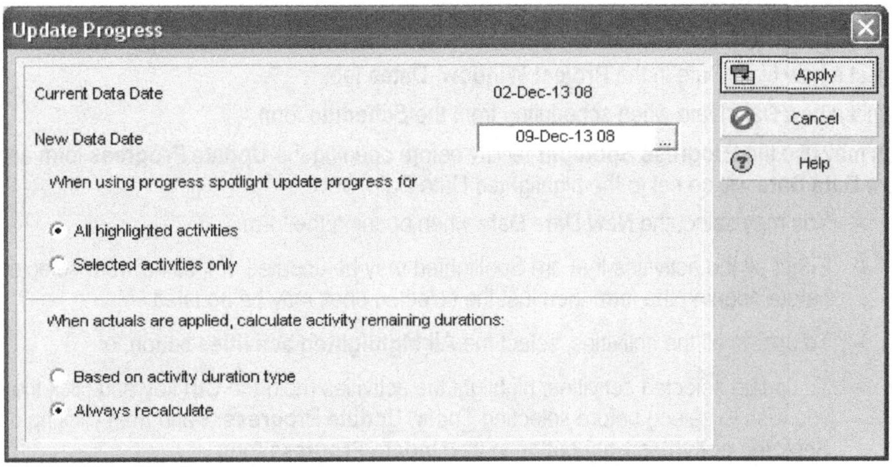

Unlike P3 and SureTrak, this Primavera **Update Progress** facility uses the **Planned Start** and **Planned Finish** dates (not the **Early Start** and **Early Finish**) for setting the **Actual Start** and **Actual Finish** dates of in-progress activities.

Thus, when the **Planned Dates** of an in-progress activity are different from the **Actual Start** and **Early Finish** dates and the activity is Automatically updated to be complete, then both these dates are set to the **Planned** dates and the **Actual Start** may be changed and the **Actual Finish** not set to the original **Early Finish**.

The following picture displays the Early bar (the upper bar) and the Current Project set as a Baseline (the lower bar) which therefore reflects the Planned Dates:

Activity Name	Orig Dur	Start	Finish
Activity A	20d	08-Sep-14 08 A	19-Sep-14 17 A
Activity B	20d	29-Sep-14 08 A	24-Oct-14 17
Activity C	20d	27-Oct-14 08	21-Nov-14 17

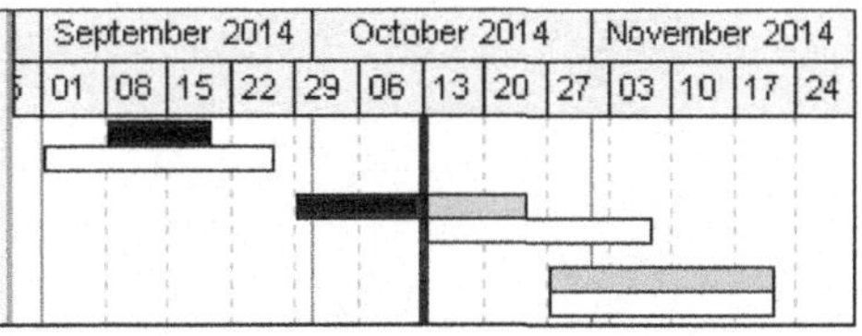

continued...

The following picture shows the effect of applying **Update Progress** to the schedule above. The Actual Start of Activity 2 has been changed and the Actual Finish of Activity 2 set to the Planned Dates, which is not the same as the original Early Finish:

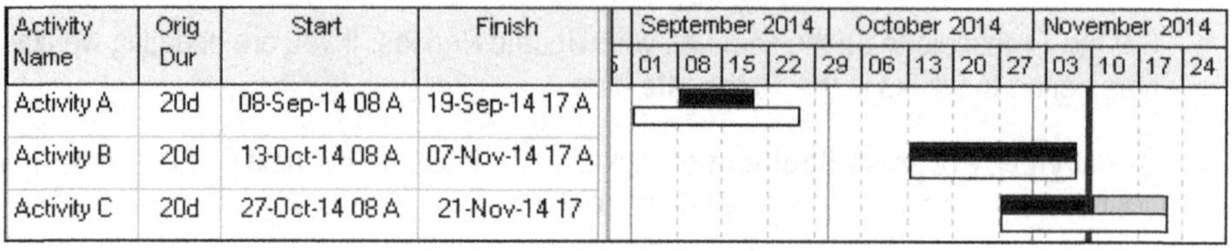

NOTE: You should not use this facility on a schedule with progress when you wish your activities to be Automatically updated to the Early dates (as in P3, SureTrak, and Microsoft Project) and not the Planned dates.

You may consider using a Global Change to set the Planned Dates to the Start and Finish dates before running Progress Spotlight, but this will also change the Original Duration and the % Duration will not calculate correctly.

There are several options for setting the **New Data Date**:

- Select a new Data Date in the **Project Window**, **Dates** tab,
- Select a new Data Date when scheduling from the **Schedule** form,
- You may use the **Progress Spotlight** facility before opening the **Update Progress** form and the **New Data Date** will be set to the highlighted Data Date, or
  - ➢ You may select the **New Data Date** when opening the form.
  - ➢ Either all the activities that are Spotlighted may be updated or if some were selected before opening the form then just the selected ones may be updated.
  - ➢ To update all the activities, select the **All highlighted activities** button, or
  - ➢ To update selected activities, highlight the activities (hold the **Ctrl** key and click the ones you wish to select) before selecting **Tools**, **Update Progress...** and then clicking on the **Selected activities only** button in the **Update Progress** form.

The option **When actuals are applied from timesheets, calculate activity remaining durations:** decides how the Remaining Duration is calculated:

- **Based on the activity duration type** will take into account activity type and hours to-date and reschedule the Remaining Duration in accordance with the activity Duration Type.
- **Always recalculate** will override the activity Duration Type and calculate the activity Remaining Durations and Hours as if the activity were a Fixed Units and Fixed Units/Time activity.
- Click [Apply] and the schedule will be updated as if all activities were completed according to the schedule.

16.5 Suspend and Resume

The Primavera Version 5.0 Suspend and Resume function enables the work to be suspended and the activity resumed at a later date. Open the **Activity Details** form **Status** tab and enter the **Suspend** and **Resume** dates. This function works in a similar way to the P3 and SureTrak function and enables only one break in an activity.

The following example shows an activity with a Suspend date and Resume date set:

- This feature works when an activity has commenced and normally the Suspend date is in the past and the Resume date in the future.
- The activity must have an actual start date before you can record a Suspend date.
- Only Resource Dependent and Task Dependent activities may be suspended and resumed.
- The suspended period is not calculated as part of the activity duration and resources are not scheduled in this period.

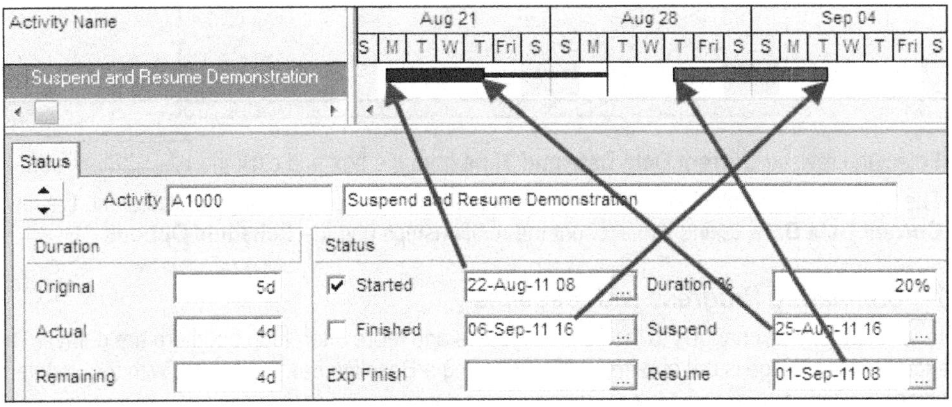

The Suspend and Resume time may be set at the incorrect time of the day. The author has found that the Suspend is usually set at the start of the day and Resume usually at the end of the day; therefore the defaults for both are illogical. Therefore you **SHOULD ALWAYS** display the time when setting Suspend and Resume dates to ensure that they are correct.

16.6 Scheduling the Project

At any time, but usually after some or all the activities have been updated, the project is scheduled:

- Open the **Schedule** form:
  - ➢ Select **Tools**, **Schedule...**, or
  - ➢ Press the **F9** key, or
  - ➢ Click on the icon.

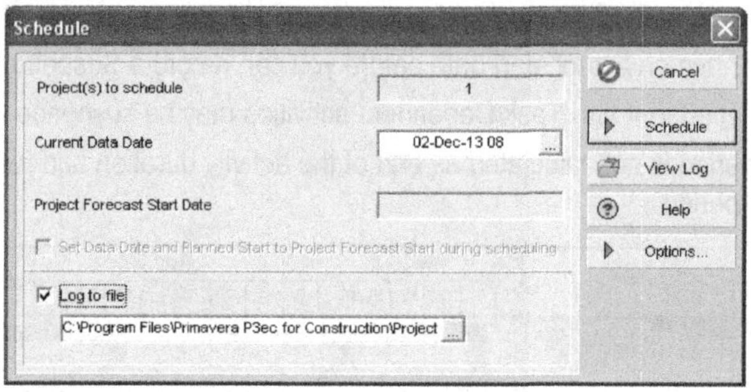

- Select the revised **Current Data Date and Time** from the box and click the Schedule icon.
- The software will recalculate all the early finish dates from the remaining durations and the new **Current Data Date**, taking into account the relationships and the **Schedule Options**.

16.7 Comparing Progress with Baseline

There will normally be changes to the schedule dates and more often than not there are delays. The full extent of the change is not apparent without having a Baseline bar to compare with the updated schedule.

To display one or more of the **Baseline Bars** in the **Bar Chart** you must open the **Bars** form and check the **Display** box of one or more baseline bars.

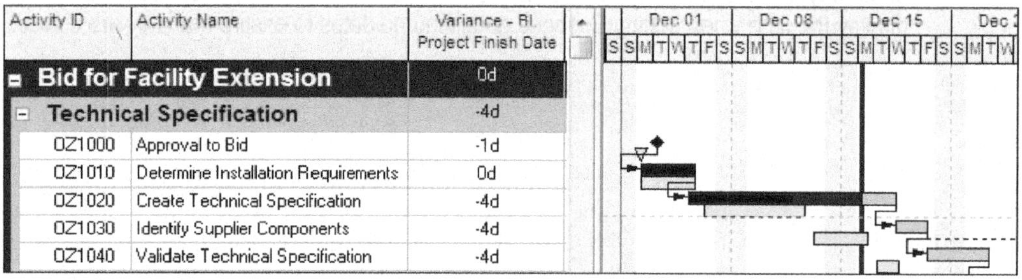

Activity ID	Activity Name	Variance - BL Project Finish Date
Bid for Facility Extension		0d
Technical Specification		-4d
OZ1000	Approval to Bid	-1d
OZ1010	Determine Installation Requirements	0d
OZ1020	Create Technical Specification	-4d
OZ1030	Identify Supplier Components	-4d
OZ1040	Validate Technical Specification	-4d

If you want to see the Start and Finish Date variances, they are available by displaying the **Variance – BL Project Start Date**, **Variance – BL Finish Date**, **Variance – BL1 Start Date**, and **Variance – BL1 Finish Date** columns.

Variance columns for Secondary and Tertiary Baseline Dates are not standard columns, but could be calculated with a Global Change.

As discussed earlier in this chapter, when a **Project Baseline** or a **Primary User Baseline** bar is displayed without a baseline being set and the **<Current Project>** (which is based on the **Planned Dates**) will be displayed. The **<Current Project>/Planned Dates** of an in-progress projects are not Baselines and may hold irrelevant data.

16.8 Progress Line Display on the Gantt Chart

This is a new feature to Primavera P6 Version 7.

A progress line displays how far ahead or behind activities are in relation to the Baseline. Either the Project Baseline or the Primary User Baseline may be used and there are four options:

- Difference between the **Baseline Start Date** and **Activity Start Date**,
- Difference between the **Baseline Finish Date** and **Activity Finish Date**,
- Connecting the progress points based on the **Activity % Complete**,
- Connecting the progress points based on the **Activity Remaining Duration**.

There are several components to displaying a Progress Line:

- Firstly the progress line is formatted using the **View, Bar,** 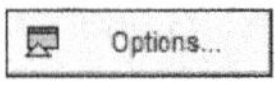

 form, **Progress Line** tab, which may also be opened by right-clicking in the Gantt Chart area:

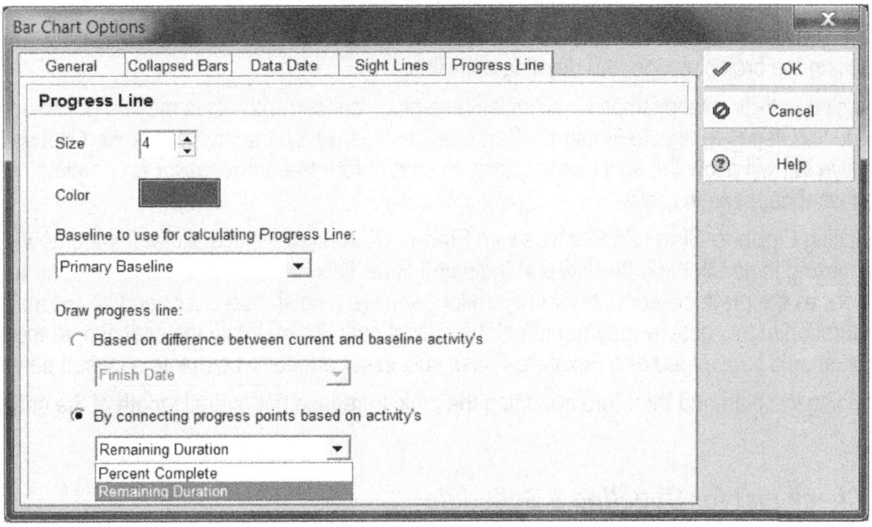

- Selecting **View, Progress Line** to hide or display the **Progress Line**.
- If you use either of the options of Percent Complete or Remaining Duration then you must display the appropriate Baseline Bar that has been selected as the **Baseline to use for calculating Progress Line:**
- The picture below shows the option highlighted above of **Percent Complete**:

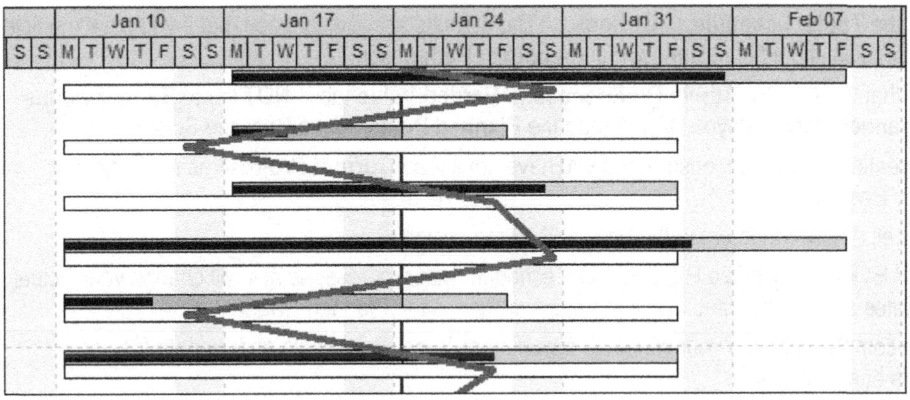

16.9 Corrective Action

Date slippage occurs when an activity is rescheduled to finish later than originally planned. There are two courses of action available:

- The first is to accept the slippage. This is rarely acceptable, but it is the easiest answer.
- The second is to examine the schedule and evaluate how you could improve the end date.

Solutions to return the project to its original completion date must be authorized by the person responsible for the project.

Suggested solutions to bring the project back on track include:

- Reducing the durations of activities on, or near, the critical path. When activities have applied resources, this may include increasing the number of resources working on the activities. Changing longer activities is often more achievable than changing the length of short duration activities.
- Providing more work time and changing calendars, say from a five-day to a six-day calendar, so that activities are being worked on for more days per week.
- Reducing the project scope and deleting activities.
- Changing activity relationships so activities take place concurrently. This may be achieved by introducing negative lags to Finish-to-Start relationships, which maintains a Closed Network. A negative lag will allow the successor activity to start before the predecessor is complete, which is often what happens in reality.
- Replacing Finish-to-Start relationships with Start-to-Start relationships. Activities are now progressing in parallel and therefore at the same time. This has the potential of creating an open network as the predecessor activity may no longer have a finish successor and an extension in the duration of this activity may not affect the critical path. To maintain the critical path then this option should be avoided or a Finish-to-Finish successor added to complete a closed network.
- Changing the plan and therefore changing the logic to reduce the overall length of the critical path.

16.10 Check List for Updating a Schedule

Before updating a schedule you should check the following items:

- Ensure you are showing the time from the **Edit**, **User Preferences...**, **Dates** tab and check that all Start and Finish dates and times are logical. You can see that these times make sense when you are updating a project.
- Check the **% Complete Type** for all the activities; the author recommends that this be set to **Physical**.
- Check the **Tools**, **Schedule...**, **Options....** The defaults are usually good, but if you have multiple calendars you should consider using the **Longest Path** option.
- Check that the **Admin**, **Admin Preferences...**, **Earned Value** tab is **NOT** set to **Budget values with planned dates**, so you will not read the **Planned Dates** from a Baseline Schedule.
- After creating a Baseline, ensure that you have not left a **<Current Project>** as the Project or Primary Baseline.
- Ensure all Actual Dates are in the past as they are assigned.
- NEVER EVER use Update Progress on a schedule with progress, as this will change your Actual Start dates and Finish dates of in-progress activities to the Planned Dates.
- Take a complete copy of your schedule including all Baseline projects after update for claim analysis at a later date.

16.11 Workshop 14 – Progressing and Baseline Comparison

Background

At the end of the first week you have to update the schedule and report progress and slippage.

Assignment

1. We are now going to update the schedule as at the end of the first week.
2. Update the project activities in the **Activities**, bottom pane **Status** tab or by adding the **Actual Start** and **Actual Finish** columns with the following information:

Activity ID	Activity Name	Actual Start	Actual Finish	Activity % Complete	Rem Dur
13 Bid for Facility Extension		04-Dec-18 08			33d
Technical Specification		04-Dec-18 08			10d
OZ1000	Approval to Bid	04-Dec-18 08		100%	0d
OZ1010	Determine Installation Requirements	04-Dec-18 08	06-Dec-18 16	100%	0d
OZ1020	Create Technical Specification	05-Dec-18 08		60%	6d

3. Reschedule the project by pressing **F9** to open the **Schedule** form:
   - ➢ Change the Current Data Date to 10-Dec-18 08:00, that will be Monday morning,
   - ➢ Open the **Schedule Options** form by clicking on the [▷ Options...] icon and ensure **Retained Logic** is selected,
   - ➢ Close the **Schedule Options** form and
   - ➢ Click on the [▷ Schedule] to reschedule,
   - ➢ Check the answer in the following pictures.

Activity ID	Activity Name	Activity % Complete	Orig Dur	Rem Dur	Start	Finish	Total Float	Variance - BL Project Finish Date
Bid for Facility Extension			38d	33d	04-Dec-18 08 A	28-Jan-19 16	0d	0d
Technical Specification			15d	10d	04-Dec-18 08 A	21-Dec-18 16	9d	-2d
OZ1000	Approval to Bid	100%	0d	0d	04-Dec-18 08 A			-1d
OZ1010	Determine Installation R	100%	4d	0d	04-Dec-18 08 A	06-Dec-18 16 A		0d
OZ1020	Create Technical Speci	60%	5d	6d	05-Dec-18 08 A	17-Dec-18 16	7d	-2d
OZ1030	Identify Supplier Compo	0%	2d	2d	18-Dec-18 08	19-Dec-18 16	7d	-2d
OZ1040	Validate Technical Spe	0%	2d	2d	20-Dec-18 08	21-Dec-18 16	9d	-2d
Delivery Plan			19d	19d	24-Dec-18 08	22-Jan-19 16	0d	0d
OZ1050	Document Delivery Met	0%	4d	4d	24-Dec-18 08	31-Dec-18 16	9d	-2d
OZ1060	Obtain Quotes from Sup	0%	8d	8d	03-Jan-19 08*	14-Jan-19 16	0d	0d
OZ1070	Calculate the Bid Estim	0%	3d	3d	15-Jan-19 08	17-Jan-19 16	0d	0d
OZ1080	Create the Project Sche	0%	3d	3d	18-Jan-19 08	21-Jan-19 16	0d	0d
OZ1090	Review the Delivery Pl	0%	1d	1d	22-Jan-19 08	22-Jan-19 16	0d	0d
Bid Dcoument			19d	19d	02-Jan-19 08	28-Jan-19 16	0d	0d
OZ1100	Create Draft of Bid Doc	0%	6d	6d	02-Jan-19 08	09-Jan-19 16	9d	-2d
OZ1110	Review Bid Document	0%	2d	2d	23-Jan-19 08	24-Jan-19 16	0d	0d
OZ1120	Finalise and Submit Bid	0%	2d	2d	25-Jan-19 08	28-Jan-19 16	0d	0d
OZ1130	Bid Document Submitte	0%	0d	0d		28-Jan-19 16*	0d	0d

continued...

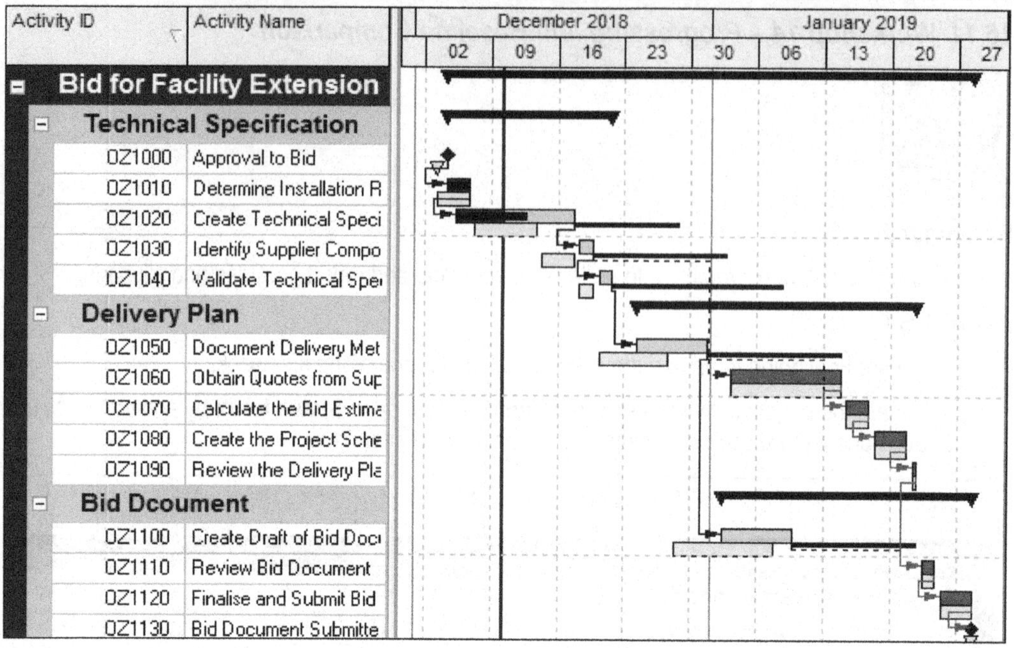

NOTE: The lower bar is the Baseline and delays to activities created by the late scheduling of the **Create Technical Specification** activity is clear in the picture above.

4. Open the **General** tab of the **Create Technical Specification** activity and change the % Complete Type to **Duration**. Reschedule and the **% Complete** will change to 0%. A link is now established between the % Complete and Remaining Duration and therefore the % Complete and Remaining Duration may not be entered independently from the Activity % Complete. The Activity % Complete Value is zero because the Remaining Duration is greater than the original duration.

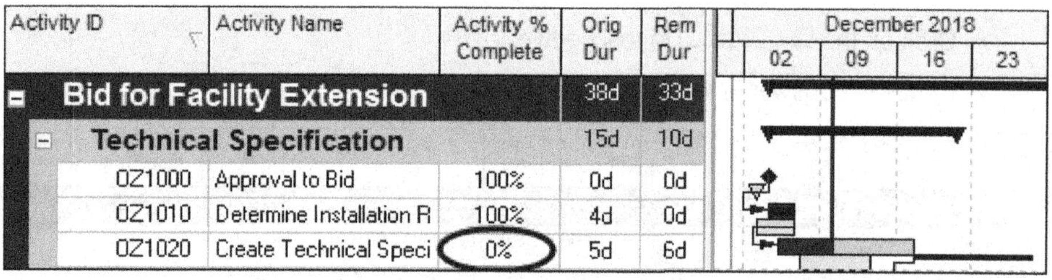

5. Enter 20% Complete against the **Create Technical Specification** activity in the **Status** tab, the Remaining Duration will reduce to 4 days and you will notice the link between the Activity % Complete and Remaining Duration.

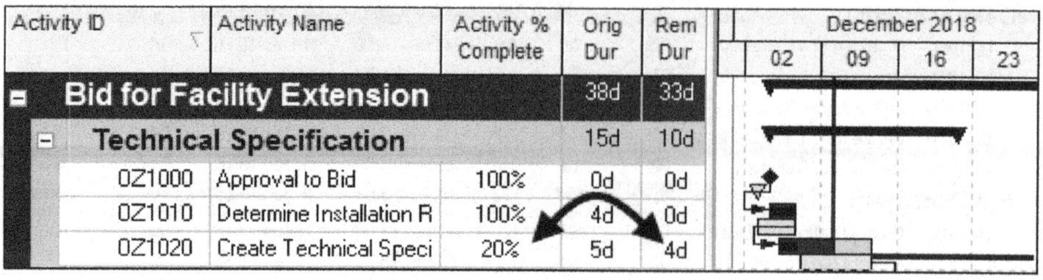

6. Now change the % Complete for the **Create Technical Specification** activity to 50%.
7. Reschedule.
8. Ensure you are showing the Duration Sub-unit of Hours by opening the **Edit, User Preferences... Time Unit** tab and check the **Duration Format Sub-unit Hours** box and check **Show Duration label**.
9. This has resulted in the Remaining Duration no longer being expressed in whole days and activities which are two days long, for example Activity OZ1030, now spanning three days because they start and finish at midday.

Activity ID	Activity Name	Activity % Complete	Orig Dur	Rem Dur	Start	Finish	Total Float	Variance - BL Project Finish Date
Bid for Facility Extension			38d	33d	04-Dec-18 08 A	28-Jan-19 16	0d	0d
Technical Specification			11d 4h	6d 4h	04-Dec-18 08 A	18-Dec-18 12	12d 4h	1d 4h
OZ1000	Approval to Bid	100%	0d	0d	04-Dec-18 08 A			-1d
OZ1010	Determine Installation R	100%	4d	0d	04-Dec-18 08 A	06-Dec-18 16 A		0d
OZ1020	Create Technical Speci	50%	5d	2d 4h	05-Dec-18 08 A	12-Dec-18 12	10d 4h	1d 4h
OZ1030	Identify Supplier Compo	0%	2d	2d	12-Dec-18 12	14-Dec-18 12	10d 4h	1d 4h
OZ1040	Validate Technical Spe	0%	2d	2d	14-Dec-18 12	18-Dec-18 12	12d 4h	1d 4h
Delivery Plan			22d 4h	22d 4h	18-Dec-18 12	22-Jan-19 16	0d	0d
OZ1050	Document Delivery Met	0%	4d	4d	18-Dec-18 12	24-Dec-18 12	12d 4h	1d 4h
OZ1060	Obtain Quotes from Sup	0%	8d	8d	03-Jan-19 08*	14-Jan-19 16	0d	0d
OZ1070	Calculate the Bid Estim	0%	3d	3d	15-Jan-19 08	17-Jan-19 16	0d	0d
OZ1080	Create the Project Sche	0%	3d	3d	18-Jan-19 08	21-Jan-19 16	0d	0d
OZ1090	Review the Delivery Pla	0%	1d	1d	22-Jan-19 08	22-Jan-19 16	0d	0d
Bid Dcoument			22d 4h	22d 4h	24-Dec-18 12	28-Jan-19 16	0d	0d
OZ1100	Create Draft of Bid Doc	0%	6d	6d	24-Dec-18 12	04-Jan-19 12	12d 4h	1d 4h
OZ1110	Review Bid Document	0%	2d	2d	23-Jan-19 08	24-Jan-19 16	0d	0d
OZ1120	Finalise and Submit Bid	0%	2d	2d	25-Jan-19 08	28-Jan-19 16	0d	0d
OZ1130	Bid Document Submitte	0%	0d	0d		28-Jan-19 16*	0d	0d

10. The situation of having durations that are not round days is often not desirable and may be prevented by using Physical % Complete and entering the Remaining Duration in whole days.
11. Save the layout as **OzBuild Workshop 14 –Baseline Comparison**.

17 USER AND ADMINISTRATION PREFERENCES AND SCHEDULING OPTIONS

This chapter will look at the following topics:

- User Preferences
- Admin menu, removed from the Optional Client
- Admin Preferences, removed from the Optional Client
- Admin Categories, removed from the Optional Client
- Miscellaneous Defaults, Set Default Project and Language

Functions removed from the Optional Client are accessed from the Web tool.

17.1 User Preferences

Select **Edit**, **User Preferences...** to open the **User Preferences** form. This form is used to set up a number of user defined parameters, which will determine how data is displayed.

The **User Preferences** form may also be opened by right-clicking in the right side of the bottom views when the **Resource Usage Spreadsheet** or **Resource Usage Profile** are displayed.

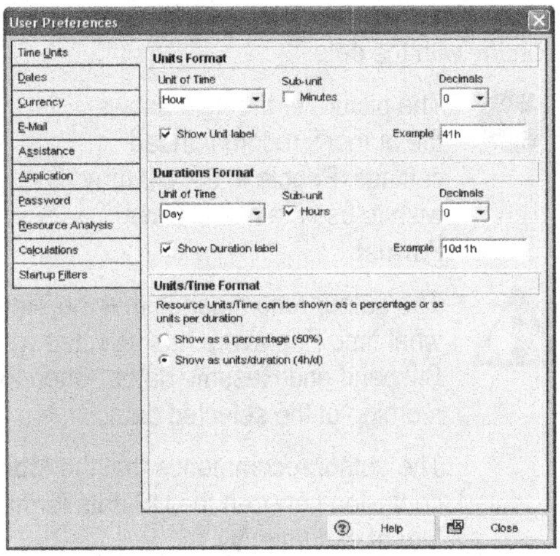

17.1.1 Time Units Tab

The **Units Format** section of the tab is used to define the **Unit of Time** format that resource information and resource assignments are displayed with, e.g., days or hours.

The **Durations Format** section of the tab is used to define the **Unit of Time** format that activity durations are displayed with, e.g., days or hours.

The picture to the right shows the author's recommended settings.

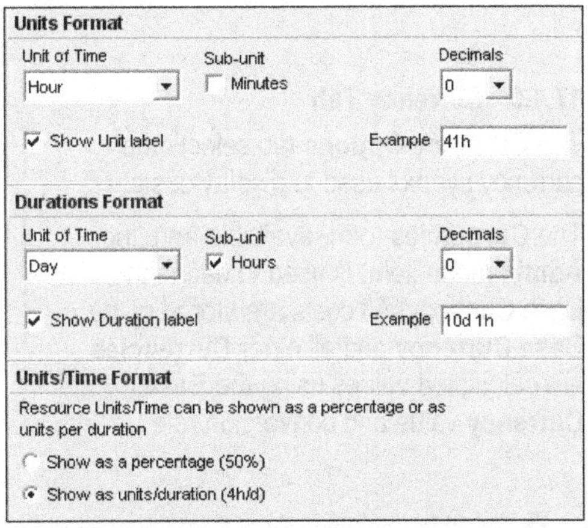

The **Units/Time Format** section of the form enables the Microsoft Project-type formatting options of **Resource/Time Format** to show Resource utilization as a percentage (50%) or as units per duration (4h/d). Therefore there are several options here; for example, three people assigned to an activity may be displayed in many formats including:

- 300%
- 24h/d
- 3d/d
- 3h/h

17.1.2 Dates Tab

The **Dates** tab is self-explanatory and is used to format the display of dates and time.

NOTE: It is not possible to display the years with 2 characters or hide the year and there always has to be a date separator, thus leading to wider date columns than otherwise could be achieved. It is also not possible to display the days in characters such as Mon or Monday with the date.

The picture to the right shows the author's recommended settings. People in the US may wish to use their local **Date Format**.

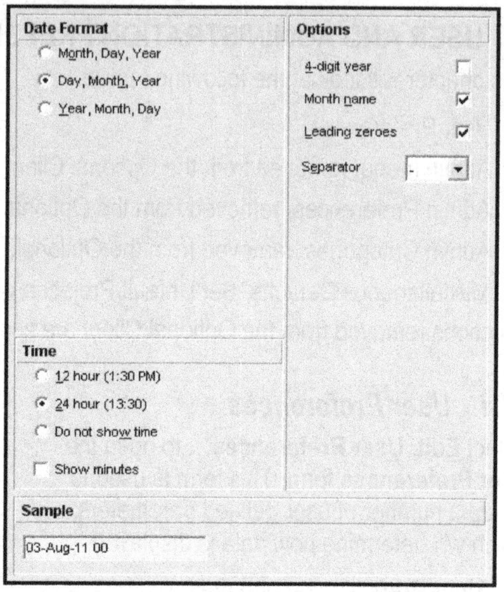

The author recommends that the **Time** should always be displayed so a user may see what time Primavera has selected when assigning Actual dates, Constraint dates, Suspend and Resume dates. Often Primavera selects 00:00, which is midnight on the morning of the selected date.

The author recommends that the **Month** name should always be displayed to avoid confusion between the US date format of mm/dd/yy and the ROW (Rest of World) date format of dd/mm/yy.

17.1.3 Currency Tab

The **Currency Options** tab selects the currency symbol used to display costs.

The **Currencies** form, available from the **Admin** menu item, is used to define the Base Currency. All costs are stored in the **Base Currency** and all other **Currencies** are calculated values using the **Base Currency** value and conversion rate.

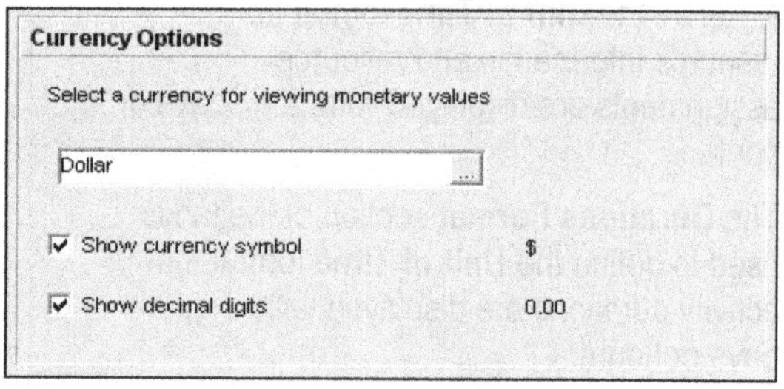

It is possible to have two currencies with the same symbol and if a user selects a different currency then all costs displayed by the user will be converted to a different value.

This option must be carefully monitored and if you do not need multiple currencies then it is suggested that you should delete all but one currency, to avoid any possible problems. If you are using multiple currencies then make sure that all have a different sign so there is no confusion.

17.1.4 E-Mail Tab

The **E-mail Protocol** tab sets up the current user's E-mail system.

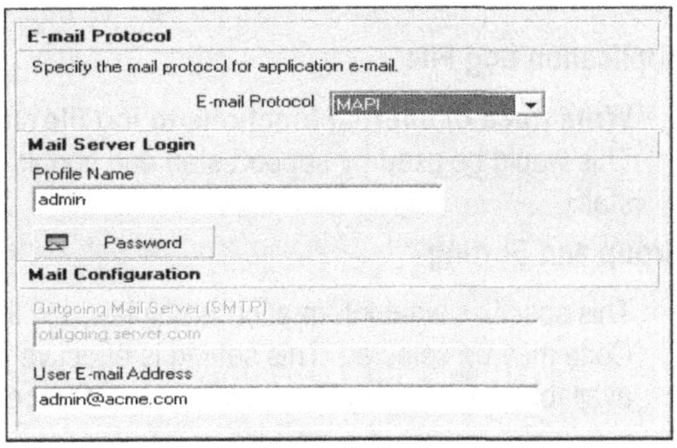

17.1.5 Assistance Tab

The **Assistance** tab specifies which wizards are run when creating **Resources** and **Activities**.

NOTE: It is suggested to turn both off as it is quicker to type the information straight into the required fields when you know how to use the software.

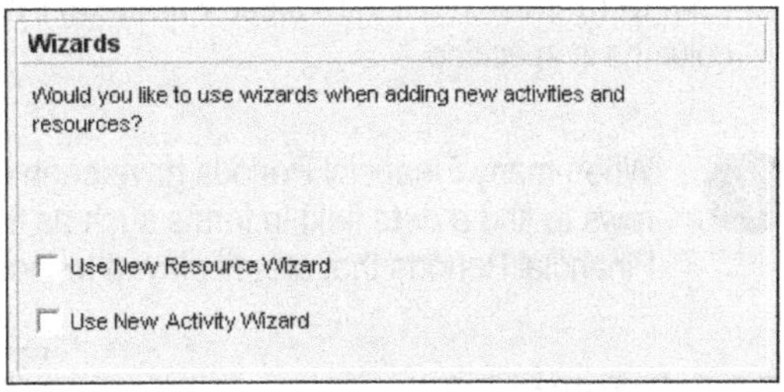

17.1.6 Application Tab

Startup Window

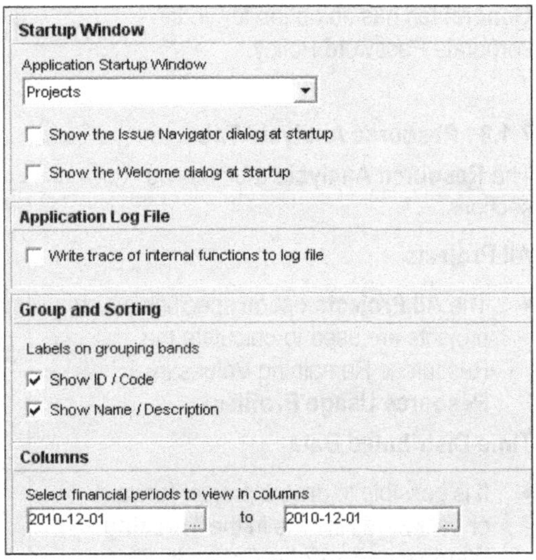

- **Application Startup Window** specifies which Primavera window is displayed when the software is started.
  - If you work in the same project all the time then set this to **Activities** and do not close the project when closing Primavera. The next time you open Primavera you will be taken to your project in the **Activities Window**.
  - If you work in different projects all the time then select **Projects** and you will be taken to the **Projects Window**.
- **Show the Issue Navigator dialog at startup** should only be checked if you wish to view the Issues when the software starts.
- **Show the Welcome dialog at startup** displays a Welcome dialog box on startup and would not usually be displayed as it slows down the user's access to the software.

Application Log File

- **Write trace of internal functions to log file** creates a log of all data entries titled ERRORS LOG. This would be used by support staff and should not be turned on unless requested by support staff.

Group and Sorting

- This specifies what information is displayed in the bands; one or both options of Description or Code may be selected. This setting is effective in situations where a Group and Sort form is not available, such as the **Predecessor** and **Successors** forms.
- Primavera Version 5.0 introduced a function titled **Reorganize Automatically**: this was removed in Version 8.1 and replaced by the **Auto-Reorganization** command.

Columns

- Primavera Version 5.0 introduced **Financial Periods** where the periods that may be displayed in columns is specified.

When many Financial Periods have been created, you may have to scroll down hundreds of rows to find a data field in forms such as the **Filter** form. You should limit the number of Financial Periods that are displayed to those that are currently being used.

17.1.7 Password Tab

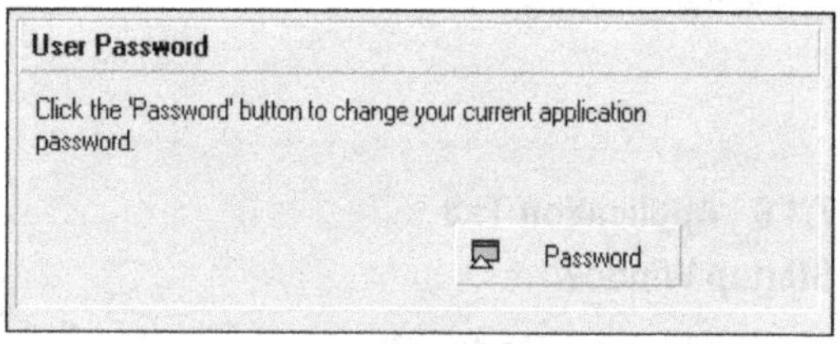

The **User Password** tab is used to change the user password.

The **Admin**, **Admin Preferences...**, **General** tab has an option for your corporate Password Policy.

17.1.8 Resource Analysis Tab

The **Resource Analysis** tab has two sections:

All Projects

- The **All Projects** option specifies which projects are used to calculate the Resources Remaining Values in **Resource Usage Profiles**.

Time-Distributed Data

- It is possible to drag a project forward or backwards in time in the **Tracking Window** or **Portfolio Analysis**. This action creates a new set of dates titled **Forecast dates**. The **Resource Usage Profile** and **Resource Usage Spreadsheet** time in the **Tracking Window** may be calculated using either the Current Schedule by checking **Remaining Early Dates** or the revised **Forecast dates**.

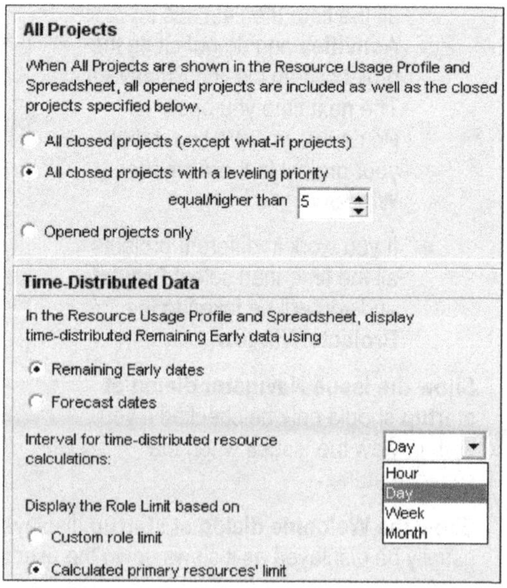

- **Interval for time-distributed resource calculations:** This option determines the time increment for displaying the Resource Usage Profile and Resource Usage Spreadsheet data.

  When this is set to days and you display time-distributed data in hours, all the hours will be displayed on the first hour:

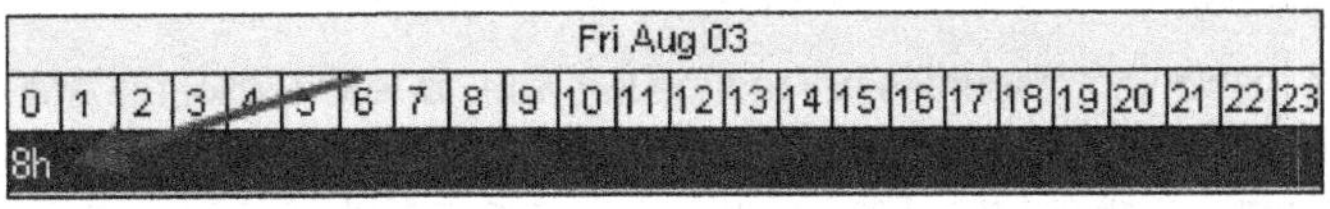

  Selecting hours will spread the resource where they are scheduled but this consumes computer resources.

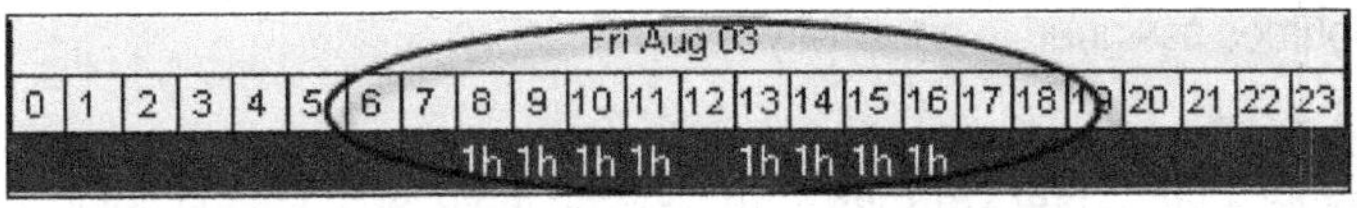

The **Interval for time-distributed resource calculations:** must be equal to or smaller than the timescale or the resource data will be displayed in the first time increment of the timescale and not distributed over the whole time period.

- **Display the Role limit based on** – Primavera introduced **Role Limits** in Version 6.0 and this enables options for displaying the **Role Limits** in **Resource Profiles**. A role may have been defined a limit of six resources but only have four Primary Resources assigned. This option allows you to decide if you wish to display a limit of four based on the resources available or six based on the limit assigned to the role.

17.1.9 Calculations Tab

IT IS IMPORTANT TO UNDERSTAND THIS OPTION.

The **Calculations** tab, Resource Assignments section has two options:

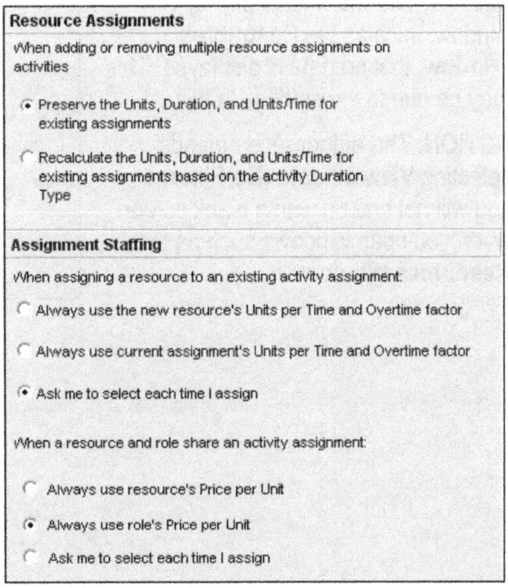

- **Preserve the Units, Duration, and Units/Time for existing assignments.** With this option, as Resources are added or deleted the total number of hours assigned to an Activity increases or decreases. The hours assigned for each resource are calculated independently.
- **Recalculate the Units, Duration, and Units/Time for existing assignments based on the activity Duration Type.** The total number of hours assigned to an activity will stay constant as second and subsequent resources are added or removed from an Activity, except when the Activity Type is **Fixed Duration and Units/Time**.

Recalculate the Units, Duration, and Units/Time for existing assignments based on the activity Duration Type is similar to making an activity Effort Driven in Microsoft Project. There is no similar function in P3 and SureTrak.

With this option as you assign or remove resources to or from a activity the total number of hours of work stay constant and the work is divided amongst all the resources.

Thus, assigning resources will reduce the work for each resource and either the activity duration will reduce or the Units per Time Period for each resource assignment will reduce. This calculation is dependent on the Duration Type.

The author prefers as a default **Preserve the Units, Duration, and Units/Time for existing assignments**. In this situation each resource work is independent on other resources assigned to an activity.

- **Assignment Staffing** are new functions to Primavera Version 5.0 options available on the **Calculations** tab of the **User Options** form allowing the user to set the defaults for:
  - Selecting the Units per Time when assigning a substitute resource to an existing resource assignment.
  - Selecting the Price per Unit for a resource which is being assigned to a Role.

The options are to select the existing resource, the new resource, or to be prompted each time a resource/role is substituted.

17.1.10 Startup Filters Tab

The **Startup Filters** option enables the selection of filters for Resources, Roles, OBS, Activity Codes and Cost Accounts, which may be applied to the current project or to all data.

You may find when you open up a window, such as the **Resources Window**, that no data is displayed. This may be due to the settings in this tab.

ACTION: The author recommends selecting **View all data (No Filter)** so you will not end up with a blank screen when you open windows such as the **Resources Window**.

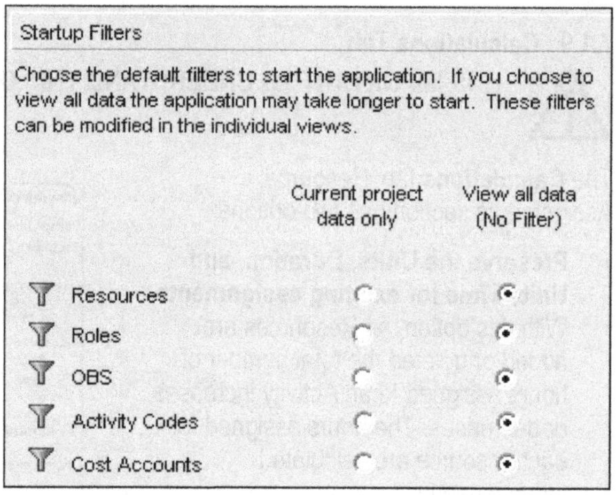

17.2 Admin Menu

The links between Users, OBS, and Projects is covered in more detail in the **Managing the Enterprise Environment** chapter. This module is an introduction to the contents of the Admin Menu.

The Admin menu is available in P6 Professional but has been removed from the P6 Optional Client and has to be accessed through the Web module when using the Optional Client.

P6 Professional

The **Admin** command opens the **Admin** form.

Depending on how Primavera has been installed and your access rights set, you may or may not have access to some or all of these menus.

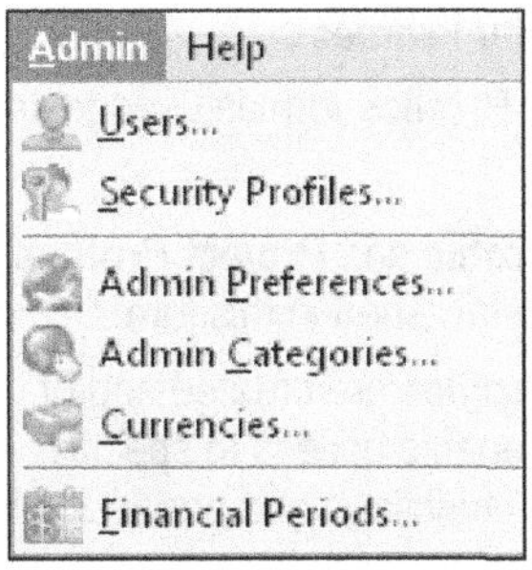

P6 Optional Client

The web **Administer** menu is where the Admin commands are located and these are all very similar to the Professional Client.

The Web commands will not covered in this book but they operate in exactly the same way.

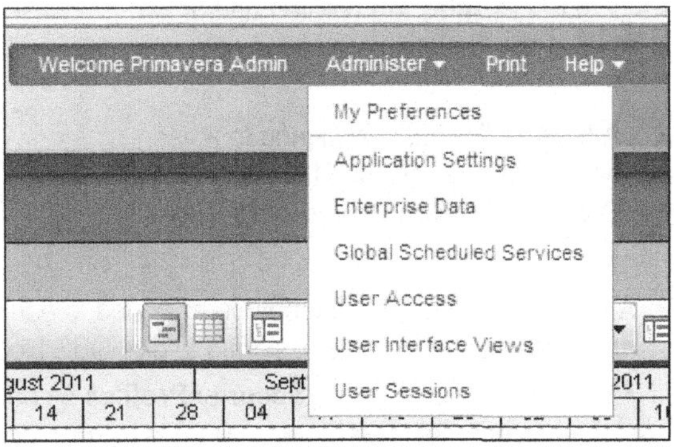

17.2.1 Users

The **Users** form is used to add and delete system users. The following information may be recorded:

- **General** tab: The Personal Name (the person's name), Login Name, Password and the Users Resource ID in the **Resources Window**.
- **Contact** tab: The person's telephone number and e-mail.
- **Global Access** tab: The Global information a user may change is specified here by assigning a **Global Profile**.

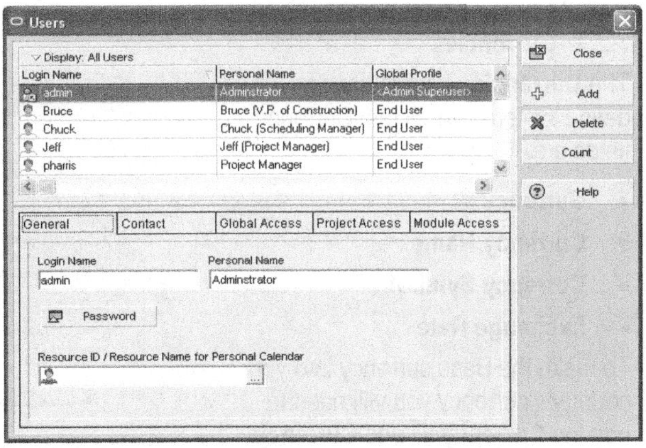

The **Global Access** tab is the location where user access to resources may be restricted.

- **Project Access** tab: This is where the **User** is assigned to one or more OBS Nodes and may only access Projects associated with those OBS Nodes. The level of user access to is projects controlled by the designated **Security Profile**.
- **Module Access** tab: This is where a person is assigned a license. A license needs to be assigned before the person may operate the system.

The User may also be assigned to an OBS Node in the **Organizational Breakdown Structure** form.

17.2.2 Security Profiles

The **Security Profiles** form is used to set up security.

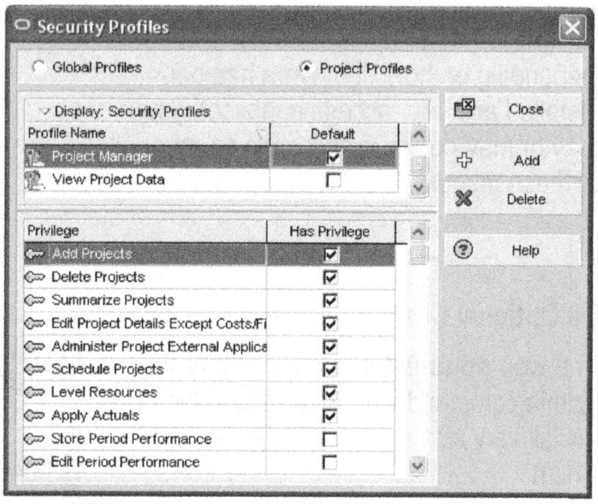

- **Global Profile** and **Project Profiles** may be established in this form.
- **Global Profiles** are created and/or edited to enable access to specific Enterprise functions and are assigned to users.
- **Project Profiles** are created and/or edited to enable access to specific Project functions.
- A **Project Profile** is assigned to a user when they are assigned to one or more **Organization Breakdown Structure** Nodes.
- A different **Project Profile** may be assigned to each user for each OBS Node, but an EPS Node and Projects may only be assigned to one OBS Node.

It is critical that the **Security Profiles** be carefully evaluated and each person assigned an appropriate level.

No one except the Administrator/s should be able to delete critical data such as project and EPS Nodes.

17.2.3 Currencies

The **Currencies** form is used to define system currencies. Currency fields are:

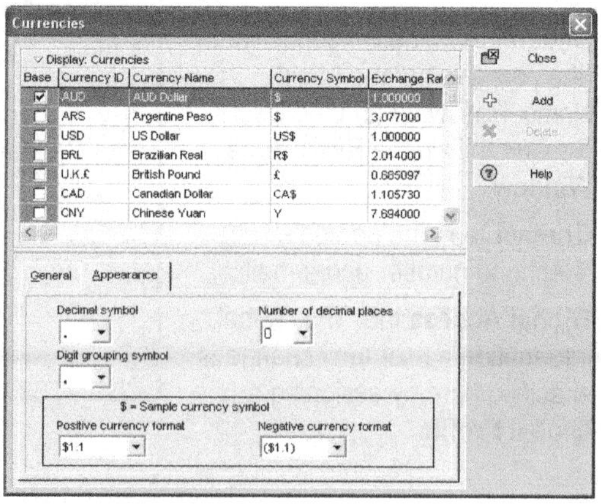

- **Currency ID**
- **Currency Name**
- **Currency Symbol**
- **Exchange Rate**

To make the Base currency into your country's currency you will need to edit the **Currency ID** and **Currency Symbol** as the first currency is permanently checked.

See the warning under Currency earlier in this chapter. Delete all unwanted currencies and make all Currency Symbols unique.

17.2.4 Financial Periods

This is where the Financial Periods associated with Storing Period Performance are created.

For details on this function see the section on Store Period Performance in the **Earned Value** chapter.

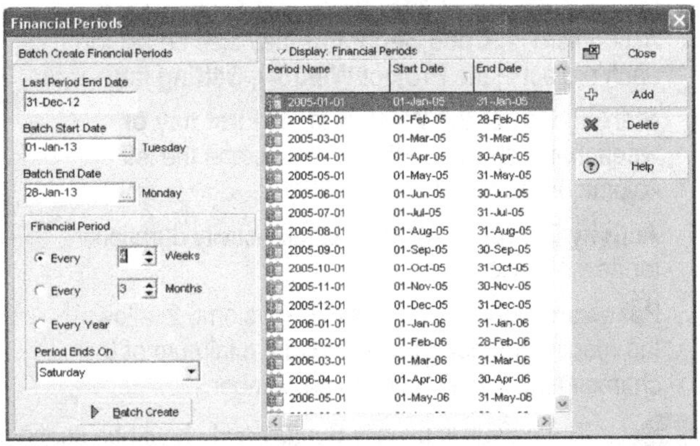

Financial Periods have to be used when it is important to have data that reflects how much work was completed or costs spent in each period and not just averaged over the periods to date. Period data is often used to create S-Curves.

17.2.5 Timesheet Dates

This option has been removed from P6 Professional. **Timesheets** may be managed in the Web application.

17.3 Admin Preferences

This form sets the default preferences for Primavera.

The **Admin Preferences** form has a number of tabs, which will be covered in more detail in the next section of this chapter.

If you do not have access to the **Admin Preferences** then these options would have been set up by the system administrator for your organization.

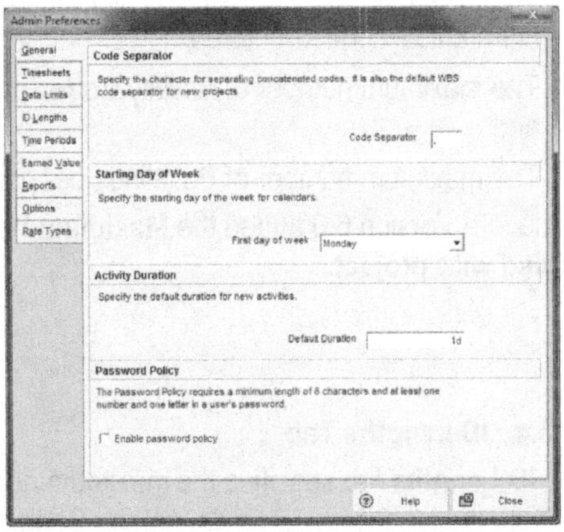

Some preferences may only be changed in this form. Items described as **defaults** may also be changed in other windows.

Select **Admin**, **Admin Preferences...** to open the **Admin Preferences** form.

17.3.1 General Tab

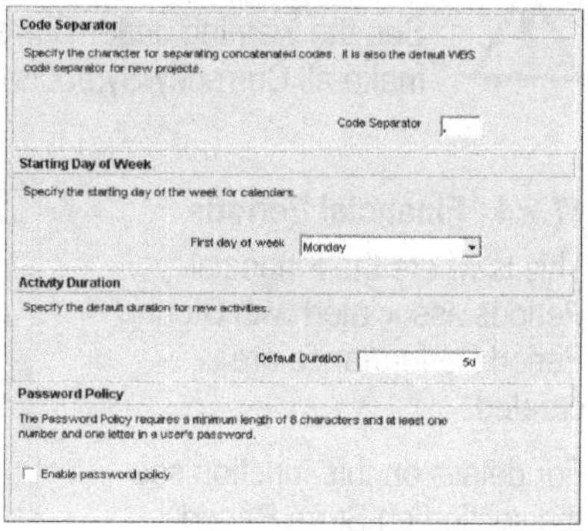

- **Code Separator** sets the default separator for new project WBS Codes and other codes such as Cost Accounts. The **Code Separator** may also be set for each project in the **Project Window**, **Setting** tab.
- **Starting Day of the Week** sets the **First day of week** that is shown on the timescale and the left column of calendars.
- **Activity Duration** sets the default Activity duration for new activities.
- **Password Policy**, introduced in Version 6.2, allows the requirement for a password of a minimum of 8 characters including a letter and number.

The default is usually Sunday and should be changed to a Monday, which results in the calendar day in the timescale representing a working day, which is often a lot more useful than a nonwork day date.

17.3.2 Timesheets Tab

The **Timesheets** tab was removed in Version 8.1 Professional, but is available in the Web application.

17.3.3 Data Limits Tab

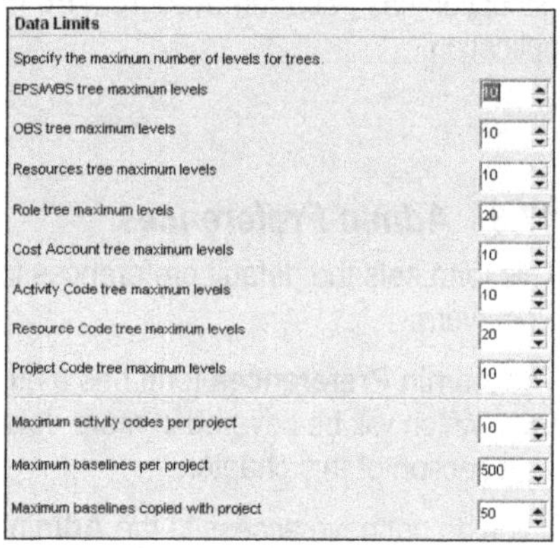

The **Data Limits** tab specifies:

- The maximum number of levels allowed in all hierarchical code structures,
- The maximum number of Activity Codes per project, and
- The maximum number of Baselines per project.

Primavera Version 6.0 added the **Maximum baselines copied with project**.

17.3.4 ID Lengths Tab

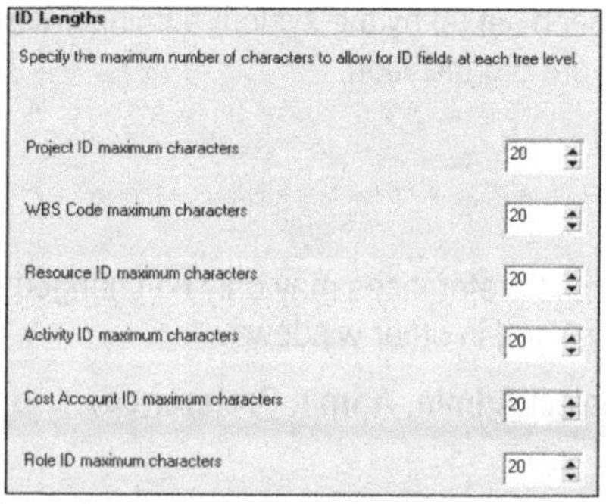

The **ID Lengths** tab specifies the maximum number of characters in the Code ID fields, not the Code Description.

17.3.5 Time Periods Tab

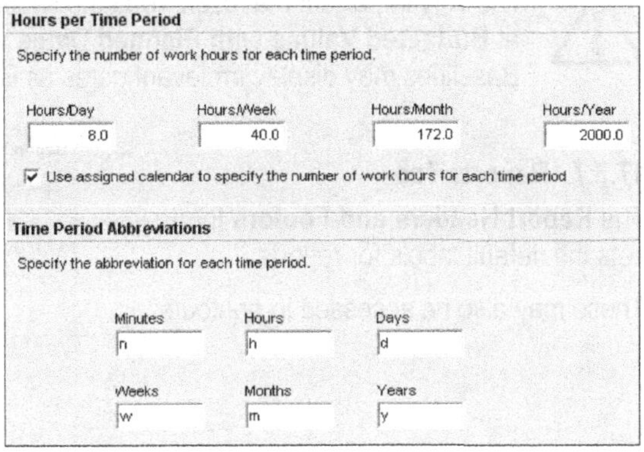

- **Hours per Time Period** values are used to convert from one time period Unit to another, for example, from days to hours. Therefore, a 40 hours activity would be calculated as 5-day with the setting displayed in the picture.
- **NOTE:** It is important that these conversions are understood. Please refer to the **Calendar** chapter for more details.
- Checking **Use assigned calendar to specify the number of work hours for each time period** enables users to edit the **Hours per Time Period** in each calendar.

It is very important when multiple calendars with different hours per day are being used that this check box is checked and the user correctly sets the **Hours per Time Period** in each calendar.

- **Time Period Abbreviations** are used to indicate the display durations.

17.3.6 Earned Value Tab

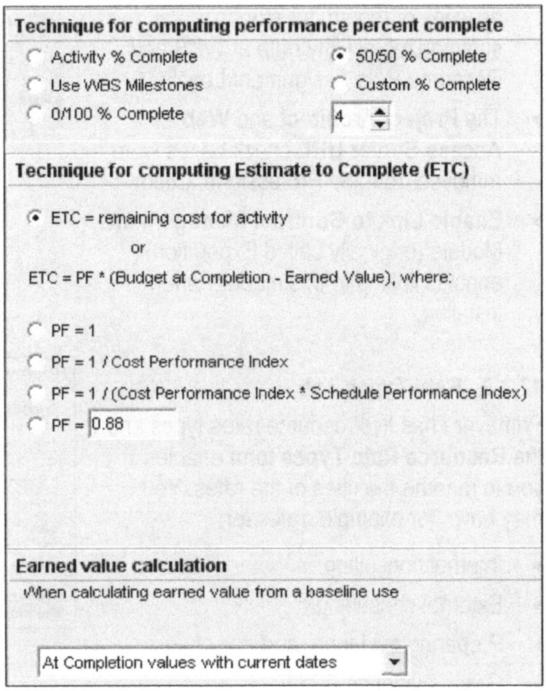

See the **Earned Value** chapter for more information.

This tab sets the WBS defaults for calculating Earned Value and may be changed individually for each WBS and apply to all activities within each WBS Node.

- The **Technique for computing performance percent complete** selects the formula for calculating the Earned Value.
- The **Technique for computing Estimate to Complete (ETC)** selects the formula for calculating the ETC. The ETC is a calculated field and is independent of the **At Completion Fields** but may contain the same value.
- **Earned value calculations** selects some options for calculating the Earned Value and displaying the Baseline Bar. The Primavera default is usually set to **Budgeted Values with Planned Dates**. This setting must never be used and please read the warning below.

It is very important that users read the sections on Planned Dates as leaving the setting at **Budgeted Values with Planned Dates** will result in the risk that all in-progress Baselines may display irrelevant dates as Baseline dates.

17.3.7 Reports Tab

The **Report Headers and Footers** form sets the default labels for reports.

These may also be accessed in printouts.

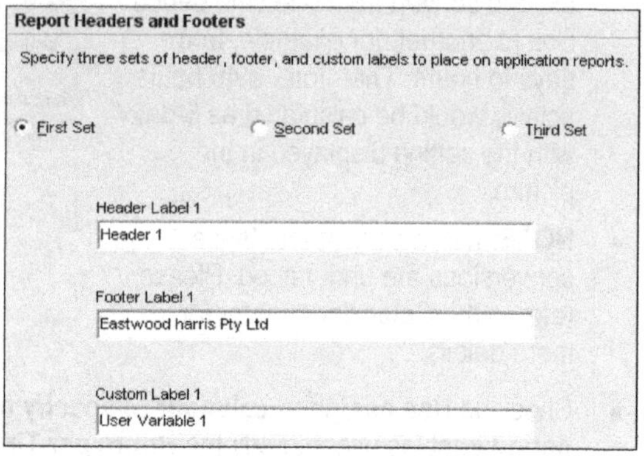

17.3.8 Options Tab

- The **Specify the interval to summarize and store resource spreads** tab sets the time period, such as week or month, for storing summarized activity data at WBS and Resource/Role Assignment Levels.
- The **Project Architect** and **Web Access Server URL** check boxes were removed from the Professional Client.
- **Enable Link to Contract Management** Module (originally called Expedition) enables linking to this module when installed.

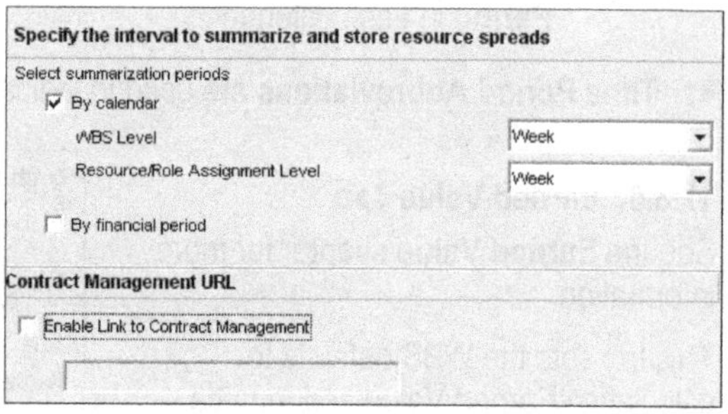

17.3.9 Rate Types Tab

Primavera has five resource rates types and the **Resource Rate Types** form enables you to rename the titles of the rates. You may have, for example, rates for:

- Internal consulting,
- External consulting,
- Preparing evidence, and
- Giving evidence.

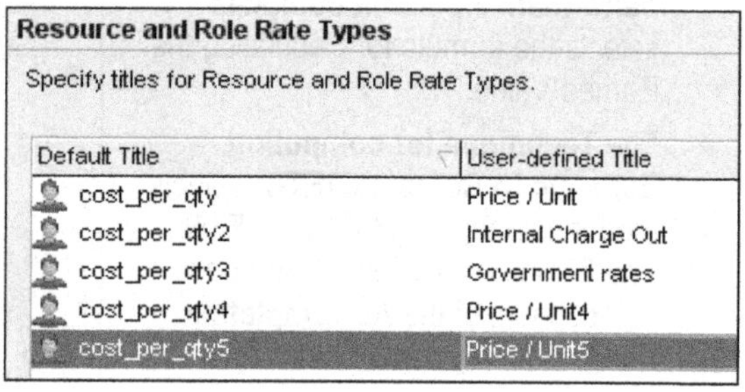

17.3.10 Industry Tab

The Industry Type determines the terminology used in some fields. In earlier versions this was set when the software was loaded. It may now be set **Admin**, **Admin Preferences...**, **Industry** tab.

You will need to restart P6 for a change to take effect:

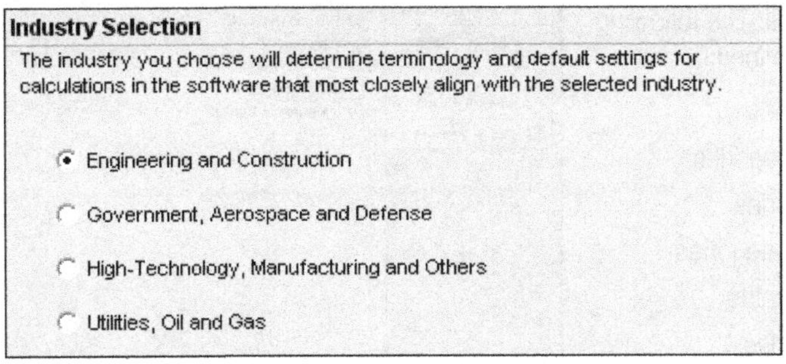

The following table displays the terminology:

Industry Type	Terminology	Name of Project Comparison Tool
Engineering and Construction	Budgeted Units & Cost Original Duration	Claim Digger
Government, Aerospace, and Defense	Planned Units & Cost Planned Duration	Schedule Comparison
High-Technology, Manufacturing and Others	Planned Units & Cost Planned Duration	Schedule Comparison
Utilities, Oil, and Gas	Budgeted Units & Cost Original Duration	Claim Digger

Engineering and Construction:

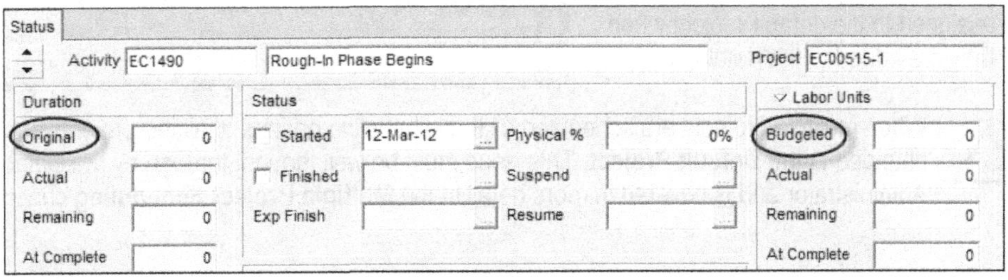

Government, Aerospace, and Defense:

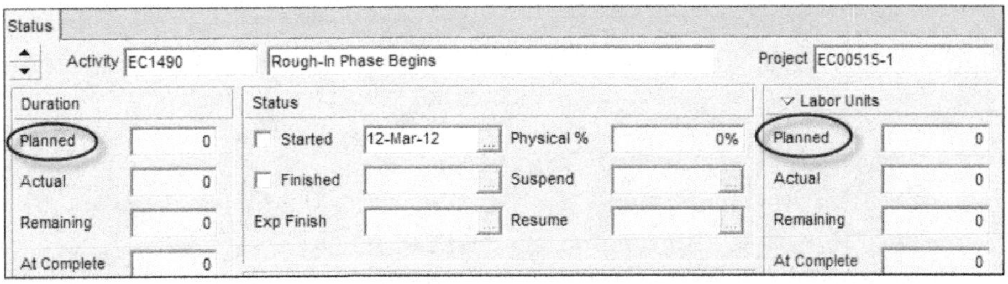

17.3.11 Admin Categories

The **Admin, Admin Categories** form is where the global data items are defined. This form is self-explanatory and will not be explained in detail. The following categories are defined:

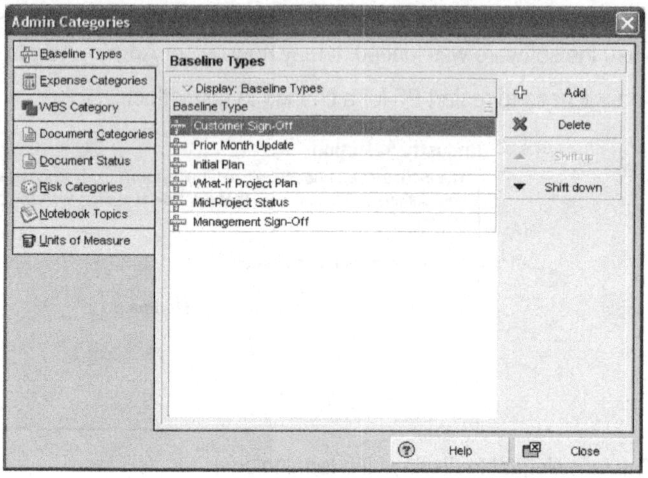

- Baseline Types
- Expense Categories
- WBS Categories
- Document Categories
- Document Status
- Risk Categories
- Notebook Topics
- Units of Measure – for Material Resources

The WBS Category defines a set of codes that may be assigned to WBS Nodes allowing the WBS structure to be reorganized under a different set of codes.

17.4 Miscellaneous Defaults

17.4.1 Default Project

Select **Project, Set Default Project...** to open the **Set Default Project** form. When multiple projects are opened the default project's settings are used to:

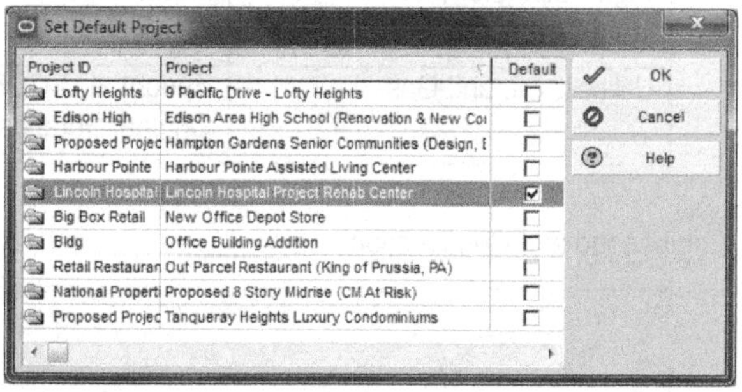

- Schedule and level all open projects.
- New data items, such as issues, are assigned to the default project when they are added to the database.

When multiple projects are scheduled all the scheduling options of all the projects are changed to the **Default Project**. This issue must be well thought through by the Database Administrator and is covered in more detail in the **Multiple Project Scheduling** chapter.

17.4.2 Set Language

Select **Tools**, **Set Language...** to open the **Set Language** form and select the language that the column headers and menu items are displayed in.

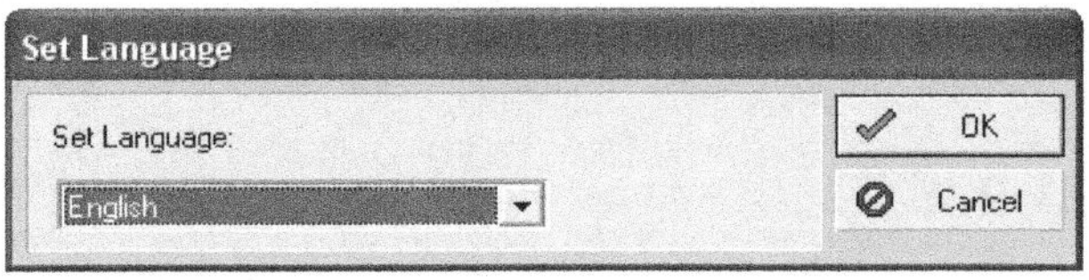

Version 15.2 move the selection of the menu language from the **Tools** menu to the Login screen.

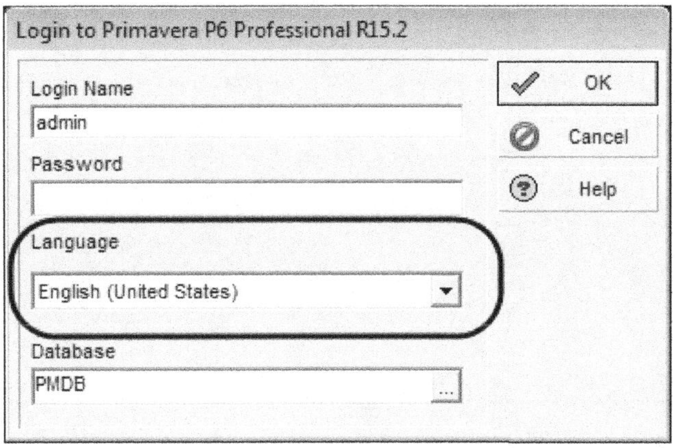

18 CREATING ROLES AND RESOURCES

Traditionally, planning and scheduling software defines a **Resource** as something or someone that is required to complete the activity and sometimes has limited availability. This includes people or groups of people, materials, equipment and money.

Primavera is able to assign Costs, a Calendar, one or more Roles and some personal information to a **Resource**.

Primavera has a function titled **Roles**. A Role is normally used at the planning stage of a project and represents a skill or position. Later, and before the activity begins, a Role would be filled by assigning a specific individual who would be defined as a Resource. Roles may be assigned to both Resources and Activities. A search by Role may be conducted on all the Resources when it is required to replace an Activity-Assigned Role with an individual from the Resource pool. Primavera allows rates to be assigned to Roles.

There are a large number of resource functions available in Primavera. Without getting into too much detail, this publication will outline the important resource-related functions that will enable you to create and assign Roles and Resources to your schedules.

This chapter will concentrate on:

Topic	Menu Command
Creating **Roles**	Select **Enterprise**, **Roles...** to open the **Roles** form.
Creating **Resources**	Open the **Resources Window**: • Select **Enterprise**, **Resources**, or • Click on the  icon on the **Enterprise** toolbar.
Editing **Resource Calendars**	Select **Enterprise**, **Calendars...** to open the **Calendars** form.

The following steps should be followed to create and use resources in a Primavera schedule:

- Create the resources in the **Resources Window**.
- Create the **Roles**, if required, in the **Roles** form.
- Assign Resources to Roles from either the **Resources Window** or the **Roles** form.
- Manipulate the Resource Calendars if resources have special timing requirements.

18.1 Understanding Resources and Roles

There are typically two methods of using the Resource function for resource planning:

- Individual Resources, and
- Group Resources

18.1.1 Individual Resources

These resources are individual people who are often responsible for completing the activity or tasks associated with activities to which they have been assigned. They are identified by name in P6.

This is typically work undertaken in an office environment, such as an IT development project, where timesheets are often completed by the people undertaking the work and the timesheet system is directly linked to the scheduling system.

In this situation, the updating of Activities that are in-progress is completed by the person assigned as a Resource to an Activity, often via the timesheet system, and the scheduler has a review function in the project updating.

18.1.2 Group Resources

These resources represent groups of people, such as trades or disciplines on a construction site. Very large projects gangs or crews, which would be made up of equipment and a number of different trades, could also be considered. The person responsible for the work is not a resource assigned to an activity and individual people doing the work will not be assigning their timesheets directly to activities in the schedule.

Also, in this environment the scheduler normally updates the activities and the resources. In this situation it is recommended that a minimum number of resources be assigned to activities. This is because every resource added to the schedule will need to be updated and as more resources are added, the scheduler's workload will increase.

Resource minimization simplifies a schedule and makes it easier to manage large schedules. This is achieved by not cluttering the schedule with resources that are in plentiful supply or are of little importance, and/or by grouping trades or disciplines into crews and gangs on large projects.

When Group Resources are used the Role function tends to become redundant but could be used to plan the contractor type and/or the actual contractor to be used on the project.

18.1.3 Input and Output Resources

When you create your resources, you may also consider them within the context of the following headings:

- **Input Resources** – These resources are required to complete the work and represent the project costs:
  - Individual people by name.
  - Groups of people by trade, discipline, or skill.
  - Individual equipment or machinery by name.
  - Groups of equipment or machinery by type.
  - Groups of resources such as Crews, Gangs, or Teams made up of equipment and machinery.
  - Materials.
  - Money.

- **Output Resources** – These could be the project deliverables or outcomes and could have a direct relationship to the project income:
  - Specifications completed.
  - Bricks laid.
  - Tons/Tonnes of material loaded with an excavator.
  - Lines of code written.
  - Tests completed.

  This type of resource is often used in the mining environment where the output in tones/tonnes or volume is scheduled and/or leveled.

The analysis of and difference between the Input and the Output resources' value and timing may be used to represent the Cash Flow, Cash Position and Project Profit (or loss).

The type of contract that the work is being conducted under would often determine if the client is more interested in the Input or Output Resources.

18.1.4 Understanding Roles

An evaluation at project or enterprise level in order to understand the long term demand for resources may be made by a combination of Roles for long term planning and Resources for short term planning.

Roles are assigned to activities for long term planning and Resources represent individual people are assigned to roles for short term planning and would represent activity assignment.

The light area to the right of the histogram below shows the unsatisfied demand of the roles titled **Unstaffed Remaining Units** and the satisfied demand from the resources is in the dark are to the left and are titled **Staffed Remaining Units**.

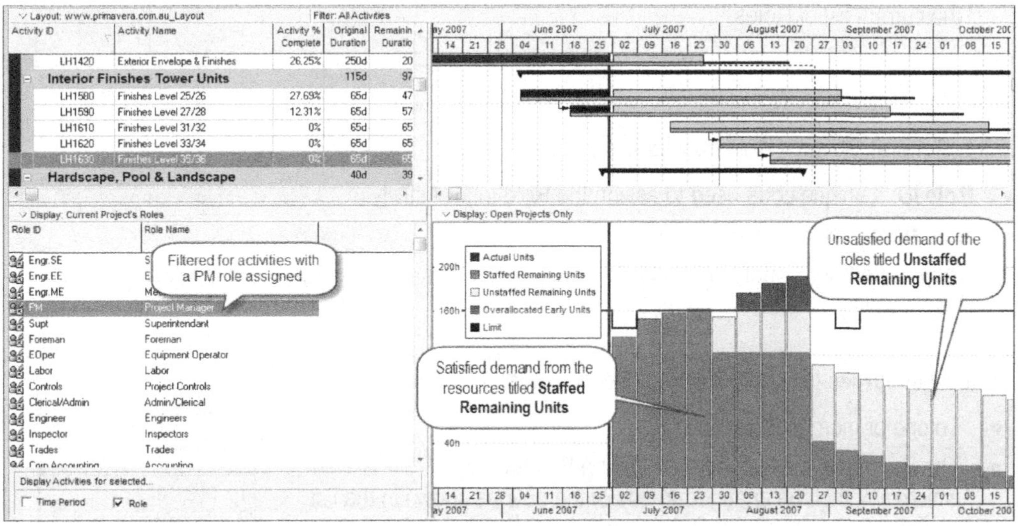

If you are a construction contractor and not assigning work to individual people then you may consider using resources only as they have more functions than roles.

18.2 Creating Roles

Roles are created, edited, and deleted in a similar method as WBSs.

To create, edit, or delete a **Role** select **Enterprise**, **Roles...** to open the **Roles** form:

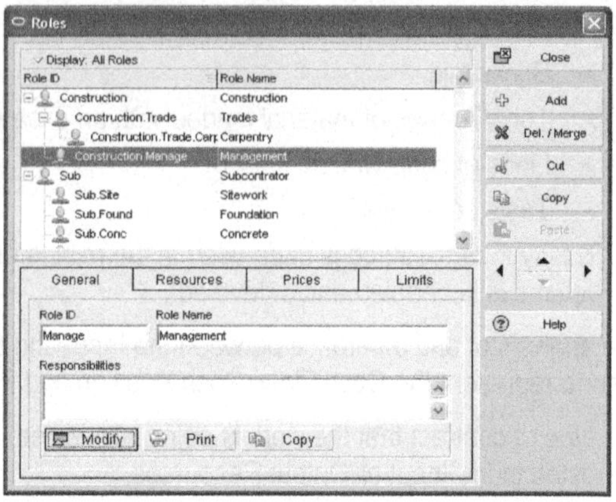

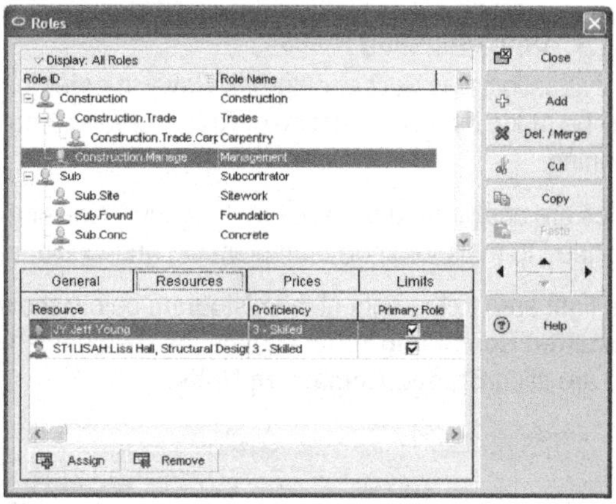

The following formatting, filtering, and sorting functions are available in the **Roles** form:

- Click on **Display: All Roles** and then the **Filter By** tab to open a menu where the roles can be filtered by **All Roles** or **Current Projects Roles**.
- Click on the **Role ID** title or the **Role Name** title to sort the Roles by **Role ID** or **Role Name**.
- **Roles** may also be displayed by the **Chart** view. The **Roles** form will have to be resized to use this function effectively.
- The **Find** function (or **Ctrl+F**) enables a Role name to be searched.
- The **Print** function opens the **Print Preview** form allowing the printing of the current list of Roles.

In the **General** tab each Role may be assigned a:

- **Role ID**, a unique code used to assign the Role to an Activity.
- **Role Name**, the Name of the Skill or Trade.
- **Responsibilities**, where you may enter text, hyperlinks, and pictures about the Role Responsibility.

In the **Resources** tab each Role may be assigned:

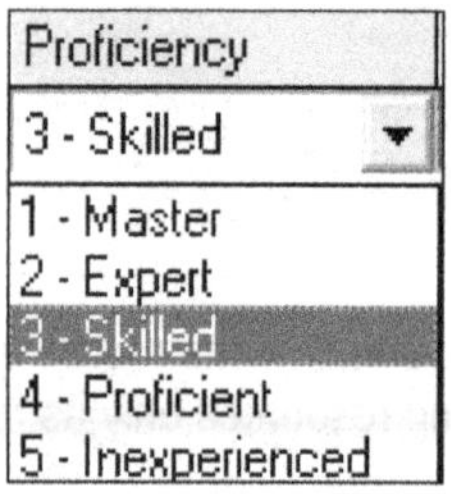

- To one or more Resources.
- The Resource is assigned by default a **Proficiency** of "3 – Skilled" which may then be changed to any of the options shown in the list.
- The Resource may be assigned a **Primary Role** which would represent the task or job they would normally be assigned.
- The **Primary Role** also links to Role availability when the option in the **Edit**, **User Preferences...**, **Resource Analysis** tab, **Display the Role Limit based** on is set to **Calculate primary resources' limit**.

Primavera supports **Rates for Roles**. Up to 5 rates (the same number of rates as resources) may be assigned to roles which may be used for estimating and cash flow forecasting of projects before the actual resource completing the work is assigned to the activity.

- Click on the **Prices** tab to edit the Role Price/Unit, and
- The **Role Rate** Type is adopted from the **Resource Rate Type** set in the **Admin**, **Admin Preferences...**, **Rate Type** tab.

Role rates may not be varied over time or leveled but Resources may be.

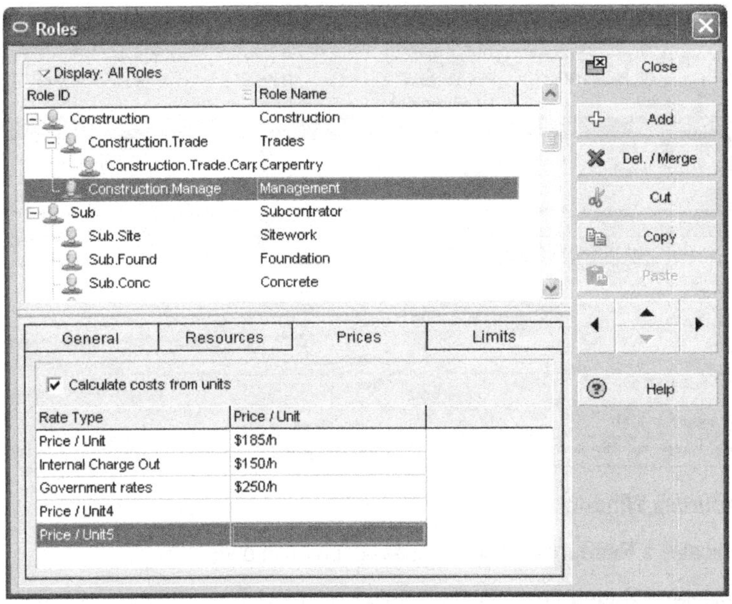

- The data columns in the **Prices** tab and **Limits** tab forms may be sorted by clicking on the column titles.
- The default rate for a project is selected when a project is created and may be changed in the **Projects Window**, **Resources** tab, **Assignment Defaults** area:

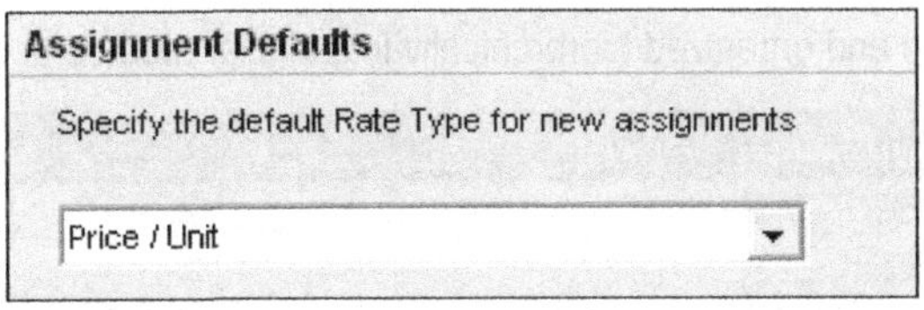

Different rates may be required for different clients such as internal project rates and rates for different types of external clients.

Five resource and role rates may not be sufficient when a company has a number of clients. There are some options which include creating a new set of resources for each project, or a new database for each project, or not selecting the option of linking costs and units.

18.3 Creating Resources and the Resources Window

To create, edit, or delete resources open the **Resources Window**:

- Select **Enterprise**, **Resources...**, or
- Click on the icon on the **Enterprise** toolbar,

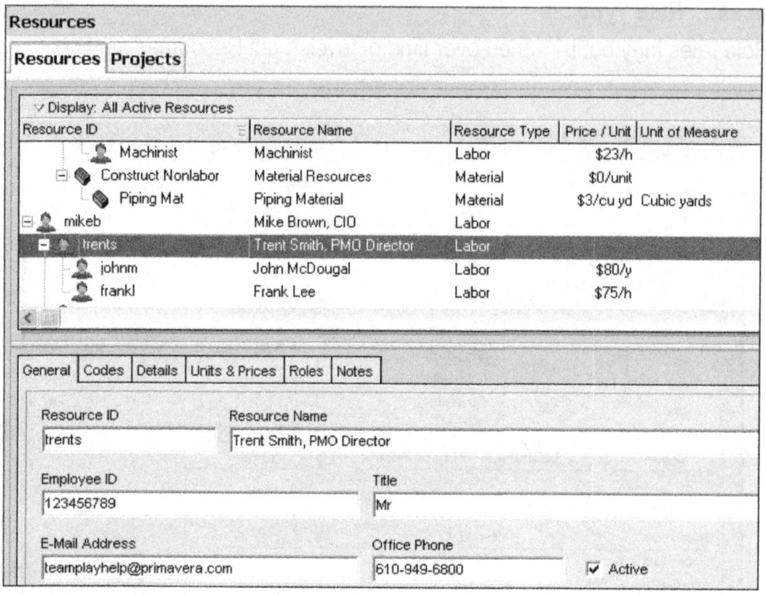

- In the **Resources Window:**
  - indicates a **Resource** which is not assigned to an open project,
  - indicates a **Resource** assigned to an open project,
  - and indicate an unassigned and assigned **Nonlabor Resource**, and
  - and indicate an unassigned and assigned **Material Resource**.

18.3.1 Resource Breakdown Structure – RBS

Resources may be added and organized hierarchically in a similar method to creating a WBS.

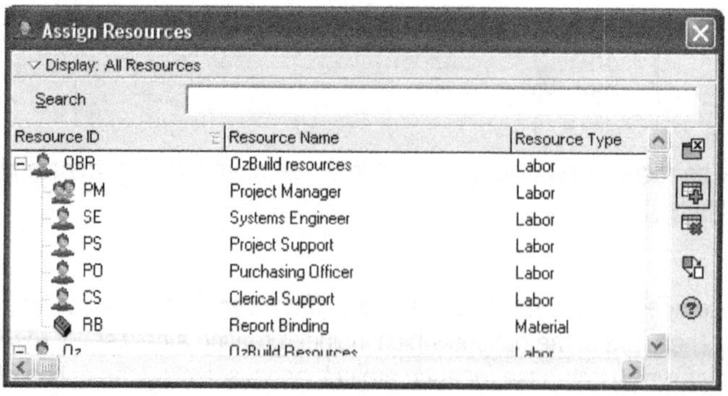

The OzBuild resources in the picture above are listed under a higher-level node titled **OzBuild Resources**. Primavera Systems calls this structure a **Resource Breakdown Structure** or **RBS**.

18.3.2 Formatting the Resources Window

The menu under the **Display: All Active Resources** has many functions that are similar to other forms:

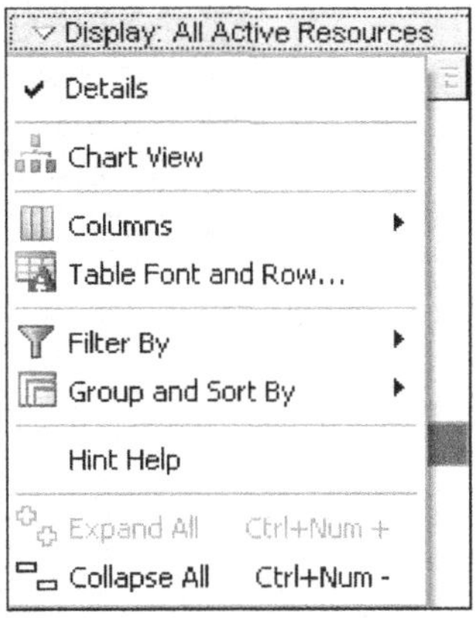

- The **Details** check box displays or hides the **Details** form in the lower pane.
- **Chart View** displays the resources as a Chart. To use this format, **Group and Sort By** must be set as **Default** or have the **Customize...** option grouped by Resources.
- **Columns**, **Table Font and Row...**, **Filter By** and **Group and Sort By** options work in a similar way to the formatting of the **Activities Window**. Click on the menus to see the options available with each.
- When the **Resources** are organized hierarchically, the **Expand All** and **Collapse All** options work in a similar way to other windows and rolls up the Resources.

18.3.3 Adding Resources

New Resources are added and deleted in a similar method to adding Activities in the **Activities Window**. Use the **Insert** key, right-click and select **Add**, or use the Add icon on the **Edit** toolbar.

18.3.4 General Tab

The fields in this tab are self-explanatory:

- The **Resource ID** has to be unique within a database and a **Resource Name** is mandatory,
- The **Employee ID**, **E-Mail Address**, **Title** and **Office Phone** are optional, and
- When the **Active** box is unchecked, the Resource is inactive and indicates that the resource is not available. When assigning Resources to Activities there is a filter to display only active Resources.

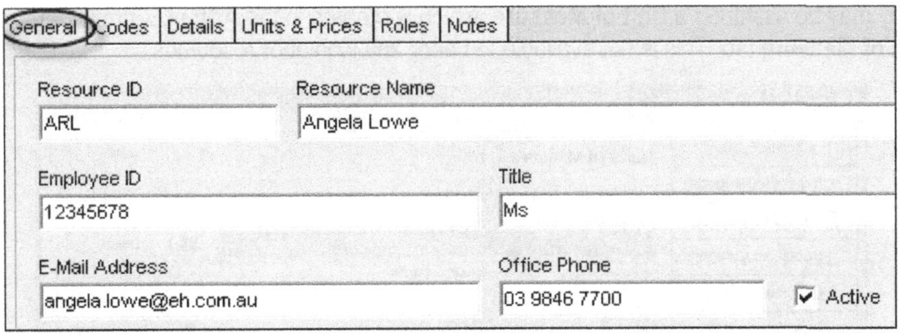

18.3.5 Codes Tab

Resource Codes are assigned to Resources allowing additional facilities to sort and report on them in the **Resource Usage Spreadsheet** and **Resources Window**.

- **Resource Codes** may be defined in the **Resource Code Definition** form, which is opened by selecting **Enterprise**, **Resource Codes...** and clicking on the Modify... icon.
- Individual **Resource Code Values** may be added to a **Resource Code** in the **Resource Codes** form by selecting **Enterprise**, **Resource Codes...**.

- Resource Codes may then be selected in a layout to sort and group Resources.

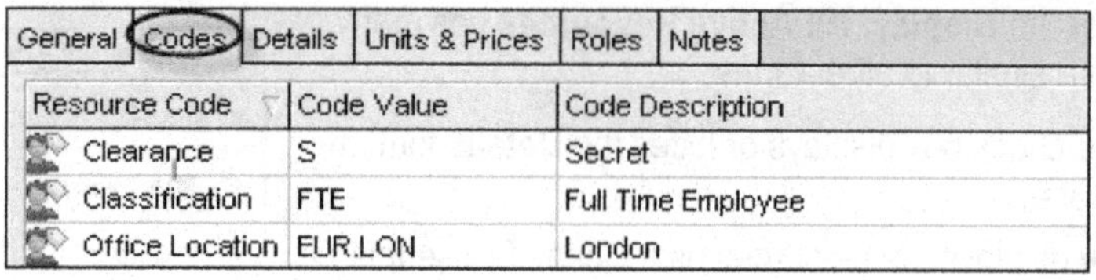

18.3.6 Details Tab

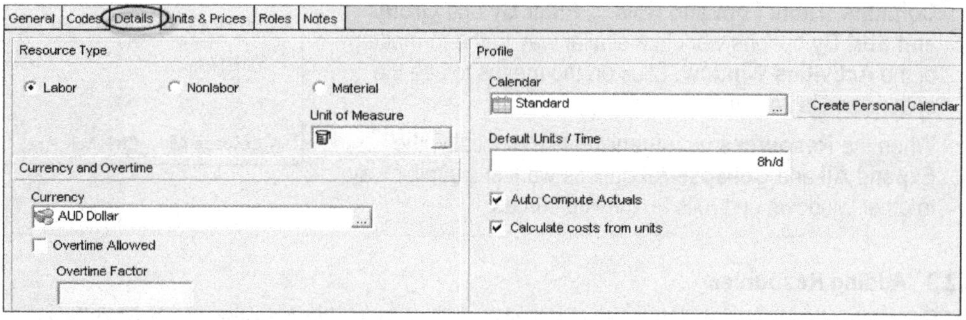

Resource Types

There are three types of Resources:

- **Labor**, intended for people
- **Nonlabor**, intended for equipment used to perform project work
- **Material**, intended for materials/supplies.

Material Resources

May be leveled and have the following differences from other resources:

- They may be assigned a **Unit of Measure**, which is created in the **Admin**, **Admin Categories...**, **Unit of Measure** tab. This is not available to Labor and Nonlabor resources.

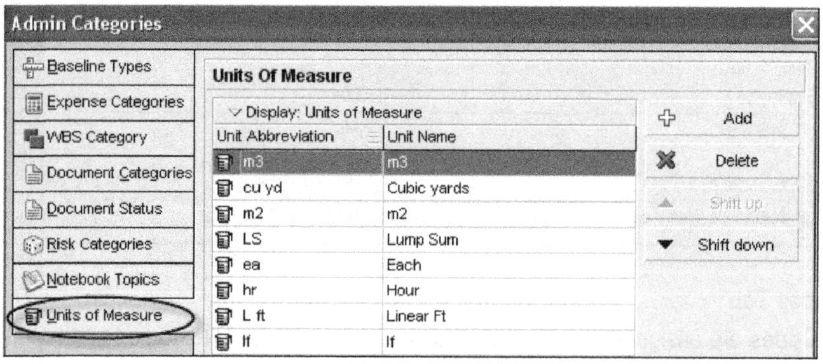

- They may not be assigned a Role.
- They may not log Overtime.

⚠ Material resources do not display units (quantities) in the **Activities Window**, as with many other products like P3, SureTrak, and Asta Powerproject. These values may be displayed in other views such as the **Resource Assignments Window** and in reports.

Currency

An alternate **Currency** may be associated with a resource. This will not affect how the Resource Unit Rates costs are entered but provides a further tagging mechanism for sorting and reporting. The costs are stored in the default currency but are displayed using the conversion rate in the currency selected for the resource.

Overtime

A **Labor Resource** may be allowed to record **Overtime** in the **Primavera timesheet** system when the **Overtime Allowed** box is checked and the costs derived from the **Unit Rates** are multiplied by the **Overtime** Factor.

Calendar

The Resource is assigned a **Global** or a **Shared Resource Calendar** in this form.

- A **Shared Resource Calendar** may be created and assigned to more than one Resource. This topic is covered in more detail in the next section of this chapter.
- Click on the [Create Personal Calendar] icon to create a **Personal Calendar** for this resource.

NOTE: The **Resource** calendar is used to display the resource limits irrespective of the calendar assigned to an activity.

Default Units/Time

The **Default Units/Time** is the value that a resource adopts when it is first assigned to an activity. In a similar way to Microsoft Project, the **Units per Time Period** may be displayed as a **Percentage** or in **Units/Time**.

- Select **Edit**, **User Preferences...**, **Time Units** tab and select the preferred display from the **Units/Time Format** section:

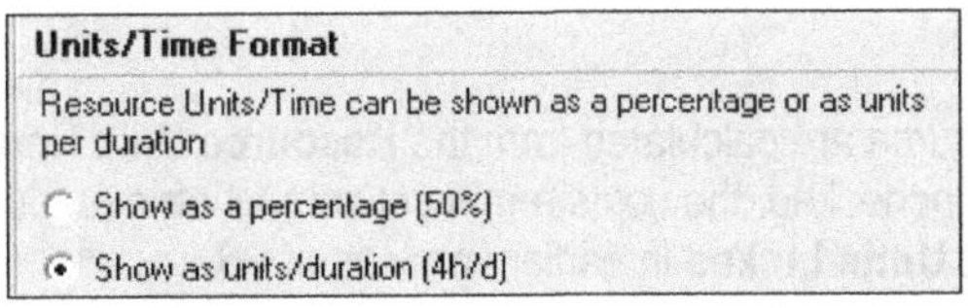

For example you may have a fleet of 12 trucks and you usually assign four trucks to each loader. In this situation you would assign the **Default Units/Time** as 400%, or 4 d/d, or 32h/d if the trucks are working 8 hours per day.

Resource and Activity Auto Compute Actuals

When a Resource **Auto Compute Actuals** field is unchecked, the work for a resource may be read from the Primavera Timesheet system or manually entered.

But when the **Activity Auto Compute Actuals** field is checked, this makes all the activity resource assignments to be **Auto Compute Actuals** irrespective of their settings in the Resource Window.

When the User uses the **Apply Actuals** function and activities or resources are set to **Auto Compute Actuals** Primavera calculates the Remaining Units based on the Remaining Duration and the Actual Units by subtracting the Remaining Units from Budgeted Units.

There are several places where the Resource **Auto Compute Actuals** field in Primavera is displayed:

- Against each resource in the **Resources Window**, **Details** tab,
- In a column in the **Resources Window**, when displayed, and
- Against each resource after it has been assigned to an activity and is displayed in the **Resources** tab of the bottom window in the **Activities Window**.

The option may **ONLY** be switched on or off against a resource in the **Resources Window** and if changed in the **Resources Window** it will affect all resource assignments for all projects for this resource.

The **Activity Auto Compute Actuals** field may be displayed as a column in the **Activities Window**:

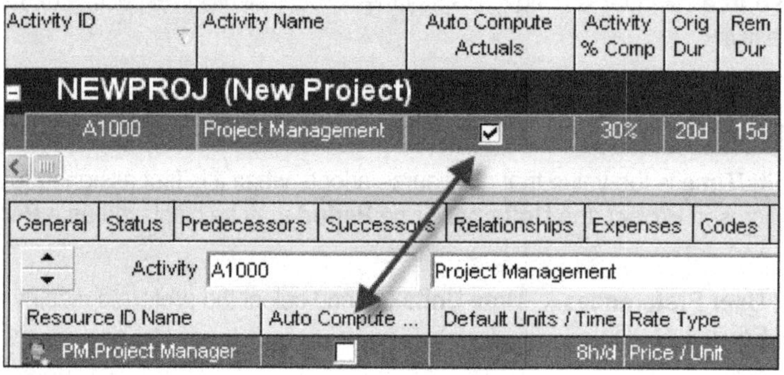

Calculate Costs from Units

With this option checked, the costs for a resource are calculated from the **Resource Unit/Time** when a resource is assigned to an activity. When unchecked, the costs remain at zero when a resource is assigned to an activity. This was called **Cost Units Linked** in earlier versions of P6.

When a resource has been assigned to an activity, there is a Resource Assignment field available in the **Resources** tab of the **Activities Window** titled **Calculate Costs from Units**. This is checked to match the **Calculate Costs from Units** field in the **Resources Window**.

The **Activities Window** field titled **Calculate Costs from Units** is not linked to the **Calculate Costs from Units** field in the **Resources Window** and only adopts the setting when a resource is assigned to an Activity.

The following picture shows a resource with the **Calculate Costs from Units** field unchecked; therefore, the costs are not calculated from the **Resource Unit Rate**.

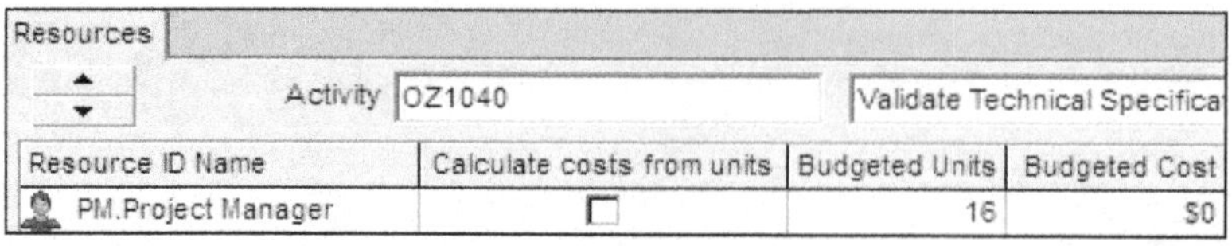

18.3.7 Units and Prices Tab

Effective Date and Rates

Each Resource may have up to five rates (Price/Unit) and these rates may be varied over time.

- The **Effective Date** represents a change in Rate or availability at that point in time.
- To display the other rates their columns should be displayed in the **Units and Prices** tab.
- The column titles of **Price/Unit 1** to **Price/Unit 5** may have their descriptions edited in the **Admin**, **Admin Preferences...**, **Rate Type** tab. These titles are shared with Roles.
- When a rate is added the effective date is the date from which the rate is applied.

Shifts

Resource Shifts are used in conjunction with leveling and should not be assigned unless they are being used. **Resource Shifts** are covered in the **Resource Optimization** chapter:

- **Resource Shifts** are created in the **Resource Shifts** form which is opened by selecting **Enterprise**, **Resource Shifts...**,
- The **Resource Shifts** and the number of shifts a resource works are assigned in the **Units and Prices** tab, **Shifts Calendar:**.

18.3.8 Roles Tab

- A Resource may be assigned more than one Role, and their **Proficiency** for the Role, in this tab.
- When multiple Roles are assigned, one is assigned as the **Primary Role**.

Role ID	Role Name	Proficiency	Primary Role
Oz.BM	Bid Manager	3 - Skilled	☑
Oz.SC	Scheduler	4 - Proficient	☐

18.3.9 Notes Tab

Notes may be added here but there are no Notebook topics available.

18.3.10 Progress Reporter Tab

Originally called **Progress Reporter** tab then changed to **Timesheets** and now back to **Progress Reporter** and has been removed from P6 Professional.

When Timesheets are implemented, the user must be added as a system user through the **P6 Web Administer**, **User Access** form where the user is assigned to a P6 Resource, thus providing the link from the timesheet user to the Primavera resource. This is covered in the **Admin Menu**, **Users** section.

For timesheets to operate, the **Uses timesheets** box in the **Progress Details** tab must also be checked and the **Timesheet Approval Manager** selected.

18.4 Workshop 15 – Adding Resources to the Database

Background

This workshop will only use Resources and these must now be added to the database.

We have updated our current project, but we need a project that has not been updated for the next activity of assigning resources. Therefore, we will have to restore the Baseline schedule saved prior to updating the current schedule to provide an unprogressed schedule for this exercise.

NOTE: If you are working in a database with other people completing this workshop then each person's Resource ID will have to be unique, say by adding your initials at the end of each Resource ID. A training course leader or database administrator should advise here.

Assignment

1. Select **Project**, **Assign Baselines...** and remove all project Baselines by setting the Baselines to the **<Current Project>**.
2. **NOTE:** Baseline Bars in the Gantt Chart will now display the Planned Dates and these should be removed, using the Bars dialogue box.
3. Restore the project using **Project**, **Maintain Baselines...**.
4. Go to the **Projects Window** where the restored baseline file will be visible.
5. Rename the restored Baseline project **Bid for Facility Extension – Resourced Schedule** and change the Project ID to **OZB-R**.
   NOTE: Users sharing a database will need to use unique Project IDs.
6. Open the restored project.
7. Open the **User Preferences** form, set the **Calculations** and **Time Units** tab as per the following pictures.

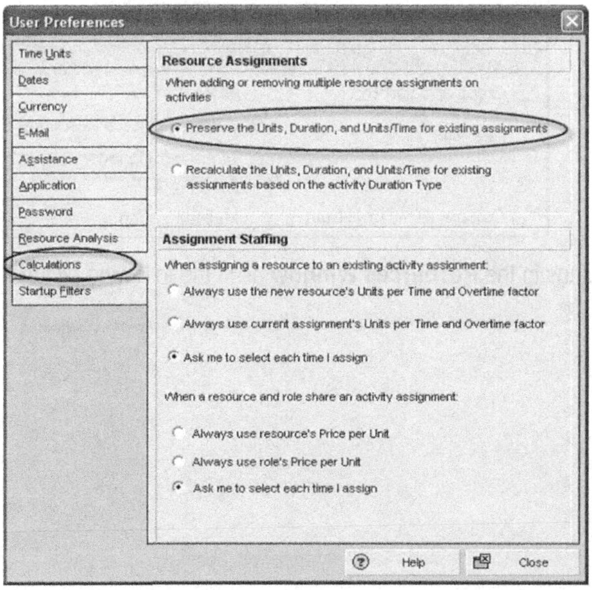

continued...

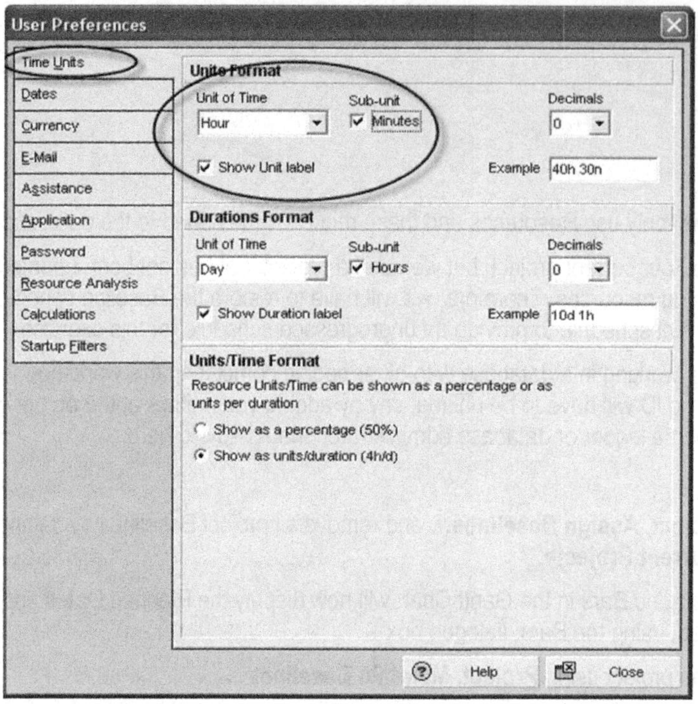

8. Now open the **Resource Window**.
9. If no resources are displayed then select all resources from the **Display:** menu:

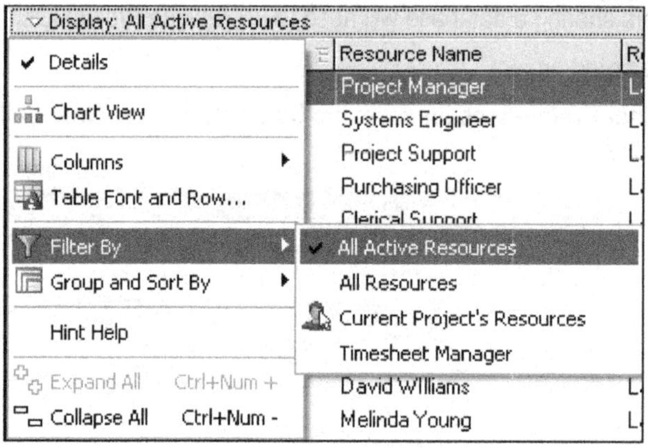

10. Format the columns in the **Resources Window** as in the following picture.

11. Add the resources as in the following picture:
    - If the **New resource Wizard** is displayed then close it as it is quicker just to type in resources.
    - The **Unit of Measure** may not be available in your database, so either add it in the **Admin**, **Admin Categories...**, or do not assign one if you do not have the access right to create a **Unit of Measure**.
    - **Price/Unit** must be entered in the bottom pane, it may be viewed but not added in a column.

    NOTE: If you are working in a database with other people completing this workshop then each person's Resource ID will have to be unique, say by adding your Initials at the end of each Resource ID.

Resource ID	Resource Name	Resource Type	Price/Unit or Standard Rate	Unit of Measure
OZB	OzBuild Resources	Labor		
PM	Project Manager	Labor	$120.00/h	
SE	Systems Engineer	Labor	$90.00/h	
PS	Project Support	Labor	$80.00/h	
PO	Purchasing Officer	Labor	$70.00/h	
CS	Clerical Support	Labor	$50.00/h	
RB	Report Binding	Material	$100.00/ea	Each

12. You may need to use the arrows on the **Move** toolbar to move the resources to the correct indent location:

13. Set the **Default Units/Time** to 8 hours per day for all the resources.
14. Set the calendar for all resources to be a Global **5-**Day Workweek, with 8 hours per day, yours may be called a Standard 5 Day/Week or similar.
15. Check **Calculate Costs from units** and **Auto compute actuals** for each resource.
16. Ensure that the resource **Effective Date** in the **Units & Prices** tab is set to 1 December 2018 or earlier otherwise the Resource will be delayed beyond this date when Leveling the resources in the Resource Optimization Workshop.

19 ASSIGNING ROLES, RESOURCES AND EXPENSES

During the planning stage, **Roles** may be assigned to Activities to gain an understanding of the long-term resource demand and they are later replaced by a **Resource** when it is known who will be undertaking the work. If you are not using named resources then you should consider not using Roles, as Resources have more functionality than Roles. A Resource may be assigned:

- Directly to an Activity, or
- To a Role which has been assigned to an Activity.

There are three types of resources, **Labor**, **Nonlabor** and **Material**, as discussed in the previous chapter. A Labor Resource has additional functionality including Overtime, Resource Calendars, Shifts and user defined Autocost rules. The **Labor** and **Nonlabor** resources are similar to the Microsoft Project **Work Resources**. A **Material** resource is similar to Microsoft Project **Material Resources**, but may not have the units displayed in **Activities Window** columns.

Primavera also has a function titled **Expenses**, where costs may be assigned to activities without resources and may be assigned a quantity and the default quantity is one. This function is similar to the **Cost Resource** function in Microsoft Project. As the project progresses, Actual and To Complete Units and Costs may be assigned to Expenses in the same way as resources. Expense units may not have the units displayed in **Activities Window** columns, may not be assigned Resource Curves, but may have costs assigned before the activity has started, may have Remaining Costs when the activity is complete, and may be assigned to Milestones.

This chapter will cover the following topics:

- Understanding Resource Calculations and Terminology
- Project and Activities Windows Resource and Role Preferences
- Details Status Form
- Activity Types and Duration Types
- Assigning and Removing Roles and Assigning Resources
- Resource and Activity Duration Calculation and Resource Lags
- Expenses
- Suggested Setup for Assigning Resources

Topic	Menu Commands
• Set **Units/Time Format** and **Resource Assignments**	Select **Edit**, **User Preferences...** to open the **User Preferences** form and select the **Time Units** tab and **Calculations** tab.
• Set **Default Duration Type** and **Default Activity Type**	Set these defaults in the **Defaults** tab in the **Projects Window**.
• Assign a **Role** to an Activity	Select the Resources tab in the Activity Details form and click on the icon on the **Assign** toolbar to open the Assign Roles form.
• To assign a **Resource** to a **Role** that has been assigned to an activity	Select the Role to be assigned a Resource from the **Resources Details** tab and click the icon on the **Assign** toolbar to open the **Assign Resources By Roles** form.
• To assign a **Resource** to an activity without a **Role**	Select the Activity to be assigned the Resource and click the icon on the **Assign** toolbar to open the **Assign Resource** form.

19.1 Understanding Resource Calculations and Terminology

A Resource has three principal components after it has been assigned to an Activity:

- **Quantity**, in terms of **Work** in hours or days or **Material** quantities required to complete the activity, which are referred to as **Units** by Primavera,
- The **Resource Unit Rate** is termed **Price/Unit** in Primavera, and
- **Cost**, which is calculated from the **Resource Unit Rate** x **Units**.

Each Resource and Expense has the same four fields for **Costs** and **Units**, which are **Budget**, **Remaining**, **Actual** and **At Completion**. The relationship among these fields changes depending on whether the activity is Not Started, In-Progress or Complete.

- When an activity is Not Started and the % Complete is zero then:
  - **Budget** is normally linked to **Remaining** and **At Completion** and therefore a change to one will change the other two and they will always be equal, and
  - **Actual** will be zero.
- When the activity is marked Started and would normally be In-Progress and the % Complete is between 0.1% and 99.9% then:
  - **Budget** becomes unlinked from **Remaining** and **At Completion**, thus allowing progress and the **At Completion** value to be compared to the **Budget** value (of the current schedule), or a **Baseline Budget** value or a **Baseline At Completion** value, and
  - **At Completion** = **Actual** + **Remaining** and have a link to **% Complete**, where a change in value to one will result in a change to the other values.
- When the activity is Complete and the % Complete is 100% then:
  - **Remaining** is set to zero, and
  - **At Completion** = **Actual**.

The Budget values for Costs and Units are linked to the At Completion values until:

- An Activity has been marked as Started or has a % Complete, or
- The **Link Budget and At Completion for not started activities** in the **Project Window Calculations** tab is unchecked, see the following picture:

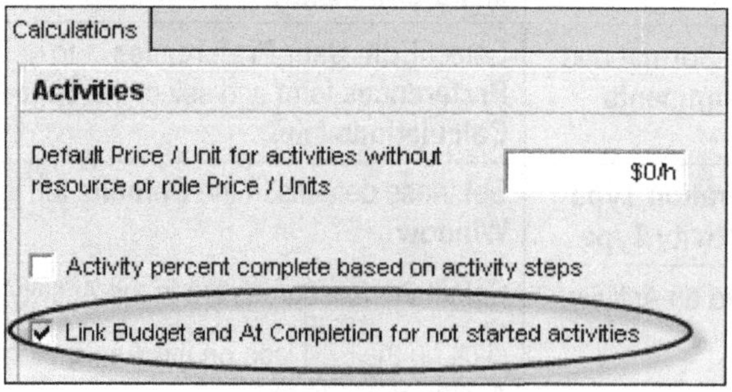

In P3 one would often unlink **Budget and At Completion** when a project has been approved and a re-estimate is required while maintaining the Budget.

This function in P6 also unlinks the **Original Duration** from the **At Completion Duration** for un-started activities which adds another complication that should be avoided.

The comparison of the current At Completion Costs is normally made with the Baseline project Budget or Baseline project At Completion values. Therefore the Budget value in the current schedule is effectively a redundant value and probably should not be displayed.

19.2 Project Window Resource Preferences

Preferences set in the **Activities Window** decide how each individual activity and resource is calculated and are covered in the next section.

Preferences and defaults (which may be changed for each resource assignment) that affect how all resources in a project are calculated are set in the **Project Window** and pertain to all activities and resources.

19.2.1 Resources Tab

The **Resources** tab in the P6 Professional **Projects Window** has had the Progress Reporter (called Timesheets in Version 6.2 and earlier) removed.

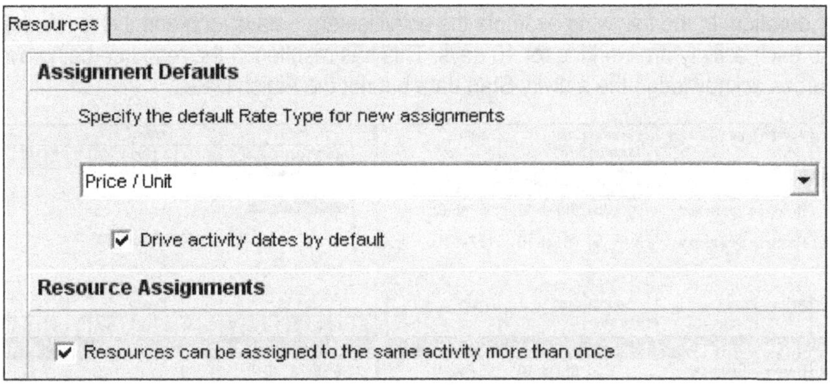

Assignment Defaults

- There are five Resource Rates available in Primavera. One rate may be set as a project default. After assignment to an activity, the Resource Rate may be changed using the **Rate Type** field in the **Resources** tab of the **Activities Window**.

Drive activity dates by default

- This is covered in more detail in the next section.

Resource Assignments

- Checking the **Resources can be assigned to the same activity more than once** box enables a resource to be assigned to an activity more than once. This is useful if it is required to assign a resource at the beginning of an activity and later at the end of an activity with a lag.

  For example, one may want to assign a crane on the first day of the activity to assist in erecting and one the last day to assist in dismantling. This check box needs to be checked for a resource to be assigned twice to an activity.

19.2.2 Understanding Resource Option to Drive Activity Dates

A resource has the following fields that are linked and a change to the **Original lag** or **Original Duration** will make a change to one or both dates:

- **Original Lag**. The duration from the Activity Start Date to the Resource Start Date, which is the date the resource commences work.
- **Original Duration**. The duration that a resource is working.
- **Start**. The Resource Start Date=Activity Start Date + the Resource Original Lag.
- **Finish**. This date is calculated by the addition of the Activity Start Date + Original Lag + the Original Duration.

When the **Drive Activity Dates** option is switched off it is possible for a resource to calculate outside the activity duration. In the following example the activities are 5 days long and the resources assigned to each activity are working for 10 days. This has resulted in the resource being overloaded. The Resources acknowledge the activity Start date but not the Finish Date.

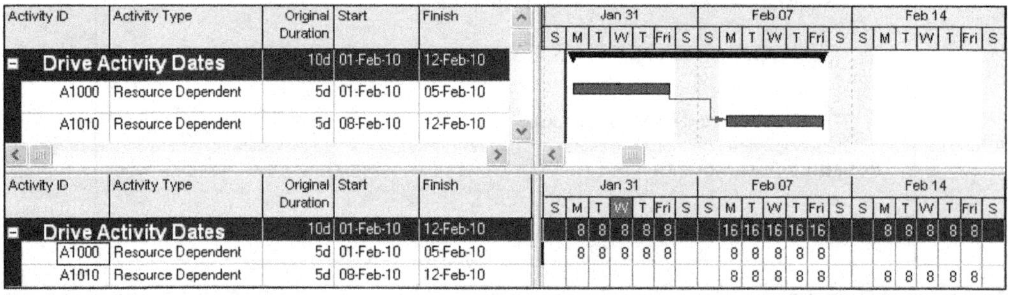

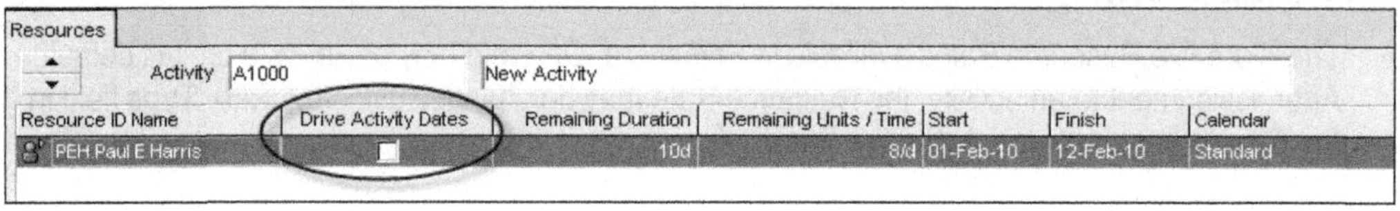

Now the **Drive Activity Dates** option has been checked against each activity, the activities are now 10 days long, and the resource is not overloaded.

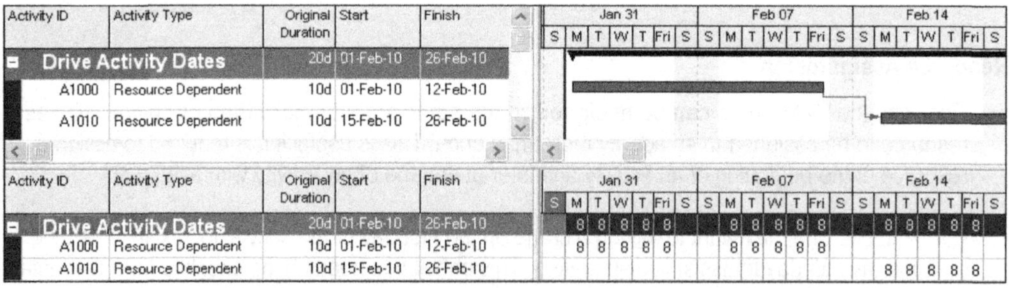

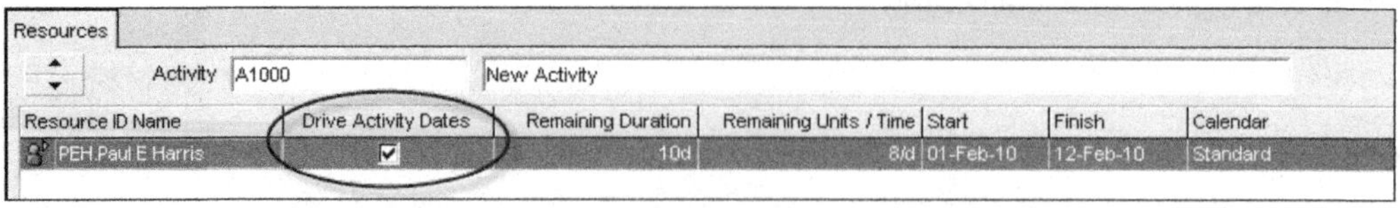

It is recommended that the **Drive activity dates by default** box is always checked, thus Resources will be assigned as **Drive Activity Dates** and this ensures that all work is contained within the duration of an activity.

The Activity Start is controlled by the Activity Calendar, therefore when an activity is Resource Driven it is important to set an Activity Calendar that will allow the resource to start work when it is required to start. Thus if there is a morning shift starting at 4:00 am, the Activity Calendar should start at 4:00 am or earlier.

In schedules with complex resource calendars may wish to consider placing all the Resource Driven activities on a 24x7 calendar and then all resource work will be controlled by the resource calendars.

19.2.3 Calculations Tab

The **Calculations** tab in the **Projects Window:**

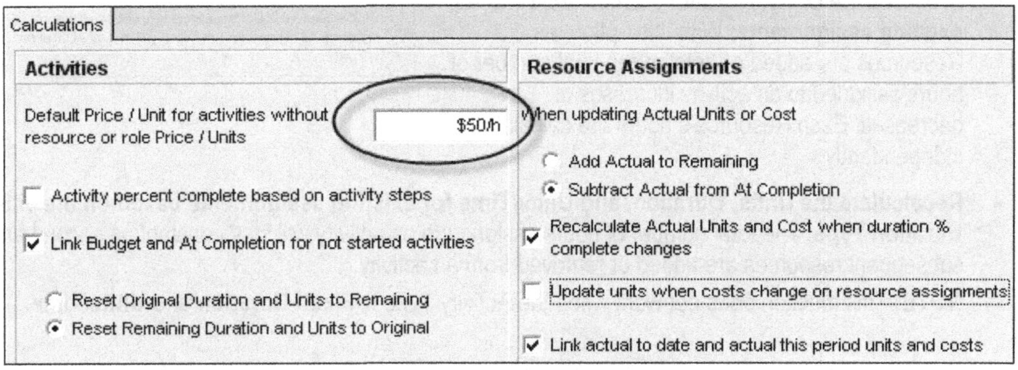

Activities – Default Price/Unit for activities without resource Price/Units.

This rate is also used to calculate the resource costs when an activity is not assigned roles or resources but is assigned a quantity in the **Activities Window**, **Status** tab.

The other functions in this tab affect the updating of resourced activities and are covered in the **Updating a Resourced Schedule** chapter.

19.3 User Preferences Applicable to Assigning Resources

Select **Edit**, **User Preferences…** to open the **User Preferences** form:

19.3.1 Units/Time Format

Select the **Time Units** tab. The **Units/Time Format** enables Microsoft Project-style formatting of **Resource/Time Format** showing Resource utilization as a percentage or as units per duration.

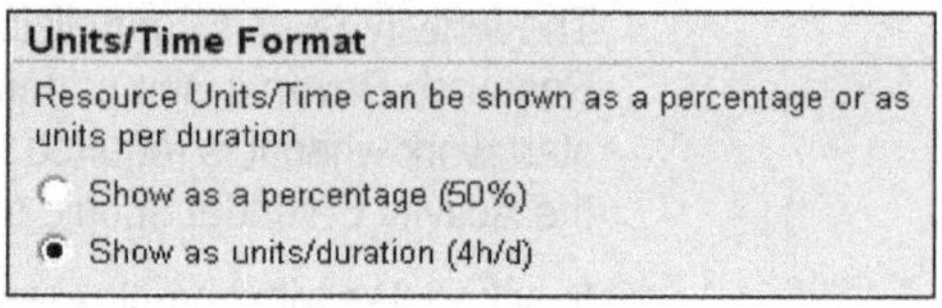

19.3.2 Resource Assignments

The **Calculations** tab has two **Resource Assignment** options:

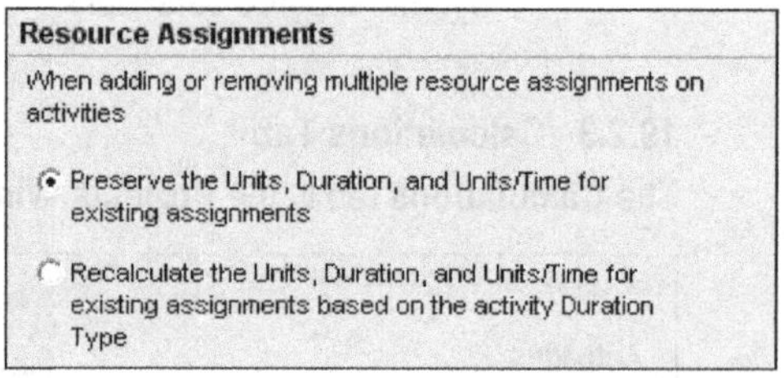

- **Preserve the Units, Duration, and Units/Time for existing assignments**. With this option, as Resources are added or deleted the total number of hours assigned to an activity increases or decreases. Each Resource's hours are calculated independently.
- **Recalculate the Units, Duration, and Units/Time for existing assignments based on the activity Duration Type**. The total number of hours assigned to an activity will stay constant as second and subsequent resources are added or removed from an activity.

  NOTE: This function does not work when the Activity Type is **Fixed Duration and Units/Time**.

The **Recalculate the Units, Duration, and Units/Time for existing assignments based on the activity Duration Type** function is similar to the Microsoft Project Effort Driven function and the **Preserve the Units, Duration, and the Units/Time for existing assignments** is the same as Non Effort Driven.

There is no similar function in P3 and SureTrak.

It is recommended that **Preserve the Units, Duration, and Units/Time for existing assignments** be used as a default as each individual resource assignment does not change as resources are added or removed from an activity.

19.3.3 Assignment Staffing

The **Assignment Staffing** option is self-explanatory and should be considered carefully when resources and roles have different rates. If it is not understood and set correctly the resource may end up with the incorrect unit rate when assigned to a Role or existing Resource.

When two users have different settings this may result in a schedule having two different rates for the same resource.

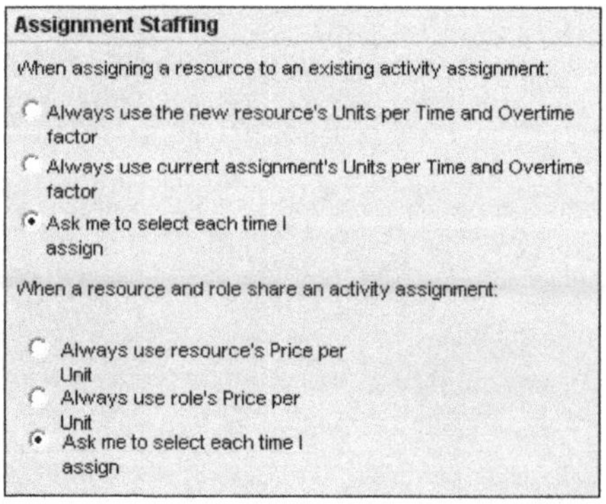

19.4 Activities Window Resource Preferences and Defaults

19.4.1 Details Status Form

This form has a section titled **Labor Units** at the right side as seen in the following picture. The drop down menu enables you to select which data is to be displayed in this section of the form.

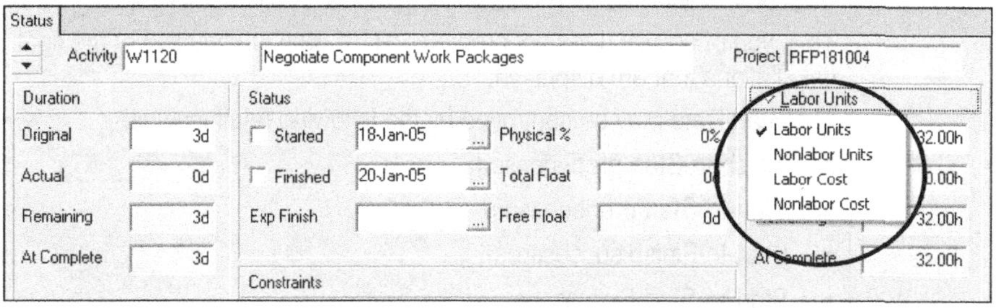

There is a link between the entries in this form and the values that are assigned to resources:

- The values in this form are the sum of the values assigned to Resources and Roles.
- When these values are edited, they will change the values assigned to Resources and Roles.

NOTE: It is possible to enter a **Labor Unit** value in the **Status** tab and not assign a resource. When a resource is assigned the resource will adopt this value in the **Status** tab. This rate is set in the **Calculations** tab in the **Projects Window, Activities tab – Default Price/Unit for activities without resource or Roles Price/Units** field.

19.4.2 Activity Type

There are five **Activity Types** assigned in the **General tab** in the **Activities Window**:

Activity Type	Notes
Task Dependent	Activities assigned as Task Dependent acknowledge their **Activity Calendar** when scheduling and the Finish Date is calculated from the Activity Calendar.
Resource Dependent	Activities assigned as Resource Dependent acknowledge their **Resource Calendar** when being scheduled. This is similar to an Independent Activity Type in P3 and SureTrak and the resources work independently and do not have to be available at the same time. The Activity Finish Date is calculated based on the longest Resource Duration when the resource option of **Drive Activity Dates** is checked against the resource assignment. ⚠ **NOTE:** The activity start date calculated on the activity calendar, not the resource calendar, may delay the start of an activity when the resource calendar has longer working hours than the activity calendar.

<table>
<tr><th>Activity Type</th><th>Notes</th></tr>
<tr><td>Level of Effort (LOE)</td><td>
This Activity Type spans other Activities. Therefore the Start Date, Finish Date, and Durations may change as the start or finish date of activities that it is dependent upon change during scheduling or updating. LOE Activity Type is similar to a Hammock in P3 and SureTrak, but more relationships may control the Start and Finish Dates. There is no equivalent in Microsoft Project.
This type of activity does not create a critical path irrespective of the float calculations that are displayed.
The Start Date may be controlled by the following relationships:
<ul>
<li>Finish-to-Start predecessors</li>
<li>Start-to-Start predecessors</li>
<li>Start-to-Finish successors</li>
<li>Start-to-Start Successors</li>
</ul>
The Finish Date may be controlled by the following relationships:
<ul>
<li>Finish-to-Finish predecessors</li>
<li>Start-to-Finish predecessors</li>
<li>Finish-to-Start successors</li>
<li>Finish-to-Finish successors</li>
</ul>
Resources assigned to a Level of Effort activity are not considered in calculations when a schedule is Leveled.
Level of Effort activities may not be assigned a Constraint.
When creating a LOE activity and the bar is not displayed, check the Bars form to ensure a LOE bar has been created and is being displayed.

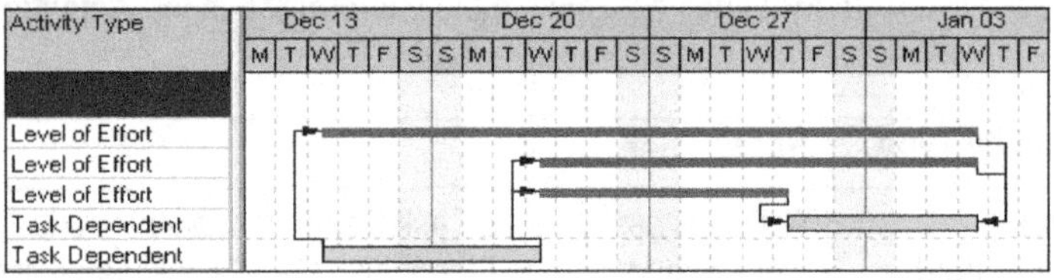

</td></tr>
<tr><td>Start Milestone</td><td>
This Activity Type is used to indicate the commencement of a Phase, Stage, or a major event in a project.
<ul>
<li>It has only a Start Date and no Duration or Finish Date.</li>
<li>It may only have Start Constraints assigned.</li>
<li>It may not have time-dependent resources assigned but may have:
<ul>
<li>An Owner assigned from the list of users to indicate who is responsible for the activity. “Owner,” enables a user who is NOT a resource to be assigned responsibility for an activity.</li>
<li>A Primary Resource assigned from the Activities Window, General tab who may update the Milestone, but no effort is assigned or recorded.</li>
</ul></li>
</ul>
</td></tr>
<tr><td colspan="2">

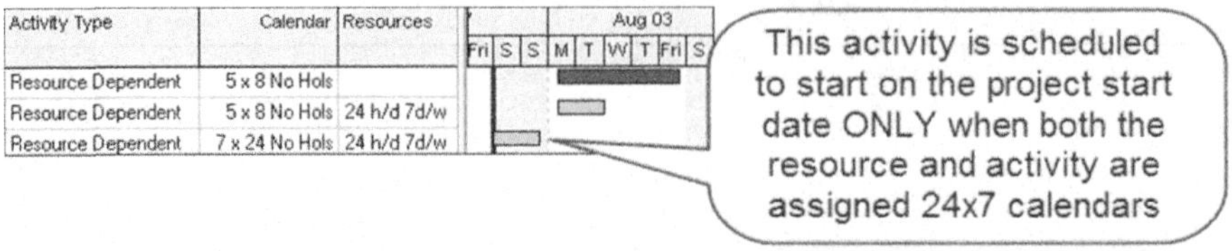

</td></tr>
</table>

Activity Type	Notes
Finish Milestone	This Activity Type is used to indicate the completion of a Phase, Stage, or a major event in a project. • It has only a Finish Date and no Duration or Start Date. • It may only have **Finish Constraints** assigned. • It may not have time-dependent resources assigned but may have: ➢ An **Owner** assigned from the list of users to indicate who is responsible for the activity. "Owner," the new activity field in Primavera Version 6.0, enables a user who is **NOT** a resource to be assigned responsibility for an activity. ➢ A **Primary Resource** assigned from the **Activities Window**, **General** tab who may update the Milestone, but no effort is assigned or recorded.
WBS Summary Activity	The new Primavera Version 5.0 **WBS Summary Activity** is an activity that spans the duration of all activities which are assigned exactly the same WBS Code and, unlike a Level of Effort Activity, do not have any predecessors or successors. 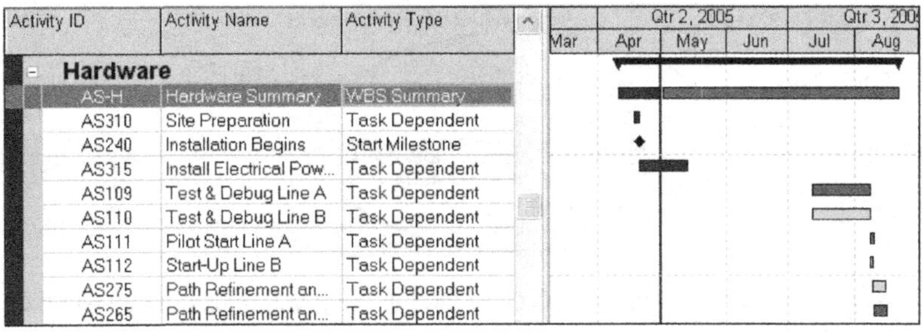 Therefore a WBS activity will change duration when either the earliest start or latest finish of activities that it spans is changed. This may happen as the project progresses and activities do not meet their original scheduled dates, or the duration of an activity is changed, or logic is changed, or the schedule is leveled. This function calculates the WBS Activity Duration in the same way as WBS activities in P3 or SureTrak, or Topic activities in SureTrak. It is similar to the way Summary activity durations are calculated in Microsoft Project, except the activities do not need to be demoted below the detailed activities in as Microsoft Project. WBS activities may be used for: • Reporting at summary level by filtering on WBS activities, • Entering estimated costs at summary level for producing cash flow tables while the detailed activities are used for calculating the overall duration for the WBS and day-to-day management of the project, and • Recording costs and hours at summary level when is it not desirable or practical to record at activity level, especially when the detailed activities are liable to change. It does not matter how activities are Grouped as they always span activities with the same WBS Code.

19.4.3 Duration Type

The Duration Type becomes effective after a resource has been assigned to an activity.

The **Duration** Type for all new activities is set in the **Defaults** tab in the **Projects Window** and all new activities are assigned this Duration Type.

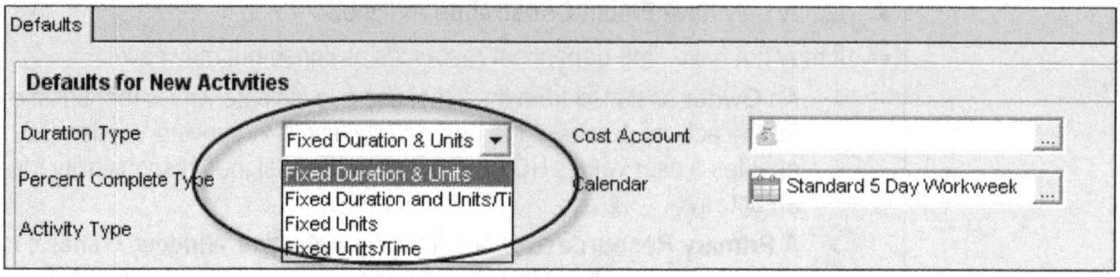

The **Duration Type** for each new activity may be changed in the **General** tab in the **Activities Window** or by displaying the **Duration Type** column:

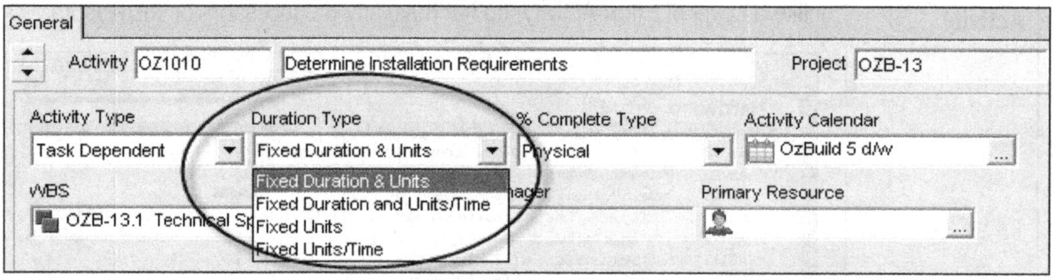

The Duration Type determines which of the following variables change when one of the others is changed in the equation:

- Resource Units = Resource Units per Time Period x Duration

For example, a 40-hour activity with 2 people working 8 hours per day will take 20 hours or 2.5 days:

- 40 hours of work = 2 people per hour x 20 hours

When an activity is in-progress this equation is modified to:

- Remaining Resource Units = Resource Units per Time period x Remaining Duration

Primavera has four options for Duration Type, Microsoft Project has three options, and P3 and SureTrak have two options (which are a lot easier to understand).

The Primavera terminology that describes the way the software treats the relationship between Durations, Resource Units and Resource Units/Time Period is different from Microsoft Project, P3, and SureTrak. Primavera has more options than all the other products and this gives the product more flexibility. The following table should clarify these options.

Purposes of the Duration Types

Duration Type	Purpose
• **Fixed Duration & Units**	**Option 1** This option is used when the Duration of an activity should not change when Resources are added or removed or Units/Time changed. For example, when the time to complete an activity is fixed, the resources may be manipulated until a satisfactory resource loading is established without the activity duration changing. **Option 2** A change to the Duration will change the Units/Time; however, the Units will remain constant. If one person is assigned to an activity for 8 hours per day and the activity is doubled in duration, there will be now be one person working on the activity for 4 hours per day and the activity will require the same number of hours to complete. **IMPORTANT POINT:** The Estimate at Completion **WILL NOT** change when the activity duration is changed and the number of resources **WILL** change.
• **Fixed Duration & Units/Time**	This **Duration Type** disables the **User Preferences**, **Calculations** tab option **Recalculate the Units, Duration, and Units/Time for existing assignments based on the activity Duration Type**. **Option 1** This option is used when the Duration of an activity should not change when Resources are added or removed or Units/Time changed. For example, when the time to complete an activity is fixed, the resources may be manipulated until a satisfactory resource loading is established without the activity duration changing. **Option 2** A change in the Duration will change the Units; however, the Units/Time will remain constant. For example, when there are two people assigned to an activity and the activity is increased in duration, there will still be two people working but for a longer period of time. **IMPORTANT POINT:** The Estimate at Completion **WILL** change when the activity duration is changed and the number of resources **WILL NOT** change.
• **Fixed Units**	This option is used when the amount of work required to finish an activity is constant. For example, if there are 8,000 bricks to be laid and a bricklayer is able to lay 100 bricks per hour, there are 80 hours of work for one bricklayer, 40 hours for 2 bricklayers and 20 hours for 4 bricklayers. Changing the Duration or the Units/Time will not change the number of hours required to complete the activity.
• **Fixed Units/Time**	This option is used when the same number of people are required to complete an activity irrespective of the activity duration. For example, if a machine requires two people to operate it and therefore a Resource is assigned to the Activity at 200%, changing either the Units or the Duration will not change the Units/Time and there will always be two people operating the machine.

The duration of both **Fixed Units** and **Fixed Units/Time** activities will change if the resource Units/Time Period or Remaining Units are changed. It is the author's preference to use:

- **Fixed Duration & Units** when the estimate at completion must not change, and
- **Fixed Duration & Units/Time** when the crew size must remain constant.

The following table displays what happens to the relationship in each of the four options when one variable is changed and

- The **User Preferences**, **Calculations** tab option **Preserve the Units, Duration, and Units/Time for existing assignments** is selected:

Duration Type	Labor Units Change in Status Tab	Activity Duration Change	Resource Units Change	Units/Time Period Change	Add or Remove Resources
Fixed Units/Time	Duration Change	Units Change	Duration Change	Duration Change	Activity Units Change, Resource Units Constant, Duration Constant
Fixed Duration & Units/Time	Units/Time Change	Units Change	Units/Time Change	Units Change	Activity Units Change, Resource Units Constant, Duration Constant
Fixed Units	Duration Change	Units/Time Change	Duration Change	Duration Change	Activity Units Change, Resource Units Constant, Duration Constant
Fixed Duration & Units	Units/Time Change	Units/Time Change	Units/Time Change	Units Change	Activity Units Change, Resource Units Constant, Duration Constant

The following table displays what happens to the relationship in each of the four options when one variable is changed and

- The **User Preferences**, **Calculations** tab option **Recalculate the Units, Duration, and Units/Time for existing assignments based on the activity Duration Type** is selected:

Duration Type	Labor Units Change in Status Tab	Activity Duration Change	Resource Units Change	Units/Time Period Change	Add or Remove Resources
Fixed Units/Time	Duration Change	Units Change	Duration Change	Duration Change	**Activity Units Constant**, **Resource Units Change**, **Duration Change**
Fixed Duration & Units/Time	Units/Time Change	Units Change	Units/Time Change	Units Change	Activity Units Change, Resource Units Constant, Duration Constant
Fixed Units	Duration Change	Units/Time Change	Duration Change	Duration Change	**Activity Units Constant**, **Resource Units Change**, **Duration Change**
Fixed Duration & Units	Units/Time Change	Units/Time Change	Units/Time Change	Units Change	**Activity Units Constant, Resource Units Change**, Duration Constant

- Bold descriptions in the right column in the table indicate the differences from the upper table.
- The **User Preferences**, **Calculations** tab option **Preserve the Units, Duration, and Units/Time for existing assignments** will not freeze the Activity Units when the **Duration Type** of **Fixed Units** is selected.

19.5 Assigning and Removing Roles

To assign a Role to an activity:

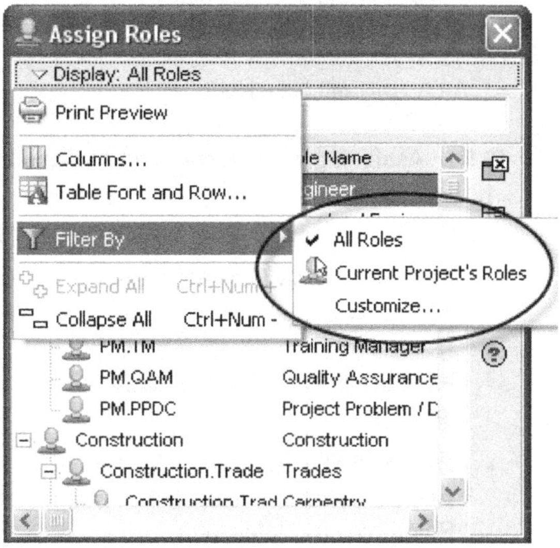

- Select the one or more activity to be assigned the Role,
- Select the **Resources** tab in the **Activity Details** form,
- Click on the **Roles... Assign** toolbar icon to open the **Assign Roles** form,
- Use the **Display:**, **Filter By** menu to select either:
  - **All Roles**, which will display all Roles in the database,
  - **Current Project's Roles**. This option will only display Roles that have been assigned to this project, or
  - **Customize**, which opens a **Filter** form enabling the user to limit the number of displayed Roles by creating a filter.
- Select one or more Roles to be assigned to an activity using the **Ctrl**-click function,
- Then to assign a Role:
  - Click on the icon, or
  - Double-click one of the Roles.

To achieve the following picture you may need to format the columns in the **Resources Details** form.

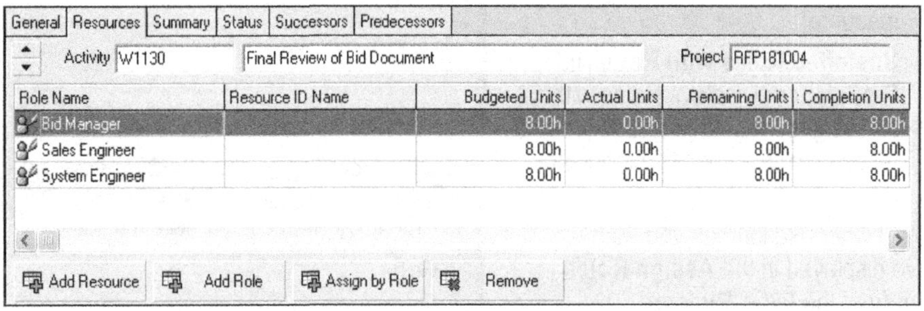

At this point, the Roles hours and costs may be edited as required.

To remove a Role:

- Select the Role, and
- Click on the Remove icon.

19.6 Assigning and Removing Resources

Resources may be assigned directly to:

- An activity that has an Assigned Role, or
- An Activity without a Role.

19.6.1 Assigning a Resource to an Assigned Role

To assign a Resource to a Role assigned to an activity:

- Select the activity to be assigned a Resource,
- Select the Role to be assigned a Resource from the **Resources Details** tab,
- Click on the **Resources by Role... Assign** toolbar icon to open the **Assign Resources By Roles** form,
- Click on the **Display:** menu and select **Filter By** to open the **Filter By** form,
  - **All Roles Required**: Chooses to view all roles assigned to the activity.
  - **Staffed Roles:** Displays Roles with an assigned resource.
  - **Unstaffed Roles Required:** Displays Roles without an assigned resource.
  - **Unstaffed Roles with Required Proficiency:** Displays Roles without an assigned resource and requires a resource with a specific proficiency level.
- Select which Resources you wish to have displayed in the **Assign Roles** form from the **Filter By** form,
- Select Apply to return to the **Assign Resources By Role** form,
- From the **Assign Resources By Role** form click the Resource you wish to assign,
- To assign the Resource either:
  - Double-click the Resource, or
  - Click on the icon.

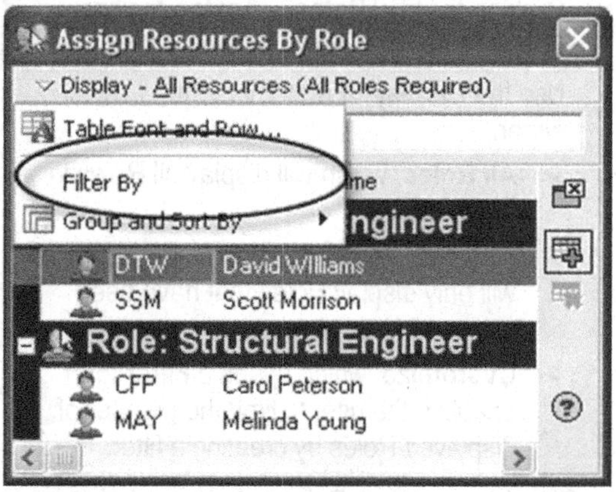

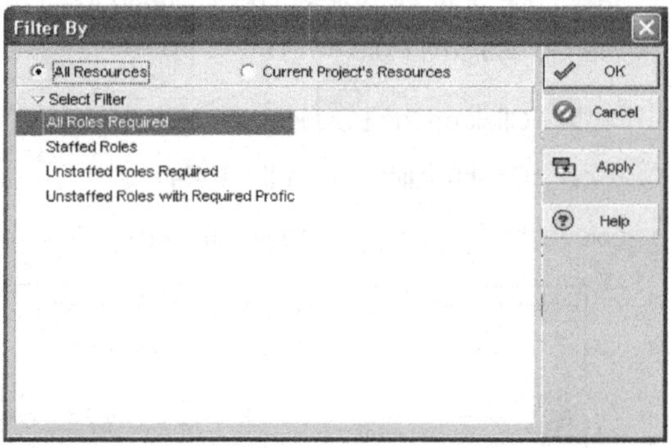

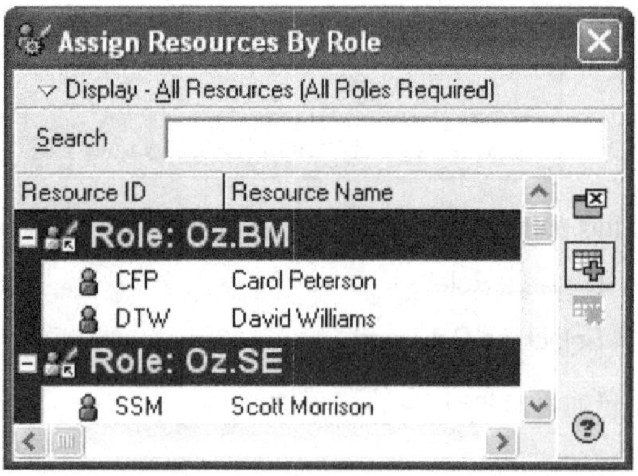

19.6.2 Assigning a Resource to an Activity Without a Role

To assign a Resource to an activity:

- Select the activity to be assigned the Resource,
- Click on the **Resources... Assign** toolbar icon to open the **Assign Resource** form,
- Click on the **Display:** menu and select **Filter By** and then select from the three options which resources you wish to display in the **Assign Resources** form,

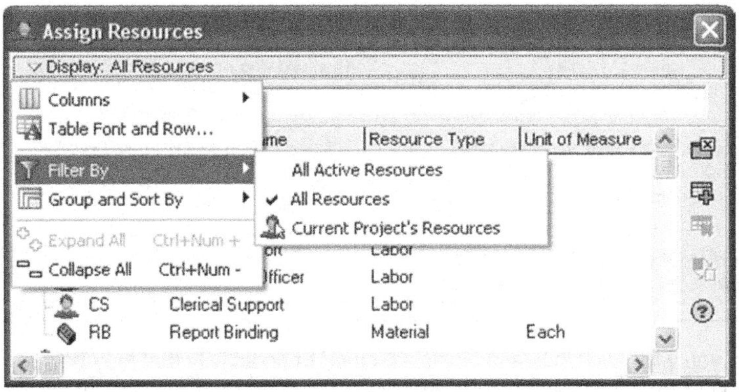

- To assign the Resource either:
  - Double-click the Resource, or
  - Click on the icon.

You may now edit the hours or Units/Time Period for each resource.

19.6.3 Removing a Resource

Before you remove a Resource from an activity that has more than one resource assigned to it, you must be aware of your **Resource Assignment** preferences. These preferences determine if the total number of Units assigned to the activity (or work) will be reduced or remain constant as resources are deleted.

To remove a resource, select one or more Resources in the bottom pane Resource tab and either:

- Strike the **Del** key, or
- Click on the Remove icon at the bottom of the screen, not the on the **Edit** toolbar.

After the last resource is removed there will be the message:

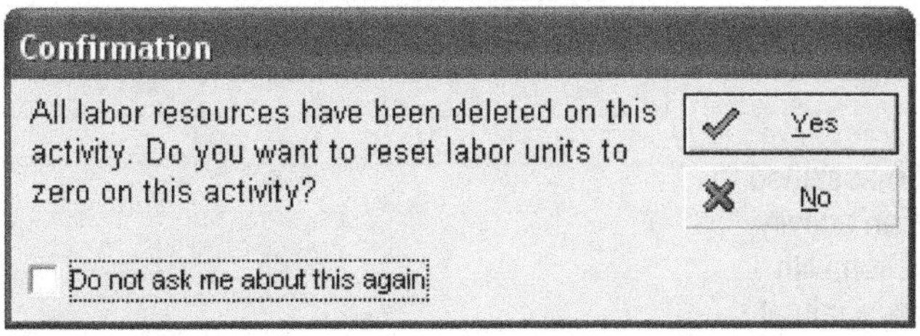

- If you select Yes then the Resource Units values in the **Activities Window**, **Status tab** will be set to zero, and the Resource Costs in the **Activities Window**, **Status tab** will be calculated from the value entered.

If you select 

then:

- The Units values in the **Activities Window**, **Status tab** will be set to equal the Resource values before they were deleted, and
- The Cost values in the **Activities Window**, **Status tab** will be calculated from the value set in **Calculations** tab in the **Projects Window.**

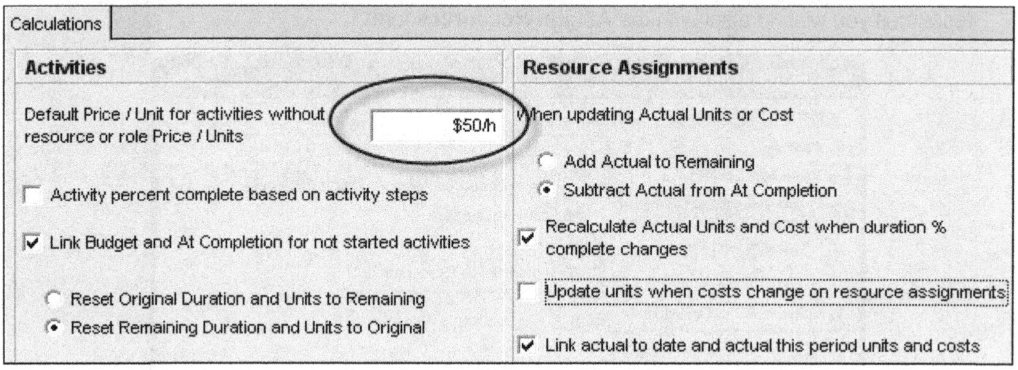

- At this point you will have Units and Costs assigned to an activity that may be seen in the **Activities Window**, **Status tab** without any assigned resources, which may not be desirable.

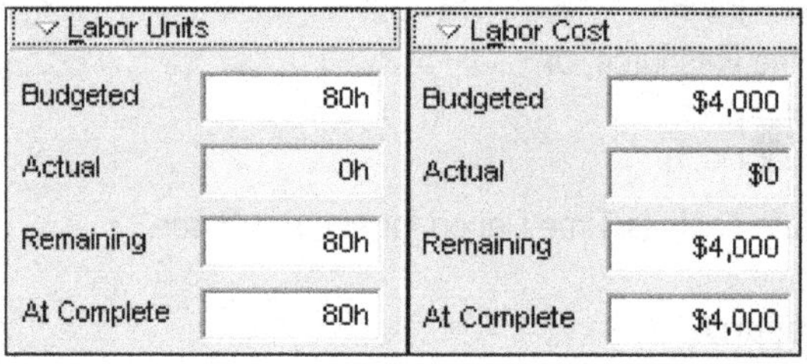

When you assign a resource to an activity in this condition the resource will adopt the Units value from the **Activities Window**, **Status tab**, ignoring the **Default Units /Time Period** set in the **Resource Window**, but normally calculate the resource value from the resource Rate.

19.6.4 Assigning a Resource to an Activity More Than Once

The option in the **Projects Window Resources** tab under the **Resources Assignments** heading enables a resource to be assigned more than once to an activity.

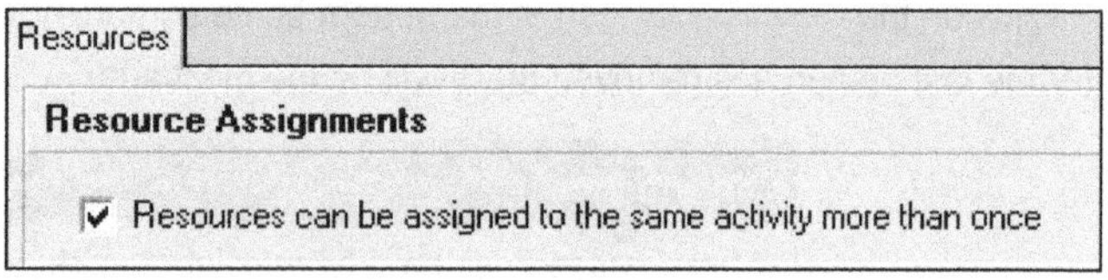

A resource could be assigned to work at the start of an activity and then in conjunction with **Resource Lag** work again at the end of an activity.

19.7 *Resource and Activity Duration Calculation and Resource Lags*

19.7.1 Activity Duration

An Activity Duration (or Activity Remaining Duration of an In-Progress Activity) is adopted from the longest Resource Duration (or Resource Remaining Duration of an In-Progress Activity) when more than one resource has been assigned to an activity.

In a situation where more than one Resource has been assigned to an activity with different Units and/or Units/Time, the Resources may have different durations.

In the following example the Activity Duration is 10 days, which is calculated from David William's **Resource Original Duration** of 10 days:

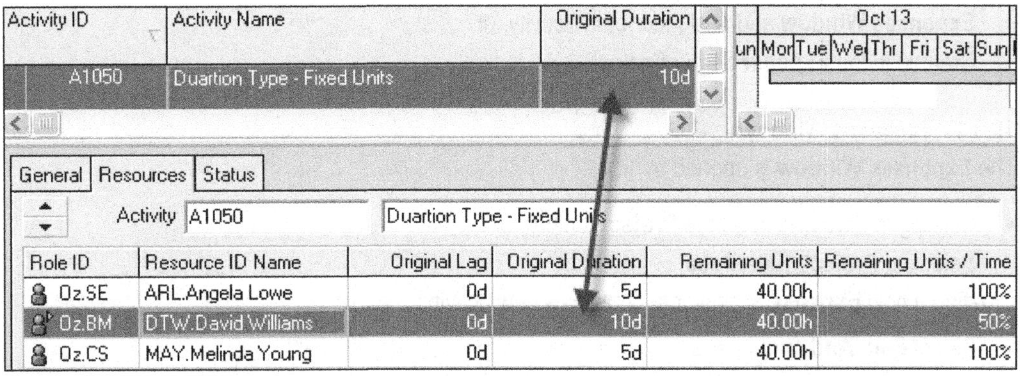

This is calculated in a similar way to P3 and SureTrak when all Resources are set to Driving.

19.7.2 Resource Lag

A Resource may be assigned a Lag, the duration from the start of the activity to the point at which the Resource commences work.

In the following example the Activity Duration is 12 days, which is calculated from Angela Lowe's **Resource Original Lag** of 7 days and **Resource Original Duration** of 5 days:

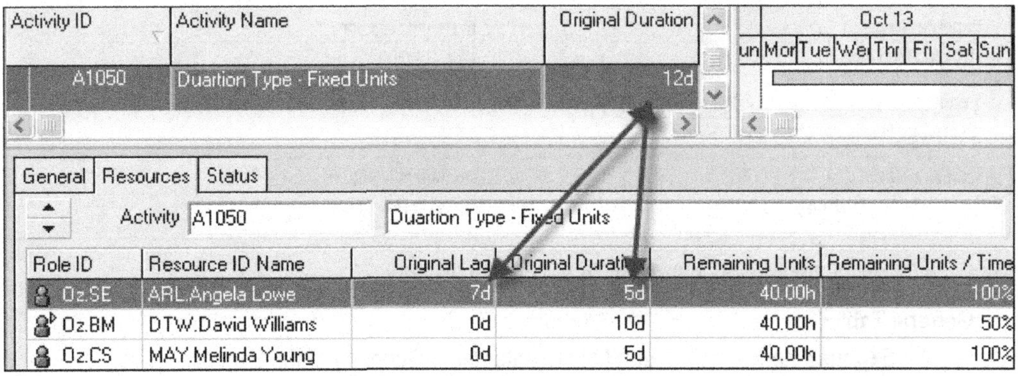

19.8 Expenses

Expenses are intended to be used for one off non-resource type costs and could include:

- Purchase of office equipment to set up a project office,
- Travel costs,
- Payment for a consultant's report,
- Insurance costs, and
- Training courses.

Expenses may be created using the:

- **Expenses Window** and assigned to an activity, or
- Created in the **Expenses tab** of an activity.

19.8.1 Expenses Window

The **Expenses Window** is opened by:

- Clicking in the icon on the **Project** toolbar, or
- Selecting **Project**, **Expenses**.

Creating a new **Expense** is similar to creating a new activity:

- Select **Edit**, **Add**, and
- The **Select Activity** form will then be displayed and the activity the expense is to be associated with is selected.

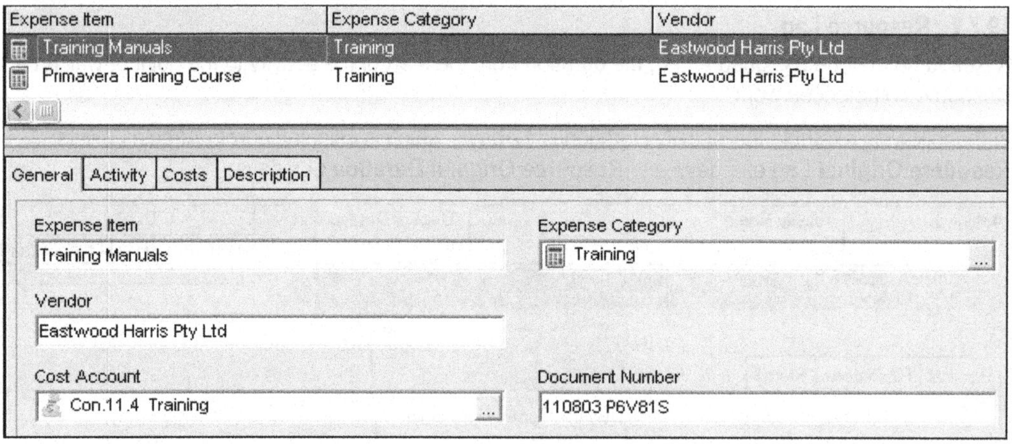

Enter the following Information in the tabs in the bottom window:

- **General Tab**
  - **Expense Item** – A free form field to enter the description of the Expense.
  - **Vendor** – A free form field to enter the vendor or supplier name.
  - **Expense Category** – Select the Expense Category; these are created in the **Admin Categories** form.

  - **Cost Account** – Select a Cost Account should you wish to see or report the costs against a Cost Account. Costs accounts are created in a similar method to other hierarchical structures in Primavera, such as the WBS, by selecting **Enterprise**, **Cost Accounts...**.
  - **Document Number** – A free form field to enter the document number that could represent the Purchase Order, Contract, or Invoice Number.

- **Activity** tab displays information mainly adopted from an activity, the Accrual Type, is editable:
  - **Accrual Type** – this enables you to select if the costs are accrued or cash flowed at the beginning, end, or uniformly over the duration of the activity.
- **Costs** tab is mainly self-explanatory. The following information is entered:
  - **Budgeted Units, Actual Units**, **Remaining Units** and **At Completion Units** – the quantity of the Expense item. When an Expense is created it is set a default value of 1. If set to zero then the costs are set to zero and costs may now not be entered.
  - **Price/Unit** – the cost per Expense item,
  - **Unit of Measure –** the units of the Expense; for example, each, foot, meter, etc.
  - Check **Auto Compute Actuals** to allow the software to calculate the Actual and Remaining Costs and Units (quantities) based on the **Remaining Duration**,
  - The remainder of the fields are used when the activity is progressed.

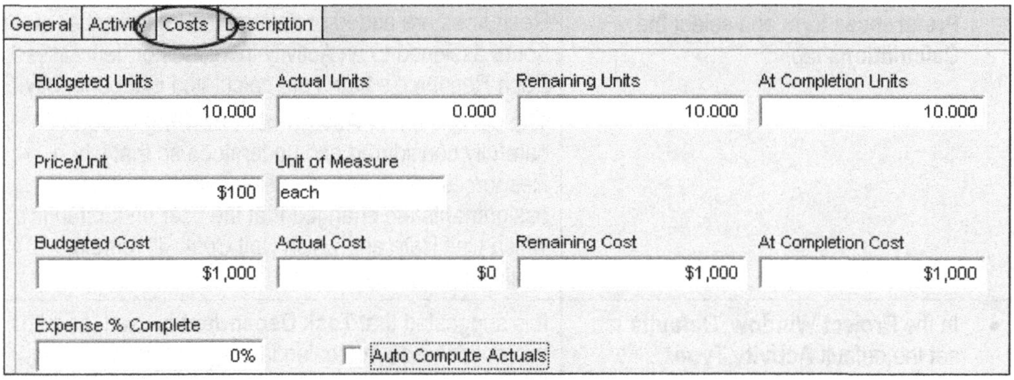

- **Description** tab is where you enter an extended description of the Expense item.

19.8.2 Expenses Tab in the Activities Window

This tab may have all the columns of data available in the **Expenses Window** displayed. All the fields may be edited from this tab:

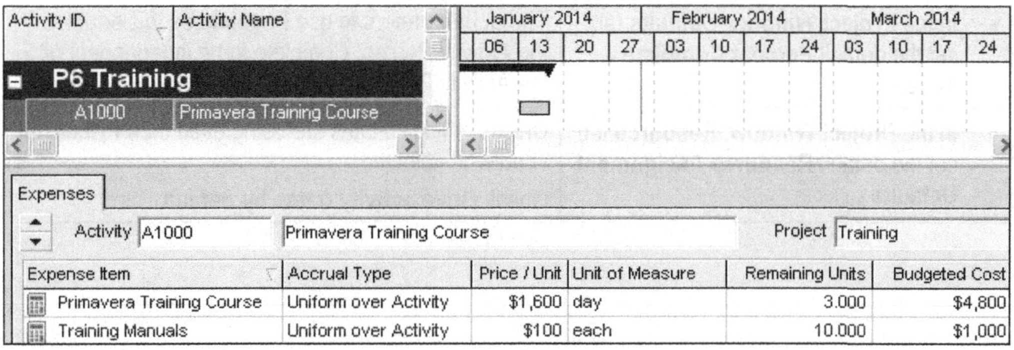

19.9 Suggested Setup for Creating a Resourced Schedule

The order that topics are introduced in this chapter is also a satisfactory order of actions that should be considered when preparing to assign resources to activities.

The simplest calculation options should be used as a default, and more complex options considered only when there is a specific scheduling requirement.

The table following lists processes and suggested options that could be considered when creating a resourced schedule. It is important to set all the parameters before the activities are added otherwise a lot of time is wasted changing parameters on a number of activities. These are not intended to suit every project but are a starting point for less experienced users.

Step	Suggested Settings
• Set the **Units/Time** format by selecting **Edit**, **User Preferences...** to open the **User Preferences** form and select the **Time Units** tab.	There is a choice of **percentage (50%)** or **units/duration (4h/d)**. This should be set on personal preference. The author prefers **(4h/d)** as this reduces typing.
• Set the **Resource Assignments** option by selecting **Edit**, **User Preferences...** to open the **User Preferences** form and select the **Calculations** tab.	It is suggested that the **Preserve the Units, Duration, and Units/Time for existing assignments** is selected. With this option as Resources are added or deleted the total number of hours assigned to an Activity increases or decreases. Each Resource's hours are calculated independently. The options under **Assignment Staffing** need to be carefully considered and understood so that when Resources are assigned to Roles and resource assignments are changed that the user understands which Unit Rate and which Unit Cost will remain against the activity.
• In the **Project Window**, **Defaults** tab set the default **Activity Type**.	It is suggested that **Task Dependent** is used, as with this option Resource calendars are not used making the schedule simpler.
• In the **Project Window**, **Defaults** tab set the default **Duration Type**.	It is suggested that **Fixed Duration & Units** is used. With this option the Activity Duration does not change when resource assignments are altered, and when an Activity Duration is changed the Units do not change, so your estimate of hours and costs will not change.
• In the **Project Window**, **Defaults** tab set the default **Percent Complete Type**.	The author prefers to use **Physical** as this enables the Activity Percent Complete to be independent of the Activity Durations.
• In the **Project Window, Resource** tab set the default **Resource Assignment Defaults**.	Unless multiple Rates are being used then **Price/Unit** should be selected. Check **Drive activity dates by default**.

19.10 Workshop 16 – Assigning Resources and Expenses to Activities

Background

The Resources must now be assigned to their specific activities.

Assignment

Open the OzBuild with Resources project and complete the following steps.

1. Apply the **OzBuild Workshop 10 – Without Float** layout and save as **OzBuild Workshop 16 – Assigning Resources** layout.
2. In the **Activities Window** display the **Gantt Chart** in the top view and **Resources** and **Expenses** tab of the **Activities Details** form in the bottom view.
3. Assign an Expense to the **Create Technical Specification** activity as per the picture below:

Expenses

Activity OZ1020 Create Technical Specification

Expense Item	Budgeted Cost	Accrual Type
Specialist Consultant	$5,000.00	Uniform over Activity

4. Format the **Resources** tab with the columns shown in the following picture:

Resources

Activity OZ1010 Determine Installation Requirements

Resource ID Name	Price / Unit	Default Units / Time	At Completion Units	At Completion Cost
PM.Project Manager	$120.00/h	8/d	32	$3,840.00
SE.Systems Engineer	$90.00/h	8/d	32	$2,880.00

5. Set your **User Preferences** as in the picture below:

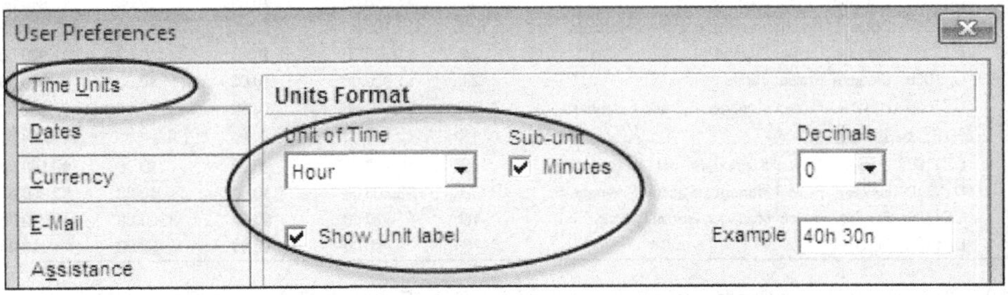

continued....

6. Add the **Resources** column to the Gantt Chart per the picture below.
7. Assign the following Resources to the Activities using the **Resource** tab [Add Resource] icon:

Activity ID	Activity Name	Resources
Bid for Facility Extension		
Technical Specification		
OZ1000	Approval to Bid	
OZ1010	Determine Installation Requirements	Project Manager, Systems Engineer
OZ1020	Create Technical Specification	Systems Engineer
OZ1030	Identify Supplier Components	Purchasing Officer
OZ1040	Validate Technical Specification	Project Manager, Systems Engineer
Delivery Plan		
OZ1050	Document Delivery Methodology	Project Manager
OZ1060	Obtain Quotes from Suppliers	Purchasing Officer, Project Manager
OZ1070	Calculate Bid Estimate	Project Support
OZ1080	Create the Project Schedule	Project Support
OZ1090	Review the Delivery Plan	Project Manager, Systems Engineer
Bid Document		
OZ1100	Create Draft of Bid Document	Clerical Support, Project Manager
OZ1110	Review Bid Document	Project Manager, Systems Engineer
OZ1120	Finalise and Submit Bid Document	Project Manager, Report Binding
OZ1130	Bid Docuement Submitted	

8. Enter 3 as the Budgeted Units and At Completion Units for the Report Binding.
9. Add the columns per below and your answer should look like this:

Activity ID	Activity Name	Resources	At Completion Labor Units	At Completion Labor Cost	At Completion Expense	At Completion Material Cost	At Completion Total Cost
Bid for Facility Extension			520h	$49,760.00	$5,000.00	$300.00	$55,060.00
Technical Specification			152h	$14,800.00	$5,000.00	$0.00	$19,800.00
OZ1000	Approva		0h	$0.00	$0.00	$0.00	$0.00
OZ1010	Determir	Project Manager, Systems Engineer	64h	$6,720.00	$0.00	$0.00	$6,720.00
OZ1020	Create T	Systems Engineer	40h	$3,600.00	$5,000.00	$0.00	$8,600.00
OZ1030	Identify :	Purchasing Officer	16h	$1,120.00	$0.00	$0.00	$1,120.00
OZ1040	Validate	Project Manager, Systems Engineer	32h	$3,360.00	$0.00	$0.00	$3,360.00
Delivery Plan			224h	$21,520.00	$0.00	$0.00	$21,520.00
OZ1050	Docume	Project Manager	32h	$3,840.00	$0.00	$0.00	$3,840.00
OZ1060	Obtain C	Purchasing Officer, Project Manager	128h	$12,160.00	$0.00	$0.00	$12,160.00
OZ1070	Calculat	Project Support	24h	$1,920.00	$0.00	$0.00	$1,920.00
OZ1080	Create tl	Project Support	24h	$1,920.00	$0.00	$0.00	$1,920.00
OZ1090	Review	Project Manager, Systems Engineer	16h	$1,680.00	$0.00	$0.00	$1,680.00
Bid Document			144h	$13,440.00	$0.00	$300.00	$13,740.00
OZ1100	Create C	Clerical Support, Project Manager	96h	$8,160.00	$0.00	$0.00	$8,160.00
OZ1110	Review	Project Manager, Systems Engineer	32h	$3,360.00	$0.00	$0.00	$3,360.00
OZ1120	Finalise	Project Manager, Report Binding	16h	$1,920.00	$0.00	$300.00	$2,220.00
OZ1130	Bid Doc		0h	$0.00	$0.00	$0.00	$0.00

10. Change the **User Preferences, Time Units, Units Format, Units per Time** to **Days** and see the difference:

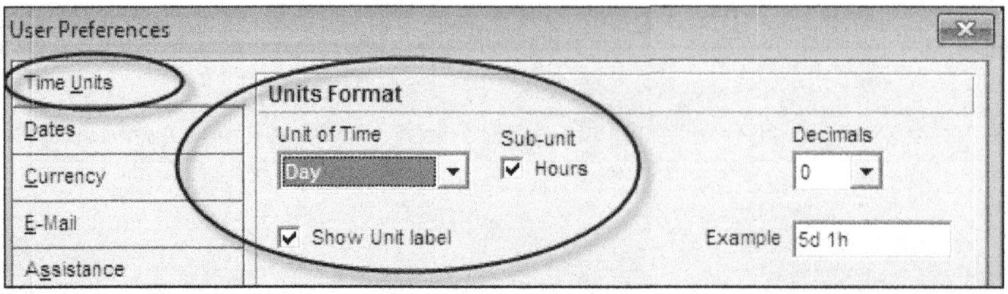

11. You will notice that there is no column to display the Materials quantity at completion.

Activity ID	Activity Name	Resources	At Completion Labor Units	At Completion Labor Cost	At Completion Expense	At Completion Material Cost	At Completion Total Cost
Bid for Facility Extension			65d	$49,760.00	$5,000.00	$300.00	$55,060.00
Technical Specification			19d	$14,800.00	$5,000.00	$0.00	$19,800.00
OZ1000	Approva		0d	$0.00	$0.00	$0.00	$0.00
OZ1010	Determir	Project Manager, Systems Engineer	8d	$6,720.00	$0.00	$0.00	$6,720.00
OZ1020	Create T	Systems Engineer	5d	$3,600.00	$5,000.00	$0.00	$8,600.00
OZ1030	Identify !	Purchasing Officer	2d	$1,120.00	$0.00	$0.00	$1,120.00
OZ1040	Validate	Project Manager, Systems Engineer	4d	$3,360.00	$0.00	$0.00	$3,360.00
Delivery Plan			28d	$21,520.00	$0.00	$0.00	$21,520.00
OZ1050	Docume	Project Manager	4d	$3,840.00	$0.00	$0.00	$3,840.00
OZ1060	Obtain C	Purchasing Officer, Project Manager	16d	$12,160.00	$0.00	$0.00	$12,160.00
OZ1070	Calculat	Project Support	3d	$1,920.00	$0.00	$0.00	$1,920.00
OZ1080	Create tl	Project Support	3d	$1,920.00	$0.00	$0.00	$1,920.00
OZ1090	Review	Project Manager, Systems Engineer	2d	$1,680.00	$0.00	$0.00	$1,680.00
Bid Document			18d	$13,440.00	$0.00	$300.00	$13,740.00
OZ1100	Create C	Clerical Support, Project Manager	12d	$8,160.00	$0.00	$0.00	$8,160.00
OZ1110	Review	Project Manager, Systems Engineer	4d	$3,360.00	$0.00	$0.00	$3,360.00
OZ1120	Finalise	Project Manager, Report Binding	2d	$1,920.00	$0.00	$300.00	$2,220.00
OZ1130	Bid Doc		0d	$0.00	$0.00	$0.00	$0.00

In a multi-user environment it is important that all users have the same User Preferences otherwise each person may display different Quantities at completion.

12. Change the **User Preferences, Time Units, Units Format, Units of Time** to **Hours**.

13. Save your layout as **OzBuild Workshop 16 – Assigning Resources**.

20 RESOURCE OPTIMIZATION

The schedule may now have to be resource optimized to:

- Reduce peaks and smooth the resource requirements, thus reducing the mobilization and demobilization costs, or to reduce the demand for site facilities, or
- Reduce resource demand to the available number of resources, or
- Reduce demand to an available cash flow when a project is financed on income.

20.1 Reviewing Resource Loading

There are a number of facilities for reviewing resource loading which consist of either displaying a Layout or running a report. The Timescale interval affects the displays. Layouts will not be covered in detail, as they are self-explanatory.

20.1.1 Activity Usage Spreadsheet

This window is displayed by clicking on the icon or selecting **View**, **Show on Bottom, Activity Usage Spreadsheet.**

- This displays a total of all the resource costs or units assigned to activities:

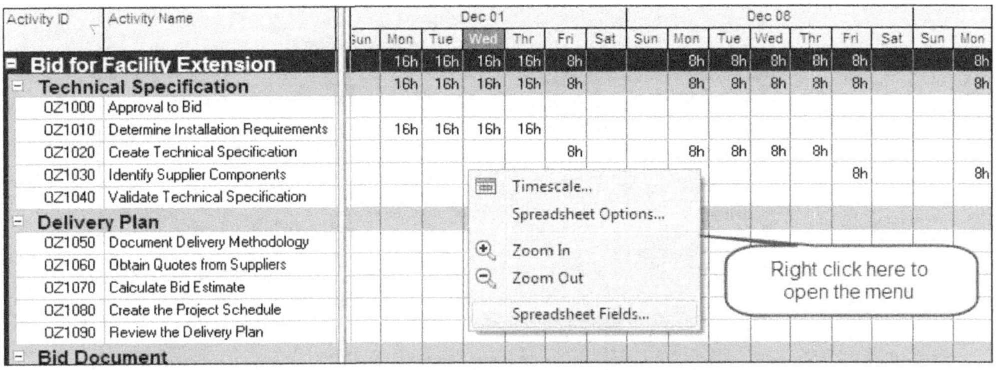

- Right-clicking will display a menu and the **Spreadsheet Fields...** option allows the selection of Cumulative and Time Interval display of Resource and Expenses information.

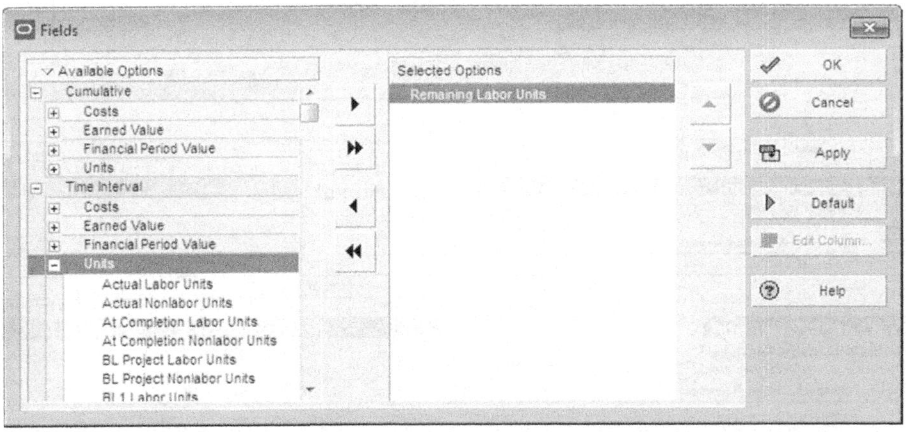

⚠ Cumulative **Expense Units** and **Material Resources Units** are not available in this view.

- **Spreadsheet Options...** allows the calculation of the average number of resources:

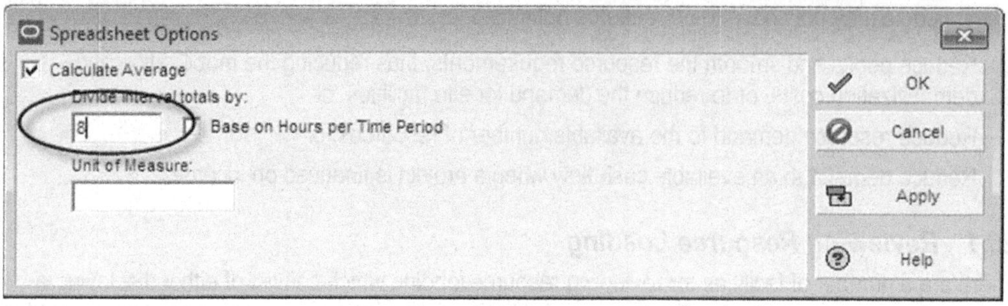

The units are formatted using the **User Preferences**, **Time Units** tab. If the minimum time unit is an hour, ensure the **User Preferences**, Resource Analysis **Interval for time-distributed resource** calculations is set to one hour; otherwise, the data will not be displayed correctly when the timescale is opened up to hours:

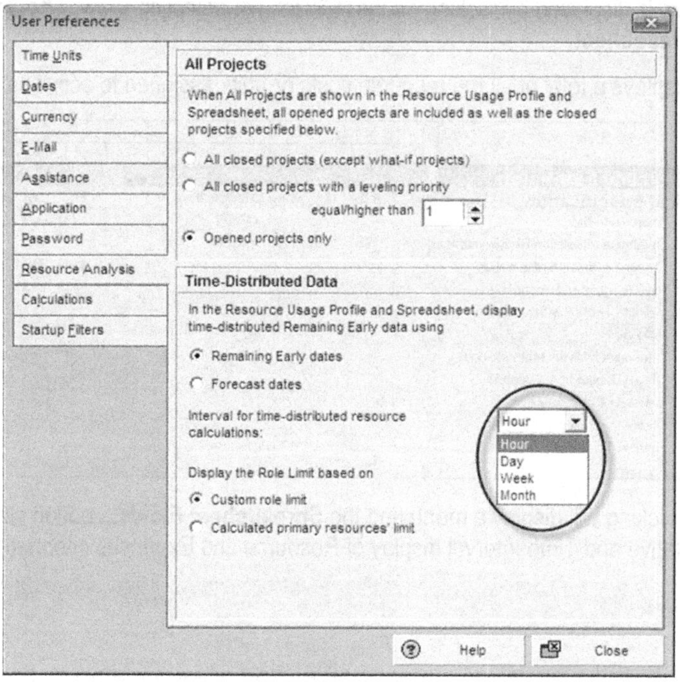

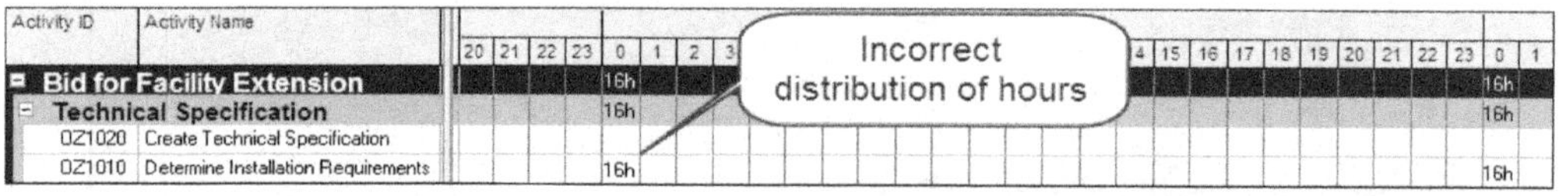

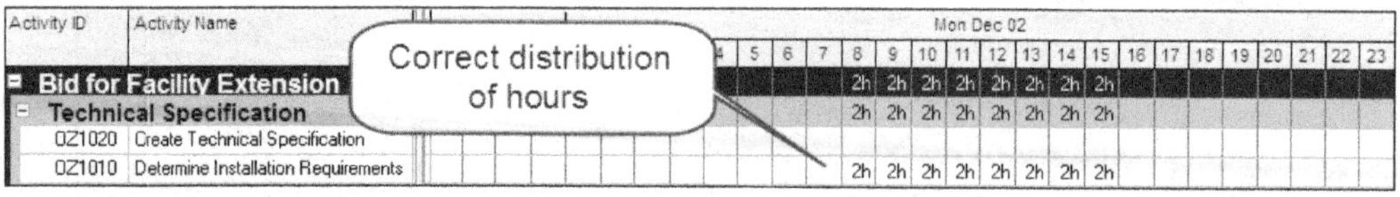

20.1.2 Activity Usage Profile

This is displayed by clicking on the icon or selecting **View**, **Show on Bottom, Activity Usage Profile**.

- It displays the total resource histogram for selected or all activities. Right-click the Histogram for the display options:

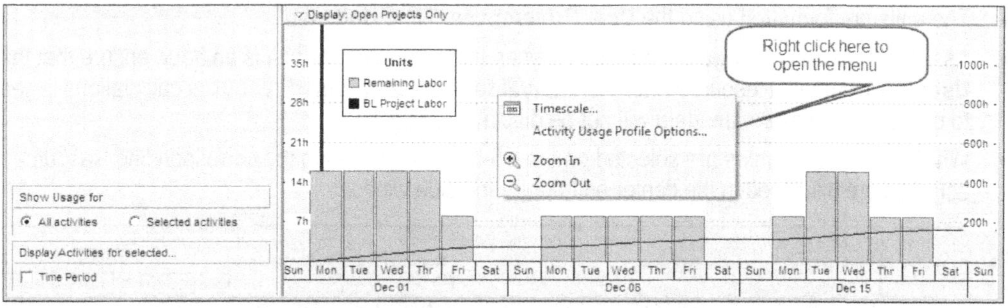

- The **Activity Usage Profile Options...** menu opens up the **Activity Usage Profile Options** form:

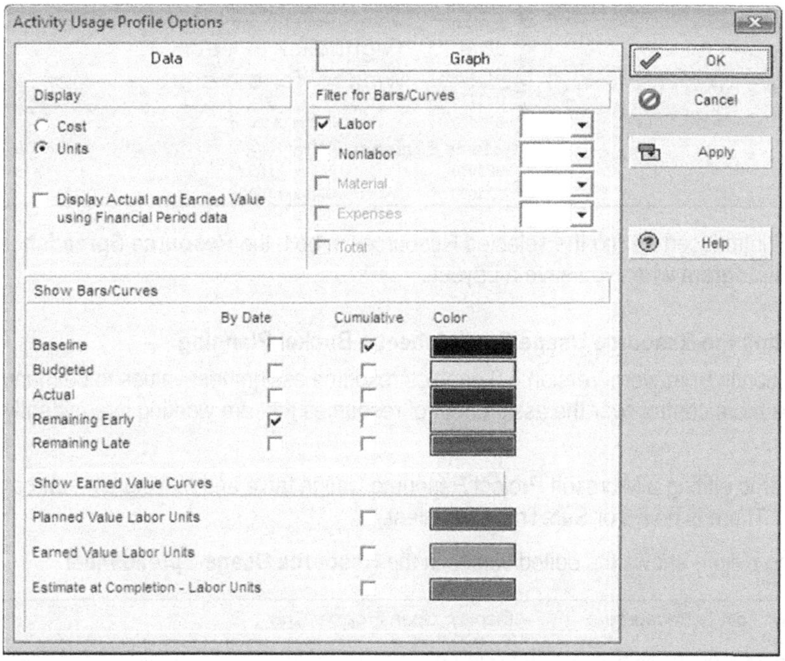

It may not be clear where these options are drawing their information from by reading the descriptions in the **Activity Usage Profile Options** form. The **Earned Value** chapter covers these options in more detail. The following functions affect the graphs display:

- The project Baseline/s,
- **User Preferences**, **Time Units** settings,
- **Projects Window**, **Settings** tab, **Project Settings** section, **Baseline for earned value calculations,**
- **Admin**, **Admin Preferences...,Earned Value Tab**, **Earned value calculation** section.

20.1.3 Resource Usage Spreadsheet

This is displayed by clicking on the icon or selecting **View**, **Show on Bottom, Resource Usage Spreadsheet**.

- This form has three windows showing the resources that are assigned to activities.
- Each window has a menu when right-clicking in the window.
- The units are formatted using the **User Preferences**, **Time Units** tab.
- As with the **Activity Usage Spreadsheet**, when the minimum time unit is an hour, ensure that the **User Preferences**, Resource Analysis **Interval for time-distributed resource** calculations is set to one hour; otherwise, the data will not be displayed correctly.
- When multiple resources are selected on the left-hand window then the corresponding Resource activities are displayed in the center and right-hand side window:

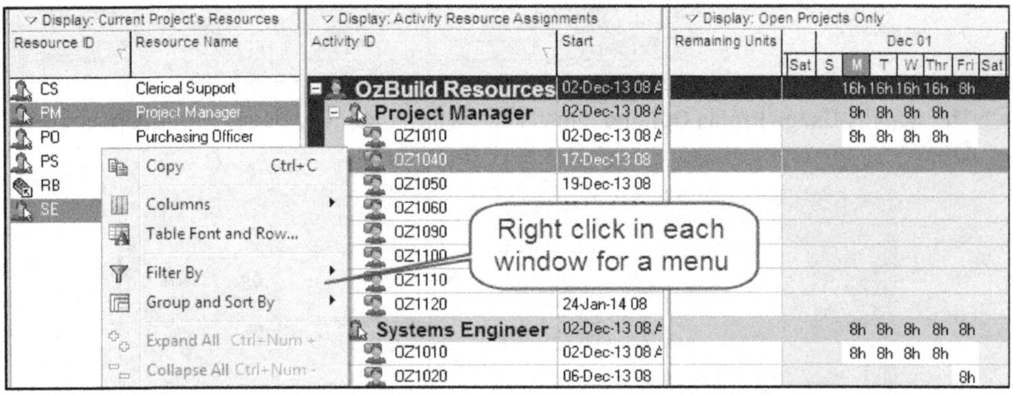

Version 15.2 introduced saving the selected Resources in both the **Resource Spreadsheet** and **Resource Histogram** when you save a Layout.

20.1.4 Editing the Resource Usage Spreadsheet – Bucket Planning

This new option in Primavera Version 6.0 enables resource assignment values to be manually edited. This enables more control over the assignment of resources that are working intermittently on an activity.

This is similar to editing a Microsoft Project Resource Usage table and making a resource assignment "Contoured." There is no P3 or SureTrak equivalent.

The following picture shows the edited values in the **Resource Usage Spreadsheet**.

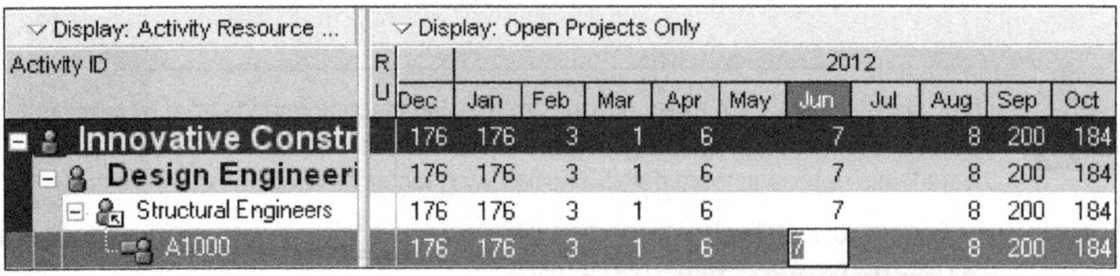

Each time period, therefore, may contain a different value.

⚠ It is recommended that you experiment with this function if you plan to progress Bucket Planned Resources as the author has found this process gives some interesting results for the incomplete portion of an in-progress activity.

20.1.5 Resource Usage Profile displaying a Resource Histogram

Click on the icon or select **View**, **Show on Bottom, Resource Usage Profile**.

- The options in this form are similar to the ones covered in the previous paragraphs,
- Stacked or individual histograms are available from the menu:

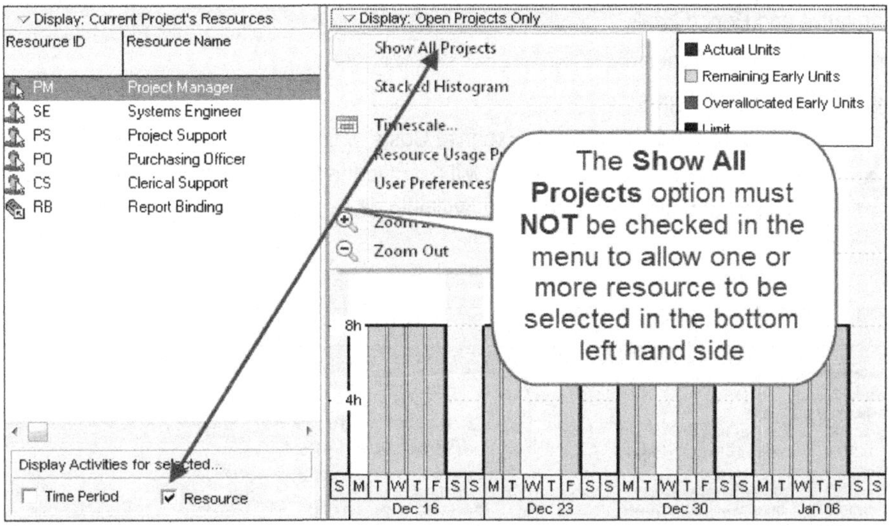

Version 15.2 introduced saving the selected Resources in both the **Resource Spreadsheet** and **Resource Histogram** when you save a Layout.

The resource availability is displayed using the Resource Calendar when the **Activity Type** is set to **Task Dependent** and the activity is scheduled using the Activity Calendar.

20.1.6 Activity Usage Profile Displaying S-Curves

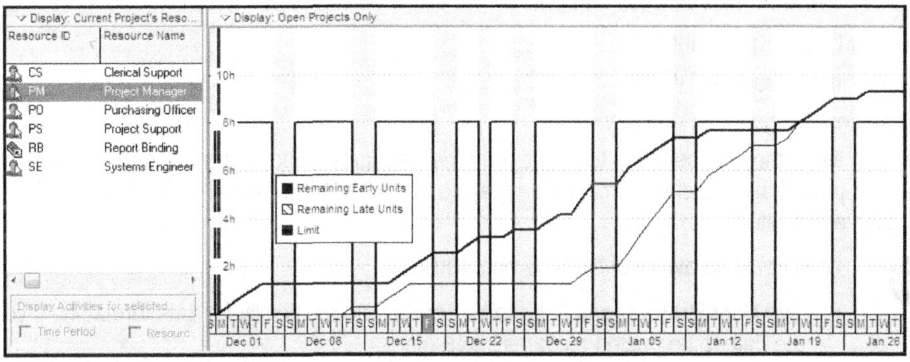

You must be prepared to experiment with the formatting menus by right-clicking in each of the windows of the above displays to understand all the many options, which include:

- Roles or Resources,
- All Resources, All Active Resources and Current Projects Resources only,
- Options to show period and cumulative values, or an average by dividing by a number,
- Options to filter, and
- Options to Group and Sort.

20.2 *Resource Assignments Window*

The **Resource Assignments Window** has some functions that are very useful especially when you wish to copy and paste data into Excel.

This view is essentially a time-phased view that is grouped by default by Resource, Role, or Activity and allows the display of:

- Cumulative and Period totals
- Cost of all Resource Types
- Units of all Resource Types

This view does not show either Expense Costs or Expense Units. So using this view for a cash flowing project with Expenses will not give the full value of the project. Resource Units Totals, say at project level, are only available when one resource type is displayed by using a filter.

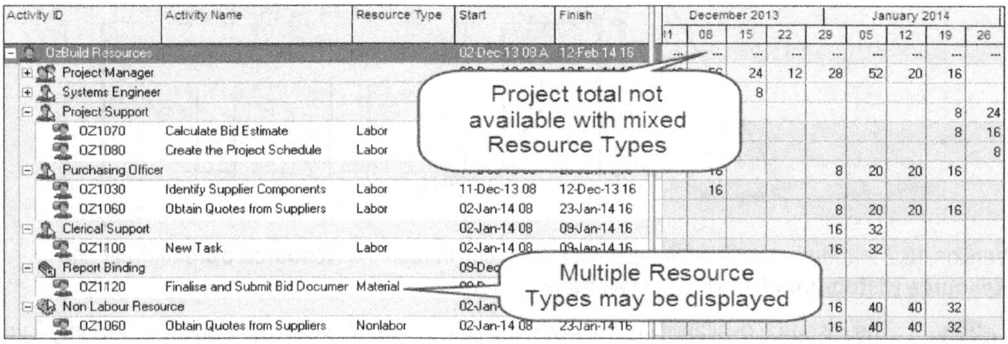

20.3 *Copying and Pasting into Excel*

The following data may be copied and pasted into Excel:

- Activity data from the Activities Window
- Activity Usage Spreadsheet
- Tables in the Tracking Window
- Resource Assignments Window

It has been the author's experience that data from the Resource Usage Spreadsheet may NOT be copied and pasted into Excel but similar data may be obtained in the Resource Assignments Window and copied and pasted.

You should be aware of the following issues:

- The **User Preferences** need to be appropriate especially for date formatting if you wish the data to be pasted as dates into Excel.
- Dates that are pasted with an "A" at the end may be removed with the Excel command of **Find and Replace**. You may need to put a space before the "A" so you do not lose the "A" in front of August.
- To remove the "*" at the end of a date you must use the syntax of "~" in the Find and Replace command as a "*" on its own will replace all the data in the spreadsheet.

20.4 Other Tools for Histograms and Tables

Oracle Primavera also sells a reporting add-on software package titled **Primavera Earned Value Management** which allows the production of a number of reports such as time-phased table, bubble, and period variance.

Contact your local Oracle Primavera distributor or go to the Oracle Primavera web site for more information.

20.5 Methods of Resolving Resource Peaks and Conflicts

Methods of resolving resource overload problems are:

- **Revising the Project Plan**. Revise a project plan to mitigate resource conflicts, such as changing the order of work, contracting work out, or using off-site pre-fabrication, etc.
- **Duration Change**. Increase the activity duration to decrease the resource requirements, so a 5-day activity with 10 people could be extended to a 10-day activity with 5 people.
- **Resource Substitution**. Substitute one resource with another available resource.
- **Increase Working Time**. This may release the resource for other activities earlier and is created by working more days per week or hours per day.
- **Split an activity around peaks in demand**. Some software enables the splitting of activities, which in turn enables work to be split around peaks in resource demand. The split function is not available in Primavera, however, an activity may be split in two individual activities to allow the work to cease in times of peak demand. If one needs to relate back to a baseline then two new activities may be created to represent the split and the original activity made into a hammock to span the two new activities, but remember to display the LOE Baseline Bar.
- **Leveling the schedule**. This technique delays activities until resource(s)are available.
- **Resource Curves** or **Manually Editing the Resource Spreadsheet** may assist in some instances.

20.6 Resource Leveling

20.6.1 Methods of Resource Leveling

After resource overloads or inefficiencies have been identified with Resource and Tables, the schedule may now have to be leveled to reduce peaks in resource demands. Leveling is defined as delaying activities until resources become available. There are several methods of delaying activities to level a schedule:

- **Turning off Automatic Calculation and Dragging Activities**. This option does not maintain a critical path and reverts to the original schedule when recalculated. This option should not be used when a contract requires a critical path schedule to be maintained, as the schedule will no longer calculate correctly.
- **Constraining Activities**. A constraint may be applied to delay an activity until the date that the resource becomes available from a higher priority activity. This is not a recommended method because the delay of the higher priority activity may unlevel the schedule.
- **Sequencing Logic**. Relationships may be applied to activities sharing the same resource(s) in the order of their priority. In this process, a resource-driven critical path is generated. If the first activity in a chain is delayed then the chain of activities will be delayed. But the schedule will not become unleveled and the critical path will be maintained. In this situation, a successor activity may be able to take place earlier and the logic will have to be manually edited.

- **Leveling Function**. The software Resource Leveling function levels resources by delaying activities without the need for Constraints or Logic, and finds the optimum order for the activities based on user defined parameters. Again, as this option does not maintain a critical path developed by durations and relationships, it should not be used when a contract requires a critical path schedule developed in this way. The Leveling function may be used to establish an optimum scheduling sequence and then Sequencing Logic applied to hold the leveled dates and to create a critical path.

The Resource Leveling function enables the optimization of resource use by delaying activities until resources become available, thus reducing the peaks in resource requirements. This feature may extend the length of a project.

The leveling function should be used by novices with extreme caution.

- It requires the scheduler to have a solid understanding of how the software resourcing functions calculate.
- Leveling increases the complexity of a schedule and requires a different approach to building a schedule. In principle, the sequencing logic is replaced by Priorities but a Closed Network should still be maintained.

Your ability to understand how the software operates is important for you to be able to utilize the leveling function with confidence on larger schedules. It is recommended that you practice with small simple schedules to gain experience in leveling and develop an understanding of the leveling issues before attempting a complex schedule.

20.6.2 Resource Leveling Function

This section outlines the software Resource Leveling functions including:

- **Level Resources** form,
- Leveling Examples, including Resource Shifts,
- Guidelines on Leveling, and
- What to look for if resources are not leveling.

20.6.3 Level Resources Form

The **Level Resources** form enables you to assign most of the Leveling prerequisites. Select **Tools, Level Resources...** to open the **Level Resources** form:

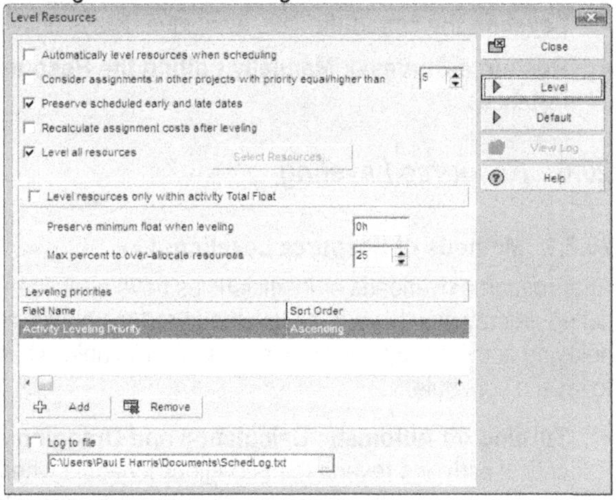

- **Automatically level resources when scheduling** – levels the schedule each time the schedule is recalculated and is not recommended.
- **Consider assignments in other projects with priority equal/higher than**. – levels resources and at the same time considers the demands of other projects. The leveling priority is set in the **Projects Window, General** tab.
- **Preserve scheduled early and late dates** – in simple terms, when unchecked enables the option of **Late Leveling**. This is explained in more detail in the following paragraphs as the computations are a little more complicated. **Late Leveling** pushes forward in time activities from their late dates to meet the resource availability and provides the latest dates the activities may be started and finished without delaying the finish date of the project.

- **Recalculate assignment costs after leveling** – is used with the resource **Effective date** and **Price/Unit**. These facilities allow a change in the cost of a resource over time. The Resource Costs are recalculated based on the resource **Price/Unit** if an activity is moved into a different price bracket when this check box is marked.
- **Level all resources** – if checked, the schedule levels all the resources; if unchecked, enables the **Select Resources** form to be opened and one or more resources selected for leveling.
- **Level resources only within activity Total Float**
  - When checked, the leveling process will not generate negative float but may not completely level a schedule. Thus, the activities will only be delayed until all float is consumed and leveling will not extend the finish date of the project. This option will also check the **Preserve scheduled early and late dates** option.
  - When unchecked, leveling will allow activities to extend beyond a **Project Must Finish By date**, when assigned in the **Projects Window Dates** tab, or beyond the latest date calculated by the schedule and may create **Negative Float**.
  - **Preserve minimum float when leveling** – works with **Level resources only within Total Float** and will not level activities if their float will drop below the assigned value.
  - **Max percent to over-allocate resources** – works with **Level resources only within activity Total Float** and enables the doubling of the resource availability, although this new limit is not displayed in the histogram limits.
- **Leveling priorities** – sets leveling the priorities, and activities are assigned resources according to the Data item chosen in the first line. If two activities have the same value in the first line then the priority in the second line is used. The Activity ID is the final value used to assign resources. There are many options for leveling priority and the following are some to consider:
  - **Activity Leveling Priority** is a field that may be set from 1 Top to 5 Lowest; the default is 3 Normal. Those with a priority 1 Top are assigned resources first.
  - **Activity Codes** or **User Defined Fields** and many other data fields such as **Remaining Duration**, **Early Start**, **Total Float**, and **Late Start** may be used to set the priority for leveling.

20.7 Leveling Examples

Two simple examples can assist you in understanding how the software works:

- The first will allow the schedule to level with positive float, and
- The second will NOT allow the schedule to level with positive float and may generate negative float.

It is recommended that you set up a small schedule and try the various options until you understand what the software is doing and how it operates before trying your hand with a large schedule.

You should then look at leveling more complex schedules only after you have mastered leveling a small schedule like the examples in this chapter.

20.7.1 Leveling with Positive Float

The following picture displays the schedule unleveled:

- A project **Must Finish By Date** of 27 Feb has been set.
- The histogram shows both the Early and Late resource histogram is overloaded.
- The bars displayed are the **Early**, **Remaining**, the **Late** and **Total Float**:

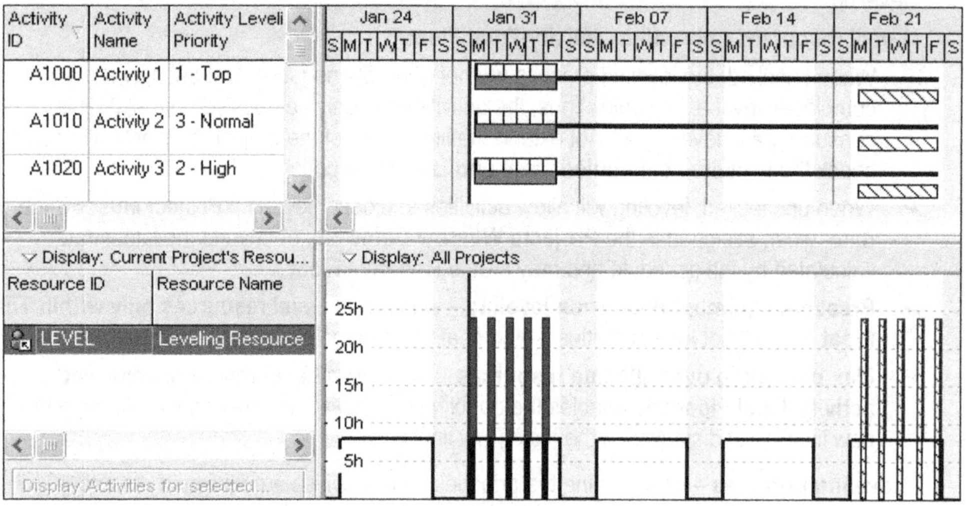

Early Bar –

Remaining Bar –

Late Bar –

After Leveling with all the Leveling options off except the **Select Resource...** option:

- Early and Late leveling has taken place and the Early and Late histogram are leveled.
- The Early and Remaining Bars have the same dates and are leveled.
- The Total Float is the difference between the Late and Early Finish and provides a similar result if there is a relationship between the activities.

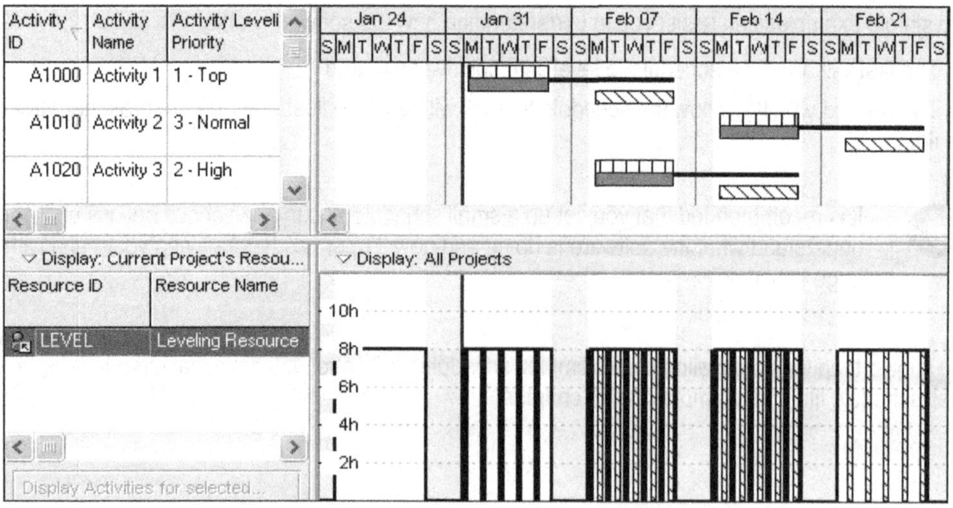

With **Preserve scheduled early and late dates** option checked:

- Early leveling of the Remaining dates has taken place and the Early histogram is leveled.
- Late leveling has NOT taken place and the Late histogram is NOT leveled.
- The Early and Late Bar have NOT been leveled.
- The Total Float is the difference between the Late and Remaining Finish dates and provides a similar result if there is NO relationship between the activities.

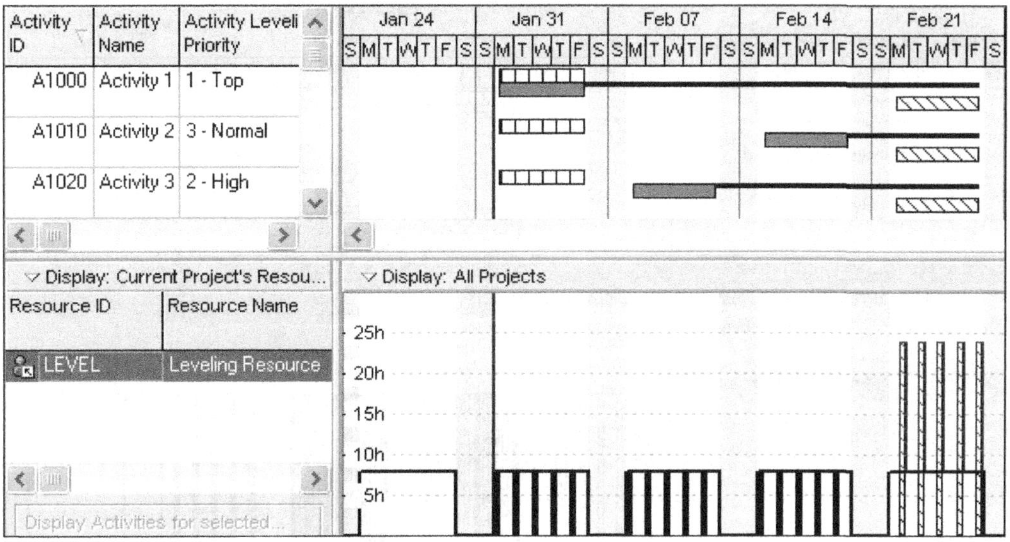

20.7.2 Leveling without Positive Float

The following picture displays the schedule unleveled:

- A project **Must Finish By Date** of 13 Feb has been set.
- The histogram shows both the Early and Late resource histogram are overloaded.

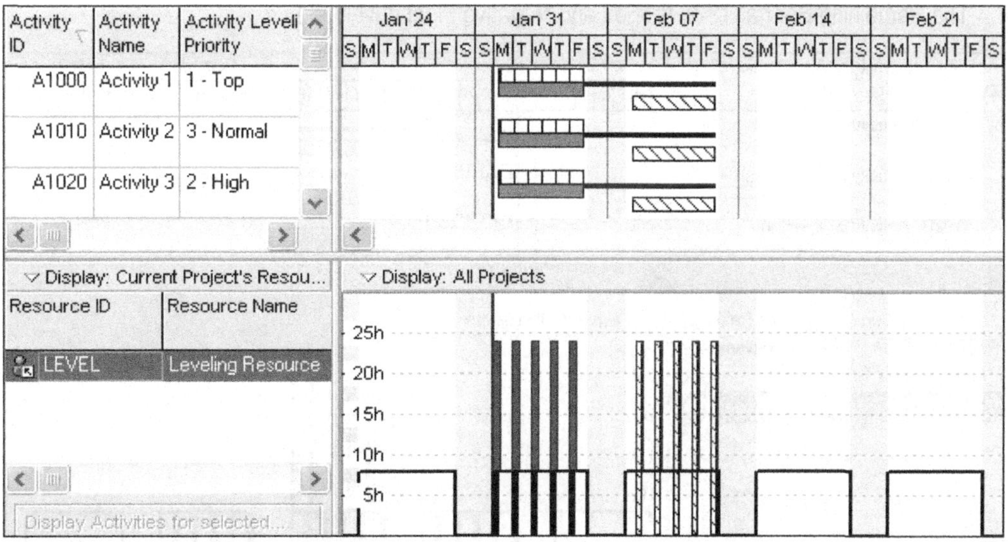

After Leveling with all the options off except the **Select Resource...** option:

- Early and Late leveling has taken place and the Early and Late histogram is leveled.
- The Early and Remaining Bars have the same dates and are leveled and Negative Float developed.
- The Total Float is the difference between the Late and Early Finish and provides a similar result if there is a relationship between the activities.

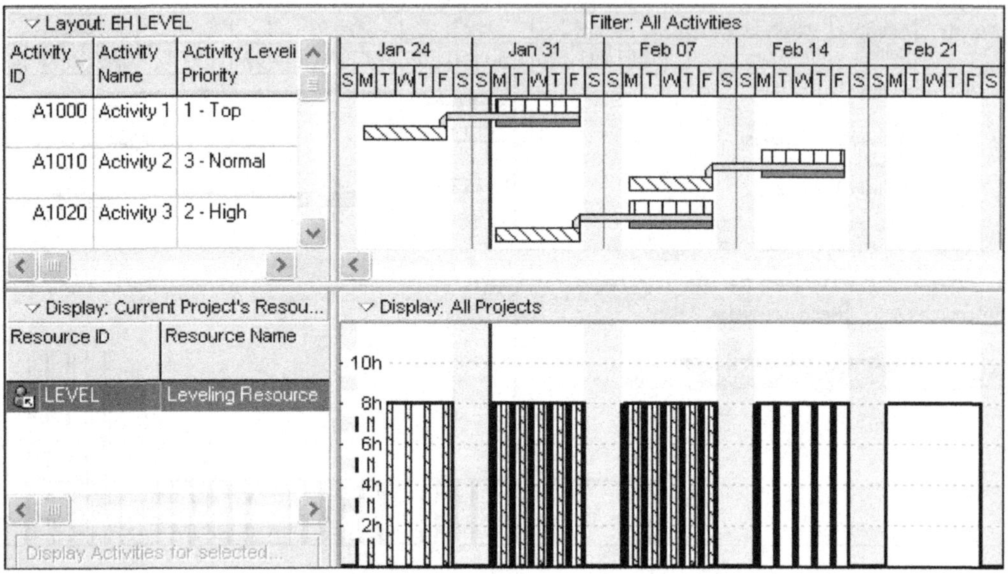

With **Preserve scheduled early and late dates** option checked:

- Early leveling has taken place and the Early histogram is leveled.
- Late leveling has NOT taken place and the Late histogram is NOT leveled.
- The Early and Late Bar have NOT been leveled.
- The Remaining Bar has been leveled and Negative Float developed.

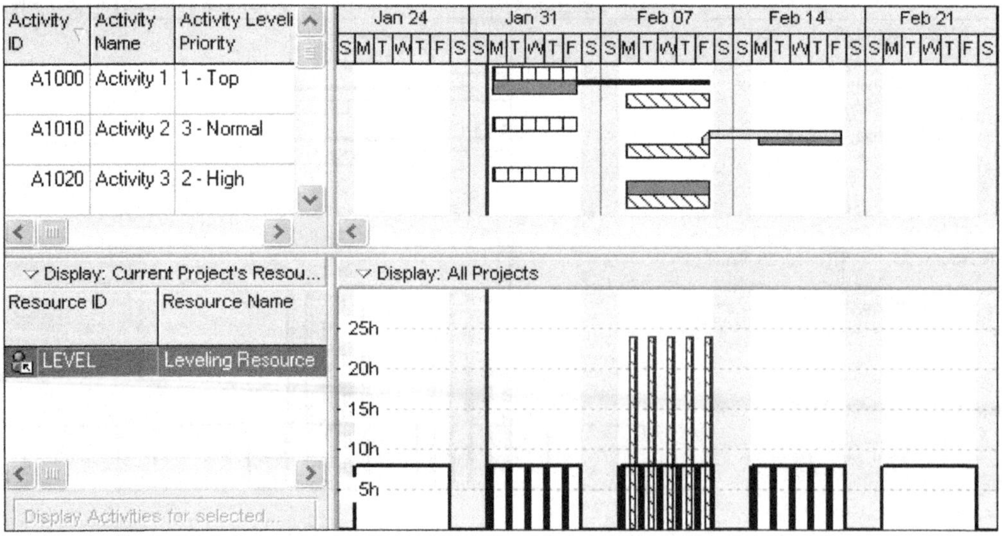

With **Preserve scheduled early and late dates** and the **Level resources only within activity Total Float option** checked:

- Early leveling on the Remaining dates has taken place as much as possible without creating Negative Float.
- Activity 2 with the lowest priority has been left on the Data Date.
- Late leveling has NOT taken place and the Late histogram is NOT leveled.
- The Early Bar has NOT been leveled

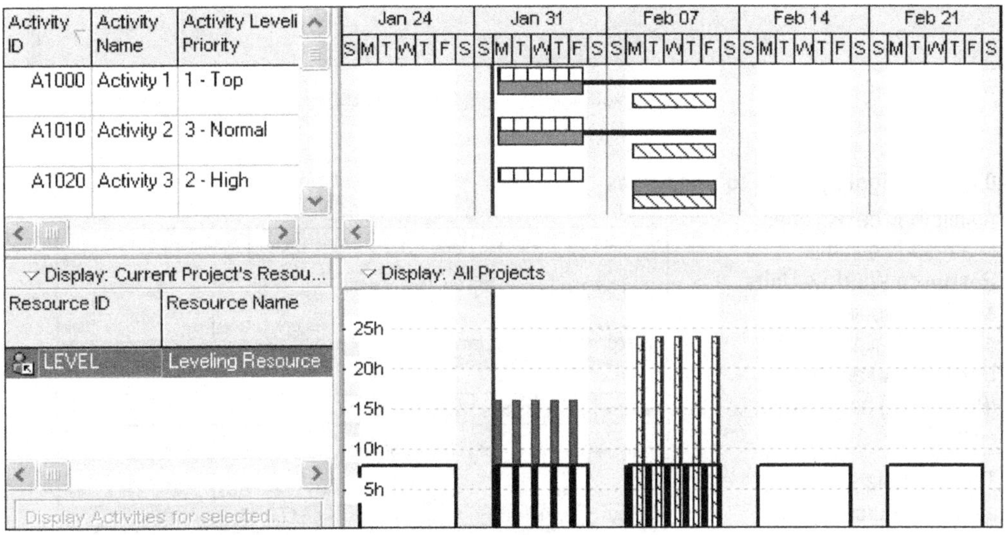

20.8 Resource Shifts

Resource shifts enable the modeling of resource availability when a different number of resources may be available on various shifts. Some key points are covered in the following text:

Resource shifts should be used with:

- Resource Dependent tasks, and
- Resources set to Drive Activity Dates after they have been assigned to activities.

Unlike other products, when an Activity is made Resource Dependent the Activity Calendar is still acknowledged for the start of a Task, but not the finish.

Before attempting to use shifts, a user should have considerable familiarity with the software or work with someone experienced.

20.8.1 Creating Shifts:

Select **Enterprise**, **Resource Shifts...** to open the **Resource Shifts** form:

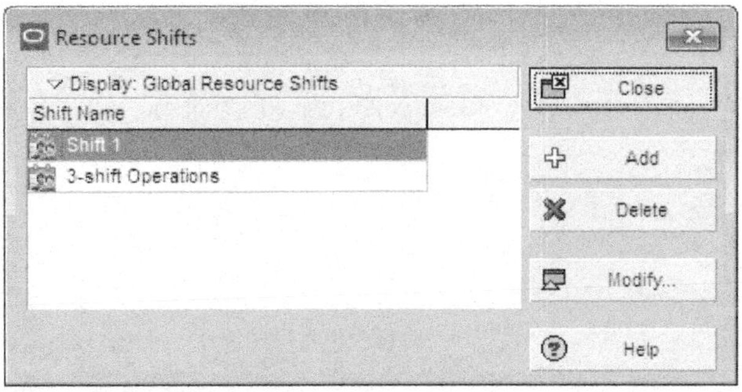

When a shift is added it must total 24 hours:

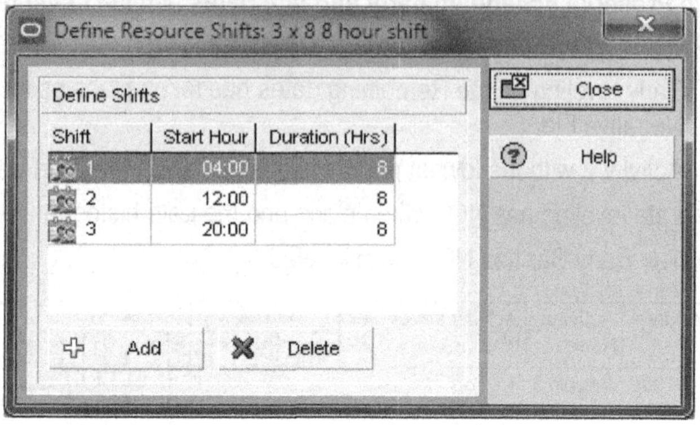

20.8.2 Assigning Shifts to Resources

A shift may be assigned to a resource in the **Resource Window Units & Prices** tab, with a different availability (**Max Units/ Time**) and rate (**Price/Unit**) assigned for each shift.

This example shows there are no resources assigned to shift 3, therefore representing a two-shift environment.

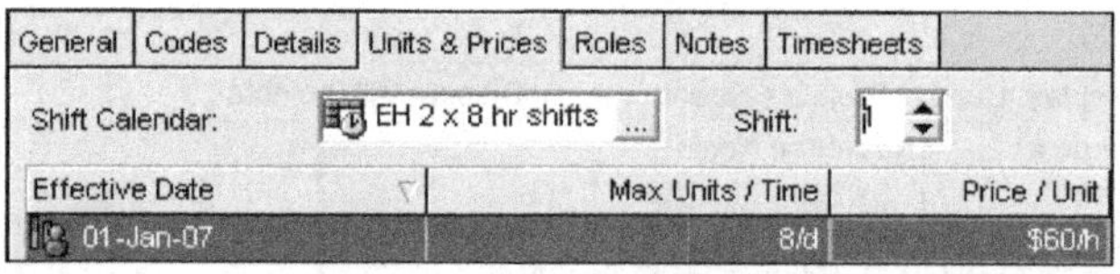

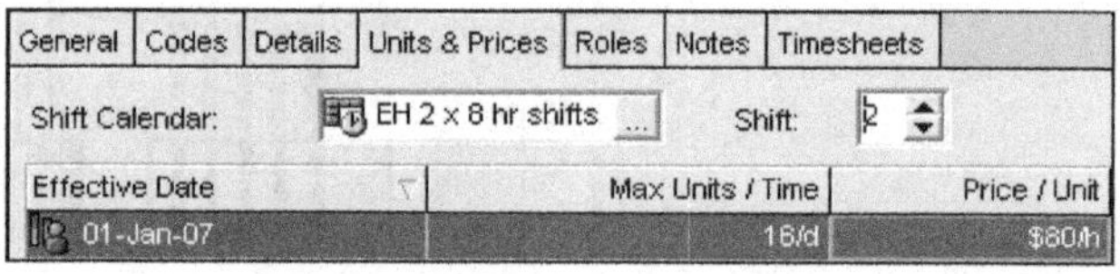

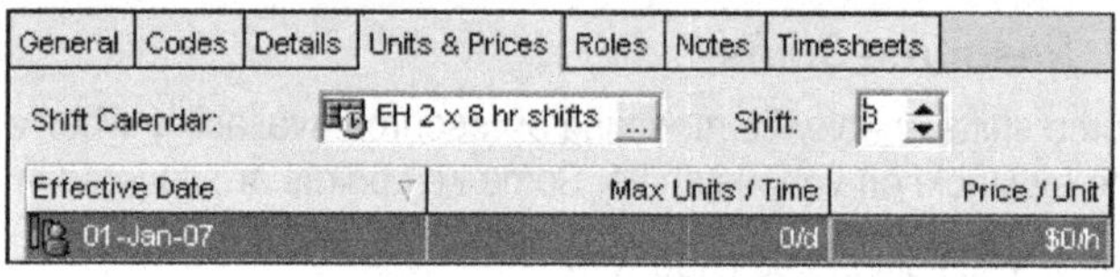

A Resource will have a little arrow in a box pointing to its head when assigned to an activity of an open project:

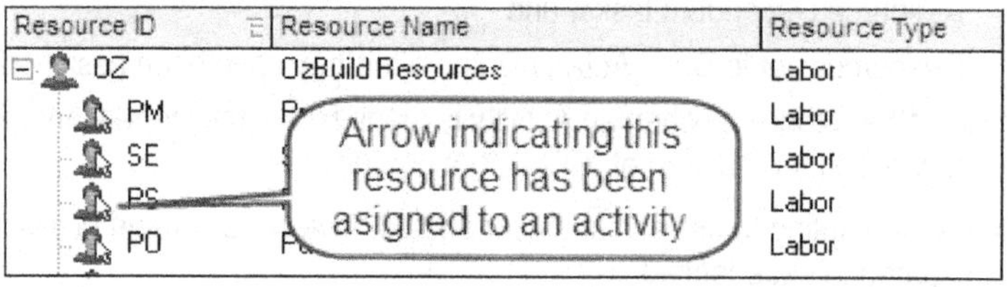

20.8.3 Leveling With Shifts

Shifts are acknowledged when the leveling function is used. The following example shows activities on a 24-hour per day, 7-day per week activity calendar, with shifts set up as on the previous page, with all activities set as Resource Dependent and Drive Activity Dates. The situation before leveling with the Resource Limit displayed according to shift availability:

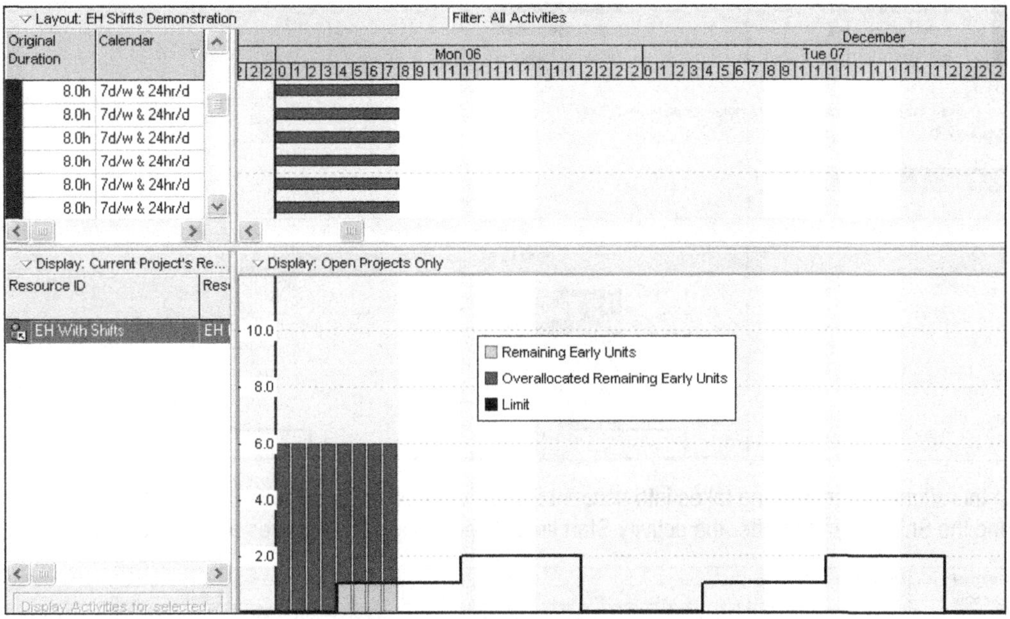

After Leveling with all leveling options **NOT** checked:

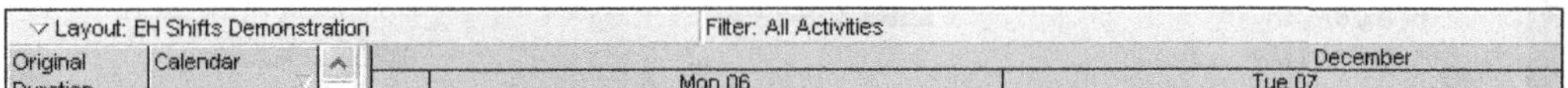

The following example has the activities on an 8-hour per day, 7-day per week calendar:

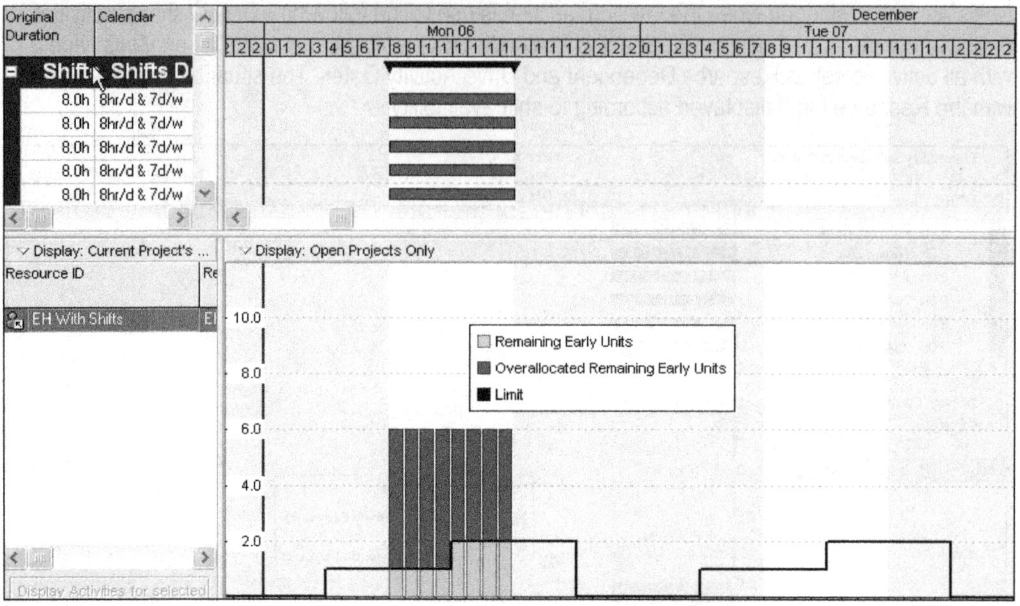

In this situation, the leveling takes into account the Activity Calendar for each Start of each activity and the Shifts operated after the activity Start time. Even though the activities are Resource Driven:

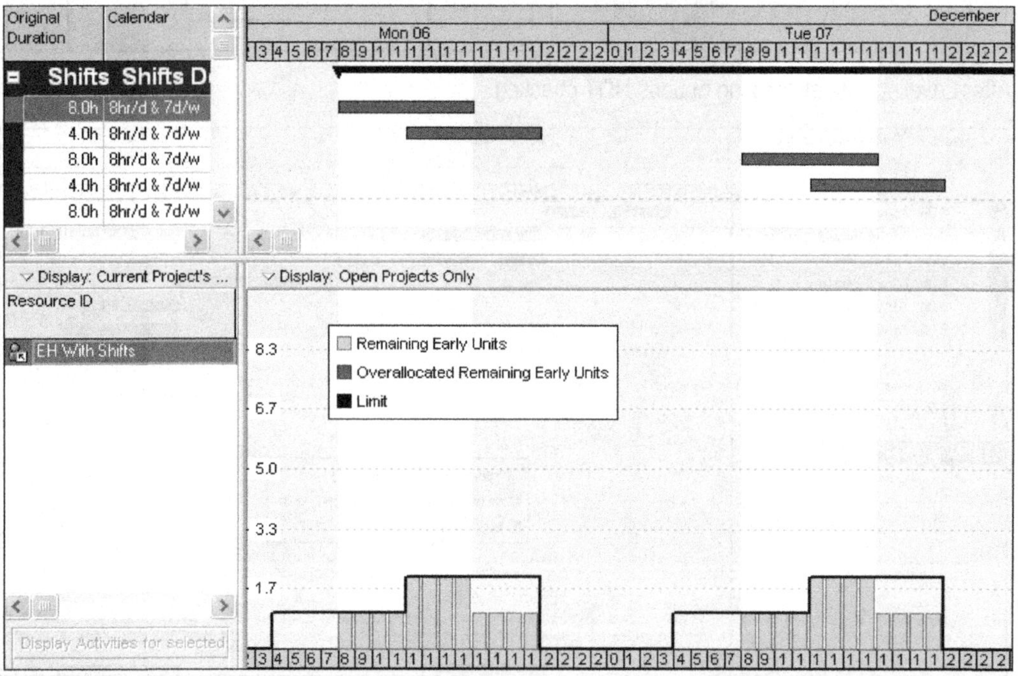

When the Resources are set to **NOT Drive Activity Dates** the resources still level, but:

- Work begins on the start date and time of the first activity, not at the start of the resource shift.
- The Activity Bars do not show when the work is taking place.
- The activities also do not begin on the shift start time when the **Default Calendar** is set 7 days per week, 24 hours per day.

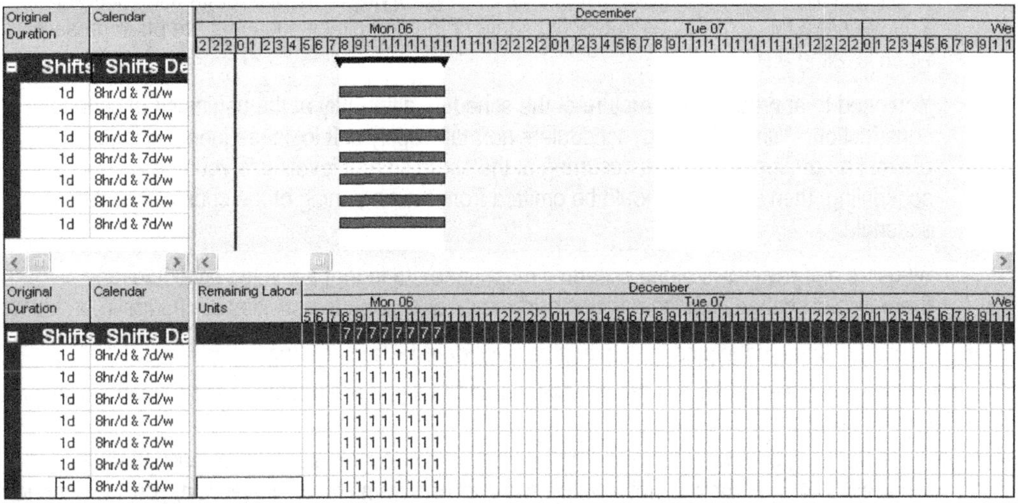

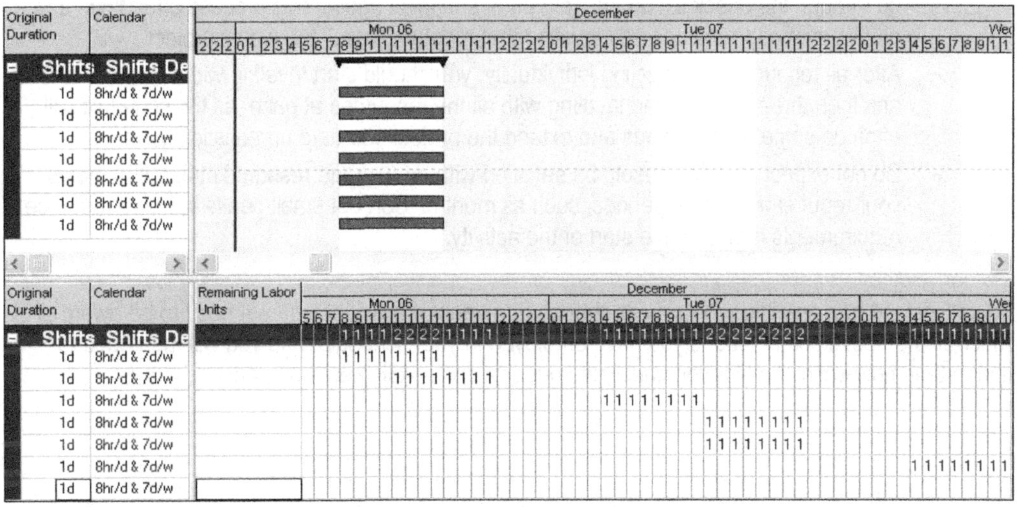

It appears the best option to make resources calculate correctly when using shifts is to:

- Put the activities on a calendar that has the same or greater working hours than the Resource Shifts, so the start of the resource work is not delayed,
- Set the resources to **Resource Driven**, to acknowledge the resource calendars,
- Set the resources to **Drive Activity Dates**, to ensure the Activity Bars move with the Leveled Resources,
- Create a small schedule and experiment to make sure the schedule is behaving the way you think it should and you understand what is happening.

20.9 Guidelines for Leveling

Leveling a schedule is a skill that is acquired through practice and experience and there are a few fundamentals that a user must bear in mind before attempting to level a complex schedule.

- If you are not an experienced scheduling software user then it is strongly suggested that you obtain some serious experience in using Primavera with resources before attempting to use leveling on a complex schedule, especially if you are trying to level a progressed schedule. You will need this experience to resolve some of the complex issues that are often present when leveling a schedule.
- You need to approach the structure of the schedule differently at the beginning of schedule construction. Without leveling, schedulers normally apply soft logic (sequencing logic) to prevent a number of activities occurring at the same time. If leveling is your method of scheduling, then soft logic should be omitted from the beginning of the construction of the schedule.
- All users and reviewers of the schedule must understand that a leveled schedule may dramatically change with the addition or removal or change to activities or change in priorities.
- There are some principles that should be considered when leveling:
  - Only level resources that are overloaded and that you are unable to supplement easily or that have an absolute limit.
  - Try leveling one resource at a time and view the histograms to ensure each resource is leveling. If a resource is not leveling and the histograms display overload, you will need to go through the check list on the next page and level again. This process often finds a driving overload resource and leveling that resource levels the whole project.
  - After all resources are leveling individually, you should start leveling with two resources and then three. Do not start leveling with all the resources at once, as the schedule will often do some drastic things and extend the project end date unrealistically.
  - Do not expect a perfect result; be satisfied with an average resource usage that meets your requirements over periods, such as months. Sort out small peaks in future resource requirements nearer to the start of the activity.

To understand how leveling will delay or change durations of activities you will need to be aware of which of the above combinations you have employed in your schedule, and you will then need to understand how each combination calculates under a non-leveling environment.

20.10 What to look for if Resources are Not Leveling

It is very frustrating if you have a project that will not level. Try some of these options when your schedule will not level:

- Have you selected a resource to level in the Select Resources form? The resources to be leveled must be selected in the Select Resources form.
- Have you set the Limits in the Resource Window? A resource needs a limit to level.
- A resource will not be leveled when you assign a resource to an activity with a Units per time period greater than value set in the resource dictionary. This may occur when:
  - The **Resource Limit** in the **Resource Window** is reduced, or
  - An activity has been assigned a resource with a **Unit per Time Period** that is greater than the **Limit**, or
  - When the activity has **Fixed Units** and the duration of an activity has been reduced, thus increasing the assigned **Units per Time Period** over the maximum available in the **Resource** form.
- Have you assigned a **Mandatory Constraint** to an unleveled activity? Activities with a Mandatory constraint will not be leveled.
- Have you checked **Level resources only within activity Total Float** option? This option enables activities without float to level.

20.11 Resource Curves

Resource Curves enable a non-linear assignment of resources to schedules in the same way as P3 and Microsoft Project. These are often used on long activities where there is not a requirement for a linear assignment of resources.

Resource curves are assigned in the **Curve** column in the **Resources** tab of the **Activities Window**:

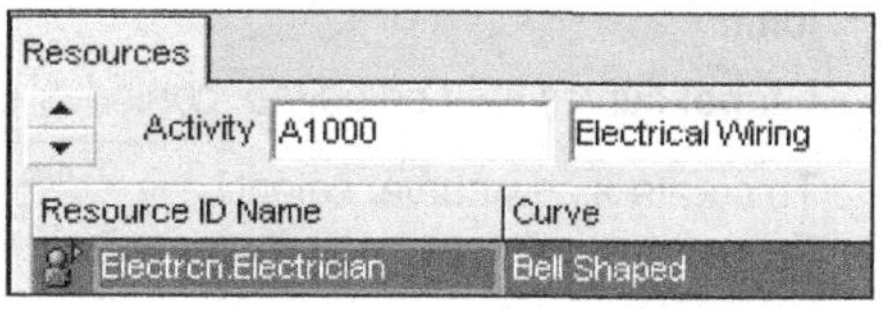

The Electrical wiring activity in the following picture has a bell-shaped Resource Curve assigned to it:

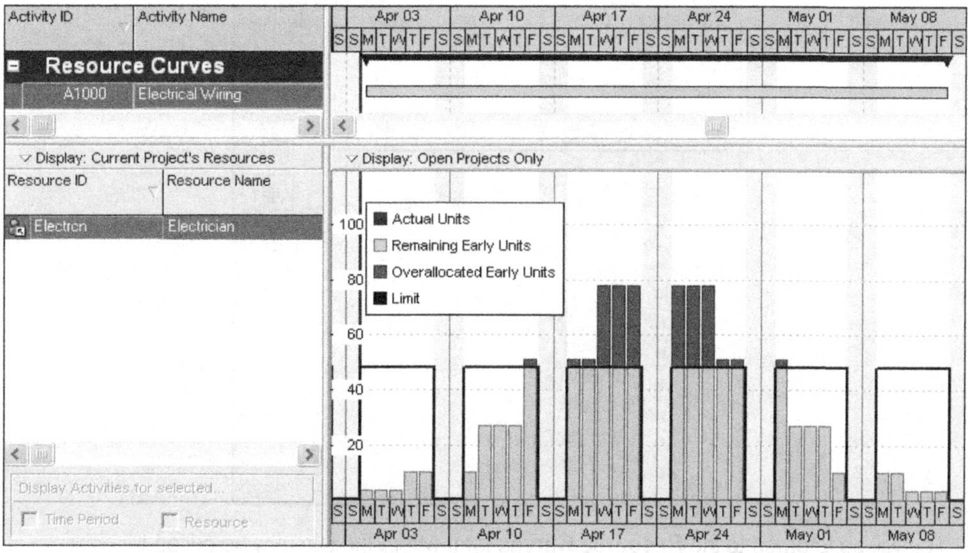

To create and use **Resource Curves**:

- Select **Enterprise**, **Resource Curves...** to open the **Resource Curves** form:

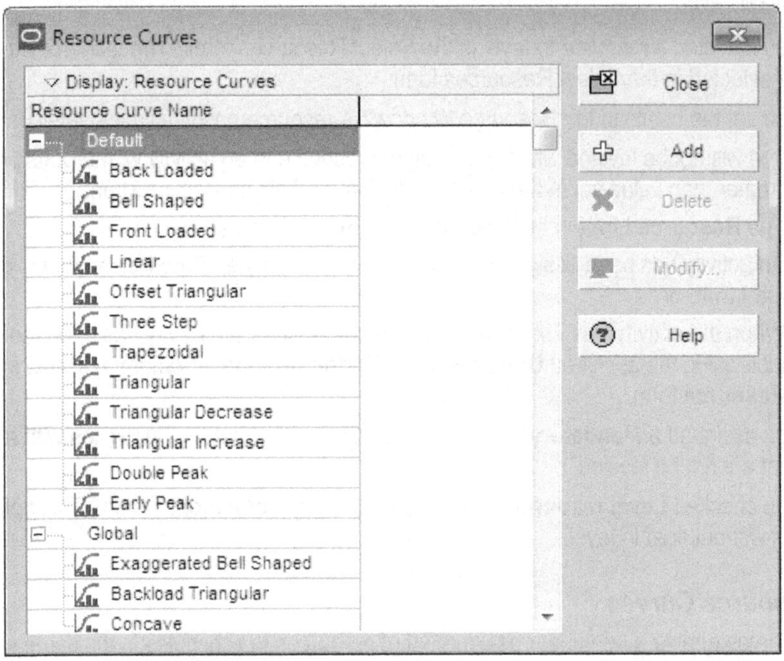

- **Default** curves may not be deleted or edited but may be copied in the **Modify Resource Curves** form.
- **Global** curves may be edited, copied or deleted.
- To create a new curve, select Add to open the **Select Resource Curve To Copy From** form and select a curve to copy.

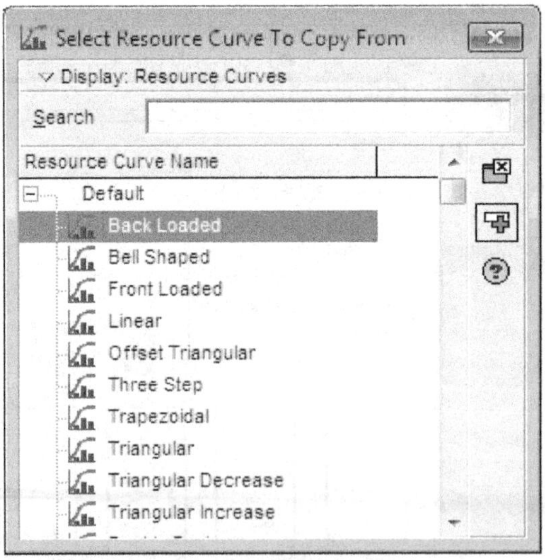

- You will be returned to the **Resource Curves** form where the title may be edited.

- Click the Modify... icon to open the **Modify Resource Curves** form:

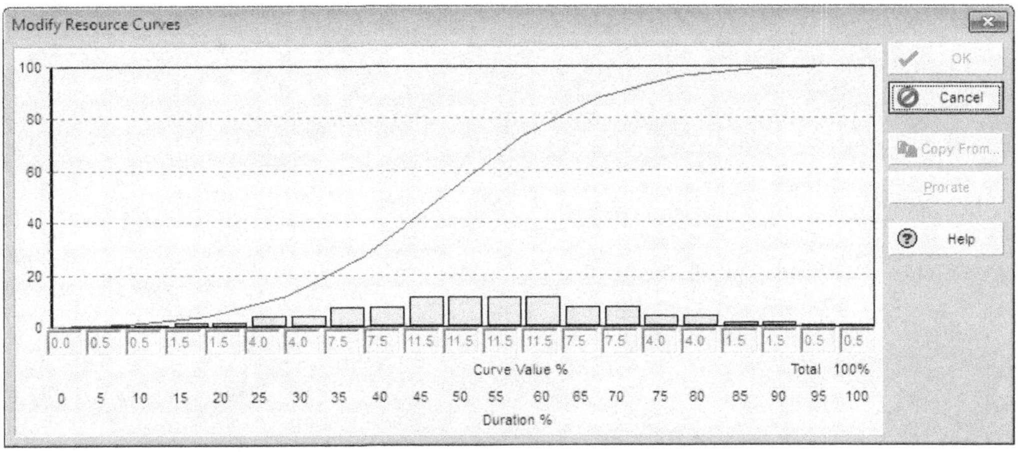

- Edit the percentages to achieve the desired shape:

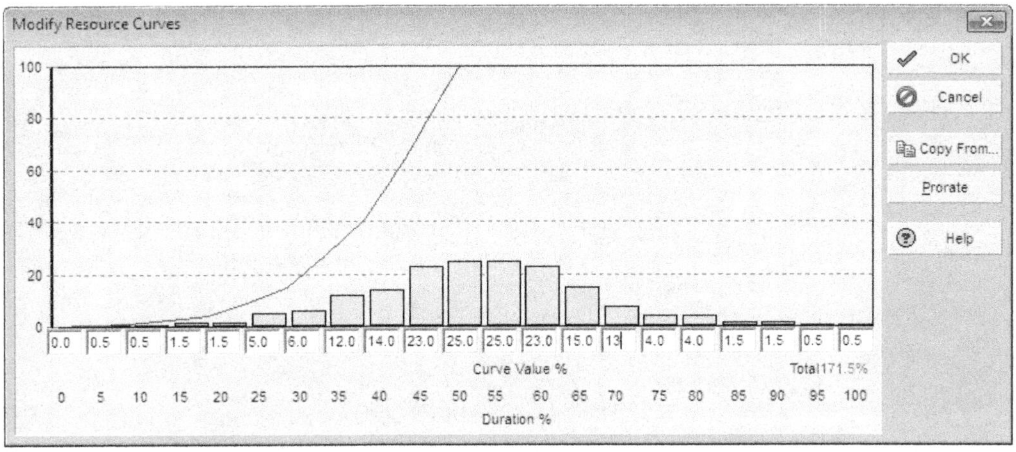

- Click on Prorate to make the percentages add to 100%:

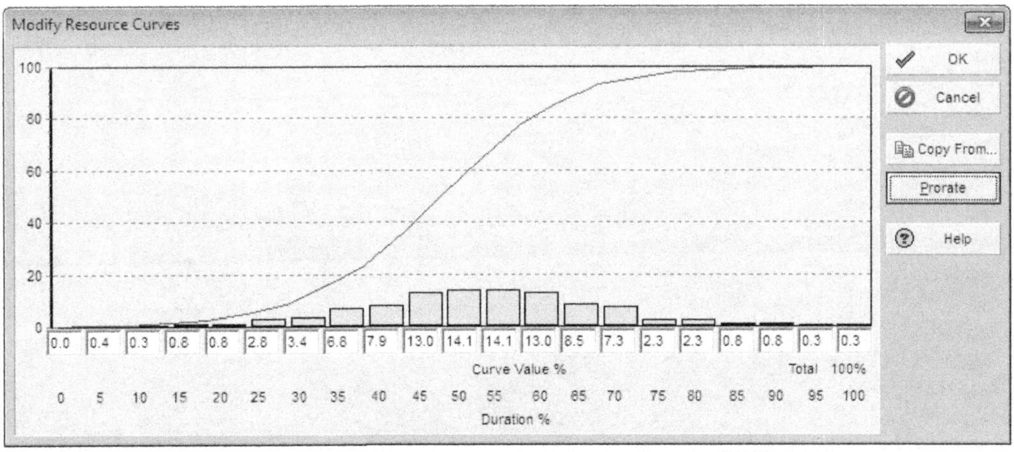

You may now assign this curve to an activity.

20.12 Workshop 17 – Resources Optimization

Assignment

1. Open the OzBuild schedule and apply the **OzBuild 10 – With Float** Layout,
2. Display the **Activity Usage Spreadsheet** by clicking on the icon. The following picture shows the number of hours per week per task, adjust the timescale to weeks:

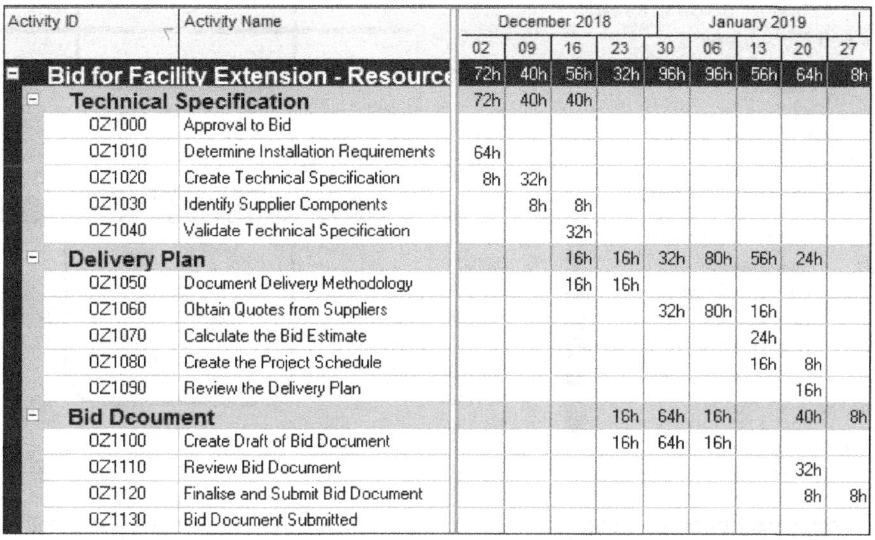

Activity ID	Activity Name	Dec 2018 02	09	16	23	30	Jan 2019 06	13	20	27
Bid for Facility Extension - Resource		72h	40h	56h	32h	96h	96h	56h	64h	8h
Technical Specification		72h	40h	40h						
OZ1000	Approval to Bid									
OZ1010	Determine Installation Requirements	64h								
OZ1020	Create Technical Specification	8h	32h							
OZ1030	Identify Supplier Components		8h	8h						
OZ1040	Validate Technical Specification			32h						
Delivery Plan				16h	16h	32h	80h	56h	24h	
OZ1050	Document Delivery Methodology			16h	16h					
OZ1060	Obtain Quotes from Suppliers					32h	80h	16h		
OZ1070	Calculate the Bid Estimate							24h		
OZ1080	Create the Project Schedule							16h	8h	
OZ1090	Review the Delivery Plan								16h	
Bid Dcoument					16h	64h	16h		40h	8h
OZ1100	Create Draft of Bid Document				16h	64h	16h			
OZ1110	Review Bid Document								32h	
OZ1120	Finalise and Submit Bid Document								8h	8h
OZ1130	Bid Document Submitted									

3. Display the **Resource Usage Sheet** by clicking on the icon.
4. Use the **Display**, **Filter** option in the bottom left window to display the **Current Project's Resources** only,

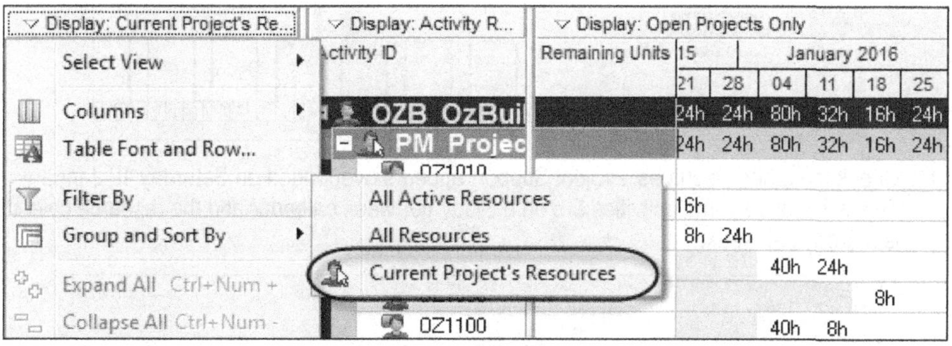

5. Select **Resource** for the option **Display Activities for selected...** (in the bottom left corner of the screen), this will display only the activities assigned to this resource.
6. Increase the timescale to a daily interval.

continued...

7. Select the **Project Manager** (in the bottom left window), which will display the Project Managers Resource Table,

8. Select **Resource** (at the bottom of the bottom left window), which will select the activities Project Manager is assigned,

9. The **Projects Manager** is overloaded (16 hours per day) on a number of days where he/she is working two activities at a time:

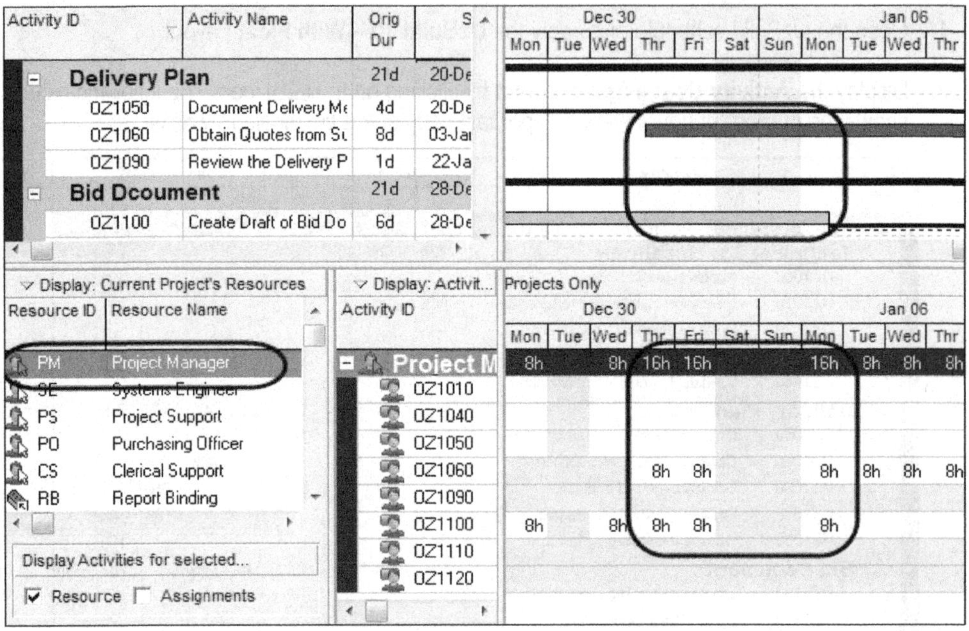

10. Display the **Resource Usage Profile** by clicking on the icon; you will also see that the Project Manager is overloaded from the end of December to start of January.

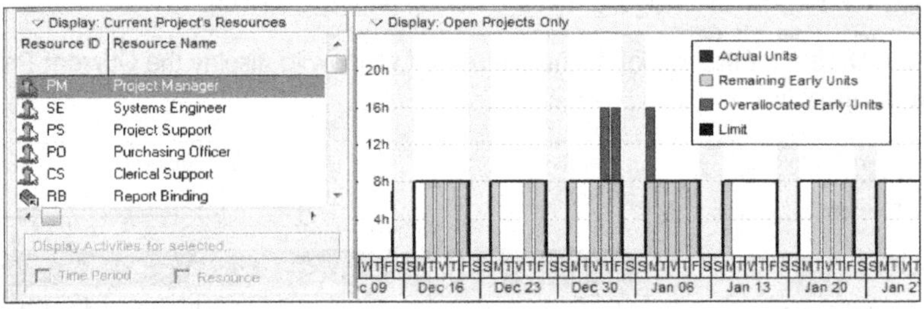

11. Check the other resources. Project Support appears overloaded on Saturday 18 January. This is because some activities are on a 6-day per week calendar and the resource calendar is a 5-day per week:

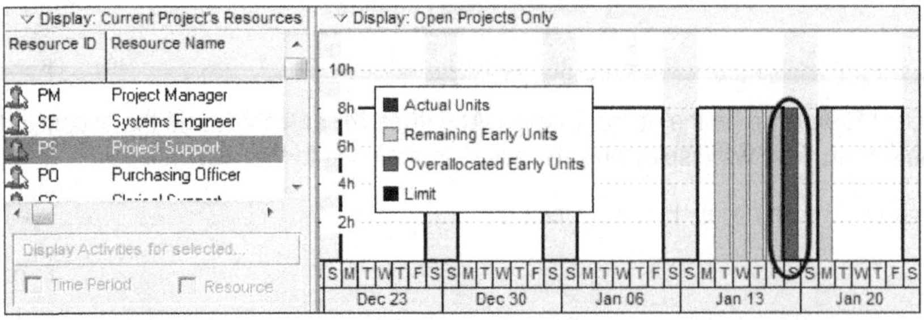

12. At this point in time resources may be optimized by a number of methods including:
    - Assigning a different resource, or
    - Reducing the assignment against the activities, or
    - Adding sequencing logic to level the schedule, or
    - Splitting activities, this has to be done by creating two activities in P6, or
    - Using the Bucket Planning function, or
    - Using the Primavera leveling function.
13. We will try using the leveling function to resolve the Project Managers overload.
14. Firstly we will create and assign a baseline and display the Baseline bar by:
    - Select **Project**, **Maintain Baselines...** and create a Baseline by saving a copy of the existing project,
    - Select **Project**, **Assign Baselines...** and select this as both your **Project Baseline** and **Primary User Baseline**, thus ensuring the baseline bar will either be blank or display the **Baseline** and not the **Planned Dates**.
    - Apply your **OzBuild Workshop 13 – Baseline** layout and the Baseline bar should be displayed,
    -
    - If there is a yellow vertical band then this is created by the **Progress Spotlight** line. Drag the **Progress Spotlight** line back to the **Data Date**.
15. Display the **Resource Usage Profile** by clicking on the  icon,
16. Select **Current Projects Resources**.
17. Increase the timescale to a daily timescale.

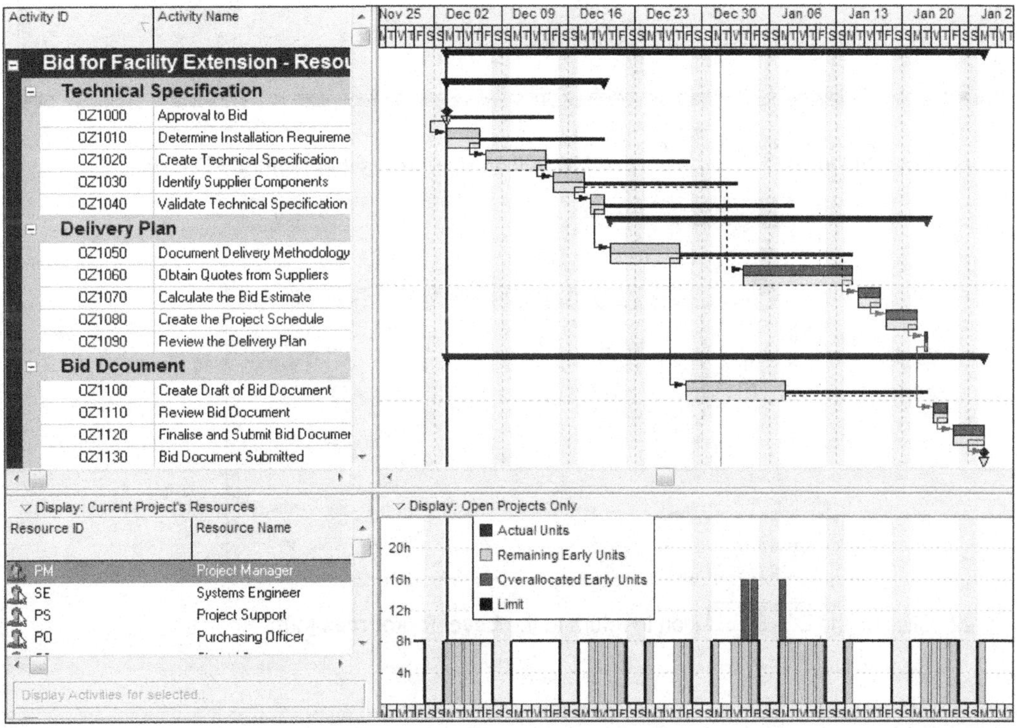

continued...

18. Save the layout as **OzBuild Workshop 17 – Leveling**.
19. Select **Tools**, **Level Resources**.
20. Set options as per the picture below:

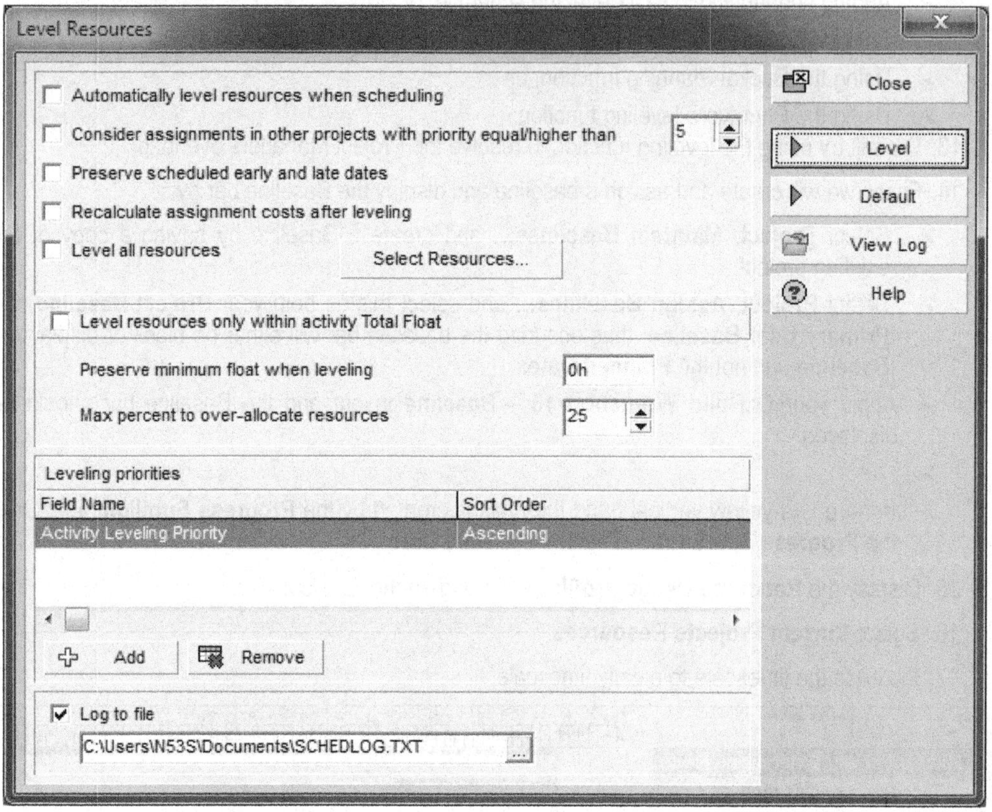

21. Click on the [Select Resources...] icon and select only **Project Manager** to level:

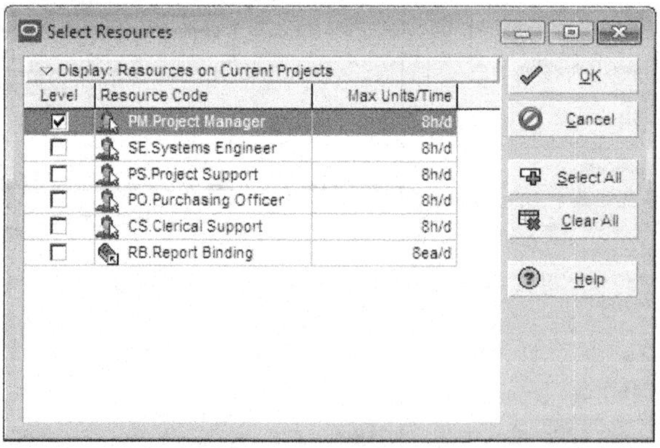

22. Click on the [OK] icon to return to the **Level Resources** form,

23. Click on the 

icon to level **Project Manager's** resource assignment:
   - The **Project Manager's** assignment will be leveled,
   - There should be Negative Float as your schedule should have a **Late Finish Constraint** on the last activity, and
   - There will be a Baseline variance.

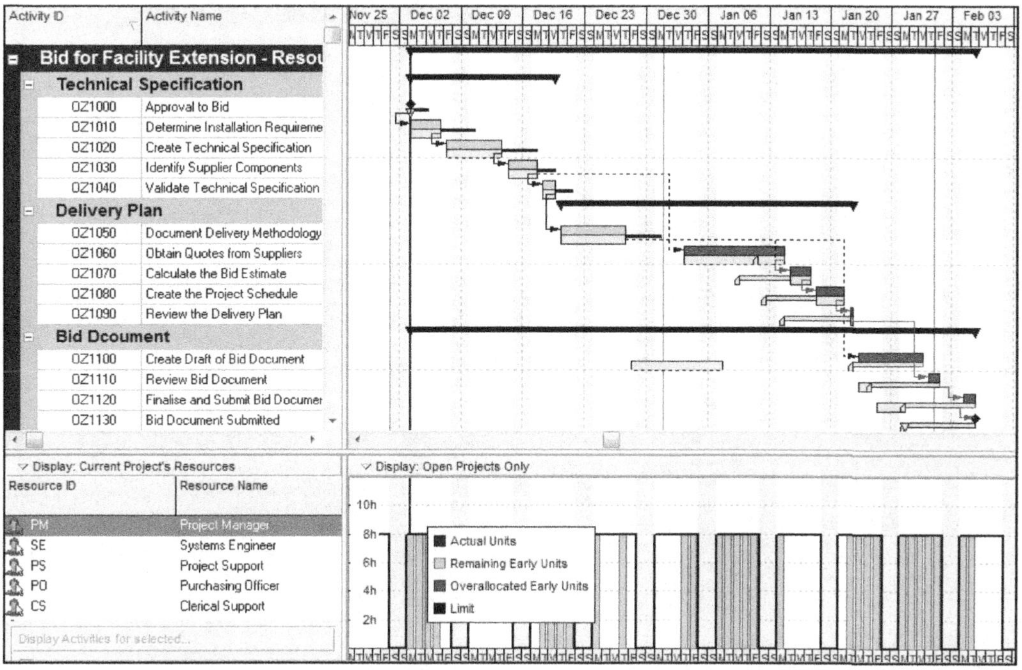

24. Reschedule and therefore un-level by pressing **F9**.
25. You may now wish to work through and recreate some of the other examples in this chapter.
26. At the end of the workshop, schedule the project so it is not leveled.

21 UPDATING A RESOURCED SCHEDULE

It is often considered best practice to update a project between 10 and 20 times in its lifecycle. Some companies update schedules to correspond with accounting periods, which are normally every month. This frequency is often too long for projects that are less than a year in duration, as too much change may happen in one month. Therefore, more frequent updating may identify problems earlier.

Updating a project with resources employs a number of preferences and options, which are very interactive and will require a significant amount of practice by a user to understand and master them.

After reading this chapter and before working on a live project, inexperienced users should gain confidence with the software by:

- Creating a new project and setting the **Defaults**, **Preferences**, and **Options** to reflect the method in which you wish to enter information and how you want Primavera to calculate the project data.
- Creating two or three activities and then assigning two or three resources to each activity.
- Updating the Activities and Resources as if you were updating a schedule and observe the results.
- Alter the preferences and defaults if you are not receiving the result you require. Re-update and note the preferences and defaults for future reference.

Some of these settings may have been set by your organization and you may not be assigned access rights to change the settings. You should still go through the updating process in a test project with dummy data similar to your real project data and be prepared to change those settings to which you do have access, as required.

Updating a project with resources takes place in two distinct steps:

- The dates, durations and relationships are updated using the methods outlined in the **Updating an Unresourced Schedule** chapter, and
- The Resource, Expenses Units (hours and quantities) and Costs, both the Actual to Date and To Complete, are then updated. These values may be automatically updated by Primavera from the % Complete or imported from accounting and timesheet systems or updated by the Primavera Timesheet system.

A decision needs to be made about what data is to be entered or imported into the schedule and what data is to be calculated by the software and the software options set appropriately.

This chapter covers the following topics:

- Understanding **Budget** Values and **Baseline Projects**
- Understanding the **Current Data Date** with respect to resources
- Information required to update a resourced schedule
- Project and Activities Windows Defaults
- Updating Resources and Expenses
- Reviewing the updated schedule

21.1 Understanding Budget Values and Baseline Projects

21.1.1 Cost and Units Budget Values

The Budget Values in Primavera are assigned to both Units and Costs for each Resource and Expense at the time the Resource or Expense is assigned to an Activity.

Budget Values reside in the current project and in all Baseline Projects.

The Budget values normally by default are linked to the At Completion values when an activity has not commenced but after the activity is in-progress by being marked as Started or having a % Complete these values become unlinked.

Should you wish to re-estimate the cost of a project and compare it to a previous value when activities have not started you could either:

1. Create a Baseline Project before re-estimating the project and compare your revised costs to the Baseline, or
2. In the **Project Window**, **Calculations** tab and uncheck the **Link Budget and At Completion for non started activities** which will unlink:
   - **Budget Costs** from **At Completion Costs**
   - **Budget Units** from **At Completion Units**
   - **Original (Planned) Durations** from **At Completion Durations**

   This option to unlink Original and At Completion Durations may not be desirable, but this option does not involve setting a baseline. This therefore adds further complications and it is recommended that it is not used except in advanced scheduling.

21.1.2 Baseline Project and Values

A Baseline project is a complete copy of a project including the relationships, resource assignments and expenses.

The creation and assignment of a Baseline Project was covered in the **Updating an Unresourced Schedule** chapter.

- **Baseline Dates** are also known as Target Dates and are normally considered to be the approved Project Early Start and Early Finish dates of an unprogressed project, which are recorded by saving a Baseline project.
- **Baseline Duration** is the original planned duration of an activity, calculated from the Early Start to the Early Finish of an Activity. This is not the P6 Planned Duration Value.
- **Baseline Costs** are also known as Budgets and represent the original project cost estimate. These are the figures against which the Actual Costs and Cost at Completion (or Estimate at Completion) may be compared.
- **Baseline Units** are also known as Budgeted Quantity and represents the original estimate of the project quantities. These are the quantities against which the consumption of resources may be compared.

The Baseline values are values against which project progress is measured. All these values may be read by and compared with the current project values and show variances from the original plan.

A Baseline would normally be created prior to updating a project for the first time.

The Primavera Variance columns use Baseline data from Baseline Projects to calculate variances.

21.2 Understanding the Current Data Date

The **Data Date** is a standard scheduling term. It is also known as the **Review Date**, **Status Date**, **Report Date, As of Date**, **Time Now**, and **Update Date**.

- The **Data Date** is the date that divides the past from the future in the schedule. It is not normally in the future but is often in the recent past due to the time it may take to collect the information required to update the schedule.
- **Actual Costs** and **Quantities/Hours** or **Actual Work** occur before the Data Date.
- **Costs** and **Quantities/Hours to Complete** or **Work to Complete** are scheduled after the Data Date.
- **Actual Duration** is calculated from the **Actual Start** to the **Current Data Date**.
- **Remaining Duration** is the duration required to complete an activity. It is calculated forward from the **Current Data Date** and the Early Finish date or an in-progress activity is calculated from the **Current Data Date** using the:
  - **Activity Calendar** when the Activity Type is Task Dependent or is Resource Dependent but no Resources have been assigned, or
  - **Resource Calendar** when the Activity Type is Resource Dependent and uses the longest Resource Duration.

Primavera has one Data Date, the **Current Data Date,** which operates in the same way as the P3 and SureTrak Data Date. Microsoft Project has four dates associated with updating a schedule. The Microsoft Project Status Date is similar in function to the Primavera **Current Data Date**.

21.3 Information Required to Update a Resourced Schedule

A project schedule is usually updated at the end of a period, such as each day, week, or month. One purpose of updating a schedule is to establish differences between the plan, which is usually saved as a Baseline, and the current schedule.

The following information is required to update a resourced schedule:

Activities completed in the update period:

- **Actual Start** date of the activity.
- **Actual Finish** date of the activity.
- **Actual Costs** and **Quantities** (Units) consumed or spent on **Labor Resources**, **Material Resources** and **Expense**. These may be calculated by the software or collected and entered into the software.

Activities commenced in the update period:

- **Actual Start** date of the activity,
- **Remaining Duration** or **Expected Finish** date,
- **Actual Costs** and/or **Actual Quantities**. Only when these are to be entered into the software,
- **Quantities to Complete** and **Costs to Complete**. Only when these are to be entered into the software,
- **% Complete**.

Activities Not Commenced:

- Changes in Logic, Constraints, or Duration, or
- Changes in estimated **Costs**, **Hours** or **Quantities** and
- Add or remove activities to represent scope changes.

The schedule may be updated after this information is collected.

Other Considerations

Primavera normally by default calculates:

- The Units to Complete and in turn the Actual Units by the relationship between the Remaining Duration and Resource Units.
- The Costs to Complete and the Actual Costs by the relationship between the Resource Unit Rate and Resource Units.

When these relationships are turned off then the Units and Costs may be entered manually.

A marked-up copy of the schedule recording the progress of the current schedule is often produced prior to updating the data with Primavera. Ideally, the mark-up should be prepared by a physical inspection of the work or by a person who intimately knows the work, although that is not always possible. It is good practice to keep this marked-up record for your own reference. Ensure that you note the date of the mark-up (i.e., the data date) and, if relevant, the time.

Often a Status Report or mark-up sheet is distributed to the people responsible for marking up the project's progress. A page break could be placed at each responsible person's band, and when the schedule is printed, each person would have a personal listing of activities that are either in-progress or due to commence. This is particularly useful for large projects. The marked-up sheets are then returned to the scheduler for data entry into the software system.

Other electronic methods, such as the Primavera Timesheet system or an e-mail based system with spreadsheet or pdf attachments, may be employed to collect the data. Irrespective of the method used, the same data needs to be collected.

It is recommended that only one person update each schedule. There is a high probability for errors when more than one person updates a schedule.

21.4 Project Window Defaults for Updating a Resourced Schedule

The **Project Window** settings affect all activities in a project that is being updated. When more than one project is open, the settings of the **Default Project** are used to calculate all open projects when they are scheduled or leveled. The Default Project is set in the **Set Default Project** form opened by selecting **Project**, **Set Default Project...**. Please read the **Multiple Project Scheduling** chapter for more details.

The **Calculations** tab in the **Projects Window** sets some important resource defaults:

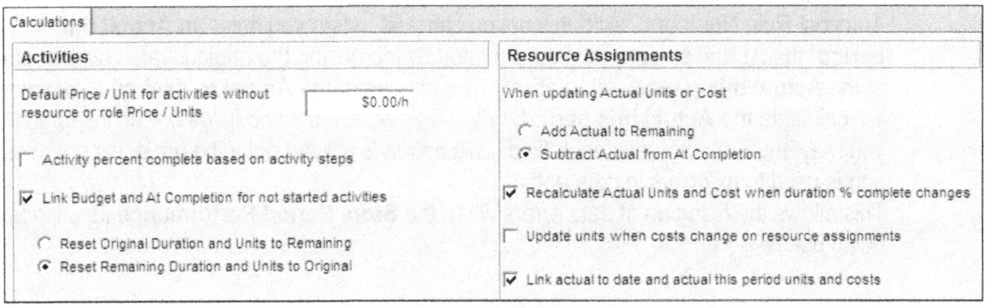

- **Activities**
  - **Default Price/Unit for activities without resource or role Price/Units**. When an activity is assigned a quantity in the **Activities**, **Status** tab but no resource is assigned, then this rate is used to calculate the cost against Labor and Nonlabor units.
  - **Activity percent complete based on activity steps**. The Primavera **Step** function enables activities to be broken down into elements called Steps. Each element earns a designated % Complete when the Step is marked as complete. Physical % Complete Type must be selected to use Steps.
  - Unchecking **Link Budget and At Completion for not started activities** enable the user to re-estimate the cost or quantities of un-started activities while preserving the **Original Budget** of an activity. This also unlinks the **Original Duration** from the **At Completion Duration** for un-started activities. This is similar to the P3 Autocost Rule Number 6 and was new to Primavera Version 4.1.
  - The next two options **Reset Original Durations and Units to Remaining** and **Reset Remaining Duration and Units to Original** determine how the Original Duration and Units are set when progress is removed from activities. This was new to Primavera Version 4.1.
- **Resource Assignments**
  - **When updating Actual Units or Costs**. There are two options, which are the same as the P3 Autocost Rule Number 3:

    Add Actual to Remaining. When Actual Costs are entered, the At Completion increases by the amount of the Actual Costs.

    Subtract Actual from At Completion. When Actual Costs are entered, the At Complete does not change and the To Complete is reduced by the value of the Actual. This is the author's preferred option, as the At Completion does not change until the At Completion is exceeded by the Actual.
  - **Recalculate Actual Units and Cost when duration % complete changes**. This option links the Duration % Complete to the Budget and To Complete, thus an increase in Duration % Complete will increase the Actual and decrease the To Complete values keeping the At Completion constant.

- **Update units when costs change on resource assignments.**

  With this option checked a change in Costs will recalculate the Units.

  With this option unchecked, a change in costs may be made independently of units after units have been changed.

  This allows the importation of Costs from an accounting system and hours from a timesheet system separately.

- **Link Actual to date and Actual This Period Units and Cost**. This is the same as the P3 Autocost Rule Number 6. With this option checked, when you enter an **Actual this period**, the **Actual to date** will be calculated by increasing the original value by the value of the **Actual this period**. Alternatively, you may enter the **Actual to date** and Primavera will calculate the **Actual this period**. When unchecked, the two fields are unlinked and you may enter any figure in each field. This option is grayed out if the project is not open and is used to fix errors in data entry.

  This allows the fixing up of data errors when the **Store Period Performance** function is being used.

21.5 Activities Window – Percent Complete Types

There are three **% Complete** types which may be assigned to each activity. The default is adopted from the setting in the **Defaults** tab in the **Projects Window**.

- **Physical**
- **Duration**
- **Units**

21.5.1 Assigning the Project Default Percent Complete Type

A project default **Percent Complete Type** is assigned in the **Defaults** tab of the **Projects Window** to each new activity created in a project. This may be changed at any time and only affects new activities created from that time onward:

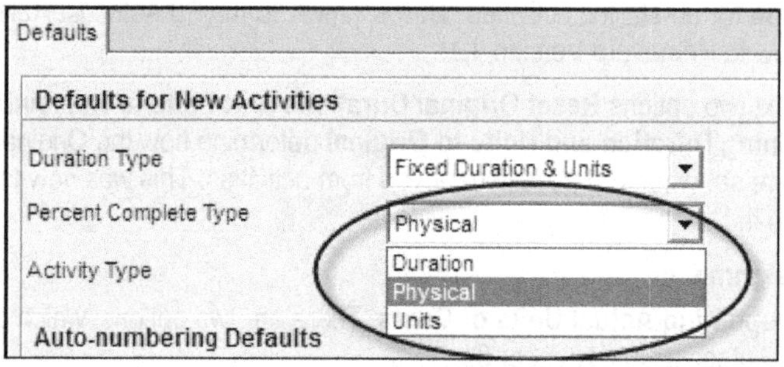

After an activity has been created, the **Percent Complete Type** may be changed in the **General** tab of the **Activities Window**:

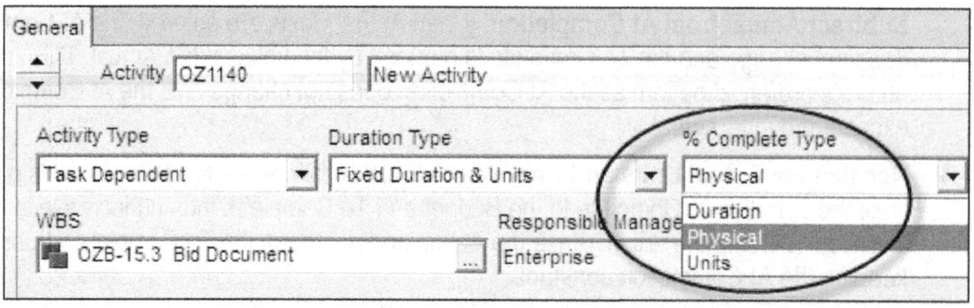

The Activity Percent Complete may be updated in the **Status** tab of the **Activities Window** where the **Percent Complete Type** is also displayed:

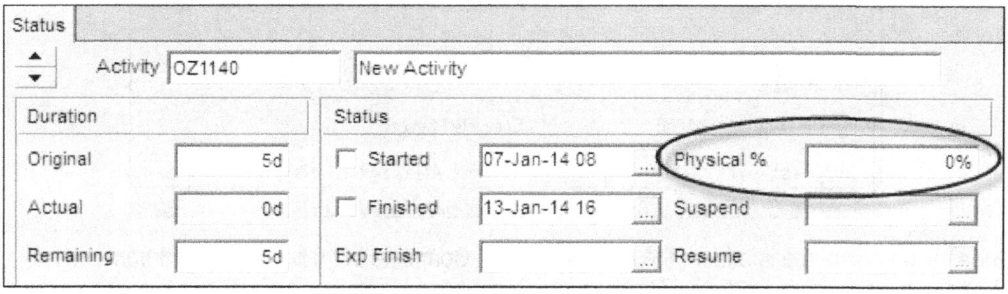

Each **Percent Complete Type** has its own data column and is always calculated.

There is also an **Activity % Complete** column which is linked to and displays the value from the **Percent Complete Type** column that has been assigned to the activity. See the following picture:

Activity ID	Activity Name	Percent Complete Type	Activity % Complete	Physical % Complete	Duration % Complete	Units % Complete
AA1000	% Complete Physical	Physical	50%	50%	0%	0%
AA1010	% Complete Duration	Duration	50%	0%	50%	0%
AA1020	% Complete Units	Units	50%	0%	0%	50%

The **Activity % Complete** is in turn linked to the Bar Percent Complete, therefore in effect the **Percent Complete Type** determines the way the percent complete is displayed on the bars.

21.5.2 Physical Percent Complete Type

An activity assigned Physical Percent Complete Type may have the % Physical Complete entered in the **Physical % Complete** or the **Activity % Complete**. This field has no impact on schedule calculations and is not linked to either the Resource Units or the Actual and Remaining Durations of the Activity.

Physical % Complete must be used when **Steps** are being used to record progress.

The **Physical Percent Complete** type is often used when the progress of an Activity is being measured outside Primavera. For example, an activity representing the installation cable that is measured by length of cable installed would have the percent complete calculated by:

- % Complete = Qty. of Cable Installed/Total Qty. of Cable to be Installed

For example, the activity may only have the installation labor assigned to it, and therefore the installation labor parameter may not be used for the measurement of the Activity % Complete. In addition, because the percent complete of the activity is based on the length of cable installed, the Activity % Complete (the progress of the work) may be compared to the resource **Units % Complete** (the amount of labor used) which is calculated from the formula:

- Units % Complete = Actual Units/At Completion Units

This example is demonstrated in the following picture:

- The Activity Physical % Complete is set at 50%.
- The Activity Unit % Complete of 20% is calculated from the At Completion Units of 12.00 hrs and At Completion Units of 60.00 hrs and not the Budget Units of 48.00 hrs.

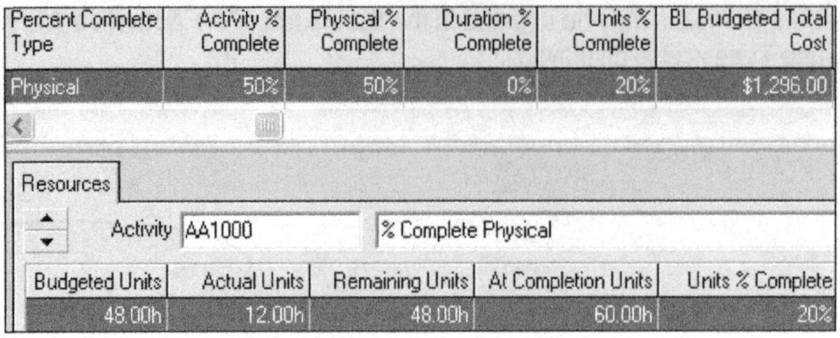

After a second resource is added, the Activity Units % Complete of 40% is calculated from the addition of the two resource Actual Units and At Completion Units:

- Activity Unit % Complete = Actual Labor Units/At Completion Labor Units
- Therefore, 40% = (12 + 36)/(60 + 60)

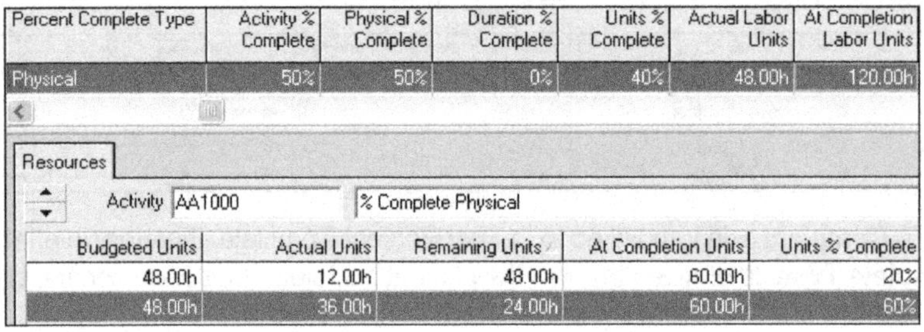

21.5.3 Duration Percent Complete Type

With Duration Percent Complete there is a link established between:

- **Duration % Complete**
- **Original Duration**
- **Remaining Duration**

A **Duration % Complete** may only be entered after an Actual Start Date has been assigned and should be in the past with respect to the Current Data Date.

A change in one parameter will change one other:

- A change in the **Duration % Complete** will change the **Remaining Duration,** and
- A change in the **Original Duration** or **Remaining Duration** will change the **Duration % Complete**:

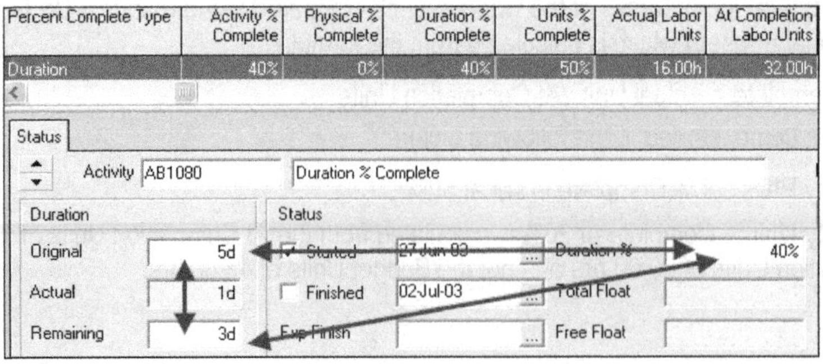

The **Actual Duration** is calculated from the duration of **Actual Start** to the **Current Data Date**.

The Activity **Units Percent Complete** is still calculated from the Resource Units.

21.5.4 Units Percent Complete Type

When **Units Percent Complete** type is selected:

- This option creates a link between the **Activity % Complete** and the activity **Units % Complete**, and
- The **Units % Complete** is calculated from the relationship between the **Actual Units** and **At Completion Units**.

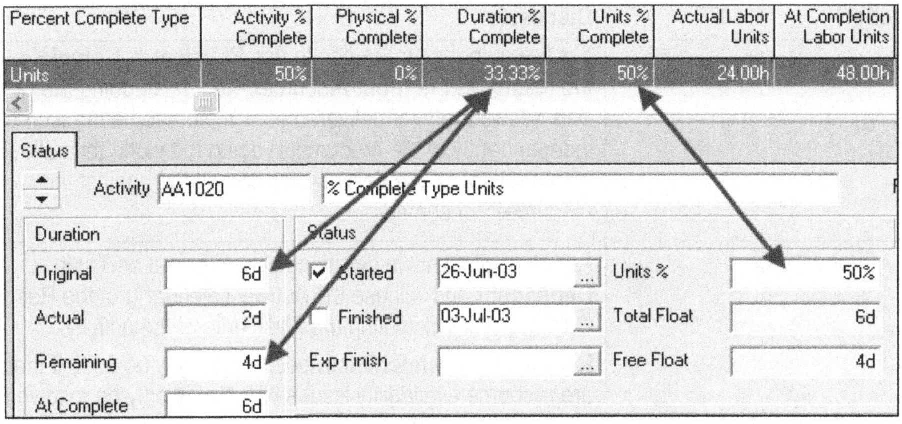

21.6 Using Steps to Calculate Activity Percent Complete

An activity percent complete may be defined by using steps. A Step is a measurable or identifiable task required to complete an activity. In summary, to use steps:

- A Step template may be created by selecting **Enterprise**, **Activity Step Template...** to open the **Activity Step Templates** form.
- Add as many steps as required and assign their weight which will be used to apportion the percent complete of an activity.
- Check the **Activity percent complete based on steps** check box in the **Projects Window**, **Calculations** tab,
- Select the **Physical** in the **% Complete Type** for each activity that is to be measured by steps in the **General** tab of **Activities Window**,
- Select the **Steps** tab in the **Activities Window**,
- Format the columns you wish to display,
- Add the number of steps you require or import from a Step Template,
- Edit the descriptions as required,
- Edit the **Step Weight** so the **Step Weight Percent** reflects the desired value of the Step,
- Check the **Completed** check box as each step is completed and this will update the percent complete.
- The **Remaining Duration** may be updated from the **Step % Complete** via the **Physical % Complete** using a **Global Change**.

Step Name	% Complete	Step Weight	Step Weight Percent	Completed
Specify Document Composition	100%	10.0	10.0	☑
Document First Draft	100%	40.0	40.0	☑
Final Draft and Internal Approval	0%	25.0	25.0	☐
Client Approval	0%	25.0	25.0	☐

21.7 Updating the Schedule

21.7.1 Preferences, Defaults and Options for Updating a Project

Most Primavera Options are good, but there are some that should be changed. The options to be considered and checked before updating a schedule:

Function	Discussion
• **% Complete Type**	It is the author's preference to use **Physical % Complete** when the resources are **Input** resources, i.e., those doing the work. This allows the % of deliverables complete to be measured independently of the resource(s) doing the work, thus allowing a comparison of the deliverables completed against the resources consumed.
• **Activity Type**	Activities with known durations should be set as **Task Dependent** and will use the Activity calendar (not the Resource Calendar) for calculating the finish date of the activity. **Resource Dependent** activities should only be used if there are resource availability issues which may only be resolved by the use of **Resource Calendars**. **Level of Effort** and **WBS** activities are useful but should be avoided by the novice user as these add an additional level of complexity that is not required.
• **Project Window Calculations tab**	The **Calculations** tab in the **Projects Window** sets some important resource defaults that should be reviewed, understood, and set so the schedule calculates the desired way. The **Link actual to date and actual this period units and Costs** option found in the **Calculations** tab of the **Project Window** should be checked if it is intended to **Store Period Performance**.
• **Duration Type**	It is the author's preference to use **Fixed Duration and Units** because the estimate to complete is not altered by changing the Activity Duration or Units/Time.
• **User Preference Calculation Tab**	This duration type also sets the **Resource Assignments** option in the **User Preferences**, **Calculation** tab to **Recalculate the Units, Duration, and Units/Time for existing assignments based on the activity Duration Type**.
• **Timesheets**	Timesheets may be used to update actuals for none, some, or all resources. Organizations using timesheets should have procedures managing their use. Timesheets are out of the scope of this publication but if they are being used the actual values should be carefully checked before being applied to ensure they are logical.

Function	Discussion
• **Resources Cost Calculation**	Resource Costs may be calculated from the Resource Unit Rates for each individual resource assignment. Each resource assignment has a field titled **Calculate cost from units**. When this is checked the resource costs are calculated from the resource units. The **Calculate costs from units** check box in the **Resource Window**, **Details** tab sets the default value for **Calculate cost from units** for new resource assignments. The two fields are not linked and the resource assignment setting may be changed at any time.
• **Resource Window Details Tab**	• **Auto Compute Actuals** This field is linked to all resources assignments. When this option is checked for a resource Primavera calculates the Remaining Units based on the Remaining Duration and the Actual Units by subtracting the Remaining Units from Budgeted Units. An unchecked resource assignment option may be overridden by applying the **Activity Auto Compute Actuals** option. • **Calculate Costs from Units** There is a field available when a resource is assigned to an activity titled **Calculate cost from units.** With this option checked the costs for a resource are calculated from the **Resource Unit/Time** when a resource is added to an activity and whenever the Resource Units are changed.
• **General Schedule Options**	One of the more important options to review is the **When scheduling progressed activities use** options, as these affect how out-of-progress sequence is handled. These options should be reviewed to ensure that when the schedule is recalculated you will understand what is happening. The author prefers **Retained Logic** as this gives a more conservative schedule and those relationships that need editing may be edited to reflect retained logic as required.
• **Steps**	Should it be decided to use Steps to update a schedule the **Projects Window Calculations** tab should have the **Activity percent complete based on activity steps** option checked and the Activity must be assigned **Physical % Complete Type** in the **General tab** of the **Activities Window** for each activity.
• **Earned value calculation**	The **Admin**, **Admin Preferences...**, **Earned Value** tab, **MUST NOT BE SET TO "Budgeted values with planned dates"** when a Baseline has progress, otherwise the Planned Dates will be displayed in the Baseline and these may contain irrelevant data when the schedule has progress.

21.7.2 Updating Dates and Percentage Complete

The schedule should be first updated as outlined in the **Updating an Unresourced Schedule** chapter. In summary, this is completed by entering:

- The **Actual Start** and **Actual Finish** dates of **Complete** activities.
- The **Actual Start**, **% Complete** and/or **Remaining Duration** of **In-Progress** activities.
- Adjust **Logic**, **Constraints** and **Durations** of **Un-started** activities.

Before updating the **% Complete**, the **% Complete Type** should be checked to ensure that the Actual and Remaining Durations, Costs, and Units calculate as required. This ideally should be done by setting the project defaults at the time the project is created and adjusting the settings as activities are added and resources assigned.

21.8 Updating Resources

There are many permutations available for calculating resource data. Due to the number of options available in Primavera, it is not feasible to document all the combinations available for resource calculation.

Resource units and costs may be updated using one of the following methods:

- Entering Progress Automatically from the timesheets, a process titled **Applying Actuals**, or
- Using the function titles **Update Progress**. This is **NOT** recommend due to the risk that your **Actual Start** and **Early Finish** may be changed by P6 when the schedule has progress, or
- Entering the data using the **Resource** tab in the **Activities Window**, or
- Entering the data using the right section of the **Status** tab in the **Activities Window**, or
- Importing from Excel. Actual dates and Remaining Durations may be imported but Suspend and Resume may not.

21.8.1 Resources Tab

The **Resources** tab may be used to update the resource **Units** (and Costs if the Units and Costs have been unlinked with the **Calculate cost from units** field). An updating layout could be created and the columns in the Resources tab formatted to your updating method; see the following picture:

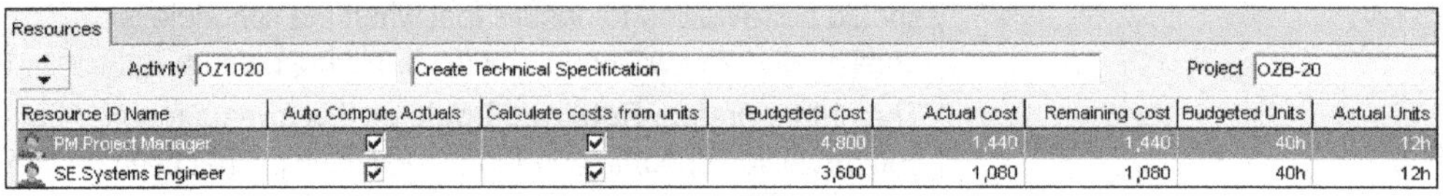

21.8.2 Status Tab

The right window may be used for updating the resources.

- When there is one resource there will be a direct link between this form and the values assigned to the resource.
- When there is more than one resource there will be a proportional change to all the resource values when a change is made in this form.

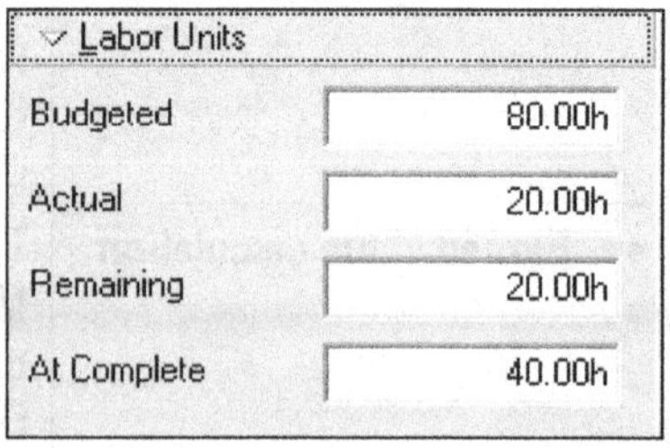

21.8.3 Applying Actuals

This functions automatically:

- Statuses activities with resources as if they went according to the Planned Dates (this may change Actual Dates and current schedule dates) and only updates activities in the period from the old to the New Data Date, or
- Applies actuals entered in the Primavera Timesheet system.

To Apply Actuals:

- Select **Tools**, **Apply Actuals...** to open the **Apply Actuals** form,
- Enter the **New Data Date** and click  icon.
- If more than one project is open a different data date may be selected for each project.
- The Activity requires the Activity **Auto Compute Actuals** field checked for this function to apply to an Activity and all the Resources assigned to an activity.

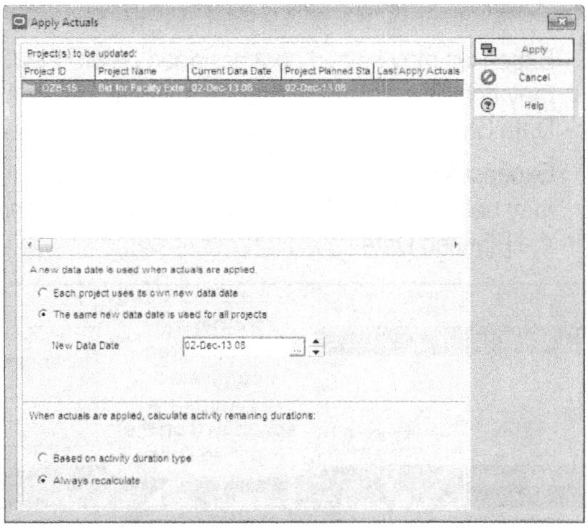

- When the Activity **Auto Compute Actuals** field is not checked only the resources that have the Resource **Auto Compute Actuals** field checked in the **Resource Window** will be updated. If one resource is checked and one not, then the checked resource will be updated and the unchecked resource work will be delayed until after the **Current Data Date**.

There are some important issues with using **Apply Actuals** that must be understood:

- This function uses the **Planned Dates**, not the current schedule dates, to progress a schedule so Actual Start Dates and the Early Finish dates may be changed by this function. This calculation process makes this function of little use to most schedulers.
- The Apply Actuals function does not work in the same way as the P3/SureTrak function "Update Progress" or the Microsoft Project function "Update Project" which both update all activities and resource assignments as if the project progressed exactly according to current schedule. They do not change any existing Actual Dates in the way the Primavera Update Progress and Apply Actual functions change dates to the Planned Dates which may hold irrelevant data.
- When the **Activity Auto Compute Actuals IS NOT** checked only activities with resources that are assigned **Auto Compute Actuals** will have their dates updated to their Planned Dates and resource assignments recalculated. Unresourced activities are scheduled after the Data Date.
- When the **Activity Auto Compute Actuals IS** checked then these activities will have their dates updated to their Planned Dates and resource assignments recalculated.
- With the introduction of **Progress Spotlight** there would initially appear to be no need to use **Apply Actuals** to automatically update a project and **Update Progress** and/or **Progress Spotlight** could be used. But as the **Update Progress** function also resets **Actual Dates** to **Planned Dates** this feature makes this function also of little use to many schedulers.
- A **Global Change** may be run first to set the **Planned** dates to the **Start** and **Finish** dates before Appling Actuals or Updating Progress, but this results in a change to the Original Duration and therefore the % Duration will calculate incorrectly and there is a risk that the user will forget to run the Global Change.

21.9 Updating Expenses

Expenses are updated in a similar way to resources in the **Activities Window**, **Expense** tab. Expenses will not be covered in detail, but here are some notes about Expenses that you may find useful:

- Expenses do not automatically update from any % Complete and have to be manually updated.

The Expense **Auto Compute Actuals** option works only with the **Apply Actuals** function, which is used when bringing in data from the Primavera Timesheets module.

- Expenses may have a cost assigned before their activity is marked started or complete; resources may not. This is useful to represent contractor's mobilization costs. These are scheduled on the Data Date.
- Expenses may have a cost to complete before their activity is NOT marked started; resources may not. This is useful to represent contractor back charges or retention. These are scheduled on the Planned Dates:

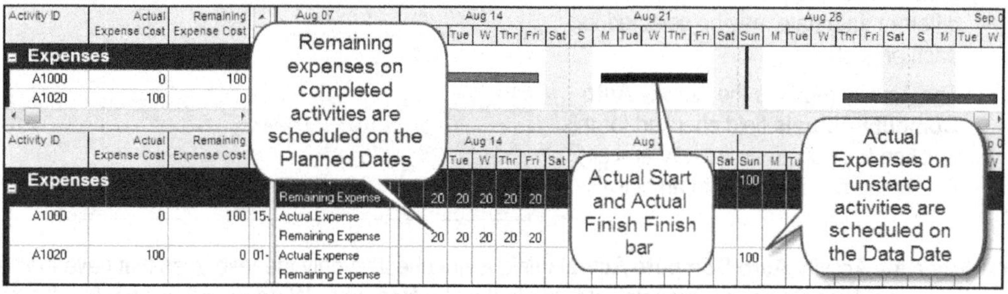

- Expenses must be assigned a quantity and unit rate. The quantity is by default a value of one.
- Expense quantities may not be displayed in the:
  - **Activities Window** columns, or
  - **Resource Usage Spreadsheet**, or
  - **Resource Usage Profile**, or
  - **Activity Usage Spreadsheet**, or
  - **Tracking Window**, or
  - **Resource Assignment Window**.
- Expense Quantities may be displayed in:
  - **Reports,** or
  - **Activity Details**, **Expenses** tab, or
  - **Expenses Window**.

Thus it is simple to get Expense Data into the system but difficult to get **Expense Quantity** data out of the system.

Remaining Expenses assigned to a complete activity are Cash Flowed on the Planned dates, which would normally result with an incorrect Cash Flow with Remaining Costs in the past.

21.10 Workshop 18 – Updating a Resourced Schedule

Background

We now need to update the activities and resources as of 14 Dec 18.

Assignment

1. If you did not complete the previous Leveling Workshop you will need to create and assign a baseline and display the Baseline bar:
   - Select **Project**, **Maintain Baselines...** and create a Baseline by saving a copy of the existing project,
   - Select **Project**, **Assign Baselines...** and select this as both your **Project Baseline** and **Primary User Baseline**, thus ensuring the baseline bar will either be blank or display the Baseline and not the **Planned Dates**.
2. Apply your **OzBuild Workshop 13 – Baseline** layout and the Baseline bar should be displayed.
3. Go to the **Project Window**, **Calculations** tab ensure your settings are as per the following picture. These are the standard settings:

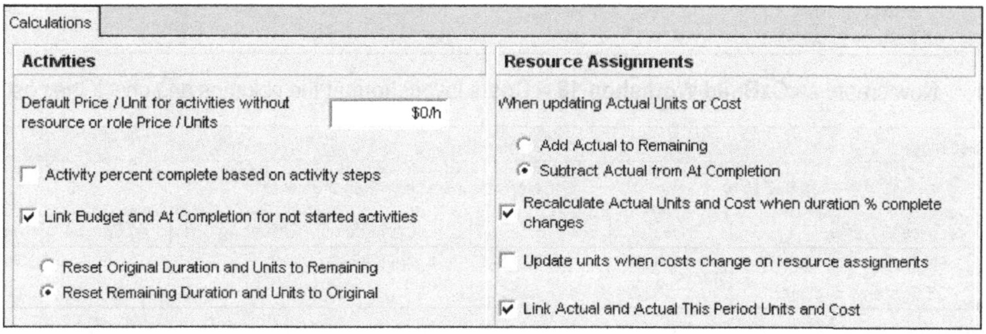

4. Assign the **Project Manager** to the **Create Technical Specification** activity as this resource was missed out at the estimating stage and will give an immediate difference between the Current Schedule and the Baseline Units and Costs.
5. Save the Layout as **OzBuild Workshop 18 – Updating Resources** and format the columns as in the following picture. Display the Primary Baseline bar.
6. Update this schedule manually by entering the following data in the **Activities**, **Status** tab or columns.

Activity ID	Activity Name	Actual Start	Actual Finish	Remaining Duration	Activity % Complete
Bid for Facility Extension - Resour(		03-Dec-18 08		33d	
Technical Specification		03-Dec-18 08		6d	
OZ1000	Approval to Bid	03-Dec-18 08		0d	100%
OZ1010	Determine Installation Requirements	03-Dec-18 08	05-Dec-18 16	0d	100%
OZ1020	Create Technical Specification	05-Dec-18 08		2d	80%

continued...

7. As you work through this workshop you should create several layouts, one for Actual Dates and Durations, one for Units, one for Costs, and one for Percentages. The Costs layout would display costs in the Activity columns and the Resources tab. The Units layout would display units in the Activity columns and the Resources tab.

8. Schedule and move the **Data Date** to 10-Dec-18 08:00.

Activity ID	Activity Name	Actual Start	Actual Finish	Rem Dur	Activity % Complete
Bid for Facility Extensior		03-Dec-18 08		33d	
Technical Specification		03-Dec-18 08		6d	
OZ1000	Approval to Bid	03-Dec-18 08		0d	100%
OZ1010	Determine Installation	03-Dec-18 08	05-Dec-18 16	0d	100%
OZ1020	Create Technical Spe	05-Dec-18 08		2d	40%

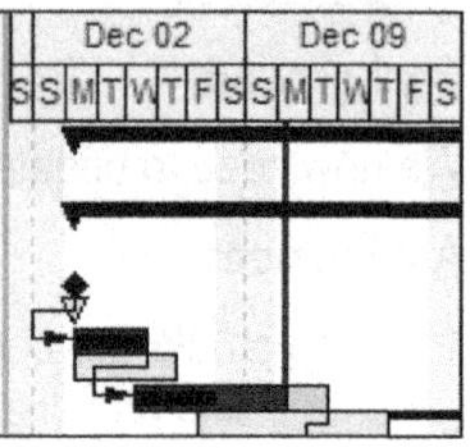

9. Create an **OzBuild Workshop 18 – Units** layout and display the columns shown in the Resources tab as shown below. See how the resources have been updated.

10. OZ1010 is complete so there are no Remaining Costs or Remaining Units and the Actuals have been set to equal the Budget, but may be manually adjusted.

Resources — Activity OZ1010 — Determine Installation Requirements

Resource ID Name	Remaining Units / Time	Budgeted Units	Actual Units	Remaining Units	At Completion Units
PM.Project Manager	8h/d	32h	32h	0h	32h
SE.Systems Engineer	8h/d	32h	32h	0h	32h

11. Now create an **OzBuild Workshop 18 – Costs** layout, format the columns and check the costs:

Resources — Activity OZ1010 — Determine Installation Requirements

Resource ID Name	Price / Unit	Budgeted Cost	Actual Cost	Remaining Cost	At Completion Cost
PM.Project Manager	$120/h	$3,840	$3,840	$0	$3,840
SE.Systems Engineer	$90/h	$2,880	$2,880	$0	$2,880

12. OZ1020 is in progress and the Remaining Units and Costs have been calculated from the Remaining Duration and the Remaining Units/Time, but may be manually adjusted.

Resources — Activity OZ1020 — Create Technical Specification

Resource ID Name	Price / Unit	Budgeted Cost	Actual Cost	Remaining Cost	At Completion Cost
PM.Project Manager	$120/h	$4,800	$2,880	$1,920	$4,800
SE.Systems Engineer	$90/h	$3,600	$2,160	$1,440	$3,600

13. Now display the **Workshop 18 – Units** layout and check the units:

Resources — Activity OZ1020 — Create Technical Specification

Resource ID Name	Remaining Units / Time	Budgeted Units	Actual Units	Remaining Units	At Completion Units
PM.Project Manager	8h/d	40h	24h	16h	40h
SE.Systems Engineer	8h/d	40h	24h	16h	40h

14. Check the expenses for the Specialist Consultant assigned to OZ1020; they do not auto update. Update the Actual Costs to $2,000.00 and the remaining to $4,500.00.

Expenses — Activity OZ1020 Create Technical Specification

Expense Item	Budgeted Cost	Actual Cost	Remaining Cost	At Completion Cost
Specialist Consultant	$5,000	$2,000	$4,500	$6,500

15. Now create an **OzBuild Workshop 18 – Percentages** layout and display the Percent Complete columns as per the following picture. Ensure Group Totals are displayed:

16. Enter 80% against the Physical % Complete of Create Technical Specification and see the Activity % Complete change to 80% as the activity % Complete Type is Physical:

Activity ID	Activity Name	Activity % Complete	Physical % Complete	Duration % Complete	Units % Complete
Bid for Facility Extension - Resourced Schedule				13.16%	20%
Technical Specification				45.45%	58.33%
OZ1000	Approval to Bid	100%	100%	100%	100%
OZ1010	Determine Installation Requirements	100%	100%	100%	100%
OZ1020	Create Technical Specification	80%	80%	60%	60%

17. Select the Create Technical Specification activity, open the Status tab, and change the Actual Labor Units from 48h to 24h in the box on the right side. Notice the Units % Complete change to 30% as fewer hours have been used, but the Remaining has increased to 56 hours:

Activity ID	Activity Name	Activity % Complete	Physical % Complete	Duration % Complete	Units % Complete
Bid for Facility Extension - Resourced Schedule				13.16%	15.71%
Technical Specification				45.45%	45.83%
OZ1000	Approval to Bid	100%	100%	100%	100%
OZ1010	Determine Installation Requirements	100%	100%	100%	100%
OZ1020	Create Technical Specification	80%	80%	60%	30%

18. Now open the **OzBuild Workshop 18 – Units** layout and both resources now show 12h Actual and 28h remaining each. The **Remaining Units/Time** is now 14 hours/day because the **Activity Type** is **Fixed Duration and Units**:

Resources — Activity OZ1020 Create Technical Specification

Resource ID Name	Remaining Units / Time	Budgeted Units	Actual Units	Remaining Units	At Completion Units
PM.Project Manager	14h/d	40h	12h	28h	40h
SE.Systems Engineer	14h/d	40h	12h	28h	40h

19. Now open the **OzBuild Workshop 18 – Costs** layout and the Actual Costs and Remaining Costs should be recalculated:

Resources — Activity OZ1020 Create Technical Specification

Resource ID Name	Price / Unit	Budgeted Cost	Actual Cost	Remaining Cost	At Completion Cost
PM.Project Manager	$120/h	$4,800	$1,440	$3,360	$4,800
SE.Systems Engineer	$90/h	$3,600	$1,080	$2,520	$3,600

continued...

20. Now open the **OzBuild Workshop 18 – Units** layout and change the **Remaining Units** of **Create Technical Specification** in the **Status** tab from 56 to 24. Note the change in the Units and Costs against the resources.

Resources

Activity OZ1020 Create Technical Specification

Resource ID Name	Remaining Units / Time	Budgeted Units	Actual Units	Remaining Units	At Completion Units
PM.Project Manager	6h/d	40h	12h	12h	24h
SE.Systems Engineer	6h/d	40h	12h	12h	24h

21. Now open the **OzBuild Workshop 18 – Costs** layout and the Actual Costs and Remaining Costs should have been recalculated:

Resources

Activity OZ1020 Create Technical Specification

Resource ID Name	Price / Unit	Budgeted Cost	Actual Cost	Remaining Cost	At Completion Cost
PM.Project Manager	$120/h	$4,800	$1,440	$1,440	$2,880
SE.Systems Engineer	$90/h	$3,600	$1,080	$1,080	$2,160

22. Create a new View titled **OzBuild Workshop 18 – Baseline Comparison** and edit the columns so you are able to see the **At Completion Variances** against activity OZ1020, the Technical Specification WBS Node, and the Project:

Activity ID	Activity Name	Activity % Complete	BL Project Labor Units	At Completion Nonlabor Units	Variance - BL Project Labor Units	BL Project Total Cost	At Completion Total Cost	Variance - BL Project Total Cost
Bid for Facility Extension - Resou			520h	0h	-8h	$55,060.00	$58,000.00	($2,940.00)
Technical Specification			152h	0h	-8h	$19,800.00	$22,740.00	($2,940.00)
OZ1000	Approval to Bid	100%	0h	0h	0h	$0.00	$0.00	$0.00
OZ1010	Determine Installation	100%	64h	0h	0h	$6,720.00	$6,720.00	$0.00
OZ1020	Create Technical Spe	80%	40h	0h	-8h	$8,600.00	$11,540.00	($2,940.00)
OZ1030	Identify Supplier Comp	0%	16h	0h	0h	$1,120.00	$1,120.00	$0.00
OZ1040	Validate Technical Sp	0%	32h	0h	0h	$3,360.00	$3,360.00	$0.00
Delivery Plan			224h	0h	0h	$21,520.00	$21,520.00	$0.00
OZ1050	Document Delivery Me	0%	32h	0h	0h	$3,840.00	$3,840.00	$0.00
OZ1060	Obtain Quotes from Su	0%	128h	0h	0h	$12,160.00	$12,160.00	$0.00
OZ1070	Calculate the Bid Estin	0%	24h	0h	0h	$1,920.00	$1,920.00	$0.00
OZ1080	Create the Project Sch	0%	24h	0h	0h	$1,920.00	$1,920.00	$0.00
OZ1090	Review the Delivery P	0%	16h	0h	0h	$1,680.00	$1,680.00	$0.00
Bid Dcoument			144h	0h	0h	$13,740.00	$13,740.00	$0.00
OZ1100	Create Draft of Bid Do	0%	96h	0h	0h	$8,160.00	$8,160.00	$0.00
OZ1110	Review Bid Documen	0%	32h	0h	0h	$3,360.00	$3,360.00	$0.00
OZ1120	Finalise and Submit Bi	0%	16h	0h	0h	$2,220.00	$2,220.00	$0.00
OZ1130	Bid Document Submitt	0%	0h	0h	0h	$0.00	$0.00	$0.00

23. At this point you may experiment with this activity. Uncheck **Auto Compute Actuals** will allow you to change the Costs and they are not recalculated from the Resource Rate.

24. You may also look at some of the other tabs such as the **Summary** tab.

22 OTHER METHODS OF ORGANIZING PROJECT DATA

The **Work Breakdown Structure – WBS** function was discussed earlier as a method of organizing projects and activities under hierarchical structures. There are alternative features available in Primavera for grouping, sorting and filtering activities, resources, and project information:

- Activity Codes
- User Defined Fields (UDF)
- WBS Categories
- Resource Codes
- Cost Accounts
- EPS Level Activity Codes

There are no Activity ID Codes in Primavera like the function found in P3 and SureTrak. In Primavera each activity must have a unique Activity ID but no logical code system may be associated with the Activity ID. Some users double-code activities so some Activity ID characters are the same as an Activity Code.

22.1 Understanding Project Breakdown Structures

A Project Breakdown Structure represents a hierarchical breakdown of a project into logical functional elements. Some organizations have highly organized and disciplined structures with "rules" for creating and coding the elements of the structure. Some clients also impose a WBS code on a contractor for reporting and/or claiming payments. The following are examples of such structures:

- WBS **Work Breakdown Structure** breaks down the project into the elements of work required to deliver a project.
- COA **Code of Accounts**, also known as **Cost Breakdown Structure**. Often this contains costs that are not included in a schedule, such as insurances and overheads. The WBS would in this situation represent part of the COA.
- OBS **Organization Breakdown Structure** shows the hierarchical management structure of a project. Primavera has a predefined field for this breakdown structure.
- CBS **Contract Breakdown Structure** shows the breakdown of contracts into elements.
- SBS **System Breakdown Structure**, a **System Engineering** method of breaking down a complex system into elements.
- PBS **Product Breakdown Structure**, a **PRINCE2** term used for the breakdown of project deliverables under two headings of Project Management and Specialist products.

22.2 Activity Codes

Activity Codes may be used to Group, Sort, and Filter activities from one or more open projects.

- **Activity Codes**, such as Phases, Trades, or Disciplines, are often defined in the **Activity Codes Definition** form.
- **Activity Code Values** are defined in the **Enterprise**, **Activity Codes...**form, such as:
  - Phases of Design, Procure, Install and Test,
  - Trades of Brickwork, Plumbing and Electrical, and
  - Disciplines of Concrete, Mechanical, Pipework.
- **Activity Codes** are assigned from the **Activities Window** using the **Codes** tab in the lower pane or displaying the appropriate Activity Code column.

P3 and SureTrak have one WBS Code Dictionary with a hierarchical structure of WBS Codes, effectively producing an unlimited number of WBS Codes with a maximum of 20 levels. Microsoft Project 2002 introduced Custom Outline Codes, which is a hierarchical coding structure that may be assigned to activities and enables the activities to be Grouped under these codes. There are 10 codes available with every project that may be renamed to suit the project requirement. The Primavera Activity Code function operates similarly to both the P3 and SureTrak WBS Code functions and the Microsoft Project Custom Outline Codes, yet enables an unlimited number of Code Dictionaries and Values for each Code Dictionary and, unlike P3 and SureTrak, may be hierarchical.

22.2.1 Understanding Activity Codes

There are three types of Activity Codes:

- **Global Activity Codes** that may be created at any time and applied to any project.
- **EPS** which are created for projects associated with one EPS Node and may only be assigned to project activities that are associated with that EPS Node. Thus you may wish to create Railway EPS Activity Codes for projects in the Railway EPS and Software Development EPS Activity Codes for projects in the Software Development EPS.
- **Project Activity Codes** that may only be created when a project is opened and applied only to the project they were created for. These may be made Global by clicking the Make Global icon in the **Activity Codes Definition – Project** form.

Activity Codes may be added, deleted, or modified in the **Activity Codes** form:

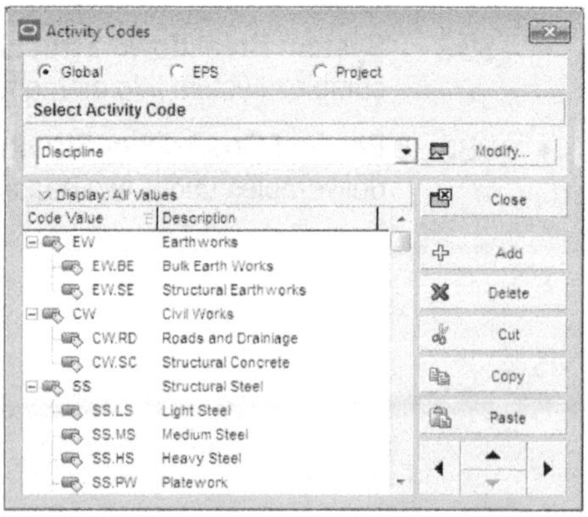

- Select **Enterprise**, **Activity Codes...** to open the **Activity Codes** form,
- Select either **Global**, **EPS** or **Project** radio button depending on whether the codes are for a specific project or available to all projects,
- Select from the drop down box under **Select Activity Code** which code structure is to be edited.
- The code structure is modified in a similar way to WBS codes.
- Each Activity Code has a Code value and a Description. The length of the Code is defined when the code is created; see the next section.

22.2.2 Activity Code Creation

This process creates a field in the database where the Activity Codes may be added.

- Open an **Activity Codes Definition** form from the **Activity Codes** form by selecting either:
  - **Global**,
  - **EPS,** or
  - **Project**,

  Each form is slightly different.
- Click the [Modify...] icon to open the **Activity Codes Definition** form.
- The Activity Codes may be created, deleted, or made into Global and reordered in these forms.
- The **Maximum Length** is the maximum number of characters a code may be assigned when it is created in the **Activity Codes form**.
- The **Secure Code** allows access to be controlled through the Users Security Profile.
- The **Activity Codes Definition – Project** form has the following icons:
  - [Make Global] that makes a Project Activity Code a Global Activity Code, and
  - [Make EPS] that makes a Project Activity Code an EPS Activity Code.

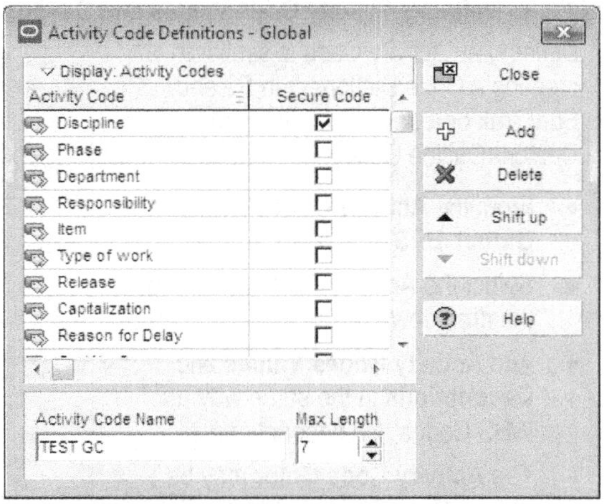

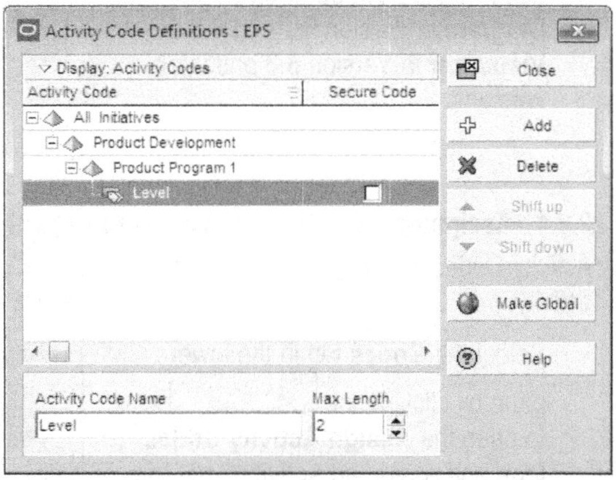

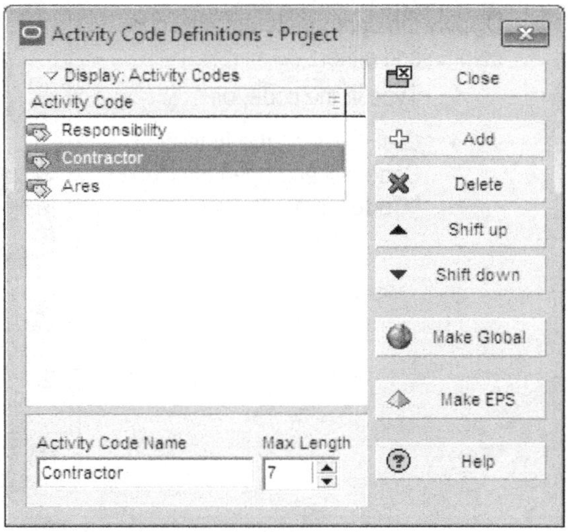

22.2.3 Defining Activity Code Values and Descriptions

Defining an Activity Code is similar to creating a Code Dictionary in P3 and SureTrak or renaming a Microsoft Project Custom Outline Code:

- From the **Activity Codes** form select **Global**, **EPS** or **Project**,
- Select the **Activity Code** to edit from the drop down box,
- Add **Activity Codes Values** and **Descriptions** in the same way as WBS Codes and descriptions.
- The **Activity Code Color** may be used with the **Timescaled Logic Diagram** in Version 8.1 and 8.2 or **Visualizer** in Version 8.3 and later versions.

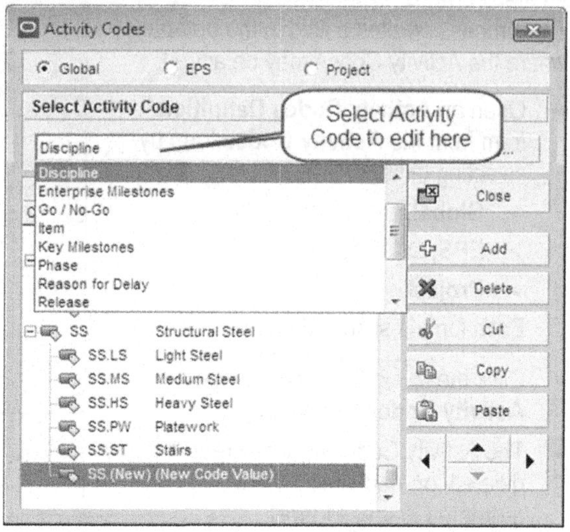

22.2.4 Assigning Activity Code Values to Activities

Activity Codes may be assigned to an activity:

- Select the **Codes** tab in the lower pane by clicking the Assign icon to open the **Assign Activity Codes** form and assign an Activity Code, or
- Display the appropriate activity code column and either:
  - Type in the code, or
  - Click twice on the Activity Code cell and open the **Select "Code"** form.

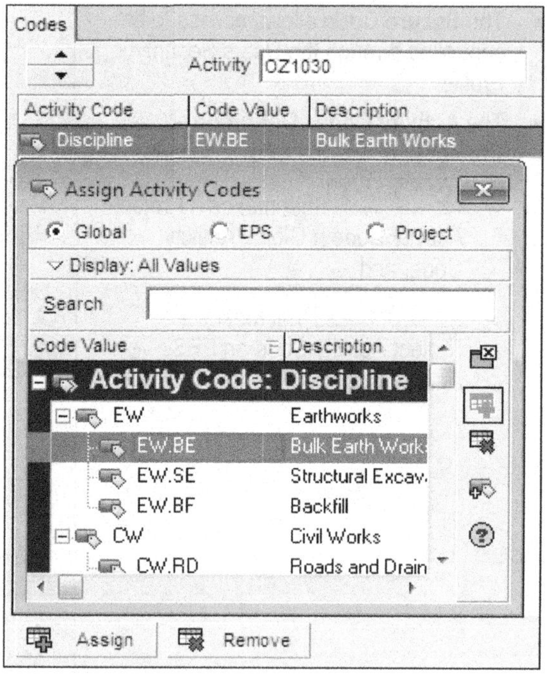

22.2.5 Add Activity Codes When Assigning Codes

Activity Codes may be added on the fly, as there is a new icon titled **New** on the **Assign Activity Codes** form that allows Activity Codes to be created as they are assigned:

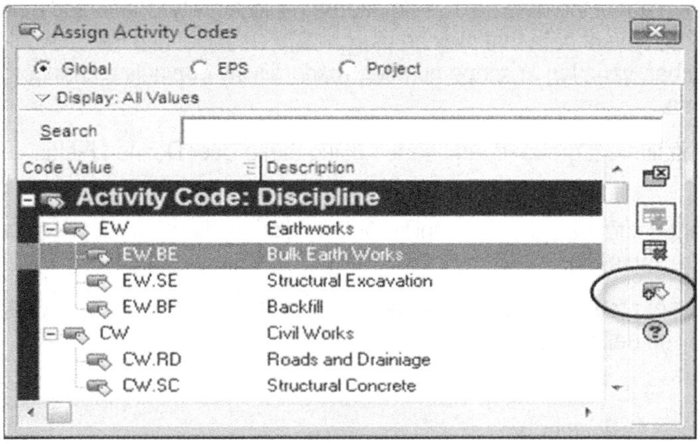

Click on the icon to open the **Add Code Value** form and enter the new Code Value and Code Value Description.

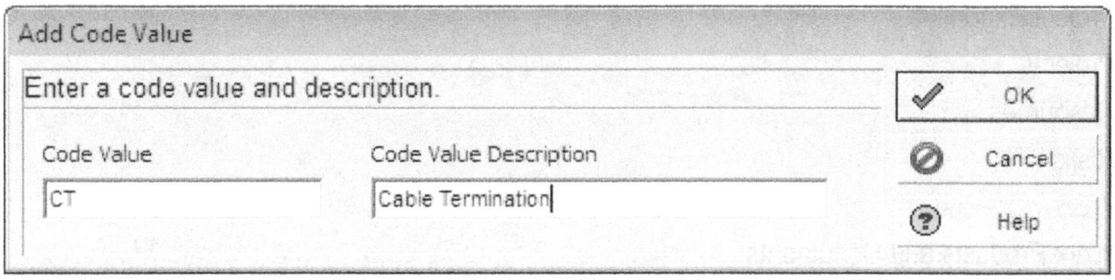

22.2.6 Grouping, Sorting and Filtering with Activity Codes

When more than one project is open an Activity Code may be used to group activities from all the open projects under one code structure.

Activity Codes are Grouped and Filtered in the same way as WBS codes.

22.2.7 Importing Activity Codes with Excel

If an Activity Code is to be imported with activities using the Primavera Excel Import function, it must exist in the database before it is imported; otherwise, the code will not be imported.

Activity Codes may be imported by loading the Software Development Kit (SDK) and using an Excel spreadsheet available from the Oracle Primavera Knowledgebase. Instructions for loading the SDK are available from the Administration Guide.

22.3 User Defined Fields

User Defined Fields are similar to Custom Data Items in P3 or Custom Fields in Microsoft Project and provide the ability to assign additional information to database records. They may be used for recording information about the data field as an alternative to Activity Codes and other predefined Primavera fields. The type of data that may be assigned to User Defined Fields would be equipment number, order number, variation or scope number; road, railway or pipeline changes; address and additional costs data.

Activity data may be filtered, grouped, and sorted using these User Defined Fields in a similar way to Activity Codes.

Data may be imported into the fields and, unlike Activity Codes, the data item does not have to exist in the database before importing.

There are a number of predefined fields that may be renamed and new ones may be created. User Defined Fields may be defined for:

- Activities
- Activity Resource Assignments
- Activity Steps
- Issues
- Project Expenses
- Projects
- Resources
- Risks
- WBS
- Work Products and Documents

The fields are assigned a **Data Type** from the following list:

- Text – maximum of 255 characters
- Start Date and Finish Date – which may be used to create bars
- Cost
- Indicator – select from 
- Integer
- Number

After some data has been entered against a field in any project, the **Data Type** may not be changed.

One advantage of **User Defined Fields** over **Notebook Topics** is that they may be also displayed in columns and be cut and pasted into other programs like Excel.

Also User Definable Field data may easily be imported from Excel and will not change your project data. You may consider importing data into User Defined Fields and then Global Change the information into the appropriate location as a second step.

- Thus Resource data needs to be imported into Resource User Defined Fields, and
- Activity data needs to be imported into Activity User Defined Fields.

You must be careful that you do not make a User Definable Field with the same name as a P6 field, otherwise you will not know which is which when creating filters.

You may consider adding a full stop at the end of each User Definable Field name so it is clear which is a User Definable field and which is a P6 field.

Select **Enterprise**, **User Defined Fields...** to open the **User Defined Fields** form:

- Select the **Subject Area** in the drop down box in the top left-hand side of the form.
- Use the Add and Delete icons to create and delete fields.
- Select the **Data Type** from the drop down list.

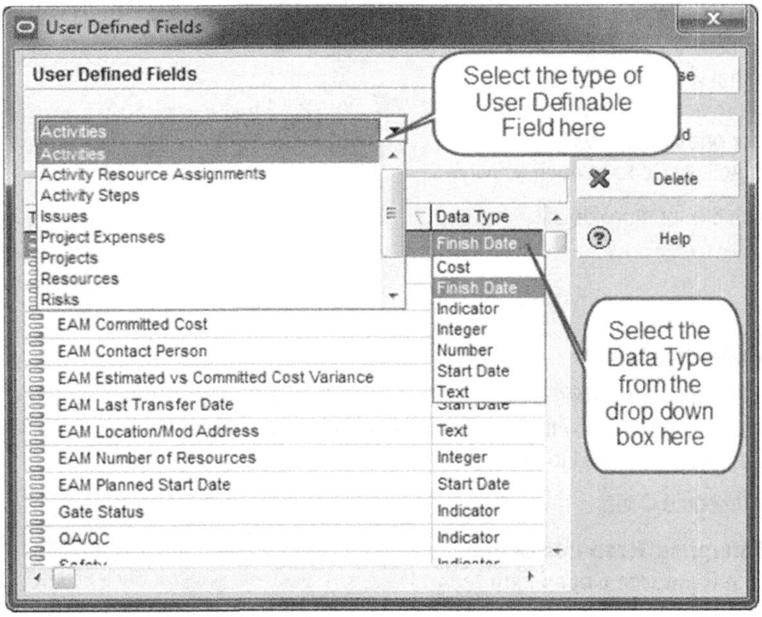

The list of User Defined Fields will re-sort as soon as a new field is added or the title edited and you may have to scroll up or down to find it in the list

To display or edit data in a User Defined Field the column should be displayed in the appropriate window. For example, if an Activity User Defined Field has been created then the Activities Window should be selected and the field will be displayed under **User Defined**.

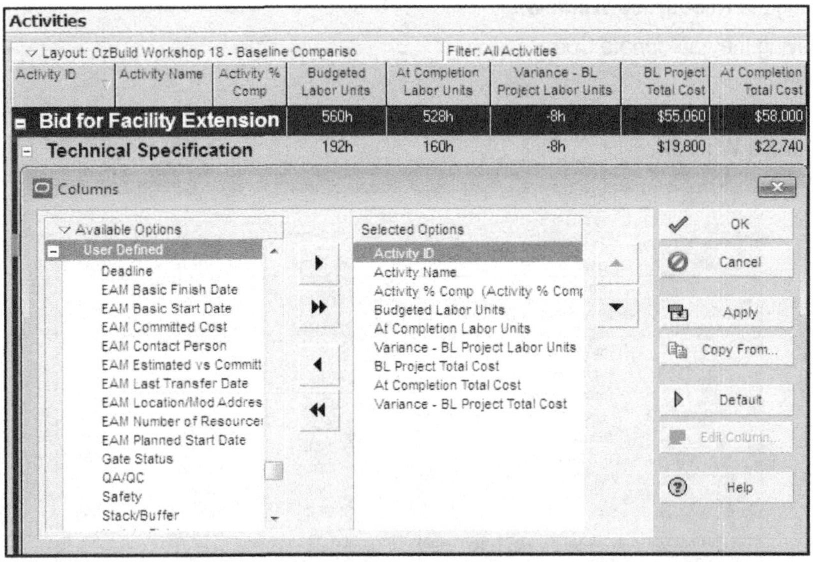

22.4 WBS Category or Project Phase

The **WBS Categories** is assigned to **WBS Nodes** in the **WBS Window** and may be used to Group and Sort WBS Nodes under a different set of headings in a similar way to Project Codes in P3.

This would enable, for example, all design WBS Nodes that were distributed throughout a project WBS to be grouped together under one heading without assigning an Activity Code to each activity.

See paragraph 6.5 for more details.

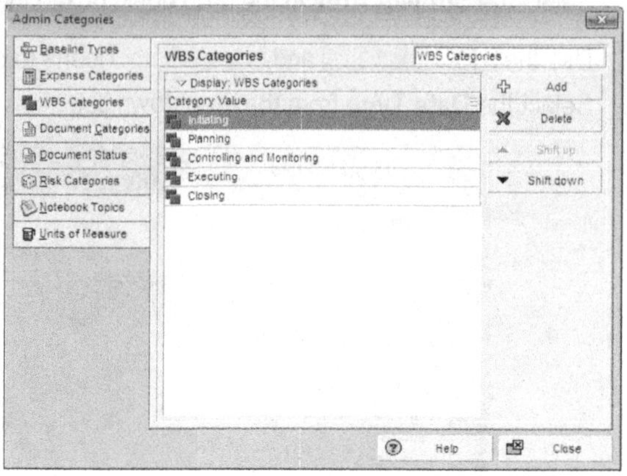

22.5 Resource Codes

Resource Codes are to resources as Activity Codes are to activities and allow resources to be Grouped, Sorted, and Filtered by these codes. Resources may have codes such as Office, Location, or Employment Status assigned to them.

To create a Resource Code:

- Select **Enterprise**, **Resource Codes...** to open the **Resource Codes** form.
- The Resource Codes are created, edited, and deleted in a similar way to Activity Codes.

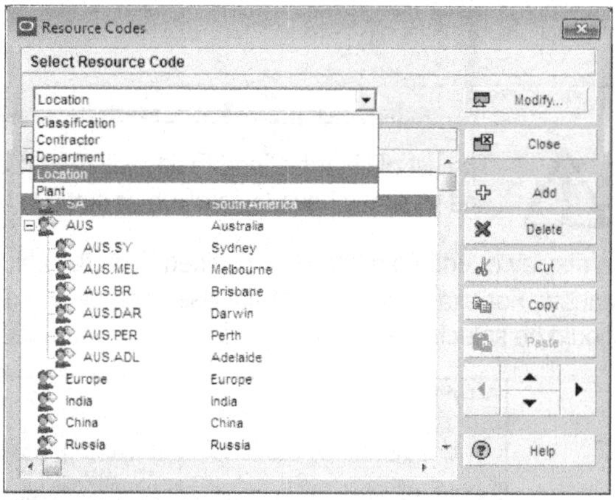

Resource Codes may be Assigned to Resources in a similar way to Activity Codes by:

- Opening the **Resources Window**,
- Displaying the appropriate Code Column,
- Opening the **Codes** tab in the **Resources Window**.

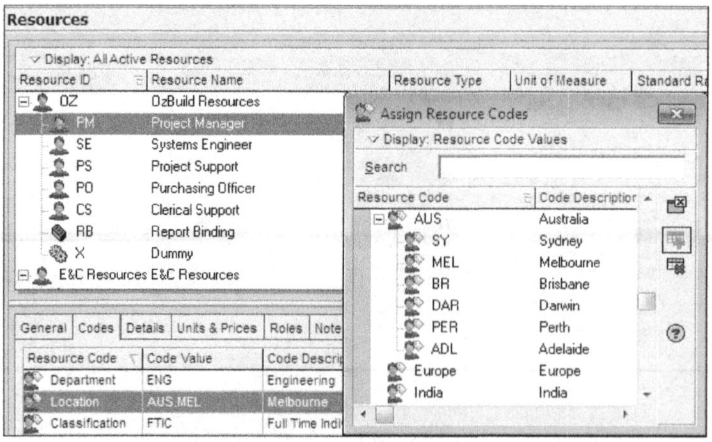

22.6 Cost Accounts

Cost Accounts are to resource assignments as Activity Codes are to activities and are intended to reflect the accounting code structure of a project. As in P3, a Cost Account in Primavera is assigned to a resource. They enable the grouping and reporting of resource data into Cost Accounts which would allow budgets to be calculated and used to update Corporate Budgets.

Cost Accounts have additional functions that Activity Codes do not have:

- A default Cost Account for each new Resource or Expense may be specified in the **Projects Window**, **Defaults** tab. This is used for each new Resource or Expense and does not affect existing assignments. The **Project Default Cost Account** may be changed at any time:

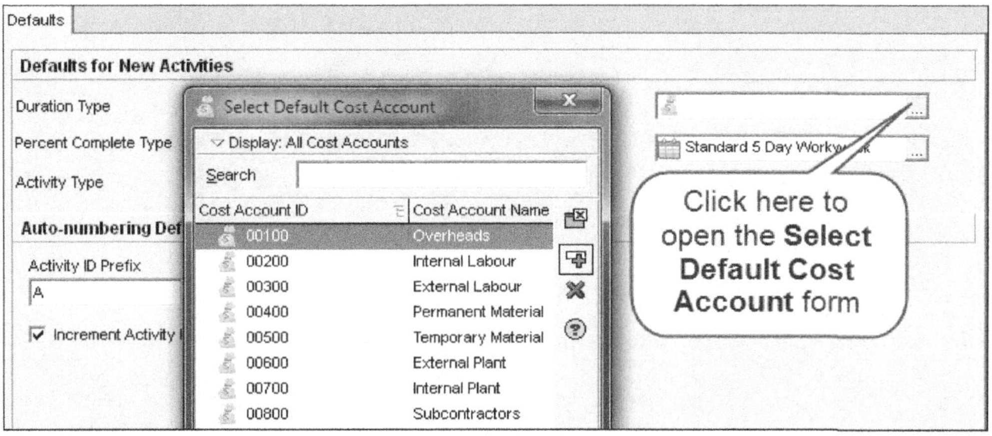

- Cost Accounts may be reassigned and merged.
- Cost Accounts may have descriptive fields when they are created.

Costs accounts are created:

- In the Professional version **Cost Accounts** form by selecting **Enterprise**, **Cost Accounts...** and opening the **Cost Accounts** form, and
- In the Optional Client by selecting **Administer**, **Enterprise Data**, **Activities**, **Cost Accounts**.

Cost Accounts are assigned to Resources or Expenses by displaying the Cost Account column in the **Activities Window** lower pane **Resources** and **Expenses** tabs.

22.7 Owner Activity Attribute

"Owner," the new activity field in Primavera Version 6.0, enables a user who is not a resource to be assigned to an activity. This now enables the person responsible for an activity to be assigned from the list of users. This function may be used in combination with a Reflection project.

22.8 Workshop 19 – Activity Codes and User Defined Fields (UDF)

Background

This workshop will look at creating an Activity Code and some UDFs. In the next workshop you will populate the UDFs using a Global Change.

We will create an activity code to represent the departments' responsibilities for the Project.

Assignment – Activity Codes

1. Select **Enterprise**, **Activity Codes...** to open the **Activity Code** form,
2. Click on the **Project** button at the top of the form.
3. Select Modify... to open the **Activity Code Definitions – Project** form.
4. Select Add to create a new code titled **Melbourne Department** and assign a **Max Length** of 3.
5. Click on Close to close the form.
6. Create the Activity Code Values and Descriptions as in the picture on the right.
7. Apply the **OzBuild Workshop 10 – Without Float** layout.
8. Add the **Melbourne Department** column per the picture and save the layout as **OzBuild Workshop 19 – Assign Codes** layout.
9. Assign the **Melbourne Departments** using all the methods available as in the following picture:

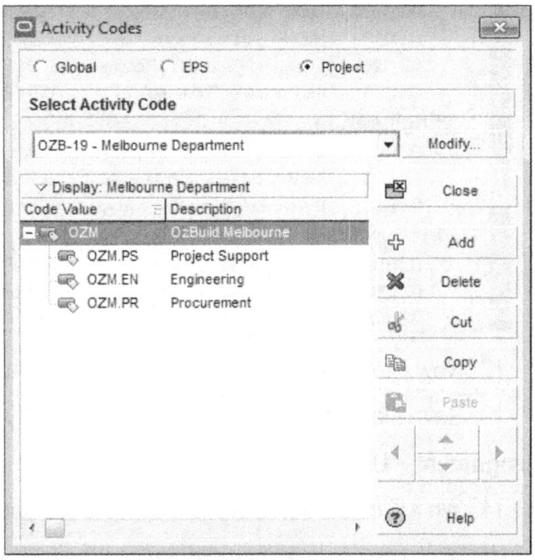

Activity ID	Activity Name	Melbourne Department
Bid for Facility Extension - Resourced Schi		
Technical Specification		
OZ1000	Approval to Bid	OBM
OZ1010	Determine Installation Requirements	OBM-EN
OZ1020	Create Technical Specification	OBM-EN
OZ1030	Identify Supplier Components	OBM-PR
OZ1040	Validate Technical Specification	OBM-PS
Delivery Plan		
OZ1050	Document Delivery Methodology	OBM-EN
OZ1060	Obtain Quotes from Suppliers	OBM-PR
OZ1070	Calculate the Bid Estimate	OBM-PR
OZ1080	Create the Project Schedule	OBM-PS
OZ1090	Review the Delivery Plan	OBM-PS
Bid Document		
OZ1100	Create Draft of Bid Document	OBM-PS
OZ1110	Review Bid Document	OBM-PS
OZ1120	Finalise and Submit Bid Document	OBM-PS
OZ1130	Bid Document Submitted	OBM

continued...

10. Now Group and Sort by the **Activity Code: Melbourne Department**, sort by Activity ID. The Milestones are now at the top of the screen.
11. Display the Project Baseline Bars and Project Baseline Milestones and move them both to the bottom of the form to ensure the relationships would be displayed on the Current Schedule bars:

Activity ID	Activity Name	Melbourne Department
OzBuild Melbourne		
OZ1000	Approval to Bid	OZM
OZ1140	New Activity	OZM
Project Support		
OZ1040	Validate Technical Specification	OZM.PS
OZ1080	Create the Project Schedule	OZM.PS
OZ1090	Review the Delivery Plan	OZM.PS
OZ1100	Create Draft of Bid Document	OZM.PS
OZ1110	Review Bid Document	OZM.PS
OZ1120	Finalise and Submit Bid Document	OZM.PS
OZ1130	Bid Document Submitted	OZM.PS
Engineering		
OZ1010	Determine Installation Requirements	OZM.EN
OZ1020	Create Technical Specification	OZM.EN
OZ1050	Document Delivery Methodology	OZM.EN
Procurement		
OZ1030	Identify Supplier Components	OZM.PR
OZ1060	Obtain Quotes from Suppliers	OZM.PR
OZ1070	Calculate the Bid Estimate	OZM.PR

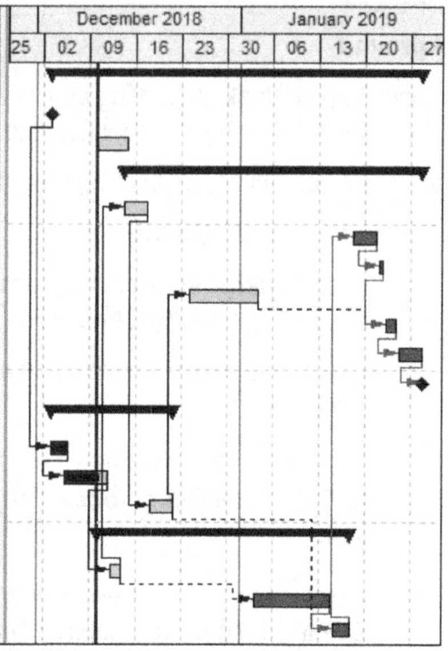

12. Now Group and Sort by the **WBS**, sort by Activity Id.
13. Save the layout as **Workshop 19 – Activity Codes**.

Assignment – UDFs

14. We will create some UDFs which we will populate using a Global Change.

NOTE: If you are in a shared database the instructor will create these UDFs.

15. Select **Enterprise**, **User Defined Fields…** to open the **Used Defined Fields** form,
16. Select **Activities** in the drop down box at the top of the form,
17. Add three UDFs titled:
    - **Last Period Start** as a **Data Type** of **Start Date**
    - **Last Period Finish** as a **Data Type** of **Finish date**
    - **Last Period AC Dur** (Last Period At Completion Duration) as a **Data Type** of **Number**.
18. Display the columns and Group by WBS as in the following picture:

Activity ID	Activity Name	At Completion Duration	Last Period AC Dur	Start	Last Period Start	Finish	Last Period Finish
Bid for Facility Extension		38d	0.00	03-Dec-18 08 A		28-Jan-19 16	
Technical Specification		11d	0.00	03-Dec-18 08 A		17-Dec-18 16	
OZ1000	Approval to Bid	0d		03-Dec-18 08 A			
OZ1010	Determine Installation	3d		03-Dec-18 08 A		05-Dec-18 16 A	
OZ1020	Create Technical Spe	5d		05-Dec-18 08 A		11-Dec-18 16	
OZ1030	Identify Supplier Comp	2d		12-Dec-18 08		13-Dec-18 16	
OZ1040	Validate Technical Sp	2d		14-Dec-18 08		17-Dec-18 16	
Delivery Plan		23d	0.00	18-Dec-18 08		22-Jan-19 16	

19. Save the Layout as **Workshop 19 – UDF**.

23 GLOBAL CHANGE

23.1 Introducing Global Change

Global Change is a facility for changing more than one data item in one step. Examples of uses of Global Change are:

- Assigning Resources to Roles
- Increasing or decreasing durations of selected activities by a factor
- Creating new activity descriptions by placing activity codes at the beginning or at the end of the original description
- Removing constraints
- Changing Calendars.

At the time of writing this publication, Global Change could not be used in the **Projects Window** as this project data may not be accessed by Global Change.

This chapter is intended as an introduction to **Global Change** and covers the following topics:

- The Basic Concepts of Global Change
- Specifying the Change Statements
- Simple Examples of Global Change
- Selecting the Activities for the Global Change
- Temporary Values and Global Change Functions
- More Advanced Examples of Global Change.

After you understand the basics you will then develop some interesting ways of using Global Change.

It is very easy to specify a Global Change that will not change data in the way you intended.

You must consider your Autocost rules when using Global Change on resources, percentages complete, and durations. For example, changing Original Durations will have no effect on the Early Finish of activities that have commenced when Remaining Duration and Percent Complete are unlinked.

Be careful when using Global Change, as the changes may not be undone. Consider copying your project or making a Reflection project if you are using Primavera before making Global Changes. Study the **Global Change Report** to review your changes before making permanent changes.

23.2 The Basic Concepts of Global Change

A Global Change may be created, saved, and used at a later date.

A Global Change may not be "Undone."

Select **Tools**, **Global Change...** to open the **Global Change** form:

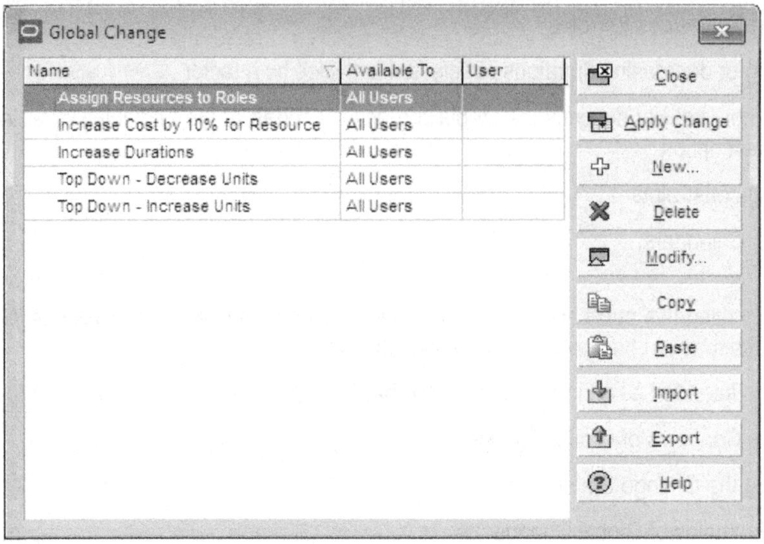

The **Global Change** form displays the list of Global Changes available in the project.

- 

enables the effects of a Global Change in the **Global Change Report** before finalizing changes to the project data by selecting 

in the **Global Change Report.**
- 

creates a new Global Change.
- 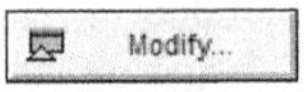

enables you to modify the highlighted Global Change.
- 

deletes the highlighted Global Change.
- 

and 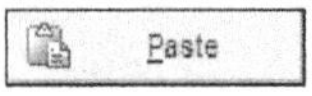

create a copy of an existing Global Change that may then be edited.
- 

and 

are used to import from or export to a Global Change from another database in the **Primavera Change File pcf** file format.

It is ***STRONGLY*** recommended that you always review the **Global Change Report** to review your changes before making permanent changes by running a Global Change.

It is ***STRONGLY*** recommended that you consider making a copy of your project before using a Global Change: copy the project in the Enterprise Window, make a Baseline or use a Reflection Project.

After creating Global Change using the New... option or Copy and Paste or by selecting Modify..., you will be presented with the second **Modify Global Change** form. This is where you select the data to be changed and where the operation to the data is specified.

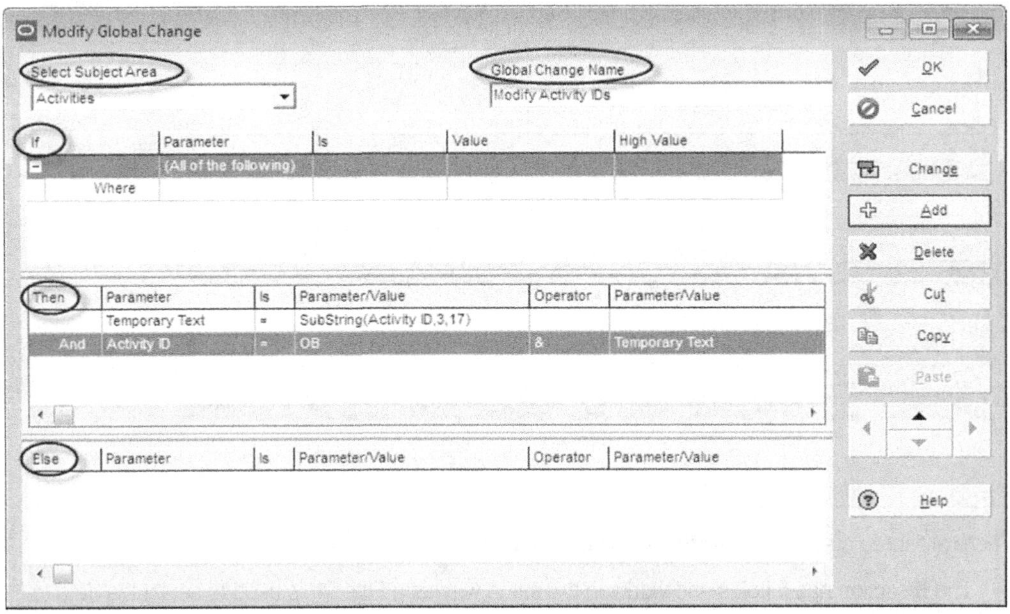

There are boxes at the top of the form:

- **Select Subject Area** enables the option of Activities, Activity Resource Assignments, or Project Expenses, and
- **Global Change Name** is the name displayed in the **Global Change** form.

The form has three lower sections. You will need to click into each area and then use Add and Delete icons to add or remove criteria or operation lines:

- **If** area is where you create a criteria for selecting the data on which to be operated. This is similar to creating a filter.
- **Then** area is where you specify the operation to be applied to the selected data.
- **Else** area is where you have an option to specify an operation to data that has not been selected.
- OK accepts edits to the Change but does not execute it.
- Cancel cancels any edits to the Change.
- Change enables you to see the results of your action in a **Global Change Report** before changing the database.
- The other commands are self-explanatory and are used to create and edit lines in the Global Change, but you will need to click into the **If** or **Then** or **Else** sections that you wish to work on.

23.3 Specifying the Change Statements

The basic Global Change in the following picture will add 5 days to the Remaining Durations of activities, where the Original Duration is greater than10 days, and increase all others by 20%.

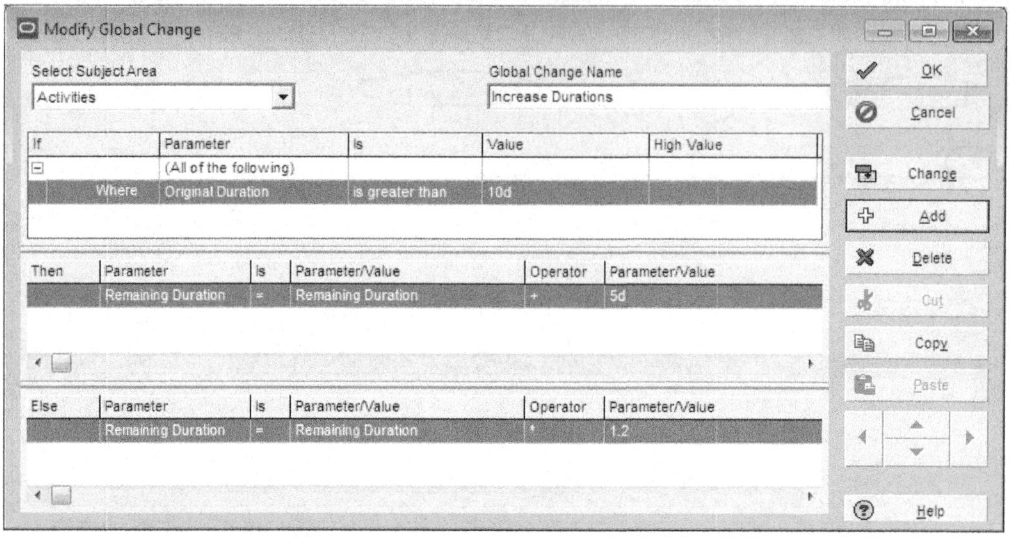

There are three areas in the **Modify Global Change** form:

- The **If** section has 5 fields and works in the same way as a Filter. It is used to select the data to be changed.
- The **Then** section has 5 fields:
  - **Parameter** – This is the data field(s) that is(are) to be modified when the **If** statement is satisfied.
  - **Is** – This is a statement.
  - **Parameter/Value** – This is the source data for the change and may be the same field as the **Parameter** when it is intended to change the parameter value.
  - **Operator** – This is how the Parameter Value is to be changed.
  - **Parameter/Value** – This is the value or other parameter that will be used to make the change.
    To enter a number, text, or value you will need to select **{Custom}** from the **Parameter/Value** drop down box:

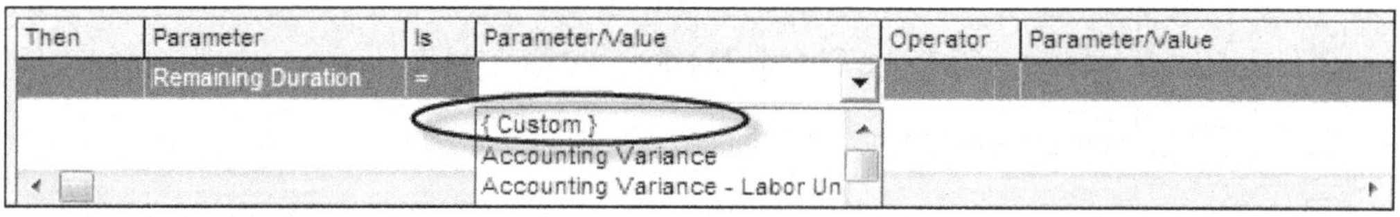

- The **Else** section operates in the same way as the **If** section when the **If** statement is NOT satisfied.

23.4 Examples of Simple Global Changes

The following examples are very simple Global Changes.

Increase Original Durations

This Global Change will increase the Original Duration field value by 20% by multiplying the original duration by 1.2.

Select Subject Area: Activities

Global Change Name: Increase Durations by 20%

If	Parameter	Is	Value	High Value
⊟	(All of the following)			
Where				

Then	Parameter	Is	Parameter/Value	Operator	Parameter/Value
	Original Duration	=	Original Duration	*	1.2

Copying Dates and Durations

This example will copy the Start, Finish, and Original Durations into custom data item fields:

Select Subject Area: Activities

Global Change Name: Copy Dates and Durations

If	Parameter	Is	Value	High Value
⊟	(All of the following)			
Where				

Then	Parameter	Is	Parameter/Value	Operator	Parameter/Value
	Last Period Start Date	=	Start		
And	Last Period Finish Date	=	Finish		
And	Last Period AC Dur	=	At Completion Duration		

Removing Actual Dates

Setting a field to be blank will remove data in some situations:

Select Subject Area: Activities

Global Change Name: Remove Actual Dates

If	Parameter	Is	Value	High Value
⊟	(All of the following)			
Where				

Then	Parameter	Is	Parameter/Value	Operator	Parameter/Value
	Actual Start	=			
And	Actual Finish	=			

23.5 Selecting the Activities for the Global Change

Often you will want to make a Global Change to data that meets a specific criteria. The **If** statement lines are used to select the data. The operations defined in the **Then** lines will be executed. Data that does not meet the **Then** criteria may be changed with operations defined in the **Else** statement lines.

The following example will double Remaining Durations if the percent complete is greater than 50%.

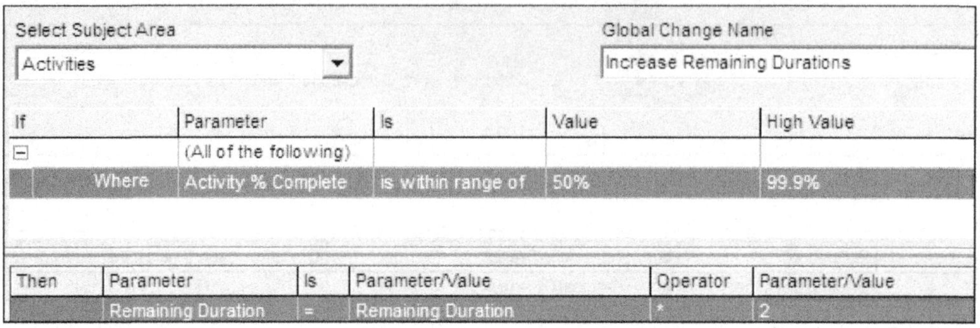

The following example will add 5 days to the Original Duration of activities over 10 days and increase by 20% those less than 10 days

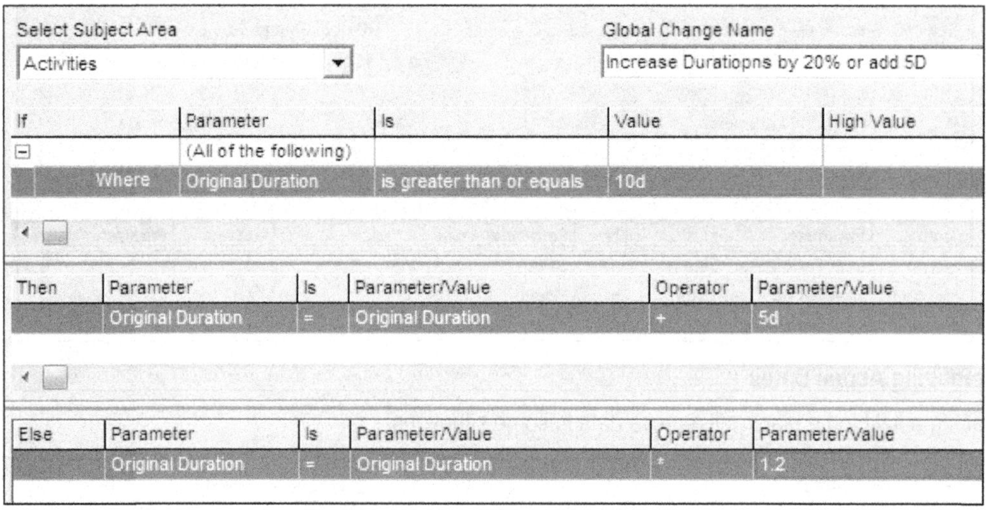

23.6 Duration Calculations with Global Change

When calculating Durations remember that P6 calculates in hours and if you are displaying durations in days then you will need to divide or multiply as appropriate the durations by 8 to obtain the correct duration.

23.7 (Any of the following) and (All of the following)

There are two options under the **Parameter** title in the **If** section, **(Any of the following)** and **(All of the following)**.These are used with the **If** statements in the same way as with filters.

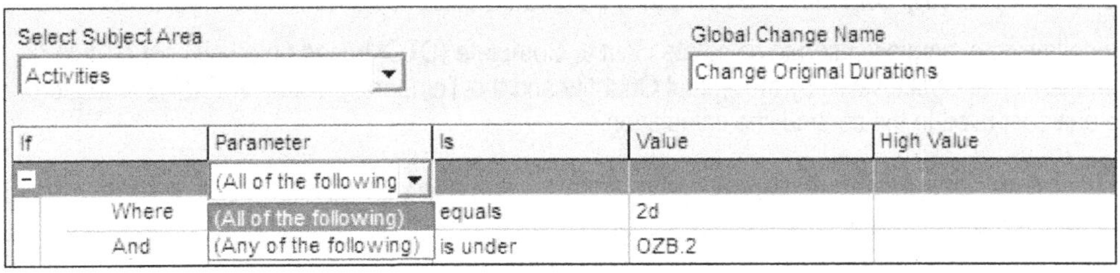

When **(Any of the following)** is selected, the Global Change will operate when any of your selection criteria is met.

In the example following, any activity with the Original Duration greater than 2 days, or an activity that is assigned to the WBS Node OZB.2, will be doubled.

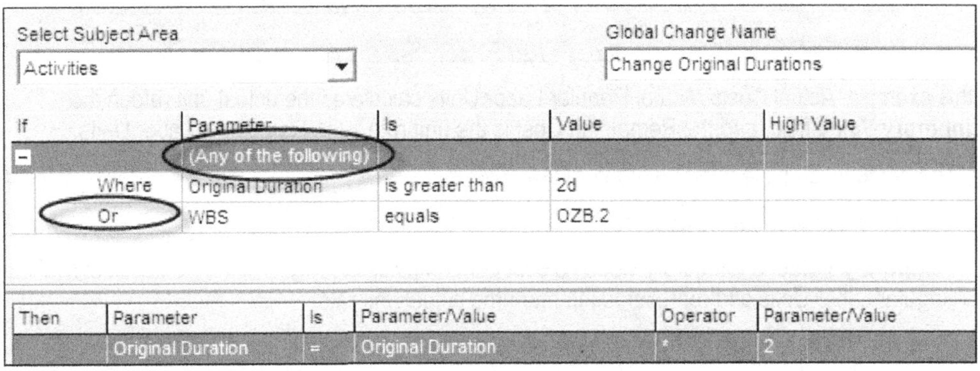

Every selection criteria has to be met when **(All of the following)** is selected for the Global Change to operate on the data.

In the example following, only activities with the Original Duration greater than 2 days and an activity that is assigned to the WBS Node OZB.2, will be doubled.

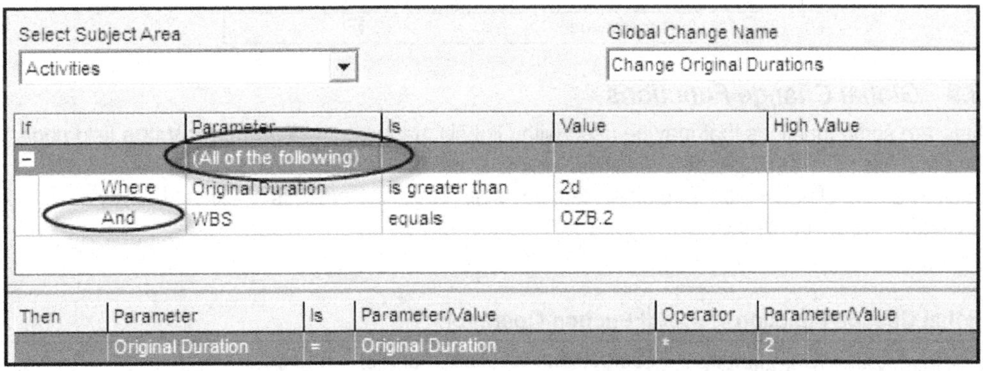

23.8 *Temporary Values*

Some calculations require more than one operation to achieve the required change. A **Temporary Value** may be stored in a **User Defined Field**. This **Temporary Value** may then be used on a subsequent line. Any **User Defined Field** may be created and used as a Temporary Value.

The following example is used to calculate Cost to Complete (CTC) based on a unit cost calculated from the Actual Cost divided by the Actual Quantity and the Temporary Value UDF is used to store the unit cost used in the second line calculation.

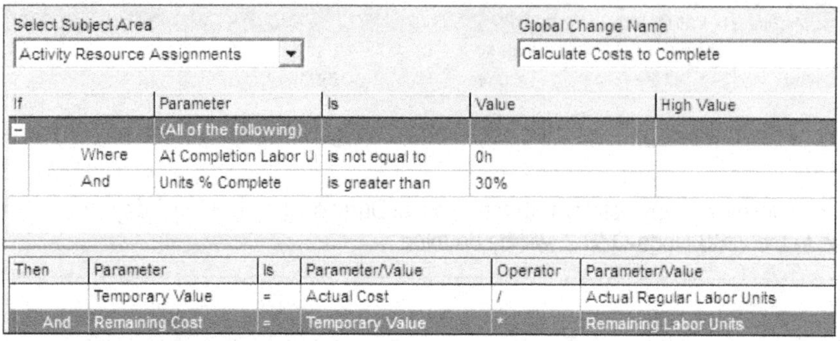

In this example, Actual Costs /Actual Regular Labor Units calculates the actual unit rate in the **Temporary Value** field, and the Remaining Cost is the unit rate x the Remaining Labor Units.

- The percent complete must be greater than 30%.
- The resource must have a quantity.
- **Temporary Value**, a temporary value, is cost per unit calculated by dividing Actual Cost by Actual Regular Labor Units and represents the resource actual unit rate.
- Remaining Cost is equal to Remaining Labor Units multiplied by the actual unit rate.

It is important that you consider the Autocost rules that you have assigned to the activities and resources, otherwise your Global Change may not work. In this situation you would not want **Cost Linked** checked.

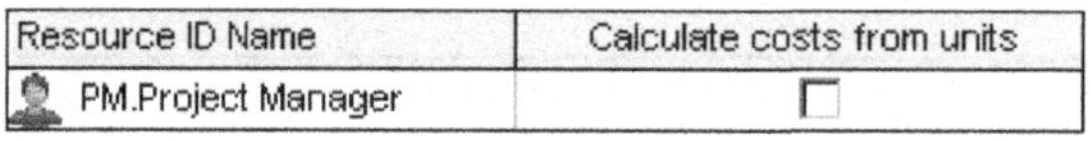

23.9 *Global Change Functions*

There are some functions that may be used with Global Change in the **Parameter/Value** field under **Then** and **Else** and that operate in a similar way to Excel or P3. These functions may be used to populate User Defined Fields from other data fields as part of the process of editing Activity Descriptions and Activity IDs.

Global Change Function	**Function Operation**
• DayOfWeek (Parameter)	Selects the weekday number of the date.
• LeftString (Parameter,*)	Selects * of characters from the start of a field.
• RightString (Parameter,*)	Selects * of characters from the end of a field.
• SubString (Parameter,a,b)	From character "a" selects "b" number of characters.

23.10 More Advanced Examples of Global Change

At the time of writing this publication, Global Change may be used to assign resources to roles, replace resources, but not assign resources to activities.

Changing Activity ID by Adding a Middle Character

The following Global Change adds a "C" after the second character of the Activity ID:

Select Subject Area: Activities

Global Change Name: Modify Activity ID's

If	Parameter	Is	Value	High Value
⊟	(All of the following)			
Where				

Then	Parameter	Is	Parameter/Value	Operator	Parameter/Value
	Temporary 1	=	LeftString(Activity ID,2)	&	C
And	Temporary 2	=	SubString(Activity ID,3,20)		
And	Activity ID	=	Temporary 1	&	Temporary 2

Adding Resources with Global Change

The following example assigns a resource, ARL Angel Lowe, to the Sales Engineer Role when the Start Date is greater than the Current Data Date.

Select Subject Area: Activity Resource Assignments

Global Change Name: Assign Resources to Roles

If	Parameter	Is	Value	High Value
⊟	(All of the following)			
Where	Role	equals	Sales Engineer	
And	Start	is greater than	CD	

Then	Parameter	Is	Parameter/Value	Operator	Parameter/Value
	Resource ID Name	=	AR.Angel Lowe		

Other Global Change Uses

Global Changes may be used for the following purposes and you may wish to inspect some of the sample Global Changes provided in the sample database:

- Add a middle character in an Activity ID or other field by using two User Defined fields and the **Concatenation** operator, which is the **"&"** character.
- Add a prefix to an Activity ID.
- Replace a resource with another. Ensure that you check the **Assignment Staffing** setting in the **User Preferences**, **Calculations** tab.
- Update the **Remaining Duration** from a **Step Percent Complete** by setting the **Duration Percent Complete** equal to the **Physical Percent Complete**.
- Edit the Activity Name using Global Change Functions.
- To set the **Planned Dates** to equal the **Start** and **Finish** dates before applying **Update Progress** so **Actual** dates are not changed by **Update Progress**.

23.11 Workshop 20 – Global Change

Background

We wish to copy the current update information to the User Defined Fields created in the previous workshop.

Assignment

1. Apply the **Workshop 19 – UDF** Layout.
2. Create a Global Change titled Set Last Period Data and add the following parameters:
   - ➢ Last Period Start to equal Start
   - ➢ Last Period Finish to equal Finish
   - ➢ Last Period AC Dur to equal At Completion Duration divided by 8 as P6 calculates in hours:

Select Subject Area: Activities

Global Change Name: Set Last Period data

If	Parameter	Is	Value	High Value
⊟	(All of the following)			
Where				

Then	Parameter	Is	Parameter/Value	Operator	Parameter/Value
	Last Period Start	=	Start		
And	Last Period Finish	=	Finish		
And	Last Period AC Dur	=	At Completion Duration	/	8.00

3. Run the Global Change and commit the changes with the icon at the bottom of the screen:

Activity ID	Activity Name	At Completion Duration	Last Period AC Dur	Start	Last Period Start	Finish	Last Period Finish
Bid for Facility Extension		38d	46.00	03-Dec-18 08 A	03-Dec-18 08	28-Jan-19 16	28-Jan-19 16
Technical Specification		11d	12.00	03-Dec-18 08 A	03-Dec-18 08	17-Dec-18 16	17-Dec-18 16
OZ1000	Approval to Bid	0d	0.00	03-Dec-18 08 A	03-Dec-18 08		03-Dec-18 08
OZ1010	Determine Installation	3d	3.00	03-Dec-18 08 A	03-Dec-18 08	05-Dec-18 16 A	05-Dec-18 16
OZ1020	Create Technical Spe	5d	5.00	05-Dec-18 08 A	05-Dec-18 08	11-Dec-18 16	11-Dec-18 16
OZ1030	Identify Supplier Comp	2d	2.00	12-Dec-18 08	12-Dec-18 08	13-Dec-18 16	13-Dec-18 16
OZ1040	Validate Technical Sp	2d	2.00	14-Dec-18 08	14-Dec-18 08	17-Dec-18 16	17-Dec-18 16
Delivery Plan		23d	19.00	18-Dec-18 08	18-Dec-18 08	22-Jan-19 16	22-Jan-19 16
Bid Dcoument		33d	15.00	10-Dec-18 08	10-Dec-18 08	28-Jan-19 16	28-Jan-19 16

You will notice that the WBS and Project Last Period Durations are not correct and are a mathematical addition of the values below. To resolve this you may either:

- Hide the **Group Total** in the **Group and Sort** form, or
- Use a further Global Change Line to put the Durations in a Text UDF that will not add up in the WBS and Project fields.

continued...

4. Create and display a gray bar showing from **Last Period Start** to **Last Period Finish** in position 3.

Display	Name	Timescale	User Start Date	User Finish Date	Filter	Preview
☑	Last Period	User Dates	Last Period Start	Last Period Finish	All Activities	

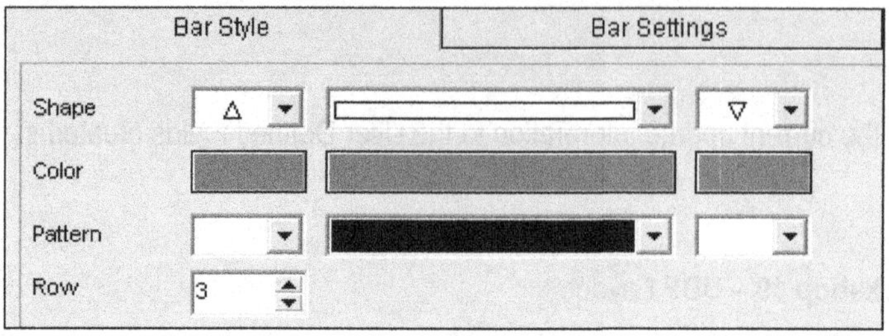

5. Adjust the row height as required and your schedule may look like the following picture with three bars.
6. Save the layout as **OzBuild Workshop 20 – Last Period Bars**.

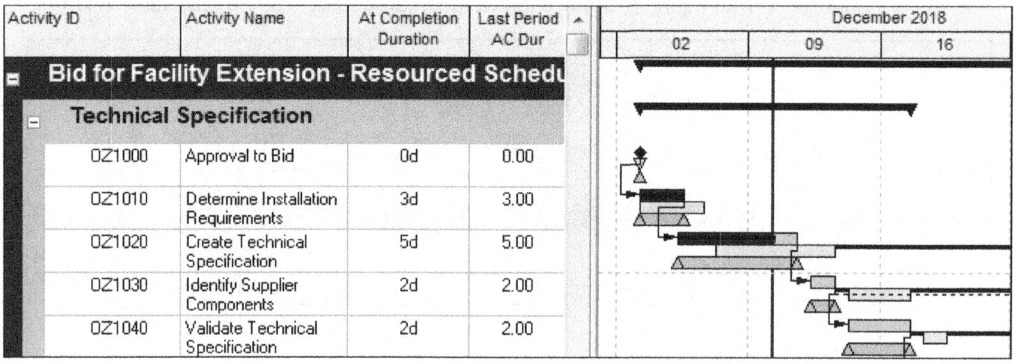

7. Create and run a Global Change to multiply the Original Durations of Activities in the Delivery Plan Phase by 2.

Select Subject Area	Global Change Name
Activities	Increase Durations by 2

If	Parameter	Is	Value	High Value
⊟	(All of the following)			
Where	WBS	equals	OZB.2	

Then	Parameter	Is	Parameter/Value	Operator	Parameter/Value
	Original Duration	=	Original Duration	*	2

8. Schedule your project:

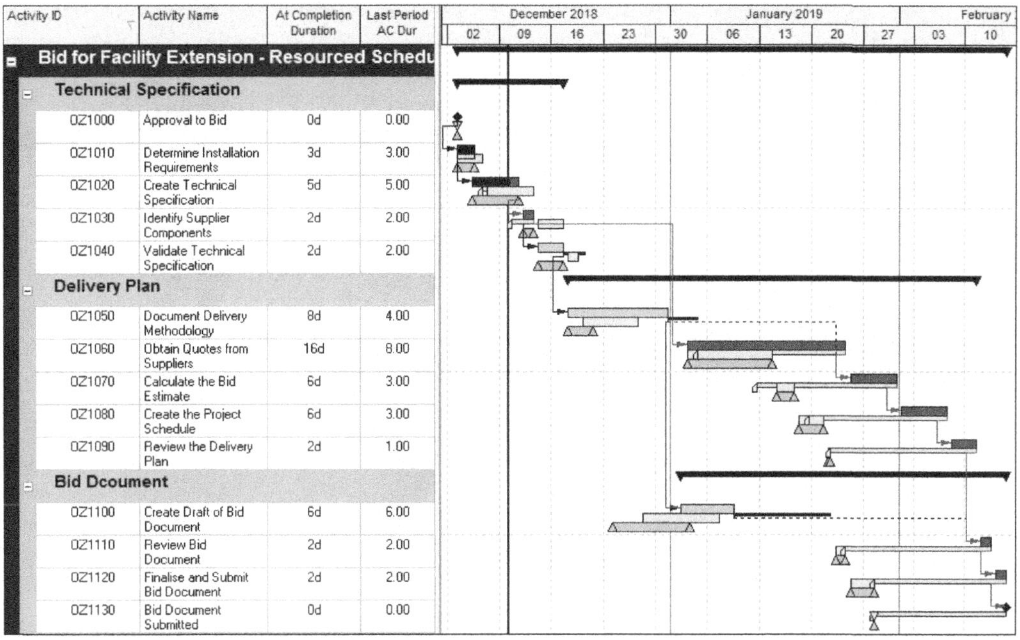

Activity ID	Activity Name	At Completion Duration	Last Period AC Dur
Bid for Facility Extension - Resourced Schedu			
Technical Specification			
OZ1000	Approval to Bid	0d	0.00
OZ1010	Determine Installation Requirements	3d	3.00
OZ1020	Create Technical Specification	5d	5.00
OZ1030	Identify Supplier Components	2d	2.00
OZ1040	Validate Technical Specification	2d	2.00
Delivery Plan			
OZ1050	Document Delivery Methodology	8d	4.00
OZ1060	Obtain Quotes from Suppliers	16d	8.00
OZ1070	Calculate the Bid Estimate	6d	3.00
OZ1080	Create the Project Schedule	6d	3.00
OZ1090	Review the Delivery Plan	2d	1.00
Bid Dcoument			
OZ1100	Create Draft of Bid Document	6d	6.00
OZ1110	Review Bid Document	2d	2.00
OZ1120	Finalise and Submit Bid Document	2d	2.00
OZ1130	Bid Document Submitted	0d	0.00

9. You will notice that Negative Float has been created and the change in durations is observed in the bars and from the differences in the Duration values.

24 MANAGING THE ENTERPRISE ENVIRONMENT

This section introduces the management of an Enterprise environment and discusses more thoroughly some subjects that have been addressed earlier.

It is important to appoint a database manager who is responsible for security and maintenance of the database for all databases that have more than one user. A database will very quickly degenerate into a mess if it is not strictly controlled. Typical problems include multiple Resources representing the same person, excessive numbers of Layouts, Filters, Calendars and other codes, the deletion of important data, and a misunderstanding or total ignorance of how the software works. The database manager should be responsible for maintaining the database, including but not limited to the following responsibilities:

- Ensuring all users are trained in the software
- Users and Security Profiles
- Enterprise Breakdown Structure
- Organizational Breakdown Structure
- Project Codes
- User Defined Fields
- Global and Resource Calendars
- Roles and Resources
- Global Layouts and Filters
- Creating Projects including setting defaults
- Importing Projects and other data.

Some areas of responsibility that are frequently used by administrators are:

Topic	Menu Commands
• Users	A **User** is created by selecting **Admin**, **Users....**
• Security Profiles	**Security Profiles** are created by selecting **Admin**, **Security Profiles....**
• Enterprise Project Structure (EPS)	Select **Enterprise**, **Enterprise Project Structure...** to open the **Enterprise Project Structure (EPS)** form.
• Portfolios	To create, edit or delete a **Portfolio** select **Enterprise**, **Project Portfolios...** to open the **Portfolio** form. The **File**, **Open** (project) form also allows the selection of a **Portfolio.**
• Organizational Breakdown Structure – OBS	Select **Enterprise**, **OBS....**to open the **Organizational Breakdown Structure** form..
• Project Codes	Select **Enterprise, Project Codes...** to open the **Project Codes** form.
• Job Services	A Job Services may be set up by selecting **Tools**, **Job Services** to open the **Job Services** form.

24.1 Multiple User Data Display Issues

The following issues **MUST** be managed by the Database Administrator and have been covered in this publication in other sections:

- Any user, with access rights, may reset the database **Default Calendar** in the **Enterprise**, **Calendar** form, but this option will reset all users to the same calendar. When an organization has projects with different hours per day and days per week then you may wish to select a Default Calendar of 5 days per week and 8 hours per day.
- By default more than one person may open a project unless the **File**, **Open**, **Read Only** option is used or access is limited through **Security Profiles**. Thus, two people may make changes and create two versions of a project. Depending on who closes what and when, the final saved version may not be what it is thought to be. The **File, Refresh Data** option enables a user to refresh project data to see what other users changed. Trials by the author indicate that only changed data is saved, thus the final version of the project may be a hybrid of both users' versions.
- When multiple projects are opened together and each project has different **Scheduling Options**, then the **Scheduling Options** of all the projects will be changed and set to the same as the **Default Project** permanently without warning. It you are intending to open multiple projects together then it is be best to ensure all projects have the same scheduling options.
- **User Baselines** are not **Project Baselines**. When a second user opens a project which has a **Primary User Baseline** set by the first user, then this baseline will not be assigned to the second user. When the same layout is used to display the project, the **<Current Project> Baseline**, which displays the **Planned Dates**, will be displayed as the **Primary User Baseline**. Again, two users opening the same project and using the same Layout may display different data.
- It is possible to have two **Currencies** with the same symbol and if a user selects a different currency then all costs displayed by the user will be converted to a different value. This option must be carefully monitored and if you do not need multiple currencies then it is suggested that you should delete them all, to avoid any possible problems. If you are using multiple currencies then make sure that all currencies have a different sign so there is no confusion.
- Users with different **Units Format** in their **User Preferences** will display different values for their units values which may be confusing when two users report two different resource values for the same project.

It is critical for contractors to appoint a database manager who understands these issues and keeps an eye on what is being sent to clients and makes sure that any display issues are either hidden or explained to the client in writing. Contractors may wish to consider making the system user and the project the same, as this resolves a number of issues. For example, User Filters and Layouts, including headers and footers, are by default the project's, reducing the possibility of sending out a report with the incorrect header or footer. User defaults become project defaults resolving display issues. Access to the project may be easily restricted to the one user and therefore only one person may have the project open at one time.

24.2 Enterprise Project Structure (EPS)

It is likely that your organization has defined an EPS (unless you have a standalone load of Primavera) that is available for new projects to be created in, but:

- You may need to add an additional EPS Node for your project, or
- If you are starting with a blank database and an EPS has not been defined, you will need to create at least one EPS Node to assign to your projects.

To add, delete, or modify the EPS Node structure:

- Select **Enterprise**, **Enterprise Project Structure...** to open the **Enterprise Project Structure (EPS)** form, or
- **Project**, **EPS**, **Add Sibling EPS** in the Web for the Optional Client users.
- The picture shows the EPS of a demonstration database supplied with Primavera.
- The  icon is used to create a new EPS Node.
- The node is then assigned an:
  - **EPS ID**,
  - **EPS Name**, and
  - **Responsible Manager**.

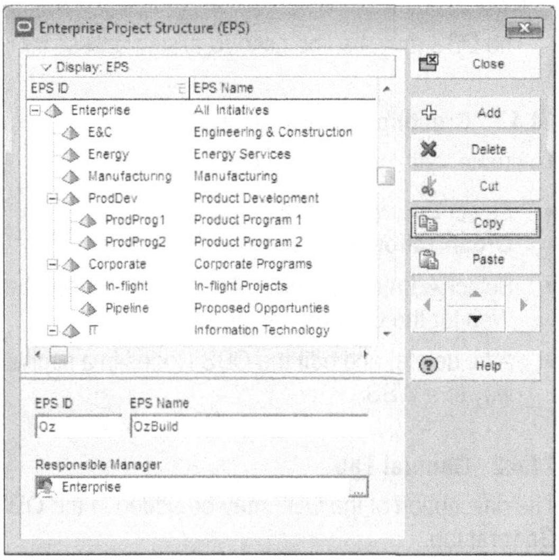

- The arrows under the 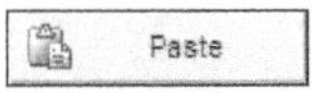 icon are used to reorganize the EPS Nodes.
- The remainder of the icons are for modifying the structure, as you require.

24.3 Project Portfolios

The **Project Portfolio** function reduces the number of Projects that are viewed in the **Projects Window**:

- To create, edit, or delete a **Portfolio** select **Enterprise**, **Project Portfolios...** to open the **Portfolio** form.
- Create a portfolio and add projects using this form. A **Portfolio** may be **Global** and all users have access or just be available to the assigned user.
- The **File**, **Open...** (project) form also allows the selection of a **Portfolio**, which reduces the number of projects that are displayed in the **Open** (project) form.
- After a **Portfolio** has been selected using **File**, **Open...**, **Select Project Portfolio...**, only those projects in the Portfolio will be displayed in the **Projects Window**.

i This feature is essential when you have a database with a large number of projects.

24.4 Organizational Breakdown Structure – OBS

The OBS is an Enterprise hierarchical structure that is intended to represent the company's OBS.

> The OBS function is the security gateway and does not have to mirror your company's OBS. Any structure that enables you to assign user access to projects is usually satisfactory and some companies just duplicate their EPS as the OBS and use a project code for the OBS.

- A user may be assigned to projects or nodes in the EPS or to a WBS Node from the OBS form.
- A user assigned an EPS is normally responsible for all projects associated with all elements of the EPS.
- The OBS may also be used to assign access by individual people to projects and WBS Nodes.

24.4.1 Creating an OBS Structure

To create, edit, or delete an OBS:

- Select **Enterprise**, **OBS...** to open the **Organizational Breakdown Structure** form, or
- Select **Administer**, **User Access**, OBS from the Web for the Optional Client users.
- Add, delete, and edit the OBS Nodes in a similar way to a WBS.

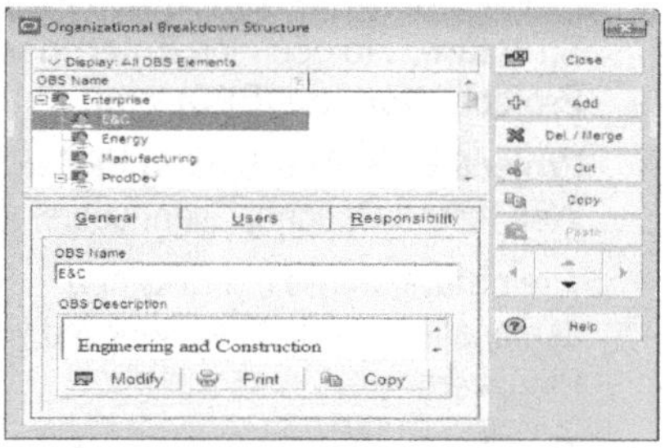

24.4.2 General Tab

The description of the OBS may be added in the **OBS General** tab.

24.4.3 Users Tab

The Login Name is assigned to the OBS in the OBS **Users** tab. Users should therefore be assigned:

- A resource for when they are assigned to work on an activity, and
- An OBS Node for the work they are responsible for or should have access to, and
- A Security Profile assigning their access rights.

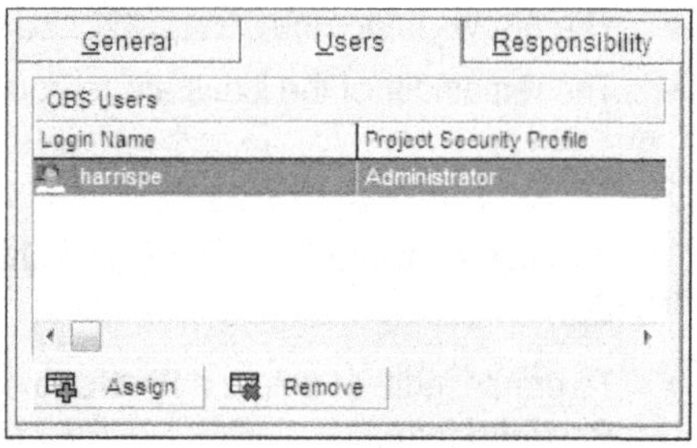

24.4.4 Responsibility Tab

The OBS **Responsibility** tab is used to indicate to which EPS or WBS Node a person has been assigned. The person is assigned to:

- A Project in the **General** tab of the **Projects Window**.
- An EPS Node in the **General** tab of the **Projects Window**.

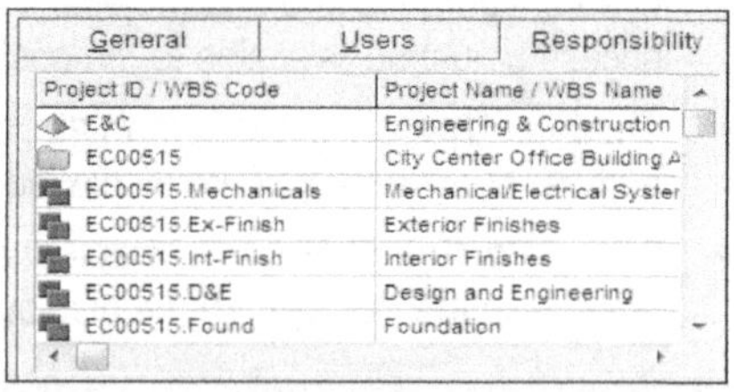

- A WBS Node in the **General** tab of the **WBS Window**. Assigning responsibility at the WBS Node controls access to the activities under the WBS Node, but does not prevent the user from seeing the entire project's data.

24.5 Users, Security Profiles and Organizational Breakdown Structure

This section is intended to introduce this topic. Please refer to the Primavera Administration Manual for full details.

The full picture and processes for creating users and assigning access are:

- The **EPS** is created, allowing projects to be created under each Node. This often mirrors the company's network drive hierarchy.
- The **OBS** is created and acts as a security gateway for users to access projects. This may not need to represent your company's **OBS** and often this is set up to mirror the **EPS**.
- A **User** is created by selecting **Admin**, **Users...** and each User is assigned:
  - A **Global Security Profile** which allows access to Global data such as EPS, OBS, etc.
  - A **Project Security Profile** for each assigned OBS Node which allows access to one or more EPS Nodes, Projects, or WBS Nodes within a project.
  - Access to all or one **Resource Nodes** is assigned to a user from the **Resource Window**. The user can only see and assign resources from this node, but may see any resources and their associated costs once they are assigned to activities.
  - Access to a software license, allowing the user to login and start the software.
  - The user may be assigned to a resource in the **Resource Window**, thus allowing timesheets to be used.
  - One or more **Resources** may be assigned to one or more **Roles**.

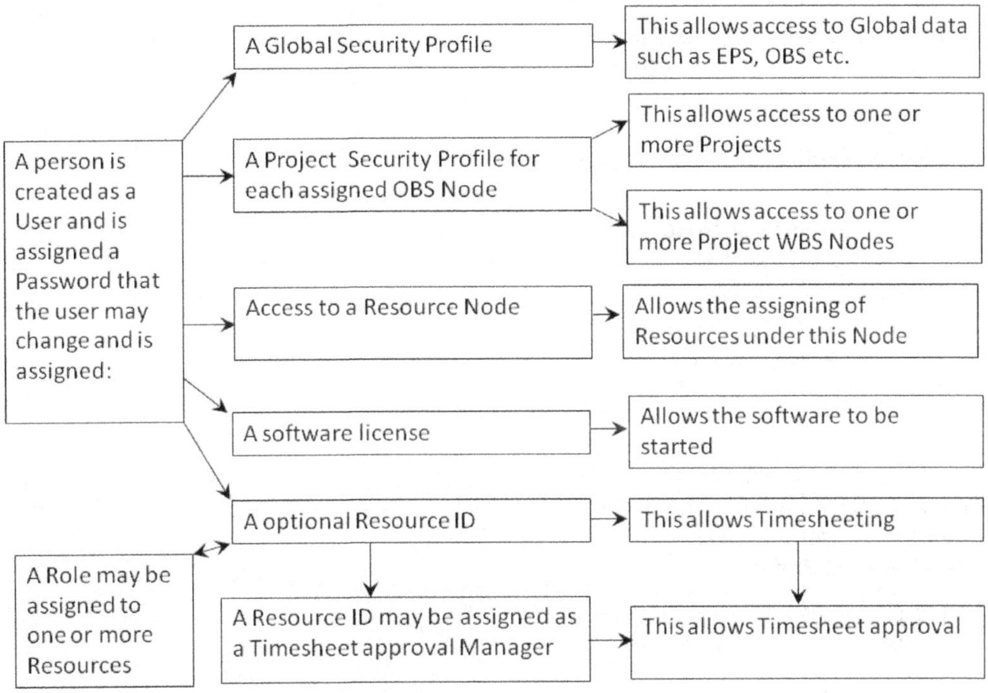

Security Profiles are created by selecting:

- **Admin**, **Security Profiles....**, or
- **Administer**, **User Access**, **Global** or **Project Security** profiles from the Web for Optional Client users.

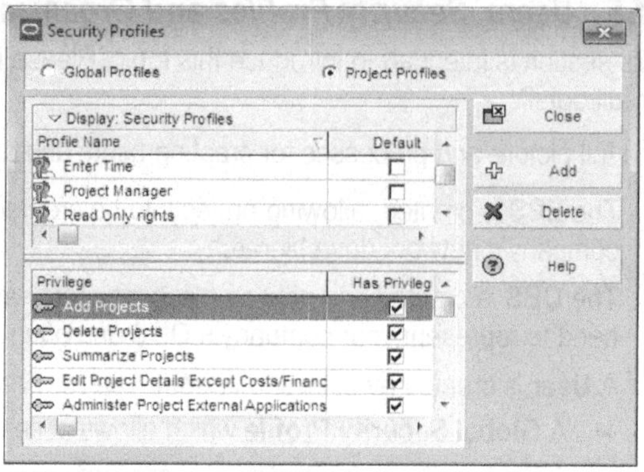

There are two types of profiles, **Global Profiles** and **Project Profiles**, which are assigned to Users allowing access such as Read Only, Create, Delete, etc.:

- Access to **Global Data** is controlled through **Global Profiles**, and
- Access to one or more **OBS Nodes** is controlled through **Project Profiles** by assigning **Users** to one or more **OBS Nodes** and assigning an applicable **Project Profile**.

A **User** is created by selecting:

- **Admin**, **Users...**, or
- **Administer**, **User Access**, **Users** in the Web for Optional Client users.

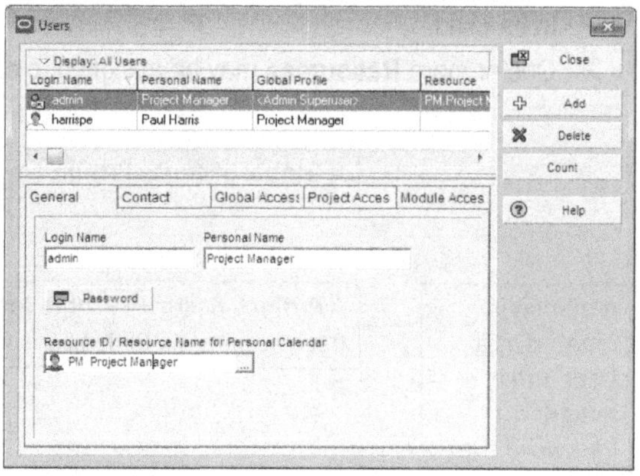

Each User is assigned:

- A **Global Profile** that enables access to Global data,
- An optional **Resource Node** thus limiting access to an area of the **Resource Window**, and
- One or more **OBS Nodes** and an applicable **Project Profile** for each **OBS Node**.

Therefore, access to projects is controlled through the **OBS**. Each **OBS Node** that is assigned to a User may be assigned a different **Project Profile**.

As a result, a User may have read-write access to some projects and read-only to others.

The OBS is edited by selecting **Enterprise**, **OBS....**

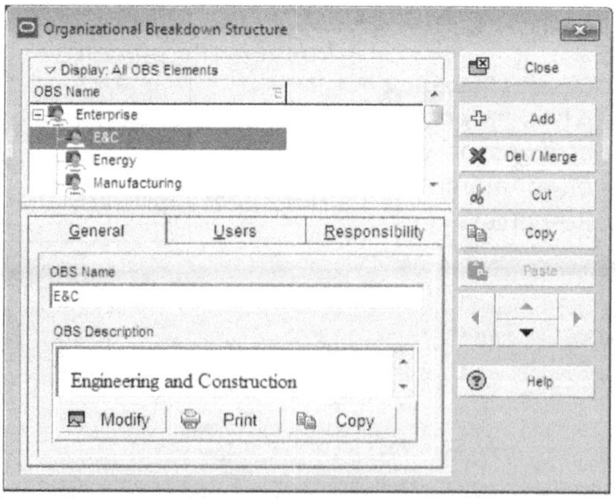

Projects are assigned to an OBS when they are created and the OBS Node must provide the required access rights to the project data.

WBS Nodes may be assigned to individual users which, although does not prevent them from viewing all the project data, will limit their access to just the node they have been assigned to in the **WBS Window**.

24.6 Project Codes

Project Codes in Primavera work in a similar way to Project Codes in P3. The codes are assigned to projects and enable projects to be Grouped and Sorted under an alternative structure to the EPS.

For example, when an EPS represents the physical location of offices by country, state/county and city, the Project Codes enables projects to be given tags, such as Reason for the Project, Safety, Compliance, New Product, and Increase Production. The Projects may be grouped under these headings.

Therefore, project codes are used to Group and Sort Projects in a similar way that Activity Codes are used to Group and Sort Activities.

To create a Project Code:

- Select **Enterprise**, **Project Codes...** to open the **Project Codes** form, or
- **Administer**, **Enterprise Data**, **Project**, **Project Codes** from the Web for Optional Client users.
- The Project Codes are created, edited, and deleted in a similar way to Activity Codes.

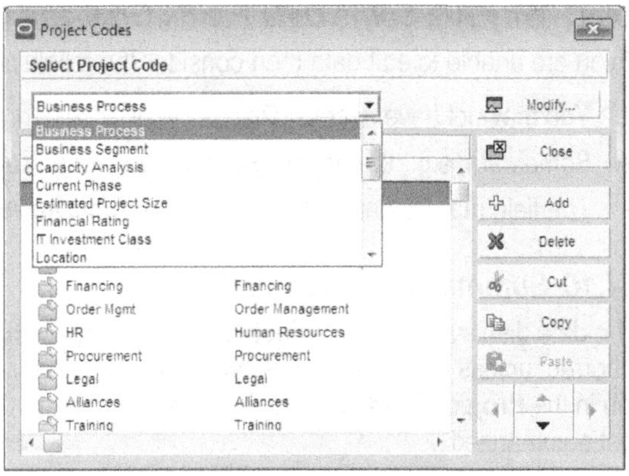

Project Codes may be assigned to projects in the **Projects Window** in a similar way as Activity Codes are assigned to activities by:

- Displaying the appropriate Code Column, or
- Opening the **Codes** tab in the **Projects Window**.

Projects may be Grouped, Sorted and Filtered in the **Projects Window** using the Group and Sort and Filter functions.

24.7 Filtering, Grouping and Sorting Projects in the Projects Window

Projects are Grouped and Sorted and filtered in the **Projects Window** in the same way as activities are in the **Activities Window**. Layouts, Filters, columns and bar formatting work in the same way in both windows.

Projects may be Grouped by fields such as **OBS**, **Responsibility**, **Project Codes** and many other fields. See the **Group, Sort and Layouts** chapter for more detail on this subject.

Projects may be filtered by similar fields, but some of the more useful fields to filter projects by are the **Status**, **Responsible Manager**, and **Project Code** fields.

24.8 Project Durations in the Projects Window

The project durations in both the **Projects Window** and **Activities Window** are calculated based on the Project Default calendar.

The summary durations of bands in the **Projects Window** are calculated on the **Enterprise**, **Calendars..., Default Calendar**.

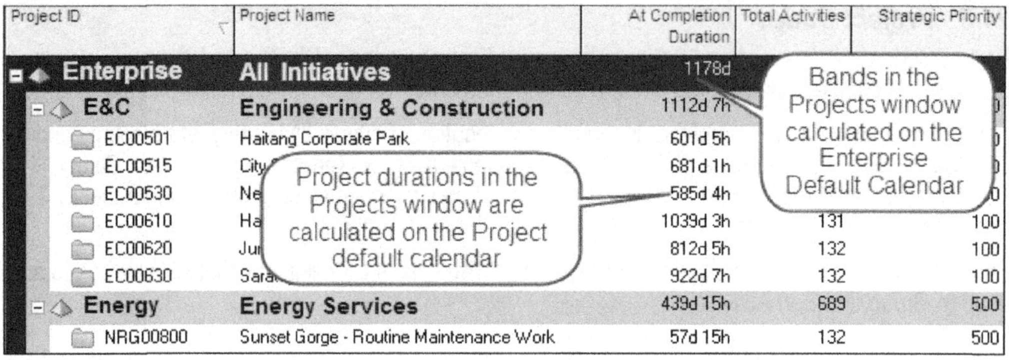

24.9 Why Are Some Data Fields Gray and Cannot Be Edited?

If you are unable to edit data then consider the following points:

- You may not have access. Discuss your access rights with your administrator.
- Some data, e.g., the project **Status**, needs the project open before the data may be edited.
- The field may be calculated, such as **Actual Duration**, and cannot be edited.

24.10 Summarizing Projects

The data displayed in the **Projects** and **Tracking Windows**, such as Durations, Dates, etc., may be incorrect unless the projects have been summarized by selecting **Tools**, **Summarize**. The **Settings** tab in the **Project Window** specifies to what level the data is summarized and indicates when it was last summarized.

A large database takes a significant amount of time to summarize and may be summarized automatically using Job Services.

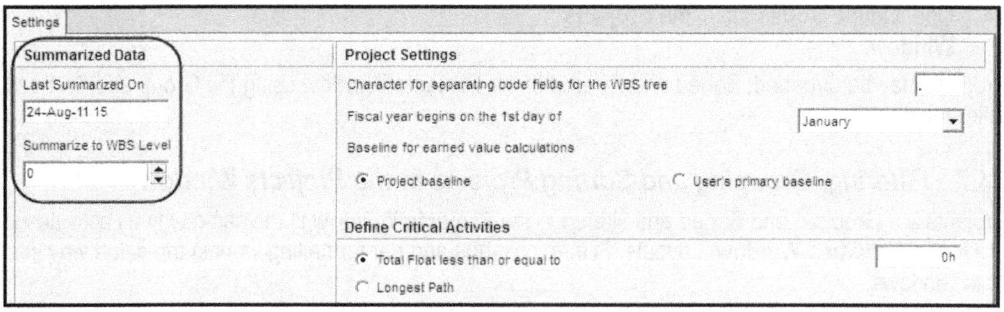

In the picture above, selecting **Summarize to WBS Level** is set to zero so all levels of the WBS will be summarized.

24.11 Job Services

A Job Services may be set up by selecting **Tools**, **Job Services...** to open the **Job Services** form, which can perform the following functions on one or more selected projects or EPS Nodes:

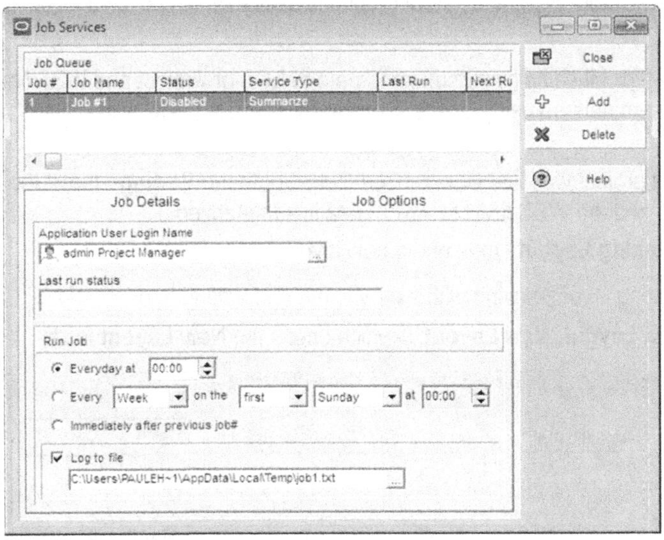

Select **Administer, Global Scheduled Services** in the Web for Optional Client users.

- **Apply Actuals** to projects when timesheets are used,
- **Batch Reports**. In the **Reports Window** a **Batch** may be created by selecting **Tools, Reports, Batch Reports...** to open the **Batch Reports** form. This creates one or more reports simultaneously. A Batch may be run on a regular basis using a job service:

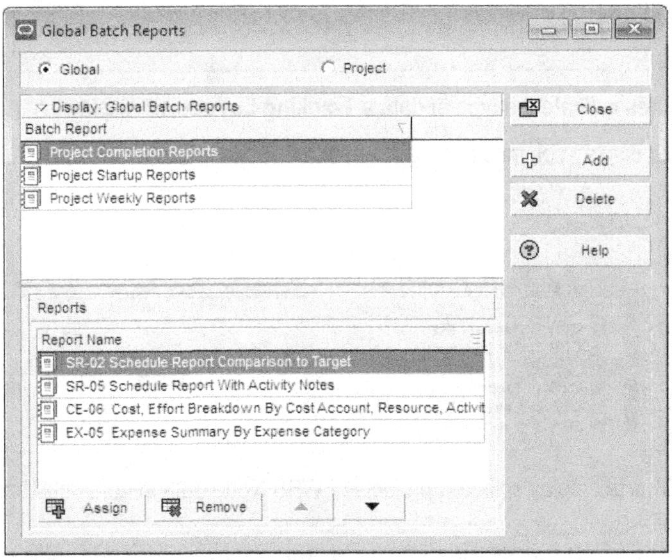

- **Export** one or more projects on a regular basis, or
- **Schedule** one or more projects on a regular basis.
- **Summarize** projects.

24.12 Tracking Window

Tracking Layouts are used for the resource, cost, and schedule analysis of multiple projects. This section introduces the concepts but does not go into the detail of using this function. You should experiment with the Group, Sort, and Filtering options available, which all function in a similar way to other windows.

- These layouts typically display summarized data to EPS or Project and WBS Node level. The data must be summarized using **Tools**, **Summarize** or using **Job Services** to display the latest current data.
- To see when a project was last summarized, select both the **Settings** tab in the lower **Projects Window** pane and the WBS level to which data is summarized.

There are four **Tracking Layout** types and a new layout is created by:

- Saving an existing layout, saving with a new name and editing it, or
- Selecting **View, Layout, New Layout...** which opens the **New Layout** form:

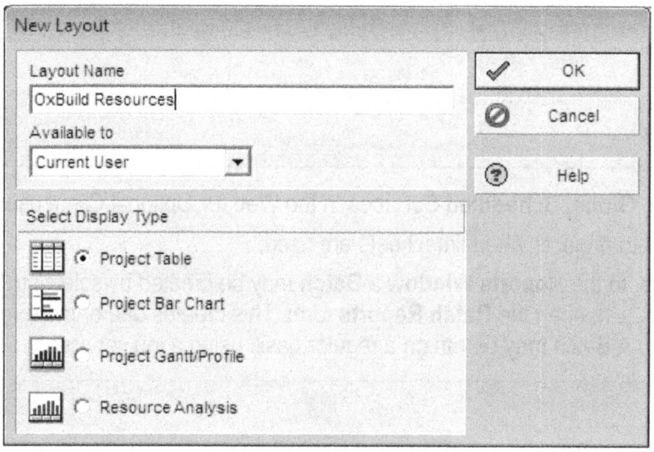

The following pictures indicate the type of data a **Tracking Layout** will display:

- **Project Tables** display columns of data for selected Projects or WBS Nodes:

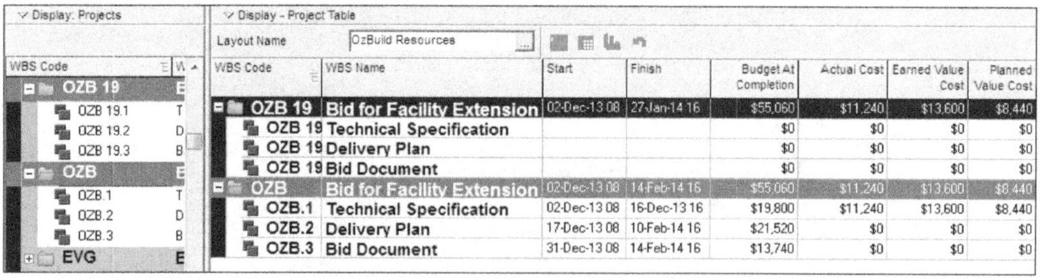

- **Project Bar Charts** display selected projects of WBS Node data in horizontal bars:

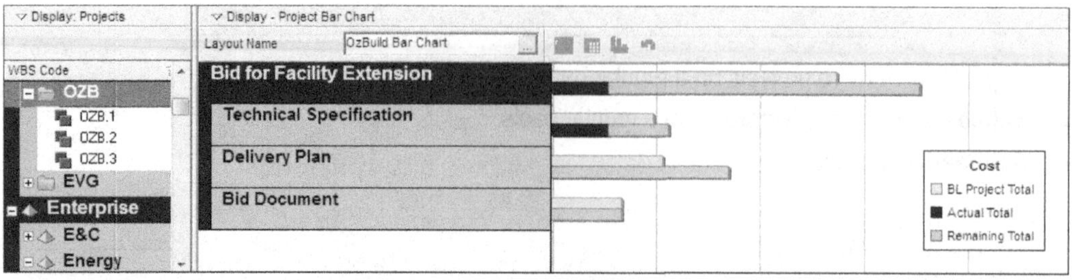

- **Project Gantt/Profiles** display three panes, with bars in the top right pane and either a spreadsheet or a profile in the bottom pane.

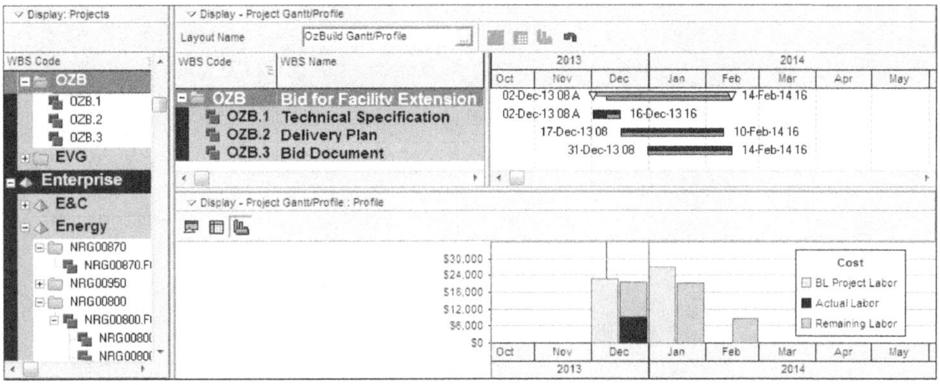

- **Resource Analysis** displays four panes:
  - ➢ The projects to be analyzed are selected in the top left-hand pane,
  - ➢ The resources to be analyzed are selected in the bottom left-hand pane,
  - ➢ Bars, a Resource Profiles or a Resource Table may be displayed in the top right-hand pane, and
  - ➢ The bottom right-hand pane may display either a Resource Profile or a Resource Table:

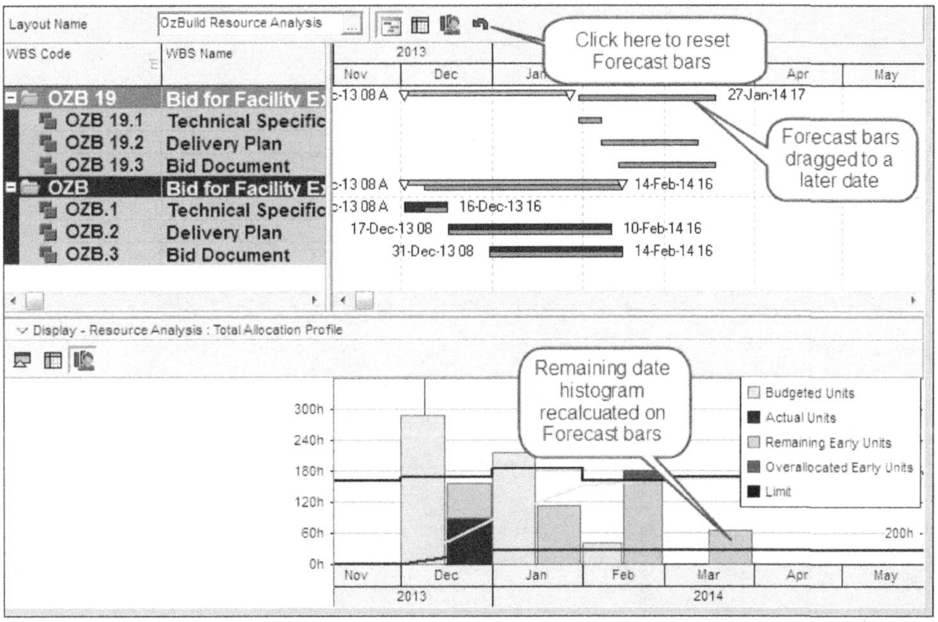

- ➢ An existing layout may be seen by opening the **Open Layout** form. Select **View, Layout** or click the icon in the top right-hand pane.
- ➢ The **Forecast Bars** have been dragged to a new location and the **Edit**, **User Preferences…**, Resource Analysis, Time-Distributed Data option set to **Forecast dates** allows the **Resource Remaining Early units/costs** to be recalculated on the **Forecast dates**.
- ➢ The bottom pane of a Tracking Layout may be hidden, as with other windows.
- ➢ You should experiment by right-clicking in all the panes to see all the display options.

25 MULTIPLE PROJECT SCHEDULING

25.1 Multiple Projects in One Primavera Project

When there are many small projects that need to be managed, it would be logical to create a Primavera Project for each project.

On the other hand, one should also consider putting a number of small projects in one Primavera Project and have the projects identified by the first level WBS Node or some other coding, such as Activity Codes or Project Phase/WBS Category. This is especially practical when there are many projects with a very small number of activities or when an organization only realizes benefits from a number of completed projects when they are all finished. This option is also practical when one scheduler is managing all the small projects. The only problem with this approach is that P6 does not allow partial projects to be Baselined.

25.2 Multiple P6 Primavera Projects Representing One Project

Normally, one Primavera Project would be created for each of an organization's projects. There may be a requirement to break a Project down into Sub-projects, these reasons include:

- The project is large enough to require a number of schedulers and therefore a Primavera Project could be created for each scheduler to delineate each scheduler's area of responsibility.

  Two or more schedulers may open one project and access may be assigned down to WBS Node but the User Access has to be set up to allow them to be able to schedule and they are not able to link to other WBS Nodes.

  There could be a requirement to keep an individual organization's financial information confidential and as security and access is set at project level, information in one project may be hidden from specific users. This situation may exist when there are two or more contractors scheduling parts of a project and they require their cost to be kept confidential from other contractors.

- A project may have separable parts or multiple clients but it is necessary to report the project parts separately, yet allow resource management project-wide. Again, a Primavera project could be created for each separate part of the project. In this situation each user may be given access to only one **Resource Node** from the **Global Access** tab of the **Admin**, **Users** form.
- A sub-project could be created as a Primavera Project for the security of sensitive financial information. The cost may be assigned to resources in the financial sub-project with access given to specific individuals. Activities in the financial sub-project may be LOE (Level of Effort) activities, spanning activities in other non-cost sub-projects. This method is generally suitable for high level cost planning and management while allowing the detailed planning of a project in a non-financial sub-project without the burden of managing costs.

When a Primavera Project is created for each sub-project, it would be logical to keep all the Primavera Projects located under one "project" EPS Node and assigned a single Project Code. All the Primavera Projects could be opened at one time for scheduling and reporting by selecting the EPS Node.

The decision to break a project into two or more Primavera Projects must have a sound basis and be well thought out. The environment chosen should be well piloted and tested to ensure the desired results are obtained from the software. Planning and scheduling software is hard enough to use without adding the burden of creating multiple projects. There is a large amount of analysis that may be completed without using multiple projects. Filters may be used to isolate parts of a project and sub-net critical paths may be generated a number of ways, such as using the **Calculating Multiple Paths** function. You must ensure that the requirement to break a project into sub-projects using individual Primavera projects is well-founded.

Some people suggest that sub-contractors should run their own sub-projects within a master schedule. My experience is that smaller or new sub-contractors often are very inexperienced at scheduling and many do not know the basics of scheduling. It is therefore unreasonable and risky to expect sub-contractors to drive strange and complex scheduling software and get it right. Some industries are better equipped to manage complex software, with skills found more likely in industries such as IT, but less likely to be found in the construction-related sector.

It is also my experience that it is better to reduce the number of schedulers working on a project schedule to the absolute minimum required to manage a project. In large complex projects, these people need to be trained in the use of the software, be reasonably experienced running the software (or working under a person who is experienced), and run the schedule by an agreed-upon and documented set of guidelines.

Managing the inclusion of sub-contractors' schedules always becomes an issue. Alliances tend to help resolve this problem as the schedules then become a joint responsibility.

25.3 Setting Up Primavera Projects as Sub-projects

There are a number of issues to be considered when moving to this environment. Be aware that Primavera does not have the sub-project options that are found in other products. For example there are EPS Activity Codes but there are no EPS Filters, Layouts, Resources or Scheduling Options and a WBS may not be shared with more than one P6 project. There is no inbuilt "P3 Project Group" calculation option, which may result in some interesting float calculations that result from inter-project relationships. This section explains some workarounds.

25.3.1 Opening One or More Projects

Enterprise and Project data may be accessed in the **Projects Window**. To access Project activity information, such as activities, resources, and relationships, a project must be opened and the **Activities Window** displayed. One or more projects may be opened at the same time by selecting one or more projects and/or selecting one or more EPS levels and then:

- Right-click and select **Open Project**,
- Select **Ctrl+O**,
- Select **File**, **Open...** to open the **Open Project** form:

The **Open** form enables the options of opening as **Exclusive**, **Shared** or **Read Only**.

A project may only be opened as **Exclusive** (meaning that only the current user may edit it) by using the **Open Project** form. All other methods will result in the project's being opened in the **Shared** mode and all users with access to the project may open and edit the project(s) at the same time. The **Shared** option may result in one user's edits overwriting another user's edits, depending on who saved what and when. In addition, opening in the **Shared** option may result in different users seeing different values for Activity, WBS Nodes, and Project durations in days or hours if the users have different **User Preferences Time Units**.

25.3.2 Default Project

When multiple projects are opened:

- The system selects the **Default Project** when two or more projects have been opened at the same time.
- The **Default Project Scheduling Options** are used to calculate all the open projects.
- Select **Project**, **Set Default Project...** to open the **Set Default Project** form where you may change the default project:

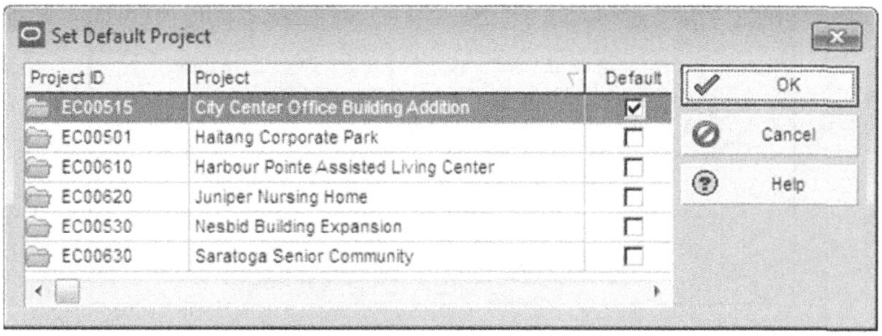

- All open projects **WILL** have their **Scheduling Options** set to the same as the **Default Project** after the projects have been scheduled.

The Help file indicates that the **Default Projects** scheduling and leveling settings are used for scheduling. It is also the default project for new data such as activities or issues when the projects are not grouped by WBS.

NOTE: When more than one Primavera project is opened at the same time and each project has different scheduling options, then the non-default project's scheduling options are changed to be the same as the default project's, without warning. These non-default projects may calculate differently when opened with other projects. In addition, the next time a non-default project is opened in isolation it may calculate very differently from the previous time it was opened in isolation. To prevent this, either all projects in each database must have the same scheduling options, or access to projects carefully restricted, or ensure users only open one project at a time.

An example of changing the default project when each project has different options is demonstrated in the following picture. The first has retained logic and the second has progress override. Activity PG3-2 has moved forward in time as it is now being scheduled with Progress Override after initially being scheduled with Retained Logic. These types of unexpected changes may significantly affect your project and may occur when two or more projects, each with different scheduling options, are opened together.

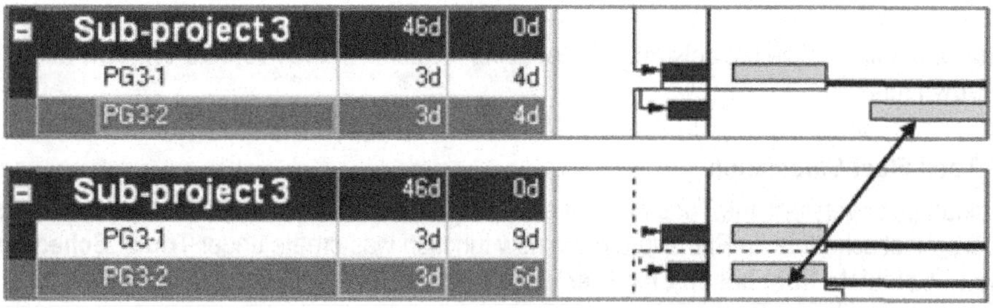

25.3.3 Setting the Projects Data Dates

The default project does not set the Data Date for all projects. In the example following:

- The default project is Sub-project 1, which has had the Data Date set to 7 Feb,
- Sub-project 2 Data Date is set to 3 Feb,
- Sub-project 3 has a Data Date of 1 Feb.

When scheduling, the following message is received:

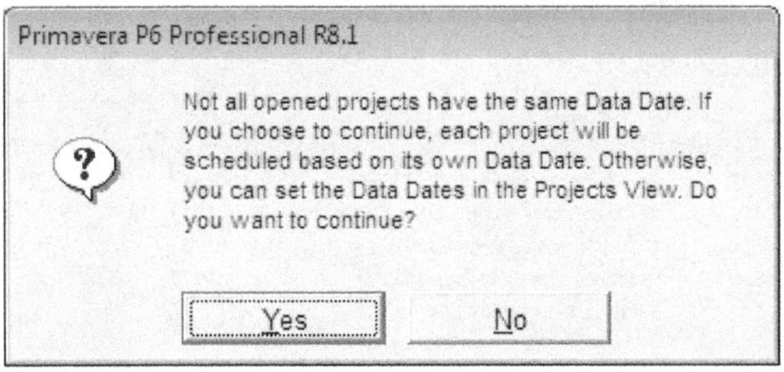

Unlinked activities, PG1-6, PG2-6 and PG3-4, have been added to each project and it may be seen in the following picture:

- All projects are scheduled according to their own Data Dates,
- The Data Date line is shown on the earliest project Data Date.

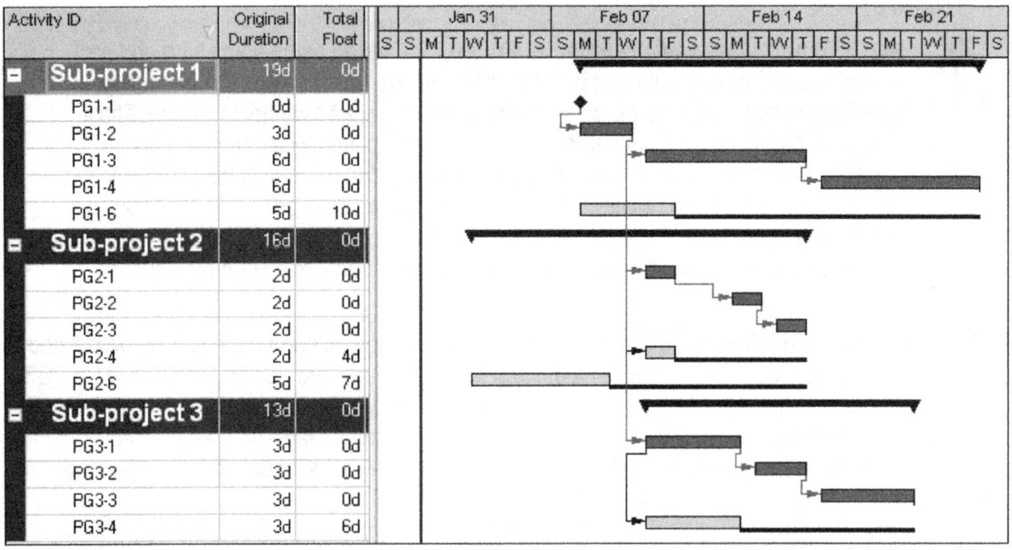

The **Data Dates** of multiple projects may be set using a column in the **Projects Window** and utilizing the **Fill Down** function.

25.3.4 Total Float Calculation

In P6.1 and earlier versions the Total Float of each project is calculated to the last activity of each individual project schedule. In Primavera 6.2 a new function was create under **Tools**, **Schedule...**, **Options...**, **Calculate float based on either** which resolves this problem. See paragraph 15.2.10 for full details on how this function operates.

25.4 Refresh Data and Commit Changes

The **File**, **Refresh Data** option is used when two or more people are working on the same project. It ensures that the latest data is displayed, which enables one user to see the latest edits made by another user. This includes resetting the Global Calendar if another user changes it.

The **File**, **Commit Changes** option is used to write any schedule changes to the database.

25.5 Who Has the Project Open?

When a project is opened with Primavera using the **File**, **Open** option the **Open Project** form has Access Mode options to open the project as **Exclusive**, **Shared**, or **Read Only**.

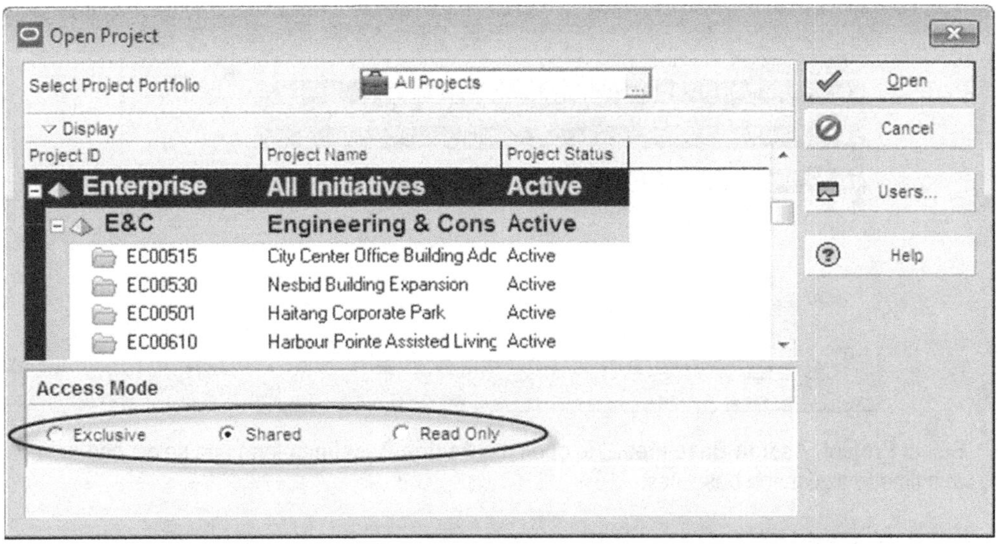

Select 

to open the **Project Users** form and see who else has the file open.

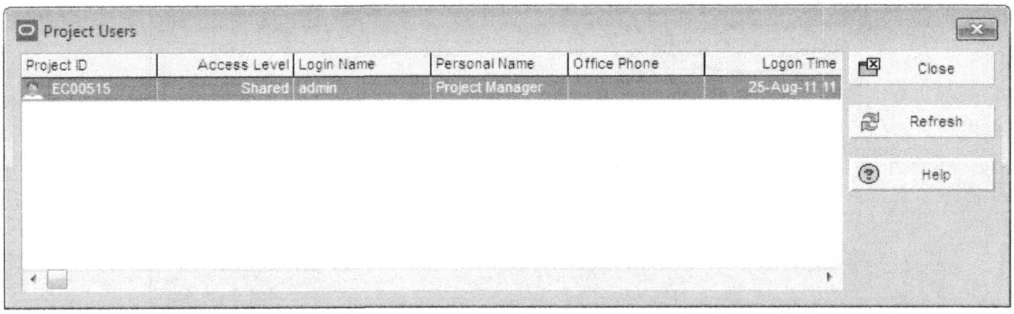

The default option is **Shared** and that means any project that is not opened with the **Open Project** form will be opened as Shared. Anyone who has access may also open the project, calculate and display with their **User Preferences**, and report different data from the same project at the same time.

25.6 Setting Baselines for Multiple Projects

Baselines may be set for all the projects using the **Maintain Baselines** form (when multiple projects are open) and the **Assign Baselines** form. The following picture show the process of setting multiple project baselines:

- Open the **Maintain Baselines** form by selecting **Project**, **Maintain Baselines...**:
  - Either all projects may be selected and a copy of all projects set as the Baselines at one time, or
  - Other current projects may be converted from the database one at a time.
- Select [Add] to open the **Add New Baseline** form and create the new baselines,

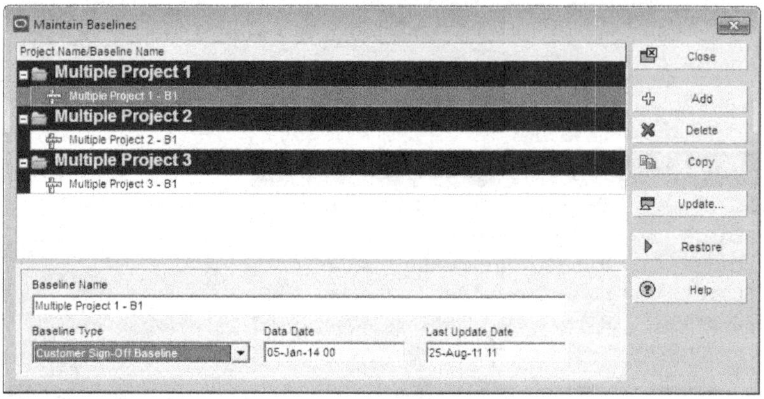

- Select **Project**, **Assign Baselines...** to open the **Assign Baselines** form and select one project at a time to assign the baselines.

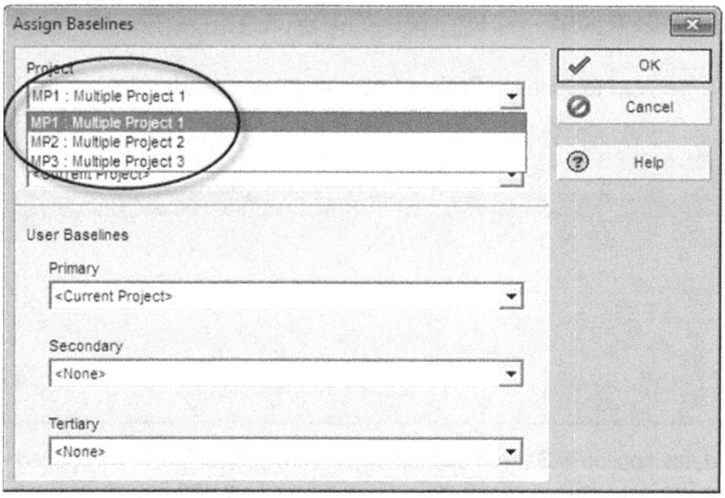

Remember, a User Baseline set by one user will not be displayed when another user opens the project. The **<Current Project> Baseline** displays the **Planned Dates** from the current schedule and will be shown as a baseline.

25.7 Restoring Baselines for Multiple Projects

The process identified in the previous page results in one interesting issue when Baseline projects are restored. The software creates Ghost relationships and External Dates, both of which must be avoided at all costs, as there is a risk that neither the Baseline nor Current projects would calculate correctly once Multiple Project Baselines are restored.

The example below explains what happens when three simple projects are baselined together:

- The three projects were opened together and baselined and restored:

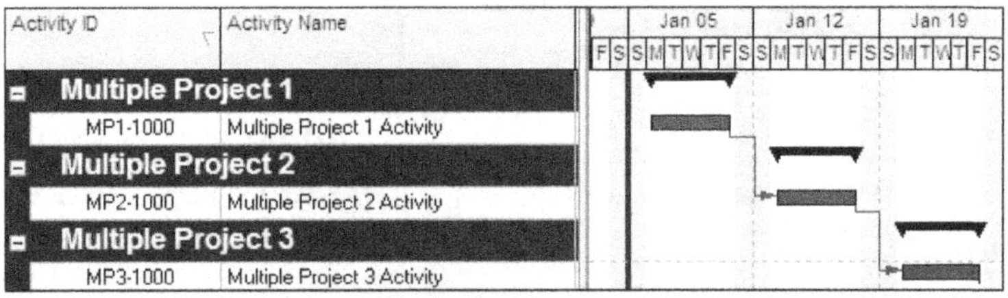

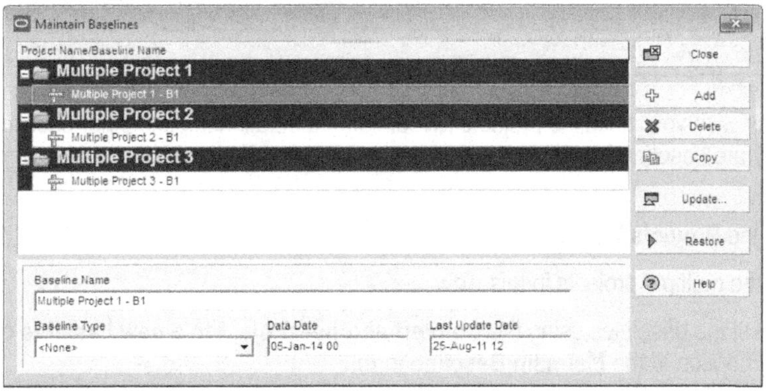

- When the current and baseline projects are opened there are relationships between the Current and Baseline projects added by the system without warning.

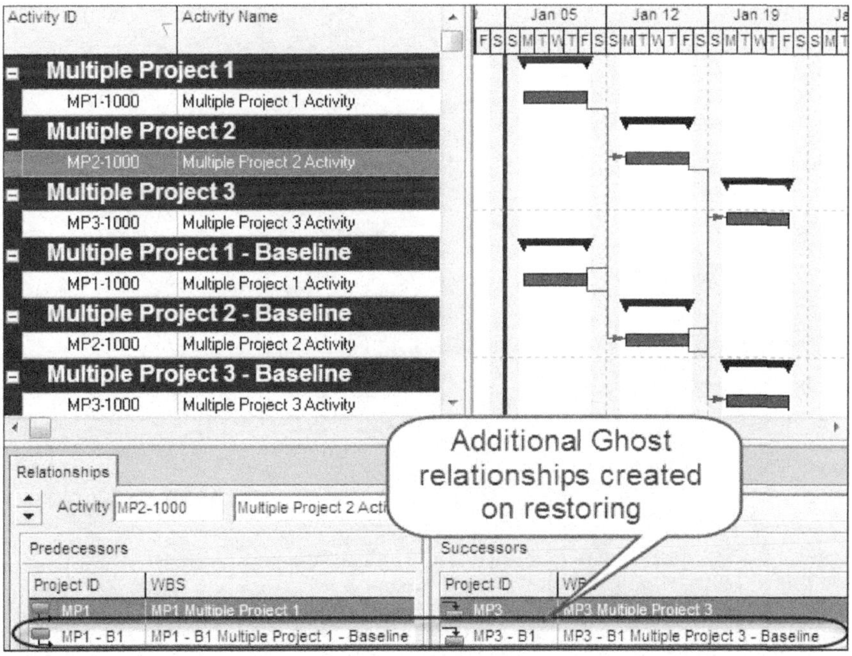

- When the current project is opened and activity durations shortened you will see that the schedule does not calculate correctly:

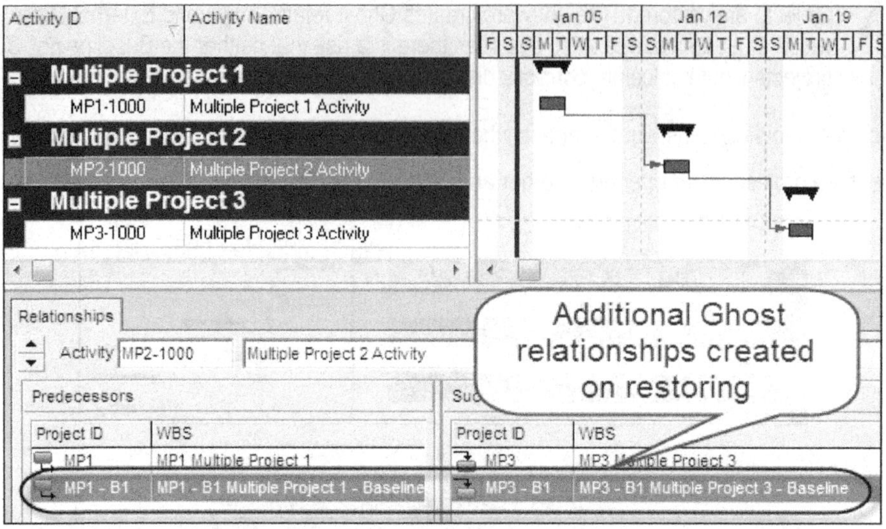

Therefore if you wish your baseline projects to maintain the relationships to other baselined projects only when they are baselined at the same time and not create relationships to other current projects then you must:

- Open the **Projects Window**,
- Copy the multiple projects in this view,
- Then set the baselines using the **Convert another project to a new baseline of the current project** option in the **Maintain Baseline** form.

Now if the baselined projects are restored then their relationships will be related to the correct other baseline.

26 UTILITIES

26.1 Reflection Projects

Primavera Version 6.0 created a Reflection project function. A Reflection is a "What-if" copy of a project that may be edited and then merged back into the original project, as the changes made are required to be kept may be incorporated into the original project and those not required may be ignored.

The **Reflection project** may be shared with a wider audience and people asked to view and make changes to the project. The **Reflection project** may be exported and sent to a customer who may make changes and then imported back into the database.

To create a Reflection:

- In the **Project Window** highlight the project and right-click,
- Select **Create Reflection....**

The Reflection project is created with a new ID and the term Reflection added to the Project Name.

To merge an edited Reflection project:

- Open the Reflection project,
- Highlight the Reflection project and right-click,
- Select **Merge Reflection into source project...**,
- This opens a form that will allow a choice to be made about which changes should be kept, if a backup XER file should be made, and if the Reflection project is to be kept or deleted:

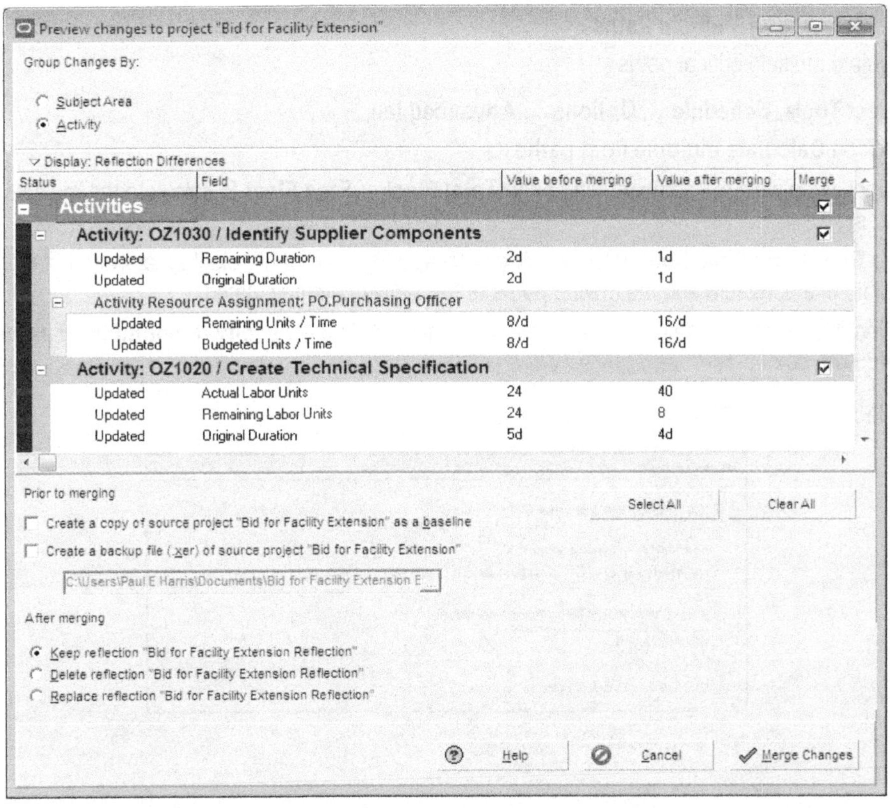

26.2 Advanced Scheduling Options

Primavera Version 5.0 has a new option that enables individual critical paths to be banded as in the following picture and is useful when analyzing larger projects that have more than one critical path. This is similar to Grouping by Total Float but this function numbers the Paths and each path contains activities that are linked, whereas banding by Total Float may group unlinked activities.

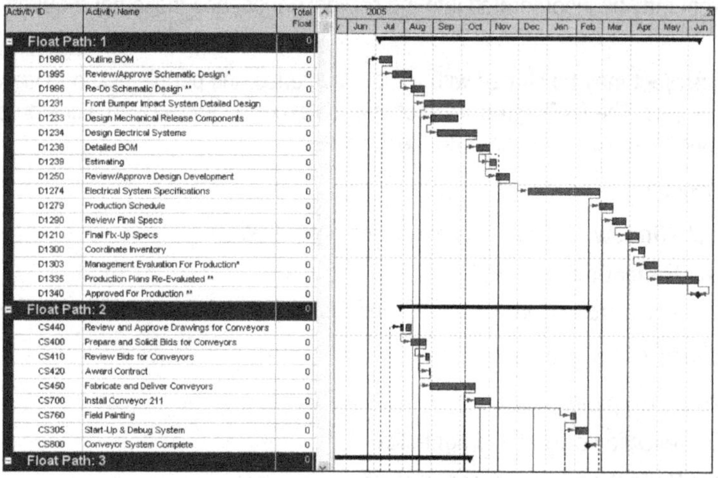

There are two steps involved, firstly calculating the multiple paths and secondly displaying the multiple paths:

26.2.1 Calculating Multiple Paths

To calculate multiple critical paths:

- Select **Tools**, **Schedule...**, **Options...**, **Advanced** tab,
- Click on **Calculate multiple float paths**,
- Select if you wish the software to use the **Total Float** or **Free Float** to calculate the multiple paths.
- The **Display multiple float paths ending with activity** is used to select an activity that is in the middle of a schedule and the driving paths of this activity are calculated.
- Select the number of paths for the software to calculate in the **Specify the number of paths to calculate** box.
- Select 

 and schedule the project.

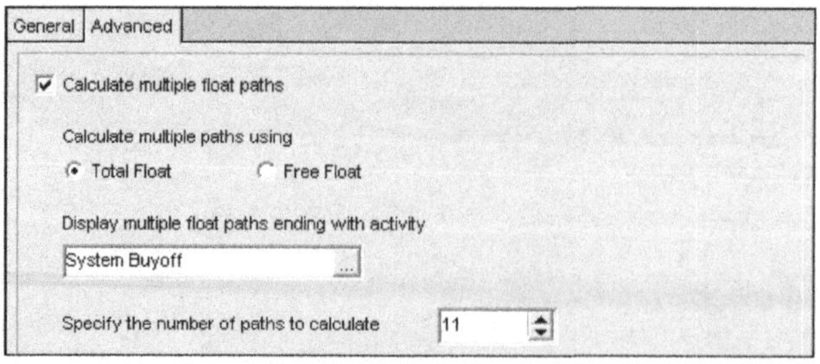

26.2.2 Displaying Multiple Paths

There are two fields that are populated in this process:

- **Float Path**, and
- **Float Path Order**

Either select multiple path Layout or create a Layout that Groups by **Float Path** and Sorts by **Float Path Order**, as in the following examples which show a before and after grouping:

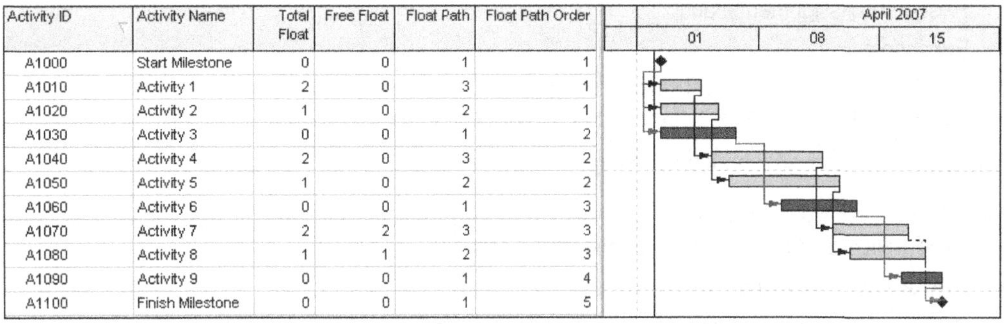

Activity ID	Activity Name	Total Float	Free Float	Float Path	Float Path Order
A1000	Start Milestone	0	0	1	1
A1010	Activity 1	2	0	3	1
A1020	Activity 2	1	0	2	1
A1030	Activity 3	0	0	1	2
A1040	Activity 4	2	0	3	2
A1050	Activity 5	1	0	2	2
A1060	Activity 6	0	0	1	3
A1070	Activity 7	2	2	3	3
A1080	Activity 8	1	1	2	3
A1090	Activity 9	0	0	1	4
A1100	Finish Milestone	0	0	1	5

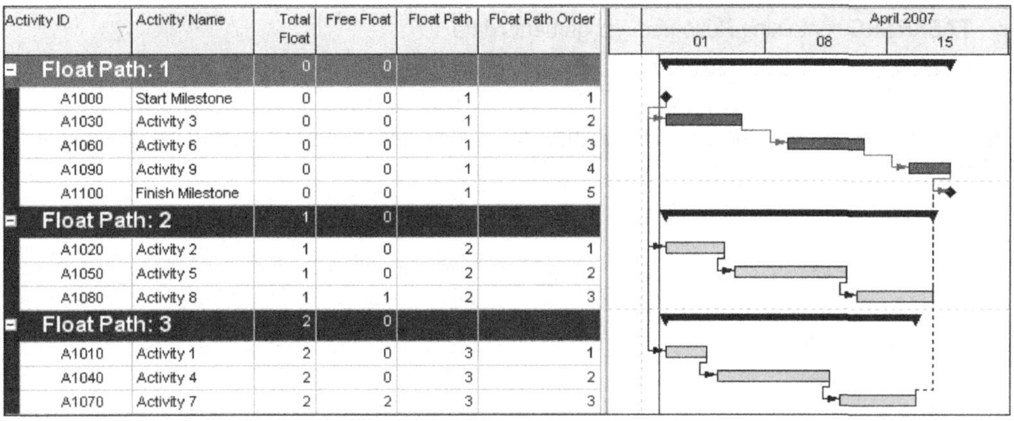

Activity ID	Activity Name	Total Float	Free Float	Float Path	Float Path Order
Float Path: 1		0	0		
A1000	Start Milestone	0	0	1	1
A1030	Activity 3	0	0	1	2
A1060	Activity 6	0	0	1	3
A1090	Activity 9	0	0	1	4
A1100	Finish Milestone	0	0	1	5
Float Path: 2		1	0		
A1020	Activity 2	1	0	2	1
A1050	Activity 5	1	0	2	2
A1080	Activity 8	1	1	2	3
Float Path: 3		2	0		
A1010	Activity 1	2	0	3	1
A1040	Activity 4	2	0	3	2
A1070	Activity 7	2	2	3	3

The reader may wish to read the Help file or experiment with the software to see the results.

26.3 Audit Trail Columns

Primavera Version 5.0 introduced four basic audit trail columns that may be displayed in the Activities Window, which display the date and user who added the activity and by whom and when it was modified:

- **Added By** – the user who added the activity,
- **Added Date** – the date the activity was added,
- **Last Modified By** – the user who last modified the activity, and
- **Last Modified Date** – the date the activity was last modified.

Primavera Version 6.0 introduced two new resource assignment fields available in the **Activities Window**, **Activity Details**, **Resources** tab:

- **Assigned by**, and
- **Assigned Date**.

26.4 Excel Import and Export Tool

Primavera has a built-in tool for importing to and exporting from Excel the following data when the user is assigned a Superuser security profile:

- Activities
- Relationships
- Resources
- Resources Assignments, and
- Expenses.

To import or export data to Excel select **File**, **Import...** or **Export...** and follow the instructions in the wizards. **Export Templates** may be created and re-used at a later date with this tool.

The following sheets are created upon export and these sheet names must not be changed:

- **TASK** containing Activity data
- **TASKPRED** containing Activity Relationships data
- **PROJCOST** containing Expenses data
- **RSRC** containing Resources data
- **TASKRSRC** containing Resource Assignments data
- **USERDATA** containing user data that should not be changed.

These templates allow the user to specify what data is to be imported and exported; an example is below:

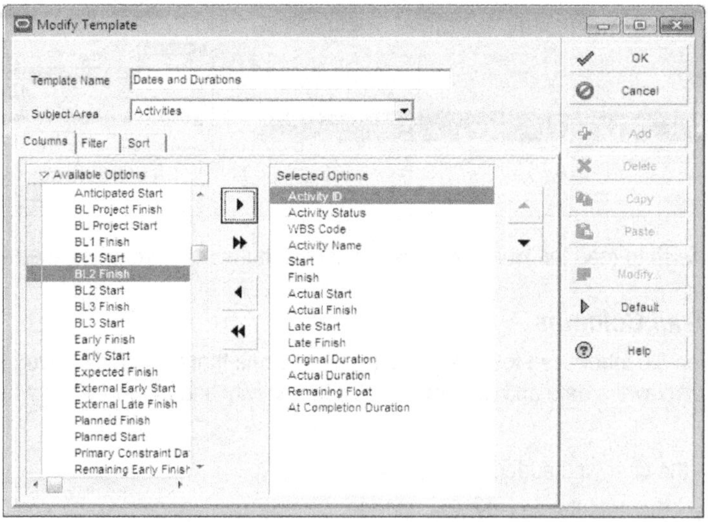

26.4.1 Notes and/or Restrictions on Export

A few points to understand when using the Primavera Excel Import function:

- The following sheets are created on export and these sheet names must not be changed:
  - **TASK** containing Activity data
  - **TASKPRED** containing Activity Relationships data
  - **PROJCOST** containing Expenses data
  - **RSRC** containing Resources data
  - **TASKRSRC** containing Resource Assignments data
  - **USERDATA** containing user data that should not be changed.
- Do not change the language between importing and exporting.
- The first row of data in each sheet that is exported contains the database field name. The first row must not be changed otherwise the data will not be imported.
- The second row in the spreadsheet contains **Captions** that are deleted on spreadsheet import by the **"Delete This Row"** entry in the right column of the spread sheet. This entry may be copied to and line of data that is to be deleted from the project.
- Dictionary data such as Activity Codes being imported must exist before the data is imported.
- Only Activity Codes may be imported, if you wish to import the Activity Code descriptions then you will have to use the Software Developers Kit (SDK).
- Only a maximum of 200 columns of data may be exported.
- **Sub-units** of time are not supported and the Sub-unit check boxes in the **Edit**, **User Preferences...**, **Time Units** tab should be unchecked.
- **Percent Completes** must be a value of between 0 and 100.
- Anything listed as a field may be exported.
- The User Preferences will affect how your data is exported and may give different values for resources.

26.4.2 Notes and Restrictions on Import

When attempting to import data using this type of tool there are some guidelines that apply to many applications, not just to this Primavera tool:

- Create a test project and experiment with this function before using it on a live project.
- Export some data first as this exports the correct column headings and sheet names.
- Change or add data to the exported spreadsheet and import new data into the test environment. Then review that the data is importing correctly and that the schedule is calculating as expected.
- Back up or take a copy of your live project before importing into a live project.
- It is often better to import into User Defined Fields to ensure the data gets into the database and then Global Change into the desired place.
- Activity data must have the Activity ID and WBS Code as these are the unique identifiers for each activity within a database.
- The **delete_record_flag**, in the far right hand column, titled **Delete titled this row** against line 2 of the Excel spreadsheet deletes the line 2 activity on import.
- The **Delete This Row** flag may be placed against any spreadsheet line and the activity will be deleted on import.

Calculated fields may not be imported and are marked with an (*). See picture below:

	A	B	C	D	E	F	G
1	task_code	status_code	wbs_id	task_name	start_date	end_date	act_start_date
2	Activity ID	Activity Status	WBS Code	Activity Name	(*)Start	(*)Finish	Actual Start
3	OZ1030	Not Started	OZB.1	Identify Supplier Components	11/12/2013 8:00:00 AM	12/12/2013 4:00:00 PM	
4	OZ1040	Not Started	OZB.1	...n	13/12/2013 8:00:00 AM	16/12/2013 4:00:00 PM	
5	OZ1000	Completed	OZB.1		2/12/2013 8:00:00 AM		2/12/2013 8:00:00 AM
6	OZ1010	Completed	OZB.1	...nents	2/12/2013 8:00:00 AM	4/12/2013 4:00:00 PM	2/12/2013 8:00:00 AM
7	OZ1020	In Progress	OZB.1	...n	4/12/2013 8:00:00 AM	10/12/2013 4:00:00 PM	4/12/2013 8:00:00 AM

These may not be imported

- To see if the data field you wish to import may be imported, export the field and see if the field has an (*) by the second line description in the spreadsheet. Fields that may not be imported include but are not limited to:
  - Most dates except the Actual Start and Actual Finish
  - Expected Finish
  - Actual, Remaining, and At Completion Durations
- Therefore if you wish to import dates to create un-started activities without importing the Original Duration then you will have to import the activity with **Actual Start** and **Actual Finish** dates where you want the activity to lie and use a Global Change to take-off the Actual Dates:

	A	B	C	D	E	F
1	task_code	wbs_id	task_name	act_start_date	act_end_date	delete_record_flag
2	Activity ID	WBS Code	Activity Name	Actual Start	Actual Finish	Delete This Row
3	OZ1140	OZB.3	New Activity	5/01/2014 8:00:00 AM	17/01/2014 4:00:00 PM	

Then	Parameter	Is	Parameter/Value	Operator	Parameter/Value
	Original Duration	=	Actual Duration		
And	Primary Constraint	=	Start On		
And	Primary Constraint Dat	=	Actual Start		
And	Actual Start	=			
And	Actual Finish	=			

- When only exporting some data on an occasional basis then it may be easier just to copy and paste the data into a spreadsheet.

There is more information in the Help file under **Reference**, **Importing and Exporting**.

Earlier versions of P6 allowed Activity Codes and other data may be imported by loading the Software Developers Kit (SDK) and using a spreadsheet available from the Oracle Primavera Knowledgebase. You will need to create a Support Login at the Oracle web site.

There is an article at **www.primavera.com.au** or **www.eh.com.au** under Technical Papers that describes in detail how to use the SDK.

If you wish to import dates into a database then you need to use the API. This has been removed from the P6 V8 Professional Client but is still available in the P6 V8 EPPM (Web) version.

26.5 Project Import and Export

Project data may be imported and exported from and to the following formats:

- **XER**, which is a Primavera proprietary format, used to exchange projects between Primavera Version 6.0 databases regardless of the database type in which it was created.
- **Primavera Contractor XER**. This is the format produced by Primavera Contractor.
- **Project (*.XML).** This is the file format that Microsoft Project now recommends for export and import from other products like Primavera. Version 8.3 included some enhancements to this function which are outlined in the What's New chapter, para 28.18
- **MPX (*.mpx).** This is a text format data file created by Microsoft Project 98 and earlier versions. MPX is a format that may be imported and exported by many other project scheduling software packages.
- **Primavera Project Planner P3** and **SureTrak** files saved in **P3** format. A SureTrak project should be saved in Concentric (P3) format before importing. Importing P3 files requires P3 to be installed on the same computer as P6 and later Windows operating systems do not support the loading of P3, effectively making this function in operable on some operating systems.
- With Primavera Version 6.0 the importation of P3 files has been improved:
  - One or more individual sub-projects may now be imported, and
  - The import EPS locations specified, which may be different for each sub-project

  Select **File**, **Import...** or **Export...** to open the appropriate form.
- **Primavera PM – (XML)** is a new format introduced with Primavera Version 6.0 which is industry standard and enables the export of most data for single project only.
- **UN/CEFACT XML** format. P6 Version 8.3 supports UN/CEFACT XML format. This format is mandated by many US Government agencies.

Project (*.mpp). This is the default file format that Microsoft Project uses to create and save files is not supported by later version of P6.

When projects are imported or exported to other scheduling packages they will often calculate differently due to the different methods of calculation of each package. Do not expect to import from Microsoft Project or any other software and expect to see the same dates when scheduling. There are some articles on **www.primavera.com.au** and **www.eh.com.au** that explain the issues.

Importing a file from another Primavera database may give different results depending on the database and user preferences in each database and these should be carefully checked.

Importing a project into a working P6 database must be carefully planned to ensure that existing projects are not impacted by the imported data and the options available on the import wizard are fully understood. Updating or overwriting existing data may affect existing schedules.

A sacrificial database may be the best option for reviewing schedule submitted by subcontractors so as to not corrupt you own working database.

26.6 Check In and Check Out

Check In and Check Out function is similar to the P3 and SureTrak function of the same name, which enables a project to be copied from a database, worked on in a remote location such as a client's database, and then be checked in to the original database at a later date and the original schedule updated with the changes.

- Select from the **Project Window**, **General** tab, **File**, **Check Out...** to check out a project:

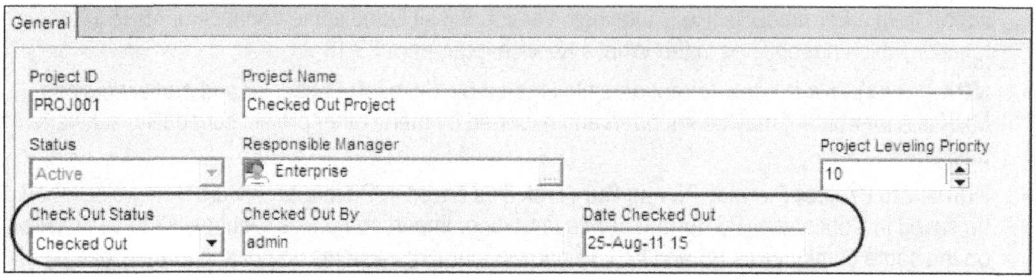

- The project XER file may then be sent to another person or organization, imported into another database and edited.
- On import to another database, **External Dates** are created where there are inter-project relationships in the source database.

These **External Dates** act like Early Start and Late Finish constraints and will affect the schedule calculation. You should always check for **External Dates** when importing a project. See paragraph 15.2.1 for an example of External date.

The file format of a Checked Out file is the same as a project exported in XER format, but checking out a project places a **Read Only** attribute on the project, and then it may be opened but not edited.

To remove the **Read Only** attribute on the project either:

- Select **File**, **Check In...** to check in a project, or
- Select change the status to **Checked In** in the **Project Window**, **General** tab:

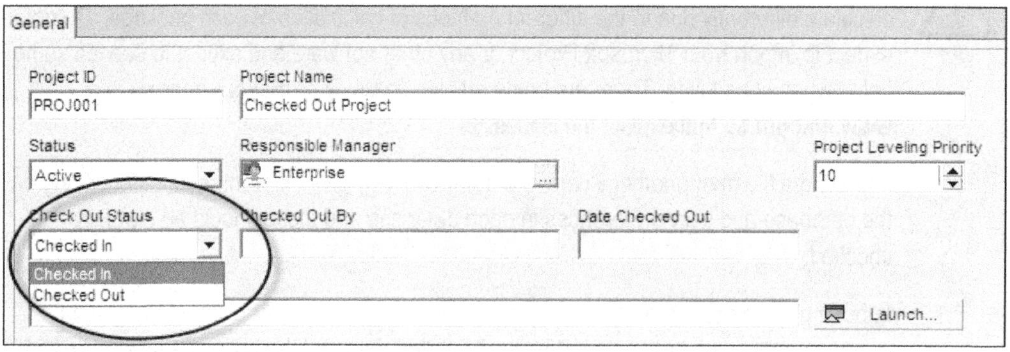

Also ensure you check what has happened to any original external relationships on re-import of a Checked Out project.

- The original inter-project relationships normally get re-linked on import, and
- Then your project may calculate differently when you have Checked In a Checked Out project that now has External Dates and different calculated dates.

26.7 UN/CEFACT XML format

P6 Version 8.3 supports UN/CEFACT XML format from the **File**, **Export** menu. This format is mandated by many US Government agencies.

26.8 Online HTML Help

The Help menu in P6 Version 8.3 has an additional menu option titled **Online Help** which will display the information in HTML format assisting people with disabilities who may access additional browser functions.

The **Admin Preferences**, **Options** tab has a new P6 Online Help section which sets the default for the F1 key. The URL is set to the Oracle Technology Network (OTN):

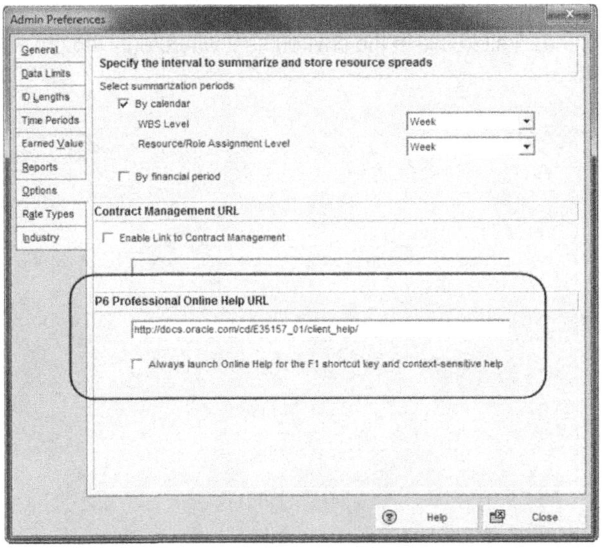

26.9 Activity Discussion Feature

A new tab has been added to the **Activities Window** in P6 Version 8.3, titled **Discussion** which enables:

- Users to create a discussion thread for each activity,
- Each entry is saved with the date of entry and user name and the entire thread is recorded allowing and interactive discussion between users who have access to P6,

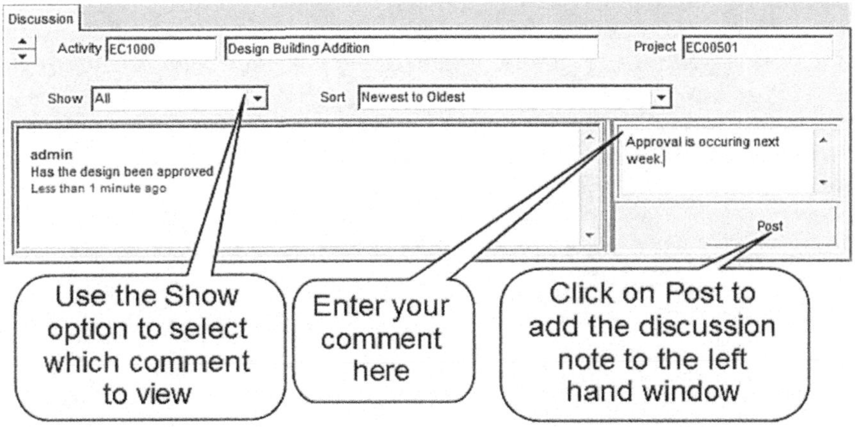

A new field titled **Unread Comments** has been created so users may identify activities with new comments that they have not read. This may be accessed through Team Member Web, the Team Member for iPhone app, and P6.

This function has limited use in the environment where only the project scheduler has access to P6.

27 EARNED VALUE MANAGEMENT WITH P6

This chapter does not teach Earned Value but it explains how P6 Earned Value functions operate. Therefore, before you read this chapter you will need to have a very good understanding of Earned Value Performance Measurement and the associated terminology. If you do not then you should consider reading some of the following documents:

- Some current EVM Standards:
  - AS 4817 Project performance using Earned Value 2006
  - Defence Material Supplement to AS 4187
  - ANSI/EIA-748-A-1998 Earned Value Management Systems
  - PMI Practice Standard for Earned Value Management
- Other material:
  - Earned Value Management APM Guidelines
  - Earned Value Project Management – Quentin W. Fleming and Joel M. Koppelman

Furthermore, readers must have a clear understanding of and experience with the following topics:

- The P6 options and preferences associated with resources, and
- Updating a resourced schedule.

This chapter will outline:

- Which P6 functions may be used for EVM,
- What P6 settings are used in these calculations,
- What options are available and how Earned Value calculations may be performed in P6,
- How this information may be reported.

The main Curves that are used in EVM are:

- **Performance Measurement Baseline** (PMB) which is a time-phased BAC.
- **Planned Value** (PV), or Budgeted Cost of Work Scheduled (BCWS), is the value of planned work at a point in time derived from the PMB.
- **Earned Value** (EV), or Budgeted Cost of Work Performed (BCWP), is the value of work completed at a point in time.
- **Actual Costs** (AC), or Actual Cost of Work Performed (ACWP), is the expenditure at a point in time to complete the work.
- **Estimate to Complete** (ETC), a revised estimate of the remaining work.

Some important points:

- No cost or resource data may be held at WBS level. All cost, resource, and expense data is held at Activity Level and summarized at WBS Node.
- If Actual Costs and Units are to be collected at WBS level then it may be appropriate to use a WBS or LOE activity to store this information and detail timing activities created under these.
- P6 will easily create the Planned and Earned values.
- If P6 is used to record Actual Values then your organization will require some mature system to import actual values from other corporate systems (accounting, procurement, time sheeting and contract management) in order that the scheduler does not become a data entry clerk.

⚠ Users should design their system and test their system with P6 to ensure that it is producing the expected results before working on a live project.

27.1 Performance Measurement Baseline

The PMB in Primavera may be read from either the Budget or At Completion values of a Baseline Project.

- At the start of a project the Performance Measurement Baseline (PMB) is usually read from the Baseline project Budget values, which normally are equal to the At Completion values.
- When a project is re-baselined in the mid-point of the project from a project that has progress, then at this point in time some activities will have progress and the At Completion values would normally be different from the Budget values.

Careful consideration needs to be given here as to which Baseline setting is to be used to ensure the correct values are reported as the PMB.

The P6 functions that decide which value is read as the Performance Measurement Baseline:

- The **Project**, **Assign Baselines...** form selects the Baselines projects to be read as the **Project Baseline** and the **Primary User Baseline**:

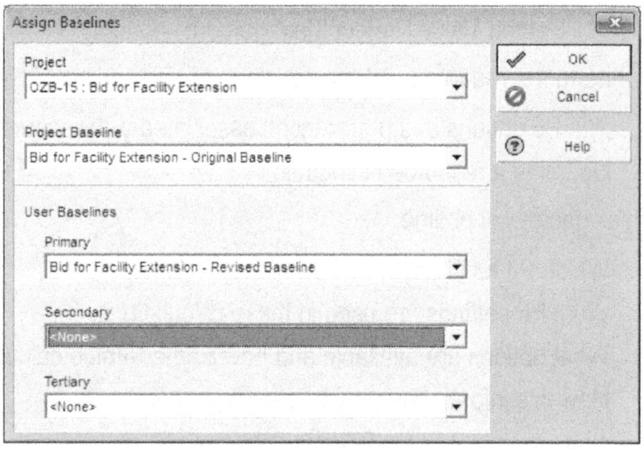

- The **Projects Window**, **Settings** tab, **Project Settings**, **Baseline for earned value calculations** decides which of the **Project baseline** or **User's primary baseline** is read for P6 Planned Values:

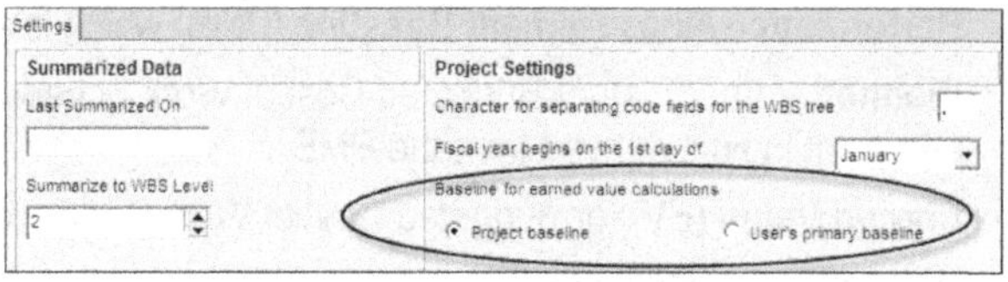

  The **Admin**, **Admin Preferences..., Earned Value** tab, **Earned value calculation** section, **When calculating earned value from a baseline use**, you should select either the:

  - **At Completion values with current dates**, or
  - **Budgeted values with current dates.**

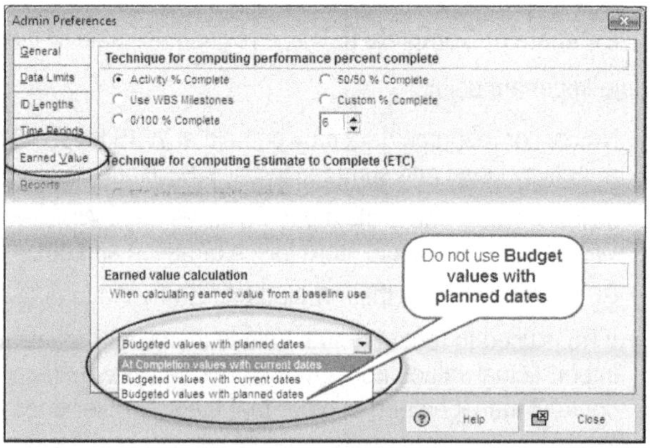

It is recommended that you do not select or use **Budgeted values with planned dates**, see paragraph 15.1.5 for details of the P6 Planned Dates issues.

27.2 Planned Value

The Planned Value is the value of the work at a point in time that was planned to be completed and is usually represented by the value calculated at the **Current Data Date**.

In P6 there are several options for displaying Planned values that may be confusing. They are:

- **Planned Value Cost** and **Planned Value Units** are read from the Performance Measurement Baseline settings as outlined in the previous paragraph:
  - These values acknowledge the **Admin Preferences**, **Baseline for earned value calculations**, and
  - These values acknowledge the **Project Settings**, **Baseline for earned value calculations**
- **BL Project** and **BL1** which may display **Expense**, **Labor**, **Nonlabor**, **Material** and **Total Costs** or **Labor** and **Nonlabor Units**. (**Expense Units** or **Material Units** are usually not available).
  - These values acknowledge the **Admin Preferences**, **Baseline for earned value calculations**, and
  - These **DO NOT** acknowledge the **Project Settings**, **Baseline for earned value calculations** and read the **Project Baseline** and **Primary User Baseline** values, respectively.
- **Budgeted Expense Costs**, **Budgeted Labor Costs**, **Budgeted Nonlabor Costs**, **Budgeted Material Costs, Budgeted Labor Units** and **Budgeted Nonlabor Units (Budgeted Expense Units** or **Budgeted Material Units** are usually not available) are **NOT** read from a Baseline schedule as one might expect but from the **Current Schedule Budget** and the **Current Schedule Planned Dates**.

All **Budgeted** values should be used with caution as they are always read from the current schedule Baseline and Planned Dates.

The **Planned Value** may be displayed as:

- **Tabulated Data** in locations such as the:
  - **Activity Usage Spreadsheet**
- **Graphical Data** in locations such as the:
  - **Activity Usage Profile**
  - **Tracking Window** by creating a **Project Gantt/Profile**.
- **Columns Data** in locations such as the:
  - **Tracking Window** by creating a **Project Table**,
  - **Activities Window** using **Planned Value Cost** or **Planned Value Labor Units**:

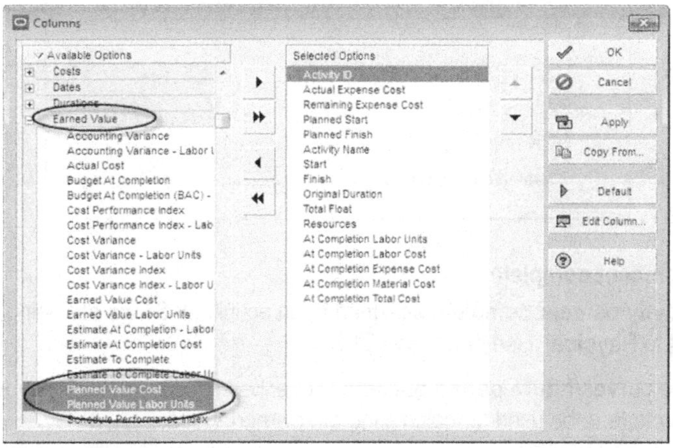

There are no options for selecting and displaying from a progressed schedule for the following:

- The **Late Baseline** values as a standard option. Many people like to show the Early and Late Baseline curve to display an envelope that progress should stay within.
- **Planned Material Units**
- **Planned Expense Units**

Planned data in the following windows or panes display the Budgeted field values which read the **Current Schedule Planned** dates and **Current Schedule Budget** values and should be used with caution:

- **Resource Usage Spreadsheet**
- **Resource Usage Profile**
- **Resource Assignments**

27.3 *Earned Value*

The Earned Value is the value of completed work expressed in terms of the budget. The normal calculation is **Earned Value** = **Budget** x **% Complete**.

27.3.1 Performance % Complete

P6 has a field titled **Performance % Complete** which is used to calculate the **Earned Value** for each activity. This may be displayed as a column or a bar in the Gantt Chart.

In P6 there are some options for calculation of the **Performance % Complete** for all activities in each **WBS Node** which is, in turn, used to calculate the **Earned Value**.

- The defaults are set in the **Admin**, **Admin Preferences...**, **Earned Value** tab,
- The options are managed at WBS Node value for all activities assigned to a WBS Node, and each WBS Node may have different values.
- Open the **WBS Window**, **Earned Value** tab to see the options which are mainly self-explanatory:

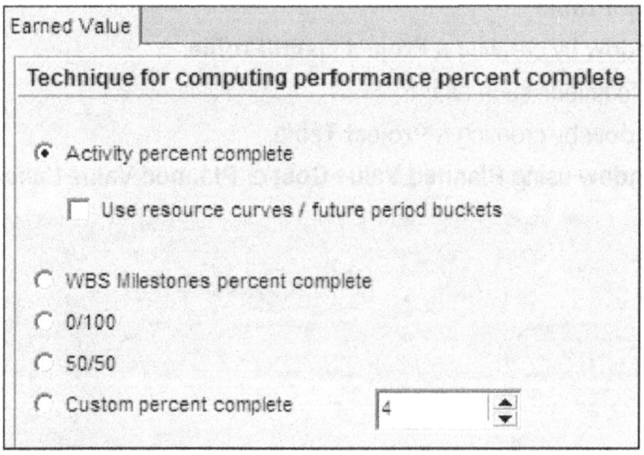

27.3.2 Activity percent complete

This uses the **Activity percent complete** assigned to an activity. If **Steps** are being used then this will have to be set to **Physical**. See paragraph 21.6.

The **Use resource curves/future period buckets** is checked to allow either **Resource Curves** or **Future Period Buckets** to be used for calculating the Earned Value.

27.3.3 WBS Milestones percent complete

WBS Milestones are created in the **WBS Window**, **WBS Milestones** tab and enable a predefined way of measuring progress against all the work assigned to a WBS Node.

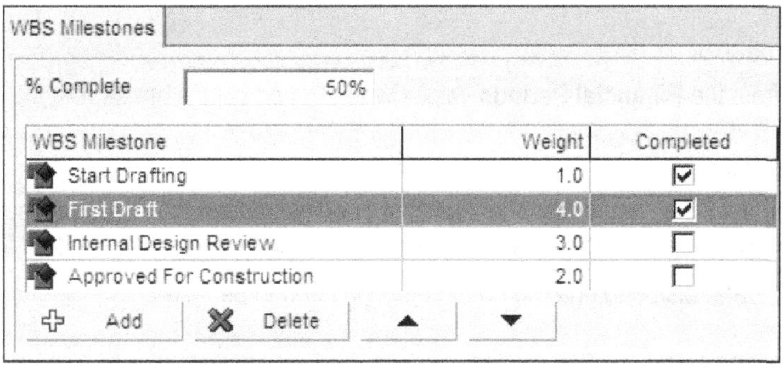

27.3.4 0/100

The **0/100** option assigns a value of zero for an in-progress activity and assigns 100% when the activity is complete.

27.3.5 50/50

The 50/50 option assigns a value of 50% for an in-progress activity and assigns 100% when the activity is complete.

27.3.6 Custom percent complete

The Custom percent complete allows a further percent complete option if the others do not suit your requirements.

27.3.7 Example of the Calculation of the Earned Value

The example below displays:

- 5 WBS Nodes with their description identifying the option for the **Technique for computing performance percent complete**, i.e., the method of calculating the Earned Value,
- 5 activities, one for each WBS Node each progressed by 50% in duration, hours, and cost,
- The % Complete bar displays the **Performance % Complete**.

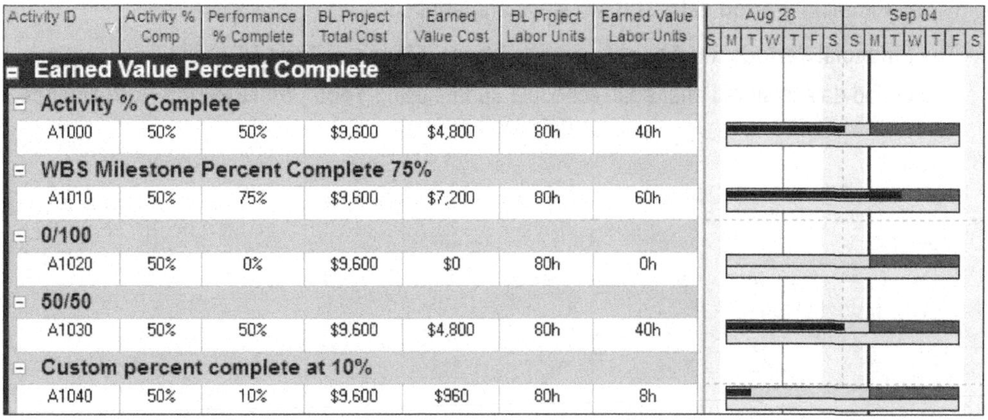

Activity ID	Activity % Comp	Performance % Complete	BL Project Total Cost	Earned Value Cost	BL Project Labor Units	Earned Value Labor Units
Earned Value Percent Complete						
Activity % Complete						
A1000	50%	50%	$9,600	$4,800	80h	40h
WBS Milestone Percent Complete 75%						
A1010	50%	75%	$9,600	$7,200	80h	60h
0/100						
A1020	50%	0%	$9,600	$0	80h	0h
50/50						
A1030	50%	50%	$9,600	$4,800	80h	40h
Custom percent complete at 10%						
A1040	50%	10%	$9,600	$960	80h	8h

27.4 Actual Costs

These are the costs actually incurred in performing the work. This is often calculated from the amount paid plus accruals. Actual Costs and Actual Units may be recorded in Primavera and displayed in two methods:

- The total to date, or
- Calculated from the **Financial Periods** values when Period values are stored.

27.4.1 Total to Date

When the total to date is selected then the total cost or units are assigned to each resource or expense and these are spread linearly from the activity **Actual Start** date to the **Data Date**.

Once the total to date has been entered no more action need to be taken.

27.4.2 Financial Periods

A more accurate option is to use **Financial Period** values to see a true picture of how much was spent in each period.

The decision to use **Financial Periods** must be made early as the period values must be saved at each schedule update.

This process takes substantially more time and should have a procedure for people to follow so no steps are missed.

This new function to Primavera Version 5.0 enables:

- The creation of user definable financial periods, say monthly or weekly, and
- The ability to record the actual and earned costs and quantities for each period.

Therefore, actual costs and quantities which span over more than one past period will be accurately reflected per period in all reports. If **Store Period Performance** is not used then the actual costs or units are spread equally over the actual duration of an activity, which may not accurately reflect when the work was performed and what was achieved in each period.

These Periods apply to all projects in the database.

If one project requires financial periods of months and one of weeks then it would be best to consider setting up two databases, one for each project.

This function is similar to the **P3 Store Period Performance** function.

To display **Financial Period data** then two steps are required:

- The **Financial Periods** must be set up using **Admin**, **Financial Periods...**, and
- The period data is stored after each schedule update using **Tools**, **Store Period Performance...**.

The steps required to store period performance are:

- Ensure that the user has the necessary privileges to edit **Financial Period Dates**, **Store Period Performance**, and **Edit Period Performance** when past actuals need to be edited.
- Create the **Financial Periods**:
  - In the Professional Version by selecting **Admin, Financial Periods....** which will open the **Financial Periods** form:

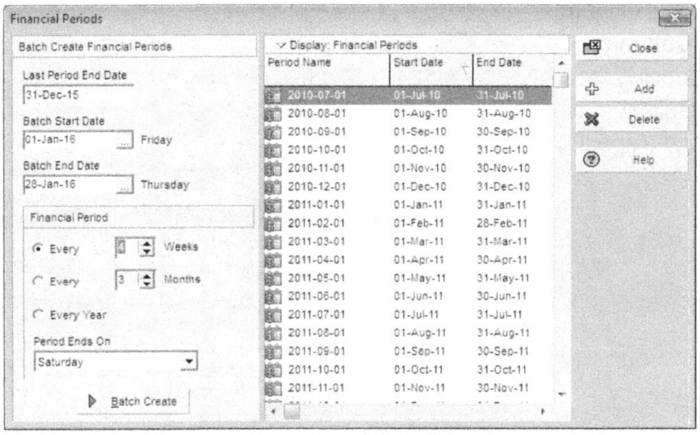

  - In the Optional Client from the Web using **Administer**, **Enterprise Data**, **Financial Data** menu.
- Open the appropriate project, select the **Calculations** tab in the lower pane of the **Projects Window**, and ensure **Link Actual to date and Actual This Period Units and Cost** is enabled by checking the check box. This option is grayed out if the project is not open:

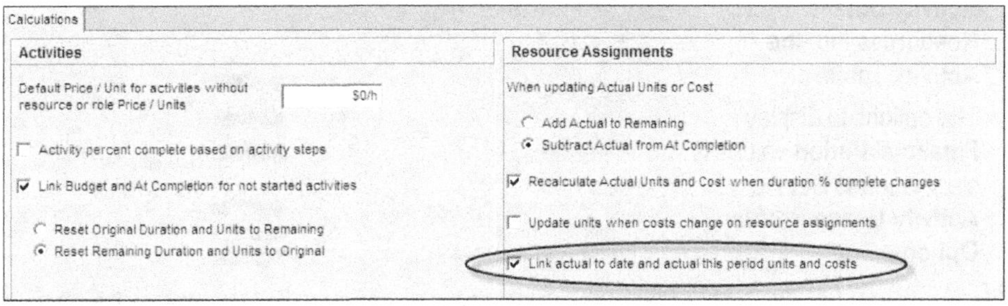

- To store the period performance select **Tools, Store Period Performance...** to open the **Store Period Performance** form, select the projects to have the period performance stored and click the  icon.

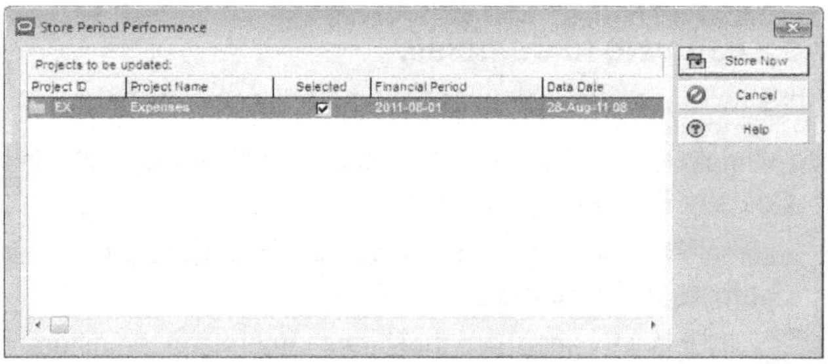

- The **Edit**, **User Preferences**, **Application** tab, **Columns** section, **Select financial periods to view in columns** enables the user to restrict the number of columns that are displayed in forms such as the **Columns** form, thus reducing the amount of scrolling required to find a specific column:

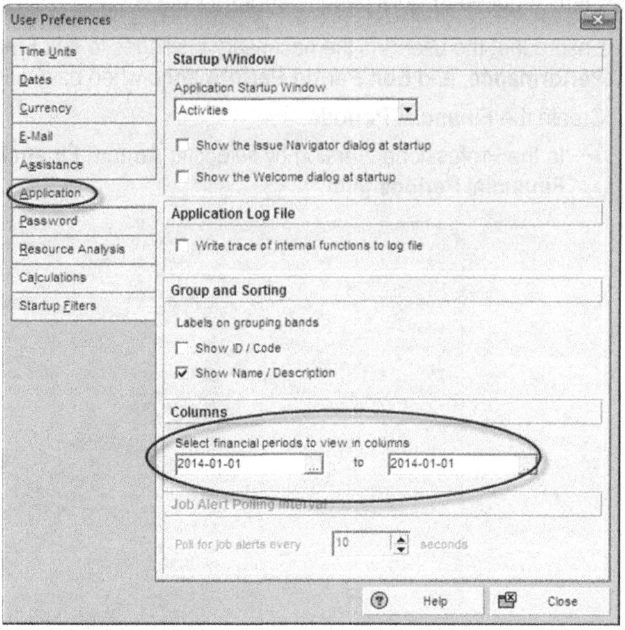

- Finally these results may be viewed and edited in the **Past Period Actuals** columns of the **Resources Assignments Window**, **Activity Details Resources** tab, **the Activity Table**, etc.
- The options to display **Financial Period** values is clear in forms like the **Activity Usage Profile Options**:

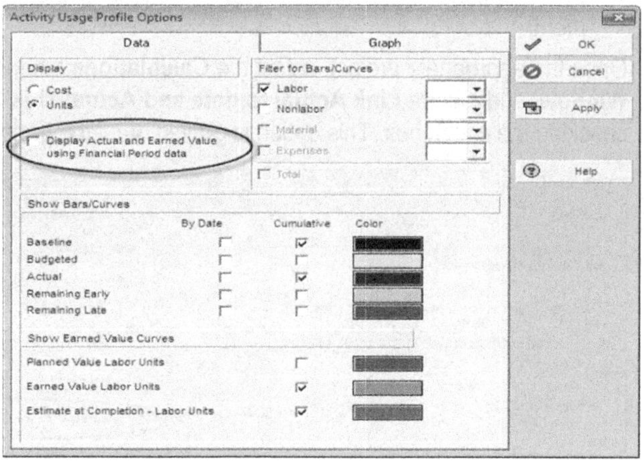

27.5 Estimate to Complete

P6 has two separately calculated estimate to complete fields:

- Estimate to Complete from Resource and Expense Units and Costs, usually titled **Remaining Costs** or **Remaining Units**.
- Estimate to Complete from P6 Earned Value Calculations, titled **Estimate to Complete** (costs) or **Estimate to Complete Labor Units**.

It is very important that users understand the differences between these two fields and know which they are using and displaying.

27.5.1 Estimate to Complete from Resource Data

This process calculates the Estimate to Complete directly from Activity Resource Assignments and Expense Remaining Costs and Units.

- The **Remaining Cost** and **Remaining Units** columns read from Resource and Costs values:

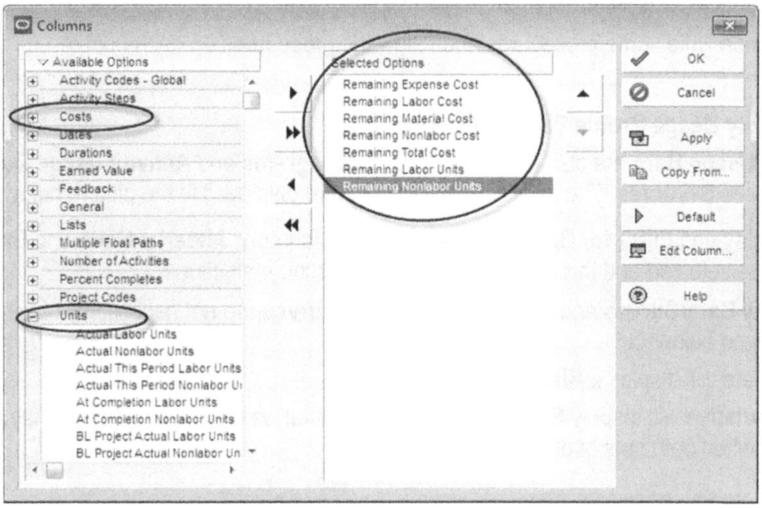

27.5.2 Estimate to Complete from P6 EV Calculations

- The Earned Value **Estimate To Complete** (Cost) and **Estimate To Complete Labor Units**:

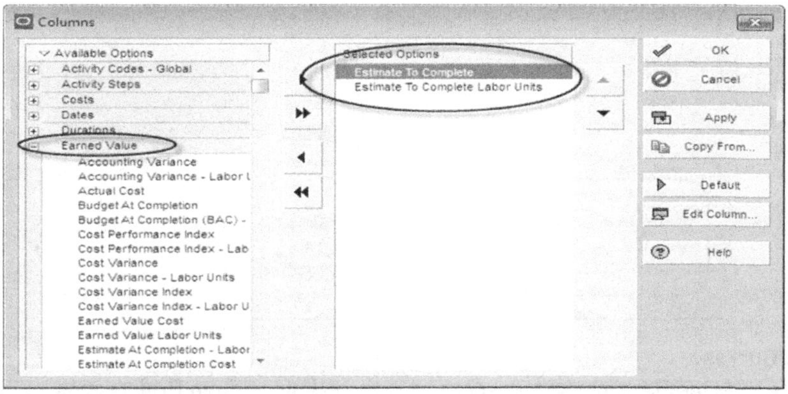

These values are calculated from the **WBS Window**, **Earned Value** tab, **Techniques for computing Estimate to Complete (ETC)** options, which are mainly self-explanatory if you understand Earned Value. **PF** stands for **Performance Factor**.

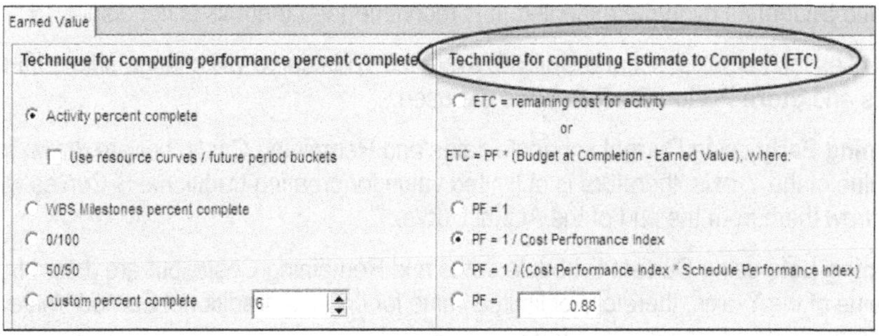

27.6 *Activity Usage S-Curves*

This section will shed some light on the graphical capabilities of P6 with some examples.

Users must spend a significant amount of time experimenting with the software so they are confident that the software is doing what they expect it to do. A small schedule with predictable results should be used to gain confidence with the software.

Then write some procedures and follow the procedures on each update.

27.6.1 Activity Usage Profile Bars and Curves

The **Activity Usage Bars** are also commonly called **Histograms** and **Activity Usage Curves** are commonly called **S-Curves**. The activity usage options are displayed in the picture below:

- The **Display** and **Filter for Bars/Curves** are self-explanatory. **Material Units** and **Expense Units** may not be selected and this creates significant reporting restrictions.
- The **Show Bars/Curves** and **Show Earned Value Curves** are not necessarily obvious and will be explained below:
  - ➢ **By Date** will display a **Histogram**, and
  - ➢ **Cumulative** will display **S-Curves**, in the same color as the Histogram so it may be difficult to read when both sets of data are displayed.

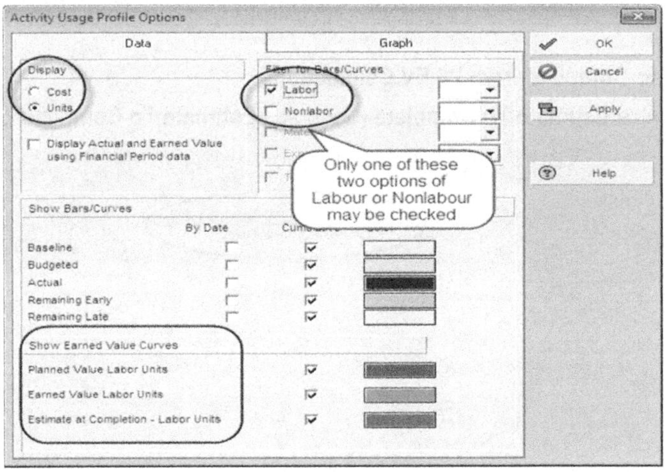

Show Bars/Curves

- **Baseline** uses the Baseline data as specified in the **Admin**, **Admin Preferences...**, **Earned Value** tab, **Earned value calculation** section tab. This is an Early Curve only and drawn from the **Project Baseline** dates.
- **Budgeted** uses the Current schedule Planned dates and Current schedule Budget, not Baseline dates and Budget as might be expected. It is recommended that this is not displayed.
- **Actual** uses the actual Costs and Units as expected. This curve will change shape if **Financial Periods** and **Store Period Performance** are used.
- **Remaining Early** using Current schedule dates and Remaining Costs, but are drawn from the zero value of the Y-axis, therefore is of limited value for creating traditional S-Curves where one would draw them from the end of the Actual Curve.
- **Remaining Late** using Current schedule dates and Remaining Costs, but are drawn from the zero value of the Y-axis, therefore of limited value for creating traditional Earned Value S-Curves drawn from the end of the Actual Curve.

27.6.2 Show Earned Value Curves

- **Planned Value Cost** is determined by the combination of two functions:
  - The **Project Window**, **Settings tab**, **Project Settings** section **Baseline for earned value calculations option** selects which Baseline is being read. This curve is usually the same as the **Baseline** curve when the **Project Baseline** is selected but will read different values if the default option is changed to the **User's primary baseline** as shown in the picture below:

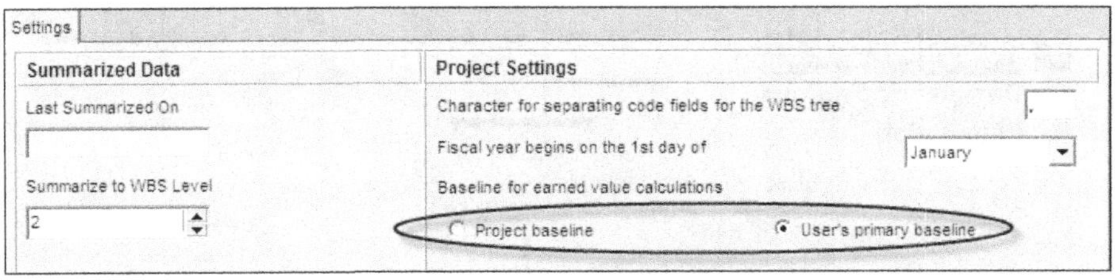

  - The Baseline Dates and Costs selected from the **Baseline for earned value calculations option** as set in the **Admin**, **Admin Preferences**, **Earned Value** tab **Earned value calculation** section and may be one of the following options:

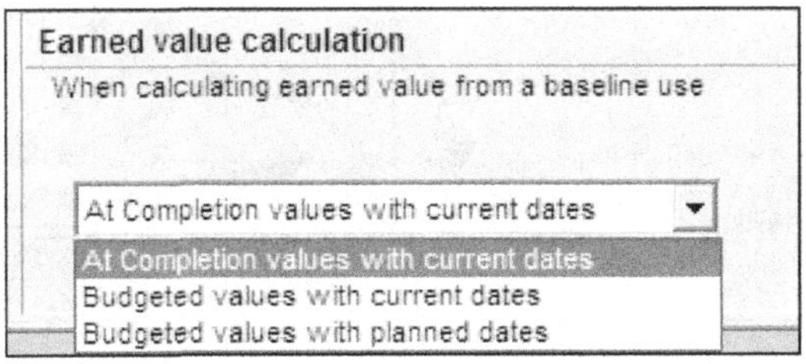

- When the **Display** option of **Units** is selected the **Show Earned Value Curves** description changes to Labor units.

Thus, in addition to Expense units and Material units, **Nonlabor** units may also not be displayed as P6 **Earned Value Curves** in the **Activity Usage Profile**.

Restrictions with the Graphical Display

It is easier to plan your EV System if you understand the system restrictions at the start, the following restrictions should be considered when planning your system:

- Multiple Histograms may not be created through the user interface.
- Late Planned data read from Baselines is restricted and the drawing Late curves difficult to achieve in the user interface.
- Time-Phased Material Resource Units are only available in the Resource Assignment Window where no EV data is available. Thus, the traditional Commodity based EV curves used in the Process Industry are difficult to produce with Material resources. In this situation, users revert to using Nonlabor resources for materials.
- The Bars and Curves functions have some formatting restrictions, such as a low level of control on the vertical axis, colors, and gridline formatting.

27.7 Sample Graphical S-Curves

The following pictures are created from the City Center Office Building Addition project available from the demonstration database available when the software is loaded:

- The curves in the picture below show that the **Remaining** and **Late Remaining** curves are drawn from the zero point not from the end of the **Actual** curve:

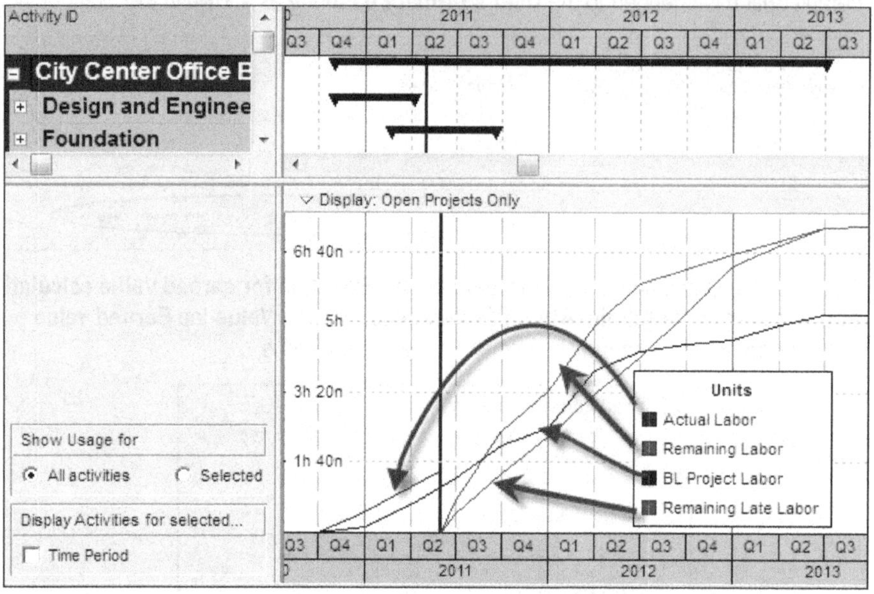

- The picture below is displaying the traditional Earned Value Curves.

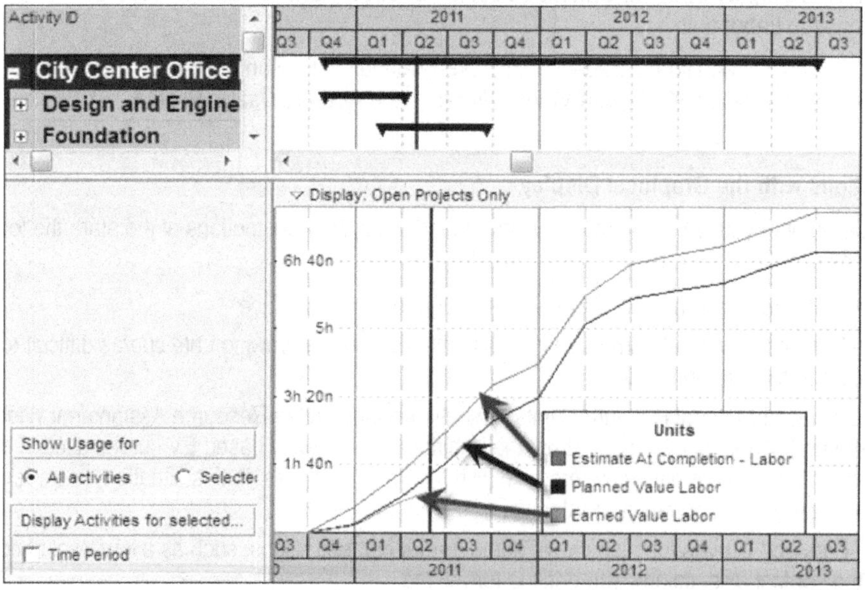

28 WHAT IS NEW IN P6 VERSION 8.1 to 15.2

There are differences in the number of functions available in P6 Professional Client and P6 Optional Client.

28.1 User Interface Update

The user interface in the Client has been overhauled to allow user defined toolbars and menus:

28.1.1 New Customizable Toolbars

All the old P6 toolbars have been removed and all new toolbars operate in a similar way to Microsoft Office 2003. Many toolbar icons have been changed.

Toolbars will not be covered in detail but significant productivity improvements may be made by ensuring that functions frequently used are available on a toolbar.

- There are many built-in toolbars in Primavera P6. These may be displayed or hidden by:
  - ➢ Using the command **View**, **Toolbars** or right-clicking in the toolbar area and then checking or un-checking the required boxes to display or hide the toolbars, or
  - ➢ Using the command **View**, **Toolbars**, **Customize...**, **Toolbar** tab and then un-checking the required boxes to display or hide the toolbars.

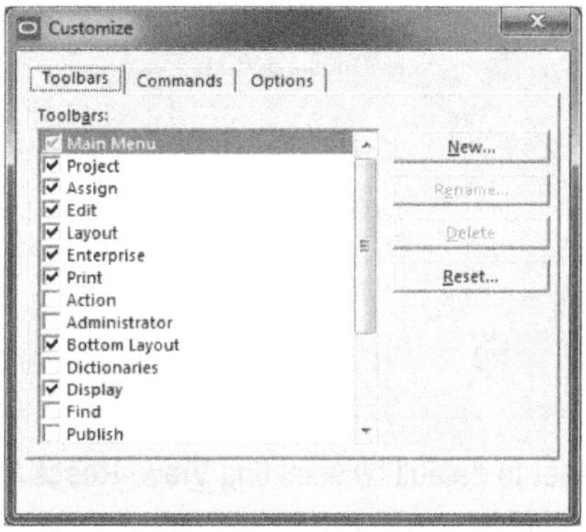

- Individual toolbar icons may be reset to default by selecting **View**, **Toolbars**, **Customize...**, **Toolbar** tab and clicking on Reset... .
- Icons may be added to a Toolbar by selecting **View**, **Toolbars**, **Customize...**, **Toolbar** tab **Commands** tab. **Toolbar Icons** may be selected from the dialog box and dragged onto any toolbar.

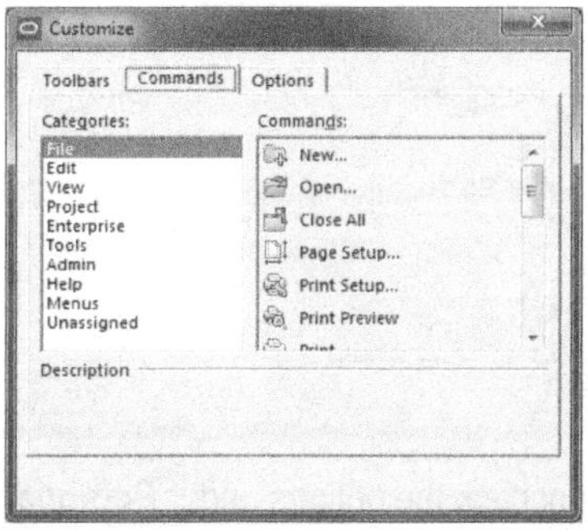

- Icons may be removed from the toolbars after the **Customize** (Toolbar**)** form is opened by holding down the left mouse icon on the icon and dragging them off the toolbar.

- Icons may also be added or removed when a toolbar is dragged into the center of a window and this reveals a further menu for editing the icons:

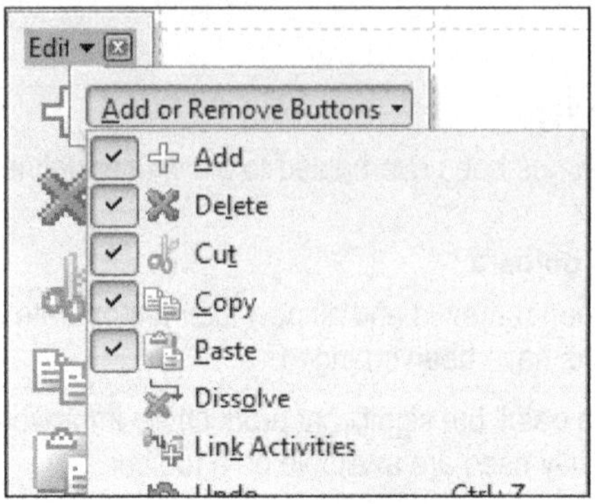

- Icons may also be added or removed by clicking on the down arrow at the right-hand end of each toolbar:

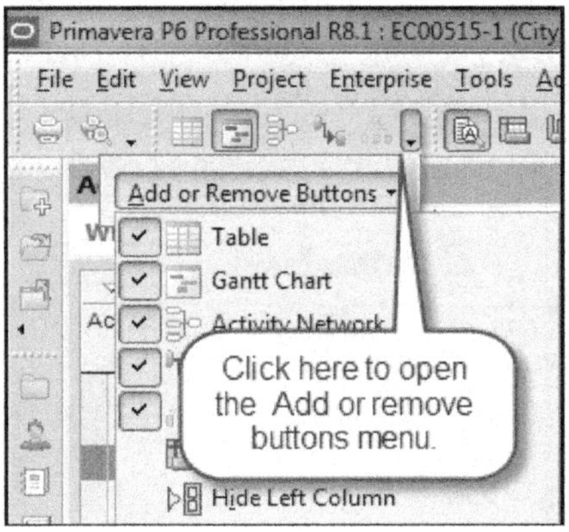

- All toolbar icons may be reset to default by selecting **View, Reset All Toolbars**.
- Toolbars may be locked so they may not be dragged by selecting **View, Lock All Toolbars**.
- Other toolbar display options are found under **View**, **Toolbars...**, **Customize**, and then selecting the **Options** tab.

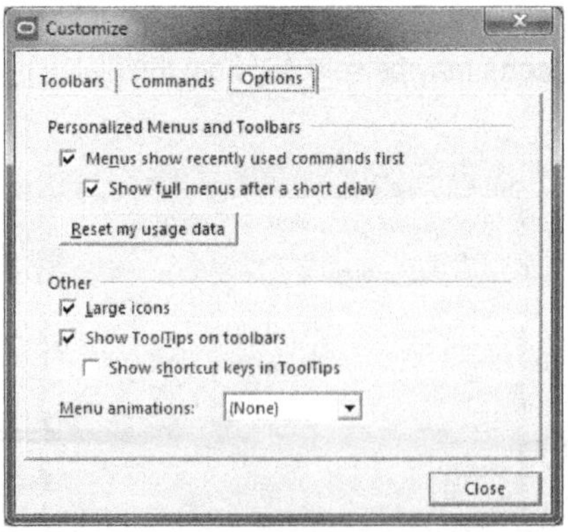

It is recommended to uncheck the options under **Personalized Menus and Toolbars** in the **View**, **Toolbars...**, **Customize**, **Options...** tab to ensure full menus are always displayed. This saves time waiting for the menu item you require to be displayed.

28.1.2 Customizable menus

The menus may also be edited:

- Open the **Customize** form,
- Then with the **Customize** form open move the mouse to the menu on the top left-hand side of the screen,
- Right-click on a menu header to reveal a menu:

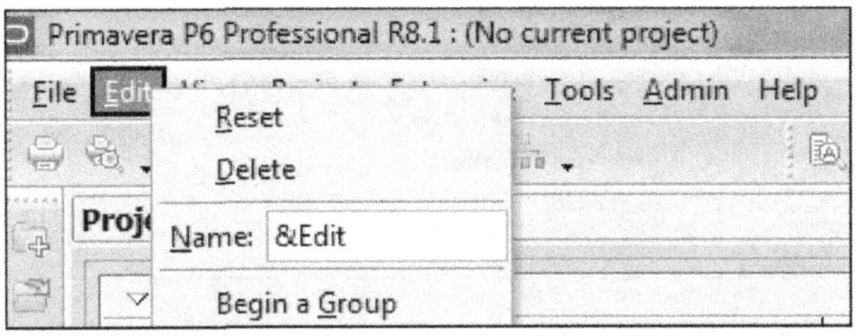

- Right-click on a menu item and you may now edit or drag the command up or down in order:

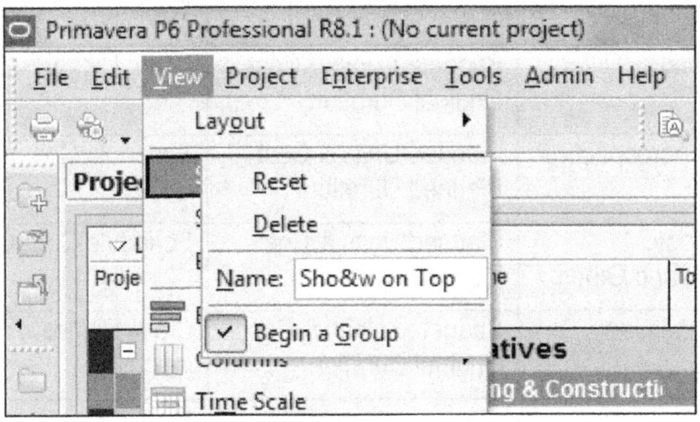

28.2 Admin Preferences - Set Industry Type

The Industry Type determines the terminology used in some fields and in earlier versions was set when the software was loaded. This now may be set in the **Admin**, **Admin Preferences...**, **Industry** tab:

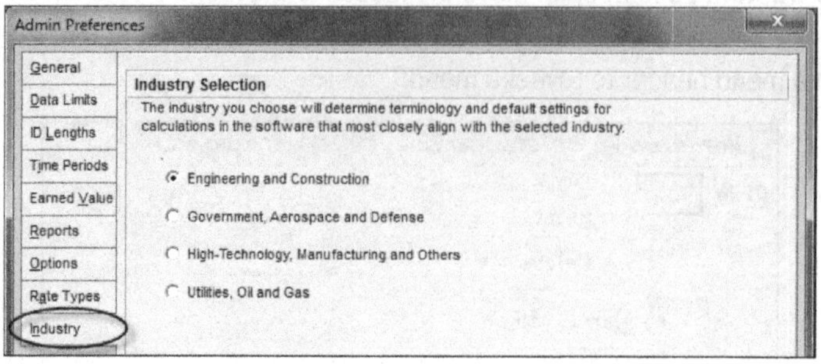

The following table displays the terminology:

Industry Type	**Terminology**	**Name of Project Comparison Tool**
Engineering and Construction	Budgeted Units &Cost Original Duration	Claim Digger
Government, Aerospace, and Defense	Planned Units & Cost Planned Duration	Schedule Comparison
High-Technology, Manufacturing and Others	Planned Units & Cost Planned Duration	Schedule Comparison
Utilities, Oil, and Gas	Budgeted Units & Cost Original Duration	Claim Digger

"Engineering and Construction" and "Utilities, Oil, and Gas":

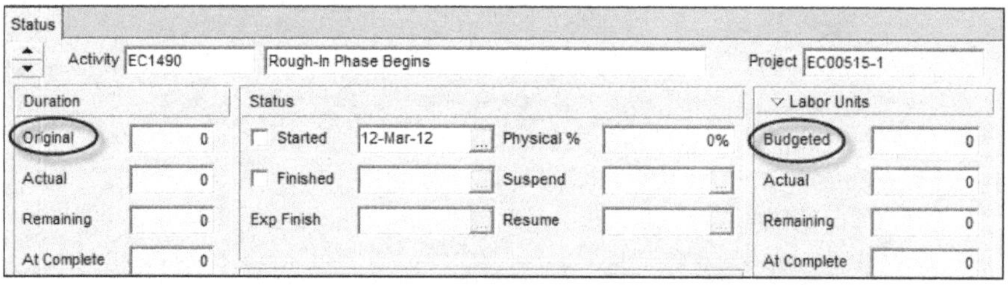

Government, Aerospace, and Defense:

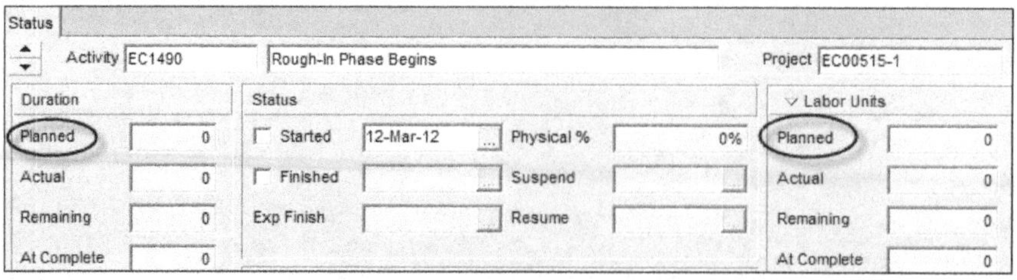

P6 has to be restarted to see the changes.

28.3 Tabbed Window Layouts

As windows are opened they are displayed as tabs. The picture below displays many tabs.

- The tabs may be dragged across left to right by clicking and dragging:

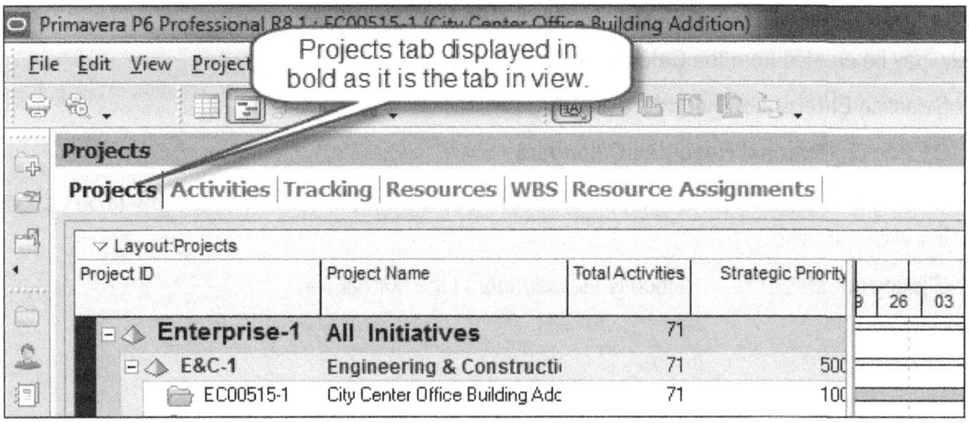

28.4 Tiled Windows

Windows may be tiled vertically or horizontally by:

- Selecting **View**, **Tab Groups** and selecting either Horizontal or Vertical split,
- Tabs in the upper window may be dragged to the lower window,
- Multiple windows may be made both vertical and horizontal as in the picture below:

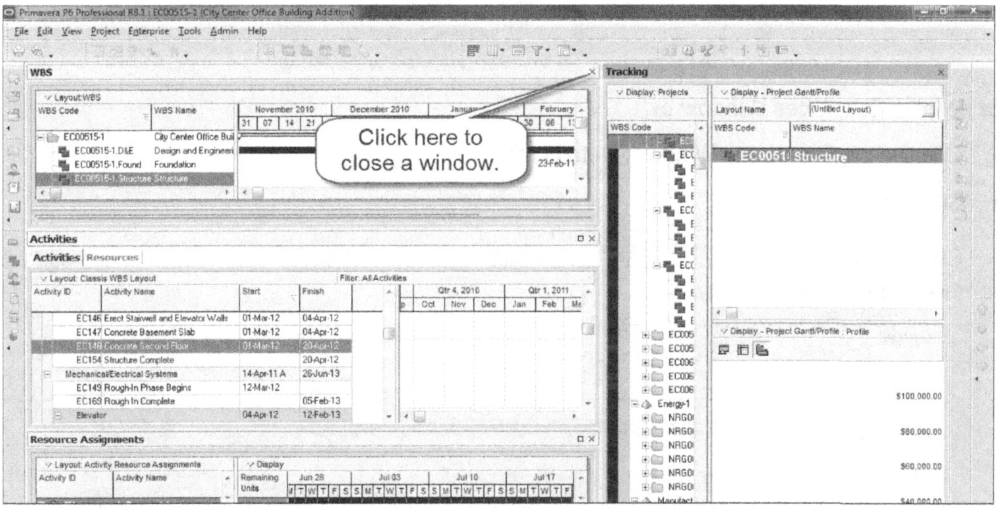

- **View**, **Tab Groups** and selecting **Merge All Tabbed Groups**, and
- Click the X at the top right-hand side of a window to close it.

28.5 Personal and Shared Resource Calendars

There are now two types of resource calendars: **Personal**, new to Primavera Version 8.1, and **Shared**, which is the same as the earlier Resource calendar.

28.5.1 Personal Resource Calendars

They may be created from the **Calendars** form by:

- Selecting **Enterprise**, **Calendars...**,
- Clicking on **Personal Resource Calendars**,
- Clicking on Add to open the **Select Resource** form to select the resource to be assigned the calendar, and
- Clicking on Modify... to modify the calendar in the normal way.

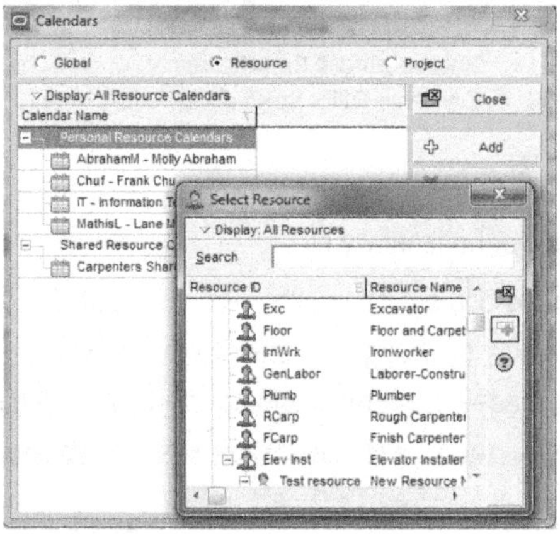

Or from the **Resources Window** by:

- Opening the **Resources Window**, **Details** tab,
- Selecting the resource,
- Clicking on the Create Personal Calendar icon to open the **Resource Calendar** form and edit the calendar in the normal way.

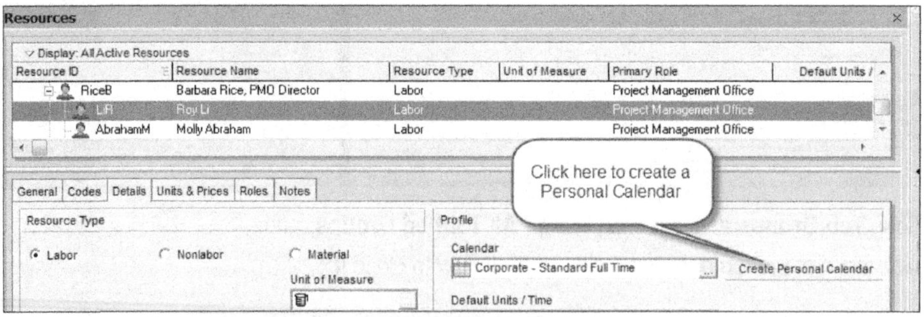

28.5.2 Shared Resource Calendars

These operate in the same way as the earlier Resource calendars and may be assigned to multiple resources.

28.6 *Auto-Reorganization*

This function reorganizes data based on the current **Group and Sort** order when an activity's attributes are changed.

For example, when an activity WBS code is changed in the Activity Details pane, then the activity will automatically be moved to the newly assigned WBS band when the activities are grouped by WBS when this option is turned on.

This function was called **Reorganize Automatically** in earlier versions and was set by each user in their **User** Options.

This has now been moved to the menu and may be turned on and off and is uniquely set for each window. To activate this function or de-activate this function:

- Select **Tools**, **Disable Auto-Reorganization**, or
- Click on the **Tools** toolbar icon.

When the icon is a dark shade then the function is disabled and the command on the menu still states **Disable Auto-Reorganization** when it means **Enable Auto-Reorganization.**

When a new Layout or Filter is applied then the data is also automatically reorganized.

28.7 *Set Page Breaks in the Group and Sort Form*

In earlier version of P6, page breaks could only be set at the first band in the **Group and Sort** form from the **Page Setup**, **Options** tab. The option of being able to set page breaks at any level has been added to P6 Version 8.1.

Select **View**, **Group and Sort by**, **Customize** or click on the icon to open the **Group and Sort** form:

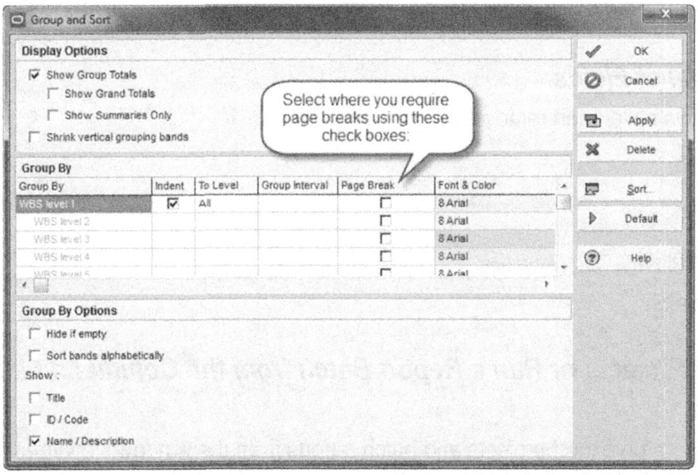

28.8 *HTML editor*

There is a new HTML editor which provides additional formatting options in forms such as the Notes tab, Steps tab, and many other details tabs.

28.9 *E-mail when printing a report or report batch*

When printing a report or printing a report batch, you can elect to automatically e-mail the report as an attachment. See Print a report and Print a report batch.

28.10 Timescaled Logic Diagrams

Timescaled Logic Diagram exports open projects from the Activities Window to the Primavera Timescaled Logic Diagram application and creates a Timescaled logic diagram in a separate application. This was superseded by Visualizer in Version 8.3.

Select **Tools**, **Timescaled Logic Diagram** to operate this function.

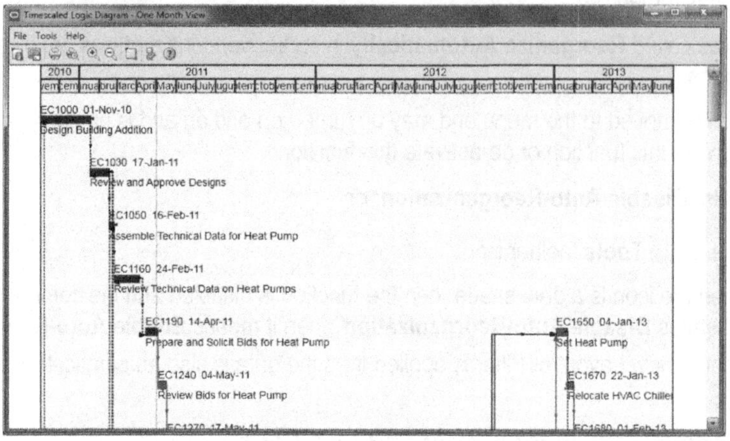

Version 8.2 introduced the following functions:

- Filter saving,
- Sight Line display and formatting functions,
- Assigning activity code colors to bars,
- Timescale Logic Diagram templates that may be shared amongst users, and
- Grouping activities under User Defined Fields.

28.11 Removal of Fields

The following fields have been removed:

- Review Finish,
- Review Status,
- Integrated Project,
- Estimated Weight.

28.12 Export Projects or Run a Report Batch from the Command Line as a Service

It is now possible to run export projects and batch reports from the window's command line, a service using an XML editor to create the command.

28.13 Activity Details Feedback Tab

Enhancements have been made to the **Activities Window**, **Details Feedback** tab to allow additional information to be entered.

28.14 Risk Module Rewrite

The risk module has been rewritten allowing compliance with more internationally recognized standards.

The Risk module is not available to users using the **Optional Client**.

When using the **Optional Client** and a user copies and pastes an activity, this action will also copy and paste any risks assigned to the copied activity and the user will be unaware that the risk has been copied.

28.15 Line Numbers

Version 8.2 introduced a Microsoft Project style **Line Numbers**. Select **View**, **Line** Number to display or hide the Line Number.

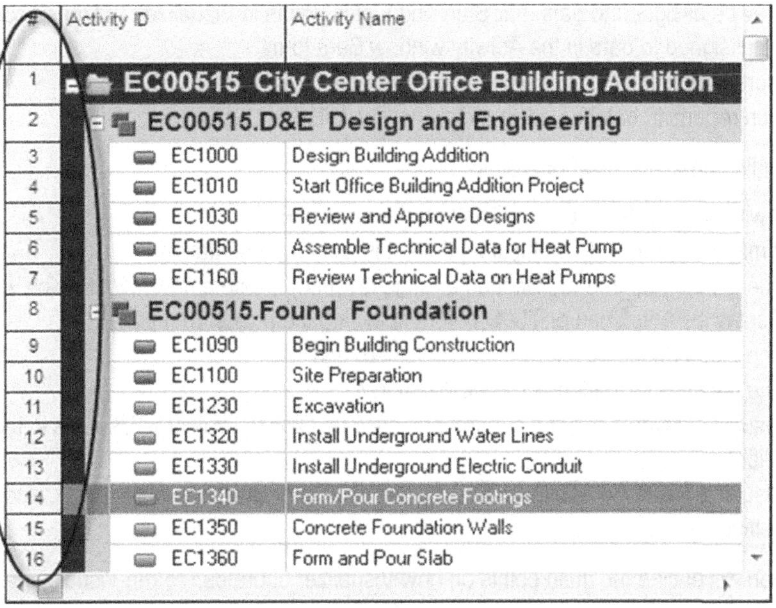

This is a very use full feature for reviewing a schedule to ensure that everyone in a meeting is looking at the same activity.

But as in Microsoft Project this is an order and the number will change if the schedule is reordered.

28.16 Visualizer

Visualizer is new to P6 Version 8.3 and is an update of the P6 Version 8.2 **Timescale Logic Diagram** module and is add on piece of software that allows a higher level of Gantt Chart customization than available from the Activities Window.

It may be run from P6 or the Windows Start Menu and also allows the creation of Timescale Logic Diagrams (TSLD) and includes the following functions:

- Printing of Layouts imported from P6 and the creation of new Visualizer layouts,
- Notebook topics and steps may be displayed as fields in the activity table or as bar labels,
- Stack columns and use word wrapping in the Gantt Chart,
- Multiple Activities on one row in the TSLD reducing the number of rows,
- Formatting of fields and labels,
- Use functions such as Baseline Bar display, Filters, Group and Sort,
- The Enterprise, Activity Code form allows Activity Codes colors to be defined. These colors may be assigned to bars, bar Start and Finish points in Visualizer, but these colors may not be assigned to bars in the Activity window Bars form.
- More shape choices and other formatting options for bars,
- Run reports in batches using programs like Windows Scheduler,

Understanding how Visualizer operates:

- It will not operate on the projects that are open in P6,
- It may not be used to manipulate data, it is just for presentation,
- The user is required to select an existing layout or create a new layout which will either display a Gantt Chart or TSLD before selecting the project to report,
- Then the projects to report on are selected, and
- The layout is formatted and save if required,
- Visualizer layouts may be created and save as Global, Project or User, as in the Windows Client,
- Visualizer uses P6 Admin Preferences for Calendar Start Day of the week, and online help setting.

This section will outline the main points on how Visualizer operates. To run Visualizer either select:

- **Tools**, **Visualizer**, or
- Open from the Windows Start Menu without opening P6.
- Select from the buttons at the top of the window what type of output you require:

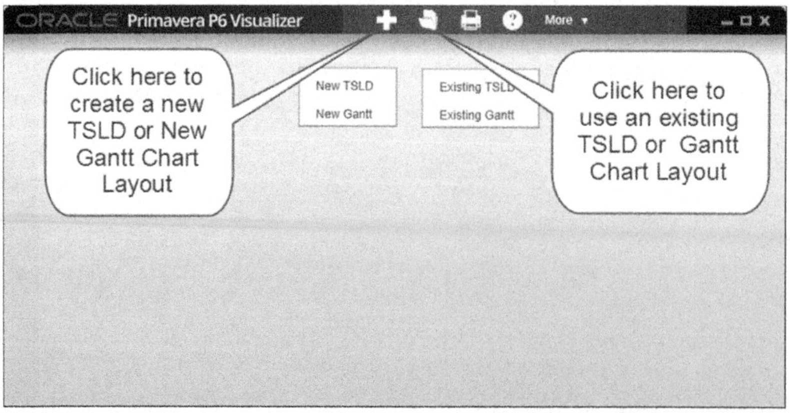

- You will then select which projects to report on, the picture below displays the option available to create a new TSLD:

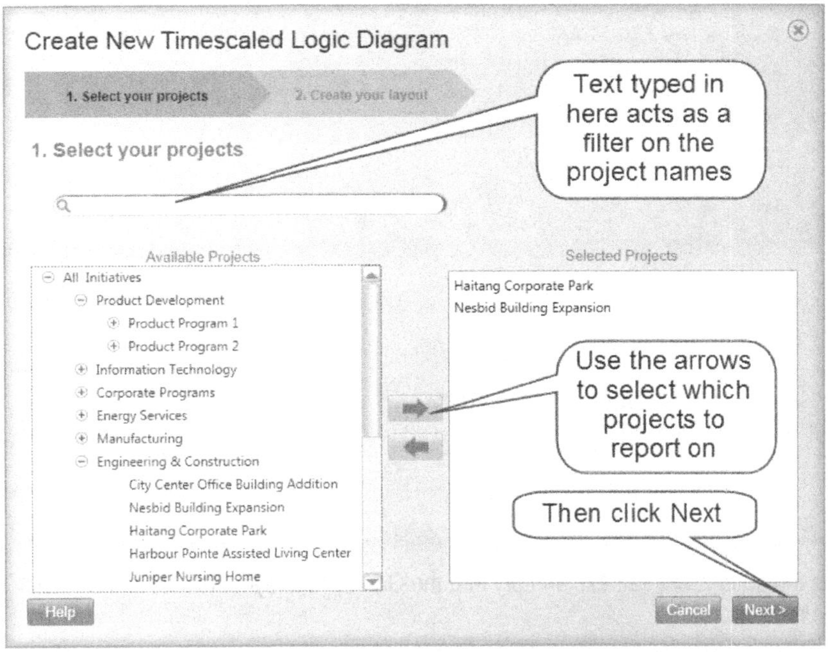

The Project ID is NOT displayed in the list of projects so you need to make sure all your project names are unique.

- Name the layout:

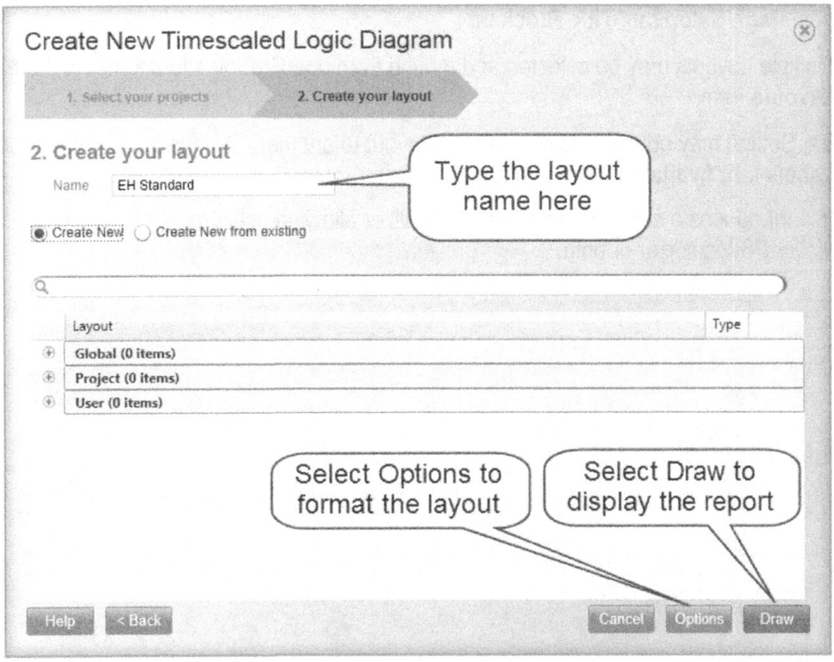

- The Options form allows a large number of formatting options:

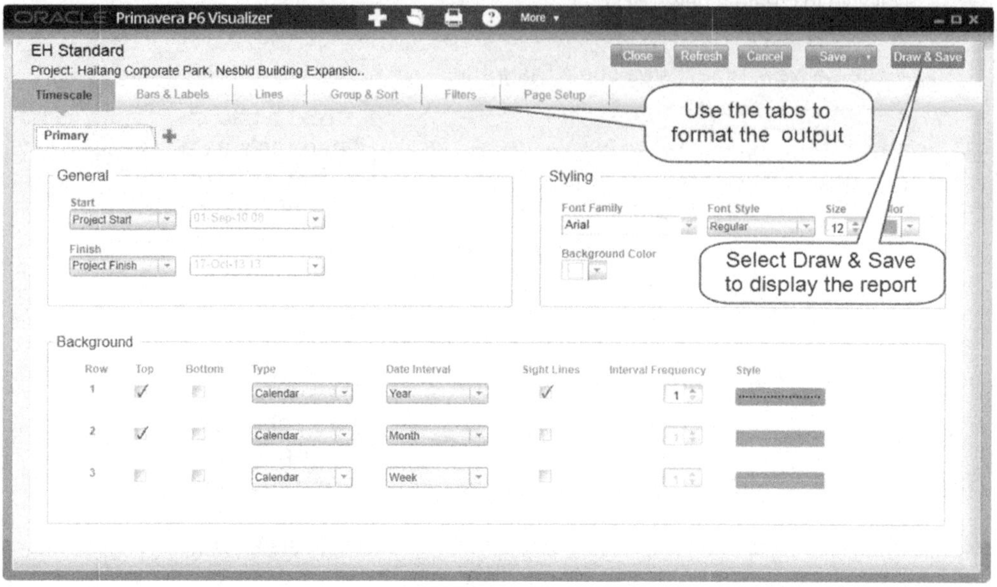

Most of the tab options are self-explanatory and the Gantt Chart layout functions are similar and will not be covered separately.

Version 8.4 introduced some new functions including:

- Display **Shifts** as a **Date Interval**. This function is accessed from the **Timescale** tab **Date Interval** list.
- The ability to add a customized legend in headers and footers. This function is accessed from **Page Setup** tab, **Title Block** tab.
- Multiple Layouts may be selected and moved from one Grouping to another in the **Manage Layouts** form.
- Bar Setting may now be copied from one layout to another. This function is accessed **Bars & Labels** tab, **Available Bars** section.

Version 15.1 introduced a separate access for Visualizer allowing users to be given access just to P6 Professional or P6 Visualizer or both.

28.17 Activity Discussion Feature

A new tab has been added to the **Activities Window** in P6 Version 8.3, titled **Discussion** which enables:

- Users to create a discussion thread for each activity,
- Each entry is saved with the date of entry and user name and the entire thread is recorded allowing an interactive discussion between users who have access to P6,

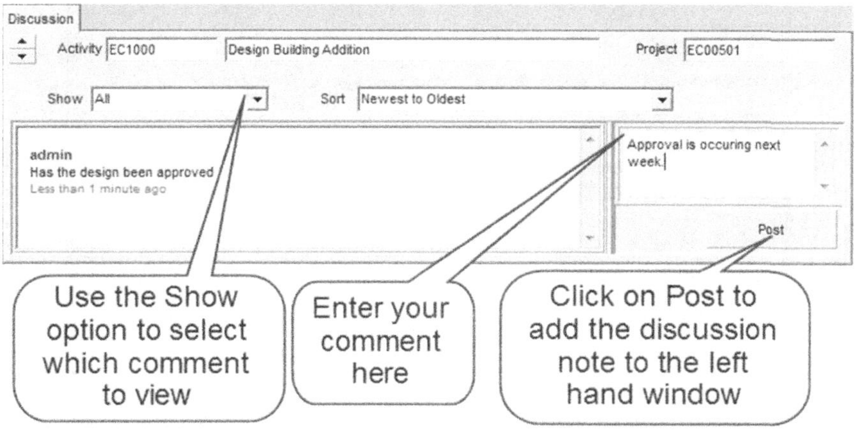

- A new field titled **Unread Comments** has been created so users may identify activities with new comments that they have not read. This may be accessed through Team Member Web, the Team Member for iPhone app, and P6.

This function has limited use in the environment where only the project scheduler has access to P6.

28.18 XML Import/Export Enhancements

The XML import/export functionality has been improved in Version 8.3:

- XML files may be exchanged with Primavera Version 6.2 Service Pack 4 and later.
- The following functions are now supported on import,
  - Constraining of external relationships,
  - Price/Unit in resource assignments,
  - Past Period Actuals,
  - Multiple projects in a single file,
  - Review of the imported data before importing data such as calendars, codes, resources, and UDFs, with the new import options window:

- The ability to import data into existing fields in database that the file is to be imported into. This will assist in resolving many issues that currently exist which result in data being corrupted by importing projects into a database by allowing mapping data to user selected fields and the renaming of fields.

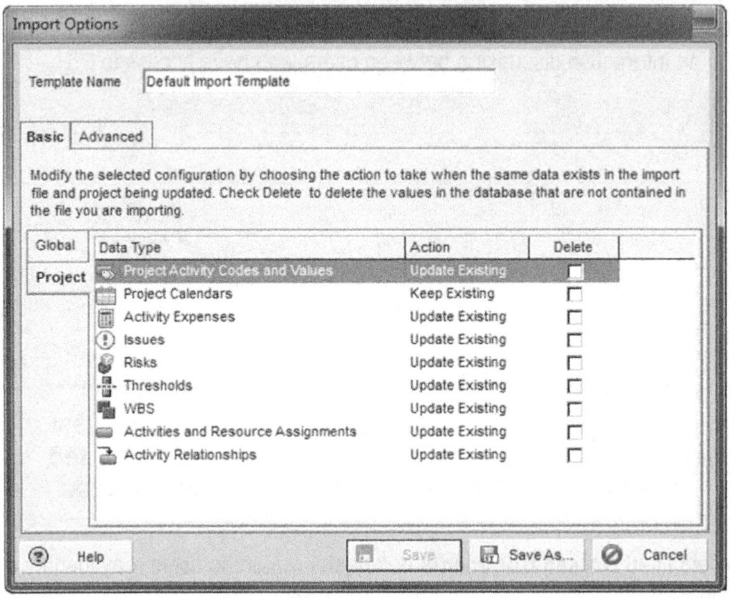

28.19 XML Import/Export Baseline Import and Export in Version 15.1

The XML import/export functionality has been improved in Version 15.1 allowing the import and export of Baseline projects. Previously Baseline projects had to be Restored, before they could be exported.

New fields exist in the Import and Export forms:

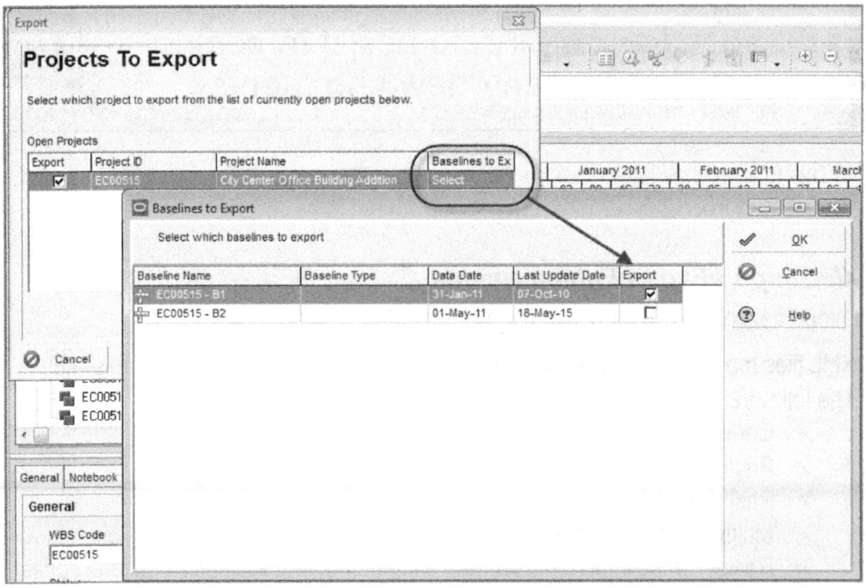

28.20 UN/CEFACT XML format

P6 Version 8.3 supports UN/CEFACT XML format from the **File**, **Export** menu. This format is mandated by many US Government agencies.

Version 15.1 added additional functionality supporting UN/CEFACT XML Format 6.

28.21 Loading Resource Summary Data on Startup

The **User Preferences**, **Startup Filters** tab in P6 Version 8.3 has a new **Resource Summary Data** check box which allows the operator to select if this data is loaded on start up. This may slow down the starting up of software and will affect the option on the use resource and role data during project summarization:

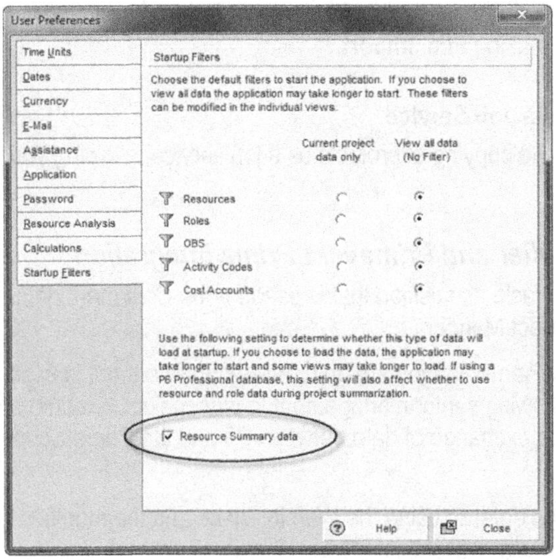

28.22 SQLite Database Available for Stand Alone Installation

SQLite database is used instead of an Oracle XE database for Standalone installations in Version 8.4. This should make it simpler to install a Standalone version of P6.

The following functions have been disabled:

- Users and Security Profiles as there is only one user
- Options to select All Users and Another User
- Project Issues e-mail notifications
- XML import Advanced options
- Project Check In and Check Out
- Job Services
- Update Baseline
- Risk Analysis
- Claim Digger
- Projects are opened in Shared mode.

28.23 Job Service Enhancements – Version 8.4 and 15.2 Enhancements

28.23.1 Manage Baselines

In Version 8.4 you may now Update, Copy or Add a Baseline using Job Services. You will receive a notification when the process is complete allowing you to continue working during the processing. This function is accessed from the Maintain Baselines form and is not available with standalone installs.

28.23.2 XML File Import

In Version 8.4 both P6 and Microsoft Project XML files may be imported as a Job Service. This is not initially available with a Professional install but is now available with Version 15.2.

This function is accessed using **File**, **Import**.

28.23.3 Copy Project as a Job Service

Version 15.2 introduced the copying of projects as a job service, allowing you to continue working as projects are being copied.

28.24 Primavera Unifier and Primavera Prime Integration

Primavera Unifier is an Oracle acquisition that is used for the Cost management of projects and is intended to replace Contract Manger.

Primavera Prime Capital Plan Management an Oracle acquisition that is used for the management of portfolios and projects allowing senior management to plan, select, execute and monitor projects. The Prime interface allows the exchange of data between P6 and the Prime Scope Management and Risk Analysis modules.

- Risk data must be entered using the Web interface and the modified dates from the Risk Analysis in Prime are available in P6.
- Activity Costs in Primavera are mapped to Prime Work Packages allowing costs and scope data to be exchanged.

28.25 Administration Menu Changes in Version 15.1

Originally when P6 Professional was connected to a EPPM database many of the enterprise administration functions were lost and these functions had to be administered from the Web tool. P6 Professional was originally called "P6 Optional Client" when it was used to open a EPPM database. The following Enterprise functions lost in Version 8.1 have been returned to Version 15.1 when it is connected to an EPPM Database therefore in the Optional Client mode.

- EPS
- OBS
- Project codes
- Activity step templates
- Cost accounts
- Funding sources

Opening a PPM Database with all Versions

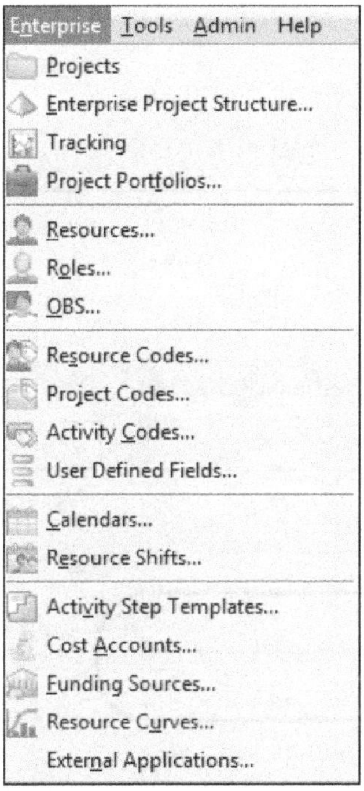

Opening a EPPM Database with Versions 8.1- 8.3

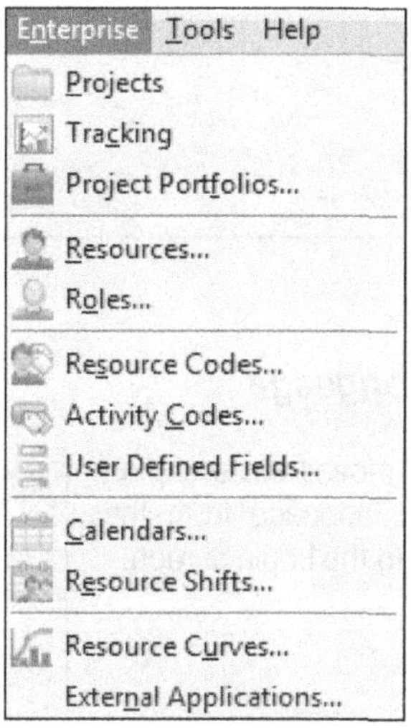

MENU OPTIONS REMOVED IN 8.1 – 8.3 WHEN OPENING A EPPM DATABASE:

Enterprise Project Structure

OBS

Project Codes

Activity Steps

Cost accounts

Funding Sources

28.26 Microsoft Project 2013 Compatibility

Version 15.2 introduced Microsoft Project 2013 compatibility with the export of Microsoft Project files in XML format:

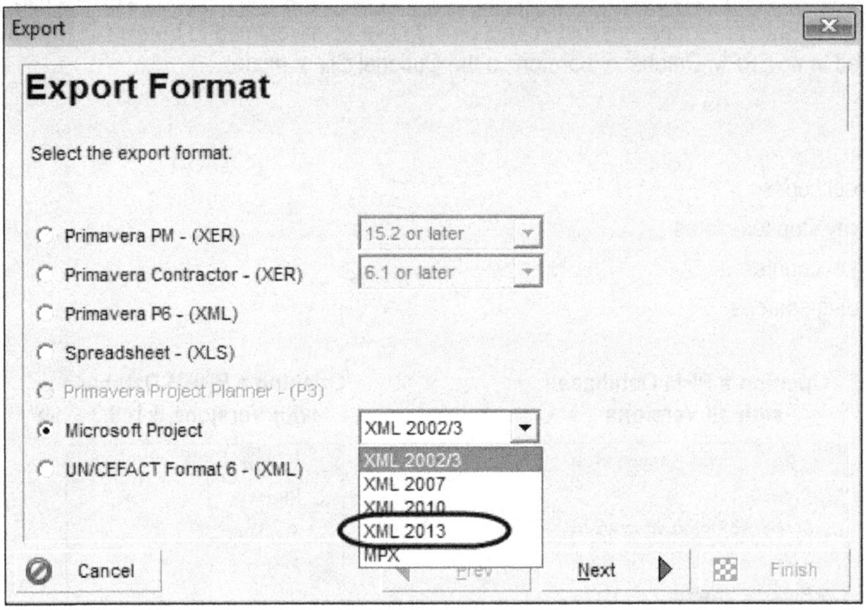

28.27 Set Language

Version 15.2 moved the selection of the menu language from the **Tools** menu to the Login screen.

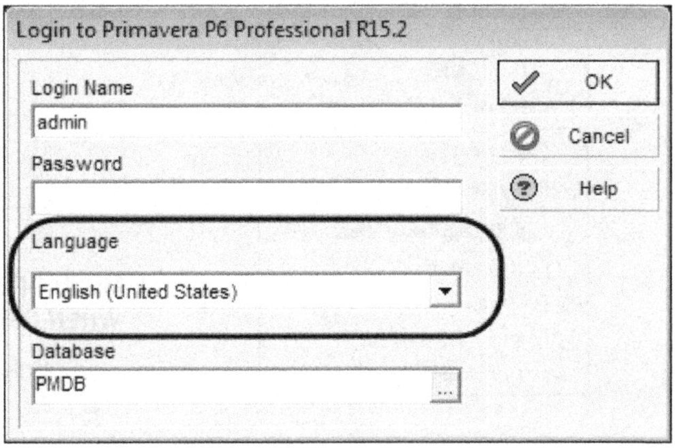

29 WHAT IS NEW IN P6 VERSION 7

29.1 Calendars – Hours per Time Period

In earlier version of P6 the calculation of the durations in hours for all calendars was set either by the Administrator in **Admin**, **Admin Preferences...**, **Time Periods** tab or by the User in the **Edit**, **User Preferences...**, **Time Units** tab.

These options calculated the duration in days correctly when all database calendars were assigned the same number of work hours per day. When activities are scheduled with calendars that do not conform to the **Edit**, **User Preferences...**, **Time Units** tab settings (e.g., when settings are for 8 hours per day but there are activities scheduled on a 24 hour/day calendar), then the Activity durations in days or weeks will be displayed incorrectly. These results often create confusion for new users and people reviewing the schedule.

This issue has been resolved in Release 7 by the removal of the user option above and the creation of a new calendar function titled **Hours per Time Period**.

When creating or editing a calendar there is a new 

icon in the **Enterprise**, **Calendars...**, **Modify** form that allows the definition of the number of hours per day, which in turn will enable the duration in days to be calculated and displayed correctly as long as the number of hours per day is the same for each work day in the calendar.

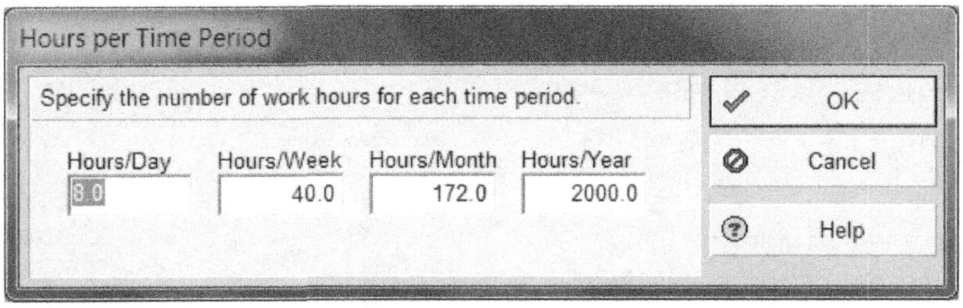

29.2 Calendars for Calculating WBS and Other Summary Durations

The calculation of the duration in days for WBS and other summary durations such as Project and Activity Code bands in Version P6.2 and earlier was calculated by a combination of the User or Administrator Hours/Day and the Global Calendar. These options calculate correctly when all database calendars have the same number of work hours per day and days per week. When activities are scheduled with calendars that do not conform to the **Edit**, **User Preferences...**, **Time Units** tab settings (e.g., when settings are for 8 hours per day but there are activities scheduled on a 24 hour/day calendar), the Activity durations in days or weeks will be incorrect. These results often create confusion for new users and people reviewing the schedule.

These summary durations are calculated in a similar way as in SureTrak:

- When all the activities in a band share the same calendar then the summary duration is calculated on the calendar of the activities in the band, and
- When they are different then the summary duration is calculated on the Project Default calendar.

The picture below has the Project Default Calendar set as 8hr/d & 5d/w and the picture shows that when the calendars are different this calendar is used to calculate the summary duration:

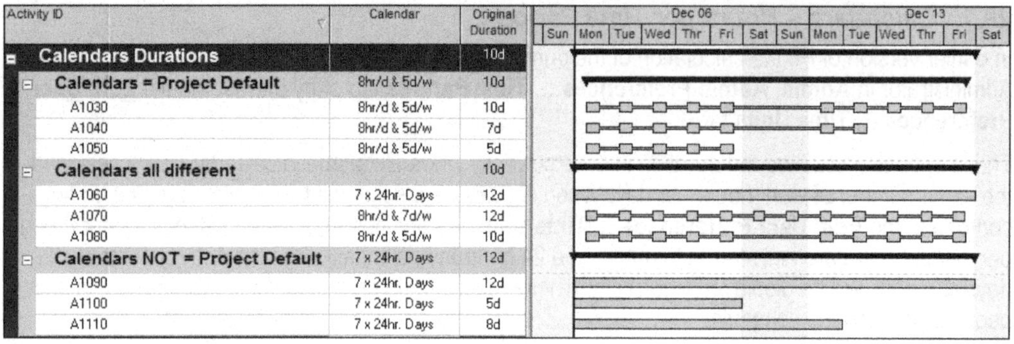

29.3 *Renumbering of Activity IDs with Copy and Paste Copy*

The new function allows the renumbering of pasted activities; the options are self-explanatory:

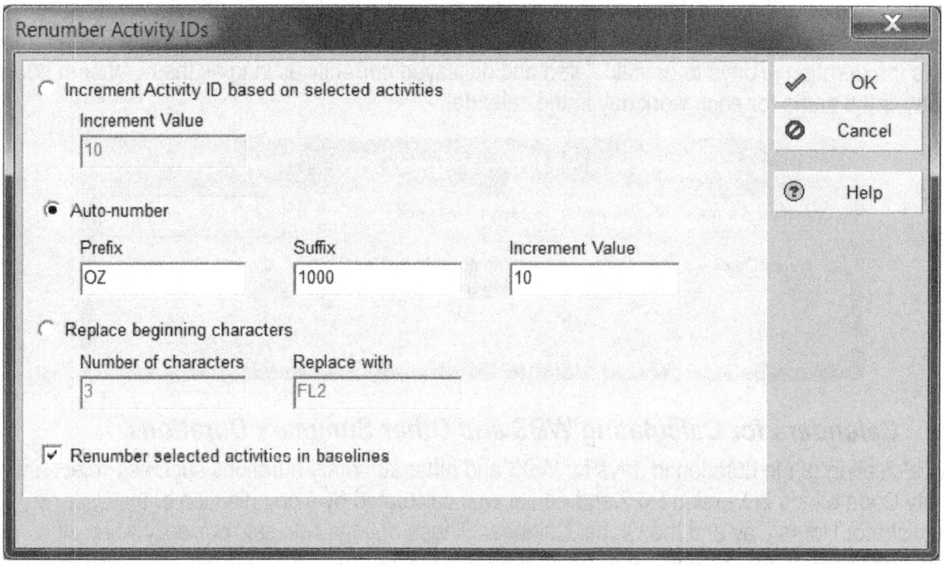

Should you attempt to renumber Activity IDs that exist then a further form is presented to allow manual renumbering:

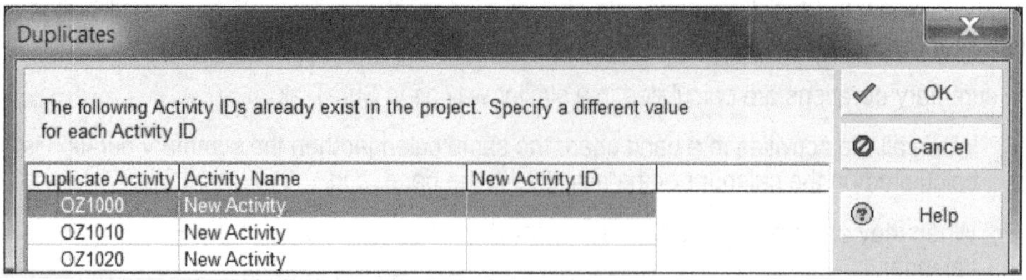

29.4 Renumbering Activity IDs

There is a new function allowing the renumbering of activities. To use this function:

- Select the activities that are to be renumbered,
- Select from the menu **Edit**, **Renumber Activity IDs** or right-click in the columns area and select **Renumber Activity IDs**,
- This opens the **Renumber Activity IDs**, as in the earlier picture, allowing renumbering of the activity IDs.

29.5 Progress Line Display on the Gantt Chart

A progress line displays how far ahead or behind activities are in relation to the Baseline. Either the Project Baseline or the Primary User Baseline may be used and there are four options:

- Difference between the Baseline Start Date and Activity Start Date,
- Difference between the Baseline Finish Date and Activity Finish Date,
- Connecting the progress points based on the Activity % Complete,
- Connecting the progress points based on the Activity Remaining Duration.

There are several main components of displaying a Progress Line in P7:

- Firstly, the progress line is formatted using the **View, Bar,** 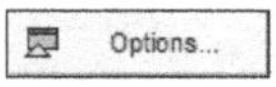

form, **Progress Line** tab, which may also be opened by right-clicking in the Gantt Chart area:

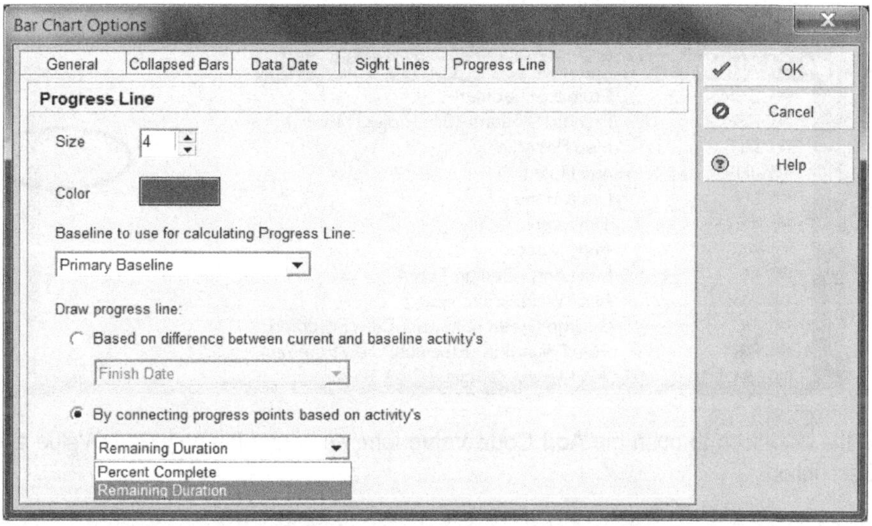

- Selecting **View, Progress Line** to hide or display the **Progress Line**.
- If you use either of the options of Percent Complete or Remaining Duration then you must display the appropriate Baseline Bar that has been selected as the **Baseline to use for calculating Progress Line:**.

- The picture below shows the option highlighted above of **Percent Complete**:

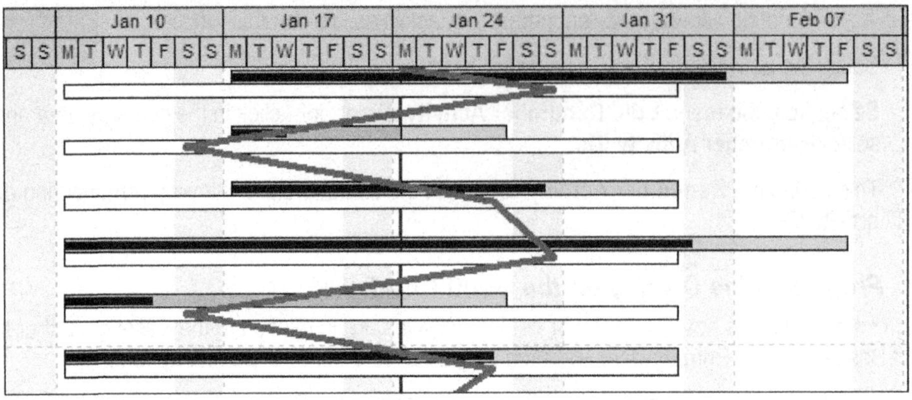

29.6 Add Activity Codes when Assigning Codes

Activity Codes may be added on the fly, as there is a new icon titled **New** on the **Assign Activity Codes** form that allows Activity Codes to be created as they are assigned:

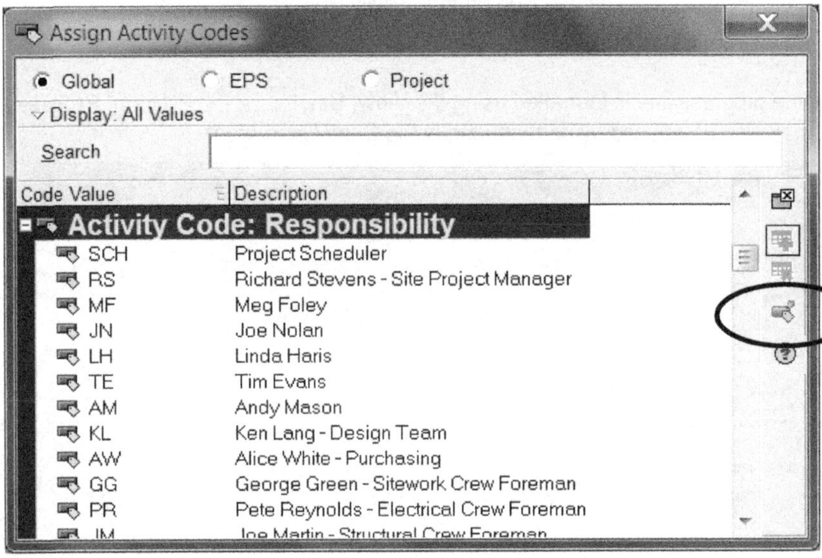

Click on the  icon to open the **Add Code Value** form and enter the new Code Value and Code Value Description.

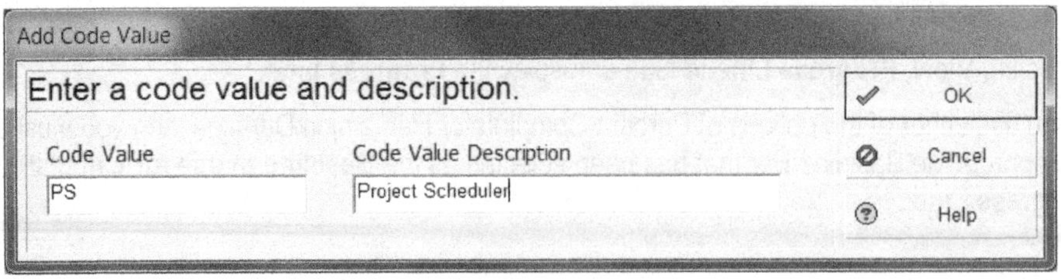

29.7 *Copy Baseline When Creating a Baseline*

A new baseline may be created by copying an existing baseline in the **Project**, **Maintain Baselines** form:

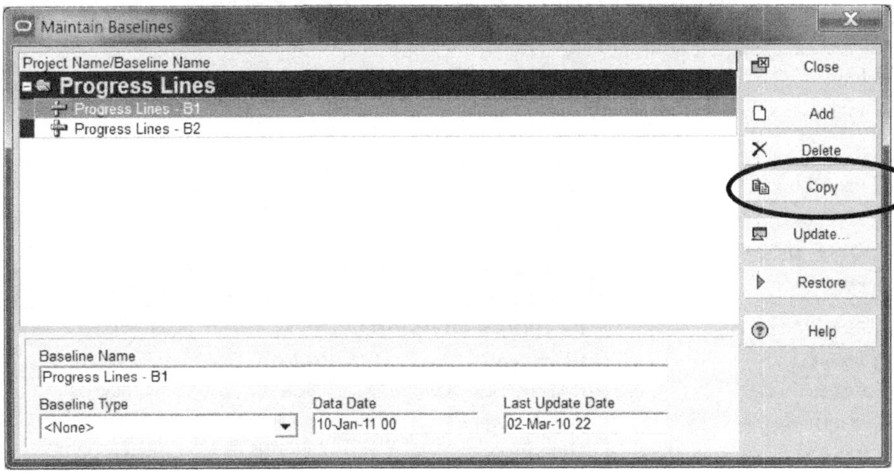

This new baseline may then be updated using the **Update** function.

29.8 *License Maintenance Changes*

The **Module Access** has been changed and the Current and Named Licensing options removed and replaced by a single access option:

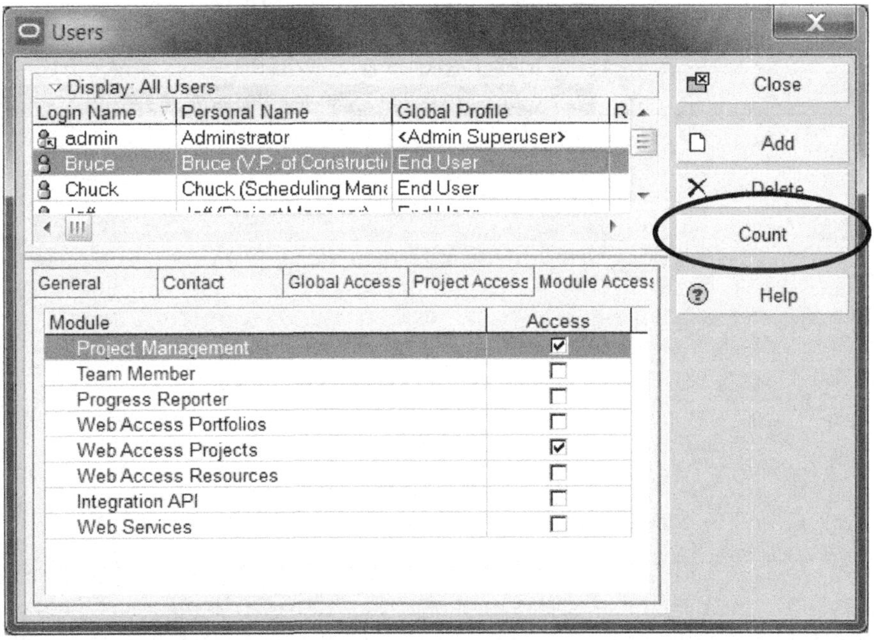

There is also a new 

icon which allows the administrator to easily count how many licenses have been assigned.

29.9 Recently Opened File List

When opening a file one can select a file from the recently opened list at the bottom of the **File** menu:

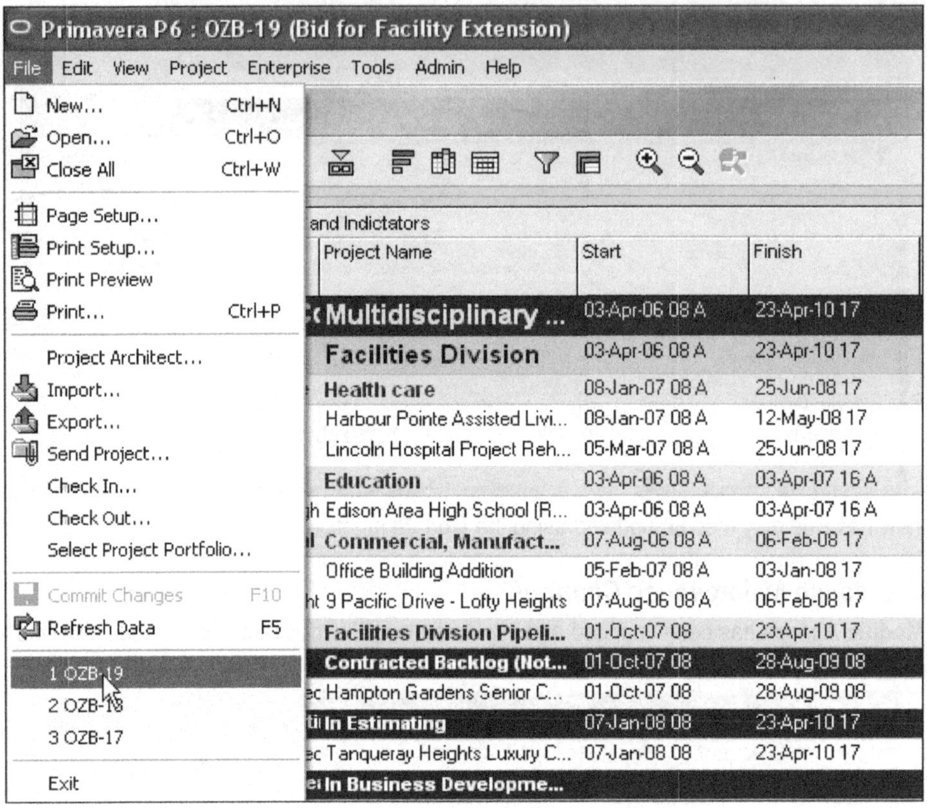

30 TOPICS NOT COVERED IN THIS PUBLICATION

The following topics are not covered in this publication:

- Budgets, including
  - Budget Summary
  - Budget Log
  - Funding
  - Spending Plan
- Thresholds
- Issues
- Risks and Risk Calculation
- External Applications
- Timesheets
- Timesheet Date Administration
- Claim Digger

31 INDEX

Made in the USA
Las Vegas, NV
13 April 2026

45279211R00249